The Black Woman
Cross-Culturally

Women comprise this work crew which is working on a cross-country road from east to west in Lesotho. Photo: United Nations, No. 118420. (1969)

The Black Woman Cross-Culturally

Edited by

Filomina Chioma Steady

SCHENKMAN BOOKS, INC.
Cambridge, Massachusetts

Library of Congress Cataloging in Publication Data

Main entry under title:

The Black woman cross-culturally.

  Bibliography: p.
  1. Women, Black—Africa—Addresses, essays, lectures.
2. Women, Black—Caribbean Area—Addresses, essays,
lectures. 3. Women, Black—Latin America—Addresses,
essays, lectures. 4. Afro-American women—Addresses,
essays, lectures. I. Steady, Filomina Chioma.
HQ1787.B56   305.4'08896   80-17214
ISBN 0-87073-345-1
ISBN 0-87073-346-X (pbk.)

Printed in the United States of America.

ACKNOWLEDGEMENTS

The author would like to thank the following publishers and contributors for
permission to reprint articles in this volume.

"Female Employment and Family Organization in West Africa" by Niara Sudarkasa
originally appeared in *New Research on Women and Sex Roles* edited by Dorothy McGui-
gan. Reprinted by permission of the University of Michigan Center for Continuing
Education of Women and the author.

"Tanzanian Women and Nation Building" by Joyce Ladner originally appeared in *The
Black Scholar*, Vol. 3, No. 4 (December 1971): 22-28. Reprinted by permission of the
publisher and the author. Copyright © 1971 The Black World Foundation.

"The Second Sex in Town" by Josef Gugler originally appeared in the *Canadian Journal
of African Studies*, Vol. VI, No. ii (1972): 289-301. Reprinted by permission of the
publisher and the author.

"Definitions of Women and Development: An African Perspective" by Achola O. Pala originally appeared in *Signs*, Vol. 3, No. 1 (Autumn 1977): 9-13. Reprinted by permission of the University of Chicago Press and the author. Copyright © 1977 University of Chicago Press.

"Racism and Tradition: Black Womanhood in Historical Perspective" by Joyce A. Ladner originally appeared in *Tomorrow's Tomorrow: The Black Woman*. Copyright © 1971 by Joyce A. Ladner. Reprinted by permission of Doubleday and Company, Inc. and the author.

"Female Slave Resistance: The Economics of Sex" by Darlene Hine and Kate Wittenstein originally appeared in the *Western Journal of Black Studies*, Vol. 3, No. 2 (Summer 1979): 123-127. Reprinted by permission of the publisher and the authors.

"Discrimination Against Afro-American Women in the Woman's Movement, 1830-1920" by Rosalyn Terborg-Penn originally appeared in *The Afro-American Woman: Struggle and Images* edited by Sharon Harley and Rosalyn Terborg-Penn. Copyright © 1978 Kennikat Press. Reprinted by permission of Kennikat Press and the author.

"Sex Roles and Survival Strategies in an Urban Black Community" by Carol B. Stack originally appeared in *Woman, Culture and Society* edited by Michelle Zimbalist Rosaldo and Louise Lamphere. Reprinted by permission of Stanford University Press and the author.

"Black Women and Music: A Survey from Africa to the New World" by Irene V. Jackson originally appeared in *Minority Voices*, Vol. 2, No. 2, pp. 15-27. Reprinted by permission of the publisher and the author.

"Images of Black Women in Afro-American Poetry" by Andrea Benton Rushing originally appeared in *The Afro-American Woman: Struggle and Images* edited by Sharon Harley and Rosalyn Terborg-Penn, Copyright © 1978 Kennikat Press. Reprinted by permission of Kennikat Press and the author.

"Social Inequity and Sexual Status in Barbados" by Constance Sutton and Susan Makiesky-Barrow originally appeared in *Sexual Stratification: A Cross-Cultural View* edited by Alice Schlegel. Reprinted by permission of Columbia University Press and the authors.

"Female Status, the Family, and Male Dominance in a West Indian Community" by Yolanda T. Moses originally appeared in *Signs*. Vol. 3, No. 1 (Autumn 1977): 9-13. Reprinted by permission of the University of Chicago Press and the author. Copyright © 1977 University of Chicago Press.

"Economic Role and Cultural Tradition" by Sidney W. Mintz originally appeared under the title "Les rôles économiques et la tradition culturelle" in *La Femme de Couleur en Amérique Latine* edited by Roger Bastide. Reprinted by permission of Editions Anthropos and the author.

"West Indian Characteristics of the Black Carib" by Nancie L. Solien Gonzalez originally appeared in the *Southwestern Journal of Anthropology* (now the *Journal of Anthropological Research*) Vol. 15, No. 3 (1959): 300-307. Reprinted by permission of the publisher and the author.

"The Spread of Capitalism in Rural Colombia: Effects on Poor Women" by Anna Rubbo originally appeared in *Toward and Anthropology of Women* edited by Ranya R. Reiter. Copyright © 1975 by Ranya R. Reiter. Reprinted by permission of Monthly Review Press and the author.

To Azania

Contents

Introduction

Filomina Chioma Steady

This anthology brings together for the first time in a cross-cultural perspective a body of relevant but previously fragmented and scattered literature on the black woman. It discusses common themes in her experience which serve to synthesize the growing literature on the subject. The studies presented here are representations of the black woman in Africa, the Caribbean, South America, and the United States of America.

There are several reasons why studies of the black woman deserve some comparative review. In the first place she had been a subject of study long before women's liberation came into vogue. It can even be claimed that to some extent she was used, directly or indirectly, as a guinea pig for the development of a significant body of anthropological theory in Africa and sociological theory in the United States and the Caribbean.

British functionalism, the school of anthropology which propelled the discipline for almost half a century, focused on a wide array of subjects dealing with kinship and marriage systems. The important position of women in maintaining the corporate structure of the enduring groups of various societies in Africa was implicit in the various analyses, even though women as a group received only superficial attention. A number of these studies were conducted during the colonial period, but colonialism was either ignored or considered as a given. Partly as a result of this, but more directly in response to the recent wave of feminism, neo-Marxist

1

thought and dependency theory, some scholars have focused specifically on an analysis of the impact of colonialism on African women. This has resulted in the adoption of new theoretical positions and a methodology of social change which contrasts sharply with functionalism. The historical perspective used served to demonstrate the deleterious effects of colonialism on the status of African women.

Also of interest to scholars of women's studies is the fact that the continent of Africa contains societies with varying degrees of sexual egalitarianism. This representation provides situations with significant variations for the study of sex roles in cultural contexts. Africa is also one of the few areas in the world where matrilineal societies exist in significant numbers.

Social change is occurring at an accelerated rate in Africa and is manifested primarily through rapid urbanization. This represents a process whereby sex roles are constantly being redefined and altered. The emerging patterns of social action arouse the interest of scholars who are seeking a better understanding of changing sex roles.

With regard to the black woman in the Caribbean, studies of the family and household have led to insights of family organization, and pointed out the need for a redefinition of traditional concepts of ' family ' and 'household.' Also within this West Indian context several patterns of social organization characteristic of, but not unique to West Indian society, have been explored. These include female-headed households, common-law marriages, and the interaction between class and color in West Indian family structure.

For the black woman in the United States variables such as race and class have been significant, as has the influence of slavery, institutional racism, and the paralyzing welfare system on black families and on the lives of black women. The controversial theory of the black matriarchy is an outcome of American functionalism and has had a great impact on sociological theory. Its significance for the future will be reflected in the growing dialectic between those who seek an explanation in Marxist analysis and those who propound a dysfunctionalist-cum-racial interpretation. Whatever the outcome of these analyses, some modern forms of matriarchy are features of the social organization of poverty and are good indicators of economic marginalization. Consequently, a study of the conditions of the majority of black women is important in understanding economic problems and their effects on the poor. The experience of the suffering of the majority of black women and their struggle for survival will clearly become more relevant for humanity as the worsening economic conditions produce similar states of poverty in other groups previously unaffected by economic hardship.

The relevance of the women's movement to black women has been a controversial topic. In my view, since sexism exists in the black community as well, sexism is relevant to the black woman, although some aspects of its analysis can best be conducted within a framework of what I term 'intraethnic feminism' —that is, within the black groups' experience. However, by studying the black woman cross-culturally we become more aware of the complex nature of oppression. The experiences of the majority of black women represent multiple forms of oppression rather than simple sexual oppression. Race and class are important variables in her experience and are significantly more important barriers to the acquisition of the basic needs for survival than is sexism.

Recognition of the operation of racism and class is important in preventing false polarizations between men and women. Rather than seeing men as the universal oppressor, women will also be seen as partners in oppression and as having the potential of becoming primary oppressors themselves. Above all, by studying the black woman we can avoid isolating sexism from the larger political and economic forces operating in many societies to produce internal colonialism, neocolonialism and economic dependency—all of which affect *both* men and women in Africa, the Caribbean, South American and the impoverished sections of the United States.

Women's studies have raised a whole set of issues concerning the ' male bias ' in our stock of knowledge. These have collided with similar challenges about research imperialism from members of Third World groups, both in the Third World and in the United States. Black scholars in particular have unmasked the middle class and oftentimes 'white' mind set which have informed a number of studies of the black family and black social life. By studying the black woman cross-culturally this bias can better be perceived as cultural than being one of gender per se. Regardless of sexual affiliation, a researcher cannot really escape the ideological and cultural influences that are contributory factors in the formulation of concepts, value orientations, and methodologies. Realizing this, I have sought to include articles by black women and men, and the majority of the papers presented here are by black authors.

A black identity is important for blacks from both political and economic standpoints, and becomes a *sine qua non* for the liberation of all blacks oppressed for reasons of their race. Consequently, a cross-cultural review of black women is in keeping with the concept of the African diaspora which provides a framework for black unity. Black consciousness will continue to reproduce itself, partly as a result of oppression, but also as a reflection of black pride. Movements such as Garveyism, the Négritude movement, Pan-Africanism, and to some extent Rastafarianism will rise to challenge racism—mankind's most persistent and stubborn form of prejudice. Its most extreme form, apartheid, will always provide a unifying focus for blacks.

Some personal factors also influenced the editing of this book. I am black and African, and identify strongly with black oppression throughout the world. My personal detestation of racism stems from the fact that it has demoralized not only the black victims, but also the whole human race.

Finally, a book such as this is of value also in a practical way. It can provide a handy text to be used for Afro-American studies, African studies, and women's studies. The book is intended not only for students but also for social scientists and for lay people. A comprehensive bibliography with useful references on the subject has been included.

Several people have influenced the editing of this book in different ways. Notable among them are Dr. Bolanle Awe, Dr. Niara Sudarkasa, Dr. Achola Pala Okeyo, Dr. Irene V. Jackson-Brown and prize-winning author June Jordan. To all these outstanding black women I offer my deep gratitude. One wonderful black man, my husband, has been a continuous source of support and inspiration in my work. He alone knows the gratification realized and the frustrations encountered in the writing and editing of this book, and in a very personal way I thank him for his help, encouragement and devotion. I would also like to thank Ms. Rosetta Young of Wesleyan University for typing sections of the manuscript, and Ms. Lisa Lipshires and Ms. Emily Hunt of Schenkman Publishing Company for their editorial assistance.

Proceeds from the royalties of this book will be donated to the United Negro College Fund for the establishment of a scholarship fund for black women, and to the Association of African Women for Research and Development (AAWORD) to promote indigenous research collaboration of African women researchers.

Woman on her way to do her laundry in a nearby stream in Bobo-Dioulasso, Upper Volta. Photo: United Nations, No. 104,579. (1967)

The Black Woman Cross-Culturally: An Overview

Filomina Chioma Steady

Male chauvinists come in all colors but ...

This pioneering volume is an attempt to present a cross-cultural view of the black woman. From the available literature it is readily apparent that the black woman, within a cross-cultural perspective, represents much diversity in terms of nationality, class affiliation, generational differences, and particular historical experience. The aim of this book is not to present a uniform profile or elicit a monolithic image but to discuss common themes which can be considered significant in the experience of the majority of black women in various parts of the world. These themes have been elucidated from discussions of the black woman's position in traditional, historical, and contemporary society and are reflected in the chapters presented here. The importance of the black woman in the understanding of changing sex roles, racial and economic exploitation, human survival and the development of a self-reliant feminism are also discussed. Although some black women belong to the middle class and a few have achieved national and international prominence, these are the exceptions. Consequently, the book focuses on the majority of black women who generally live in rural or depressed urban areas, have a low income and are more severely victimized by economic and racial oppression. In this overview, I have tried to integrate the ideas presented in the various articles into a number of recurring and related themes. I consider these themes to be of critical importance in the lives of the majority of black women when viewed from a cross-cultural perspective.

AFRICAN HERITAGE

The primary unifying theme of the black women in this anthology is their common African heritage. The studies presented are of black women on the African continent and in the African diaspora, notably the Caribbean, South America and the United States of America. Some of the articles, particularly those by Ladner, Staples, Jackson, and Mintz reflect this diasporic theme. Black women in Europe, particularly in Great Britain, no doubt share some experiences similar to those presented here, but have not been included in this anthology mainly because the majority of them represent second stage migrations rather than the primary and major dispersal of Africans through slavery. Furthermore, very few studies exist of the black woman in Europe, although Emecheta's novel *Second-Class Citizen* is written with such consumate skill that it poignantly portrays the black woman's experience in England. A number of studies can be found of immigrant groups in Britain,[1] but these are mainly studies of communities and families rather than of the black woman *per se*. Similarly, in the case of South America studies of the black woman are strikingly rare, and when available are often in a language other than English.[2]

ECONOMIC EXPLOITATION AND MARGINALIZATION

The second unifying theme is that of economic exploitation and marginalization manifested historically through slavery and colonialism, and at the present time through neocolonialism in Africa, the Caribbean and South America and 'internal colonialism' in the United States. The single most important factor in the dynamics of the African dispersal was the slave trade. Over a period of four hundred years about fifteen to twenty million Africans were shipped regularly across the Atlantic Ocean to work as slaves in the Americas and, to a lesser extent, in Europe. When, during the nineteenth century, it was no longer profitable for some countries to have slaves, the slave trade was abolished, first by Denmark, then Britain followed by the United States. Portugal and Spain continued until the eighteen-sixties to import slaves to work on the plantations in Brazil and Cuba.[3] The majority of black women in the diaspora are descended from black women brought from Africa as slaves.

The black woman from Africa became a key factor in the production of capital because of her capacity to reproduce slave labor. Closely linked with economic exploitation is sexual exploitation, rampant during slavery, and evident today in various forms ranging from sexual harassment to the use of prostitution as a means of survival in depressed urban areas. Other versions of economic and sexual exploitation of the black woman are apparent in certain types of tourist activities in the Caribbean and in Africa that encourage prostitution. Some of these activities in Africa are controlled and operated from Europe for tourists notably from the Scandinavian countries and Germany.

The sexual exploitation of the black woman during slavery which is well documented, gave rise to much resistance as discussed in the chapter by Hine and Wittenstein. No doubt it also stimulated some female consciousness-raising, not only for the black woman but also for the white woman to whom these acts must have posed a threat. According to one writer, the white man's lust for the black woman was one of the most serious impediments to the development of morality during slavery.[4] It is interesting to note here a well-known fact that the feminist movement of the nineteenth century in the United States developed from the abolition movement. How much more effective it would have been had the movement developed across racial lines and challenged the economic system (the very root of female exploitation) in its infancy. Instead, racial discrimination was widely practiced in the women's move ment as Terborg-Penn's chapter clearly points out.

The slave trade was only the beginning of a complex system which led to direct colonization of Africa and the survival of colonialism through economic dependency. Some pertinent theories of underdevelopment have shown how colonialism and neocolonialism led to the underdevelopment of Africa.[5] There is no need for elaboration here but a brief commentary is in order. Through colonization by European nations (notably Britain, France, Belgium, and Portugal) Africa was brought into the world economic system. It became a reservoir from which surplus was drawn in the form of raw materials, food crops, mineral resources and cheap labor. In this process a number of traditional institutions were destroyed, some of which had guaranteed women greater political participation and higher status. Aidoo's chapter on Asante Queen mothers examines this important executive role of women in nineteenth-century Asante society. Okonjo discusses some of the deleterious effects of colonialism on the political participation of African women which was guaranteed in precolonial society. Not surprisingly, African women were active in resisting colonialism in a number of ways, and played an important role in the movements for independence from colonial rule.[6] Urdang's study chronicles women's role in this struggle in Guinea-Bissau, formerly a Portuguese colony. One aftermath of independence is depicted by Ladner in her study of women's role in nation building in Tanzania.

Under colonialism several new institutions were set up, mainly for moving goods to and from the colonies. These included colonial trading companies, shipping companies and banks. Of crucial importance for the success of these economic operations was the existence of a conducive political climate. This was made possible by the colonial administration and its military and policing machinery. Not only did these institutions guarantee optimum conditions under which private companies could exploit African resources, they also imposed a system of taxation whereby the colonial administrative structure could be maintained. The African economy has therefore functioned essentially to develop countries outside of Africa and to make profits for people who belong primarily to the Caucasian race. The aftermath of colonial administration was political independence, but economic dependence continues in full force and links both men and women in dependency relationships to the main European and American metropolitan cities of central capital.

The question of women's status relative to their participation in production has been studied as early as 1891 by Engels and more recently by several scholars, notably Leacock and Sacks.[7] Central to this whole issue and to the recent studies of sex roles from various perspectives and paradigms is the attempt to arrive at an understanding of the sexual division of labor in its various economic, social, cultural and ideological dimensions.[8] Taking into account the complex conceptual problems surrounding the term 'egalitarianism' one can accept that, in general, there is greater sexual egalitarianism in societies where gathering, hunting, and horticulture are the main economic activities. Serious problems of inequality occur when a capitalist mode of production is imposed on these societies as part of the process of incorporation of peasants into a market economy.

Historical processes which integrated Africa into the world economic system upset the balance in the sexual division of labor which had given women in traditional societies a great deal of autonomy and independence. The chapter by Sudarkasa examines different aspects of this autonomy in precapitalist African societies. Since all societies in Africa have been influenced in varying degrees by the capitalist mode of production, it is necessary to understand its total effect on women's roles and work. The unequal relations to production which developed were manifest in the sexual division of labor. This process is not unique to Africa and is being replicated in many parts of the underdeveloped world. Rubbo's chapter is a study of the effects of capitalism on poor black women in Colombia.

With regard to the question of labor output in agricultural production and its relation to the sexual division of labor, women's labor output in subsistence farming in Africa far surpasses that of men. A United Nations Economic Commission for Africa study estimated that women comprise 60 to 80 percent of the labor force in African agriculture.[9] In most cases the new organization of the means of production reinforced existing patterns of division of labor along sexual lines, but with differential value being given to women's work. Traditionally, in Africa, both male and female labor was necessary in food production. Communal ownership of the means of production assures the woman a certain degree of control over her labor and some decision-making power relative to her labor input. The sexual division of labor was essentially along parallel rather than hierarchical lines, thereby giving, in general terms, equal value to male and female labor.

The growth and processes of capitalist modes of production and the concomitant value orientations resulted in the reinforcement of patriarchal systems in which command of women's labor and children's labor became absolutely essential. Through this command a hierarchy developed in the labor processes which led to different values being placed on male and female labor. With wage labor, unlike subsistence agriculture, the production unit became the individual rather than the family. The market's demand for wage labor was primarily for male labor, consequently male labor was given an 'exchange value' whereas female labor was given a 'use value.' The labor shortages in agricultural production, resulting from the demands of male wage labor, and new skills that led to the migration of the young, were remedied by women. This led, in many instances, to the feminization of the labor force in subsistence agricultural production. In the final analysis the use value of female labor is a necessary concomitant of capital development, since it subsidized male labor, increased profits for owners of the means of production, and contributed to greater capital accumulation.

These processes also led to the decline of indigenous systems of production, with serious nutritional consequences. Through the use of forced labor initially, and by seizing land for cash crops, colonial powers developed plantation systems. In addition, family-based cash crop production of necessity developed, and because of the taxes imposed on Africans a system of wage labor also developed. Other methods involved the use of the best land for cash-crop production and the deliberate importing of food crops so as to compete with local production, as in the case of Senegal where rice was imported. There were several deleterious effects on women, namely the reduction in some cases of women's rights to land, a greater increase in women's workload, the imposition of a wage system which excluded women, and the cultivation of commercial crops primarily by men. These processes continue until the present day and have far-reaching consequences, not only in terms of women's roles in production, but also with regard to nutrition.[10]

The critical issue with regard to the African situation, therefore, is not so much which sex is growing what crop but the danger of food shortages, given the greater emphasis on cash crop production. Malnutrition and undernutrition are grave problems in many parts of Africa and in depressed areas of the Caribbean, South America and the United States. A large percentage of the 1.3 billion people who, according to one estimate,[11] are short of calories and suffer from malnutrition, are black. Women and children are particularly vulnerable. Since malnutrition increases the risk of infection, serious problems of collective ill health are created for many blacks who live in situations of poor environmental sanitation, have inadequate housing and water supply, and are exposed to infectious diseases.

Other manifestations of these processes of economic marginali- zation can be seen in the study of the internal marketing system in urban areas and the precariousness of such marketing activities when dominated by powerful world economic forces. The precar- ious nature of the internal marketing system is a feature of under- development which undermines local efforts, as discussed in part by Simms in her study of women entrepreneurs in Africa. The African situation is somewhat parallel to other areas in the diaspora. One study has examined this phenomenon in Haiti by analyzing the employment of scarce capital among Haitian women traders within the constraints of a precarious internal marketing system.[12]

The processes of marginalization of the poor, especially women, reflect the nature of underdevelopment in these countries as out- lined in Pala's chapter on African women and devlopment. An unequal dual economic system inevitably develops which favors the modern urban sector at the expense of the traditional rural sector. Additionally, within the modern sector there exists formal and informal labor markets. The unemployed and recently arrived immigrants to the city become absorbed in the informal labor market and eke out a living as hawkers, domestics, prostitutes, etc. Some of the contributions, most notably that by Gugler, examine the problems of urbanization and job scarcity for African women.

Through what has been termed 'internal colonialism' in the United States a similar process of economic marginalization takes place and adversely affects poor, urban, black women. Institutional racism in the United States further aggravates the problem for black women. A number of authors in this volume, notably Ladner, Stack, Staples, and French, address the issue of the multiple effects of poverty, economic exploitation and institutional racism on the lives of black families, and especially of black women, in the United States. French's chapter in particular shows institutional racism in its extreme manifestation in prisons where black women become less than third-class citizens.

NEGATIVE LITERARY IMAGES

Closely linked to the theme of economic exploitation and marginali- zation is the projection in literature of negative stereotypes of the black woman. In the United States, with the exception of Afro- American literature which according to Rushing has presented some positive images focussing on the moral, intellectual and political aspects, the most common stereotypes of black woman are the 'mammy', the 'matriarch', the 'tragic mulatto' and the 'sensuous whore'.[13] Very often these images are presented by males from other racial groups. The image of the black woman as a sensuous sex object was not uncommon in the works of Faulkner.[14]

Nunes' chapter discusses the obsession of Brazilian male writers with the sexuality of the woman of color, and sees this as an expression of exploitation. Since the black woman is marginal in Brazilian society she lacks the protection that comes from being of a higher socioeconomic class. Latortue's study shows how in nineteenth and early twentieth century Haitian literature, the Haitian woman was seen as a sex object closely related to nature.

In the African context female sexuality has been used as an index of social change. One study has examined the image of African women as portrayed mainly by male writers.[15] It shows how in the traditional context very little emphasis is given to the African woman's sexuality. The focus is generally on women's role in the family, the issue of polygamy versus monogamy, and the importance of children. Women's sexuality characterized by loose morals, surfaces more in the cities, and is often a result of rapid social change. The image of the prostitute or mistress is centrally projected. Career women on the other hand become the tragic heroines, often doomed to psychological and familial problems, and are likely to end up victims of suicide. The fact that these images are presented within the context of social change indicates a breakdown is social control which regulated the sexual behavior of men and women in traditional society.

The obsession with female sexuality by male writers is not unique to the black woman. What is unique is the fact that by presenting the black woman as a sensuous whore, her sexuality can be exploited with justification. Undoubtedly, the image of the black woman as sex object is linked to her sexual exploitation, but what is of utmost importance is her fertility, which is seen at one and the same time as profitable and threatening, and is nearly always subject to manipulation.

The manipulation of the fertility of the black woman is a good indicator of her exploitation. During slavery her fertility was highly valued, since it was necessary to reproduce slave labor. A young slave woman of childbearing age was valuable property, and one of her selling points was her 'breeding' potential. Today the reverse is the case. Slave labor is no longer needed to create wealth. Furthermore, the trend is towards capital-intensive rather than labor-intensive industrialization which may likely one day render labor—even cheap labor—obsolete. Consequently, the fertility of the black woman, though still necessary to produce cheap labor, is increasingly viewed as unprofitable and from a racist perspective as threatening. The emphasis on the contraceptive aspects of family planning in the Third World is one outcome of the desire to control black fertility. Many Europeans seek to promote fertility in their own countries. At the same time a number of aid-related programs from European and American countries, dealing with health, women's issues and nutrition, discreetly aim at reducing the population growth of the Third World, particularly of the black race. The black woman then, whether in Africa, the Caribbean or the United States, has been a main target of most family-planning programs. Some of these programs are aggressively carried out and include sterilization without informed consent. The image of the black woman as a sensuous whore becomes fused with the image of the black woman as prolific breeder.

SELF-RELIANCE AS A NECESSARY IDEOLOGY

The theme of self-reliance as an ideology common in the experience of the black woman varies according to the economic context. In some situations, where the economic infrastructure supports this ideology and provides certain safeguards for women, the effects have been positive. In other contexts the economic infrastructure works against this ideology and produces economic marginalization of black women with correspondingly negative results.

Traditional African societies by their very structure encouraged the development of self-reliance among women. This is particularly marked in the pivotal role women play in the traditional economy regardless of the mode of obtaining a livelihood. It is customary for women in Africa to make an economic contribution to the family or household. Implicit in this self-reliant ideology is the reliance of others on women. Horticulture and agriculture are the predominant economic activities in Africa in which the role of women is paramount.[16] Since from all available evidence women spend more time on agricultural activities than men, women not only develop an ideology of self-reliance but can be said to have 'food power' in that they make certain decisions with regard to food production, processing and distribution.[17] In most countries women own the food crops they produce. Consequently, decisions about the disposal of food, especially in terms of family consumption, are essentially theirs. These decisions give women some degree of autonomy and leverage in terms of their relationship with men. Patterns of resistance and protest against males have often taken the form of refusal to feed men. Ousmane Sembène, the Senegalese filmmaker, is quite outstanding in capturing this element of 'food power' which African women possess. In the film *Emitai* he shows how Senegalese women resisted the French order to give up to the soldiers the supply of rice which they, the women, had grown and harvested. In another film, *Mandabi*, the wives of the protagonists refused to give away the last bag of rice even though the husband had ordered them to do so. Pala has pointed out that women may refuse to work on a crop if they receive no share of the income from it. 'In situations where a cash crop like cotton competes for labor with food crops, women will tend to neglect work on the cash crop until work on the food crop is finished. Thus late weeding and failure to apply fertilizers have caused a reduction in cotton yields from time to time.'[18]

Some African traditional institutions facilitated the development of a self-reliant ideology among women. Ironically polygyny, viewed from some perspectives as oppressive to women, in many ways contributed to the development of this ideology. Polygyny, an institution which is on the decline, is the traditional form of marriage in many African societies. Its function is essentially economic. Traditionally, land was communally owned and distributed according to the ability of a man to farm a certain area. Polygyny increased the number of wives and also the potential of having large numbers of children to work on the farm. In theory a man divided his time equally among his wives, and the basic unit comprised a mother and her children. Patriarchal authority in polygynous families, unlike monogamous families, could therefore be regarded as 'limited' rather than 'absolute,' since it could not be exercised over all women on a continuous basis, and men could be viewed as peripheral to each wife/child unit. In fact the double standard of morality characteristic of monogamous marriages was not the rule. It was quite acceptable in many societies for women in polygynous households to have lovers. Social organization being communal, rather than composed of nuclear family units, ensured a certain amount of socioeconomic security and cooperation among members of the polygynous household. Polygyny also guaranteed the social and economic responsibility of males for their children. As a result women did not have to struggle for their survival or bear the sole responsibility for their children's care, but could at the same time have a certain amount of independence from absolute male dominance.

Matrilineal societies also provide good examples of the development of an infrastructure which makes female self-reliance a positive ideology. These societies exist in many parts of Africa and encourage greater self-support among women and female kin. In these societies the mother is the central figure in kinship, family and household organization, since descent is traced through women. The Asante of Ghana are a good example of a matrilineal society. Marriage bonds are generally weak and the husband can be regarded as having limited authority in the household. Males who are members of the matrilineage are, however, very important as agents of socialization of their sister's children and as guardians of their sister's property. Indeed it can be said that in matrilineal societies males exist to ensure the continuity of the matrilineage.

In the absence of a conducive economic infrastructure female self-reliance has had negative effects. This is particularly true of situations where the larger socioeconomic structure creates chronic unemployment among black males, and fosters male absenteeism through male migration and seasonal migration. In these instances self-reliance has produced a hardship effect on women who have had to take on additional burdens in meeting subsistence needs under conditions of extreme poverty, and have had to assume the sole responsibility for their children. These developments reflect consequences of economic changes which continue to marginalize the poor, especially blacks, erode family ties and render the black family a cheap source of labor. In these instances female self-reliance becomes synonymous with male peripherality.

Some of these processes date back to slavery, a system that ensured the maximum exploitation of black labor. The preservation of the unity of the slave family had low priority, and males were peripheral to the family unit. The stability of the black family was continually threatened because of the frequency of separation of husbands and wives. Although monogamous marriage was stressed the father could be sold off at any time. Moreover, the father's peripherality was institutionalized by the slave system under which he had no status and was regarded as the property of his master. Family life, though valued, was precarious, and slave biographies profusely and resentfully recount the separation of family members.[19]

Male peripherality during slavery was also marked in Maroon societies which were rebel communities set up as a result of flight from slavery, or 'maroonage.' These communities existed throughout the areas of the New World where slavery was practised. They were constantly under attack, and defense was given the highest priority. Men had to be free to defend their territory, and therefore became peripheral to the household with women and children forming the core. Bilby and Steady discuss the importance of women in the survival of Maroon societies.

A new type of male peripherality producing a hardship effect on women is a result of the economic changes taking place in Africa. As stated earlier, in many traditional African societies men and women were important in agricultural production. Changes in the mode of production altered the sexual relations of production, and the introduction of wage labor for males led to male employment and male migration to urban areas. Male migration and seasonal employment, in many cases, led not only to male peripherality for long periods, but to the complete breakdown of the family or household unit.

Today in many African countries, because of the rapid rate of rural-urban migration of both men and women, family life is undergoing tremendous transformation. The acceleration of urban growth and rural decay is a result of the unequal development of a modern sector (urban) at the expense of the traditional sector (rural). This pattern of urban growth is not in response to labor demands of the city and, as a result, the cities cannot absorb the large influx of migrants. Unemployment rates are high, and many of the migrants and urban poor live in slum areas that are increasing in size. Female-headed households are growing in number, and men are becoming increasingly peripheral to family and household units.[20]

South Africa, through its policy of apartheid, provides the most extreme example of male peripherality among black families. Through a pass system migration to urban areas is strictly controlled. Men who migrate to work in the mines and in other industrial complexes are often not permitted to bring their families with them. Women, children, and the old are left behind in the 'homelands.' Long periods of separation of family members inevitably lead to the breakdown of the family. The imposition of the Bantustans can be seen as reinforcing male peripherality. The chapter by Rivkin provides some examples of the oppressive conditions of black women under the system of apartheid in South Africa, and Lapchick's chapter examines various mechanisms used by women in their struggles against apartheid. One study has dealt specifically with the effect of male migration on black women in South Africa and poignantly illustrates the adjustment of black women to male absenteeism.[21]

Male peripherality in the Caribbean and the United States, as in African societies undergoing industrialization, is also the result of economic marginalization and imposed poverty. Even when the ideology is one of male dominance as in Montserrat, according to the study by Moses, men are peripheral to the family unit because of their inability to obtain employment. Sutton and Makiesky-Barrow mention some of these aspects of male peripherality in Barbados.

In the Caribbean the occurrence of female-headed households, the dispersal of members of a nuclear family in different residential units, and the incidence of concubinage have all been shown to occur particularly in low income families. So widespread are these patterns in the West Indies that Solien, in this volume, has offered some useful definitions of the family and household in the West Indian context. The chapter by Justus discusses the issue of matrifocality in the West Indies, and some of the chapters on the black woman in the United States, notably those by Staples and Ladner, examine the controversial thesis of the black matriarchy. All of these authors challenge the thesis of the black matriarchy in a number of ways but essentially for its simplistic stance in 'blaming the victim'.[22] Clearly, a feature which is characteristic of one of the poorest groups in a society must have its raison d'être in the structural bases of the economic relations in that society.

Because of the high rates of unemployment among black males in the United States black women, the majority of whom are poor, have often lacked the economic support which the society delegates to males. These women for their survival have had to develop a greater reliance on their own resources and on the resources of women in similar situations, as the chapter by Stack points out. The black female-headed household ultimately serves a very important economic function, namely, the reproduction of cheap labor. Meanwhile the state provides her with a surrogate husband, i.e., 'Welfare,' who jealously guards and ensures her permanent dependency on the state. One writer states the problem as follows:

> There is nothing wrong with being a black single parent . . . But there is something wrong with why a black woman is so much more likely to experience the single-parent situation, why one race can freely imprison, send off to military duty, unemploy, underemploy and otherwise destroy the oppressed black woman's eligible male supply.[23]

CREATION OF SURVIVAL IMPERATIVES

Black women have consistently had to ensure not only their economic, political and social survival, but their physical survival as well. Because of poverty, racial and sexual discrimination and a generally low status in society, most black women are constantly exposed to health hazards. As a result black women generally have a lower life expectancy than white women. Many women in Africa die before reaching their forty-fifth birthday.[24] In the United States the life expectancy of black women is lower than that of white women.[25] Black women also suffer child loss more frequently than white women. In Africa the mean infant mortality rate is 147 per thousand live births.[26] In the United States there is a higher mortality rate for black infants than for white infants.[27]

Factors which contribute to poor health, such as inadequate housing, lack of access to health care facilities, inadequate nutrition, and poor environmental sanitation, are characteristic of the living conditions of the majority of black women. Chronic anxiety, despair and desperation are likely to result from the life of hardship that most black women face. The work patterns of black women, involving long hours of hard physical labor and back-breaking tasks, particularly in the rural areas of Africa, create tremendous risks to their health. Women in these rural areas walk to the farms, plant, weed, harvest, fetch firewood and water, pound grains, and constantly perform a number of strenuous tasks. As much as eight to ten hours a day may be spent on back-breaking tasks without the nutritional intake commensurate with the energy expended.[28] The majority of black working women in the United States perform tasks involving heavy physical output in the lower ranks of service professions and as domestics and washerwomen.[29]

Black women are also more prone than white women to hypertension and sickle cell anemia, both of which can lead to complications during pregnancy. Infertility and pregnancy wastage are serious problems in many parts of Africa.[30] In spite of this wastage of black lives, black women have been the targets of aggressive population control activities. The health of black women and children is increasingly being jeopardized through activities involved in the transfer of technology. Black women are among Third World women used in experimentation with new contraceptives. Black infants are more likely than white infants to die as victims of marasmus, an extreme form of malnutrition often resulting from the early abandonment of breastfeeding. The role of the infant food industry in seducing women in the Third World into adopting bottle feeding, through aggressive and unethical promotional activities, is well known. Furthermore, if the attempt by Western industries to dump industrial waste products in Africa succeeds, the black woman is likely to become the most vulnerable victim.[31]

In order to ensure their physical survival black women have had to develop survival imperatives, one of which is the provision of health care. During slavery black women performed healing roles, including midwifery. This is also true of Africa, the Caribbean and South America where women traditionally provide primary health care services and deliver babies. During slavery infections diseases and gynecological problems were prevalent, and black women had to rely on a number of home remedies for survival. Some of this knowledge, particularly of medicinal herbs, was derived from Africa.[32]

Black women have had to rely on their own resources and to be ingenious with the meager resources at their command in order to survive in other ways as well. According to one study, rural women in Kenya generally experiment with different varieties until they produce a successful crop.[33] In another context a study of Haitian market women shows how, in a situation where capital is scarce, women substitute labor for capital and utilize a whole range of traditional institutions and social networks for economic survival.[34] The survival of Maroon societies depended to a large extent on the creative responses of women who, with their children, formed the core of Maroon societies as Bilby and Steady point out in this volume.

The chapter by Mintz examines the cultural tradition of trading among women in Afro-Caribbean societies which gave women a great deal of independence and autonomy, and enabled them to survive economically after emancipation. Justus shows how the relations among females in the West Indies are emphasized and highly prized, and how group solidarity and sharing among women are important survival imperatives. Rubbo points out that the change in the mode of economic production works to the disadvantage of Colombian women, who lose their economic independence while retaining sole responsibility for raising their children. Stack provides a study of survival strategies among black urban women in the United States who are faced with chronic male unemployment, male marginality, and poverty. Economic resources are increasingly controlled by women, thereby enhancing the precarious domestic network, and the sad and demoralizing welfare system. Irene Jackson looks at the creativity of black women as expressed in music, and discusses how music has been used by black women for cathartic purposes. She also contends that black women are the essential bearers of certain musical traditions. The chapter by Jules-Rosette is a study of the role of women in indigenous African cults and churches as creative responses to urbanization.

The dichotomy between the public (male) and private (female) spheres has been offered as an explanation of the subordinate position of women.[35] However, Sudarkasa argues that in precapitalist societies in West Africa this dichotomy did not correspond to masculine and feminine domains. It can also be argued that in societies where survival is crucial, as in many black societies, the exigencies of survival transcend the need for dichotomies between the public and private spheres. This was particularly true of slavery and the subsequent development of Barbados' society as Sutton and

Makiesky-Barrow indicate. In the United States, men were depicted in slave narratives as performing roles of cooking, serving and child-rearing. As Perkins points out, the disenfranchisement and oppression of all blacks during slavery left little room for male chauvinism. One study has observed that during slavery men and women were equal both in production outside the household context and also 'under the whip.' [36]

Black women can and do participate in the public sphere often as cheap sources of labor. Correspondingly, men's inability to maintain their spouses as 'housewives' can necessitate their involvement in the private sphere. Also, the failure of males to secure employment in urban areas would naturally reduce their capabilities to participate effectively in the public sphere. The dichotomy between the private and public spheres and the corresponding association with feminine and masculine domains is, therefore, a "luxury" more characteristic of white middle-class family structures.

A LESS ANTAGONISTIC 'FEMINISM'

Black women generally portray a less antagonistic brand of feminism. Some, in fact, feel quite alienated from the women's movement, as Reid shows in 'Together' Black Women. [37] There are several reasons for this, some of which are discussed in this volume, particularly by Staples and Ladner.

Regardless of one's position, the implications of the feminist movement for the black woman are complex. Within the framework of what can be regarded as a universal feminism, black women share similar problems with other women. These are problems that fall within the sphere of discrimination against women. Problems surrounding the roles of childbearing, women's health and nutritional status, and female participation in the labor force, have not been satisfactorily resolved in many parts of the world. Additionally, numerous injurious practices such as wife-beating, rape, female circumcision, sexual harrasment, and forced marriage exist in many societies. [38] These problems have inspired a number of United Nations declarations and actions, so that they are now fairly well recognized as global problems. Above all, sexism can be manifested in various forms, and male chauvinists *do* come in all colors.

However, several factors set the black woman apart as having a different order of priorities. She is oppressed not simply because of her sex but ostensibly because of her race and, for the majority, essentially because of their class. Women belong to different socio-economic groups and do not represent a universal category. Because the majority of black women are poor, there is likely to be some alienation from the middle-class aspect of the women's movement which perceives feminism as an attack on men rather than on a system which thrives on inequality. Bourgeois feminism fails to deal with the major problem of equitable distribution of resources to all socioeconomic groups. Such an approach leads to a concentration of energies on sexual symbolism rather than on more substantive economic realities.

It is not surprising, therefore, that, despite claims about similarities between the black civil rights movement and the women's movement, many black women in the United States do not seem to support the priorities of the women's movement. Ladner, for instance, feels that the black woman's vision of liberation transcends the relatively narrow, white, middle-class female goals of equalization of sex roles, and insists that all of the energies and resources of black males and females are necessary to obliterate institutional racism.

> Black women do not perceive their enemy to be black men, but rather the enemy is considered to be oppressive forces in the larger society which subjugate black men, women and children.[39]

Similarly, Reid's study of black women[40] concludes that, despite the generalized praise for women's liberation efforts, few women in her study sample saw a valid connection between the elimination of sexism and the cessation of racism. 'Even if sex discrimination were eliminated, most of the women concluded the demise of race discrimination would not necessarily follow.'[41]

In discussing the 'feminist literature' and its relevance to black women, Cade raises the following questions: 'How relevant are the truths, the experiences, the findings of white women to black women? Are women, after all simply women? I do not know that our priorities are the same, that our concerns and methods are the same, or even similar enough so that we can afford to deal with this new field of experts (white, female).'[42] Even Wallace, who comes closest to the movement's line of reasoning, deals intensely with the civil rights issues rather with women's issues per se.[43] Some black women, in fact, have had to ensure that black women's contributions and triumphs to American life receive their proper recognition. The very title of Noble's book, *Beautiful, also, are the Souls of my Black Sisters*, bears this message.

The women's movement in the West has displayed, in some instances, a neocolonialist aspect by producing a group of women who seek to dominate or become patrons and mouthpieces for Third World women. Development experts working in the field of foreign aid have become the new missionaries of Africa. More often than not their research and development policies are externally derived and top-heavy with highly salaried foreign 'experts'. They have little or no impact on the lives of the poor people they claim to help, and in every respect their activities can be regarded as new types of colonialism and business enterprises. Aid business perpetuates dependency relations; and certain academic activities, including research on ' integrating women into development ', can be seen as integral components of aid business. Pala's chapter deals with the role of research, inspired by feminism within the dependency context of African societies, and outlines their constraints on development for the African woman. In the United States there appears to be an attempt by the women's movement to co-opt the black consciousness painfully raised prior to and during the civil rights movement of the sixties. A movement which claims to fight for women's rights but fails to deal with the exigent needs of the black woman in a racist society is not a movement in the best interests of black women.

Finally, the most unattractive feature of the women's movement is its missionary aspect. Women of the Third World and in Third World communities in the United States find this feature patronizing at best, and at times insulting, especially when this brand of feminism has emerged from an economic system which defines the relationship of men and women to the means of production as unequal. In this system, masculine values have been given to spheres which have monopolies over economic and political power. Characteristics such as competitiveness, selfishness, and rugged individualism are great assets. Women feminists in this context are uncritical emulators of these features, and seek integration into a system based on inequality. The fact that alternative systems exist which recognize other loci of power, authority, and rewards, are often overlooked. This male-dominated system is being transmitted to many areas of the Third World through the transfer of technology, etc., but whether it will develop into the full-blown version best exemplified in the United States is still uncertain. Hopefully, the type of male-dominated system which has its basis in the evolution of the modern capitalist state, in organized religion, and in the commercialization of the female body, will have a less controlling influence in many Third World countries. Becoming westernized is not a necessary precondition for female emancipation. On the contrary, one consequence of this system is the subordination of women and the denigration of the female body. One study of male/female dynamics in a muslim society summarizes the Western woman's dilemma.

> One of the main obstacles Western women have been dealing with is their society's view of women as inferior beings. The fact that generations of university-educated women in both Europe and America failed to win access to decision-making is partly due to the deeply ingrained image of women as inferior.[44]

RACISM, SEXISM, AND CLASS

In the final analysis, the issue of black women's oppression and racism are part of the ' class issue ', but there is a danger of subsuming the black woman's continued oppression to class and class alone. For even within the same class there are groups that are more oppressed than others. Blacks are likely to experience hardship and discrimination more severely and consistently than whites, because of racism. In fact, there is a sense in which the white working classes in the United States and South Africa can be regarded as a 'labor aristocracy' when compared with the black working class. In general, it can be argued that the subordinate position of women is attributed largely to the unequal relations to production that capitalism fosters. The condition of black oppression in America is also related to capitalism. Beale feels that with regard to the question of women's liberation, capitalism must be seen as the enemy to both black and white women alike.

> If the white groups do not realize that they are, in fact, fighting capitalism and racism, we do not have common bonds.[45]

Without any doubt there is a great potential for class alignments through the struggle for women's liberation, but this alliance cannot be forged as long as women belong to different social classes and transmit their class identities to their children through socialization. The fact is that the majority of black women belong to the working class and, given the history of blacks, race has been and continues to be an important factor in the oppression of blacks.

In considering the interaction between racism and class, therefore, it can be argued that the Marxist analysis has failed to deal adequately with the racial question. Theoretically, the black/white variety of racism can be seen as a feature of capitalism, but racism remains the most stubborn and persistent form of oppression, with apartheid as its most extreme manifestation. With the exception of Cuba, many socialist and socialist-inspired countries cannot be declared free of racism. As for self-avowed Marxists in the West, I personally know many who are outright racists. Racism has been a serious obstacle in the development of class alignments. Racism is no accident but part of a systematic process used to ensure that certain phenotypically distinct members of the population never achieve equality with the rest. Highly visible factors, such as racial differences, make for greater expediency in the execution of the rules of inequality. Affirmative action is only a palliative used in an attempt to contain the internal contradictions inherent in systems that thrive on the maintenance of a permanent underclass.

Racism, sexism, and class are manifestations of systems that oppress. As part of the syndrome of inequality, polarizations and hostilities develop along lines of race, sex and class. The significance of racism, sexism and class for the majority of black women is that *they* can experience all three types of oppression.

In discussing problems of racism and sexism as they apply to the black woman, several conceptual difficulties are bound to become apparent, regardless of the unit of analysis used. 'Women' as units of analysis can be shown to perform certain sex-specific roles which may limit their full participation in the political and economic spheres of society. Moreover, regardless of the nature of the roles played by men and women, there exist, in many societies, tensions between the sexes as well as sexual discrimination and oppression. However, racial discrimination and oppression are problems of a different order, for the maintenance of racial privilege by one group implicitly establishes a bond between males and females of the privileged group. For the black woman in a racist society, racial factors, rather than sexual ones, operate more consistently in making her a target for discrimination and marginalization. This becomes apparent when the 'family' is viewed as a unit of analysis. Regardless of differential access to resources by both men and women, white males and females, as members of family groups, share a proportionately higher quantity of the earth's resources than do black males and females. There is a great difference between discrimination by privilege and protection, and discrimination by deprivation and exclusion.

AN AFRICAN BRAND OF FEMINISM

The problem with Western feminist interpretations of women's positions in Africa is that they have often been projections of male/female antagonisms that derive from Western middle-class experiences. There is often very little concern shown for the oppression by world economic systems on African *men* as well as women. Rather than presenting the problem as one of economic stratification supporting male dominance and female dependence, the concern should focus more on the effect of neocolonialism and the economic, political, and cultural domination of African societies. One often feels even more uneasy when analyses of changing sex roles in Africa have been given sexist interpretations by some men. To a certain extent, one can say that Western men and women have used African women as pawns in their sex war.

To a large extent, it is true to say that African women have evolved their own brand of feminism based on the tradition of autonomy in the performance of sex roles. As a result of this there are several points of departure in terms of Western interpretations of women's subordination. This will be discussed briefly under the following headings: Female Autonomy and Cooperation, Nature versus Culture, The Role of Ridicule in Women's Worldview, and The Centrality of Children.

Autonomy and Cooperation

Autonomy and cooperation provide a more appropriate framework in which to examine the question of sex roles in Africa than a framework of competition and opposition which Western feminism fosters. In traditional society the African woman had definite social, political and economic roles which enabled her to achieve a measure of independence and autonomy. This is more clearly expressed in societies organized on the basis of descent through females, in which the males are more dispersed and where inheritance and transfer of property and office are affected by the matrilineal principle. In such societies life is organized around the mother.

With regard to societies organized on the basis of patrilineal descent, males are more localized and can develop strong corporate groups with a greater degree of control over females. But even in these societies there is often a paradox: male dominance on the one hand conflicts with the structural significance of women as 'mothers' on the other. As a result, even women in male-dominated societies have a certain degree of autonomy. This may account in part for the prevalence of women's groups in patrilineal societies.[46] Pala has examined the postion of Luo women in precolonial Kenya and establishes the existence of various loci of women's power and influence within the patrilineage.[47] Sibisi has examined this question from the point of view of the woman's relationship to her ancestors in Zulu society.[48]

No doubt the most important factor with regard to the woman in traditional society is her role as *mother* and the centrality of this role for society as a whole. Even in strictly patrilineal societies, women are important as wives and mothers since their reproductive capacity is crucial to the maintenance of the husband's lineage and it is because of women that men can have a patrilineage *at all*.

The importance of motherhood and the valuation of the childbearing capacity by African women is probably the most fundamental difference between the African woman and her Western counterpart in their common struggle to end discrimination against women. For African women, the role of mother is often central and has intrinsic value. Most novels by African writers capture the essence of this maternal or female principle. Thus, in Achebe's *Things Fall Apart*[49] we see that despite the apparent formal male dominance in Umuahia, Okonkwo, the strong and brave hero, is under the complete control of the owner of life, the earth goddess Ani, and her priestess. The difficulty in reconciling the ultimate control of the earth goddess and Okonkwo's striving for the attainment of the male values of prowess, strength and courage may serve to explain the chronic nature of his anger.

Sibisi has pointed out that the formal ritual sphere need not be the exclusive domain of one sex. 'Whereas in some societies, a calling to the priesthood is reserved for men only, in other societies such a calling is reserved for women. Viewed in this light, diviners among the Zulu play a role which is set for them by the society for the benefit of the society. They are not primarily looking for outlets in an unequal, male-dominated society, as many anthropologists have suggested.' [50] In some societies the birth and death of women are celebrated with more elaborate ritual then the birth and death of men.[51] Women's roles as child-bearers and food-producers are often associated with fertility of the land, and this is implicit in much of the ritual. This life-giving quality endows women not only with much prestige but equates them with the life-giving force itself.

Several points of departure can also be seen in the dichotomy between the 'public sphere' and the 'domestic sphere' as expressed by Rosaldo, Lamphere and others in *Woman, Culture and Society*.[52] Much of the criticism of the application of this model to precolonial societies in Africa has been made by Sudarkasa in this volume. She contends that the public and private spheres need not be dichotomized or attributed to one sex or the other. Moreover, there was considerable overlap between the spheres indicating some degree of cooperation.

One can also look at the concept of power in the same light. Several definitions have been given of power centering around the ability to control one's actions and/or the actions of others; the ability to control scarce resources, make decisions, and use coercion in one form or another. In general, however, formal political power is often seen by some Western feminists as the most important indicator of power. Since men dominate formal political power, it is often assumed that domination in all other spheres is inevitable in traditional society. In my view, it might be necessary to distinguish between effective power and formal power when discussing colonial and postcolonial realities in Africa. Chiefs and lineage heads may have power but lack opportunities to use this power. During colonial times, some chiefs lost their power and their position or had ineffective formal power. In the neocolonialist period, it is not unusual for political leaders to become pawns and lackeys in big power politics in Africa. In southern Africa, whites in the near future are bound to lose formal political power to Africans but will no doubt attempt to control economic and military power with the help of their allies.[53]

With this distinction between formal power and real power, one can say that in societies where most of the activities are geared towards survival and where women's roles are pivotal to this survival, it is women who have the real and relevant power, especially if there are not many opportunities for men to be politically active. Power is defined here not as 'the control over one's own action and the action of others' or 'the control over scarce resources,' but as *control over one's existence and the existence of others*. Women in Africa are the chief providers of food and they play a crucial role from production to processing, distribution and consumption. Their arduous labor output is what ensures the existence of many communities. Power need not be defined strictly in terms of formal political power, for in the African context much of the effective elements of this type of power, in fact, resides outside the continent.

Nature versus Culture

Another point of departure from Western interpretations involves the viewpoint that nature is necessarily inferior to culture and consequently, in keeping with views of female inferiority, correlates female with nature and male with culture. When one thinks of how, in the name of culture, technology will very nearly destroy all that is natural and good on the planet earth and replace it with nuclear technology and pollution, one wonders why there has been such overvaluation of so-called progress. This is evident in the present controversy over breast milk and bottled milk (formulas) in infant feeding,[54] and the use of chemicals in processed foods. The increasing popularity of organically grown foods and the new trend towards breastfeeding and natural childbirth are not necessarily inferior, nor it is necessary to control them at all costs because they represent nature. And have we really controlled nature? If so, how can we explain the crippling effects of the New England blizzard of 1978, or the massive starvation caused by the Sahelian drought, or the devastating effects of the Guatemalan earthquake? Through the blind worship of technology we have wholeheartedly accepted the myth that humankind has controlled nature. Our energies might be better spent if we focus on the more critical fact, namely that the earth's resources (nature), on which technology (culture) depends, are finite.

The connection between biology and female inferiority facilitates the exploitation of the female body and is a sexist mode of thinking which Western men have unfortunately got their women to accept. Despite the fact that pollution rules surround women's menstruation in some African societies, this does not imply female inferiority as Aidoo points out. After all, semen also can be seen as polluting.[55] One study has indicated a main obstacle to Western woman's liberation. 'American women will get the right to abortion, but it will take a long time before they can prevent the female body from being exploited as a marketable product.' [56] Symbolically, in many African societies, the female body has always been viewed as an asset, as a sacred vessel carrying life, and as a source of strength and pride. As has been stated, the woman is of intrinsic value in the ideology of many African societies and represents the ultimate value in life, namely the continuity of the group.

Speaking as an African woman, I can say that we are quite at home with our bodies and have achieved a sense of balance with the hormonal composition and processes. Consequently, as African women we can only work out our emancipation within the framework of being women. We believe that we can be emancipated without being castrated; that we can strive for equality and still remain female.

The Centrality of Children, Multiple Mothering, and Kinship Ties

Another factor which tends to minimize the conflict between men and women in Africa is the value placed on children by both sexes. Men generally play an important role in socialization, especially of boys, since childhood ends earlier in many African societies than in Western societies. Children are structurally quite central in that they ensure the continuity of groups and provide links among the living, the dead, and those yet to be born. Children are also important as one form of social security for parents in their old age.

Infant mortality rates are high for most countries in Africa[57] and the survival of children becomes an all-absorbing goal. A great deal of emotional and physical energy is expended on keeping children alive and ensuring their survival, and this is a preoccupation of men and women alike. Pro-fertility values are, in part, a result of the high incidence of infant mortality and fetal wastage. A woman without a child is stigmatized in many societies in Africa, and barrenness is seen as a punishment for sin. For men, fecundity is often equated with potency and virility. This valuation of fertility and motherhood are reflections of the centrality of children.

Another important element in this is the importance of relationships between the consanguinal (blood) kin group which gives rise to multiple mothering. The isolation of the nuclear family is not the typical pattern among blacks in Africa nor in the diaspora. As a result, the extended family system in its many forms and close kin networks are more characteristic and tend to encourage greater reliance on one's blood kin than on one's spouse. Consequently, ties with one's kin are ultimately far more important than ties with one's spouse. Moreover, the greater reliance on one's kin together with the centrality of children tend to reduce emotional dependency of women on men and the likelihood of inducing greater male control through such dependencies.

The Role of Ridicule in Women's Worldview

Tensions have always existed between the sexes, and African societies traditionally have developed mechanisms to regulate these tensions. Apart from the more publicized protests and boycotts by women, institutionalized mechanisms for releasing tensions between the sexes exist in most societies and provide opportunities for striking back. In Sierra Leone and Liberia, there are secret societies—the Poro (male) and the Bondo or Sande (female)—found principally among the Mende and Temne but also among other groups. Both societies perform the function of instruction and initiation of the adolescent into the status and role of adulthood. A bond is thereby created with sanctions to ensure loyalty to the group. Both Bondo and Poro respect each other's rules which control behavior between the sexes, and thereby provide institutionalized means of diffusing tensions that might arise in the domestic sphere and between men and women. Even in areas such as Freetown where, on account of urbanization much of the sacred aspect of Bondo societies is diluted rendering them more like voluntary associations and social agencies, these societies still serve to regulate relationships between the sexes through the maintenance of sororal bonds.[58]

Ridicule and scapegoating are also used as effective mechanisms for neutralizing tensions between the sexes. These can take the form of direct taunts, group pressure or ritual satire. By using humor and ridicule in this way in the daily contacts between men and women, much of the tensions between the sexes is released. In Nigeria, among the Ekperi and Edo-speaking people in the Midwest

State, songs of ritual license are often used to release tensions between the sexes. 'The songs themselves represent an occasion of ritualized verbal license in which men and women ridicule each other's genitalia and sexual habits. Normally, such ridicule would be an antisocial act in the extreme, an offense against the continuity of life. In the ritual context, however, the songs provide recognition, acceptance, and release of that tension which exists between the sexes in all cultures.' [59] A Western version of this tension-releasing mechanism is Erica Jong's *Fear of Flying*. Part of this book's success is due to Jong's overt ridicule of the sexual habits of men.

An analysis of African women's worldview is likely to reveal that women use their importance in reproduction and food production to gain the upper hand or force compliance not only by the use of pressure or coercion but also by praising the virtues and powers of motherhood and food production. Thus, among the Nso of Cameroon women are praised as follows:

> A woman is an important thing. A man is a worthless thing indeed, because a woman gives birth to the people of the country. What work can a man do? A woman bears a child, then takes a hoe, goes to the field and is working there. A man buys palm oil. Men only build houses.

> Important things are women. Men are little. The things of women are important. What are the things of men? Men are indeed worthless. Women are indeed God. Men are nothing. Have you not seen? [60]

In a modern context in Sierra Leone, women were seen by a female political leader as owning men. According to her, 'We give birth to men so in a way we own them.' [61] During my research in Sierra Leone in 1978, I asked a group of women about their views of the women's movement of the West. According to one woman,

> The very language and style of the women's movement of the West is an admission of the women's belief that they are inferior to men. [62]

CONCLUSION: BLACK WOMAN—THE ORIGINAL FEMINIST

For the majority of black women, liberation from sexual oppression has always been fused with liberation from other forms of oppression, namely slavery, colonialism, neocolonialism, racism, poverty, illiteracy and disease. Consequently, her feminism has relevance in human terms rather than narrow sexist terms. The manifold nature of her oppression not only heightens her consciousness about the economic basis of oppression but also indicates its roots. For the black woman, the enemy is not black men but history.

The black woman's condition, as has been discussed, is linked with the history of the black race and with the importance of the African continent and its peoples in the diaspora for the development of Western capitalism. Processes which destroyed and distorted African social systems led directly or indirectly to the dispersion of Africans to various parts of the world. These processes have even greater relevance for the black woman, who has shouldered the heavier part of the burden of ensuring the survival of the black race. For the black woman, the issue is not increasing participation in the labor force, for she is already overburdened with participation. Unlike the typical white middle-class 'housewife', the black woman has had to work outside the home for the survival of herself and her family. While white middle-class women complain about the oppression of affluence, the majority of black women struggle against the oppression of poverty.

In the black woman's experience, it is crystal clear that survival and liberation are synonymous, and that she must be the main activist in the struggle to ensure both. For this she can draw inspiration from the continent of Africa. The birthplace of human life must also be the birthplace of human struggles, and feminist consciousness must in some way be related to the earliest divisions of labor according to sex on the continent. But even more significant is the fact that the forms of social organization which approach sexual equality, in addition to matrilineal societies where women are central, can be found on the African continent. African women have also participated in the struggles against colonialism and in liberation movements against racism. The experience of exploitation, racism, poverty and sexism create a multiple form of oppression which fully justifies the black woman's anger and puts her among the most oppressed peoples in the world. Her struggle for survival has necessitated the development of certain survival skills. Lack of guaranteed male support has increased her capacity for self-reliance. True feminism is an abnegation of male protection and a determination to be resourceful and self-reliant. The majority of the black women in Africa and in the diaspora have developed these characteristics, though not always by choice. The essence of feminism is not hatred of men or blaming men, some of whom after all are also victims of oppression. True feminism springs from an actual experience of oppression, a lack of the socially prescribed means of ensuring one's wellbeing, and a true lack of access to resources for survival. True feminism is the reaction which leads to the development of greater resourcefulness for survival and greater self-reliance.

Above all, true feminism is impossible without intensive involvement in production. All over the African diaspora, but particularly on the continent, the black woman's role in this regard is paramount. It can, therefore, be stated with much justification that the black woman is to a large extent the original feminist.

NOTES

1. See Little 1972; Patterson 1963; Watson 1977.

2. For example Bastide 1974.

3. Numerous publications document this history. See for example, Williams 1944; Curtin 1969; Blassingame 1972; Kilson and Rotberg 1976.

4. Blassingame 1972, p. 82.

5. For example Amin 1976, 1977; Rodney 1974; Kofi 1977.

6. The most well known female resistance is probably the Igbo women's war against the British. Also notable is the Senegalese women's resistance against the French, documented in Ousmane Sembene's *God's Bits of Wood*.

7. Leacock 1971; Sacks 1974.

8. See for example E. Ardener 1972; S. Ardener 1975; Leacock 1972; Chinas 1973; Rosaldo and Lamphere 1974; Reiter 1975.

9. UN/ECA 1974.

10. George 1977; Steady 1978.

11. IBRD 1975.

12. Mintz 1964.

13. These negative stereotypes are also presented in the mass media with Hollywood's contribution being the most persistently racist. See Bogle 1978.

14. Kent 1974, 1975.

15. Mutiso 1977.

16. Boserup 1970.

17. See PAG Report 1977.

18. Pala 1975, p. 7.

19. Blassingame 1972, p. 87.

20. A number of studies document this trend. See also UN Demographic Yearbook 1977 figures for Lesotho and Botswana. Males from a number of countries in southern Africa migrate to South Africa to work in the mines.

21. Sibisi 1977.

22. Moynihan 1965.

23. Hare 1978, p. 2.

24. *United Nations Demographic Yearbook 1977*. The mean life expectancy for women in sub-Saharan Africa is forty-four years.

25. See *Statistical Abstract of the United States 1979*. Figures for blacks are combined with other nonwhite groups, but the rate is still lower than that for Whites.

26. *1978 World Population Data Sheet*. In comparison, other mean infant mortality rates are, for Europe 20, and for North America 15.

27. See *Statistical Abstract of the United States 1979*.

28. Eide and Steady 1980.

29. See Noble 1978, chapter 4.

30. World Health Organization, "The Epidemiology of Infertility."

31. For accounts of this controversial issue, see *The New York Times* 25 January 1980, p. A13 ("U.S. Aroused by Industry Plans to Ship Toxic Wastes Overseas"); *The Washington Post* 26 January 1980, p. A4 (U.S. Fights Export of Hazardous Waste"); *West Africa* No. 3264, 11 February 1980 ("Matchet's Diary"); *Africa* Magazine (London) No. 104, April 1980, p. 37 ("Sierra Leone: Stevens Bows to Pressure").

32. Savitt 1978.

33. See PAG Report 1977.

34. Mintz 1964.

35. Rosaldo, "Theoretical Overview" in Rosaldo and Lamphere 1974.

36. Mathurin 1975.

37. Reid 1975.

38. *Crimes Against Women*, 1976. The United Nations Economic Commission for Africa's Second regional conference on the Integration of Women in Development held in Lusaka, Zambia Dec. 3-7, 1975 (in preparation for the mid-decade conference of the World Conference of the United Nations Decade for Women) passed a resolution condemning female circumcision and called on governments and women's groups to bring an end to this practice. The resolution also condemned foreign interference and sensationalization of this practice.

39. Ladner 1972, pp. 277-278.

40. Reid, op. cit.

41. Ibid. p. 51.

42. Cade 1970, p. 9.

43. See Wallace 1979.

44. Mernissi 1975. p. 108.

45. Beale 1970, p. 99.

46. Leis 1974.

47. Pala, "Women in Precolonial Luo Society", mimeographed paper, 1977.

48. Sibisi, "The Position of a Zulu Married Woman in Relation to Her Ancestors and to her Natal Family," mimeographed paper, 1975.
49. Achebe 1959.
50. Sibisi 1977, pp. 174-175.
51. Kaberry 1952, p. 50.
52. Rosaldo and Lamphere 1974.
53. Zimbabwe gained its independence in 1980 under the leadership of Prime Minister Robert Mugabe whose party, ZANU, won an overwhelming majority in Parliament.
54. Numerous studies document this. For a comprehensive volume see Jelliffe and Jelliffe 1978.
55. Sibisi 1977.
56. Mernissi 1975, p. 109.
57. 160-170 per thousand live births in some countries.
58. Steady 1974.
59. Borgatti 1976, p. 66.
60. Kaberry 1952, p. 60.
61. Steady 1975, p. 61.
62. Miss A. John, personal communication, May 1978.

REFERENCES

Achebe, Chinua. *Things Fall Apart*. New York: McDowell, Obolensky, 1959.
Amin, Samir. *Neocolonialism in West Africa*. New York: Pathfinder Press, 1976.
———— . *Imperialism and Unequal Development*. New York: Monthly Review Press, 1977.
Ardener, Edwin. "Belief and the Problem of Women," in J. S. Lafontaine (ed.) *Interpretation of Ritual*. London: Tavistock, 1972.
Ardener, Shirley (ed.). *Perceiving Women*. New York: Halstead Press, 1975.
Bastide, Roger (ed.). *La Femme de Couleur en Amerique Latine*. Paris: Editions Anthropos, 1974.
Beale, Frances M. "Double Jeopardy: To be Black and Female," in Toni Cade (ed.) *The Black Woman: An Anthology*. New York: New American Library, 1970.
Blassingame, John. *The Slave Plantation*. New York: Oxford University Press, 1972.
Bogle, Donald. *Tom, Coons, Mulattoes, Mammies and Bucks: An Interpretive History of Blacks in American Films*. New York: Viking Press, 1978.
Borgatti, Jean. "Songs of Ritual License from Midwestern Nigeria," *Alcheringa* new series 2 (1976): 66-71.
Boserup, Ester. *Women's Role in Economic Development*. London: George Allen and Unwin, 1970.

Cade, Toni (ed.). *The Black Woman: An Anthology.* New York: New American Library, 1970.

Chinas, Beverly. *The Isthmus Xapotecs.* New York: Holt, Rinehart and Winston, 1973.

Crimes Against Women. Proceedings of the International Tribunal, compiled and edited by Diana E. H. Russell and Nicole Vandeven. Millbrae, CA: Les Femmes, 1976.

Curtin, Philip D. *The Atlantic Slave Trade.* Madison: Wisconsin University Press, 1969.

Eide, Wenche Barth and Steady, Filomina Chioma. "Individual and Social Energy Flows: Bridging Nutritional and Anthropological Thinking about Women's Work in Rural Africa: some theoretical considerations," in Jerome, N., Kandel, R.F. and Pelto, G.H. (eds) *Nutritional Anthropology.* New York: Redgrave Publishing Co., 1980, pp. 61-84.

Emecheta, Buchi. *Second-Class Citizen.* New York: George Braziller, 1975.

George, Susan. *How the Other Half Dies: the real reasons for world hunger.* Montclair, NJ: Allanheld, Osmun, 1977.

Hare, Nathan. "Revolution without a Revolution: the psychology of sex and race," *Black Scholar* (April 1978): 2-7.

International Bank for Reconstruction and Development, 1975.

Jelliffe, Derrick B. and Jelliffe, E.F. Patrice. *Human Milk in the Modern World: psychological, nutritional and economic significance.* New York: Viking Press, 1978.

Kaberry, Phyllis M. *Women of the Grassfields: a study of the economic position of women in Bamenda, British Cameroon.* London: Her Majesty's Stationery Office, 1952.

Kilson, Martin L. and Rotberg, Robert I. (eds). *The African Disapora: interpretive essays.* Cambridge: Harvard Univ. Press., 1976.

Kent, George E. "The Black Woman in Faulkner's Works, with the exclusion of Dilsey.
Part I." *Phylon* 35 (1974): 430-441.

_____ . "The Black Woman in Faulkner's Works, with the exclusion of Dilsey. Part II." *Phylon* 36 (1975): 55-67.

Kofi, T. A. "Peasants and Economic Development: Populist Lessons for Africa," *The African Studies Review* 20(3): Waltham, MA: African Studies Association, 1977.

Ladner, Joyce. *Tomorrow's Tomorrow: The Black Woman.* Garden City, NY: Anchor Books (Doubleday), 1972.

Leacock, Eleanor. "Introduction," in Frederick Engels, *The Origin of the Family, Private Property and the State.* New York: International Publishers Co., 1972.

Leis, Nancy. "Women in Groups," in Rosaldo, M.Z. and Lamphere, L. (eds). *Woman, Culture and Society.* Stanford: Stanford University Press, 1974.

Little, Kenneth. *Negroes in Britain: study of racial relations in English society*, revised edition. London: Routledge and Kegan Paul, 1972.

_____ . *African Women in Towns: a study of African social evolution*. Cambridge: Cambridge University Press, 1973.

Mathurin, Lucille. *The Rebel Woman in the British West Indies during Slavery*. Kingston: African-Caribbean Publications, 1975.

Mernissi, Fatima. *Beyond the Veil: Male-Female Dynamics in a Modern Muslim Society*. Cambridge, MA: Schenkman Publishing Co., 1975.

Mintz, Sidney W. "The Employment of Capital by Haitian Market Women," in Firth, R. and Yamey, B. (eds) *Capital, Saving and Credit in Peasant Society*. Chicago: Aldine Publishing Co., pp. 256-286, 1964.

Moynihan, Daniel Patrick. *The Negro Family: The Case for National Action*. Washington, DC: Government Printing Office (March 1965); reprinted in Rainwater, L. and Yancey, W. L., *The Moynihan Report and the Politics of Controversy*. Cambridge, MA: M.I.T. Press.

Mutiso, G.C.M. "Women in African Literature," *East African Journal* (March 1977): 4-14.

Noble, Jeann. L. *Beautiful, Also, are the Souls of my Black Sisters*. Englewood Cliffs, NJ: Prentice-Hall, 1978.

Pala, Achola O. "A preliminary survey of avenues for and constraints on women in the development process in Kenya." Discussion Paper no 218, Institute of Development Studies, University of Nairobi, Kenya, 1975.

_____ . "Women in Precolonial Luo Society,' chapter 3 in "Changes in Economy and Ideology: A Study of Joluo of Kenya with special reference to women." Ph.D. dissertation, Harvard University, 1977.

Patterson, Sheila. *Dark Strangers*. London: Tavistock, 1963.

Reid, Inez. *"Together" Black Women*. New York: The Third Press, 1975.

Reiter, Rayna (ed.). *Towards an Anthropology of Women*. New York: Monthly Review Press, 1975.

Rodney, Walter. *How Europe Underdeveloped Africa*. Washington, DC: Howard University Press, 1974.

Rosaldo, Michele Z. "Theoretical Overview" in Rosaldo, M.Z. and Lamphere, L. (eds) *Woman, Culture and Society*. Stanford: Stanford University Press, 1974.

Rosaldo, Michele Z. and Lamphere, Louise (eds). *Woman, Culture and Society*. Stanford: Stanford University Press, 1974.

Sacks, Karen. "Engels Revisited: Women, the Organization of Production, and Private Property," in Rosaldo, M.Z. and Lamphere (eds) *Woman, Culture and Society*. Stanford: Stanford University Press, 1974.

Savitt, Todd L. *Medicine and Slavery: the diseases and health care of Blacks in antebellum Virginia*. Urbana: University of Illinois Press, 1978.

Sembene, Ousmane. *God's Bits of Wood: a novel of the independence struggle in French Africa*. Garden City, NY: Anchor Books (Doubleday), 1970.

Sibisi, Harriet. "The position of a Zulu married women in relation to her ancestors and to her natal family," mimeographed paper, 1975.

———— . *Mind and Body in Zulu Medicine.* New York: Academic Press, 1977.

Statistical Abstracts of the United States. (1979) U.S. Bureau of Census (100th edition), Washington, DC.

Steady, Filomina Chioma. "The Structure and Function of Women's Voluntary Associations in an African City: a study of the associative process among women of Freetown." Unpublished D. Phil dissertation, Oxford University, 1974.

———— . "Urban Malnutrition in West Africa: a consequence of abnormal urban growth and underdevelopment." Paper presented at the Tenth International Congress of Anthropological and Ethnological Sciences, New Delhi, India, December 1978.

United Nations Demographic Yearbook, 1977. (Twenty-ninth Issue) United Nations Publishing Service, New York, 1978.

United Nations Economic Commission for Africa (UN/ECA). "Africa's Food Producers: The Impact of Change on Rural Women." Paper prepared by the Women's Programme Unit, Human Resource Division for the American Geographical Society, 1974.

United Nations Protein-Calorie Advisory Group (PAG). *Women in Food Production, Food Handling and Nutrition, with special emphasis on Africa.* New York: United Nations, 1977.

Wallace, Michelle. *Black Macho and the Myth of the Superwoman.* New York: Dial Press, 1979.

Watson, James L. *Between Two Cultures: Migrants and Minorities in Britain.* Oxford: Basil Blackwell, 1977.

Williams, Eric. *Capitalism and Slavery.* Chapel Hill: University of North Carolina Press. Reprinted 1966, New York: Capricorn Books, 1944.

World Health Organization. "The Epidemiology of Infertility." Technical Report Series no. 582 (Geneva, 1975).

World Population Data Sheet. Population Reference Bureau, Inc., Washington, DC, 1978.

A woman works the land in the foothills of the Ruwenzori Mountains, South West Uganda. Photo: United Nations, No. 107,961. (1967)

Part I:
AFRICA

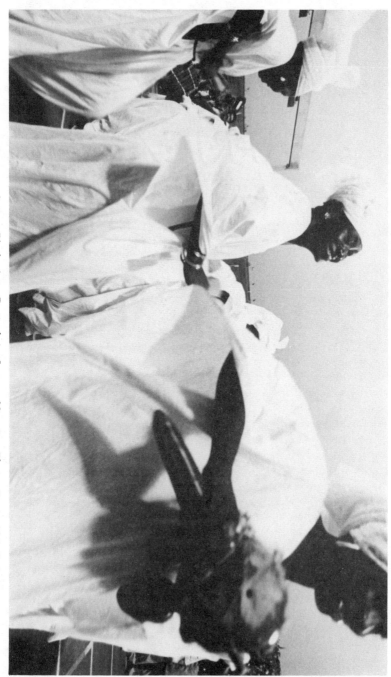

Guinea performers during Black Arts Festival in Lagos, Nigeria. Photo: Reginald L. Jackson.

Africa

INTRODUCTORY SUMMARY

Africa is a continent of great diversity, and traditional cultures have been greatly influenced by colonialism. These different colonial experiences transformed many African societies and affected the traditional relations between the sexes. Sudarkasa points out that in precolonial states and stateless societies in West Africa the 'domestic sphere' was an integral part of the 'public sphere'. Consequently power, authority, and influence within the 'domestic sphere' was *de facto* power, authority and influence at certain levels within the 'public sphere', especially since there was considerable overlap between the two spheres. She concludes by discussing the changes brought about in women's work and their position within the lineage structure as a result of westernization.

Aidoo analyzes the dynamics of the position of the Asante Queen Mothers in government and politics in nineteenth century Ghana. She examines the career of three Queen Mothers, and highlights the great personal strengths of these women. She also makes the important point that their power is derived from the 'constitution' rather than from the fact that they represented women.

Okonjo examines the changes brought about by colonization on women's political participation. She discusses the traditional pattern of dual sex roles in political organizations and their decline under colonial administration. She proposes a quota system based on sex which would guarantee women political office in the future.

The history of Africa is a history of struggle against colonial domination, economic exploitation and racial oppression. Consequently, some countries in Africa have chosen a policy of development along socialist lines as a way of ensuring self-determination through self-reliance. Women are seen as important contributors to the development process. This need is often articulated by the leaders and by national women's associations. Ladner's chapter on women in Tanzania discusses the role of women in the building of a socialist state and sees the association *Umoja wa wanawake wa Tanzania* (United Women of Tanzania) as a potential political force which also seeks to involve women in economic development.

Among countries that have chosen the socialist path to development are the former Portuguese colonies which gained their independence only after protracted guerilla warfare with Portugal, the most reluctant country to end its colonialism in Africa. The role of women in the liberation struggle in Guinea-Bissau is discussed by Urdang. Implicit in this struggle is their own struggle for women's liberation, which is seen as an overall program for building a new socialist society free of any form of exploitation.

In the nineteen-sixties and seventies most countries in Africa gained independence from colonial rule. Economic colonialism continued through unequal trade and aid agreements and dependency relations. Pala succintly analyzes the implications for development from an African perspective. She argues that the position of women in contemporary Africa must be seen in the context of an on-going process which both responds to and resists economic exploitation and cultural domination.

Following this line Simms gives comprehensive treatment to the problems and prospects for development with reference to the African woman as entrepreneur. She examines the traditional role of women in commerce, particularly in West Africa, and comments on their primary contribution to the system of food production, processing and distribution. She advances some suggestions for basic research and policy analysis in an attempt to move beyond the inequities in the dependency relationships that historically have conditioned these societies.

Urbanization is taking place in Africa at an explosive rate, and in some countries more than 50 percent of the population now live in urban areas. The consequences of urbanization are often deleterious in countries with dependent economies. Peasants are pushed off the land into urban areas in search of work, and not as a result of labor demands of the city. Urban unemployment is high, and many migrants to the city live under deplorable conditions. Previous research on African urbanization has tended to glorify this process as a sign of development, and African women were seen as being better off in town than in rural areas. Gugler dispels this myth and points out the precariousness of the informal labor market in which many migrant women make a living. He argues that although some women have fared well in professional activities and commerce, all too frequently illicit activities, such as prostitution, and brewing and selling liquor, provide the major opportunities for women to support themselves. Sex discrimination in education and employment operates in the urban areas to further limit the occupational opportunities available to women.

Various adaptive mechanisms to urbanization have emerged in new forms of religious and secular associations. Jules-Rosette examines women in indigenous African cults and churches as a feature of this process. One of the consequences of the inimical urban growth process in Africa is a deterioration of the health and nutritional status of the urban poor. Some of the new religious cults and churches perform a much-needed role of healing and prophecy. Women play an important role as healers. Jules-Rosette also looks at the development of female leadership, and points out that though the goal of some type of sexual equality in religious terms is expressed as an ideal, ceremonial leadership is more accessible to women than formal political leadership.

No study of the black woman in Africa will be complete without a look at her position in southern Africa. South Africa continues to defy humanity with its racist apartheid policies despite worldwide condemnation. Lapchick's contribution is a historical analysis of women's struggles against apartheid and the various institutions that were designed to sustain it, such as the Bantu system of education. He discusses among other activities, resistance to the pass system, boycott of the bus services, and protests against forced migration. The chapter also explores the range of techniques of resistance from violent confrontations to passive resistance, and notes that women's struggles against apartheid also involved activities in the trade unions and various women's organizations. Rivkin presents a poignant picture of the deliberate and systematic oppression of the black majority in order to maintain the white minority in a position of privilege. The heaviest burden falls on the black woman, who is often left in the 'homelands' while her husband migrates to the city in search of work. The 'homelands' constitute the worst arable land, and many of the inhabitants live in abject poverty. Malnutrition is acute, and the infant mortality rate is more than five times higher for blacks. One can justifiably claim that with poor medical facilities, malnutrition, and general economic deprivation the 'homelands' can be regarded as mechanisms designed for the elimination of blacks.

1
Female Employment and Family Organization in West Africa

Niara Sudarkasa

Wherever and whenever women work extensively "outside the home," there must be supporting structural arrangements to enable them to combine their domestic roles with their extra-domestic occupational roles. We know from oral and written historical sources that for centuries in West Africa women have been extensively involved in farming, trading, and other economic activities, while at the same time taking care of their responsibilities as wives and mothers. Moreover, during the pre-colonial period in many West African societies, women had important political and religious roles that entailed their working extensively "outside the home." In contemporary West Africa virtually all adult females are engaged in some type of money-making activity that involves them in the "public," in addition to the "domestic," arena.

In this paper I want to discuss the relationship between the economic roles of West African women and their overall position in the kinship and residential groupings to which they belong. The paper will highlight some of the domestic patterns that facilitate the involvement of women in money-making pursuits. The discussion is prefaced by a comment on the involvement of women in the "domestic" and "public" spheres of traditional West African societies, inasmuch as an appreciation of the roles of women in the traditional societies is essential to an understanding of the widespread participation of contemporary West African women in employment "outside the home."

THE ROLE OF WOMEN IN THE "PUBLIC" AND "DOMESTIC" SPHERES IN TRADITIONAL WEST AFRICA.

The distinction between the activities and responsibilities of women "in the home" and "outside the home" underlies many of the current cross-cultural comparisons of the status and roles of women. One of the recurring themes in the articles that comprise the book *Woman, Culture, and Society*[1] is the proposition that most societies distinguish between the *domestic* and the *public* sphere of activity, and that this distinction is critical to any discussion of the status of women in a given society or in different societies. Michelle Rosaldo draws the distinction between the two spheres as follows:

> "Domestic," as used here, refers to those minimal institutions and modes of activity that are organized immediately around one or more mothers and their children; "public" refers to activities, institutions, and forms of association that link, rank, organize, or subsume particular mother-child groups. (1974:23)

Peggy Sanday states:

> The domestic domain includes activities performed within the realm of the localized family unit. The public domain includes political and economic activities that take place or have impact beyond the localized family unit and that relate to control of persons or control of things. (1974:190)

All the contributors to the volume *Woman, Culture, and Society* seem to agree with Rosaldo (1974:17-42) that the nature and extent of authority (and, secondarily, power)[2] wielded by women in the *public sphere* is the key measure of their overall status in any given society and across societies. Rosaldo suggests that the status of women is lowest in those societies which "firmly" differentiate between the public and domestic spheres and confine women to domestic activities, cutting them off from other women and from the public sphere dominated by men (1974:36, 41). She suggests further that women's statuses are "raised" in societies where they either "enter the men's world" or "create a public world of their own" (1974:36). Both Rosaldo (1974:36) and Louise Lamphere (1974:112) characterize "the most egalitarian of societies" as those in which the public and domestic spheres are only weakly differentiated, and males and females share authority in both.

The few references made to West African societies in Rosaldo's article indicate that she interprets them as societies in which public and domestic spheres, and male and female roles, are "firmly differentiated." However, in her view women in that part of the world were able to "achieve considerable status and power" by (a) manipulating men and influencing their decisions, (b) creating a public world of their own in which they exercised authority and power, and (c) taking on "men's roles" such as that of chief or monarch (1974:37-38).

It is not my intention in the present paper to undertake a full scale discussion of the utility of the various suggestions and hypotheses put forth by Rosaldo, Lamphere, and their colleagues for an understanding of the status and roles of women in West Africa. This is being done in another essay. Here I simply want to pursue the question of the separation of the public and domestic spheres in traditional West African societies, pointing out in particular the relation between women's roles in their domestic groups and their overall participation in the "public" arena of the societies in which they live.

A factor which must be kept in mind in any discussion of the separation of the domestic and public spheres in West Africa (and indeed throughout the world) is that this separation has been greatly heightened in the late nineteenth and twentieth centuries. With the spread of the nation-state as the predominant form of political organization and of capitalism as the predominant form of economic organization, much of the "traditional" overlap between the domestic and public spheres was eroded. The state arrogated to its bureaucracy many of the political functions that had been carried out by domestic units. The capitalist (i.e., "market") economic system redefined "labor" so as to make it virtually synonymous with work for which cash or other forms of remuneration was paid. Whereas in traditional economies in West Africa (and elsewhere) all productive work was recognized as such, under the capitalist economic system productive activities carried on "within the home" by females (and to some extent by males and by children) who received no pay—came to be regarded as something other than "strictly economic" activities. In short, the growth of the contemporary nation-state and of the "market economy" accentuated and accelerated the divergence of the public and domestic spheres in societies throughout the world. Whereas from the perspective of the twentieth century the publc sphere of a society can be defined, as Sanday has done, in terms of political and economic activities that extend "beyond the localized family unit," when one looks at the preindustrial, precapitalist, and precolonial world, it becomes obvious that many such political and economic activities were in fact embedded, albeit not exclusively, in domestic units.

In considering the issue of the separation of the domestic and public spheres in traditional West African societies, it is convenient to divide the discussion into two parts: looking first at the relation between the domestic sphere and the political realm of the public sphere, and secondly, at the relation between the domestic sphere and the economic realm of the public sphere.

When one examines the political or governmental realm of these societies, it can be demonstrated that in both precolonial state societies (such as the Yoruba and the Asante) and in precolonial non-state societies (such as the Ibo [Igbo]), the "domestic sphere" was an integral part of the "public sphere." Power, authority, and influence within the "domestic sphere" was *de facto* power, authority, and influence at certain levels within the "public sphere." This is not to say that the two spheres were coterminous, but rather that there was considerable overlap between them.

To understand this point it is only necessary to recall that in precolonial West Africa, and in the more traditional areas of contemporary West Africa, domestic groups were (and are) extended families built around segments of marti- or patri-lineages. The predominant type of domestic grouping consisted of an extended family comprising male members of a lineage, their wives, and children (see, e.g., Sudarkasa 1973:97-116). These groups resided in dwellings normally referred to as compounds.

Within compounds, which range in size from about twenty or thirty persons to several hundred persons, both males and females have roles of authority. Members of the compound are usually ranked according to seniority, with order of birth being the usual determinant of seniority within the lineage core of the compound, and order of marriage into the compound being the determinant of seniority among the wives of the male members of the lineage (Bascomb 1942; Marshall 1970; Oppong 1974:28-34; Uchendu 1965:39-41, 84-87). Within each polygamous subdivision of the extended family (i.e., within the group comprised of one man and his wives and children), wives are also ranked according to the same principle of seniority. There is normally an official male head of the compound and a female counterpart whose primary responsibility is the safeguarding of the welfare of the women of the house.

This latter point notwithstanding, it would be misrepresentation of the dynamics of compound organization to say that males have authority over adult males and females, whereas females have authority only over other females. Because of the importance of seniority in ordering relationships within the compound, male and female elders have authority over junior members of both sexes. The relationship between males and females of approximately the same age is not usually one of superordination/subordination, but rather one of complementarity of functions one of purview.[3]

In traditional West Africa the compound was usually the minimal unit of political organization, and decisions within the compound had implications for the wider political units, whether this was a village or a town. Thus wives, mothers, sisters, or daughters could exert direct political influence over males, or they themselves could play important political roles by virtue of their positions of authority, power, or influence in their natal and/or affinal compounds.

Traditionally, senior members of the compound constituted the "court of the first instance" for the settlement of many issues that have come to be defined by the nation-state as falling within the jurisdiction of the "public domain." These issues were extra-domestic as well as domestic in their scope and implications. The settlement of disputes, the investigation of charges of theft, adultery, "witchcraft," or of other offenses involving members of the same compound was usually carried out in the first instance by the elders of that compound. When members of different compounds were involved, these matters were normally handled first by the elders or leaders of the compounds in question. Only when such matters could not be settled on the compound level, would they be referred to higher authorities. The involvement of women in the various matters that came before the compound leadership represented *de facto* involvement in the "public sphere."

The overlap between the public and domestic spheres in traditional West African societies is demonstrated by an examination of the functin of lineages as well as the function of compounds. Lineages, around which compounds were (and usually are) organized, were corporate groups which normally controlled the use of land,

provided access to various political and/or religious offices, regulated marriages, and performed a wide range of political and economic functions which fell within the "public sphere." For example,
they often controlled access to certain occupational groups within
the society (see, e.g., Lloyd 1953). It was common for women to
have important roles within patrilineages as well as within matrilineages in West Africa, and in their roles as sisters and daughters of
the lineage, they often exercised *de facto* authority and/or power
within the "public sphere" (Fortes 1950:256-57; Lloyd 1955; Sudarkasa 1973:111).

When one looks at the realm of economics, one also finds that
there was considerable overlap between the domestic and public
spheres in traditional West African societies. In fact, there was no
clear cut differentiation in most instances between "domestic" economic roles and "public" economic roles.

In most societies it was usual for females as well as males to be
engaged in activities—such as farming, trading, craft production, or
food-processing—which involved them in their society's "wider
economy." Yet most of the economic activities which females (and
males) performed were as much part of their "domestic" roles as
they were separate "occupational roles." To be a good husband and
father, a male not only had to support his family (by means of an
occupation that took him into the "public sphere"), but he also had
to fulfill specific domestic obligations such as participating in the
socialization of children and attending to the upkeep of the physical
dwellings in which the family resided. To be a good wife and
mother, a woman had not only to cook and attend to her husband
and children, but she also had to farm, trade, or otherwise contribute to her household's livelihood.

The general point here is that the important economic roles of
women in traditional West Africa were part and parcel of the overall
domestic roles of wife, mother, sister, and daughter, around which
the lives of most females were ordered. At the same time, through
their economic roles, women played an important part in the "public
sphere." Not only were they physically prominent in the public
world of the market, they were also vital contributors to the economy in their roles as farmers, food processors, weavers, potters,
etc. Moreover, through their trade and craft associations, and
through what might be termed the economic chieftancies which
some females held, women actually played a significant role in the

regulation of the economy in many societies (see, e.g., Nadel 1942:147-56; Sudarkasa 1973:57-64).

When the overall political and economic roles of the majority of West African women operating within their domestic and kinship groups are understood, it becomes apparent that the existence of female chiefs and of other female leaders in the public sphere should not be interpreted as evidence of their achieving status by "entering the world of men." This formulation misses the essential point that the "public sphere" in most West African societies was not concep-tualized as "the world of men." Rather it was one in which both sexes were recognized as having important roles to play.[4]

FEMALE EMPLOYMENT AND DOMESTIC ROLES IN CONTEMPORARY WEST AFRICA

Over the past century the specific economic roles of women in West Africa have changed, but the general pattern of female involvement in the "public" as well as in the "domestic" economic sphere has continued. Throughout West Africa, most women regularly work at some occupation which directly or indirectly involves them in the "cash economy." Even women in seclusion in Muslim areas carry on a variety of trade activities from which they earn cash incomes (Hill 1969 and 1971). The majority of working women in West Africa are self-employed, i.e., they work "on their own account" as farmers, food processors, traders, crafts-producers, seamstresses, purvey-ors of cooked foods, hair dressers, etc. Females are also employed as wage earners in clerical and professional occupations such as typists, office receptionists, teachers, civil servants, nurses, law-yers, physicians, and university lecturers. A small percentage of salaried females are also employed in the factories that are begin-ning to be a feature of the West African economic landscape.

Most women who are not self-employed or salaried workers should not be considered "housewives" in the sense that that term is used in America, although in recent years the term has come into vogue in West Africa as a label for married females who do not work for cash remuneration. Usually, however, these females work with relatives, or with their husbands, in small businesses or in other trading enterprises. Some women who engage in food processing on a small scale (e.g., some of those who make gari [cassava meal] or who work on the farm for part of the year may also be referred to as "housewives" in censuses and in other statistical compilations. The point, however, is that virtually all these women are engaged in pursuits that would, in America, be termed "work outside the home."

The working women of West Africa are as numerous in the urban areas as they are in the rural areas. They are also found within all the socio-economic groupings in that part of the world. Even the wives of high salaried males and of wealthy businessmen are usually "working women." In fact many of these females are wealthy businesswomen in their own right or they are professionals who themselves fall into the "elite" group by virtue of their own occupations and earnings.

Generally speaking, self-employed women manage their own business affairs, with little or no input from males other than from those whom the women specifically ask for advice or whom they employ. Of course, the scale of business operations of the vast majority of self-employed women (most of whom are "petty traders" with operating capital of less than $100) does not enable them to have employees, although they normally have dependent female or male children working with them. However, throughout West Africa there are well-to-do businesswomen with annual incomes in the thousands of dollars, who have male and female employees working under them. A number of the wealthy females who are not literate in English hire male clerks or managers to keep their accounts and to deal with the European firms with which they often have business connections.

Women in West Africa do not work to get away from their "domestic" situations; they work because it is considered an integral part of their domestic responsibilities. In fact, West African women do not draw the sharp distinction, made in America, between "domestic duties" and "work outside the home." Females regard employment in money-making occupations as necessary components of their roles as wives, mothers, sisters, and daughters. It is by earning money that women help to fulfill the responsibilities they have not only toward the immediate family (polygamous or monogamous) into which they are born or into which they marry, but also toward members of the extended networks formed by their consanguineal ("blood") and affinal (in-law) kinsmen.

For the most part women in West Africa still function within the context of families that transcend the conjugally-based nuclear family. Women are born into lineages and most of them still grow up in compounds. When they marry, they move into compounds or otherwise join families that include many significant actors other than their husbands. Women become linked not only to their husbands' lineage members, but also in some instances to other wives of their husband's compounds. (In some patrilineal societies, women married into the same compound, i.e., to males of the same lineage, are collectively referred to as "wives of the house.") Thus, a woman in the role of "wife" occupies a position of many more dimensions and facets than is the case in the West.

In all their kinship roles, females have placed upon them obligations that are independent of those placed upon their husbands, brothers, fathers, or sons. In other words, within the lineage, and within the compound, women quite literally "pull their own loads." This is both a reflection of the relatively high status of women in West Africa, and a response to the reality that in the past as in the present, women, like men, have had independent resources as a result of their roles in the production and distribution networks in their economies.

In the modern context, the obligations that fall to women include bearing some of the financial responsibility for the upbringing of their children, and, where they can afford it, of children of less fortunate relatives. The most substantial cash outlays in this regard are usually those associated with the formal education which these children receive in schools, and/or as apprentices to skilled craftsmen. Women also contribute substantially to their immediate family's requirements of food, clothing, and shelter; however, women do not normally pool their resources with those of their husbands, but rather a husband "does his part" and each wife does hers. On all ceremonial occasions, such as those associated with the marriage or death of relatives or friends, or the birth of children, females make substantial financial contributions to the costs of the events, and/or take time off from their work to help with the preparations that are made for the entertainment of the crowds that assemble for the occasions.

The various kin groups to which females belong provide the most important structural supports for the involvement of women in economic endeavors. There are elaborate child-rearing networks that operate among women in most West African societies as a result, for the most part, of the involvement of women in employment outside the home. The number of children whom a woman has living with her, or for whom she is financially responsible at any given time, is seldom a reflection merely of the number of children to whom she has given birth. Older women assist their daughters, sisters, or daughters-in-law in caring for their children when these women's occupations do not permit them to care for their own children. It is very common to find women looking after the children of relatives while some or all of their own children are being looked after by others. Childless women often rear children who have been placed in their care by relatives or by friends.

These situations arise because women take in or disperse children depending on the point at which they are in their own domestic and occupationsl life cycles, and depending on the responsibilities which they feel toward their kinsmen and close associates (Sudarkasa 1973:132-44, and 1974; Schildkrout 1972). A woman's age, education, place of residence, marital status, financial status and that of her relatives with children, are all variables which operate in determining the number, ages, and relationship of the dependent children for whom she is responsible. In turn, women are assisted in their work by the children for whom they take financial responsibility. When these dependents are not in school, they are usually busy working with their mothers or guardians.

In addition to assistance from kinsmen, there are at least two other important types of social structural support for the involvement of West African women in employment outside the home. First of all, relatively inexpensive household help is still available in most areas. Women who do not have enough dependents to help them with their day-to-day housework, usually have "houseboys" or "housegirls" who are paid by them or by their husbands to help with cooking, washing and ironing, house cleaning, and child care. Secondly, there are in all West African countries, a number of males and females who make their living from service occupations (such as laundering) that help to allow others the freedom to pursue their "extra-domestic" occupations. Perhaps the most important of the specialists in service occupations are the women who prepare inexpensive meals for sale in various locations throughout the towns (and villages) of West Africa (see, e.g., Hill 1971:303-304; Sudarkasa 1973:79-81). It is common for working men and women and for school children to buy one or more of their daily meals from these cooked food sellers. Some of these women specialize in making staple dietary items which take a relatively long time to prepare, and they sell them to women who add to these staples the stews, vegetables, and other items that would make up the main family meal for the day.

The interplay between West African women's domestic and economic roles cannot be concluded without mention of the implications of women's employment for the decision-making process "in the home." I have already intimated that the phrase "in the home" must be divested of its Western implications. The West African wife is actively involved in a number of decision-making domestic and kinship networks, only one of which is the immediate conjugal unit comprised of herself, her husband, and in some instances, her co-wives. Although it cannot be undertaken here, a full discussion of West African women's decision-making role in their "domestic situations" must take into consideration their power, influence, and/or authority within their natal compounds, within their affinal compounds, and, in some cases, within the domiciles established and headed by the women themselves. As Christine Oppong's very informative study of marriage among Ghanaian civil servants abundantly documents, even the process of decision-making within the immediate conjugal unit itself is intricately tied to the roles which husbands and wives play within their wider kinship networks (Oppong 1974).

If there is any single generalization that can be made concerning the decision-making process within West African conjugal units, it is that husbands and wives often make independent decisions concerning the allocation of their resources. In fact, outside the relatively small circle of "elite" families whose households tend toward the Western nuclear family ideal, day-to-day joint decision-making by husbands and wives concerning household affairs seems to be the exception rather than the rule.[5] It appears rather that from the onset of most West African marriages, the husbands assume responsibility for certain domains within the household, and the wife or wives assume responsibility for others.

I noted among families of traders and farmers in Western Nigeria, for example, that husbands and wives did not normally consult each other concerning the day-to-day disbursement of their respective incomes (Sudarkasa 1973:117-132). However, they usually discussed the major responsibilities (such as paying for the education of a child or building a house) that either one was about to undertake in any given period. There would of course be consultation on all projects that required the resources of both. The separate management of "the family purse" definitely appeared to be a response to a situation in which the members of conjugal units had independent obligations to persons outside these groups. However, it was also a way of minimizing the risks involved in the expenditure of money by disbursing it among potentially beneficial investment options, as perceived from the vantage point of the different persons concerned (Sudarkasa 1973).

CONCLUSION

This brief overview of the relationship between women's familial and economic roles in West Africa began with a comment on the overall position of women in the "domestic" and "public" spheres in traditional West African societies. The discusssion emphasizes the continuity in the roles of women in so far as their participation in the economic realm of the public sphere is concerned. It has also emphasized the continuity in the way in which women's familial roles have reflected and been affected by their involvement in economic activities outside the home.

It must be emphasized in conclusion that the other side of the picture, namely the discussion of the changes in women's occupational and familial roles that have resulted from overall changes in the economic, political, and demographic patterns in West Africa, must be analyzed in order to understand the variations in domestic structures and in patterns of domestic behavior evident in West Africa today (see e.g., Okediji and Okediji 1966; Oppong 1974). This task was beyond the scope of the present paper; however, three important points that shed light on the nature and direction of changes in women's domestic and occupational roles should be noted.

(1). Females are being employed in increasing numbers in salaried occupations that are much more disruptive of established domestic patterns than is work in the market place or on the farms. To cite one example: traditionally the first two or three years of a Yoruba child's life was spent in very close proximity to its mother. Yoruba women normally took their young children with them on their backs to the market, to the places where they processed foodstuffs, and to their craft worksites. Today most women traders maintain the tradition of taking their young children with them to the market; however, women in salaried positions in the "modern" business or governmental sector of the society must make arrangements for the care of their infants in their homes or elsewhere.

(2). Traditional compound-based living patterns are being undermined by the increasing migration of men and women to cities within their countries of origin and to urban and rural areas in other countries where economic opportunities are available. A high percentage of men and their wives live in modern derivatives of compounds (which are essentially large rooming houses), wherein reside persons from different lineages, different towns, and, in many cases, different ethnic groups. Moreover, in a number of instances, particularly where the migrants live outside their regions or countries of origins, husbands with more than one wife find rooms for their spouses in a number of different compounds [i.e., rooming houses] (see Sudarkasa 1974). These changes in patterns of domicile, along with other such changes also present, are having far-reaching implications for husband-wife relationships, co-wife relationships, child-rearing patterns, and relationships of spouses to their wider kin networks.

(3). More and more, young females and males are being exposed to westernized education, western values and life styles as communicated through the media, and western commercial and academic propaganda which tends to identify "modernization" with westernization. This exposure, which is buttressed by the fact that in many places westernization is perceived to be the primary path to social mobility, is changing the very nature of what are considered to be suitable occupations, and is undermining the traditional value placed upon maintaining lineage and extended family ties which were the traditional bases of personal identity and social security.

NOTES

1. Michelle Z. Rosaldo and Louise Lamphere, eds. *Woman, Culture and Society* (Palo Alto, California: Stanford University Press, 1974).

2. The contributors utilize M. G. Smith's observation that authority is "the right to make a particular decision and to command obedience" whereas power is "the ability to act effectively on persons or things" regardless of whether this ability is legitimized by the society or some segment thereof. Authority "entails a hierarchical chain of command and control," but "the exercise of power has no positive sanctions, only rules that specify 'the conditions of illegality of its operation.'" (Rosaldo 1974:21).

3. The question of the relative rank of males and females within the lineage and compound is a complex one which cannot be adequately handled in a few sentences. It can be noted that Fortes observed "a high degree of equality between male and female members of the lineage" among the matrilineal Asante [Ashanti] or Ghana (Fortes 1950:256-57). Among the patrilineal Yoruba, a person's sex and relative seniority are among the factors which determine relative rank in any given situation (Marshall 1970). Nevertheless, the ideology of the Yoruba holds that in general males out-rank females; and in general females do show deference toward males of their own age and older by kneeling or curtsying in their presence. It is misleading, however, to attempt to assess the overall status of females in any West African society on the basis of the deference behavior they display toward males. Thus Rosaldo is mistaken in implying that Yoruba females have low status because they traditionally kneel before their husbands (Rosaldo 1974:20). Her reference to the "bowing and scraping of the Yoruba wife" (1974:22) is a particularly misleading statement. Just as females kneel before their husbands, so do males prostrate themselves before their mothers, older sisters, and other females whose age or position demand that they do so.

4. Moreover, the fact that females organized their own political, economic, and convivial associations did not mean that their statuses rested primarily on their "creation of a public world of their own." These associations separated females from males but they did not insulate females from a "public world of men." Female associations, like male associations, were vehicles through which a pattern of complementarity of action, rooted in domestic groupings, was continued in the wider public arena. Of course the notion of "complementarity of action" implies recognition of difference, and it is clear that males and females in West African societies conceptualized their roles—and in many situations, their interests and objectives—as being different from one another. It is also true that through their associations, females sometimes collectively pursued objectives and interests that brought them into temporary conflict with males. However, it is misleading to focus, as many writers do, on the instances when women used their associations as "weapons" in conflicts with men, rather than to recognize that for the most part these associations were used as vehicles for cooperation or collaboration with the males of the society.

5. This is not to imply that all "elite" families tend toward the nuclear-type household, nor that joint decision-making is prevalent among all of those households that are modeled after nuclear families. First of all, most "elite" families include one or more dependents other than children of the couples who head them. Secondly, in some "elite" households many major decisions regarding allocation of resources and/or household tasks and responsibilities are made independently by husbands and wives, or they are made primarily by the husbands (see, e.g., Oppong 1974).

BIBLIOGRAPHY

Bascom, William R. "The Principle of Seniority in the Social Structure of the Yoruba." *American Anthropologist*, vol. 44, No. 1, 1942, pp. 37-46.

Fortes, Meyèr. "Kinship and Marriage Among the Ashanti" in *African Systems of Kinship and Marriage*, A. R. Radcliffe-Brown and D. Forde, eds. Oxford: Oxford University Press, 1950.

Hill, Polly. "Hidden Trade in Hausaland." *Man*, vol. 4, No. 3, 1969, pp. 392-409.

_____ . "Two Types of West African House Trade" in *The Development of Indigenous Trade and Markets in West Africa*, Claude Meillassoux, ed. Oxford: Oxford University Press, 1971.

Lloyd, Peter C. "Craft Organizations in Yoruba Towns." *Africa* vol. 23, No. 1, 1953, pp. 30-44.

_____ . "The Yoruba Lineage." *Africa*, vol. 25, No. 3, 1955, pp. 235-51.

Marshall, Gloria A. [Niara Sudarkasa]. "In A World of Women: Field Work in a Yoruba Community" in *Women in the Field*, Peggy Golde, ed. Chicago: Aldine, 1970.

Nadel, S. F. *A Black Byzantium*. Oxford: Oxford University Press, 1942.

Okediji, O. and Okediji, F. "Marital Stability and Social Structure in an African City." *Nigerian Journal of Economic and Social Studies*, vol. 8, No. 1, 1966, pp. 151-163.

Oppong, Enristine. *Marriage Among a Matrilineal Elite*. Cambridge: Cambridge University Press, 1974.

Rosaldo, Michelle. "Woman, Culture, and Society: A Theoretical Overview" in *Woman, Culture, and Society*, M. Rosaldo and L. Lamphere, eds. Palo Alto, California: Stanford University Press, 1974.

Rosaldo, M. and Louise Lamphere, eds. *Woman, Culture and Society*. Palo Alto, California: Stanford University Press, 1974.

Sanday, Peggy. "Female Status in the Public Domain" in *Woman, Culture, and Society*, M. Rosaldo and L. Lamphere, eds. Palo Alto, California: Stanford University Press, 1974.

Schildkrout, Enid. "The Fostering of Children in Urban Ghana." Presented in a symposium on *Transactions in Parenthood* at the Annual Meeting of the American Anthropological Association, Toronto, 1972.

Sudarkasa, Niara. *Where Women Work*. Ann Arbor: University of Michigan, Museum of Anthropology, 1973.

_____ . "Commercial Migration in West Africa, with special reference to the Yoruba in Ghana" in *Migrants and Strangers in Africa*, N. Sudarkasa, ed. *African Urban Notes* Michigan State University, East Lansing, Winter 1974-75.

Uchendu, Victor. *The Igbo [Ibo] of Southeast Nigeria*. New York: Holt, Rinehart and Winston, 1965.

Crowd singing the party song at the rally of the JUVENTO party on election eve in Lomé, Togoland. Photo: United Nations, No. 62084. (1958)

2

Asante Queen Mothers in Government and Politics in the Nineteenth Century

Agnes Akosua Aidoo

Asante queen mothers were very often eclipsed and overwhelmed by the numerically superior male actors in the political arena. This is perhaps the reason why historians have largely neglected them. The picture we have of these women corulers has been drawn mainly by anthropologists and sociologists such as R. S. Rattray, M. Fortes, M. Manoukian and K. A. Busia. Their picture is a static one which depicts the position and status of the queen mothers. The operational dynamics of their position and the scope and modalities of their power within actual social and political processes have not been fully studied. But there is sufficient data from the nineteenth century at least to reconstruct the history of some queen mothers in government and politics.

Like all Akan women, the queen mother derived her position from the matrilineal social organization. The Akan trace descent through the female line. The woman is the genetically significant link between successive generations. The *mogya*, "blood" or life force, which she bestows or transmits to her children determines their succession, inheritance, rights, obligations and citizenship. Even though political offices in the lineage and state are held almost exclusively by men, political status is conferred by women. Thus the Asante never tire of pointing out in proverbs: *Obaa na owoo obarima; Obaa na owoo ohene* (It's a woman who gave birth to a man; it's a woman who gave birth to a chief).

The recognition given to the crucial role of women in Asante social and political organization has impressed many observers.

After his extensive research in the early 1920s, Rattray concluded that, but for "the natural physical inferiority of woman from a physical standpoint" and for the ritual prohibitions surrounding menstruation, the Asante woman "would easily eclipse any male in importance."[1]

In spite of this importance, there was only *one* political office in the Akan chiefdom or state held by women. This was the office of the *ohemaa*, literally female ruler. The *ohemaa* occupied the senior of two stools in the state which served jointly as the visible repository of political authority. She was a coruler and had joint responsibility with the male chief for all affairs of the state. In the absence of a male ruler or heir, she ruled alone as chief.

The *ohemaa* was either the natural or classificatory mother or sister of the male chief. She could also be the senior female in the royal lineage. The anthropological literature places very heavy emphasis on the aspect of motherhood implied in the position. Rattray claimed, for example, that "the Queen Mother is to an Ashanti the personification of motherhood."[2] Fortes wrote in 1950: "a queen mother's authority depends on moral rather than legal sanctions and her position is a symbol of the decisive function of motherhood in the social system."[3] This emphasis is misleading. The office of the queen mother was not merely an elevated domestic position. It was a vital political office in the public domain and the occupant was an active political being. The queen mother's obligation to advise and guide the chief, including her right to criticize and rebuke him in public, was a constitutional duty. It differed from the maternal responsibility towards children. A queen mother who failed to perform the counselling duty was liable to deposition or destoolment.

As a full member and cochairman of the governing council or assembly of the state, the queen mother's presence was required whenever important matters of state were to be decided. She also had to hear all judicial cases involving the sacred oaths of the state. She was entitled to, and did have, her own separate court where she was assisted by female counsellors and functionaries. Her independent jurisdiction covered all domestic matters affecting women and members of the royal family. In certain cases, however, male litigants could apply to have their civil cases transferred from the chief's court to the queen mother's where fees and fines were generally lower.

The queen mother was the royal genealogist and she had the right to determine the legitimacy of all claimants to a vacant stool. In the case of the Asantehemaa (Queen Mother of the Asante union), she had the first right to nominate a candidate for the Golden Stool. She could exercise this prerogative three times, but her nominee had to be approved and accepted by the chiefs of Kumase and the federated states. When a successful candidate was selected the Asantehemaa played a key role in the rites and ceremonies of enstoolment. When the king died she also had responsibility for certain essential funeral rituals.[4]

As a political actor, the queen mother operated in two arenas: the royal lineage and the state. Lineage and state politics were a highly competitive business. Competition became endemic because there were no fixed rules of succession to the chiefship, the highest political office. The sons of all the women in the royal lineage were eligible. No royal person had the presumptive right to succeed. Rotation of the office among the segments of the lineage followed the vagaries of effective political power.

Given the open nature of succession, incumbent and prospective queen mothers had to use all available resources to secure optimum benefits from the structures of power in Asante society. Success of the women in politics, like their male counterparts, depended to a large extent on personal qualities of tact, leadership, intelligence, and political acumen. It also depended on personal and family assets which could be deployed to influence the political process. Like all Asante women, the queen mother was entitled to her independent wealth and property. The personal assets of many nineteenth-century queen mothers were known to be very considerable. T. E. Bowdich and Rev. T. B. Freeman, for example, commented in the early part of the century on the vast estates and whole villages owned by the Asantehemaa. Huge farms on these estates were cultivated by personal slaves and dependents.[5] In the middle years, several queen mothers throughout the kingdom became wealthy gold, kola and rubber traders.

It should be noted that certain structural and ideological limitations inhibited the effective exercise of power by the Asante queen mother. Although she had a general supervisory authority over women, she did not represent women's interests *as such* in the state government. Her hereditary royal position immediately raised her above women commoners who had no direct control over her conduct in office. The situation of the queen mother was thus very different from, say, that of the Iyalode in the Yoruba states where the latter was elected to represent women in government.[6] The structurally elevated position of the queen mother depended on the prestige of her ascribed status and not on her representative power.

Ideological constraints applied to all Asante women. Although the social system was characterized by a very high degree of equality between male and female members of a lineage, there were cultural attitudes which restricted the *modus operandi* of women in public life. One such attitude was the abhorrence of aggressiveness in public behavior in women but not in men. The aggressive female was sharply put down as *obaa-barima* (a "he-woman"). A much more significant ideological constraint was the ritual disability of women emanating from menstruation. This disability restricted the queen mother's participation in public life. During her menstruation she could not perform any religious rites for the ancestors, or go to the chief's court, or associate with any of the male functionaries in government.

Ritual disqualification and the fear of menstrual contamination (rather than physical inferiority) prevented all Asante women from serving in the state armies. Scholars of Asante have so far not appreciated the implications of women's military exclusion for the distribution of power between men and women. After the war of liberation from Denkyira in 1701, Osei Tutu, the founder of the Asante union, effected a complete integration of the military with government and politics. He appointed his successful military commanders as his principal councillors and assigned major administrative responsibilities to them. In fact, the military organization evolved for the Denkyira war and the earlier foundation wars became the framework for the distribution of state functions and administrative portfolios throughout the kingdom. Thus the seven military divisions with their commanding generals—Konti, Adwamu, Adonten, Nifa, Benkum, Kyidom and Gyaase—became the locus of political and administrative power.[7] I suggest that the conception and distribution of political and administrative power in a military framework operated to prevent women from acquiring political office in the state. Their ritual exclusion from military activity denied them a major opportunity for direct political participation.

There have, of course, been outstanding fighting queen mothers in Asante history. The state of Dwaben boasts of the energetic Ama

Seewaa (1841-c. 1850) who fought with her sons against Kumase in
the 1830s and returned from exile ten years later to rebuild her
state. The Kokofu recount the actions of Kokofuhemaa Ataa Birago
who fought in the turbulent civil wars of the 1880s and lost her life
in 1884. Then there is the well-known record of the very famous
Edwesohemaa Yaa Asantewaa (c. 1888-1922) who instigated and
commanded the determined war against the British in Asante's
final resistance in 1900. There is one common fact, however, about
all the known fighting queen mothers. They had all reached the
menopause. Rev. Freeman who visited Ama Seewaa in Dwaben in
1842 estimated her age between sixty and sixty-five.[8] Estimates
from oral traditions and documentary sources place Yaa Asantewaa's age in 1900 around sixty. In fact a remarkable aspect of the
elderly fighting women is that they could actually be so effective in
war when they had had no systematic practice or experience in their
prime.

A picture that emerges from a survey of some nineteenth-
century queen mothers is that of very dynamic women who skillfully blended a sense of history, politics, that is power politics, and
responsibility towards the preservation of their society. Their
careers reveal the modalities of their power in national affairs. A
brief summary of the activities of three of them will be given here to
illustrate the point.[9]

Asantehemaa Afua Kobi (1860-84) came to the stool after a major
purge by Asantehene Kwaku Dua I (1834-67) in which her mother,
Afua Sapon, and her brother, Osei Kwadwo, lost their lives. In 1867
her son Kofi Kakari became Asantehene after some unsuccessful
sharp manouevres by his opponents in the royal family. The joint
rule of Afua Kobi and her son took place in most critical circumstances which determined most of the Asantehemaa's actions and
responses.

First, the royal lineage in Kumase witnessed a growing lack of
unity and internal competition. Rivalry was intensified because of a
proliferation of royal women with numerous descendants, all of
whom sought power. Afua Kobi herself had three sisters who had
eligible sons for the kingship. Her daughter Yaa Akyaa (b. 1842),
who was later to challenge and depose her, had four sons and nine
daughters who were used as a major political resource.

Secondly, the death of the autocratic Kwaku Dua I in 1867
released a great number of ambitious, competitive and rivalling
military politicians on the national scene. These were men like the

powerful Generals Owusu Koko, Amankwatia IV and Adu Bofo who represented key administrative divisions and factions in Kumase. Their counterparts from the federated states who shared the national government were equally powerful and intractable. They included Mamponhene Kwabena Dwumo, Dwabenhene Asafo Agyei and Bekwaehene Yaw Opoku. They are hereditary chiefs of wealthy and populous states within the Asante union and they commanded great prestige as outstanding soldiers in their own right. The large collection of great military politicians quite overwhelmed the amiable but inexperienced Asantehene. Their actions and decisions precipitated the disastrous war of 1873-1874 with the British.

Eye witnesses and contemporary accounts agree that Asantehemaa Afua Kobi showed considerable tact and judgment in the difficult political circumstances of her times. Described as "a woman of great ability and shrewdness," she won the affection of the peope while she tried hard to influence her son and the other councillors. She judged correctly that a full-scale war with the British in 1873 would be disastraous for Asante. Consequently she counselled caution, peace and moderation. A "stout, energetic old lady" who looked very regal and much younger than her fifty-five years, Afua Kobi impressed witnesses who observed her at meetings of the Asante national assembly. She forcefully argued against the war policies of the ambitious military chiefs. She was always conscious of the judgement of posterity. Her sense of history was emphasized in her speech of 20 November 1873 to the assembled chiefs. In repudiating the war she said:

> From olden times it has been seen that God fights for Ashantee if the war is a just one. This one is unjust. . . . I am old now; I lived before Kwakoo Dooah, and I have now placed my son on the Ashantee throne. . . . I do not wish for our successors to say my son was the cause of the disturbance of the sixty *nkurow* [towns; i.e. the whole of Asante].[10]

Afua Kobi was not merely a pacifist. She perceived the suicidal nature of the war politics of the competing chiefs. She believed with some justification that many of the conflicts between Asante and the British could be resolved by negotiation. However, she did not completely eschew war as a possible and ultimate means of conflict resolution. The Elmina-born British envoy, Henry Plange, was made aware of this fact when he went to Kumase in 1872 to negotiate the cession of Elmina. Plange, who had a well-known antipathy to Asante, used very abrupt language and bold threats of British take-over in his discussions with Kofi Kakari and the chiefs. At the national assembly meeting of 2 September 1872 the Asantehemaa put a stop to the envoy's annoying threats when she rose to her feet and declared: "I am only a woman, but would fight the governor with my left hand."[11]

In 1873 Afua Kobi's counsels were overriden by the powerful and unscrupulous warlords surrounding her son. They went to war, fought brilliantly but lost. In the defeat and aftermath of 1874 the Asantehemaa recommended the deposition of Kakari. He had indeed revealed no noticeable political or administrative skills, and he had become quite profligate. It was a sad but courageous decision for Afua Kobi. She was observed in July 1874 to be "in a most pitiable and dejected state" on account of the ruin of Asante through the war and her son's actions. Nevertheless, she hoped to maintain her power and that of her branch of the royal lineage. Consequently, she proposed her younger son, Mensa Bonsu, as successor to Kakari "so that the kingship might at least be preserved for her dynasty."[12]

In spite of Afua Kobi's personal exertions the reign of her second son proved even more problematic. She formed useful alliances with the senior chief in Kumase, Bantamahene Awua II and the Omanhere of the Kokofu state, Yaw Berko. Both men were instrumental in securing Mensa Bonsu's election. However the stiffest challenge came from the Asantehemaa's own daughter, Yaa Akyaa. Starting from the late 1870s Yaa Akyaa built up a powerful political base from which she sponsored the claims of her own children to the Golden Stool.

It was unfortunate that Mensa Bonsu (1874-83) proved incompetent to deal with the oligarchic and factional politics of Kumase. He also failed to provide decisive leadership. Many well-intentioned administrative and social reforms that he sponsored in the postwar reconstruction failed or floundered because of his incompetence and the challenges and obstructionist tactics of the powerful councillors. In a deepening political crisis marked by secession, palace coups and assassination attempts, Mensa Bonsu's personality rapidly deteriorated. He instituted a bloody terror in the kingdom and resorted to flagrant extraconstitutional and extralegal means to maintain his position. On 8 March 1883 he was deposed and exiled in a coup that was cleverly managed by two leading Kumase politicians, Akyempemhene Owusu Koko and Akwamuhene Asafo Boakye. These two men were firm supporters of the Asantehene's ambitious sister, Yaa Akyaa, to whom they were linked by marriage.

Asante oral traditions today tend to gloss over the complexities of mid-nineteenth-century politics. They oversimplify the causes of the failures of Kofi Kakari and Mensa Bonsu, and they constantly blame their mother for failing to give them "good advice." As has been pointed out, Afua Kobi was very much alive to her responsibilities. Her contemporaries attest that she advised her children on matters of policy. But she could not control the character of the grown sons (both were thirty-five when they became kings) any more than she could eliminate the endemic rivalry within the royal lineage.

The woman who achieved complete mastery of the internal power politics of Asante was Afua Kobi's eldest daughter. She was shrewd and ruthless. In 1884 Yaa Akyaa and her clique of powerful supporters ousted her mother from office and banished her. Afua Kobi went into exile with Mensa Bonsu and neither of them was allowed to enter Kumase while Yaa Akyaa and her son, Prempe I, ruled there. The other deposed brother, Kofi Kakari, made a political comeback and contested the election of 1883 against Yaa Akyaa's son, Kwaku Dua II. Yaa Akyaa's forces won. She then secured the arrest of her brother in 1884 and ordered his execution. O\. er 200 of Kakari's kinsfolk were also annihilated.

When Kwaku Dua II died prematurely after reigning for only forty-four days, his mother promptly reorganized her forces in support of her next son, Prempe I. His claim was however challenged by a maternal "uncle," Yaw Atwereboanna. The struggle lasted for four years until 1888. The political and material cost to Asante was immeasurable. Yaa Akyaa's methods and tactics in the struggle have earned her condemnation in Asante traditions as a ruthless *obaa-barima* ("he-woman"). She is today one of the most controversial persons in Asante history.

When Yaa Akyaa usurped the stool from her mother in 1884, she was forty-four; but it is clear that she had been scheming for many years before. A strategy she found particularly useful was political marriage which she fully exploited. She herself married two brothers in succession who were the sons of her powerful granduncle Kwaku Dua I. Kwaku Dua I in fact initiated the grand strategy with his own cross-cousin marriage and the marriage of his sons into his matrilineal family. The result was that his grandsons born to Yaa Akyaa established a dynasty which had strong support from numerous patrilateral relations descended from the powerful king. Yaa Akyaa pursued the policy and married off seven of her daughters to powerful and wealthy chiefs in and out of Kumase. The sons-in-law provided much needed political and material support for the Asantehemaa's campaign and wars for the kingship.

Yaa Akyaa's personal assets were a crucial factor in her success. A woman of remarkable personality, her ambition was matched by her political astuteness. Her strong will, determination and energy kept her engaged for thirty years in the turbulent politics of late nineteenth-century Asante. Her considerable personal wealth enabled her to influence the political process, bribing politicians and supporters and acquiring necessary war materials (e.g. very expensive Snider rifles and ammunition) for her succession wars. Described by informants as a "fabulously rich" woman, she derived most of her wealth from inheritance and trade. She was one of the leading *akonkofo* (commercial enterpreneurs) in Kumase and she used her money to finance wars and political campaigns for her children. Later when she gained power as a virtual ruler of Asante she used the resources of the national treasury (*sanaa*) to further her political aims even though this was contrary to tradition.

In the contest between her son Prempe I and her "cousin" ("brother" in Asante kinship terminology), Atwereboanna, Yaa Akyaa left no stone unturned in the effort to capture the kingship for Prempe. She used diplomacy to secure allies in Kumase and the federated states. Diplomacy also won her British support which had become a major factor in Asante's internal politics. She used unstinted force and terror to eliminate her opponents such as her former son-in-law Butuakwa Okyeame Dwuben and the elderly kinsman and head of the royal household, Saamanhene Akyampon Panin who were executed. She also took possession of the Golden Stool which meant that none of her opponents in the royal family could be enstooled even if he won the contest. As the political struggle intensified all parties recoursed to the consultation of shrines, oracles and Muslin diviners. This was a usual practice in Asante where supernatural forces and predictions were used as

important adjuncts to political calculation. Yaa Akyaa avidly com-
peted in the search for shrines and predictions in the 1880s. Elderly
informants recall that most predictions were unfavorable to the
queen mother and her son but she persisted nonetheless to use
them. What she did in fact was to bribe most of the noted shrine
priests and Muslim diviners with large "donations" of gold.

In the end, Yaa Akyaa's superior forces, resources and organization won the Golden Stool for Prempe I in 1888. It is remarkable,
however, that the Asantehemaa changed her high-handed tactics
and abandoned the ruthless persecution of her political opponents
once she was secure in power. Since Prempe I was only fifteen when
he won the stool Yaa Akyaa became the virtual ruler of Asante for
most of the reign. She counselled and encouraged reconciliation
with her foes, a policy which was necessary because Asante had
been hopelessly depopulated and torn apart by the civil wars.[13]

The Asantehemaa also changed her stand towards the British
once she attained power. The British authorities in the Gold Coast
Colony never looked with favor on how she ruled the kingdom "by
her strong will and resolution." They never complimented her. But
Yaa Akyaa made it quite clear that there was no love lost between
her and such men as Governors Griffith, Hodgson and Maxwell.
She opposed every one of their spying and diplomatic missions
which sought to end Asante's independence. There were times
when the queen mother could barely tolerate or be civil to the
stream of British agents to Kumase. The agents realized to their
discomfiture that the "frostily dignified old lady" had all along stood
for aims that were diametrically opposed to their own. When British imperialism, therefore, decided to end Asante independence in
1895-96, the Asantehemaa became a principal target. She was
deported along with Prempe I and several important Asante chiefs
in 1896. She died on the Seychelles Islands on 2 September 1917 at
the age of seventy-five.

The tradition of opposition to the British passed on to another
queen mother, Yaa Asantewaa of Edweso. Her dramatic career in
the War of Independence in 1900 illustrates the singular determination of the Asante queen mothers to preserve the integrity of their
kingdom. There could be no compromise on the possession of the
Golden Stool as Governor Hodgson discovered at great cost. At a
secret meeting on the night of Hodgson's fatal speech, 28 March
1900, Yaa Asantewaa made a stirring appeal to the leaderless chiefs

and people of Asante. She asked them to commit themselves to a fight for Asante's freedom. She argued that no price or sacrifice was too great to regain their usurped power and maintain their cultural identity embodied in the Golden Stool. When the men began to argue among themselves and debate the issue, Yaa Asantewaa rose to her feet and charged:

> How can a proud and brave people like the Asante sit back and look while whitemen took away their king and chiefs, and humiliated them with a demand for the Golden Stool. The Golden Stool only means money to the whitemen; they have searched and dug every-where for it. I shall not pay one *predwan* to the governor. If you, the chiefs of Asante, are going to behave like cowards and not fight, you should exchange your loincloths for my undergarments (*Montu mo danta mma me na monnya me tam*).[14]

To dramatize her determination to go to war she seized a gun and fired a shot in front of the men. The challenge was accepted. That night all the chiefs "drank the gods" and took an oath to fight to rid Asante of British rule.

It would seem that the political role of Asante queen mothers was particularly heightened in times of crisis when male leadership was either unavailable or ineffectual. The individual and personal quali-ties of the women came into greater focus then. Yaa Asantewaa's personal devotion to the Golden Stool, her determination and cour-age contributed to making the siege and guerrilla war of 1900 one of the most determined resistance movements in West African his-tory. There is no doubt that she was inspired by a sense of personal loss arising from the deportation of her grandson, Edwesohene Kwasi Afrane II, in 1896. But she was fully committed to the restoration of the Asante monarchy itself and the freedom of the nation from British control. When she became the sole ruler of Edweso in 1896 she committed all her resources to the national cause. She made enormous military contributions from the vast supplies of war materials and money which she had inherited from her exiled grandson. She took to the field from the beginning of the war and her own picked bodyguard of shock troops proved to be the best organized and most determined soldiers.

CONCLUSION

It is not possible to make any sweeping generalizations about queen mothers in Asante history. However, the careers of Afua Kobi, Yaa

Akyaa, and Yaa Asantewaa that have been sketched here reveal certain important aspects of the queen mothers' role in government and politics. First, the women were individuals with great personal strength and ability and their personal qualities contributed to their effectiveness in public life. Secondly, the political milieu and historical circumstances within which they operated greatly affected their chances of success in politics. Ideological constraints and the changing alignments of political forces in Asante's factional politics determined the scope of the queen mother's power. These conditions were crucial especially where the queen mother as a political actor was grossly outnumbered by men. She was most effective in politics and government when she was free from ritual constraints and there was no available or effective male leadership.

Finally, the queen mother in public life cannot be seen as an isolated representative of women. The structural definition of her position as a hereditary coruler from a ruling lineage limited any "representative" aspect in her position. Her participation in government and politics therefore cannot be regarded as a general index to female political activity. Many queen mothers indeed have left impressive records of this participation, but their political goals were defined and generalized from concrete lineage or family interests. Their political fields were the arenas of lineage and state and they drew their support not from "female power" but from all effective sections of Asante society.

NOTES

1. R. S. Rattray, *Ashanti* (Oxford, 1923), pp. 81.2.

2. *Ibid.*, p. 85.

3. Meyer Fortes, "Kinship and Marriage among the Ashanti," in A. R. Radcliffe-Brown and D. Forde (eds.), *African Systems of Kinship and Marriage* (London, 1950), pp. 252-84.

4. See. A. A. Y. Kyerematen, *Kinship and Ceremony in Ashanti* (Kumasi [1970]).

5. T. E. Bowdich, *Mission from Cape Coast Castle to Ashantee* (London, 1819), p. 45; T. B. Freeman, *Journal of Various Visits to the Kingdoms of Ashanti, Aku and Dahomi* (3rd ed.; London, 1968. First publ. 1844).

6. See Bolanle Awe, "The Institution of the Iyalode within the Traditional Yoruba Political System", Unpublished conference paper submitted to the ASA Annual Meeting, Chicago 1974.

7. I have discussed the implications of the military in government and politics in greater detail elsewhere. See Agnes Akosua Aidoo, "Political

Crisis and Social Change in the Asante Kingdom, 1867-1901", unpublished Ph.D. dissertation (University of California, Los Angeles, 1975); also R. S. Rattray, *Ashanti Laws and Constitution* (Oxford, 1929), chs. IX-XII, XV.

8. Freeman, *Journal*, p. 162.

9. The detailed accounts can be found in my dissertation, "Political Crisis", *op. cit.* I am currently engaged in research and writing of a collective biography of five 19th century queen mothers including the three cited here.

10. Quoted in F. A. Ramseyer and J. Kuhne, *Four Years in Ashantee* (New York, 1875), pp. 246-47.

11. *Ibid.*, pp. 180-181; "Journal of Henry Plange" in H. Brackenbury, *The Ashanti War: A Narrative* (2 vols.; London, 1874), I, 42-49.

12. *Ramseyer and Kuhne*, Four Years, p. 298.

13. See Aidoo, "Political Crisis", *op. cit.*, Ch. X: The Reconstruction of Asante under Prempe I, 1888-1896".

14. Aidoo, Field-notes: Interview with Opanin Kwabena Baako, Edweso, 24 August 1970. Opanin Baako was present at the meeting and took part in all the subsequent events.

Members of the Organization of Women of Angola (OMA) taking part at a rally on the independence day. Photo: United Nations/J. P. Laffont, No. 131278. (1975)

3

Women's Political Participation in Nigeria[1]

Kamene Okonjo

POLITICAL SYSTEMS IN THE LESS-DEVELOPED COUNTRIES OF AFRICA—AN ALTERNATIVE MODEL

Any discussion of the role which women play in politics in a less-developed country like Nigeria has to contend with two major difficulties: the general bias against women in all recorded history, and the cultural bias which is often evident in the writings of Western social scientists when interpreting non-Western cultures.

Considering the bias against women in the writing of history, Vern Bullough in his book, *The Subordinate Sex*, observes that although women have existed as long as men and have borne the vicissitudes of life side by side with them, only a few deviants from the traditional subordinate roles have managed to break into the pages of history. Prominent among them are prostitutes and dancers. Even being a queen was not enough to win a woman a place in history. In order to be historically interesting there has to be something scandalous about the queen; Cleopatra, Hatshesput, Catherine of Prussia and Queen Elizabeth I of England all attracted the attention of writers not because what they did or were was "normal" but because what they did or were was considered "not normal."[2]

Social scientists have tried to explain this selectivity in historical bias by pointing out that men have, in the main, been responsible for recording history and have consequently chronicled what to them seemed important. Perhaps if women had written history, there might have been more objective reporting. Historically and sociologically, however, there is little doubt that the patriarchal system of authority, which appears universal, has had the effect of making curios out of women who concern themselves with affairs which deviate from that of the generally accepted mandate of "housewife." This has been even more true of women engaged in politics. Thus, much that has been written about women has been less dependent on scientific objectivity than on prejudice—paraded in the garb of tradition or social heritage sanctified by religion.

Organized religion helped to create, emphasize, and perpetuate the patriarchal *status quo*—the domination of the female by the male. It is a major factor affecting, in many places, women's participation in public life.[3] The Christian religion charges women to submit themselves to their husbands as it is fit in the Lord.[4] Islamic ideas on the place of women and the institution of purdah continue to restrict women's use of their own mental and physical abilities. Hinduism and Confucianism have worked out a detailed system in which the position of women has been fixed as absolutely and unconditionally inferior to that of men. Confucianism, for example, extolls the ideal woman as one who concentrates all her efforts on her household tasks and abhors participation in outside affairs. It regards such participation as the "root of all evil and the cause of the downfall of the great dynasties."[5]

Attitudes which have led to the idea of woman as a domestic type who shrinks from participating in public life, have existed not only in medieval times and in the societies of the less-developed countries, but in western Europe and North America as well. It is one of the aims of this paper to draw attention to the ways in which these "Western" prejudices have adversely affected the participation of Nigerian women in contemporary politics.

The second difficulty in a discussion of women in Nigerian politics, is the cultural bias evident in the perception and interpretation of non-Western cultures by Western social scientists. This bias particularly affects their reporting of the role which women play in publc life in America. In their book *Cultures and Societies of Africa* Simon and Phoebe Ottenberg express the view that:

> The role of women in the political organisation of Africa is in general a limited one, and their primary concerns are productive activities. While occasionally groups of 'Amazons' have been found in African

states, such as the specialized military forces of the ruler of Dahomey in West Africa, the political significance of such groups have been overrated, and their importance in Africa has been vastly overemphasized in some popular writings. Even in African matrilineal systems, such as the Ashanti of Ghana or those found in South Central Africa, women do not dominate politics, though kin ties through females form the basis of much of the political organization and action of the men. But it is clearly the men who control the society and who have the ultimate rights over property. In some indigenous states of southern Africa, the role of the chief's mother or wife may be a very important one, and there are a few instances when a ruler has been a woman, such as among the Lovedu of the Transvaal. Nevertheless, political systems are generally dominated by males regardless of type of kinship ties or of other factors in the political system.[6]

This assessment of the role of women in political organization in Africa raises many more questions than it answers. What explanation do we have for the emergence of groups of Amazons (women warriors) in Africa? Is this a chance phenomenon or does it result from the nature and organization of the political system? What political rights did military power confer on women in a state like Dahomey and how was it exercised? If kin ties through females form the basis of much of the political organization and action of the men, how did the political system operate without the women playing an influential if not a dominating role in politics? Is it only in some indigeneous states of southern Africa that the role of the chief's mother or wife may be a very important one? Why did women rulers emerge in some states, and what type of political system made this possible?

Whatever the truth of the situation, in the light of the few questions raised here, it is clear that Simon and Phoebe Ottenberg's statement cannot be regarded as an authoritative and final assessment of the role of women in the political organization of African states. Moreover, the validity of the views typified by this statement, which are beginning to be challenged by more recent research, are contradicted by some earlier authoritative views. Herskovits, writing in 1962, states that, "psychologically and functionally the position of women in African society has been high."[7] This view, which predates the Ottenberg's observation, is confirmed by Bohannan and Curtin who, writing in 1971, state that "African women by and large have a high social position; legal rights, religious and political responsibility, economic independence. Women in Africa are not, in short, a deprived group as they were in the nineteenth century Western world."[8] In this connection, the author, working among Nigerians in 1972 and North Americans in 1973, has noted that the Western ideal, in which the husband, as the sole earner in a household with a high standard of living, provides his wife with domestic help and/or gadgets with which to tackle housework, is alien to Africa. Instead, a wife expects to contribute to the needs of her household just as her husband does. In Africa, each spouse's contributions are recognized and appreciated by the other.[9] Afigbo, discussing women in Nigerian history in 1974, maintains that African women had an honoured and recognized place in society which made it possible for the gifted ones amongst them to rise to positions of political, economic, and social eminence. He contends that this was possible because of the opportunity for vertical and horizontal mobility which indigeneous societies provided women, enabling them to contribute significantly to their way of life.[10]

These views encourage us to present an alternative model of a political system, which might better fit the facts gathered in Africa. We refer here to what we might call "a political system with bisexual functional roles"—in short, a bisexual political system, as opposed to the unisexual political system which obtains in much of the Western world. In the latter system politics is dominated by men, the only status-bearing roles are filled by men, and women can achieve distinction and recognition only in so far as they take on the public functions of men and perform these creditably. By contrast, in the bisexual political system, while specific roles in politics are assigned to men, others are given to women, and women participate fully in the political affairs of their communities by right rather than by sufferance. This alternative model for the political systems of traditional African states and societies may be more useful in considering politics both in traditional as well as modern Nigerian society.

TRANSITION AND CHANGE IN NIGERIAN POLITICS— A THEORETICAL CHARACTERIZATION

We have mentioned ideal types like "traditional" and "modern" societies without discussing their characteristics. It is therefore necessary to define the various types which we are likely to use in our analysis, especially with reference to the variable, "participation of women in politics".

Great evolutionary theorists like Comte, Spencer, and Hobhouse in sociology, and Tylor and Westermarck in anthropology, assumed that all societies pass through similar stages of development. They theorized that, unless arrested, societies move from simpler, less complex, and less differentiated forms, to more complex, more differentiated ones, culminating in the modern industrial society.

Political scientists divide these stages of social development into three phases: the traditional, the transitional, and the modern—with each stage having its distinct characteristics as shown in Table I. But such a delineation of the stages of societal development is arbitrary, for since these stages present no demarcation lines, they generally are a poor guide to reality. It is difficult to say where one stage ends and another begins and they are better viewed as a continuum with sometimes considerable overlap between one stage and another. Two of these stages perhaps require further discussion.

Under the category of African traditional political organization as shown in Table I, are subsumed a diversity of types of political systems. These systems are characterized by the factors of kinship, territoriality, and allegiance, with the significance of each factor varying from society to society. Two further characteristics of such African political systems also deserve mention: the fact that ritual and religious beliefs are an integral part of government, and that political leaders often have to carry out religious functions for the welfare of society. In such a society, as among the western Igbo for example, the role of "mother of the community" cannot be taken up by a man, nor can a man function as the interceder on behalf of the community with "Mother Earth". The religious and political functions of "mother of the community" are of necessity vested in a woman. Secondly, the traditional political group is also characterised by its legalistic emphasis; this is shown in the many regulations dealing with the rights of the group and the individual. The judicial aspects of goverment are very often coupled with the executive arm of government, and administrators are very often judges as well.[12] It follows that if a political role is conferred by virtue of one's sex, administrative as well as juridical functions are also attached to the political role. Thus, it is to be expected that in a bisexual political

system where some roles in politics are sex specific, women's participation in all levels of politics is high.

TABLE 1
NIGERIA—THE THREE PHASES OF SOCIETAL DEVELOPMENT
AND WOMEN'S PARTICIPATION IN POLITICAL LIFE

Stages in Societal Development	Political Development	Political Participation	Modernization Variables	Social Mobility
I	Traditional	High	Nil	Very High
	Transitional (a) Colonial Period	Low	(1) Literacy (2) Urbani- zation (3) Christian Religion (4) Western Ideals	Very Low
II	*Transitional* (b) Post Colonial Period	Not so low (continues to improve)	(1) Literacy (2) Urbani- zation (3) Christian Religion (4) Western Ideals (5) Indust- rializa- tion	Low (continues to improve)
III	Modern	(Projection) High to Very High	(1) Literacy (2) Urbani- zation (3) Christian Religion (4) Western Ideals (5) Higher rate of Industri- alization	(Projection) High

The size of the traditional political organization is not a matter of
importance. As Potholm has pointed out, although the traditional
political organization is generally small in size (seldom more than

100,000 persons), preliterate, possessing minimal technology, and exhibiting intermittent political activity, it should be remembered that traditional political systems perform the same functions as larger, more elaborate, and more differentiated systems. Like larger systems, traditional political systems provide a basic societal order, process demands and elicit support, establish decisions that are enforceable, and, finally, set goals. The simplicity and sporadic nature of the decision-making process, the limited numbers of goals espoused, and the generally weak capabilities of such systems, should not therefore obscure the fact that differences between them and those systems termed "developed" are in fact, more of degree than of kind.[13]

In contrast to the traditional phase of political organization with its relative stability,[14] the transitional phase in any societal development ushers in "changing demographic, economic and political patterns, increasing technology and profound attitudinal changes."[15] During this phase the primacy of the central political authority is asserted, and is recognized by a widening group of constituents as the supreme legal authority. The composition of the political elite changes as its members are drawn from a wider set of socioeconomic backgrounds. Increasingly complex political structures develop and existing institutions may take on different and more specific functions.[16] The general population, however, is more directly affected by changing societal and environmental patterns. Primacy sentiments and local attachments are replaced by more contemporary and wider identifications. The society becomes less and less traditional and more and more associational. Major social bonds become voluntary and based upon the rational pursuit of self-interest. People enter into relations with one another at this stage, not because they must or because it is natural, but as a practical way of achieving an objective. A significant percentage of the population becomes urbanized. With the introduction of new health aids, greater awareness of disease patterns, and better nutrition, the death rate declines and life expectancy increases to over 40 years. For a period of perhaps several generations, however, the birth rate continues at the high level associated with a traditional society, and the result is a marked increase in the rate of growth of the population, of perhaps up to 3 per cent a year.[17]

From the description of the transitional phase of societal development, it can be seen that traditional institutions begin to weaken as new aspects of modernization and westernization erode those variables which favoured and perpetuated traditionalism. The colonial era ushered in this phase of Nigeria's societal development.

The colonial era disturbed the functioning of traditional institutions by imposing alien systems upon the colonies. Even though in most places, earlier forms of social organization still underlie the new system imposed upon them, they have nevertheless been profoundly altered for the worse. They have been rapidly reduced to a level in which they no longer answer the needs they were designed to fulfill and the demands which are made on them. Women in Africa have suffered more from this change than men, for after having had a role in traditional forms of organization, under colonialism they discovered themselves systematically excluded from any participation in the new set-up.[18] "Completely swept aside by this new development, they found that both the material and the psychological basis upon which their authority had rested had crumbled, and that gradually their privileges were disappearing."[19]

As shown in Figure 1, the most significant forces in robbing women of most of their traditional political powers have been modernization and westernization.

These antecedent variables of literacy, Western ideas concerning the position of women, new concepts of the supernatural, urbanization, and industrialization, have all had negative effects on the role which the Nigerian woman has played in traditional political life. The traditional political role of the woman is thus depicted as shrinking with each new element of modernization and westernization introduced into the traditional system. It is against this conceptual background that the participation of women in politics in Nigeria will be examined.

THE PARTICIPATION OF WOMEN IN NIGERIAN POLITICS— THREE CASE STUDIES

With an area of 983,000 square kilometers and a 1970 estimated population of 55 million, Nigeria is Africa's most populous country.[20] The area now known as Nigeria gradually came under British rule in the latter part of the nineteenth century, with the movement toward formal political control, which began in 1861, being completed by an edict in 1914. The edict amalgamated the colony of Lagos and the protectorates of Southern and Northern Nigeria into a political entity named Nigeria. The British Colonial Government

FIGURE 1
MODEL SHOWING THE DIMINUTION OF WOMEN'S POLITICAL PARTICIPATION DURING THE TRANSITIONAL PHASE OF SOCIO-ECONOMIC DEVELOPMENT IN NIGERIA

Modernization
Variables
Dependent
Variables
Consequent
Variables

1. Industrialization
2. Literacy
3. Urbanism
4. Western Ideas
   vis-a-vis Women

Traditional
Political
Participa-
tion of
Women
Depoliticization
of women
in Social Life
Religious
Variables

1. Islam
2. Christianity

with its headquarters in Lagos firmly controlled the unitary government until the decade 1950-60. Then, with the progressive implementation of decolonization policies, representative government was introduced. The country was reorganized in 1954 and again in 1963 and 1966, before May of 1967 when it was formed into a Federation with twelve states under a Federal Military Government.

The introduction of representative government also led to the establishment of, among others, three major Western type political parties. The Action Group (AG) formed the government in Western Nigeria, the Northern People's Congress (NPC) formed that in Northern Nigeria, and the National Council of Nigeria and the Camerouns (NCNC) in Midwestern and Eastern Nigeria. Independence came on October 1, 1960. 1966 marked a new phase in the political evolution of Nigeria, for two coups-d-états occurred, with the armed forces assuming power and banning political parties. Finally, in 1967, as has already been noted, the Federal Military Government established twelve states in the country.

Because of its size, there is a considerable diversity in the geography, climate, religion and ethnic traits of Nigeria. There are some 268 ethnic groups, the principal ones being the Hausa and Fulani of Northern Nigeria, the Yoruba of Western Nigeria, and the Igbo of Eastern Nigeria. This study will concentrate its attention on these main groups.

The Participation of Women in Nigerian Politics: The Case of the Hausa

The Hausa today are one of the largest linguistic groups in Africa. They do not form an ethnic unity, but are the result of a complet historical process which extended the range of a common language and culture. Their early history is obscure. It is bound up, as Trimingham points out, with the fortunes of a number of city states which were formed during the eleventh and twelfth centuries. Tradition indicates that the distinctive cultural characteristics of the Hausa have arisen from an intermingling of diverse elements from the north and east with the original inhabitants.[21] There is evidence that at least until almost the end of the fifteenth century, the status of women in Hausa society was very high, for the cuturally dominant people belonged to the So cycle of civilization, characterized by matrilineal succession in the ruling class and walled towns. While legend implies the substitution of patrilineal for matrilineal succession, women continued to hold high political office.[22] In the fifteenth Century, Queen Amina of Zaria, after succeeding to her father's throne, conquered all the towns around Zaria as far as Kwarafa and Nupe and dominated these regions for thirty-four years. In fact, the introduction of fortifications into Hausaland is attributed to her.[23]

Although Islam had reached the Hausa states by the 14th century,[24] it made slow progress and was usually practiced by only foreign communities settled in the towns and a few of the Hausa rulers. Functioning as a class religion in the Hausa city states, Islam did not gain a hold upon the Hausa cultivators until after the Fulbe conquest of the Hausa over the period 1802-1817. Barth, writing in 1857, was able to observe that: "It is evident that the larger portion of the population all over Hausa, especially that of the country town and villages, remained addicted to paganism till the fanatic zeal of their conquerors the Fulbe forced them to profess Islam, at least publicly."[25]

By 1900, when the British took control of Northern Nigeria, some 50 percent of the Hausa were animist, although by 1959 Islam had spread so rapidly that some 75-80 percent of the Hausa had become Muslim. Large blocks of animists collectively known as Azna or Maquzawa still survive, but they are coming more and more under Islamic pressure.[26]

Thus, although as early as 1485 the ruling monarch in Kano Muhamad Rimfa had established the custom of "kulle"—or wife seclusion,[27] both Muslim and pagan women in the Hausa city states enjoyed considerable freedom and high social status. The Muslim women were especially favored because of the limitation to four wives allowable to a muslim in a largely polygynous society. All Hausa women were economically independent of their husbands, and since they were responsible for the maintenance of their children, engaged themselves in commercial activities in order to do this. Because of the progressive Islamization of Hausa society following the Fulbe conquest of 1802-17, the unstable nature of the period, increasing sexual laxity and the greater use of concubines by men, respectable citizens felt forced to adopt the Persian system of the harem. The strict seclusion and segregation of the sexes under the Persian system protected women from unwelcome male attentions. Islam now invested the Hausa husband with absolute authority to decide where the conjugal home could be; this often led to conflict where matrilocal customs existed. With their progressive seclusion and the loss of their freedom to engage in economic activities, women became more and more dependent on men. Their obligations became confined exclusively to domestic work.[29] And without an economic base women could hardly influence politics.

As has already been pointed out in Figure 1, the influence of Islam on the participation of women in traditional Hausa politics has been one of depoliticization. In terms of the three phases of societal development as outlined in Table 1, the transitional colonial period, for the Hausa, started with the Fulbe conquest. Far from liberating Hausa society from Fulani religious, economic, and political domination, British colonialism confirmed this domination. It also permitted the expansion of Islam, with its deleterious effects on the participation of women in political and economic life. With the increasing Islamic influence upon Hausa society, the customs of the nobles and the wealthy in the towns such as purdah spread to the poorer peasants in the rural areas. The participation of women in Hausa politics was minimal; only a very few cases are recorded of women participating in politics in Northern Nigeria during the colonial period. One such case was the nomination of two members, the Sagi and the Niniwaye, to the Bida Town Council in 1937.[30]

The position of the Hausa prostitute today, especially in the Hausa diaspora in southern Nigeria, is in marked contrast to the seclusion of the majority of Hausa women from current politics. Prostitutes have been it must be noted, "the freest, most versatile and often the best-educated women in Islamic West Africa."[31] The Hausa trading disapora in southern Nigeria requires for its expansion the continued recruitment of women, since, according to its rules, descent is defined bilaterally, so that a good citizen of the diaspora is one born of a Hausa man and a Hausa woman. Hausa men in the diaspora marry only Hausa women, and in view of the shortage of eligible women, the institution of prostitution is used to reach a speedy adjustment of the demographic balance between the sexes and the ages. Since the traditional Islamic institution of prostitution has freed many women from their natal settlements in the North, and rendered them mobile within the Hausa diaspora, prostitutes have thus become a fundamental source of Hausa housewives for the pioneering men.[32]

In some of these settlements, like the Sabo settlement at Ibadan, there is an officially installed "chieftainess" who attends to the welfare of these women. With the introduction of party politics to the settlements in 1950, the prostitutes organized themselves in separate branches of the two major Southern Nigeria parties—the NCNC and the Action Group. In contrast to the housewives "barred" from public life, they have been very politically active, registering their names 'on voters' lists and casting their votes in federal, regional, and municipal elections.[33]

Two interesting questions immediately arise. Why have Hausa prostitutes participated in politics in the diaspora as contrasted with housewives? Secondly, why is there the necessity to appoint a "chieftainers" of the prostitutes when a "chief" to whom all are accountable already exists? The explanation might be found in the bisexual political system. Freed from the restricting influence of the Muslim institution of purdah, the bisexual nature of traditional Hausa politics reasserts itself. It becomes necessary to have a chieftainess, who takes direct responsibility for ruling over the women who do not fall into the category of "housewives." That is, free from the restrictions of Muslim law and institutions, and in a situation where women have their own economic base independent of men, there is a reversion to bisexual political practice.

This point is important in assessing the influence of secular Western ideas on the future position and role of women in politics in Hausa communities. The influence of Western education so far has been to encourage educated Hausa women to challenge the present sociopolitical status of women in Northern Nigeria. A few Hausa women hold important positions in their states and hold them creditably. In the North Central State, for example, a woman minister, appointed by that state's military regime, has held many ministerial posts.[34] Her status and that of other women like her is likely to spur Hausa women—the female group with one of the lowest sociopolitical status in the country at present—to ask for their rightful place in Nigerian politics. Table 2 attempts a summary of the past, current, and possible future development of the participation of Hausa women in politics.

Women's Participation in Politics among the Yoruba and the Edo

The Yoruba and the Edo are discussed together here since they are geographically neighbours and were from 1954 to 1963 both grouped in what was then the Western Region of Nigeria. According to the 1973 census, the Yoruba number about eight million and the Edo about one and a quarter million. Before the advent of British rule in the latter part of the nineteenth and earlier part of the twentieth centuries, both the Yoruba and the Edo had established empires. Politics in these empires was essentially centered around the king in his capital and his palace.

Women played a very important role in politics. In the Yoruba kingdom of Oyo, these "Ladies of the Palace," as they were called, contributed greatly to the smooth functioning of the political machinery. There were eight such titled ladies as well as eight priestesses. Of the eight titled ladies of very high rank, four deserve special mention, the "Iya Oba" who was the king's "official mother," the king's biological mother, if she was still alive (being quietly "put to sleep" on her son's ascession to the throne), the "Iya Kere," who, as the custodian of the royal treasures, wielded the greatest power and authority in the palace. Her position was one of great political significance because she could sabotage any of the king's public appearances by refusing to allow him the use of his garments of office, especially if there were disatisfication with him and his leadership. A third very powerful political figure was the "Iyalagbon"—the mother of the Crown Prince—who, like the king, wielded great authority and ruled over a part of the capital city. The fourth of these important ladies of the palace was the "Iyamode" who was responsible for the king's spiritual well-being. Her function was to guard the graves of departed kings and to act as an intercessionary and intermediary between the living king and the spirits of his dead predecessors. The king's unprecedented respect

TABLE 2

THE POLITICAL PARTICIPATION OF WOMEN IN HAUSALAND AT VARIOUS STAGES OF SOCIETAL DEVELOPMENT AND THE EFFECTS OF MODERNIZATION AND SOCIAL MOBILITY

Stages of Societal Development	Political Participation	Moderni- zation	Social Mobility
(1) Traditional or pre-literate (a) Before tenth century	Very high, women fought wars, ruled states, founded kingdoms	Nil	Very high
Traditional or pre-literate (b) During and after nineteenth century.	Institution of Purdah. Very little political participation	Nil	Very low
(2) Transitional (a) Colonial era	Institution of purdah. Very little political participation No voting right	Low literacy, urbanization Western standards and ideas	Very low
(b) Post colonial era	Very little political participation. Still no voting right	Low but improved;Low Literacy, Western ideal. High urbani- zation in places some industrial- ization	
(3) Modern Projection	Right to the vote. Medium political participation	High literacy Urbanization Industrialization	Medium to High

for her exalted position was evident in the manner in which he addressed her, calling her "Baba" (father), and saluting her on his knees. No other human being enjoyed that honour.[35]

This group of women formed an effective group of spokes-women for political stability and human rule, as well as for the interest of women at the highest political level in the kingdom. Their lives were bound up with that of the ruling monarch, with whom they were expected to depart to the land of the spirits in the event of his demise. The majority of Yoruba women are also known to have established, in the precolonial period, very effective political pressure groups, through which the political authorities were per-suaded to attend to issues which were of immediate concern to women. There is evidence that this practice continued in the Yoruba kingdoms until shortly after 1914, when with the amalga-mation of the Northern and Southern Nigeria Protectorates into the Colony and Protectorate of Nigeria, Nigeria passed formally under British colonial rule.[36] It should therefore be evident that because of the bisexual nature of the political system traditional Yoruba society accorded women high political status and permitted the participation of women in politics at all levels. Moreover, it is erroneous to believe that the sociopolitical status of women was depressed in traditional Yoruba society. In fact, the depressed sta-tus of women in politics resulted from the imposition of British colonial rule on a hitherto bisexual political society.

The high sociopolitical status of women found in traditional Yoruba society can also be observed in Edo society. There, for example, the Queen-Mother always received the title "Iyoba" from her son, the king, three years after his ascension to the throne and was thereafter sent to Uselu (a part of the kingdom) where she reigned as the "Iyoba of Uselu" and sat in the king's Executive Council as one of his four most senior and important chiefs. This practice of installing a Queen-Mother, who then participated in the running of the affairs of the Benin kingdom, was begun by Oba (King) Esigie. In 1506, Esigie installed as the first "Iyoba" of Uselu his mother Queen-Mother Idia, who was reputed to be politcally shrewd, warlike, and to have helped her son win a war against the Idah kingdom. This custom continued until 1889, when the British, as one of their first steps after conquering the kingdom of Benin, abolished the post of "Iyoba".[37] However, since the end of colonial rule, tradition has partially reasserted itself. The Government of the Midwestern State of Nigeria, has lately recognized the political eminence of Queen-Mother Idia by naming the first girls secondary school in Benin City after her.

The transitional phase in Yoruba and Edo political evolution, ushered in by the simultaneous imposition of the "Pax Britannica" and British colonial rule eliminated women from their exalted institutional positions in traditional politics. A new female political elite emerged to perforce, establishing itself through its success in colonial commerce. One such Yoruba woman was Madam Tinubu.

Madam Tinubu won herself wealth, position, and power through trade in slaves and tobacco with Brazil. Because of her position, she fought with success for the return and reinstatement of "Oba Akitoye," the Oba of Lagos exiled following the British seizure of Lagos in 1861. Thereafter Madam Tinubu became the power behind the throne of Lagos, a role which she continued to play until Akitoye died and his son, Dosunmu, became king. Her political power was so great that she was seen as a threat by some prominent chiefs in Lagos, who appealed to the British colonial administration for her removal. The British complied, and she was banished from Lagos to Abeokuta, the capital of the then independent kingdom of the Egba to the north of the colony of Lagos. She quickly established herself as the political and military power behind the throne of Egbaland and through successful trading in guns and gunpowder, played a key role in organizaing the successful defense of Egbaland against the kingdom of Dahomey in the 1860s. Understandably, the Egba rewarded her for her activities in the war with the title of "Iyalode" (First Lady) of Egbaland.[38]

The colonial era proper also produced its own female political activists in Yorubaland. A living example is Mrs. Funmilayo Ransome-Kuti who made an impact on the political life of Egbaland, and with independence has continued her political activities. Leader of the Nigerian Women's Union, she led the women of Egbaland in the forties to revolt against the taxation of women by the Abeokuta Local Authority and forced the then King of Egbaland into temporary self-exile.[39]

With the introduction of party politics in 1950, Yoruba women became active politically, organizing women's wings of political parties. With the end of colonial rule and the achievement of independence in 1960, it would be expected that their political potentialities would acquire new dimensions, since they had obtained the rights to vote and to run for office.

Yet they have not benefited in the exercise of this right, for not one female has been voted in as an elected represntative of the people in the Nigerian national legislature during the decade 1950-60. The record of the political parties had been dismal in this respect, despite the efforts of women. Of the two major southern political parties operating in Yorubaland which admit that women have a right to participate in politics (the Northern People's Congress does not), only the Action Group was prepared to nominate women candidates in the preindependence Federal election of 1959. Their candidate, Mrs. Wuraola Esan, lost her fight. In the case of the N.C.N.C., the party refused to nominate Mrs. Ransome Kuti of Egba fame, who had been an N.C.N.C. women's wing organizer and leader, and instead gave the nomination to a man who had once been a clerk in the school where Mrs. Kuti's husband had been headmaster. She contested as an independent and lost.[40] Table 3 attempts to summarize past and current women's participation in politics in Yorubaland. We turn now to the third major Nigerian ethnic group—the Igbo.

The Igbo, numbering some 8.7 million, live mainly in the East Central State of Nigeria. A small group—about 0.5 million—live in the Asaba, Aboh, and Ikah Divisions of the Mid-Western State of Nigeria, and are separated from their kin in South-Eastern Nigeria by the Niger River. In this ethnic group we encounter perhaps the most illustrative examples of women's traditional participation in the political lives of their communities. Frequently characterized as aggressive, frank, and ambitious, the Igbo (especially those on the eastern side of the Niger) have a political system which can be said to belong to the Group B or segmentary category described for Fortes and Evans-Pritchad in their epochal study of the typology of African political systems.[41] The difference with the Igbo, is that unlike the classic type, the political system of the Igbo has some centralized administrative and judicial institutions as well as divisions of wealth and status corresponding to the distribution of power and authority.[42]

Meek, the classical colonial anthropologist, describes the characteristic feature of Igbo society as the "almost complete absence of any higher political or social unit than the commune or small group

TABLE 3

WOMEN'S PARTICIPATIVE EXPERIENCE IN YORUBA POLITICS AT VARIOUS STAGES OF SOCIETAL DEVELOPMENT AND THE EFFECTS OF MODERNICATION AND SOCIAL MOBILITY

Stages of Societal Development	Political Participation	Modernization	Social Mobility
Traditional or preliterate	High. Politics centered around the palace in many forms	Traditional urban towns existed. Otherwise no modernization variables	High to Very High
(a) *Transitional Era* Colonial period	Low	Literacy. Westernization. Urbanization	Low
(b) Post colonial Era.	Much improvement Party membership. Voting. Seeking nominations and elections to legislature	As above and industriali-zation.	Much improved.
Modern Era	Very High	High	Very High

Women and Politics in Eastern and Mid-Western Nigeria—The Case of the Igbo

of contiguous villages whose customs and cults are identical and whose sense of solidarity is so strong that they regard themselves as descendants of a common ancestor."[43] Green remarks that it is not possible to identify any territorial unit among the Eastern Igbo within which there is a sovereign governmental authority.[44] Leadership is achieved, not ascribed, and authority is dispersed widely within each autonomous unit. It is not easy to single out any particular individual (male or female) who plays as outstanding a role as can be played among the Hausa, Yoruba, and Edo. Afigbo points out that these segmentary political systems also depend, for the regulation of political affairs between territorial segments, on non-kinship associations like title and secret societies. Each equivalent segment within the federation of segments, which constitute the central government of each autonomous unit, retains a large measure of power and authority and regards as binding only those decisions to which it has given its assent.[45] Afigbo further distinguishes two types of these political systems: the "Constitutional Village Monarchy" type to be found among the riverine and Western Igbo, and the "Democratic Village Republic" type to be found among the rest of the Igbo. Both systems are characterized by the small size of the political units, the wide dispersal of political authority among the sexes, lineages and kinship institutions, age grades, secret and title societies, oracles and diviners and other professional groups, the lack of clear separation between judicial, executive, and legislative functions, and, lastly, the lack of distinction between politics and religion in the governmental process.[46]

In both types of political system, each sex generally managed its own affairs, had its own kinship institutions, age grades, and secret and title societies. Independent evidence exists that women had the right to manage their affairs in traditional Igbo society. Sylvia Leith-Ross, the British government anthropologist, writing in 1939, observed that Igbo women were politically and economically the equals of Igbo men and that such industrious, ambitious, and independent women were bound to play a leading role in the development of their country. She had been astounded at the way Igbo women had organized and accomplished "a movement as original, and formidable as the Aba Riots, known to them as the Women's War, which necessitated the calling in of military forces before order could be restored and the subsequent appointment of a Commission of Enquiry." Her impressions were that more than the men, the women seemed to be able to cooperate, follow a common aim, and to stand by each other, even in difficulties.[47]

The Women's War took place during the colonial era and was a protest against the rumored taxation of women and the excesses of the Indirect Rule system in Igboland. The sociopolitical factors which made an organizd protest embracing an area of about 520 square kilometers possible, however, are to be sought for in a traditional structure which recognized the rights of Igbo women to manage their own affairs.[48] In Igbo political history, as is the case in the political history of most of Africa, it is not easy to ascertain the exact dimensions of women's political powers. Yet it is obvious from their elevated sociopolitical status at the turn of the century, when Nigeria came under British rule, that Igbo women enjoyed a great deal of political independence and that they had their own Women's Councils which enacted laws.

Prominent among the institutions evolved by women for the running of their affairs in both types of political system, are the *Ikporo-Ani*, the *Umu-Ada* and the *Inyemedi*. The *Inyemedi* (wives of a lineage) comprising all women married to men of one lineage, was responsible for settling all disputes between the wives of that lineage. In meetings of the *Inyemedi*, the *Anasi*—the most senior wife in terms of length of marriage to a man of the lineage—presides. Disputes of a more serious nature of infractions of sexual morality by women were dealt with by the *Umu-Ada*. The *Umu-Ada* was composed of the widowed, married, and unmarried daughters of a lineage, village, or a village group. Because of the exogamous nature of marriages in Igboland, the married daughters acted as arbiters between their natal lineage, and the lineages into which they had married. They were thus able to prevent wars. They also took a keen interest in the local politics of their natal lineage, and village. When necessary, they took a common stand on an issue, forcing the political authorities of their villages to implement their wishes or demands. The *Ikporo-Ani*, on the other hand, was made up of all the adult women in a village, or village group, and made decisions on all matters which affected the generality of women.

Peculiar to the "Constitutional Village Monarchy" type of political system found among the riverine and western Igbo, is the female institution of the "Omu." The "Omu" has been styled by anthropologists and sociologists like Northcote Thomas, Basden, and Henderson as the "Queen" of the village, or village groups, since her role in society closely parallels that of the king.[49] Calling her "queen", however, gives a false impression of her social and political roles. The Omu is neither the king's wife, nor his relative. The word Omu is the traditional Ika Igbo salutation to a married and matured women. It is, most likely a shortened form of the word "*Omunwa*" or "*Nneomumu*"—"she who bears children," or "mother". She is, therefore, simply the "female counterpart of the king" in his role as father of the community or the traditional "mother" of the village, or village group.

As the official mother of her society, the Omu, usually a woman distinguished by her wealth, intellect, and character, had responsibility for the affairs of the women of the community and presided at meetings of the *Ikporo-Ani*. She selected her own counselors just as the king (*Obi*) did and with identical titles, and reigned from a throne just as he did. She also had the right to don the colonial-type white helmet, felt hat, or red cap (in Onitsha) to signify her political equality with her men peers. Since her major political function centered around women's affairs, and since trading was a major social and economic function of women in traditional Igbo society, she and her counselors reigned supreme in the markets—fixing prices of goods, settling quarrels arising in the market, and imposing fines, if necessary. To her, also, fell the duty of acting as a court of law for all cases involving women, encouraging traditional title-taking among women, and cleansing and releasing widows from protracted mourning. She and her counselors acted as custodians of the welfare of the village or village group, performing propitiatory rites and sacrifices to ensure the welfare of its markets and to prevent the occurrence of epidemics and wars.

It is not surprising, in the light of their action in abolishing the post and title of *Iya-Oba* of Uselu after their conquering of Benin in 1889, that the British colonial administration either failed to see or refused to recognise the political institutions evolved by Igbo women for their governance. The British were conditioned by their experience to seek in their newly-acquired territories a social organism which would evolve into the western European type of nation state. They regarded the Igbo, with their segmentary political system, as acephalous, primitive, and stateless. The British sought to create an administration modelled after the emirates of Northern Nigeria, which had formed the basis of the famous system of indirect rule. District and village heads in Northern Nigeria did not find in the democratic village republic political system of the Igbo, political figures equivalent to the Emir. They were anxious to use in their administration of the Igbo areas some variety of local administration of African antecedents. Since they had as their model of indirect rule the emirate version in the orthodox tradition of Lugard, Perham, and Mair, it is also not surprising that the British Colonial Government proceeded to create and appoint, without consulting the Igbo, Warrant Chiefs, and introduced a Native Administration system in which the Warrant Chiefs played a primary role. The Warrant Chief and Native Administration system, as proposed by the British, proved unacceptable to the Igbo. The failure of indirect rule in Eastern Nigeria, the collapse of the Warrant Chief system, and the success of the revolt of the women in

1929 known as the "Women's War," all point to the unsatisfactory nature of the colonial solution.

Not integrated into the new unisexual colonial framework of politics, Igbo women suffered a dimunition in their collective participation in politics during the transitional colonial period. Yet, as in the case of the Yoruba, new leaders emerged through achieving outstanding success in colonial commerce. These leaders attempted to unite in their persons traditional political power and colonial political influence. A case in point is the famed Madam Okwei of Onitsha and Ossomari, otherwise known as Omu Okwei (1872-1943). Using her wealth acquired in her trading with foreign merchant companies to acquire political power, she engineered the appointment of her husband as a member of the Onitsha Native Court—a position of considerable political importance in the colonial administration of the period. She finally became the Omu of Ossomari, functioning in her role of Omu as "foreign minister" or "ambassador-at-large" between her people, the foreign commercial firms, and the British colonial administration. She held her post of Omu so creditably that she is still regarded by many as the greatest Omu in Ossomari political history.[50]

In the period of the transfer of power from the British colonial administration to the hands of local politicians in the decade 1950-1960, women participated in party politics in Eastern Nigeria, mobilizing women and organizing women's wings of political parties. Again, as in Western Nigeria, despite the women's acknowledged activities which benefited their parties immensely, their parties failed to accord them the recognition which they deserved. Mrs. Margaret Ekpo, the dynamic leader of the women's wing of the N.C.N.C. in Eastern Nigeria, sought but failed to obtain her party's nomination to stand as its candidate in the Aba urban constituency. Mrs. R.T. Brown who was nominated by the Action Group to contest in Port Harcourt lost the election, while Mrs. M.R. Nwogu who stood as an Independent in the Orlu South Eastern constituency also lost.[51]

Thus, in the seven years of postindependence civilian politics, not one woman was elected into any of the national or regional legislatures. The southern parties attempted to correct this situation by appointing their party faithfuls to various legislatures. In this way, Mrs. Margaret Ekpo (N.C.N.C., Eastern Nigeria), Mrs. Kerri (N.C.N.C. Midwest), Mrs. Janet Mokelu (N.C.N.C., Eastern Nigeria) and Mrs. Elizabeth Adekogbe (Action Group Western Nigeria) were all appointed to the Senate, the Upper House in Lagos. This trend has been continued in the East Central State by the appointment of Mrs. Flora Nwakuche as Commissioner in the Military Government. Table 4 summarizes the salient variables in the discussion of the participation of Igbo women in politics in Nigeria.

TABLE 4

THE PARTICIPATION OF IGBO WOMEN IN POLITICS IN NIGERIA AT VARIOUS STAGES OF SOCIETAL DEVELOPMENT AND THE EFFECTS OF MODERNIZATION AND SOCIAL MOBILITY

Stages in Societal Development	Political Participation	Modernization	Social Mobility
1. Traditional or Pre-colonial.	Very High.	Nil	Very High.
2. *Transitional* (a) Colonial.	Very Low.	Literacy, Urbanization Western Ideas vis-à-vis women	Low
(b) Post Colonial	Low. Some improvement	Ditto Also Industrialization	Not so low.
3. Modern. (Projection)	High to Very High.	As in 2(b)	High to Very High.

SUMMARY AND CONCLUSION

The foregoing analysis has directed attention to the unsatisfactory nature of much of current Western description, categorization, and interpretation of women's political participation in Nigeria and has presented an alternative framework—the political system with bisexual functional roles—for viewing these activities. We have attempted to show that this alternative conceptual framework might better fit the reality of political activity in the traditional political system considered, since certain politico-religious roles are sex-determined in these societies. We have pointed out that with the imposition of colonial rule, whether of the local or foreign variety, women's active participation in the political life of their communities had diminished. This has been the result of the imposition of unisexual political systems on hitherto bisexual political systems, a situation reinforced by the generally anti-feminist prejudices of organized religions like Christianity and Islam.

We have presented evidence to demonstrate that the current unisexual nature of national politics, itself only a slight modification of the imported prototype of the Western governmental model, still stifles Nigerian women's political participation. National leaders, unconsciously seeking for solutions to a felt but unrecognized problem, appoint women to posts at the highest political levels, by-passing the established political machinery. We have further demonstrated that these indigeneous bisexual political systems have continued to flourish at the local and subnational levels, despite the nonintegration of women in politics at the national level.

It seems, therefore, that a departure from the imported unisexual Western representative governmental model is necessary in Nigeria. There are good reasons for this assertion. Apart from the grounds already extensively argued in this paper, demographically, women constitute about 50 percent of the world's population. If political representation in legislatures and governments reflected the actual situation in a country, it would be expected that, by and large, 50 percent of the seats in a legislature or of posts in government would be held by women. The fact that this is not the case is a clear indication that the political process, as it is now operated, is biased against women. New procedures for the selection of persons to serve on legislatures and government are therefore necessary in order to correct this bias.

In the traditional bisexual political system women chose their own leaders to run the affairs of state which were recognised to be in the province of women. It is proposed, as an approximation of the bisexual political system and to ensure adequate representation of women, that each constituency elect two persons—a man and a woman—to the legislature. In order to ensure that the total number of legislators does not unnecessarily increase, the size of a constituency should be double that of a current constituency, with the voters in each such enlarged constituency electing two persons— one woman and one man—for seats in the legislature. This would then ensure that the distribution by sex of the legislature conforms with the actual demographic situation in a country, while leaving the total number of legislators unchanged.

As there would be as many women as men in the legislature, the likelihood of a cabinet or government made up only of men would be remote, and parity of representation by sex in the government would more likely be assured. Thus, the particular needs and feelings of women, in any major decisions made about the affairs of a country would not be overlooked, and women would no longer constitute the "silent majority" of a country. Moreover, the legislature and government which would emerge in Nigeria under such a reformed electoral system would approximate the bisexual political system to which Nigerian societies are already accustomed.

It is to be seen whether Nigerian political leaders will grope their way to a correct diagnosis of the current malaise in Nigerian politics. A correct diagnosis of the source of this malaise and its subsequent removal are necessary for the successful mobilization of women in the drive for accelerated economic development. This is a goal accepted by all, both women and men, as the most important national goal after that of national integration and unity.

NOTES

1. This paper was first presented at the American Political Science Association Conference at Chicago in August, 1974, and later at the African Studies Association Meeting in San Francisco in October, 1975. The paper, however, is being published as only a slightly revised version of the 1974 paper, for although political leadership in Nigeria has changed, womens' nonparticipation in politics still remains very much an issue.

2. Vern Bullough, *The Subordinate Sex: A History of Attitudes Toward Women* (Baltimore: Penguin Books, 1974), pp. 2-4.

3. L. N. Menon, "From Constitutional Recognition to Public Office," *The Annals of the American Academy* (January, 1968):25-36.

4. Compare St. Paul the Apostle. First Epistle to the Corinthians, XI, 8-11; XIV, 34-35, *The Holy Bible* (London: The British Foreign and Bible Society, 1958), pp. 1088, 1091.

5. Bullough, *op. cit.*, pp. 230-249.

6. Simon Ottenberg and Phoebe Ottenberg, eds., *Cultures and Societies of Africa* (New York: Random House, 1969), pp. 48-49.

7. M. J. Herskovits, The Human Ractor In Changing Africa (, 1962), pp. 246.

8. P. Bohannan and P. Curtin, *Africa and Africans* (New York: Natural History Press, 1971), pp. 107-108.

9. These observations were made during field work which I conducted in Nigeria in 1972 among the Igbo, both Western and Eastern, and among North Americans in the United States in 1973.

10. A. E. Afigbo, "Women in Nigerian History," Unpublished paper, Nsukka, Nigeria, March 1974, pp. 2-4.

11. Durkheim calls the earlier stage of development, with its lack of complexity and differentiation, "the mechanically organized society" and the latter stage, with its complexity and division of labor "the organically organized society." E. Durkheim, *The Division of Labour in Society*, George Simpson, trans. (New York: The Free Press, 1969).

12. Simon Ottenberg and Phoebe Ottenberg, *op. cit.* pp. 46-48.

13. C. P. Potholm, *Four African Political Systems* (Englewood Cliffs, N. J.: Prentice-Hall, 1970), pp. 41.

14. The difference between this phase and the succeeding phases lay in the fact that change in the traditional era was change within the system itself, as opposed to change of the whole system in the transitional and modern eras.

15. C. P. Potholm, *op. cit.*, pp. 36-37.

16. *Ibid.*, p. 36-37.

17. L. Broom and P. Selznick, *Sociology: A Text with Adapted Readings* (New York: Harper and Row, 1963), pp. 46.

18. J. Van Allen "Sitting on a Man: Colonialism and the Lost Political Institutions of Igbo Women," *Canadian Journal of African Studies*, VI, ii (1972): 165-181. See also A. Lebeuf, "Women in Political Organization," *Women of Tropical Africa*, D. Paulme ed. (Berkeley: University of California Press, 1971), pp. 94.

19. A. Lebeuf, *op. cit.*, pp. 94.

20. These 1970 medium variant United Nations estimates are based on a 1962 estimate of 45.3 million for the population of Nigeria made by Chukuka Okonjo. See Chukuka Okonjo and J. C. Caldwell eds., *The Population of Tropica Africa*, (London: Longmans, Freen and Co., 1968), pp. 78-96. See also United Nations, *World Population Prospects as Addressed in 1968*, Population Studies, No. 53, United Nations document ST/SOA/ Series A/53 (1973): 29, 116.

21. J. Spencer Trimingham, *A History of Islam in West Africa* (Oxford University Press, 1962) pp. 126.

22. H. R. Palmer, *Sudanese Memoirs*, 3 vols. (Lagos, 1928) pp. 132 ff.

23. H. R. Palmer, *op. cit.*, pp. 109.

24. *Kano Chronicle* text, pp. 24-26: H. R. Palmer, *op. cit.*, pp. 105-106.

25. H. Barth, *Travels and Discoveries in North and Central Africa 1849-1855, 5 vols., vol. II, (1857), pp. 118.*

26. J. Spencer Trimingham, *Islam in West Africa* (Oxford at the Clarendon Press, 1959), pp. 16.

27. Kano Chronicle text p. 45; H. R. Palmer, op. cit. 112.

28. S. J. Hogben and A. H. M. Kirk-Greene, *The Emirates of Northern Nigeria: A Preliminary Survey of their Historical Traditions* (Oxford University Press, 1966), p. 26.

29. J. Spencer Trimingham, *Islam in West Africa, op. cit.*, pp. 176, 177, 189.

30. S. J. Hogben, and A. H. M. Kirk-Greene. *op. cit.*, pp. 279.

31. J. Spencer Trimingham, *Islam in West Africa, op. cit.*, pp. 178.

32. Abner Cohen, "Cultural Strategies in the Organization of Trading Diasporas", *The Development of Indigeneous Trade and Markets in West Africa,* Claude Meillasoux, ed. (London: Oxford University Press, 1971), pp. 266-281.

33. Abner Cohen, *Custom and Politics in Urban Africa: A Study of Hausa Migrants in Yoruba Towns* (London, 1963), pp. 63.

34. Miss D. Miller, a Hausa Christian, has held various portfolios as a Commissioner in the government of the North Central State of Nigeria.

35. Rev. S. Johnson, *The History of the Yorubas: From the Earliest Times to the Beginning of the British Protectorate.* (London, 1966), pp. 63-67.

36. N. A. Fadipe, *The Sociology of the Yoruba*, (Ibadan, 1970), pp. 253.

37. Jacob Egharevba, *A Short History of Benin.* (Ibadan, 1968), pp. 75-76.

38. S. Biobaku. "Madam Tinubu," *Prominent Nigerians of the Nineteenth Century.* (Cambridge, 1960).

39. L. R. Sklar, *Nigerian Political Parties.* Princeton: Princeton University Press, 1963), pp. 251.

40. K. W. J. Post, *The Nigerian Federal Election of 1959: Politics and Administration in a Developing Political System,* (Oxford University Press, 1963), pp. 264-265.

41. M. Fortes and E. E. Evans-Pritchard, eds., *African Political Systems* (Oxford, 1940). See the Introduction for their typology of African political systems.

42. G. I. Jones, *The Trading States of the Oil Rivers.* (Oxford, 1963), pp. 4.

43. C. K. Meek, *Law and Authority in a Nigerian Tribe: A Study in Indirect Rule* (London: Oxford University Press, 1937), pp. 3.

44. M. Green, *Igbo Village Affairs* (London: Sidgwick and Jackson, 1947), pp. 3-5.

45. A. E. Afigbo. *The Warrant Chiefs: Indirect Rule in South-Eastern Nigeria 1891-1929.* (London: Longman, 1972) pp. 13-36.

46. *Ibid.*

47. S. Leigh-Ross, *African Women,* (UK.: Reutledge Kegan Paul Ltd., 1965), pp. 19-20.

48. For a fuller discussion of the causes of the Women's War (Ogu Umunwanyi), otherwise known in Nigerian colonial literature as the Aba Riots see A. E. Afigbo, *The Warrant Chiefs op. cit.*, pp. 207-248.

49. G. T. Basden, *Niger Ibos,* (London: Seeley Service and C., Ltd., 1938), Reprinted, London: Frank Cass, 1966.; also R. N. Henderson ed., *The King in Every Man, Evolutionary Trends in Onitsha Ibo Society and Culture.* (New Haven and London: Yale University Press). and Northcote W. Thomas, *Law and Custom of the Ibo of the Asaba District, S. Nigeria, Part IV,* (London: Harrison and Sons).

50. F. I. Ekejiuba, "OMU OKWEI: The Merchant Queen of Ossomari," *Nigeria Magazine*, No. 90.

51. K. W. J. Post, *op. cit.*, p. 281.

4

Tanzanian Women and Nation Building

Joyce Ladner

*Our motto has ever been, to unite and join hands with all the women in
Tanzania of every race and creed, so that the many problems and tasks facing
us, can be shared. In this spirit, the work of adult literacy, health and child
care, better farming methods, increased incomes through cooperatives, han-
dicrafts and small trades, have all emerged in different parts of the country,
bringing hope, encouragement and confidence in the future.*

Motto of the *UMOJA WA
WANAWAKE WA TANZANIA*
(UNITED WOMEN OF TANZANIA)

Tanzanian women have been encouraged by the country's leadership to break the shackles of tradition and play an assertive role in
every phase of this young East African nation's political, social and
economic development. There are several major areas in which the
participation of women can be recognized. First, the *Umoja wa Wanawake wa Tanzania* (United Women of Tanzania) was founded in 1962
by President Julius Nyerere and the Ministry of Cooperatives and
Community Development to foster more active political involvement in the *Ujaama* villages. *Ujaama* villages are cooperative farms
and other economic development enterprises that were initiated by
the government to encourage "self-reliance" among the entire
population. Finally, young women are able to join the National
Servicemen corps whereby they undergo intensive training that
enables them to serve the nation-building efforts.

Tanzania, under the leadership of the charismatic Mwalimu Julius K. Nyerere, received its independence from Britain in 1961. As a member of the East African Community (with Kenya and Uganda), the majority of its population still survive under widespread poverty with the per capita income being roughly the equivalent of seventy American dollars. Yet, in ten short years Tanzania has gone further than most comparable developing African nations in abolishing the very small colonial-inspired elite class which was set above the teeming masses, the majority of whom still reside in rural villages.

Today Tanzania is in the vanguard of a "united" African movement, maintaining a non-aligned stance from the major Eastern and Western powers. President Nyerere is one of the most outspoken critics of white domination in Southern Africa and from the capitol of Dar-es Salaam provides a base of operation for the African freedom fighter movements.

One of the most interesting features of Tanzania's development is its "African Socialism" which determines both policies and values. President Nyerere explains the importance of this ideology:

> Modern African socialism can draw from its traditional heritage the recognition of "society" as an extension of the basic family unit . . . It was in the struggle to break the grip of colonialism that we learned the need for unity. We came to recognize that the same socialist attitude of mind which, in tribal days, gave to every individual the security that comes of belonging to a widely extended family, must be preserved within the still wider society of the nation.[1]

Through accepting the traditional concept of the extended family and its translation to a political, economic and social context, Tanzanian masses readily identify with the task of nation-building in which the country is currently engaged. Individuals feel themselves to be a vital part of this dynamic process because they can totally engage *themselves*—their bodies, minds and spirits—in this movement toward the self-reliance and national destiny.

In calling for a new beginning whereby the nation's masses would be able to overcome the poverty and the other wretched conditions produced by colonialism, Nyerere felt it necessary to involve the entire population in the struggle. It is the contention of the country's leadership that if Tanzania is to become self-reliant, no sex or group can be discriminated against and prevented from playing an active role in nation-building.

This new thrust, however, necessitated a break from the tradition of female subjagation and the establishing of an open society that would value and utilize the skills of men, women and children. Indeed, no developing country with a lack of skilled personnel can afford not to utilize all of its available manpower in the development of its political, economic, and social institutions.

However, the traditional role of Tanzanian women has been an inferior one. Confined to the background in practically every facet of their lives, they performed more than their share of the work load, and were oftentimes exploited by the male population. Some of this exploitation was described by Mrs. Sarah Nyirenda, Chairman of the Women's Rights Committee of the *Umoja wa Wanawake wa Tanzania* (U.W.T.):

> ...We know that our society is overcrowded with all sorts of problems, many of them based on tradition. Marriage is one of these problems. I...fail to see how I could give my hard-earned vote to a man who, for instance, has dropped his rightful wife simply because she has proved outmoded since the attainment of independence; or to a man whose children look neglected, underfed and underdressed while their father drives a deluxe car every day and spends his nights in nightclubs on drinking sprees. Or take the case of a polygamous peasant whose wives have been turned into working machines to bring wealth to him while all they get in return are pieces of kitenge or khanga (African print) cloth after a year's productive labour. This is what I call exploitation under the family cover. Can this be tolerated in socialist Tanzania?[2]

An additional factor which has contributed to the subjugation of women is the strong influence of the Islamic religion which requires that women assume very passive roles in both public and private life.

President Nyerere understands this situation thoroughly, in fact, no one seems to understand more clearly than he the role their sexual inequalities have played in the traditional life. He writes:

> Although we try to hide the fact...it is true that women in traditional society were regarded as having a place in the community which was not only different, but to some extent inferior.[3]

In commenting on the work load of women, he continued:

> It is impossible to deny that the women did, and still do, more than their fair share of the work in the fields and in the homes. By virtue of

their sex they suffered from inequalities which had nothing to do with their contribution to the family welfare. Although it is wrong to suggest that they have always been an oppressed group, it is true that within traditional society ill-treatment and enforced subservience could be their lot. This is certainly inconsistent with our socialist right of all to live in such security and freedom for all others. If we want our country to make full and quick progress now, it is essential that our women live on terms of full equality with their fellow citizens who are men.[4]

Nyerere has thus consistently advocated the equality of all people within the society as a necessary prerequisite for full and prosperous nation-building. At the same time, however, he has recognized the traditional inequities which characterized the lot of Tanzania's female population, and he understands the difficulties involved in breaking with tradition and immediately embarking upon this new course. Thus, one can observe deep strains, conflicts and contradictions within Tanzanian society as women move forward to assume previously forbidden roles and responsibilities. More will be said about this later.

One of the creative responses to combatting traditional inequalities has been the deliberate attempt by the country's leadership to organize Tanzanian women in relevant political and economic nation-building activities. The most visible of these is the U.W.T., an arm of Tanzania's sole Political Party, the Tanganyika African National Union, commonly referred to as TANU.

Before the U.W.T. was formed, several groups throughout the country, including the Tanganyika Council of Women, were also attempting to organize those females who wanted to play a more active role in nation-building. However, it was deemed necessary to combine all of these diverse groups under one banner and utilize them as a political force, rather than simply relegating them to the civic and social arena.

In outlining the U.W.T. platform, Bibi Titi Mohammed, former president of the organization, parliamentary secretary and members of the National Assembly, made the following comments:

> As the one and only national women's organization, we women are determined to help, not only in the fight against the three enemies— poverty, ignorance and disease but to raise the social, economic and educational status, and to make the role of women a more dynamic

one, thus enabling us to fulfill more effectively our own needs, those of our families and those of our country. The U.W.T.'s special contribution will be to encourage women to take an active part in promoting family welfare through full participation in the fields of health, education and social development.[5]

The U.W.T. immediately set about the task of organizing literacy classes, cooperative agricultural projects, public health instruction, and nursery schools. From its formation, some of the more active members have been the wives of Tanzania's top leadership. Mrs. Fatma Karume (wife of The Second Vice President), Mrs. Sophie Kawawa (wife of The First Vice President), and Mrs. Maria Nyerere are at the forefront of this organization, and are quite outspoken on the critical issues affecting Tanzanian women. In addition to advocating equal rights for women, they are also active project organizers. For example , Mrs. Maria Nyerere became upset over the large quantities of eggs that were being imported from neighboring Kenya, and established a cooperative egg farm to meet Tanzania's consumer demands. On the local level, the party draws its constituency from very active grassroots women in every region in Tanzania. Local chapters of the U.W.T. are spread throughout the countryside.

The role of the U.W.T. as a potent political force cannot be overlooked. In addition to involving women in grass-roots politics throughout the nation, they have also heeded the call of action when Tanzania has been faced with crises situations. In 1965 they led the brigade, mobilized by tens of thousands of women all over the country, against the Army mutiny, and were directly responsible for putting down this subversive action which could have caused the overthrow of the government. In 1970 the U.W.T. played a leading role in organizing a protest against the Portuguese-led invasion of Guinea, Tanzania's West African sister nation. The U.W.T. joined forces with labor, civil servants, students and peasants to protest the invasion. Realizing the vulnerability of their own country to these kinds of external attacks from hostile forces, some women even volunteered to go to Guinea and take up arms, had it been necessary.

A second major area in which one observes strong participation by females is in economic development. It is perhaps more in agriculture than in other areas that one recognizes the prominent role the masses of women play. I was personally overwhelmed by my own observations of how hard Tanzanian women work on the *shamba* (farm), often involving themselves in ways most of us would consider expressly forbidden. It was not uncommon to see women working in the fields with a young baby strapped to their backs and other young children playing nearby. President Nyerere himself recognized the vast importance of women in the agricultural economy when he stated:

> Women who live in the villages work harder than anybody else in Tanzania. But the men who live in the villages (and some of the women in towns) are on leave for half of their life. The energies of the millions of men in the villages and thousands of women in the towns ... are a great treasure which could contribute more towards the development of our country than anything we could get from rich nations.[6]

Indeed, the women could be considered the true proletarians, or the "backbone" of the agricultural economy. Although their traditional status in the society was an inferior one, they have always contributed more than their share of skills to nation-building.

Much of the active role women have played as individuals in economic development has been transferred to a group context in the *Ujaama* villages. The *Ujaama* villages are the best examples of Tanzania's grand design for the building of an ideal society. These villages were jointly organized as cooperative farms by the government and by citizens groups. Coming together to live and work as extended family units, the villages drew upon the traditional extended-family concept and translated this ancient African tradition into modern functional socio-political and economic practices.

The villages embrace the "education for self-reliance" philosophy that advocates the totality of Tanzania's socialization policies and practices. President Nyerere has stressed the integration of these institutions into one composite whole, and has consistently emphasized the necessity of formal education being related to politics and service. The government's policy advocates that in all areas of one's involvement, the individual must be taught to become self reliant. Thus, one can observe politically conscious mothers translating this philosophy to their children by training them to become independent in the home, on the *shamba* (farm), in the community and school. Indeed, many of the nation's young children are being taught to care for their own needs and to perform a service to the nation in whatever ways possible.

One young mother, who was educated in Britain, explained to me that she was teaching her three-year old daughter and five-year old son to become self-reliant by learning to put away their clothes, help with chores around the home and be responsible for their behavior, whether it be good or bad behavior. She was also teaching them some of the national songs, as well as many of the values she was taught. Many parents were translating the self-reliance philosophy to their children in similar manner, with the objective of socializing the child so that he will grow up with an understanding of an commitment to Tanzania's broader social, economic, political and cultural goals.

Unlike Western child-rearing philosophy, Tanzanians hold that the child's social values are acquired not primarily through his association with his nuclear family but equally through the extended family, of the school and society. Tanzanians stress the importance of the child's education being oriented toward community service. On this point Nyerere states:

> Our education must...inculcate a sense of commitment to the total community, and help the pupils to accept the values appropriate to our   colonial past...The educational system must emphasize co-operative endeavor, not individual advancement; it must stress concepts of equality and the responsibility to give service which goes with any special ability, whether it be in carpentry, in animal husbandry, or in academic pursuits.[7]

It is this value system which undergirds the *Ujamma* villages, and with which the women intimately involve themselves. Confined largely to the agricultural world, many actively participate in the organization and implementation of the village's total program. On one of my visits to a village, I observed that the local president of the U.W.T., a "Queen Mother" prototype, sat on the decision-making corporate body and participated in the formulation and execution of not only the political and economic policies of her village but directed the U.W.T. chapter's literacy and public health education programs as well. Such examples are numerous and can be found throughout the countryside.

The importance of women's involvement in nation-building was summed up in the statement by a U.W.T. spokesman:

> In a country like ours where the young are a great foundation for the future and the women are the majority, I think adequate representation of women and by women is very much needed. It is important and highly beneficial in all policy-making bodies...from the village and local council level to Parliament. The idea should be to make women be (come) involved and then life will be (come) smoother for everybody. In this way family problems will be considered in the right perspective...in the Ujaama style...[8]

Therefore, *Ujaama* is utilized by women as a practical working model for the solution of problems in all areas of the society.

Another area in which women actively participate is in the National Servicemen corps. The National Service was started in 1964 for the purpose of allowing the country's youth to offer a service to nation-building. Members are recruited from the nation's 18 to 25 year old males and females, although a growing number of individuals past 25 are now joining. They are required to be able to read and write Swahili as well as to display political loyalty.

They spend a total of six months in the National Service. The first three months are spent in a training program which includes acquiring military skills, constructing roads and buildings, etc. After the first three months are completed, National Servicemen are assigned to jobs in the civil service, police force, army and in a variety of other positions. When the six months training and service are completed, these young people are expected to go back into the community and establish various social services, and to establish new Ujaama village settlements. Many of the males join the army after the completion of their duties. Others who choose to go back into civilian life may be recalled to military duty.[9]

The concept of the National Serviceman is very viable in that it has institutionalized the idea of devotion and service to Tanzania's nation-building efforts. University students are unable to go through their educational training without also experiencing the practical aspects as well as the academic. In a similar manner, females are not exempt from the National Service or any of its programs including military training. This cadre of Tanzanians promises much hope for the eventual commitment of the entire population to the idea that formal education and community service must become inseparable. The National Servicemen is also aiding in breaking down the rigid sexual barriers which previously prevented females from participating in this kind of group, consequently being unable to participate fully in their nation's development.

There does not seem to be as much vitality and involvement of Tanzanian women residing in the urban areas as there is in the villages. Once the individual moves to the city, life becomes somewhat similar to urban life in other parts of the world simply because urban life tends to be similar, regardless of geographical location. One finds for example, more educated women in the towns, thereby providing a special socio-economic characteristic unknown in the rural villages.

One of the crucial problems which urban women are experiencing relates to the tension, conflicts, and contradictions which result in the society when the traditional roles and status of a group are forced to undergo changes. As Tanzanian women become more urbanized, more educated and enlightened, they must also suffer the problems which these new roles present. In traditional society, roles and relationships were more pronounced and clear. Little or no confusion existed regarding one's duties and responsibilities. Women knew that their duties were to care for their children, their husbands, the home and the *shamba*. All other functions were usually assumed by the male population. This was especially the case among females living in the coastal region where the Islamic faith is predominant and dictates the rigid, pious roles women play.

There is still much resistance by men to accept the new professional and political roles women now assume. Many women students at the University of Dar-es-Salaam find it difficult to find dates among their male peers because the women have too much education. Some males are quick to explain that they do not want a wife who has the same educational background as they but prefer a more traditional woman, and resort to dating less educated girls.

There are also many common prejudices shared by a great portion of the male population regarding the alleged inferiority and inability of women to carry out the new careers they are assuming in law, medicine, teaching, and government. Some women also experience prejudice and discrimination from their male coworkers.

A final problem has to do with the degree to which some of the educated urban population have rejected the notion of embracing traditional African culture and translating it to a contemporary context through *Ujaama*. One still finds a sizeable number of Tanzanian women adopting Western cultural patterns, values and attitudes. These are manifested in their style of dress, their straightened hair, and their use of bleaching cream and the like. This small group of women appear to be more interested in the acquisition of material goods and in affecting a type of Western life-style than in joining the nation-building movement of U.W.T. This, of course, is one of the peculiar characteristics of urban culture, where there is more exposure to alien ideas a life-styles.

In spite of these obstacles, the Tanzanian leadership has remained consistent in its belief that women should be granted every possible opportunity to be in the vanguard of the nation-building movement. Tanzanian society has a long road to travel before the traditional prejudices and discrimination against women have been totally eliminated.

Tanzania's critics would raise many questions about the way she has responded to the problem of unequal treatment of the nation's women. Some would question the wisdom of a government setting up a special political group for women. They would argue that the U.W.T. is simply another form of discrimination whereby females are once again relegated to the position of communicating and working primarily with each other instead of participating in TANU in a direct manner. Such a segregated role, they would argue, weakens any strong impact women may have upon the total political process of the country.

Some American critics may argue that Tanzanian women have taken the route of the Women's Liberation advocates in this country and may ultimately prove to be a divisive force, instead of a unifying one. Such criticisms may, of course, be endless. The fact is, however, that all of these are irrelevant because the success of the Tanzanian model for female participation has proven to be a workable solution to the problems addressed. Perhaps the *institutionalization* of women's activities was the most viable way to *assure* full female participation.

The women's movement should not be viewed from the perspective of women's liberation but within the context of every able-bodied Tanzanian being equally allowed to participate in nation-building. It is simply the realistic assumption that the work force should be—must be—open to everyone regardless of age and sex if socialism is to be achieved. In this regard no developing nation, whether it be the black colonies of the United States or the independent nations of Africa, Asia or Latin America, can afford the luxury of keeping its women in bondage.

There is a parallel, to some degree, between what is occurring in Tanzania and what our aims as Africans in the United States are. African-American women continue to play the vital roles they have always played within the para-colonies of the United States. Yet, it is not necessary to take up the "Women's Lib" banner in order to do this. After all, it has not been necessary to do so in the past. Nation-building for us has historically meant total involvement. To stop doing so, or to slow down, at this point would be unwise and ultimately detrimental. The full resources of black men, women and children are essential for the survival and ultimate prosperity of us as a people. Thus, the hope for the future of Tanzanian women and black women within the United States bears a common feature: the ability to participate fully in the home, community, and nation in eliminating the destructive forces of racism, human exploitation and every vestige of neocolonialism which remain.

NOTES

1. Julius K. Nyerere, "African Socialism," *The Black Scholar,*February, 1971, p. 7.

2. Sarah Nyirenda, "Women in Search of a Better Deal," *Tanzania Sunday News Magazine,* August 30, 1970, p. 8.

3. Julius K. Nyerere, *Freedom and Socialism,* New York, Oxford University Press, 1968, p. 339.

4. Ibid., p. 339.

5. Alexander MacDonald, *Tanzania: Young Nation in a Hurry,* New York, Hawthorne Books: 1966, p. 186.

6. Julius K. Nyerere, *Freedom and Socialism, p. 245.*

7. *Ibid.,*p. 273.

8. Sarah Nyirenda, "Women in Search of a Better Deal," p. 8.

9. Henry Bienen, *Tanzania: Party Transformation and Economic Development,* Princeton University Press: 1967, p. 375-376.

Women of the Frelimo army, Mozambique. Photo: United Nations/Van Lierop, No. 123 817. (1971)

5

The Role of Women in the Revolution in Guinea-Bissau

Stephanie Urdang

INTRODUCTION:

In September 1974, the African Party for the Independence of Guinea and Cape Verde (PAIGC) took over the government of the new Republic of Guinea-Bissau. It was a momentous occasion, not only for this small West African country, but for the continent of Africa and the Third World. For the first time in sub-Saharan Africa, a colonial power had been forced to withdraw as a result of a war of liberation. The coup which brought down the Caetano regime was a direct result of the successful armed struggle waged in Guinea-Bissau, as well as in Mozambique (by FRELIMO) and in Angola (by MPLA). The victory brought an end to one hundred years of Portuguese colonialism reputed to have been the most oppressive and brutal of all colonialisms in Africa.

The war in Guinea-Bissau ended after eleven and a half years. The achievements of the liberation movement were due not only to military successes, but to an ideology which articulated the need for an armed struggle which went beyond defeating Portuguese colonialism. The ultimate goal of PAIGC was the reconstruction of a new society based on the mass participation of its people—a society that truly eradicated all forms of exploitation.

Amilcar Cabral, founder and leader of PAIGC who was assassinated in 1973, was consistently clear and outspoken on the issues. "It is time to put an end to the suffering caused by colonialism," he told a meeting of peasants in a liberated zones of his country in

1967, "But we must also put an end to the backwardness of our people. There is no point to our struggle if our only goal is to drive out the Portuguese. We want to drive them out, but we are also struggling to end the exploitation of our people, both by whites and by blacks."[1]

Exploitation of the people does not refer only to colonialist or neo-colonialist domination. It includes exploitation of one group of people by another, whether on the basis of race, ethnic group, religion or sex.

From the beginning of the political mobilization for the war of liberation, the need for equality between men and women was made an explicit and integral part of the overall revolution. "Our revolution will not be successful, unless it ensures the full participation of women," said Amilcar Cabral. These ideas were expressed in another way by Carmen Pereira, one of the leading members of the party, when she told the author that "In Guinea-Bissau, we say that women are fighting two colonialisms—one against the Portuguese, the other against men." The party's practice, however, goes even beyond such words. In order to achieve the emancipation of women, PAIGC believes an ongoing struggle must be waged by the women themselves. Emancipation was never seen as something that would be conveniently realized at the time of independence, "because now everybody is free."

To understand how this process was set in motion, it is helpful to look briefly at the history of the country.

HISTORY:

Portuguese economic exploitation of this area of West Africa dates back 500 years, when Portugal began centuries of trading. The market in slaves being the source of a highly lucrative income. Like the other European colonizers, it was only after the 'scramble for Africa,' towards the end of the nineteenth century, that Lisbon began to entrench its political control over the colonies it had carved out of the continent in its own name. Realizing that Portugal's strength as an imperial power was rapidly dwindling, the Portuguese sought to tighten their grasp or lose out altogether. Nevertheless, they met considerable resistance from the people of Guinea-Bissau, and were only able to achieve complete domination in the late 1920s, when—with the rise of fascism in Portugal—their methods became extremely brutal.

Guinea-Bissau, unlike Angola and Mozambique, was not blessed with vast mineral resources. Its small size and comparatively difficult climate dissuaded the colonizers from establishing large plantations based on forced labor, as they had done in the other colonies. The Portuguese quest to extract wealth from this country led them to develop a latifundia in peanuts (forcing cultivation of peanuts by the people on their own land) and to impose extremely heavy taxes.

The concentration on peanuts had a dire effect on the already fragile subsistence farming of the peasants whose staple food product was rice. There was not enough time or workers to produce both, so the level of poverty increased as the cultivation of rice decreased.

The system of taxation further eroded the subsistence economy. The colonists wielded it as a double-edged sword, gaining as they did both in income from taxes as well as acquiring peanuts and rice for export at very little cost. Their coffers filled all the more as they expanded taxation to touch every aspect of peasant life: not only did they tax nuts, every pound of rice grown, every palm tree on a plot of land, palm oil livestock, but also weddings and other celebrations, festivities, dances for amusements, burials, and so fouth. The peasants had no option but to trade their produce at the Portuguese stores at prices arbitrarily set extremely low. With the pittance they received, peasant families had somehow to pay their taxes, facing forced labor, jail, beatings, and confiscation of livestock and other property if they could not.

No social services were provided for the peasants in the rural areas, where the vast majority of the population lived. What was available in the towns had to be paid for. Hence, by the beginning of the war of national liberation, the illiteracy rate was 99 percent, the infant mortality rate was 60 percent, and any form of "justice" or representative government nonexistent. The people became more and more improverished as the drain on their economy took its toll, and political repression mounted.

Against this backdrop and with the gathering momentum towards independence in the British and French colonies, PAIGC was founded clandestinely in Bissau in 1956. At first, the goal was to organize workers in the towns, under the assumption that effective demonstrations and strikes could convince the Portuguese colonialists to negotiate independence. It soon became clear that this was not going to happen. Each demonstration was met by the violence of the colonialists, until, fifty dockworkers were shot within twenty minutes as they held a peaceful demonstration at the docks in Bissau. It was a turning point for the movement, the final realization that independence could be won only through armed struggle based on the support and participation of the people. PAIGC turned its focus to the countryside and to mobilization of the peasants, who comprised 95 percent of the population.

Young cadres were trained by Amilcar Cabral in Conakry, capital of neighboring Guinea, an ex-French colony. The recruits then returned to their own country and conducted an intensive campaign in the countryside. By the end of three years they had won the strong support of the peasants and, in January 1963 the guerrilla war began. Eleven and a half years later, at the time of the coup in Portugal, PAIGC had liberated two thirds of the territory.

During the war, the Portuguese colonialists represented a visible and common enemy. In the process of fighting that enemy, differences based on religion, ethnic group and sex became less important and were submerged in a sense of national unity. This sense served to accelerate the process of social transformation. At the same time the daily conditions of the peasants were improved through the establishment in the liberated zones of medical services, schools, people's stores, a system of justice, and elected local and regional government. These helped both in gaining further support for PAIGC and in involving the people in the control of their lives.

"National liberation," to quote Cabral once more, "war on colonialism, building of peace and progress, independence—all that will remain meaningless for the people unless it brings a real improvement to the conditions of life."

The successes of PAIGC can best be measured not through military victories, though they were considerable, but from the way in which the people participated in the armed struggle and in the building of a new society. The peoples' participation affected the way in which the fundamentals of the state were built, and most importantly, the way in which a new woman and a new man began to emerge out of the revolutionary experience. It is in this context that the emphasis on the liberation of women can be looked at in more detail.

SITUATION OF WOMEN

Guinea-Bissau is a diverse society. Its one million people comprise over twelve different ethnic groups. The largest group is the

Balanta which comprises thirty percent of the population. The Balanta, like seventy percent of the population, are followers of indigenous African religions. The remaining thirty percent is Muslim, the largest group being the Fula who comprise 12 percent of the total population.

Regardless of ethnic background, it is the women in Guinea-Bissau who are responsible for well over half of the agricultural work, and for all the work in the village—cleaning, childcare, washing clothes, pounding, and cooking. It is a strenuous day's work, beginning in the early morning and continuing throughout the day, each day of the year. Women are the providers of food, but despite the fundamental importance of this work, they lack political power or real authority in the society. "In spite of the importance of women in the life of African peoples," states a PAIGC document, "it is only rarely that they take an active part in political affairs. In our country, women have almost always been kept out of political affairs, of decisions concerning the life which they nonetheless support, thanks to their anonymous daily work."

Almost without exception, it is the men who are responsible for the decision-making process, whether they are chiefs or members of councils of elders.

Along with lack of substantial authority over village life, goes a general lack of status. Men's work, whatever it may be, possesses higher status than women's work. Women in Guinea-Bissau, like most of their African sisters, are held in lower esteem than men of the same age group. They are expected to play, to a greater or lesser extent, a subservient role to the men.

The situation is not something that the women accepted without question. But there was little they can do within the traditional society to change it. Maria Sá, a member of a sector committee in the south, was one of the many women who talked to me about the situation.

> You want to know how we women suffer? First, it is the women who pound, it is the women who fish, it is the women who cook for the man. And then sometimes he says, 'ah, your food is not well cooked'. With all the work we have to do, and he protests! It is these kinds of things, this discrimination that we have suffered and continue to suffer from. When there is a lot of work to do, we women go and help the men. When the men are tilling the land, we have to cook quickly and take it to him. And we must be sure that we are not late with the food! It is our responsibility also, to find food supplements

such as fish and meat. It is very hard, our life. In addition to all of this, if his clothes are dirty, it is we women who must wash them. Nice and clean. Because if the man walks in the village wearing dirty clothes and people see him like this, who does it reflect on? Why the women! Not the men. We do not like this or want this. All these things are ways in which women suffer. As for the men, the only thing they do is till the land. Once the men have tilled the land and the rice begins to grow, we are then responsible for everything after that. The women alone harvest the rice and we have to transport it without their help to the village. This, I tell you, is how all women are suffering.

Liberating Women: The Period of Armed Struggle

The involvement of women in the revolution was a goal from the outset and not an afterthought brought about through necessity. A PAIGC directive of the early 1960's states:

> "Defend the rights of women, respect and make others respect women (whether as children, young girls or adults), but persuade the women of our country that their liberation must be their own achievement on the basis of their work, dedication to the Party, self-respect, personality, and decisiveness toward everyting that can act against their dignity."

There are some pragmatic reasons why the involvement of women was encouraged. Every member of the society—man, woman, child—was needed to fight against the tremendous force of the colonialists. But armed struggle was never viewed as the final stage of the revolution. And so it was that the concept of equality was integrated into the ideology of PAIGC at its inception, and then put into practice in numerous notable ways which would have been considered extraneous had they simply been responding to critical moments of the war.

When the first mobilizers went into the countryside in 1960, they spoke about the need for women to participate equally in the revolution and for an end to their exploitation. At first few women attended the meetings. To make sure that at least a few did, representatives were chosen from the women in each village who were to report back to the others. Slowly female participation increased.

Nonetheless, many of the first people mobilized were women. Among these was Bwetna N'Dubi, a Balanta peasant who lived in the south of the country. At the time of my visit, she held an elected position of responsibility in the local government, being a member of the regional council. As such, she acted a liaison between the people in her own area and the representatives of the assembly, among many other tasks. She spoke with confidence, articulating with emphasis the need for women to struggle for their liberation.

"I first heard about women's rights at the beginning of mobilization," she told me. "I understand what was being said immediately—that equality is necessary and possible. Today I work together with men, having more responsibility than many men. This is not only true for me. I understand that I have to fight together with other women against the domination of men. But we have to fight twice, once to convince women and the second time to convince men that women have to have the same rights as men."

Bwetna N'dubi was a member of the first elected village council. These councils were established soon after an area had been liberated to carry out local party work, to handle the daily organization of life in the village and to provide support for the war. Council members were elected by the peasants and replaced the traditional councils of elders or the chiefs. PAIGC stipulated that at least two of the five members had to be women, and so brought the question of involving women out of the realm of political education and into practice. However, given the traditions of the society, the chances were that neither men nor women would agree to this radical departure from past practices. To circumvent any resistance, PAIGC used the tactic of making the women members of the council responsible for the supply of rice for the guerrillas. As an extension of their traditional work within the society and one over which they already had considerable control, it was accepted by the men. Nevertheless, a qualitative change had taken place: the integration of women into a decision-making body, once a male preserve, brought with it recognition and increased status for women's work.

Of the many changes now transforming the lives of peasant women, one of the most important is the firm stand that PAIGC has taken against customs detrimental to women. "Oppose without violence all prejudicial customs," states another PAIGC directive, "the negative aspects of the beliefs and traditions of our people." Those pertaining specifically to women are forced marriage, no recourse to divorce, and polygyny.

Forced marriage was part of the customary law of all the ethnic groups in Guinea-Bissau. A husband would be chosen for a girl at a very early age, often—in the case of some of the Muslim groups—while she was still a baby. The girl could not refuse to marry the man even if she was very much against it. An older man was preferred by parents because he would be more economically secure. Once the husband was chosen and the "bride price" agreed upon, the man would begin to transfer these "gifts" to the girl's family. "It's just as if a woman is being sold to a man", commented one woman militant to me. "It's like selling babies or young children."

The question of forced marriage, taken up when mobilization first began, was a regular theme of speeches at mass peasant meetings. The response of many young women about to enter such marriages was immediate. They joined the party and went to work in the guerrilla bases away from the villages. Thus, by providing new places to which women could escape, PAIGC laid the practical foundation on which Guinean women could begin to change their subordinate position.

There was a similar response to the question of divorce. Women who had been forced to marry against their wishes could now leave their husbands. Before the mobilization, lack of divorce for women, like forced marriage, had been well entrenched in the customs of the people. It was extremely unusual for a woman to be given permission to return to her family, and if she did, she would have to leave her children with their father and would lose access to them. A man, on the other hand—particularly among Muslims—could "repudiate' his wife if for any reason he felt she was unsatisfactory: because she was lazy, disobedient or whatever he decided was not permissable behavior. He could send her back to her parents in disgrace and the children would remain with him.

Among Muslim groups, women are expected to be obedient to their husbands and sexually faithful. "A woman is sold for a cow or a pig," commented another woman militant of the party, "she then goes to the man's house and has no active voice whatsoever." There was considerably more flexibility, however, among followers of traditional African religions, the Balanta in particular. Although unable to divorce, Balanta women could have lovers and it was customary for them to leave home for a few months at a time and live with their lovers. Any children resulting from such a union would be considered to belong to the woman's husband and not the biological father.

People's courts were established in each village, or group of villages, some five years after the first areas were liberated. Charged with the responsibility of deciding on cases of divorce and forced marriage, and, as divorce was now legal and forced marriage illegal, the courts would invariably judge in the woman's favor. By the end of the war, the old practices were virtually nonexistent in the liberated zones.

The process of bringing an end to the custom of polygyny was a more complex one. Because forced marriage and lack of divorce were considered more oppressive in that they force women to act against their will, PAIGC took immediate action on these. A woman who is unhappy in a polygynous marriage can now get a divorce. But the total reversal of the practice will take much longer. Polygyny, basic to the social structure and economy of the village, is not something that can be quickly changed. The Commissioner of Justice said in this regard:

> For the people in the rural areas, polygyny has much significance. It is not only the pleasure of having two or three wives. No, it is an economic necessity as well. The wives do a substantial amount of work in the rice fields. If a man has two or three wives it means that he has more help in production. We understand that we cannot change the customs of the people suddenly, or they will turn against us. We have to move, but we have to move slowly. It is a custom that has existed from generation to generation and although the party is against the practice we cannot change it quickly.

As Amilcar Cabral would say, the party cannot simply pass a decree and outlaw retrograde customs. The process of transformation begins with political education. But political education in itself is insufficient—as the liberation movement understood so clearly. Ultimately, it is the economy that must be changed so as to remove the conditions which give rise to these social practices. The pace of reform the party has set is well reflected in the comment "we must move slowly or else the peole will turn against us." It is this concern for all the people, so intrinsic to the ideology and practice of PAIGC, that provides the key to the profound changes which took place over the years following the beginning of mobilization.

For women, the prospect of change is somewhat easier. They are quick to respond to the possibility of a life that does not bind them in a proscribed way. For men it is a totally different matter, they have everything to lose, and in the immediate future, seemingly little to gain. Bringing about far-reaching change can only take a long time.

Nevertheless, the changes that have taken place in the daily life of peasant women were inconceivable before the beginning of mobilization. "Before, life was very difficult for women," said Bwetna N'dubi, "The Party has brought new ways and a new life for women. But we must continue to defend ourselves."

While Bwetna sees the struggle as continuous, many peasant women are overawed by the changes they have witnessed. "My eyes have been opened to a new world," was a recurring comment. In this context, it is easy to understand why older peasant women would say to me, shaking their heads with the enormity of the thought, "now we are free." They were not liberated. The process had only begun. But I left the villages with a sense of the great strides that had been made. I felt that the impact on peasant women, due to the conscious efforts to liberate women, would continue to be strong.

Kumba Kilubali, a member of the village council of her Muslim (Fula) village, spoke for many of her sisters when she said:

> The difference between my life as a woman before and my life now is very, very big. Life is much better for women now. You see, before you were brought up to be a boy or a girl. Now things are different. For the Party says everybody is the same and we understand this. A boy can be a girl and a girl can be a boy. In other words, each can do what the other can do.
>
> Oh yes, life is very different now. For example, I sit here at this moment and men are nearby. They have listened to what I have said and they have accepted it. They have made no objection. Before it was not possible for me as a woman to sit here and talk to you, a visitor. It would have had to be a man who talked with you. It would not even have been possible for a woman to sit and listen. Before men and women could not work together doing the same work. The men had this idea that the women must work *for* the men. Not any more. Now the men and women work together.

It is the young women cadres, formed by the revolution, who are the vanguard for the future generation. In absolute terms, the number of women in positions of leadership and responsibility was small. Still, given that the number of women previously involved in political work or treated as equal to men had been nil, the participation of women cadres in the revolution was substantial. There were women members of the government, women political workers, women in education, health, and information.

These women emphasized the need to fight sexist attitudes of men towards women. Teodora Gomes, a Regional Political commissar in the South front during the war, a position of considerable responsibility, spoke to me with special feeling about this:

> It is one of the aspects of our society that has been present, still is present and will continue to be present for a long time. Men have very particular ideas about women. At the beginning of the struggle when women and men first began working together, the men brought these ideas with them from their previous experience. They found it difficult to regard a woman as a comrade or to treat her with the respect due to her—as someone who is equal in the struggle and working for the same goal. It was common to find these comrades having relationships with more than one woman, and saying blithely that he loved them all!

Teodora joined PAIGC when she was seventeen and said she had to fight continuously against such attitudes. She added:

> We continue to struggle very hard against this and I can say there has been a very perceptible change over the years. Nonetheless, we cannot deny that these problems still exist despite our efforts. but it is not just the men. Women themselves must have a clear understanding of how these attitudes affect them, because no one else can fight for our rights, other than ourselves.

Francisca Pereira, a member of the Superior Council for the Fight, had experiences similar to those of Teodora, as she too was a young adult when she joined the party.

> Now though, these difficulties seldom occur between comrades working together. Women with positions in the party, like Teordora or myself, have their opinions and decisions taken seriously and with respect.
>
> But this is not always the case with the younger women who are only beginning to work with the party. The party has given her certain tasks to perform and many times she can do the work better than a man could. But when she gives an order to a man, he feels that he doesn't have to obey it, simply because he is a man!
>
> This problem exists in the family as well, where a man will go ahead and act without consulting his wife, even though his actions affect

her. And then there is a big uproar if the woman acts without consulting him—perhaps over taking contraceptives or having an abortion. This is the sort of thing we are fighting against.

I spent a considerable amount of time in the company of women cadres. They related to each other with ease and I seldom was made aware of any overt or even subtle discrimination against women by the men.

On one occasion when I was staying at a boarding school, the director of which was a nineteen-year-old woman, the workers at the school sat around a table after supper, talking and joking together. We were five women and five men. One of the men, who had recently returned to Guinea-Bissau after six years abroad, turned to me and, with appreciation in his voice, commented that he would never have seen this six years earlier. "Maybe the women would have eaten together with the men, but after the meal they would have excused themselves and left."

In the young women of nineteen or twenty, who have grown up and been educated in the revolution, I perceived a different attitude. For them it was not the struggle it had been for women like Teodora and Francisca. By the time they were adults they had spent many years with boys and young men who also had been educated in the revolution, and whose attitudes did not appear to be of the old sort.

"Sometimes it is a problem," one young school director told me, "because some men feel that they have to make advances to women, because if they do not, they are not men. It is true that men still have these ideas. For example, a comrade came here a little while ago. He had never been here before and did not know the women. After a few hours he began making propositions. Not directly—you know how men are. Nevertheless, if a woman like him, if she has no commitment to another, she can accept if she wishes. Why not? We don't think that by accepting, it is a commitment for life. For if a man has a desire, a woman has a desire as well. That is normal and it is the same for both."

She told me this without trace of bitterness. It was not a problem for these young women, it seemed to me. The game was played on their terms, not just on the man's, so that they did not feel manipulated or as if they were treated as sex objects. They did what *they* wanted to do.

There was one area of work, however, where women were not encouraged to play an equal role: the military. I seldom saw women armed. Those who were, were generally cadres of the party armed for self-defense with revolvers.

At the beginning of the war there had been many women among fighters in the national militia. However, after five years in which the level of fighting steadily grew more fierce, the guerrillas were reorganized into a more tightly-knit national army, and the military role of women was downplayed. Instead, women were encouraged to join the nursing corps or become radio operators. PAIGC reasoning was as follows: Guinea-Bissau was a small country where there were more men who wanted to join the army than were needed. Therefore, unlike armed struggles being waged elsewhere—Mozambique and Vietnam, for instance—it was not necessary for women to take part in combat.

There was also some indication, though the evidence was inconclusive, that in the early stages of the fighting, when women were in the national militia, they did not keep up with the men in combat situations.

But a major factor influencing PAIGC thinking on women in the military turned on another matter altogether, one which had nothing to do with women's real capacity to bear arms. The party realized that, in order to recruit women as regular soldiers, and as a matter of national policy, the traditions of the society would have to be overcome—a protracted process which would have slowed down the war when the first priority was to oust the Portuguese.

The fight against retrograde social traditions was carried out on another front—behind the lines, in the liberated zones. There, time was on the side of the guerrillas, and the peasantry could be exposed to concepts of female equality in an atmosphere conducive to change because of all the other improvements in the conditions of life that were directly attributable to PAIGC.

And so it was, toward the end of the war, that women soldiers were again being trained in a camp in the east, but the armistice came before they could be incorporated into the army.

The question of women in the military, however, should be seen in the broader context of the overall revolution. PAIGC emphasized strongly that the war should be viewed as a transitory phase and that the ultimate goal for the country was the building of a new society. This goal transcended the armed struggle and, as a consequence, no heroic importance was attached to the role of the guerrilla fighter. Rather, the party emphasized that all work contributing to the new society is of equal importance, and that the work of the soldier is no more important than any other. Cabral stressed this in an address to a meeting of peasants in 1966:

> Every man and woman must learn that work is their first duty, and that all workers in the country are useful to the cause.... The armed struggle is very important but the most important thing of all is an understanding of our people's situation. Our people support the armed struggle. We must assure them that those who bear arms are the sons of our people and that arms are no better than the tools of labor. Between one man carrying a gun and another carrying a tool, the more important of the two is the man with the tool. We've taken up arms to defeat the Portuguese, but the whole point of driving out the Portuguese is to defend the man with tool.[3]

Nonetheless, the fact that women were not armed is potentially problematic. Guns and power are often equated, I wondered, seeing guns everywhere, whether this might have an effect on the girls and boys growing up in the society. On the other hand, seeing they were close to victory in the independence struggle, women had become more vigilant about men's attempts to dominate them. It is to be hoped that this determination will counteract the fact that women have not been armed as men have been.

Teodora Gomes, who for me embodies the emerging new woman of the revolution, outlined her concept of the liberation of women in response to my question:

> By a liberated woman I mean a woman who has a clear conscious-ness about her responsibility in the society and who is economically independent. I mean, by a liberated woman, one who is able to do all the jobs in the society without being discriminated against—a woman who can go to school to learn, who can become a leader.
>
> While women are fighting for their freedom at present, a new system is evolving which is preparing the young people of the next generation. And this new system is trying to change their idea of liberty, their idea of freedom and their idea of coexistence between the elements of the family and within the society in general.
>
> In conclusion, I must say that the struggle for the liberation of women has to be waged in different ways. First of all, women must fight together with men against colonialism and all systems of exploi-tation. Secondly, and this is one of the most fundamental points, every woman must convince herself that she can be free and that she has to be free. And that she is able to do all things that men do in social life. And thirdly, women must fight in order to convince men that she

has naturally the same rights as he has. But she must understand that the fundamental problem is not the contradiction between women and men, but that it is the system in which we are all living.

If we construct a society without exploitation of man by man, then of course women will have to be free in that society. Our struggle for national liberation is one way of assuring the liberation of women because by doing the same work as men, or by doing work that ensures the liberation of our country, a woman will convince herself that she is able to do the same work as men. In the process women will learn that they are able to do many things that they could not have conceived of before. They will learn that in our party there are women in the highest level of leadership and that women are working in all different sectors of our lives. This is important because it convinces women that they have potential and shows men what that potential is.

You cannot isolate the liberation of women is such circumstances as ours because there is one goal for the people of our country, which is to transform our society step by step.

Liberating Women: Postindependence

With independence at the end of 1974, PAIGC faced two problems: the development of a nonexploitative economy and "a real improvement in the conditions of life," and the continued political mobilization of the people so that government by the masses of the people can become a reality. It is one thing to talk about the need for building a just society when the society in which the people are living is an oppressive colonial one, or when it is at war. It is clearly not the same when the society is at "peace" and the visible enemy has dissappeared. It becomes more difficult to attain the goals of the revolution. Amilcar Cabral foresaw this when he said: "when we are independent, that is when our struggle *really* begins." Political mobilization continues now side by side with national reconstruction, which includes taking over a bureaucracy developed by the Portuguese colonialists, dismantling it and replacing it with a government based on the ideology of PAIGC. In every area—be it agriculture, education, justice, public works, communications, people's stores and markets, health, or housing—new systems have to be developed. Guinea-Bissau was totally neglected by the Portuguese government and PAIGC took over a country with virtually no services or elements of development from which to begin. They had to start—from scratch with an economy that afforded them no foreign exchange, not even self-sufficiency. With 95 percent of the population being peasants, the first task and the highest priority has become the development of agriculture.

What does the liberation of women mean now? Teodora Gomes's realization that it cannot be confined to involvement in the armed struggle still holds true. From impressions gained during my recent visit, I believe that the goal to liberate women is as integral a part of the ideology of the revolution as it was during the war.

It will be useful now to look at some of the ways in which that continued struggle is being guaranteed in Guinea-Bissau.

The Organization of Women was established a few months after independence. It was not the first time that PAIGC had formed a women's organization. In 1961, before the beginning of the armed struggle, the Democratic Union of Women was founded and based in Conakry, then the headquarters of PAIGC. The majority of the women involved in the organization were daughters of exiles living in the neighbouring Guinea. When the struggle intensified, many of these women resisted going inside Guinea-Bissau. Because the organization could not develop into a mass organization, it was disbanded.

The leadership of the new organization consists of a ten-member Commission of Women, which is equivalent to a ministry of the government. All ten women were active during the armed struggle, and each represents one region of the country. Some are in the leadership of the government and party, others are political workers. Five-member committees of the women's organization have been elected in all the regions and sectors of the country, and the regional president of the women's organization works closely with the corresponding representative of the Women's Commission. The latter travels regularly through her region, meeting with committee members, discussing problems related to women and addressing mass meetings.

I accompanied the youngest member of the Commission, twenty-three-year-old Satu Djassi, while she travelled for ten days to different villages in the south of the country. She grew up in a peasant village and joined the struggle in her early teens. The political line and orientation of the women's organization is exemplified in a speech she gave at a village close to the Republic of Guinea (Conakry) border. During the war the village was in the liberated zones and had been reestablished in the forest to protect it from bombing. Nevertheless, the majority of the population had left as refugees to the Republic of Guinea (Conakry) and returned only after independence.

Satu began her speech by emphasizing the need to work hard at rebuilding the country and encouraging women to help with the building of houses—work that has traditionally been done by the men.

> If the wife does not help to build the house, your husband can say; "This is my house, not yours" and, as is done so often, he can send you away. But if the husband and wife share in the building of the house, then it belongs to both. One does not have more rights than the other.

At the meeting of the National Assembly in May of this year, six new laws were passed. Three of these concerned the protection of the rights of women. One laid down conditions for divorce, so that the law has become a national one. Through the passage of another law, the categories of "legitimate" and "illegitimate" children were eliminated. As a result all children have the same status under the law, regardless of whether their parents are officially married or not. If a man has a number of children by different women, he is equally responsible for their support.

A third law gives equal status to common-law marriages and "legal" marriages. Common-law marriages are a frequent practice in the towns of Guinea-Bissau. The idea of a man and woman together without being formally married is socially acceptable in the towns, despite the Portuguese colonial—and hence Catholic—influence. However, problems arose which the law seeks to remedy. For instance, a woman who has lived with a man for twenty years might discover at his death that all his assets—which may have resulted from the work of both—are inherited by a woman he formally married before he met his common-law wife and with whom he had lost contact. Another, more urgent problem, which highlighted the need for such a law, concerned the militants who had lived with women in the liberated zones during the war. After independence, many of these young men went to Bissau or other towns to work for the party. Some met young women there, decided to marry and pushed their previous common-law marriage into the realm of the past, much as they had done with the war itself. The new law allows for a simple registration of common-law marriages which have lasted for at least three years. Once registered, it is treated as a legal marriage and can be dissolved by divorce only. A man can not simply "forget" his former spouse, but must acknowledge the commitment he made to her by having to go through a divorce procedure if he wants to leave her, and having to bear a continued responsibility for financial support.

The three laws affecting women are seen as mechanisms for developing a greater respect and sense of responsibility on the part of men. PAIGC anticipates that a man who is faced with the prospect of taking equal responsibility for all the children he brings into the world, or who cannot simply "forget" a common-law wife, is more likely to weigh his actions vis-à-vis women extra carefully in the future.

The most striking example of PAIGC's attempt to bring about a change in such attitudes as quickly as possible, as well as provide protection for women, is the regulation concerning battered wives. Because laws take some time from formulation to enactment, there is a provision for putting into immediate effect regulations which require agreement only by PAIGC. (This device is seen as a resort only in emergency situations and as yet has only been used in this one instance.) It is a phenomenon that is not found in the old liberated zones, but mainly in the towns. In Bissau, for instance, an injured wife can report the case to the Commission of Justice and if she can show marks on her body from a beating, her husband will be immediately jailed for a minimum of forty-eight hours. In explaining this regulation, the Commissioner of Justice said:

> We have to show these men that we are serious about changing these attitudes. Men must learn to respect women, and if they do not, we have to take actions to combat this. The situation was scandalous. Every single day wives would be beaten so badly that some even died. Men have been oppressed by the colonialists and took out their frustrations on their wives, even their children. It was an urgent situation that had to be dealt with strongly.

The schools, perhaps the key to the future of women's rights, continue to address the question as they did in the liberated zones. The situation is more complex now that the war is over because a dual system of education is in operation. The one is a continuation of the boarding schools established in the liberated zones, and the others are the schools that were previously run by the Portuguese administration or privately, and have been taken over by the government.

The worst aspects of the Portuguese system such as the highly inaccurate or irrelevant history and geography syllabi were replaced. In most of the smaller towns, the schools taken over by the government are responding well to the changes. The pace has been slower at the secondary school in Bissau, the only such school in the country prior to independence and where the average age is higher. The school served to educate the future colonial civil servants and to create an educated elite in the country. The attitudes inculcated in the students reflected the colonial mentality which, among other things, regarded PAIGC members as terrorists and fearsome communists. A teacher at the school, who is a member of the party, described to me some of her efforts to raise the political consciousness of the students in her English classes.

She guides the discussion for the practice of English along lines that will encourage her pupils to think politically and analytically. A story by an African writer, for example, which refers to "the woman standing outside the door," evokes the question: "Why is the woman standing outside the door and not in the room with the men?" and she goes on to develop a discussion about the role of women. The same process occurs in discussing, "why is it that only women fetch water from the well?" At the end of the first term, when a criticism/self-criticism session was held, she was criticised by the class for being "too political." A number of students said that they had come to learn English and not to have political education. Nonetheless, she persevered and, in the two years since independence, the level of political consciousness amongst the pupils—who now include youth from peasant and worker backgrounds—has increased considerably.

The differences between this school and the PAIGC secondary school and intermediary boarding schools, with regard to the level of political consciousness, is immediately apparent. In the latter, political consciousness in general, and in regard to women in particular, is extremely high. The schools operate in a collective way, with a committee elected by the students having overall responsibility for their management. A six-member committee is equally divided between boys and girls, although the percentage of girls at school is in the vicinity of 30 percent, as a way of indicating that the goal is numerical equality. I asked a fourteen-year-old student at one of the intermediary schools how she felt about the need for the liberation of women, and whether it is discussed in the school:

In school we talk a lot about the role of women in our country and the problems confronting women because of their unequal status. However, in our school the girls live and work on a completely equal basis with our male comrades. So here it is not a problem. But nonetheless, we talk about it frequently.

When I go to visit Bissau, I see immediately the difference between the role of women there and the special situation of equality that exists in our school. There, women do *all* the work. She works continuously and very hard. Men do not help with this work at all, although they could very easily. Men are of course engaged in other work, work which women cannot do although they are perfectly capable. This is because they are treated as unequal in the society, and are expected to serve the men.

In order to develop our country, in order to make the women of our country advance towards complete equality, women and men must have the same rights. We women must do the same work as the men which they believe we cannot do, and men too must free women from the enormous amount of work they have to do in the home. In this way our country will advance so that men and women will have the same responsibilities and the same rights.

CONCLUSIONS

The process of liberating women under socialism is very different from the quest for the liberation of women in capitalist society. The idea of liberating women is antagonistic to capitalism. The need for expanding profits cannot accommodate full employment and an equal role of women in production. For women to work for equality within the system does not change it. More women corporate executives or members of Congress will do nothing to eradicate the imperialist practices of the United States government and multinational corporations. Although this is not recognized by many women in the women's movement in the United States, the fight for the liberation of women under capitalism becomes a fight to end capitalism.

In Guinea-Bissau the women's struggle is precisely an effort to gain equality within the system. If separated from the revolution it would lose its meaning, regardless of the particular phase of that revolution. During the war of liberation, Portuguese colonialism presented a visible and easily identifiable enemy, and hence provided a focal point for the mobilization of the masses of the people. While the immediate priority was ousting the colonialists from their respective countries, this was only one facet of the struggle, and essentially a transitional one. The long-term goal is building a socialist society. Women who became involved in the revolution during the war were not expected to cease this struggle as soon as the national flag was raised over their independent country. The priority since independence has shifted, from liberation from colonialism, to the construction of that socialist society.

Women of Guinea-Bissau are fortunate in that their government and party supports their fight for emancipation, actively encourages it, provides it with a material base, and understands with clarity that it is essential for the success of the overall revolution.

NOTES

1. Quoted in Gerald Chaliand, *Armed Struggle in Africa*, Monthly Review Press, New York, 1971.

2. Polygamy and polygyny tend to be used interchangeably, although the term polygyny strictly refers to marrying more than one wife, while polygamy refers to marrying more than one wife or husband. I use polygyny, unless quoting from a source.

Peanuts being harvested by women in the village of Pizonou, Upper Volta. Photo: United Nations/Ray Witlin. No. 137/11. (1977)

6

The African Woman as Entrepreneur: Problems and Perspectives on Their Roles

Ruth Simms

INTRODUCTION

The African woman as entrepreneur is not a twentieth century phenomenon, but an aspect of reality deeply rooted in the history of African social, economic, and political structures. In Western Africa, in particular, women as merchants and traders have become legendary. Daaku, for example, has described one of the important trade patterns that had emerged by the beginning of the seventeenth century in Ghana.

> ... there were local community marketing places where most of the local foodstuff, crafts, and a few necessaries were sold. Almost invariably trading at this level was the women's affair, for the Akan made a subtle distinction between what was to be sold by the different sexes, ... [1]

Other images of the forerunners of contemporary female merchants may be gleaned from literary accounts of travelers to Tropical Africa in the early nineteenth century. Representative are descriptions of women and their roles in the Whydah market,[2] as well as the function of "market queens" in the so-called "silent trade" in Maiduguri.[3]

Current perceptions and role definitions of African female entrepreneurs grow out of this historical pattern of development. Consequently, the pervasive image of the entrepreneur is that of street vendor and market trader. In fact, this group is quantitatively significant and highly visible in most of Tropical Africa. On the other hand, there is also a small but emerging group of business women who are proprietors of developing industrial enterprises and retail shops. This is a group for which there is little or no systematic data and analysis, yet its existence and economic activities require a broader perspective concerning the parameters of entrepreneurship.

Within the confines of this paper, an entrepreneur is a proprietor of a business. Specifically, entrepreneur refers to any independent or self-employed person who controls the management of capital and who invests it in some enterprise to gain profit.[4] This definition, while permitting identification of the analytical population, does not preclude concern for the "entrepreneurial function,"[5] a point to be discussed later. Given this view, the discussion is oriented toward delineating some of the major issues related to study and analysis of African women entrepreneurs. It is hoped that the discussion may serve as a basis for identifying critical areas for basic research and policy analysis.

The Chapter is divided into two major parts. Some data and a social profile are presented in Part I. They provide a perspective on the question since female entrepreneurs operate within the larger context of female activity, as well as general economic activity. The second part is devoted to identifying and discussing some of the problems and issues which may be useful in acquiring a more holistic view of the development process and the relationship of women to it.

I. AFRICAN ECONOMIC ACTIVITY[6] AND THE DISTRIBUTION OF WOMEN ENTREPRENEURS

As of 1970, it is estimated that the economically active population of Africa was 132 million, in contrast to approximately 109 million in 1960. These figures represent a crude activity rate (proportion of total population) of 40.4 percent for 1960 and 38.5 percent in 1970. Based on 1960 estimates, the activity rate for females was 25.4 percent, in comparison with 55.5 percent for males. Roughly 31 percent of women in Africa were economically active, with considerable variation by country and region. Representative of this variation are Western Africa, with 38.7 percent of women in the labour force, Northern Africa, 7.4 percent, Southern Africa, 27.4 percent, Eastern Africa, 34.8 percent, and Middle Africa, 36.9 percent.

These differences can be attributed to a variety of factors, including current levels of economic development, sociocultural variables such as religion, and familism. Women in Western Africa, for example, have a history of economic independence, with trade and market relationships constituting a way of life. The opposite is the case for women in northern Africa and other parts of the continent who have traditionally played a lesser role in secular activities due to Moslem religious practices; caution, however, is necessary in this judgment, as there are many exceptions and a tendency to underestimate moslem female economic involvement. Dakar is a noteworthy exception, as a significant proportion of women traders there are Muslims. Moreover, Polly Hill has admirably documented and discussed extra-market 'house trade' of secluded Hausa women.[7]

Over three-fourths of all workers were in agriculture in 1960, with the proportion of women higher than that of men. This difference can be attributed largely to a higher rural-to-urban out-migration for men than for women, as well as to men's greater access to educational and employment opportunities.

As indicated in Table 1, countries such as Angola, Botswana, Gabon and Liberia, have a higher percentage of women in agriculture than other nations. This suggests underlying differences throughout the African economic experience, particularly with respect to types of colonial and neo-colonial dependency relations.

For most of Africa, women are underrepresented in the secondary or industrial sector (see Table 2); however, according to Denti, women are proportionately more numerous than men in the service or tertiary industries

> ...in all the countries of Northern Africa and in the territories under Spanish or Portuguese administration (except Mozambique), as well as in the following states or territories: Nigeria, Ghana, Dahomey, Togo, Southern Rhodesia, Reunion, Mauritius, Congo (Brazzaville), Republic of South Africa and Namibia.[8]

> Thus, next to agriculture the service sector accounts for a significant proportion of female workers.

Tertiary industries include economic activity such as wholesale and retail trade, storage, construction, transport and communication, domestic and personal services, banking and insurance, the profes-

TABLE 1
PERCENTAGE DISTRIBUTION OF FEMALE ECONOMICALLY ACTIVE POPULATION BY BRANCH OF ECONOMIC ACTIVITY (INDUSTRY)

Country	Agriculture Electricity Forestry Hunting Fishing		Mining Quarrying		Industrial Manufacturing		Construction		Gas, Water Sanitary Services	
	N	%	N	%	N	%	N	%	N	%
Algeria	3,302	28.3	2	.02	6,275	53.9	12	.1	1	.008
Angola	30,434	76.5	-	-	933	2.3	2	.005	-	-
Botswana	115,328	99.8	2	.001	38	.03	3	.002	-	-
Egypt	34,723	41.0	-	-	11,666	13.8	148	.17	127	.15
Gabon	4,500	78.9	-	-	-	-	-	-	-	-
Ghana	397,960	52.7	1,000	.13	86,850	11.5	110	.015	10	.001
Liberia	27,463	86.7	99	.31	515	1.6	20	.06	1	.003
Libya	424	16.2	1	.04	1,783	68.1	6	.23	1	.04
Mauritius	691	27.9	-	-	783	31.6	1	.04	-	-
Reunion	443	21.5	-	-	286	13.9	9	.44	-	-
Seychelles*	91	15.3	-	-	180	30.2	4	.67	-	-
Sierra Leone	28,450	56.6	168	.33	4,396	8.8	26	.05	22	.04
S. Rhodesia	291	23.2	5	.39	63	5.0	-	-	-	-

	Commerce N	Commerce %	Transport Storage Communication N	Transport Storage Communication %	Service N	Service %	Other Activities not Adequately Described N	Other Activities not Adequately Described %	Totals
	791	6.8	27	.23	1,159	10.0	78	.67	11,647
	-	-	7,679	19.3	-	-	714	1.8	- 39,762
	91	.08	-	-	32	.03	5	.004	15,504
	22,392	26.5	195	.23	4,302	5.1	11,024	13.0	84,577
	1,000	17.5	-	-	-	-	200	3.5	5,700
	258,090	34.1	-	-	11,690	1.5	-	-	775,710
	3,021	9.5	9	.03	378	1.2	163	.51	31,699
	119	4.5	7	.27	117	6.8	98	3.7	2,616
	565	22.8	1	.04	430	17.4	5	.20	2,476
	1,123	54.6	18	.88	173	8.4	5	.24	2,057
			1	.17	199	33.4	57	9.6	596
	16,533	32.9	39	.08	564	1.1	17	.03	50,215
	346	27.6	2	.16	545	43.5	-	-	1,252

N 63

% 10.6

*Seychelles uses slightly different classifications, i.e.: wholesale & retail trade financing, insurance, real eastate & business

Source: *1973 Yearbook of Labor Statistics*, International Labor Office, 1973, pp. 42-54.

Table 2
Proportion of Women in the Total Labour Force
By Economic Sector and by Region, 1960

ECONOMIC SECTOR	AFRICA			REGION[a]		
		Western	Eastern	Middle	Northern	Southern
All Sectors	32	39	35	39	7	26
Agriculture	34	40	37	44	5	24
Industry	15	25	16	5	9	7
Services	30	46	24	14	11	44

Source: Ettore Denti, "Africa's Labour Force, 1960-80," *International Labor Review*, 1960-1980, Vol. 104, No. 3 September 1971.

[a] Western: (Nigeria, Ghana, Upper Volta, Mali, Ivory Coast, Senegal, Guinea, Niger, Sierra Leone, Dahomey, Togo, Liberia, Mauritania, Guinea Bissau, Gambia)

Eastern: (Ethiopia, Tanzania, Kenya, Uganda, Mozambique, Madagascar, Southern Rhodesia, Malawi, Zambia, Rwanda, Burundi, Somalia, Mauritius, Reunion)

Middle: (Zaire, Angola, Cameroon, Chad, Central African Republic, Congo (Brazzaville), Gabon, Equatorial Guinea)

Northern: (UAR Egypt), Sudan, Morocco, Algeria, Tunisia, Libya)

Southern: (South Africa (Rep. of); Lesotho, Namibia, Botswana, Swaziland)

sions, and government employment. There is a high concentration of female entrepreneurs in commercial market trade and in direct private services. Often referred to as self-employed or own-account workers, they constitute close to 30 percent of the total female labor force in Africa.

Table 3 evinces variation in women's status in selected countries depending upon whether they are own-account, salaried (wage), or family workers. The problem that emerges, however, is that it is difficult to disentangle the own-account or self-employed women from those engaged in family undertakings or those in subsistence farming.[9]

In summary, distribution of women in the labor force, while varying regionally, is directly related to the level of economic activity of Africa generally. Most women are in primary industry in the agricultural sector, with the remainder distributed in the secondary and tertiary non-agricultural labor force. The majority of women in the latter are in the service sector where they are overrepresented in self-employment retail trade, and earn a living and cash income by working independently.

TABLE 3
ECONOMICALLY ACTIVE FEMALE POPULATION BY STATUS (PRECENTAGES)

County	Own Account		Salaried		Family		Other		Total
	N	%	N	%	N	%	N	%	
Algeria	11,647	10.6	73,025	66.7	14,056	12.8	10,725	9.8	109,453
Angola	39,762	35.6	68,862	61.7	2,866	2.6	88	.08	111,578
Botswana	115,504	92.2	4,850	3.9	2,628	2.1	2,219	1.8	125,201
Egypt	84,577	13.6	383,447	61.7	153,869	24.7	-	-	621,893
Gabon	5,700	5.7	5,450	5.4	60,000	60.0	28,850	28.9	100,000
Ghana	775,710	72.5	43,490	4.2	188,670	18.1	54,250	5.2	1,042,120
Liberia	31,669	21.4	5,319	3.6	111,246	75.0	-	-	148,234
Libya	2,616	13.2	6,082	30.6	9,266	46.6	1,901	9.6	19,865
Mauritius	2,476	7.4	30,191	90.6	482	1.4	167	.5	33,316
RePunion	2,057	8.8	20,336	87.4	597	2.6	258	1.1	23,248
Seychelles	596	9.1	5,769	88.5	152	2.3	-	-	6,517
Sierra Leone	50,215	15.0	6,067	1.8	274,940	82.4	2,342	.7	333,564
S. Rhodesia	1,252	3.9	29,531	92.0	566	1.8	743	2.3	32,092

Sourse: *1973 Year Book of Labor Statistics*, International Labor Office, Geneva, 1973, pp. 42-54.

Profile of Female Entrepreneurs

Specific details regarding the productive and distributive patterns of self-employed females are not covered within the parameters of this paper. Census data, ILO statistics, United Nations documents, and pioneer works of scholars such as Comhaire-Sylvain,[10]Nypan,[11] and Sudarkasa,[12] do suggest general contours which are summarized below.

1. *Scale of Activity*   Women dominate retail trade, whether in the market place, on the streets, or on the premises of their compounds. They are underrepresented in wholesale and import trading, and in other large-scale businesses that are handled and controlled by both African and non-African men. There is an increasing number of women industrialists but little is known about the range and limits of their economic activity. Moreover, there exists a small but significant group of "market queens" whose business activities have taken on international dimensions.[13]

Female dominance in market centers is well-established in Western Africa; it has also been reported that women dominate markets in many parts of Eastern Africa including Southern Rhodesia, Zambia, and Malawi.[14] Thus, while the general trading organization is that of the one-person enterprise, the scale of female entrepreneurship varies from those engaged in the wholesale-retail productive and distributive process, to those engaged in extremely small-scale local street-hawking, or market-gardening and vending. The range of economic activity expands across all industrial sectors—agricultural, manufacturing, and service.

2. *Type of Business Activity*   As commercial traders, women handle mainly foods and agricultural products: fruits, vegetables, milk, eggs, and poultry. One study reports that " ... well over half the traders deal with foodstuffs, about one-quarter sell various other goods, mainly manufactures, and about one-fifth more (tailors and traders in food prepared on the spot) combine processing and trading activities."[15] Traditionally, other self-employed women engage in market-gardening, poultry-rearing, beer-brewing and "spirit-making," hairdressing, dressmaking, and laundering. Others engage in lucrative crafts such as the making of pottery and the dyeing of cloth.

Female business proprietors work in large-scale transport activities as owners of taxies, lorries, and buses. Some are independent farmers, and there is scattered information about women who own various manufacturing and service enterprises such as restaurants and hotels, trawlers and fishing fleets, food canneries, and dress shops.

3. *Income and Wealth* Some of the women are wealthy and earn large incomes (running into four figures); they have penetrated the higher capital return wholesale and import market.[16] They are few in number, and tend to work in the secondary and tertiary sectors, mainly in transport, wholesale trade, and manufacturing.

The *majority* of women are "petty traders," working in a highly competitive market place. They deal in a variety of goods, but in quite small quantities. Their incomes are low and their average annual profit has been estimated from a low 5 to 6 percent to a high 20 to 30 percent of value of turnover.[17]

4. *Age and Education* The majority of women entrepreneurs have "little or no education," ranging from no schooling at all, to only a few years of primary school.[18] Women with higher levels of education are in larger scale business activities and tend to be better off economically.[19] Women between the ages of 30 years and 60 years are overrepresented in the entrepreneurial group, which suggests a high correlation between the high rate of illiteracy and the high average age of women traders.[20]

5. *Locality Base* Female entrepreneurship is an established reality in rural and urban areas, but the intensity and diversity of female business enterprises are more evident in cities and urban fringe areas. This rise of tertiary industries and services is linked to the process of urbanization and the changing scale of societal activity generally. This trend does not belie the significant existence of self-employed workers in villages and rural towns. Exemplary is rural Western Nigeria, (see Table 4) where it has been estimated that 26.4 percent of gainfully employed men and women are sales workers with trading as a main occupation. The percentages for women in both villages and towns is considerably higher, and they, in fact, constitute more than 85 percent of all sales workers.[21]

Given the above observations, which are representative but not exhaustive, it is possible to raise queries about the changing patterns of participation of female entrepreneurs within a larger societal context.

TABLE 4
TRADING AS MAIN OCCUPATION AND COMMERCE IN IFO, OTTO AND ILARO DISTRICTS OF WESTERN NIGERIA, 1966

Settlement Class	Estimated numbers of sales workers as percent of gainfully employed persons by sex			
		Both Sexes	Male	Female
All Villages	N	(15,497)	(1,727)	(13,770)
	%	24.4	5.7	41.4
All Rural Towns	N	(4,846)	(615)	(4,231)
(Ifo, Otto, Ilaro)	%	35.8	8.6	66.4
Total for Districts	N	(20,343)	(2,342)	(18,001)
	%	26.4	6.2	45.4

Source: *International Labor Office, Socio-Economic Conditions in the Ifo, Otta and Ilaro Districts of Nigeria,* Pilot Project for Rural Employment Promotion in the Western State, Ad hoc Technical Report (UNDP/SF - NIR - 36), 1972, p. 208.

II. PERSPECTIVES ON THE AFRICAN WOMAN AS ENTREPRENEUR

Female entrepreneurs, particularly market traders, provide essential services to consumers in urban and rural areas. They work as owners of neighborhood and community general stores, as clothiers and fashion designers, artisans, and beauticians. They make goods available to the consumer in quantities the average person can afford, and thereby fulfill an imortant public need. Women make a significant contribution to economic and social development in that they are largely responsible for the internal distribution of food and other local services.[22] It has been acknowledged

> . . . that without the day-to-day initiative of traders and lorry owners, a large part of produce would rot, the rural population would lack many modern amenities, and the main population centres would starve.[23]

The issue, therefore, is not the exclusion of women from participation in the economic sector in most of Africa. Rather, the problem is one of concern for the character and quality of their participation given the changing economic and social structures in different locations. Women are subject to institutional discrimination such as unequal access to education. Economically, they receive minimal rewards for jobs performed. As a group, women hold highly disadvantageous positions in the economic, educational, and political institutions of society.

It has been widely noted that large numbers of women engage in trading because there are limited economic alternatives for them to do other work. Moreover, the possibilities of broadening the range of employment opportunities depends on the extent to which there is expansion and diversification of the economy. These are not chance events. Rather, they suggest a structure of institutions, classes, and power arrangements—the dependency relations they have shaped the social structure of underdevelopment in Africa.[24] By dependence is meant

> ...a situation in which the economy of certain countries is conditioned by the development and expansion of another economy to which the former is subjected. The relation of interdependence between two or more economies, and between these and world trade, assumes the form of dependence when some countries (the dominant ones) can expand and can be self-sustaining, while other countries (the dependent ones) can do this only as a reflection of that expansion, which can have either a positive or a negative effect on their immediate development.[25]

The point is that any analysis of the conflicts, changes, and problems of the entrepreneur must be perceived as a reflection of a complex of historically conditioned situations directly related to Africa's position in the world economy. It can be argued from this vantage point, that nothing short of profound and fundamental change will significantly alter the "underclass" status of the small-scale entrepreneur in Africa. Ultimately, development is " ... a discontinuous process that involves changes in the fundamental institutions and structures of economy and society."[26] Yet, taking a more pragmatic and programmatic perspective, some short-term and long-term strategies could be set in motion to help alleviate some of the institutionalized disadvantages. It is therefore incumbent upon scholars, activists, and planners, to explore strategies and programs designed to move people out of poverty and social oppression.

In the discussion that follows, a number of questions are raised regarding the position of the African woman as entrepreneur, her changing patterns of participation, and the changing nature of societal relationships of which she is part. The questions, most of which are fairly general, and abstract, should serve as heuristic devices.Hopefully, new perspectives and programmatic ideas can be generated around the role of the female entrepreneur in development.

Many of the issues presented are biased in the direction of Western Africa and the problems of economically disadvantaged females in the commercial and trading sector. This bias is largely caused by historical tradition and the lack of research literature and data on the subject. The issues, however, should not be perceived as bound to physical or social space. Indeed, they should be expanded, rephrased, and reinterpreted to accommodate other general or particularistic concerns. Every opportunity should be seized to identify additional problems and broaden the scope of knowledge about female entrepreneurship in all of its dimensions.

The following discussion is divided into three parts: the impact of structural change on the female entrepreneur, techniques of change and the entrepreneurial function, and development planning and consciousness. The queries within each are indicative of the range of concerns that lead toward a more comprehensive understanding of women in development.

A. Impact of Structural Change

A plethora of historical events from precolonial to postindependent Africa have had infinite repercussions in every institutional arena in which these women operate. Structural transformations are reflected in changing forms of government, political leadership, economic relations and policies, cultural traditions, and styles of life. Changes in the composition, distribution, and location of people, for example, have altered population structures. For although the majority of the population is rural-based, there continue to occur small, but significant, shifts in the distribution and composition of populations through migration. These trends suggest changes in social processes and in the total scale of societal activity. How are women entrepreneurs affected by the various processes of change and conflict? What are the quantitative and qualitative manifestations of such processes as migration, urbanization, industrialization, indigenization or Africanization?

It has been argued that colonialism had a significant impact upon the role of African women.[27] However, as new forms of structural dependence emerge, such as the investment of multinational corporations in the internal markets of Africa, what might be the conse-

quences for small scale entrepreneurs? Some observers contend
that market women are in danger of being pushed out of the market
by big commercial enterprises.[28] While the movement toward shops
with shop assistants has had variable impact, the question is raised
as to whether such a change will strengthen the position of women
in the labor force or whether it will lead to the increased "masculini-
zation" of the trade sector.[29] Is it possible that the tradition of
women in trade will enhance and work to their advantage, or will
recruitment practices and high rates of illiteracy continue to give
men priority and mitigate against the involvement of women?
Moreover, what are the social implications of possible male/female
conflicts emerging out of such a situation? Independent African
governments are advancing new policies for development which
will have a profound effect on the future of entrepreneurship.
Some economies, with the view of fostering a more equitable distribution of goods and services, have become more institutionalized
through emerging public corporations or parastatals. Attempts
have been made to change internal distribution and transportation
systems as well as to impose stricter licensing, and import and price
controls. In this context Esther Ocloo, president of Nkulenu Industries in Ghana, paints a bleak picture of the future for women in the
trading sector of the country's economy.

> They are not finding business as easy and profitable as before. There
> are restrictions now on imported goods. And those which are being
> imported are very costly, because our Government has now with-
> drawn the subsidy on all imported essential commodities. The
> Government's price control is so much enforced that many of them
> who try to make some gain are landing in prison. Their future does
> not look very bright.[30]

Relatedly, the move by Kenya's government to limit trade-permits
and impose more rigid licensing requirements has had an adverse
effect on the activities of women:

> Unlike the women in West Africa, women in Nairobi do not appear to
> occupy a recognized place in the marketing activities of the City.
> Thus for example, of some 1,500 Hawkers' Licenses that have been
> issued annually by the City Council of Nairobi, only about 20 percent
> are issued to women. This is not necessarily in accordance with the
> wishes of the women, who significantly, account for a much larger
> percentage of prosecutions for illegal hawking, than do men, . . . [31]

What, in essence, are the ramifications of government policy and administrative change for the participation of women in economic development? How, and in what ways, if any, have women entrepreneurs as organized groups experienced a change in economic and political power relationships as a result of transformations in state institutions and national systems? What is the nature of the conflict and what are some of the specific problems?

B. *Techniques of Change and the Entrepreneurial Function*

It has been postulated that the role of the private sector in the development process is to provide enterprise.[32] Schumpeter refers to this expectation as the "entrepreneurial function," meaning

> ... to reform or revolutionize the pattern of production by exploiting an invention or, more generally, an untried technological possibility for producing a new commodity or producing an old one in a new way, by opening up a new source of supply of materials or a new outlet for products, by reorganizing an industry and so on.[33]

Any assessment of the role of female entrepreneurs should include an analysis of their contributions to change and their potential as sustained and resourceful agents of change. The study of this problem would require analysis of such issues as the availability of resources and opportunities for change, individual and structural impediments, and facilitators of change. Indeed, the issues are numerous, and as suggested by the discussion below, complex as well.

Based on research in Africa, Katzin advises that

> The primary object of most traders is not to change the system of trade but to advance their own position within the existing system, by building up trading capital, expanding the range of their trading contacts and thereby increasing their volume of trade ... typical successful women traders, most of whom do not read or write, indicate that they begun as petty traders, gradually gained experience, accumulated capital and a sound credit rating, shifted to more profitable lines and finally become wholesaler-retailers, specializing in lines that were expected to yield the highest returns.[34]

In a different contextual but related observation it has been pointed out that

> The women form themselves into powerful associations according to their particular interests, and are real powers in politics (to such a

point that there are governments which do not dare to claim the income tax justified by the size of their turnover).[35]

Can it be argued, therefore, that the goals of women entrepreneurs, individually and collectively, may be incompatible with national or societal goals? How does one get at casual relations and the possible policy implications? A significant portion of traditional African economic literature has focused on the importance of so-called "noneconomic factors" that operate as barriers to Africans performing the entrepreneurial function. Varied emphasis has been given to such variables as family, kinship and tribal obligations, titles to land, attitudes to thrift, individualism, corruption, social class, status, and mobility.[36]

This literature is not without value, but many such explications tend to be limited in explanatory value, and, as pointed out by some critics, are inclined toward exaggeration.[37] One of the main problems is their authors' failure to discuss and interrelate larger political and economic conditions of African societies stemming from a broader network of relationships. Hakam is emphatic on this point, and describes the stifling effect of expatriate and foreign groups on the growth of private indigenous enterprise.[38] Thus, a problem of historical and contemporary impact relates to improved understanding of the structural dynamics between African women and immigrant trading diasporas in the trading and commercial market. The presence of the Levantines in Western Africa, and of Indians and Arabs in Eastern Africa should enable researchers to appraise the nature of dominance and subordinance relations within different spatial and temporal contexts. While many African governments have taken restrictive measures such as the deportation of immigrants and the implementation of indigenization decrees, it is expedient to examine the overall impact of this experience, psychologically, economically, and politically.

Despite the part women have played in trade and commerce, surprisingly little attention has been directed to the problems they encounter with forming capital and credit and loan facilities. What emerges as an interesting point, nonetheless, is that this is also an area in which women have demonstrated creativity and ingenuity. Illustrative is the formation of various organizations to provide "help in times of need." Mutual benefit societies, insurance companies, and credit, savings, and loan associations, were developed to provide capital for their businesses and for other competing individual and social demands.[39]

Many of these programs emerged during the period of world depression between 1929 and 1939 and persist today, with varying levels of growth and development.[40] The principal point, however, is that these grassroots institutions provide channels of access to funds and resources not available to women in larger state-owned and/or expatriate banking institutions and development corporations.[41] The emergence of such organizations should force rethinking of the social conditions surrounding capital development, policies for capital, use incentives for seeking capital, strategies for survival, and related issues.[42]

In this connection, there are also pressing policy concerns. Given the fact that most women in business are poor and lack working capital, what is the feasibility of developing existent indigenous credit and loan associations into more responsive institutions? Are there other experimental programs that would offer less complicated conditions for loans? How can small commercial credit departments and industrial credit schemes in banks better serve women?[43]

The above examples intimate the obligation to look at linkages between so-called "economic" and "noneconomic factors" that affect the participation of women as "innovating entrepreneurs." Certainly attitudes toward thrift may relate to the ability to secure credit or accumulate capital, as well as to organizational and financial management skills. Likewise, business size and male competition, monopolies, and government and banking policy toward business, can be directly related to individualism or corruption. The point is that for analytical purposes, it is possible to identify and isolate selected economic and noneconomic variables, but it is very often their interrelated effect that is more important than their separate results.

Finally, among the remaining unmentioned problems and conflicts pertinent to entrepreneurial roles of African women, is one that should be of particular interest to those concerned with change: the possibility of broadening the scope and efficiency of productivity for women. Given women's existing entrepreneurial skills, levels of literacy, and market organization, how can the efficiency of their productivity be increased? Moreover, to what extent are there opportunities available for women? Are women encouraged and recruited to join a wider array of businesses in all economic sectors—primary, secondary, and tertiary? What can be learned from the experiences of the younger, and more literate group of emerging female industrialists. Their contributions to development, productive activity, organization, and management, deserve study and analysis.

Response to these concerns demands critical appraisal of the changing nature of the opportunity structures to which women have different access: education and training, employment, technical assistance, and social and economic resources ranging from child care to monetary loans.

Certainly, these needs and considerations have been addressed in a variety of ways, and the strategies below are those mentioned most frequently in the development literature.[44]

1. Encourage women to form cooperatives to enlarge the base of production and marketing activities, credit loan, and storage facilities.

2. Persuade governments to develop meaningful and accessible vocational and training programs directly related to the needs of women.

3. Continue to educate younger women and recruit them to pursue management training so that they can work with illiterate women in marketing, accounting, and management procedures.

4. Governments and/or private agencies should continue to create improved intrastructure in the areas of transportation, communications, marketing, and storage facilities.

Many such programs have been initiated, but there is little systematic knowledge of the relative successes or failures of these attempts. Cooperatives have been organized in diverse regions and countries of Africa, including Uganda, Kenya, Nigeria, Dahomey, and Guinea. In Tanzania, there is a developing program geared toward education for cooperatives which might provide insights regarding social and economic benefits and costs.[45] Comparative study of areas such as program implementation, effectiveness in goal attainment, and efficiency as an instrument of change, would provide valuable data for others considering such ideas and strategies. Policy makers and program planners—at all levels of government and in the private sector—are faced with competing demands for scarce resources. In order to establish priorities, there is a need for more evaluation research on existing service and support programs, as well as on social change experiments in diverse settings.

The search for alternative channels of change and the reassessment of existing arenas of participation should not be diminished. For instance, the current structures such as trade associations, may not be fully utilized to maximize benefits for women as well as the larger society. Is adequate attention being given to problems posed for women by illiteracy, such as the acquisition of knowledge of the larger social world of relations that extend beyond the boundaries of their immediate lives and marketplace encounters?[46] What of changing management procedures, supervision, and making new contacts?[47] Such problems eventually relate, directly and indirectly, to developmental perspectives geared toward broadening the productive capacity of women entrepreneurs. Success is in large part dependent upon the planning process and its relevancy to the needs of women—a problem discussed briefly below.

C. Development Planning and Consciousness

In the final analysis, the role of African female entrepreneurs will depend, in part, on whether or not their contributions are understood and perceived to be important to societal development, particularly in the economic realm. As primary actors in the production and distribution process in Western Africa, are their efforts valued and appreciated by the consuming public and those in decision-making positions who ultimately define and plan national priorities? One might glean from systematic analysis of national planning schemes, specific indicators of the weight given self-employed business women and the consequences for their long-term growth and development. Is there a priority of redefining and rethinking the notion of entrepreneurship with the view of increasing efficiency and productivity commensurate with national goals? Or has the attempt to alter structural relationships in the economy resulted in ignoring small-scale indigenous business by importing entrepreneurship and duplicating lines of production?[48] What has emerged as policy, and what are the consequences and possible alternatives?

As one observer puts it

In their concern with effecting...changes, planners have concentrated on attempting to introduce new forms of enterprise, while virtually ignoring altogether those indigenous forms which flourish under their noses. Indigenous enterprise has frequently been dismissed as 'cottage industry' (whatever that may be) which central planning offices could treat as peripheral to their main concerns.[49]

If this remark can be generalized in any sense, the study of the position of women in national development planning deserves much more attention than currently acknowledged. In the following discussion, several ideas are projected which may provide additional perspective on the general problem.

First, more systematic knowledge is required on the social and economic organization of internal trade and the various facets of indigenous enterprise.[50] Perhaps more emphasis on the changing dimensions and creative aspects of the "indigenous economic system" in relation to women would inform and help sensitize central planners to view local enterpreneurs in more creative terms.

A second set of concerns might focus on developing strategies to foster greater participation of women in development planning. What realistic possibilities emerge for reciprocal action and dialogue with central planning agencies? One idea is that to maximize congruency on national goals, central planners and women might exchange projected ideas and possible courses of action. The postulation that emerges is that the degree to which women entrepreneurs make specific contributions to economic development is directly related to their involvement in program planning and implementation. What forces, therefore, are at work to detract from or add to this process?

A third area of examination is linked to the definitions and perceptions of the women. How do female entrepreneurs define their structural position in society? What are the centers of tension and sites of conflict between these definitions and those people in positions of power? What do such observations reveal about the interpenetration of problems, and the nature of the total societal reality? From the perspective of women, what is development, and how does the definition change, temporally and spatially?

The programmatic implications are quite relevant here if one accepts the assumption that the starting point for organizing social and economic change must be the present, concrete situation, which reflects peoples' aspirations and ideals.[51] Commenting on the methodology of change, Freire makes the following plea to potential agents of change:

> We must never provide the people with programs which have little or nothing to do with their own preoccupations, doubts, hopes, and fears—programs which at times in fact increase the fears of the oppressed consciousness. It is not our role to speak to the people about our own view of the world, nor to attempt to impose that view on them, but rather to dialogue with the people about their view and ours. We must realize that their view of the world, manifested variously in their action, reflects their *situation* in the world. Educational and political action which is not critically aware of this situation runs the risk either of 'banking' or of preaching in the desert.[52]

The intention, therefore, is not to "blame the victims" and make the women merely objects of investigation, but rather to better understand that their views and ideas did not emerge in a vacuum. Certainly their definitions are a reflection of the historical-social conditions of the society in which the very ideas they project are generated.

African countries are relying more and more upon long-range development planning for effecting social change. Women entrepreneurs, in order to survive and occupy a major role in the development process, will no doubt need to become fully involved in every phase of the action. This will necessitate intelligent and organized efforts on their part to keep abreast of events; it will also require that planners develop greater sensitivity and consciousness of the major problems. In the past women have had no hesitation in pressing for solutions to their problems and making their feelings known. While there is little reason to assume that such activity will not continue, the issue is, again, not one of degree but one of *kind*—the kind of thrust for change. The action-oriented student of change is therefore faced with a plethora of problems; they range from evaluating national goals and priorities, to involving groups in reciprocal dialogue to raise the level of consciousness regarding the self-employed female entrepreneur in the process of economic development. Such persons must not only operate with an enlightened and broad perspective, but they must also have an organized plan of action that is realistic and workable.

III. SUMMARY

The African female entrepreneur holds a critical position in the internal production and distribution of goods and services to the consuming public. The major thrust of this paper has been to identify some of the critical problems and conflicts confronting the own-account business woman in the process of social change and economic development.

Without pretending to be exhaustive, suggestions have been advanced for basic research and policy analysis. They include the investigation of development planning as it relates to the role of women, ways of broadening the productive capacity and efficiency of business women, evaluation research on proposed and already existent strategies for change, and the study of the impact of structural change on the entrepreneur. Many of the issues outlined overlap in content, yet they do point to gaps in our knowledge, and call attention to the exigency to develop new and broader perspectives which may help create conditions for growth and development.

Emergent literature and data are available, but there is necessity for organized study of all facets of the problems. In particular, there is a lack of comparative data representative of the various regions of the continent. Very little is known about self-employed women in manufacturing. Also, there is need for more systematic analysis of women in agricultural and tertiary activities.

Trend data would be extremely useful in illuminating the impact and consequences of change over time. Conceivably, interdisciplinary research teams might bring rich insights to problems relevant to women in the development process.

Finally, development is perceived as a discontinuous process oriented toward developing people out of poverty and oppression. It means moving beyond the network of unequal dependency relationships that have historically conditioned African societies. The location and position of women in the economic hierarchy is invariably linked to the experiences of the total society. Thus, data analysis and interpretations must be placed within historical-cultural context, utilizing both quantitative and qualitative data.

NOTES

1. Kwame Daaku, "Trade and Trading Patterns of the Akan in the Seventeenth and Eighteenth Centuries," in *The Development of Indigenous Trade and Markets in West Africa*, ed. by Claude Meillassoux (London: Oxford University Press, 1971), p. 177.

2. John Duncan, *Travels in Western Africa in 1845 and 1846*, Vol. II (London: Richard Bentley, 1847), pp. 48-49, and, Vol. I, pp. 120-123.

3. Lars Sundström, *The Exchange Economy of Pre-Colonial Tropical Africa* (New York: St. Martin's Press, 1974), p. 47.

4. This definition is closely related to that of entrepreneur given by Keith Hart, "Small Scale Entrepreneurs in Ghana and Development Planning," *Journal of Development Studies*, VI, No. 4, (July, 1970), p. 107.

5. See. Chapter XII of Joseph A. Schumpeter, *Capitalism, Socialism, and Democracy* (3rd ed. New York: Harper and Row, 1950).

6. Unless otherwise indicated most of the data for this section are drawn from two sources: a) International Labour Office, *Labour Force Projections 1965-1985, Part II, Africa* (Geneva: International Labour Office, 1971), and, b) Ettore Denti, "Africa's Labour Force, 1960-1980," International Labour Review, 104, No. 3 (Sept. 1971), pp. 189-202.

7. Polly Hill, "Hidden Trade in Hausaland," *Man*, 4 (1969), pp. 392-409.

8. Denti, *op. cit.*, p. 191.

9. International Labour Office, *The Employment and Conditions of Work of African Women*, Second African Regional Conference, Addis Ababa, 1964 (Geneva: International Labour Office, 1964), p. 9.

10. Suzanne Comhaire-Sylvain, "Participation of Women in Industry and Commerce in African Towns South of the Sahara," Economic Commission for Africa, *Workshop on Urban Problems: The Role of Women in Urban Development* (E/CN.14/URB/14), 1963.

11. Astrid Nypan, *Market Trade: A Sample Study of Market Traders in Accra*, Africa Business Series No. 2 (University College of Ghana: Economic Research Division, 1960).

12. Sudarkasa, Niara, *Where Women Work: A Study of Yoruba Women in the Marketplace and in the Home*, Museum of Anthropology, Unviersity of Michigan, No. 53, (Ann Arbor: University of Michigan, 1973).

13. Paper prepared by United Nations Economic Commission for Africa, Human Resources Development Division, "Women: The Neglected Human Resource for African Development," *Canadian Journal of African Studies*, VI, No. 2 (1972), p. 364.

14. Ester Boserup, *Women's Role in Economic Development* (New York: St. Martin's Press, 1970), p. 89 fn.

15. Astrid Nypan, "Market Trade in Accra," *The Econmic Bulletin of Ghana*, IV 3 (March, 1960), p. 11.

16. Gloria Addae, "The Retailing of Imported Textiles in the Accra Market," West African Institute of Social and Economic Research. *Proceedings of the Third Annual Conference* (Ibadan: Nigeria, 1956), and, Boserup, *op. cit.*, p. 95.

17. Peter Garlick, *African Traders and Economic Development in Ghana* (Oxford: Clarendon Press, 1971), p. 50; Claudine and Claude Tardits, "Traditional Market Economy in South Dahomey" in *Markets in Africa*, ed. by Paul Bohannan and George Dalton (Evanston, Ill.: Northwestern University Press, 1962), p. 102; Elliot P. Skinner, "Trade and Markets among the Mossi People," in *Ibid.*, p. 265; International Labor Office, *Socio-Economic Conditions in the Ifo, Otta, and Ilaro Districts of Nigeria, Pilot Project for Rural Employment Promotion*

in the Western State, ad hoc Technical Report (UNDP/SF-NIR-36), 1972, pp. 207-212; Sudarkasa, *op. cit.*, pp. 94-95; Nypan, *Market Trade: A Sample of Market Traders in Accra*, pp. 40-55; and, Florence Aleeno Sai, "The Market Women in the Economy of Ghana" (unpublished Master's thesis, Cornell University, 1971), pp. 60-61.

18. International Labor Office, *Employment and Conditions of Work*, pp. 10-14.

19. *Ibid.*

20. Boserup, *op. cit.*, p. 95.

21. International Labor Office, *Socio-Economic Conditions*, p. 208.

22. Hart, *op. cit.*, pp. 109-111.

23. *Ibid.*, p. 110.

24. Dale L. Johnson, "Dependence and the International System," in *Dependence and Underdevelopment*, ed. by Frank Crockcroft and Dale Johnson (New York: Anchor Books, 1972), p. 73.

25. Theotonio Dos Santos, "The Structure of Dependence," *American Economic Review*, LX (May, 1970), p. 231.

26. Johnson, *op. cit.*, p. 273.

27. See the following works: United Nations Economic Commission for Africa, Women: *The Neglected Human Resource for African Development*; Denise Paulme, "Introduction" and Anne Laurentin, "Nzakara Women-Central African Republic," in *Women of Tropical Africa*, ed. by Denise Paulme (Los Angeles: University of California, 1971); Margarita Dobert, "The Changing Status of Women in French-Speaking Africa: Two Examples: Dahomey and Guinea" (unpublished paper, 1975); and, Boserup, *op. cit.*, chapt. 3 and other chapter references.

28. United Nations Economic Commission for Africa, Women: *The Neglected Human Resource*, p. 364.

29. Boserup, *op. cit.*, p. 97.

30. Esther Ocloo, "The Ghanian Market Women," unpublished paper presented before the Society for International Development, 14th World Conference, Abidjan, Ivory Coast, August 11-16, 1974).

31. Julius Carlebach, "The Position of Women in Kenya," Economic Commission on Africa, *Workshop on Urban Problems: The Role of Women in Urban Development* (E/CN. 14/URB/9), Sept., 1963.

32. D. C. Hague, "The Role and Problems of Indigenous Private Enterprise in Economic Development," *The Economic Bulletin of Ghana*, XII, 2/3 (1968), pp. 27-36.

33. Schumpeter, *op. cit.* p. 132; see also P. T. Bauer, *West African Trade* (London: Cambridge University Press, 1954), pp. 28-31, and , W. A. Lewis, *Theory of Economic Growth* (London: Allen and Unwin, 1955), p. 265.

34. Margaret Katzin, "The Role of the Small Entrepreneur," in *Economic Transition in Africa*, ed. by Melville J. Herskovits and Mitchell Harwitz (Evanston, Ill.: Northwestern University Press, 1961), pp. 180-181.

35. Marie-Helene Lefaucheux, "The Contribution of Women to the Economic and Social Development of African Countries," *International Labour Review*, 86, No. 1 (July, 1962), p. 21.

36. A. N. Hakam, "Impediments to the Growth of Indigenous Industrial Entrepreneurship in Ghana: 1946-1968," *The Economic Bulletin of Ghana*, 11, 2 (1972), pp. 6-7, and, Katzin, *op. cit.*, pp. 193-197.

37. Hakam, *op. cit.*, pp. 6-9.

38. *Ibid.*

39. Based on original research of the author in 1973, article forthcoming.

40. *Ibid.*

41. Hakam, *op. cit.*, discusses this issue as relates to African business men in Ghana.

42. For a general discussion of those issues see Raymond Firth, "Capital, Saving and Credit in Peasant Societies: A Viewpoint from Economic Anthropology," in *Capital, Saving and Credit in Peasant Societies*, ed. by Raymond Firth and B. S. Yamey (Chicago: Aldine Publishing Co., 1964).

43. Comhaire-Sylvain, *op. cit.*, p. 31.

44. Consult the following: Boserup, *op. cit.*; Lefaucheux, *op. cit.*; United Nations Economic Commission for Africa, *Women: The Neglected Resource*; International Labour Office, *The Employment and Conditions of Work*, pp. 32-34; United Nations Social Development Section of the Economic Commission for Africa, "Women at Work," *The Status and Role of Woman in East Africa*, 6 (June, 1967), pp. 19-26; and, "African Conference on the Role of Women in National Development," *International Labor Review*, 104, 6 (Dec. 1971), pp. 555-557.

45. Sven Grabe, "Tanzania: An Educational Program for Cooperatives," in *Education For Rural Development*, ed. by Manzoor Ahmed and Philip H. Coombs (New York: Praeger Publishers, 1975), p. 589-615.

46. This point is raised by Peter Marris in a discussion based on a study of businessmen in Kenya. See Peter Marris, "The Social Barriers to African Entrepreneurship," *Journal of Development Studies*, V. 1 (Oct., 1968), pp. 29-38.

47. *Ibid.*, and, Hart, *op. cit.*, pp. 115-116.

48. Hart, *op. cit.*, p. 115.

49. *Ibid.*

50. For in-depth discussion consult Polly Hill, "A Plea for Indigeneous Economics: The West African Example," Economic Development and Cultural Change, XV, 1 (Oct., 1966), pp. 10-20.

51. Paulo Freire, *Pedagogy of the Oppressed* (New York: The Seabury Press, 1973), p. 85.

52. *Ibid.*

BIBLIOGRAPHY

Addae, Gloria. "The Retailing of Imported Textiles in the Accra Market." West African Institute of Social and Economic Research. *Proceedings of the Third Annual Conference*. Ibadan, Nigeria, 1956.

"African Conference on the Role of Women in National Development." *International Labor Review*, 6 (Dec., 1971), pp. 555-557.

Ahmed, Manzoor, and Coombs, Philip H., eds. *Education for Rural Development*. New York: Praeger Publishers, 1975.

Bauer, P.T. *West African Trade*. London: Cambridge University Press, 1954.

Bohannan, Paul, and Dalton, George, eds. *Markets in Africa*. Evanston, Ill.: Northwestern University Press, 1962.

Boserup, Ester. *Women's Role in Economic Development*. New York: St. Martin's Press, 1970.

Carlebach, Julius. "The Position of Women in Kenya." Economic Commission on Africa, *Workshop on Urban Problems: The Role of Women in Urban Development* (E/CN. 14/URB/9), Sept., 1963.

Comhaire-Sylvain, Suzanne. *Femmes de Kinshasa*. Paris: Mouton and Co., 1968.

_____ "Participation of Women in Industry and Commerce in African Towns South of the Sahara." Economic Commission for Africa, *Workshop on Urban Problem: The Role of Women in Urban Development* (E/CN. 14/URB/14), 1963.

Crockcroft, Frank and Johnson, Dale, eds. *Dependence and Underdevelopment*. New York: Anchor Books, 1972.

Daaku, Kwame. "Trade and Training Patterns of the Akan in the Seventeenth and Eighteenth Centuries." *The Development of Indigeneous Trade and Markets in West Africa*. Edited by Claude Meillassoux. London: Oxford University Press, 1971.

Dalton, George, ed. *Tribal and Peasant Economies*. Garden City, New York: The Natural History Press, 1967.

Denti, Ettore. "Africa's Labour Force, 1960-80." *International Labour Review*, 104, 3 (Sept., 1971), pp. 181-203.

"Dependence et developpement: Le Statut de la Femme en Afrique Moderne." *Notes Africaines*, No. 139 (Juillet, 1973), pp. 57-66.

Dobert, Margarita. "The Changing Status of Women in French-Speaking Africa: Two Examples: Dahomey and Guinea." Unpublished paper, 1975.

Dos Santos, Theotonio. "The Structure of Dependence." *American Economic Review*, LX, May, 1970, pp. 231-236.

Ducan, John. *Travels in Western Africa in 1845 and 1846*, Vol. I and II, London: Richard Bentley, 1847.

Falade, Solange. "Women of Dakar and the Surrounding Urban Area." *Women of Tropical Africa.* Edited by Denise Paulme. Los Angeles: University of California Press, 1971.

Firth, Raymond and Yamey, B.S., eds. *Capital Saving and Credit in Peasant Societies.* Chicago: Aldine Publishing Co., 1964.

Firth, Ramond. "Capital, Saving, and Credit in Peasant Societies: A Viewpoint From Economic Anthropology." *Capital, Saving, and Credit in Peasant Societies.* Edited by Raymond Firth and B.S. Yamey. Chicago: Aldine Publishing Co., 1964.

Frankman, Myron and Charle, Edwin. "Employment in the Service Sector in Sub-Saharan Africa." *The Journal of Modern African Studies,* II, 2 (1973), pp. 201-210.

Friere, Paulo. *Pedagogy of the Oppressed.* New York: The Seabury Press, 1973.

Garlick, Peter C. *African Traders and Economic Development in Ghana.* Oxford: Clarendon Press, 1971.

Genoud, Roger. *Nationalism and Economic Development in Ghana.* Praeger Special Studies in International Economics and Development. New York: Praeger, 1969.

Grabe, Sven. "Tanzania: An Educational Program for Cooperatives." *Education for Rural Development.* Edited by Manzoor Ahmed and Philip H. Coombs. New York: Praeger Publishers, 1975.

Greenstreet, Miranda. "Employment of Women in Ghana." *International Labour Review,* 103, No. 2 (Feb., 1971), pp. 117-129.

Hague, D.C. "Private Enterprise and National Development Planning in a Developing Economy." *The Economic Bulletin of Ghana,* XII, No. 1 (1968), pp. 3-7.

_____ "The Role and Problems of Indigenous Private Enterprise in Economic Development." *The Economic Bulletin of Ghana,* No. 2/3 (1968), pp. 27-36.

Hakam, A.N. "Impediments to the Growth of Indigenous Industrial Entrepreneurship in Ghana: 1946-1968." *The Economic Bulletin of Ghana,* II, No. 2 (1972), pp. 3-16.

Hart, Keith. "Small Scale Entrepreneurs in Ghana and Development Planning." *Journal of Development Studies,* VI (July, 1970), pp. 104-120.

Herskovits, Melville and Harwitz, ed. *Economic Transition in Africa.* Evanston, Ill.: Northwestern University Press, 1961.

Hill, Polly. "A Plea for Indigeneous Economics: The West African Example." *Economic Development and Cultural Change,* XV, No. 1 (Oct., 1966), pp. 10-20.

_____ "Hidden Trade in Hausaland " *Man,* 4 (1969), pp. 392-409.

Hodder, B.W. and Ukwu, U.I. *Markets in West Africa.* Ibadan: Ibadan University Press, 1969.

International Labour Office. *Labour Force Projections 1965-1985, Part II, Africa.* Geneva: International Labour Office, 1971.

_____ *Socio-Economic Conditions in the Ifo, Otta and Ilaro Districts of Nigeria, Pilot Project for Rural Employment Promotion in the Western State,* ad hoc Technical Report (UNDP/SF - Nir - 36), 1972.

_____ *The Employment and Conditions of Work of African Women.* Second African Regional Conference. Addis Ababa, 1964.

Johnson, Dale L. "Dependence and the International System." *Dependence and Underdevelopment.* Edited by Frank Crockcroft and Dale Johnson. New York: Anchor Books, 1972.

Katzin, Margaret. "The Role of the Small Entrepreneur." *Economic Transition in Africa.* Edited by Denise Paulme. Los Angeles: University of California, 1971.

Lefaucheux, Marie-Helene. "The Contribution of Women to the Economic and Social Development of African Countries." *International Labour Review,* 86, No. 1 (July, 1962), pp. 15-30.

Lewis, W.A. *Theory of Economic Growth.* London: Allen and Unwin, 1955.

Mabogunje, Akin. *The Market Woman.* Ibadan: University College of Ibadan, 1961.

Marris, Peter. "The Social Barriers to African Entrepreneurship." *Journal of Development Studies,* V, No. 1 (Oct., 1968), pp. 29-38.

Meillassoux, Claude, ed. *The Development of Indigenous Trade and Markets in West Africa.* London: Oxford University Press, 1971.

Nypan, Astrid. Market Trade: A Sample Study of Market Traders in *Accra,* Africa Business Series No. 2., University College of Ghana: Economic Research Division, 1960.

_____ *"Market Trade in Accra." The Economic Bulletin of Ghana,* IV, No. 3 (March, 1960), pp. 7-16.

Ocloo, Esther. "The Ghanian Market Women." Unpublished paper presented before the Society for International Development, 14th World Conference, Abidjan, Ivory Coast, August 11-16, 1974.

Paulme, Danise, ed. *Women of Tropical Africa.* Los Angeles: University of California, 1971.

Polyani, Karl; Arensberg, C.M.; and Pearson, H.W. *Trade and Market in the Early Empires.* Glencoe, Ill.: Free Press, 1957.

Robertson, Claire C. "Social and Economic Change in Twentieth Century Accra: Ga Women." Unpublished Ph.D. dissertation, University of Wisconsin, 1974.

Sai, Florence Aleeno. "The Market Women in the economy of Ghana." Unpublished Master's thesis, Cornell University, 1971.

Schumpeter, Joseph A. *Capitalism, Socialism and Democracy.* 3rd ed.; New York: Harper and Row, 1950.

Skinner, Elliot P. "Trade and Markets among the Mossi People." *Markets in Africa*. Edited by Paul Bohannan and George Dalton. Evanston, Ill.: Northwestern University Press, 1962.

Sudarkasa, Niara. *Where Women Work: A Study of Yoruba Women in the Market Place and in the Home*. Museum of Anthropology, University of Michigan, No. 53. Ann Arbor: University of Michigan, 1973.

Tardits, Claude and Claudine. "Traditional Market Economy in South Dahomey." *Markets in Africa*. Edited by Paul Bohannan and George Dalton. Evanston, Ill.: Northwestern University Press, 1962.

United Nations Economic Commission of Africa, Human Resources Development Division, "Women: The Neglected Human Resource for African Development." *Canadian Journal of African Studies*, VI, No. 2 (1972), pp. 359-370.

United Nations Social Development Section of the Economic Commission for Africa. "women at Work." *The Status and Role of Women in East Africa*. 6 (June, 1967), pp. 19-26.

Vicent, J.L. *Femmes Africaines en Milieu Urbaine*. Paris: Office de la Recherche Scientifique et Technique Outre-Mer, 1966.

7

The Second Sex in Town[1]

Josef Gugler

...It is traditional in Africa to regard marriage as an active association to which the woman has her daily contribution to make—an idea
which is so recent in the West that it is still only accepted in some
sections of society. Unaccustomed to relying on anyone but herself,
the African woman will have no need to acquire a feeling of self-
confidence, since she is already rarely without one.

Paulme[2]

I want to walk beside you in the street,
Side by side and arm in arm
Just like the Lagos couples I have seen
High-heeled shoes for the lady, red paint
On her lips. And her hair is stretched
Like a magazine photo. I will teach you
The waltz and we'll both learn the foxtrot
And we'll spend the week-end in night-clubs at Ibadan.
Oh I must show you the grandeur of towns
We'll live there if you like or merely pay visits.
So choose. Be a modern wife, look me in the eye
And give me a little kiss—like this.

Teacher's love (Soyinka)[3]

It is time men started to change their thinking, for to-day's society
can no longer be regarded as yesterday's. Women will no longer be
subservient to men...May I remind you all that women need recognition, respect, privileges, participation, and their voices to be heard
in all walks of life.

Habwe, President of Maendeleo ya Wanawake[4]

This paper explores the position of women in the fast growing towns of Subsaharan Africa. An attempt is made to evaluate and to integrate the available information.

First, I will briefly discuss the changes that affect the position of women in Subsaharan Africa, in an attempt to evaluate the impact of these changes in the urban setting. Then two themes will be explored: the opportunities for economic independence of urban women, and the urban family. A short discussion of the policy implications of sex discrimination in education and occupation will conclude this article.

Before we discuss changes in the position of women, we must ask: "change from what?" What were the relative positions of the sexes in Subsaharan Africa in the past? These positions may not have been subjected to evaluation in terms of "higher" and "lower" because frequently there was a strict division of labour between men and women. In our opening quotation Paulme suggests the self-assurance women used to enjoy in Africa. In some traditional societies this differentiation went so far as to create a considerable dependence on the other sex. However, if we apply the criteria usually employed in stratification analysis, i.e., power, wealth, and status, women can be seen in most societies to have enjoyed less of these than men. In another perspective, men frequently lived to a considerable extent on the product of the work of their womenfolk.[5]

FORCES FOR CHANGE

Western ideology has been a potent factor in changing the position of women in much of Subsaharan Africa: most Christian missions propounded a doctrine of the equality of marriage partners; schools taught boys and girls; print, radio, and screen extolled the overriding importance of love; when general suffrage was introduced toward the end of the colonial era it was not "one man, one vote," but the vote for every adult.[6]

Women thus found new aspirations, and men faced pressures to reform institutions lest they be considered backward. These demands are articulated by the few educated women, like the president of the Kenyan association "Women's Progress," quoted at the beginning of this paper.[7] The discussion on national legislation on marriage, maintenance of children, divorce, custody of children, and inheritance takes account of "world opinion." However, after lengthy debate, such legislation was not enacted in Ghana in the early sixties[8]; in Kenya men have not been eager to change laws that definitely favoied them, while the Affiliation Act that required fathers of illegitimate children to provide some financial support was abolished by an all-male National Assembly in 1969;[9] and the legislation that was passed in the Ivory Coast in 1964, while a radical departure from traditional norms in several respects, recognizes the husband as the head of the household.[10]

Further, there is the gap between law and practice. Levasseur[11] reports that family legislation decreed in 1939 and 1951 for what was then French West Africa and French Equatorial Africa failed completely in its purpose.[12] A survey conducted in 1967 by the Jeunesse Ouvrière Chrétienne among Ivory Coast youths aged thirteen to twenty-five revealed that many had never heard of the Civil Code passed three years earlier; among those who had, many indicated a continued preference for marriage according to customary law. Thus even among the relatively educated young persons reached by a Christian organization, the code's impact was severely limited. In fact, Ivory Coast officials themselves expressed doubts concerning its impact.[13]

The spread of modern methods of contraception is probably a major factor for change in the position of women. The very possibility of effective birth control gives women the prospect of greater power over their futures. Spouses are induced to agree on the number of children they desire. They may deliberate what method of contraception to adopt. Most important, to the extent that family size is effectively reduced, women will be less bound by home and children and in a better position to pursue career opportunities.

THE URBAN SETTING

In Soyinka's[14] hilarious play, *The Lion and the Jewel*, it is the male teacher who seeks to convince the small-town belle of the attractions of the new life style. Nigeria's two biggest cities provide the models. Indeed, Western ideology, changes in the law, family planning—all make their strongest impact in the urban setting.[15] Not only are urban dwellers most exposed to these innovations, but an older generation that might oppose them is far away. Women have additional bargaining power in the towns, because the sex imbalance allows them to be particular in selecting more or less permanent partners. Little[16] suggests that voluntary associations allow young women to get to know young men personally in a way that ordinarily might be very difficult; they facilitate an informed choice. Meillassoux[17] reports that girls settled on permanent or semi-permanent partners in neighborhood dancing associations in Bamako, even though marriage depended largely, for the girls, on the parents' decision.

Leblanc's research in Katanga in the fifties highlights differences among urban centers, here between Lubumbashi and the more recently established and smaller town of Kolwezi. Leblanc[18] developed a sentence completion test and administered it to men primary school teachers and women social workers, part of what was then the African elite. Responses showed that changes in attitudes toward women had gone further in Lubumbashi. She also devised a thematic apperception test which was taken by the social workers. One conspicuous difference between the towns was that Lubumbashi women identified single persons in the designs more frequently as female.[19]

There appears to be general agreement that women are better off in town than in rural areas. As Mayer[20] puts it:

> Even the most fortunate rural woman has to go through a long period of subjection to men and to older women; the least fortunate, such as widows and unmarried mothers, may suffer deprived status permanently. Many Xhosa women seem to use East London as a semi-permanent escape. Most agree that it is a place "to be free," "to be independent," "to get way from the rule of the people at home." In different terminology, women have reason to like this new environment where status depends less on ascription and more on achievement.

We might quarrel, though, with the interpretation in terms of a shift to a greater emphasis on achievement as the source of status. We would suggest, rather, that the decisive shift is in the different status ascribed to women in town.

This is not to suggest that equal status is ascribed to males and females in the urban setting. Women were indeed the second sex to come to the colonial towns. Today they are clearly lagging in the key areas of economic opportunity and education. Employment continues to be preferentially offered to men. This pattern is to some extent both cause and effect of the tendency for girls to get less formal education than boys, or none at all.[21] There is some irony, then, in the recurrent comments on the attraction that idleness in town holds for rural women: "She is free from the everlasting duties of fetching water and stamping meal."[22] "Their real motive, the men say, is that they like the easier life in town. 'In town they can just sit down, eat, drink and do nothing'."[23] "It is hardly surprising that there should be a widespread desire among African women to exchange a village life of hard toil for an urban life of leisure . . ."[24]

An emphasis on the idleness of women in town appears misplaced when, in fact, many urban women are without gainful occupation, not out of choice, but because opportunities are woefully limited. As Pons[25] observed for Kisangani in the early fifties:

> . . . Urban conditions had in various ways largely released women from some of the immediate constraints of traditional life, but their economic, occupational, and educational advancement still lagged far behind their personal emancipation. Most women continued to be directly dependent on their menfolk despite their new-found urban freedom, and urban feminine roles inevitably came to be defined and evaluated as more specifically sexual and domestic than the tribal roles to which most women had been reared in youth.

OPPORTUNITIES FOR ECONOMIC INDEPENDENCE

Increasing numbers of women do find economic independence in town.[26] Some, especially those who have some formal education or training, obtain employment. Others resort to outright prostitution. However, the most striking developments have been in commerce. Here the position of women has been strengthened by the absence of restrictions on their control of land, houses, and goods such as were common in traditional societies. Noteworthy are the women traders of West Africa.[27] Their independence is frequently supported by voluntary associations that promote their economic interests.[28]

In many parts of the continent, however, concern with the "embellishment" of towns led to urban regulations severely restricting small-scale trading. All too frequently, illicit activities such as prostitution and the brewing and selling of liquor provide the major opportunities for women to support themselves.

For married women earnings have particular significance where there is a strict separation of resources between husband and wife.

In central Lagos, Marris[29] found most wives engaged in trade. Unless their parents had already provided them with the needed capital to set up stock, they expected it from their husbands. This money was often a wedding gift from the groom to bride, one of the conditions of her consent. A wife's profit was her own, and she spent it mostly on personal needs, her children, and in aiding her relatives. She might have helped her husband were he in difficulty; in fact, the initial capitalization may be seen as his "insurance" or "social security." But first and foremost, through her earnings, a wife secured economic independence which protected against the failure of her husband to support her.

From Dakar, Grandmaison[30] likewise reports that women keep their earnings separate from the household's. They are supported by the Islamic rule that places the entire responsibility for supporting the family on the husband and accords the wife the independent administration of her personal belongings. Wives may assist husbands who are in temporary trouble, though. Among the Lebou, many women own fishing boats and hire their husbands as fishermen. They rigorously apply the usual rules concerning the sharing of the catch between employer and employees. Thus, in a society where authority in law resides with men, some women manage to control the means of production and to transform their husbands into salaried workers.

Tardits[31] also emphasizes the independence illiterate women in Porto Novo, Benin, find in trade. He contrasts this with the dependency experienced by educated wives who stay at home.

For Ghana Vellenga[32] reports that no legislator, man or woman, would be prepared to come out in favor of community property within a marriage. Very few husbands let their wives know their total income. For her part, the wife is free to control and invest her capital as she wishes. Even some of the most militant women Vellenga interviewed were ambivalent concerning the idea of a common budget. Some attributed the continued viability of their marriages to the fact that the partners had not pooled their resources. With the wife's and the husband's relatives making different demands regarding school fees, funeral contributions, and the like, common property would create considerable difficulty. There were further problems in relation to inheritance, children outside the marriage, and other wives.

In the Ivory Coast, however, the new Civil Code established a matrimonial regime in which the earnings and incomes of the spouses are community property. The survey by the Jeunesse Ouvière Chrétienne referred to earlier found this to be one of the most favored aspects.[33]

THE FAMILY

Whatever their views, many men who want a woman to live permanently with them in town have to accept that she will gain a degree of economic independence since his earnings are insufficient to support a family in urban conditions. Conflict is rife, though. Southall[34] noted in his study of a low-income area in Kampala that the relations between the sexes showed every indication of tension. Neither men nor women were consistent in maintaining the attitudes appropriate to their usual behaviour. When it suited them to do so, they tended to invoke the values of the past, or of more traditional and stable rural conditions, in opposition to the urban conditions which at other times they accepted and exploited. While traditional values are still in competition with an emergent culture, they provide a ready ideological weapon whenever interests clash.

Yet, for many couples, there is a real divergence in outlook. On the one hand, women tend to be quicker than men to embrace innovations that promise to improve their position. In a sample of literate persons in Porto Novo in the early 1950s, men overwhelmingly intended to keep their young children in case of marital breakup—in accordance with the patrilineal custom. A sizeable minority of women thought, however, that their sons ought to stay with them, and a majority that their daughters should remain. Also, while the majority of men felt that girls should have a smaller part in succession than men, the majority of women pleaded for equal division.[35] The stage is thus set for a radicalization of women. In a survey of the senior students in a sample of secondary and teacher training institutions throughout Ghana in the late 1950s, women were found to be more radical than men on the subject of marriage and the family. They were more set against polygamy; they took a stronger view against inheritance from the maternal uncle; they were more determined to provide for their offspring themselves than to rely on others; and they would rather be married in church than in any other way.[36]

On the other hand, major factors are at work keeping women more secluded than their husbands from the rapid changes in urban Africa. First of all, discrimination in education means a considerable educational gap between most spouses. Second, women, tied as they are to the home because of child rearing and household chores, tend to be more restricted to their neighborhood than men. This is especially true if they have no occupational or other roles outside the neighborhood.[37] Finally, the interchange between spouses that might compensate for unequal exposure to change, tends to be limited. Lloyd[38] reports that in Ibadan husband and wife spend little leisure time together even in elite families. Women share few close friendships with their husbands and each spouse spends much of the non-working day visiting or entertaining his or her own friends, in exclusively male or female gatherings. We should not be surprised then if there are sharp differences in attitudes towards modern changes and, consequently, severe stress on the marital relationship. Such a situation is eloquently described in Okot p'Bitek's poems "Song of Lawino". Lawino laments:

> Ocol says he is a modern man,
> A progressive and civilized man,
> He says he has read extensively and widely
> And he can no longer live with a thing like me
> Who cannot distinguish between good and bad.
>
> He says I am just a village woman,
> I am of the old type,
> And no longer attractive.
>
> He says I am blocking his progress,
> My head, he says,
> Is as big as that of an elephant
> But it is only bones,
> There is no brain in it,
> He says I am only wasting his time.[39]

Plotnicov[40] emphasizes that the urban couple are more dependent upon each other for carrying out familial tasks and for emotional support. He suggests that the dependence will encourage a greater degree of equality. This assumption, that more joint relationships imply more equal relationships, may require scrutiny. The overall inequality between the sexes would seem to stand in the way of conjugal equality. To begin with, the statuses assigned to men and women in the society at large presumably have a bearing on their relative positions in the family. Second, probably related to the theme of male dominance, girls tend to get married quite young to men who are several years their elders. Third, there is the educational gap to which we have already referred.

Bernard[41] contends that male authoritarianism had even been reinforced in the teachers' families he studied Kinshasa: their wives no longer enjoyed the traditional guarantees provided in the rural setting, and they depended economically on their husbands. A teacher's wife enjoyed a relatively high social status and a higher standard of living than the women around her, sizeable advantages she would be reluctant to jeopardize by a lack of submission.

Typically, though, women in town wield increased control over the day-to-day affairs of the household. With the separation of work-place and home, most husbands are away for much of the day, leaving to their wives the running of the home and the education of the children.[42] The extreme case is the "matrifocal" family. Marwick[43] has suggested that with a few more generations of urban living the type of matrifocal family common among Blacks in diverse parts of the New World might be expected to emerge in South Africa as well, because their circumstances—particularly the determination of their social status by racial rather than economic and personal factors—are basically similar to those of Blacks in the Western Hemisphere. Pauw[44] found households with mothers as their heads in East London: some were completely fatherless; most had had legal fathers, but had lost them relatively early. There was also a trend for households to become extended in the matriline: for more kin on the mother's side to be included in the household than kin on the father's side, for unmarried daughters to join with their children.[45] In East London families without fathers seemed to manage fairly well, the husband-father was "dispendable." Pauw[46] emphasizes, however, that the father, when present, was not marginal; he often spent much of his leisure time at home and he was seldom away for long periods. There was rarely any doubt about his being head of the family, not only in name, but also in practice.

POLICY ISSUES

For the governments of the new nations of Subsaharan Africa two policy matters concerning women stand out. One revolves around the position of women in the family. It remains to be seen how effectively lawmakers can legislate in the sphere of personal status. As Zolberg[47] observes:

> ...Such activities as the registration of births and deaths, the enforcement of rules concerning marriage and divorce, the definition of personal rights, the inheritance of property, the regulation of work, are clearly important areas of policy-making...It is therefore highly significant to note that the activities of the West African party-state in this entire sphere are extremely limited. The regime is concerned with extending its authority in this direction by making laws that will affect these activities, but of course, there is a vast difference between the staking of a claim to do so and the genuine operation of allocative authority. Yet...we know that rules exist, that they are enforced, that they undergo change, that conflicts occur, and that they are settled, hence that the political system allocates values authoritatively in this sphere.

The other issue concerns the access women have to education and career opportunities. Frequently a lack of political initiative thinly veils a policy of discrimination.[48] Continued discrimination is an insult to aspirations for sexual equality to which so much lip service is paid. Furthermore, unequal access to economic opportunities in the urban setting imposes heavy costs on societies that seem so contented with the status quo. Families are separated, and/or a large segment of the population is dependent on urban services but constrained from realizing its potential contribution to the urban economy.

The separation of families is widespread in the towns of Subsaharan Africa and expresses itself in unbalanced sex ratios. We have discussed elsewhere the constraints which motivate rural-urban migrants to maintain strong ties with their areas of origin and frequently to leave their wives and children there.[49] We have also presented a case study of this pattern in Eastern Nigeria which we characterized as living in a dual system.[50] Suffice to say that more women would join their husbands in town if the urban economy offered women earning opportunities that compensated for rural income.

Few will disagree that the separation of families is undesirable, but the costs of such separation are difficult to assess. One indication is the high rates of labour turnover common until quite recently. With unemployment on the increase, the sanction of dismissal has become more effective. What used to be an economic cost to employers has become a social cost to employees: high labour turnover has been replaced by an additional strain put on the relationship between the worker and his family. Another cost of separation has become all too obvious: venereal disease is now one of the major medical problems in urban areas. Unbalanced sex ratios constitute the root cause in as much as they encourage short-lived unions and prostitution.

Where men do bring their families to town, the women have only limited or no opportunity to contribute to the urban economy. Most women become economically inactive or join the already over-crowded ranks of petty traders. There is not only a loss of rural income forgone by such families, or, to the extent that they are compensated by profits from trading, a reduction in the business of other traders, but also a considerable cost to the national economy. If women were fully integrated into the urban economy, a smaller population would have to be accomodated in urban centers to perform the same economic tasks. Accordingly a lower investment would be required in infrastructure, major elements of which are notably more expensive than their rural equivalents, e.g. housing, sewerage, provision of fuel, and distribution of staple foods.[51] As Boserup[52] points out:

> Villagers in developing countries usually build their own houses of local materials, supply themselves with water, light and fuel, arrange their own local transport . . . In towns, by contrast, public investment budgets are burdened by investment costs to provide migrant fami-lies with dwellings, light, water, sanitation, schools, hospitals, etc . . . If employment is provided for both men and women from immigrant families, this investment for infra-structure will be lower per person employed, and if employment is given only to hitherto idle wives and daughters of families already living in the towns, little additional infra-structure will be needed.

In short, sex discrimination in the urban setting carries high costs. It fosters the separation of families and/or leads to an increased demand for a costly urban infrastructure.

NOTES

1. I am ill at ease in the role of one more male chauvinist writing about women. Lest the title of this reckless essay be misconstrued, I expressly claim for it the maternity of Simone de Beauvoir's "Le deuxième sexe".

I am grateful to David Clark, William Flanagan, and Linda Lowe for comments on an earlier version of this paper.

2. Denise Paulme, in Denise Paulme (ed.), *Women of Tropical Africa* (London: Routledge & Kegan Paul; Berkeley/Los Angeles: University of California Press, 1963), p. 15.

3. Wole Soyinka, *The Lion and the Jewel* (London: Oxford University Press, 1963), p. 100.

4. Audrey Wipper, "Equal Rights for Women in Kenya?", *Journal of Modern African Studies*, 3 (1971): 433.

5. In an overview of the issue Paulme agrees that masculine dominance in the political sphere was not entirely mythical, but holds that the position of women in the kinship group was neither superior nor inferior to that of the men but simply different and complementary. She reacts in particular against outside observers who compare African practice with the Western ideal. Indeed it is tempting to speculate how European men delighted in trumpeting the inferior position of women in Africa—so as to silence the voices pointing out the gap between ideal and practice in their own societies. Denise Paulme, *op. cit.*, p. 4.

Traditional Afikpo Ibo society provides an illustration of male domination made explicit. Relations between men and women were in fact characterized by strong male domination. The ideal of the innate superiority of men over women was backed by men's control over land and the supernatural and by sanctions of the village men's society, one of whose admitted purposes was to "keep the women down" [Phoebe V. Ottenberg, "The Changing Economic Position of Women among the Afikpo Ibo", in William R. Bascom & Melville J. Herskovits (eds.), *Continuity and Change in African Cultures* (Chicago: University of Chicago Press, 1959), p. 207].

For a functionalist interpretation of the position of women in marriage in traditinal patrilineal societies, see Marlene Dobkin, "Colonialism and the Legal Status of Women in Francophonic Africa", *Cahiers d'Études Africaines*, 8 (1968): 390-405.

6. Not everywhere though: in Zaïre women were to obtain the vote only in 1970. (Suzanne Comhaire-Sylvain, *Femmes de Kinshasa hier et aujourd'hui* (Paris/The Hague: Mouton, 1968), p. 229).

7. For an account of the women's movement in Kenya see Audrey Wipper, *op. cit.*, and "The Politics of Sex: Some Strategies Employed by the Kenyan Power Elite to Handle a Normative-existential Discrepancy", *African Studies Review*, 1971, no. 14, pp. 463-482. For a brief reference to the situation in Ghana, Dorothy Dee Vellenga, "Attempts to Change the Marriage Laws in Ghana and the Ivory Coast", in Philip Foster and Aristide R. Zolberg (eds.), *Ghana and the Ivory Coast: Perspectives on Modernization* (Chicago/London: University of Chicago Press, 1971), p. 138.

8. Dorothy Dee Vellenga, *idem*, p. 141.

9. Audrey Wipper, "The Politics of Sex . . .",. *op. cit.*, p. 465.

10. Alain A. Levasseur, "The Modernization of Law in Africa with Particular Reference to Family Law in the Ivory Coast" in Philip Foster & Aristide R. Zolberg (eds.), *Ghana and the Ivory Coast: Perspectives on modernization* (Chicago/London: University of Chicago Press, 1971), p. 161.

11. *Ibid.*, p. 163.

12. Marlene Dobkin, *op. cit.*, however, summarizes accounts of the dislocating effects of the very same legislation. It is not always clear, though, to what extent such changes were effects of the legislation rather than of other forces simultaneously at work. The inflation in bridewealth in particular would seem to have to be traced to the spread of the money economy.

13. Alain A. Levasseur, *op. cit.*, p. 166.

14. Wole Soyinka, *op. cit.*

15. In his overview of research on the spread of family planning knowledge, attitudes and practices in tropical Africa, Caldwell reports that change has been greatest in the large towns. John C. Caldwell, "The Control of Family Size in Tropical Africa", *Demography* 5 (1968): 618.

16. Kenneth Little, *West African Urbanization: A Study of Voluntary Associations in Social Change* (Cambridge: Cambridge University Press, 1965), p. 133.

17. Claude Meillassoux, *Urbanization of an African Community: Voluntary Associations in Bamako* (Seattle/London: University of Washington Press, 1968), p. 127.

18. Maria Leblanc, *Personnalité de la femme katangaise: Contribution à l'étude de son acculturation* (Louvain/Paris: Nauwelaerts, 1960), p. 127.

19. *Ibid.*, p. 208.

20. Philip Mayer, *Townsmen or Tribesmen: Conservatism and the Process of Urbanization in a South African City* (2nd ed., London: Oxford University Press, 1971), p. 234.

21. For a presentation of what limited statistical data are available on women in training and in employment in developing countries, see Ester Boserup, *Woman's role in economic development* (New York: St. Martin's Press, 1970). Evans suggests that in Subsaharan Africa between 20% and 40% of the educational resources below university level are used to educate girls, and that the proportion is growing. In many African countries women are now moving into occupations that used to be held mostly by men: nursing, teaching, secretarial work, unskilled labor in light industry. David R. Evans, "Image and reality: Career goals of educated Ugandan women" in Canadian Association of African Studies (ed.), *Issues in African Development*, papers presented at the Annual Meeting, Waterloo, Ont., February 25 & 26, 1972, p. 69.

22. William Watson, *Tribal Cohesion in a Money Economy: A Study of The Mambwe People of Nothern Rhodesia* (Manchester: Manchester University Press, 1958), p. 45.

23. Philip Mayer, *op. cit.*, p. 309.

24. Ester Boserup, *op cit.*, p. 191.

25. Valdo Pons, *Stanleyville: An African Urban Community Under Belgian Administration* (London: Oxford University Press, 1969), p. 218.

26. For biographical sketches of some economically independent women in Kinshasa see Suzanne Comhaire-Sylvain, *op. cit.*, p. 312.

27. Lawson in her study of food retailing in Ghana reports that between 1963 and 1967 retail marketing services for local foods developed better in the urban centers, particularly in Accra, than in the rural centers. She goes on to suggest that markets in the large towns and cities are likely to continue to provide a low-cost service and to remain more competitive than rural retail markets—as long as there are few opportunities for the employment of urban unskilled female labor. Rowena M. Lawson, "The Supply Response of Retail Trading Services to Urban Population Growth in Ghana", in Claude Meillassoux (ed.), *The Development of Indigenous Trade and Markets in West Africa* (London: Oxford University Press, 1971), p. 390.

28. Kenneth Little, *op. cit.*, p. 122.

29. Peter Marris, *Family and Social Change in an African City: A Study of Rehousing in Lagos* (London: Routledge & Kegan Paul; Evanston, Ill.: Northwestern University Press, 1961), p. 53.

30. Colette Le Cour Grandmaison, "Activités économiques des femmes Dakaroises", *Africa* 39 (1969): 148.

31. Claude Tardits, "Réflexions sur le problème de la scolarisation des filles au Dahomey", *Cahiers d'Etudes Africaines*, 3 (1963): 274.

32. Dorothy Dee Vellenga, *op. cit.*, p. 148.

33. Alain A. Levasseur, *op. cit.*, p. 166.

34. Aidan W. Southall and Peter C.W. Gutkind, *Townsmen in the making: Kampala and its suburbs* (2nd edition, Kampala: East African Institute of Social Research, 1957), p. 72.

35. Claude Tardits, *Porto-Novo: Les nouvelles générations Africaines entre leurs traditions et l'Occident* (Paris/The Hague: Mouton, 1958), pp. 51, 68, 113, 118.

36. T. Peter Omari, "Changing Attitudes of Students in West African Society towards Marriage and Family Relationships", *British Journal of Sociology*, 11 (1960): 207. Tardits found that education of ascendants made no significant difference. Omari did not control for this factor.

37. Boswell observed in Lusaka that women of all strata tended to draw their friends and acquaintances from their neighbors and only went further afield to visit close kin: David M. Boswell, "Personal crises and the mobilization of the social network", in J. Clyde Mitchel (ed.), *Social Networks in Urban Situations: Analyses of Personal Relationships in Central African Towns* (Manchester: Manchester University Press, 1969), p. 252. Parkin describes neighborhoods in two housing estates in Kampala as arenas of socialization, particularly, though not exclusively, for women: David J. Parkin, *Neighbors and Nationals in an African City Ward* (London: Routledge and Kegan Paul; Berkeley/Los Angeles: University of California Press, 1969), p. 62.

Mayer notes that in Mdantsane, a new "homeland town" in South Africa, those who became intimate through neighborhood as such were mainly women: Philip Mayer, *op. cit.*, p. 302.

38. Peter C. Lloyd, "The Elite", in Peter C. Lloyd, Akin L. Mabogunje, and B. Awe, (eds.), *The City of Ibadan* (Cambridge: Cambridge University Press, 1971), p. 145.

39. Okot p'Bitek, *Song of Lawino* (Nairobi: East African Publishing House, 1966), p. 17.

40. Leonard Plotnicov, "Fixed Membership Groups: The Locus of Culture Processes", *American Anthropologist*, 64 (1962): 101.

41. Guy Bernard, *Ville africaine, famille urbaine: Les enseignants de Kinshasa* (Paris/The Hague: Mouton, 1968), p. 157.

42. The power of women will similarly increase in rural families where men are away in distant employment—unless the extended family is still effective in which case male relatives may take charge. Control over women by close male relatives can sometimes be found even in urban areas. *Parkin* in his study of recent immigrants in two housing estates in Kampala argues persuasively that the degree of control men exert over women is related to the system of land tenure, marriage, residence, and descent in their rural home area, David J. Parkin, *op. cit.*, p. 192.

43. M.G. Marwick, "The Modern Family in Social-anthropological Perspective", *African Studies*, 17 (1958): 153.

44. B.A. Pauw, *The Second Generation: A Study of the Family among Urbanized Bantu in East London* (London: Oxford University Press, 1963), p. 155.

45. Mphalele's autobiographical "Down Second Avenue" is a moving monument to such a matrifocal family—and to the conditions under which the oppressive racism of South Africa made it live: Ezekiel Mphalele, *Down Second Avenue* (London: Faber and Faber, 1959).

46. B.A. Pauw, *op. cit.*, p. 158.

47. Aristide R. Zolberg, *Creating Political Order: The Party-states West Africa* (Chicago: Rand McNally, 1966), p. 133.

48. For an account of the inertia displayed in this domain by the Kenya ruling elite see Audrey Wipper, "The Politics of Sex . . .", *op. cit.*, Women's representation in legislative bodies usually doesn't go beyond tokenism. The case of Guinea where 20 out of 75 deputies in 1968 were women is exceptional: Claude Riviere, "La Promotion de la Femme Guinéenne", *Cahiers d'Études Africaines*, 8 (1968): 423.

49. Josef Gugler and William G. Flanagan, *Urbanization and Social Change in West Africa* (Cambridge: , 1978), p. 167.

50. Josef Gugler, "Life in a Dual System: Eastern Nigerians in Town, 1961", *Cahiers d'Etudes Africaines*, 11 (1971): 400-421.

51. The fact that substantial numbers of unemployed men crowd into the major cities is irrelevant to the argument here. Urban unemployed are not a static group in tropical Africa; there is rather constant movement

between urban and rural areas. The number of urban unemployed is a function of rural-urban income differentials, probabilities of finding urban employment, length of such employment, and means of subsistence. For a presentation of the argument see Josef Gugler, "Migrating to Urban Centers of Unemployment in Tropical Africa," in Anthony H. Richmond and Daniel Kubat (eds.), *Internal Migration: The New World and the Third World* (Beverly Hills, Calif.: Sage, 1976), p. 67. Restricting urban employment to men, increases—for men—the probability of finding employment; hence it will encourage further male immigrants to join the ranks of the urban unemployed and to try their luck. Opening up employment opportunities to women will probably not attract any more women, given the numbers of women already in urban residence who would have considerable advantages over recent immigrants in competing for jobs.

52. Ester Boserup, *op. cit.*, p. 206.

8

Women in Indigenous African Cults and Churches

Bennetta Jules-Rosette

Indigenous African cults and churches have provided a special vehicle for women's self-expression. These groups span the spectrum from cults growing out of traditional religious concerns to charismatic movements within established mission churches.[1] They have in common an attempt to make elements of custom applicable and relevant to the changes caused by increased urbanization in Africa. For the most part, although there have been some exceptions, women have *not* been the founders of Africa's new religions, but they have held some of the most effective leadership roles. This leadership has a highly expressive dimension and women's spiritual leadership has resulted in a symbolic redefinition of the position of women in specific religious groups as well as in a larger social context. When describing the position of women in Africa's new religions, a crucial distinction must be made between various forms of leadership and adepthood.[2] Understanding the balance between these two forms of participation is essential to an assessment of women's contributions to religion and cultural change.

It is helpful to begin by differentiating betwen those religious organizations that give women official leadership positions, and those that stress their interactional skills or influence in the absence of official recognition.[3] The recognition of women's leadership skills will be referred to as ceremonial leadership. Expressive participation is a necessary background for ceremonial leadership and offers the channels through which women may potentially rise to officially recognized prominence. In the following discussion of

women's power, ceremonial leadership will be of primary importance, since women may be adepts at specialized spiritual tasks
without being able to engage in formal political leadership. In many
cases they can exercise what has been referred to as "influence"
(Parsons 1967:356; Dahl 1961). However, I will not use "influence"
to designate the contribution of women, because it is my assumption that although women do not always exercise formally legitimized authority, they directly assume two other forms of power:
(1) mystical power, which operates in a fashion rather comparable
to *mana*, and (2) direct control of situated interactions. I shall refer to
the exercise of both of these forms of power as ceremonial
leadership.

Weber, in his discussion of charisma (1947:363-370), generalized
the notion of spiritual power in a religious movement to a broader
conception of interactional leadership. Here, I am using "charismatic" in a double sense: as both direct spiritual power and as
interactional power in a religious association. Although some theorists have objected to this interpretation of charisma as not fully
recognizing the potential of charisma to become institutionalized, I
am concerned with returning the discussion to an interactional
domain.[4] For this reason, I dinstinguish ceremonial leadership,
based on spiritual and interactional charisma, from formalized
political authority. On the other hand, it is impossible to examine
the charismatic role of women in religious gropus without looking
at their authority structure, both the formal hierarchies that they
have developed and the informal structure of influential members.
Expressive participation, on the other hand, will be used to describe
adepthood and more informal types of influence.

A TYPOLOGY OF RELIGIOUS GROUPS

James Fernandez (1964:531-549) has suggested a continuum from
more traditional to more acculturative religious associations. We
may distinguish, for example, between the traditional secret societies found in the Interlacustrine region and in West Africa (for
example, the Poro-Sande complex among the Mende and other
tribes), spirit mediumship, and various forms of syncretic religious
groups influenced to different degrees by Western religions. In the
secret associations, men's and women's functions are generally
completely segregated, and a great deal of attention is devoted to
creating a ritual sense of these distinctions. These distinctions have

been referred to as a form of ritual illusion that is maintained throughout many of the societies' daily activities.[5] In this case, women become powerful leaders within their own associations, but the purview of their activities is restricted.

It is, however, possible for women to employ ritual leadership in combination with lineage and familial alliances to establish a power base that extends beyond the secret associations. Such extension of leadership was skillfully accomplished by Madam Yoko, a nineteenth-century paramount chief among the Mende. She was able to expand her control into a series of "clientship" relations through which she made alliances with a number of younger men and their families after the death of her husband, the former paramount chief.[6] Madam Yoko was able to develop both ceremonial and acknowledged political leadership through a traditional "cult" or secret association.

There are many cult associations in an intermediary position between traditional associations and more "acculturative" churches. David Barrett, in summarizing many of the histories of these groups, makes a sharp distinction between nativistic and syncretic groups that tend to preserve traditional symbols, and ritual and revivalistic groups that introduce new ritual forms into Western religions.[7] Often, the lines that can be drawn among these groups are empirically quite artificial. Many groups that the social scientists would label syncretic cults refer to themselves in the most orthodox sense as "churches." For the purposes of a discussion of women's leadership roles, a single crucial aspect of many groups who consider themselves as churches will be emphasized: the integration of men and women in the same ritual activities and decision-making processes. Particularly within Christian-based churches,[8] the ideology of equality of the sexes is central to church doctrine. Both sexes have equal access to the sacraments and to potential heavenly pardon. While such equality is not absent in cult associations, the importance of ritual separateness often makes forms of women's leadership parallel to, and insulated from, the political leadership of men.

THE IMPORTANCE OF WOMEN IN THE GROWTH OF CENTRAL AFRICAN INDEPENDENCY

As early as the eighteenth-century, women appeared as leaders of Christian-based prophetic cults and sects in Central Africa. These sects contained many of the ceremonial themes relating to their sex that subsequently appeared in independency: the acceptance of polygamy, the rejection of traditional medicines and the emphasis on spiritual purification.[9] Among the earliest prophetesses were Fumaria, a reputedly "insane" or "hysterical" seer, and Donna Béatrice-Anthony, a visionary who claimed to be the incarnation of St. Anthony.[10] Both arose in the Kongo Kingdom of San Salvador in the early 1700s. Little seems to be known about Fumaria other than her claim to have direct revelations from the Virgin Mary, enabling her to detect and punish sins. On the other hand, Béatrice's following grew large enough to be ultimately labeled as a heretical break from the Catholic Church. The prophetess protested against the Capuchin missions, stressing that followers return to polygamy, abandon the symbols of the Catholic Church, purify themselves with rain water, and oust priests from the kingdom.[11] She urged members to await the mesianic coming of princes who would "restore" Kongo kingship. Béatrice was ultimately burned at the stake with one of her followers by the Catholic Church, gaining immortality in the legends that survived her.

In the later nineteenth- and early twentieth-centuries, the Fumaria-Béatrice ritual themes reemerged in a different, more widespread form in Congolese ngunzism (prophetic cults particularly associated with the Kimbanguist group) and in similar independent churches.[12] The prophet Simon Kimbangu, who established a colony at N'Kamba in the Lower Congo, attracted vast numbers of disillusioned Christians who were seeking spiritual renewal, direct revelations from God, and charismatic healing. Although not generally preachers and catechists, women were drawn to this church in large numbers and became a major force among Kimbangu's followers.

The Déima cult, a Harrist offshoot in the Ivory Coast, might be classified as a syncretic group. Founded by Marie Dahonon Lalou, a Godié woman, in the late 1940s, the Déima emphasized healing through the use of a special form of holy water said to have been obtained from serpents.[13] Marie Lalou, like some more traditional mediums, renounced marriage and sexual contact. She virtually became a ritual male, no longer subject to the traditional roles of Godié women. Her combination of animism with other aspects of Harrist doctrine has caused many scholars to describe her group as syncretist.[14] Four aspects of this cult are important to the proposed discussion of ceremonial leadership: (1) that Lalou, its founder, was a woman, (2) that some of the activities of women were conceived of as ritually exclusive to them even though male adepthood was involved, (3) that ceremonial leadership required celibacy, and (4) that healing, often related to the women's nurturant role, was one of the cult's major concerns.

Marie Lalou's syncretist group may be compared with the Mai Chaza Church (often described as an independent church), which reportedly was started by its founder's spiritual inspiration in 1953-1954 (Martin 1971:110-111). Like Lalou, Mai Chaza left her husband and refused sexual contact thereafter. During this period, she had intense visionary experiences and acquired the ability to heal. Subsequently, she established a holy city (Guta ra Jehovah) where she and her followers specialized in the exorcism of witchcraft and the healing of barrenness and other female disorders. While the precedents for Marie Lalou's inspiration seem ambiguous in terms of local custom, Mai Chaza's teachings can be traced more clearly both to her childhood as a Methodist and to the Shona tradition of Spirit mediumship. Her "City of God" was a utopian Christian community in which her followers were soldiers of Christ and of Mai Chaza. Yet, she and her male successor Vamutenga also used the imagery of Mwari, the Shona God believed to have his mysterious abode in the mountains and caves of the area. Like one of Marie Lalou's followers, Jesus Onoi or Woman Jesus, (Walker, forthcoming:49), she was later considered a female incarnation of Moses and Christ. Hence, for those emphasizing healing, it is possible to trace the dual influence of custom and Western religion in indigenous cults and churches to define ceremonial leadership for women. Some scholars believe that the ritual male role was considerably influenced by Catholic celibacy, but ample evidence suggests customary precedents for it in spirit mediumship.

The indigenous churches heavily influenced by mission groups are often referred to as independent churches (Sundkler 1961; Barrett 1968). The position of women in these groups spans the spectrum from founding leadership to pure adepthood with little political expression. Nevertheless, the goal of some type of sexual equality in religious terms is expressed as an ideal in these groups. Independent churches provide three major outlets for women: (1) Holy communities with female founders and heads (including the Mai Chaza and Lumpa Churches), (2) spirit churches of an Apostolic type in which women are largely adepts rather than leaders (e.g., the Maranke and Masowe Apostolic Churches), and (3) revivalistic groups of various types in which women are both founders and leaders, and also adepts (from the Balokole Revival of East Africa to the Legio Maria and Gaudencia Aoko's offshoot of it). The third category might be viewed as containing its own radical subdivisions, moving from a more syncretic alternative like Aoko's Legio to revival groups that remain largely within mission churches and accept many of their definitions of feminine roles.

CEREMONIAL LEADERSHIP AND ADEPTHOOD IN INDIGENOUS CHURCHES

It seems obvious that a high degree of female leadership has been attained when a woman founds an entire religious community that includes a holy city or special place of residence for her most committed followers. In strict institutional terms, however, such leadership is often more ephemeral than it appears at first glance. The hereditary passage of leadership is difficult to sustain among women. The status of Marie Lalou's successor was ambiguous and several claims to leadership were made. Mai Chaza failed to pass on power to others and the Luo Gaudencia Aoko sustained her control of the Kenyan Legio Maria for only a few years. In all of these cases, women's contributions were based essentially on a display of extaordinary personal spiritual powers.

In addition to providing for women's leadership, the holy communities established by women redefined conceptions of family and social organization. Among the most widely known of the religious communities founded by a woman is the Lumpa church (the church that "excels all"), of Alice Lenshina Mulenga. Lenshina used the model of female chieftainship, already extant among the Bemba of Zambia, as a major basis for her claim to power. Like Lalou and Mai Chaza, Lenshina began with a strong opposition to witchcraft and traditional medicine. Her movement started within the Scotland Presbyterian mission but quickly grew beyond it. Like many other women leaders, Lenshina claimed to have mystical experiences and to have "died" before receiving her major inspiration. A millenial message of redemption was preached to her followers. Kasomo, the "holy village" or "New Zion," became the local base for new members. When they entered it, they were required to dispose of all fetishes and charms. With regard to the family, Lenshina exhorted

strict monogamy. Along with this, she stressed abandoning traditional ceremonies at the time of marriage and death (Taylor and
Lehmann 1961:253). Above all, Lenshina's group strongly espoused
the "unity of mankind," the equality of men and women, and a sense
of community.

Although Lenshina's following consisted of far more women
than men, young women functioned chiefly as singers while men
were deacons and preachers. Her group provides an example of the
redefinition of the woman's position in terms of a Christian ethos of
equality *without* full assurance of ceremonial leadership for women
in general. Familial roles were redefined without a commensurate
redefinition in terms of leadership. In rebuttal to the Zambian
government, who had accused them of affiliation with the African
National Congress, one of the country's former political parties, the
Lumpas refused to pay their taxes and in 1964 defended their village
in armed opposition to the administration. After this, many followers were exiled to the Northern Provinces of Zaire, and the church
was formally outlawed in Zambia. Now, some twenty years after its
inception, Lenshina is still confident of the church's survival despite
its dispersion and exile.

Mai Chaza's Guta ra Jehovah provides a more conventional
example of the founder's appeal to women suffering from specific
forms of tension and illness. The members of Mai Chaza's group,
like those of Lenshina's, are required to be monogamists if they are
not already in polygamous unions.[15] Similarly, her movement also
banned witchcraft. Mai Chaza herself claimed to have the divine
ability to heal blindness, barrenness, and female disorders. Her
"cities of God," located across Rhodesia, attracted women from
several countries in search of cures. Part of the group's appeal lies in
its imagery of activism. Women dress as "nurses" in uniforms of
white, while men wear a khaki uniform with shorts and a military
belt. When among the GRJ (as the Mai Chaza followers refer to
themselves), one has the impression of being in the midst of a holy
war fought by faithful soldiers and tended by their medical corps.[16]

Both Lenshina's and Mai Chaza's churches relied on the charismatic powers of individual women who failed to establish commensurate leadership positions for other women in the group. At the
time of Mai Chaza's death, no other woman rivaled her power or
renown, and no woman had threatened her authority with a major
schism. Rather than modify the woman's role from that of rank and

file adepthood, Lenshina and Mai Chaza suggested changes in the structure of the family and of customary religious practices that directly affected women. For example, the practice of taking secondary wives in a polygamous union as a result of the first wife's barrenness was forbidden in each group. Mai Chaza's group emphasized the role of healing and built the role of the traditional Shona medium. By contrast, Lenshina used the idiom of political power and chieftainship to extend her impact far beyond the religious sphere.

The two patterns of leadership emerging here include rites of power and roles of power. Women who are not priests and priestesses, however, participate largely as rank and file adepts whose duties are confined to limited spheres of activity.[17] These holy communities consist equally of men and women, but some of the highest positions of political leadership are usually staffed by men. In contrast to these communities, are the groups in which women have become influential leaders for a limited period of time. Gaudencia Aoko broke away from the Legio Maria and established her own dynamic antiwitchcraft movement. Two of her children had died in 1963 as a result of a mysterius accident that Aoko attributed to sorcery. She sought the assistance of a self-styled prophet, Marcellanius Orongo in Tanzania, and was ultimately baptized by him.

Crucifix and rosary in hand, Aoko healed the sick, burned amulets, and battled against alien spirits.[18] Her group offered, to women, curing and release from sorcery. Her example, like that of Lalou and Mai Chaza, inspired Luo women with the possibility of freedom from the domination of their husbands' families. In encouraging these reforms, Aoko's Legio also reacted to the political structure of the Catholic Church by developing a lay clergy with married priests and priestesses. In the hands of Aoko, the conventional ritual symbols of the Catholic Church became special articles of power. Nonetheless, her appeal was short lived. As her following began to decline, Aoko was unable to establish a stable church community, and her renown did not spread to the outlying Tanzanian branches of the Legio.[19] The problem of female leadership again appeared to be one of institutionalizing a ceremonial role as an official right to full-time leadership.

THE APOSTOLIC VARIATION

Bengt Sundkler (1961:142-143) asserts that spirit churches, of which Apostolic groups are one variation, offer a "real power base"

for women leaders, allowing them to use their "hysterical disposi-
tions" to attract a following. The participation of women in these
groups is formally limited, but their access to charismatic or expressive forms of participation may be far greater than it is in the holy
communities and revival groups. Sundkler documents the growth
of women's organizations with separate activities and leadership
hierarchies in the spirit churches (Ibid., 142). In this case, women
confine their activities to sewing circles, song groups, and restricted
forms of charismatic acitivity. Within two apostolic groups in the
South Central area, the Apostles of John Maranke and the Apostles
of John Masowe, women are recognized as prophetesses and healers and exercise interactive control as singers, subgroup leaders,
and midwives. Their positions in all cases are ceremonial rather
than political, for they are formally excluded from the groups'
major decision-making processes.

This exclusion takes place through specific types of formal
instruction. Young men are encouraged to develop their verbal
skills among the Maranke and Masowe Apostles. They engage in
lengthy biblical discourse, exegesis, and preaching. It is their duty to
interpret the Bible and to uncover its secrets for other members.
Women are allowed to develop these skills only in an indirect
manner. In the Maranke church, they must receive special inspiration through "tuning" or exorcism conducted by the male leaders.
Once they have been tuned, these women are eligible to become
special singers and prophetesses.

The routine role of most women among the Maranke Apostles is
that of healing. Many Maranke women stated that healing was a
"natural" function for them, the only job that they could perform in
the group. They accepted their status as a matter of course and did
not attempt to assert themselves through special ceremonial
means. These women stand in contrast to prophetesses, midwives,
special singers, and wives who share in their husbands' positions of
leadership.

The overall distinction among women in the Apostolic groups is
found between those who have been pressurd to join by husbands
and relatives, and those who are spiritually motivated to assert
themselves and obtain a measure of power within the group. Only
on one occasion do all of the Maranke women unite as a council of
elders: the virginity examination of young women. The elders
decide corporately upon those who pass. Successful candidates are

(ideally) given free choice of their marriage partners, while those who do not pass the examination are given away as secondary wives.

Among the Masowe Apostles, women are chiefly singers and prophetesses.[20] Just as in the Maranke church and in the earlier Zionist cases described by Sundkler, these women do not directly affect decision-making processes and are not instructed to challenge the overall organization of the group. The Masowe church is distinguished by its sacred sisterhood or group of virgin girls who are not allowed to marry for symbolic purposes. However, they have no influence as group leaders and are forbidden to preach or to hold higher offices within the group.

WOMEN IN RITUAL

The Apostolic groups demonstrate the subtle leadership potential of women in ceremonial settings. In the Maranke Apostles' *kerek*, or main worship ceremony, it is expected that women will sing. While the ideal of Christian equality that men and women will enter Heaven side by side influences the participation of women, this equality rests on complementary contributions. Women may intervene during sermons with songs that modify and redirect discourse. In such cases, they chastise men and suggest alternative topics and perspectives for their sermons. A relationship of mild ritual competition arises through the vehicle of song interruption and response. If women do not interrupt enough, male leaders chide them for being passive and too withdrawn from worship. When they interrupt a speaker too frequently, however, he may override their songs with continued preaching, stating, in effect, that hearing the Gospel directly from the Bible is more important than song. Insofar as women actually alter the direction of discourse, they exercise a restricted form of ceremonial leadership, didactic songs are regarded as their form of preaching. The following sermon excerpt illustrates the modification of a topic through a woman's song:

Kangaga, Zaire, 1969:

Speaker: Do you think that this baptism is a simple matter? Jesus himself said it. He stands in harsh condition until his baptism is accomplish. You see this baptism can bring division among people who were once dear to

each other. We—
We are in a hard situation—

Singer: The baptism of John is difficult
               Jesus is on one side and Satan on the other
               They fight and the whole earth needs the Holy Spirit
               Light shone on those who believed
               All the commandments are in the Bible

Speaker: Life to you Apostles. You heard how Mama did the
               Gospel. She lets you know that the baptism of John is a
               difficult problem. How easy would it be to believe in
               Jesus if he is engaged in a fight with Satan? Before you
               believe and get saved, you experience a fight within
               your consciousness, but once you join you will see
               what Spirit you get.

The woman interrupting the speaker utilized yet shifted the topic
presented by the evangelist. While he stressed the divisions and
conflicts created by baptism, she emphasized that the baptism
introduced difficult individual problems arising from the battle
between God and Satan. Through maintaining the theme of the
preaching in song interruptions, the woman both presented her
own message and caused the speaker to alter his for the remainder
of the sermon.

While men view the ritual aspects of preaching as a means of
direct teaching and visible leadership, women operate more indirectly to control reshape discourse. Women's reading and singing
groups formed outside of *kerek* increase and direct their influence
during the ceremony. A group of women whose husbands were
railroad workers often met together in Kananga, Zaire, forming a
singing and healing group with its own prophetess. These women
used their associations to enhance ceremonial leadership. When one
woman initiated a song in *kerek*, the others would join in immediately, assuring the song's survival and making it difficult for the
speaker to regain the floor until the women decided collectively to
terminate.

Women song leaders are confirmed as gifted or master singers
(maharikros) (cf. Murphree 1969:95). These women, often, although by no means always, are the wives of elders, and have a vast
repertoire of songs that they employ not only as sermon interjections, but also to interrupt or extend songs already intiated by men.

The maharikros are among the first to lead off songs in *kerek* and through their frequent interjections teach members new song versions, verses, and harmonies. On occasion, contests take place between male and female maharikros to intiate and continue special songs.

Another form of ceremonial leadership is exercised by Maranke prophetesses. They examine each member before the main ceremony to determine sins and transgressions of church laws. All members are subject to their testimonies. They also enter the sacred aisle used for preaching to give testimony once *kerek* prayers are concluded. Women in this instance may control decisions made by the male hierarchy by presenting spiritually based modifications or suggestions. In one instance, a prophetess and wife of an important elder reprimanded his policy toward the church's Rhodesian leaders and called upon him to confess past errors and change his stand. Although such confrontations are rare, prophecy is one of the arenas in which a woman's charismatic leadership can challenge political decisions. Sundkler anticipated this finding with the description of women diviners and healers in South African Zionist churches. In outlining the boundaries of leadership for women, he asserts:

> The most spectacular form of female leadership in the Zionist churches is seen when they act as media for a risen Bantu Christ. In Bantu organizations where the main requirement for a rise to leadership is possession of the 'Holy Spirit,' women of a hysterical disposition may wield very considerable influence. In close relationship with the prophet himself, these women who answer to fanciful names, such as Umphefumulo, the spirit, or Ufahaza, the Witness; or Maria Magdalene—exercise great power behind the scenes (Sundkler 1961: 143-144).

As already indicated, curing, or burapi, is the major spiritual arena for women in the Maranke group and in other spirit churches. While healing is defined as an inspired spiritual activity for which one must be especially gifted, it is also the most basic of all spiritual concerns for the Maranke Apostles. Maranke members often refer to their organization as a church of healing and prophecy. All other forms of spiritual exercise, including baptism and evangelism, are considered to contain an element of healing. In the absence of an official healer, other members routinely perform these duties. When women in one congregation protested against this overlap in functions, they were informed that most competent and spiritually powerful members of a congregation could heal. Thus, while healing is chiefly reserved for women, it is considered to be within the domain of expertise of all members.

There are several types of women healers among the Maranke Bapostolo: healer-prophetesses (baprofiti mapipi), marapi or regular healers, and midwives. All operate with the basic assumption that there are no "natural" illnesses. Evil action and demons are believed to cause sickness. Spiritual laxity, such as anger or transgression of food taboos, allows demon possession to occur. The possibility of possession is always present. Baptism, which cleanses the new member and makes a spiritual redefinition possible, is accompanied by a comparable vulnerability. Healers and exorcists help to protect the member. The mapipi are so specialized that they can diagnose illnesses and often develop a reputation for their cures. Similarly, the activities of the midwives are also charismatic, involving hearing confession, diagnosis, and delivery of the child. The routine healers, on the other hand, are instructed in a standard healing ceremony that is performed after *kerek* or when requested (cf. Lanzas and Bernard 1966:201-202). The majority of these healers confine their activities to the domestic arena.

In the standard healing ritual, the patient faces East with the healer kneeling behind. Other members of the group surround the patient to sing and pray. The healer then uses either her hands or a prayer stick to touch the points of pain from the head to the toes of the patient, taking care not to touch the very top of the head. Women perform the more "routine" healing ceremony for both sexes. Healing becomes a vehicle for women's participation. It does not challenge leadership in the manner of song intervention or prophetic reviews.

When women do not individually distinguish themselves as ritual performers, they can sometimes do so as a group. Singers often meet several times a week to discuss church matters informally and practice religious songs. These women, one group of which were briefly described, are able to develop coordination through song and to intervene in and successfully redirect ceremonies. This again points to the distinction between formally recognized (or institutionalized) ceremonial leadership found in the case of the prophetess and expressive participation noted in the instance of routine healing and in singing. Through ritual, women are able to develop various types and degrees of leadership in the Apostolic churches, but are often able to sustain this leadership only for particular settings and even then in a restricted manner.

THE CONVERSION EXPERIENCE: WOMEN EXPLAIN THEIR PARTICIPATION

The types of conversion experiences described by men in the Maranke and similar churches differ substantially from those described by women. The women who join as a result of a visionary or other religious experience may be distinguished from those coerced by relatives. The first category tend to become involved directly in ceremonial leadership while the latter group remain a more passive membership. Regardless of the avowed motivations for joining, the initial reasons given by these women differed substantially from the benefits of membership. Some women who admitted joining to follow suit with their husbands or parents stated that they remained members "to receive the hidden life of Christ" and the Holy Spirit's blessings. When these women described their responsibilities in the church, only routine healing was mentioned. Many of these women stated that they neither questioned their conversion nor their spiritual gift of healing but merely expected them to be confirmed because they were women.

Three accounts in particular epitomize the conversion experience of Apostolic women. In the first case, the woman felt pressured to join through her husband's affiliation. For seven years, she resisted membership until a final confrontation occurred. She described this experience as follows:

> While we were in the village, my husband became very ill with a stomach disease. The prophet said that he could be cured only if I were baptized. I agreed that the Apostles could baptize my body but they could not have my soul. When I approached the water and reluctantly entered it, a snake appeared out of nowhere. The baptist hit the snake and broke it in two pieces with his staff. I then said go ahead. Baptize both my soul and my body (Jules-Rosette 1975:66).

This woman was subsequently confirmed as a healer and remained a committed though not an active, member of the church. Although her husband was an evangelist and a special church judge;

she did not attend palavers or women's subgroup song sessions. Her attendance at *kerek* was also somewhat sporadic. Nevertheless, she was considered a member in good standing and a competent healer.

The second respondent was a prophetess. She described illness as the motivation for joining and stated emphatically that she had not joined through her husband's influence. She met regularly with a woman's subgroup and as its only prophetess was considered its leader. Her participation in *kerek* and in individual wilderness retreats in quest of visions was regular and active.

The third respondent, a healer, stressed the connection between a spiritual quest and physical healing. She stated that she had joined the group to seek a hidden life in Christ and to receive help in childbirth. She found relief from birth disorders through the church and proclaimed that as a result of joining she had given birth to six children without complications.[21]

Many women gave pregnancy problems and chidbirth as reasons for joining. One woman stated that she joined after losing her child in the seventh month of pregnancy; another woman said that she had joined in order to cure a menstrual disorder that had caused a continual bleeding. The latter informant recalled that for several years she had resisted her parents' request that she join the church, viewing it as incompatible with her high school and secretarial education. However, complications resulting from the birth of her first child drew her to the church, although her husband remained a nonmember. She stated that her faith had increased through the miracles of healing that she had witnessed, and she found an active outlet for church life in her parents' family. In this case, the parents' family and church activities provided some escape from the duties of her own home.

A critical element of increased commitment seems to be active participation in either familial or women's prayer and social groupings supportive of the Sabbath worship services. Those women involved in associational subgroupings seemed to find fuller outlets in both worship and leadership. However, the data allow little generalization from statements of first contact to affirmations of commitment on the basis of an initial reluctance to join. Instead, women seem equally divided in terms of interview responses in the self-motivated and "forced" categories, and they have developed very different individual forms of association in which the presence of women's subgroups seems to influence their ultimate commitment to the group.[22] The extent of a family's participation in the church also seems an important aspect of a woman's conversion and membership experience. My own observations suggest that the wives of elders were more assertive and directly involved in church activities than those women who participated neither in leadership through their husbands, nor in women's associational subgroupings. Such women were, however, unable to function as co-owners of their husbands' positions in the absence of a grouping of women that was ready to respond to their leadership.

WOMEN AND CULTURAL CHANGE: INDIGENOUS CHURCHES AS REDEFINITIONS Of FAMILY AND COMMUNITY

Implicit in all of the groups described, has been a challenge to, or modification of, family and community relationships. The holy communities have been the most insistent about establishing monogamy and an equal division of responsibility among men and women. Yet, even in these groups, the political position of women members who are not founders is weak. In addition, there is little detailed ethnographic data on the relationship of daily community and household life to the overall political structure of these communities. There is evidence that the requirement of radical separation from outsiders, including one's former family, in these groups forces upon participants a sharp redefinition of tradition. This separation is certainly evident in the case of the Mai Chaza community and, to a certain extent, in the case of Lenshina holy villages.

The reformist groups which had women as founders offered female members the promise of freedom from certain types of familial subservience and jealousy. However, the precedents established by these groups are ephemeral. They were able to attract small numbers of women to make innovative social responses but were not able to sustain their appeal or impact.

Churches of the Spirit or Apostolic type vary considerably in their overall effect in opening new alternatives to women. They do offer women restricted expressive channels for leadership. The extent to which leadership responsibilities build on existing ritual roles for women is a productive topic for further research and cannot be fully assessed on the basis of the present data. The more basic question of the importance of the persistence of polygamy and of models for expressive leadership can be examined. The present data on Apostolic groups suggest that: (1) women are excluded from political decision making and hold lower positions within the groups than men, (2) women can nevertheless exercise political checks or controls upon the central decision-making units in the group, (3) voluntary polygamy offers women several family options and ways in which to "influence" religious activities through the family, and (4) voluntary polygamy also swells the ranks of many spirit churches with adepts who join to support their husbands and who are content to exercise minimal influence in the group.

Thus, the problem of alternate life options and leadership in spirit churches is complex. The possibility for individual distinction is present through a particular woman's abilities and through familial support. On some occasions, the women in these groups unite for ceremonial purposes but the effects of such cooperation are more expressive and symbolic than lasting. The institutionally recognized powers of women in these groups are minimal and yet possibilities for creating alternate family, community, and leadership styles abound. Like the holy communities, the spirit groups tend to be encapsulated[23] and therefore provide an open opportunity to redefine traditional conceptions of the family without a great deal of pressure from outsiders. In these groups, religious training for children is also stressed. Women consistently list proper care and instruction of children as one of their major reasons for joining the Apostolic groups. Indigenous churches, in this case, redirect the type of legitimate choices available in constructing family relationships. The tone of these relationships, in turn, influence the participation and assertiveness of women in ceremonial activities outside of the home.

When the women in the Apostolic groups described are compared with those in other spirit churches (for example, Rhodesian Zionists), their official positions appear lower yet considerably more active (cf. Aquina 1967:206; Aquina 1969:130). The opportunity to become prophetesses, to interrupt sermons through song, and to preach, are apparently denied women in some of the other groups, even though singing and healing are their major outlets. In these Zionist groups, the dichotomy between leadership and adepthood, and between the participation of men and women, is one of the most important aspects of the groups' ritual and social life. Women in all of the spirit churches are much more likely than men to remain strictly in the status of adepts and as marginal members. As secondary wives of male leaders, they are often shadow members who silently swell the ranks of nominal followers. In these cases, women view adepthood as their "natural" and "habitual" role in the group and are able to alter this conception of themselves chiefly through claims of spiritual ordination, and secondarily through their own subgroup associations.

It is important to note that subgroup association for the Maranke members interviewed appeared to be completely independent of participation in polygamous or monogamous households. It is *not* the case that monogamy leads to increased active participation for women. Even in the holy communities that required monogamy, women were placed largely in adept rather than leadership positions. On the other hand, polygamous marriages in some of the indigenous churches, for example, the Maranke and Masowe communities, bring women together with direct control over children and crucial household resources.[24] Even though many women in these churches do not hold office, those that are able to achieve ceremonial leadership often have structured households (whether monogamous or polygamous) in which they were able to establish economic independence as small merchants or as participants in cottage industries.

CONCLUDING STATEMENTS

Instead of deriving explanations for the participation of women in indigenous churches solely from their familial or their ritual status in terms of putative psychological aims, it has been suggested that an analysis of ceremonial leadership be used for this purpose. Ceremonial leadership refers to the possibilities for women to exercise virtual power in ritual interactions. In some cases, this form of leadership is accompanied by rights of office or is supplemented by political leadership. In other cases, it is replaced by expressive participation through which women exercise some influence over a ritual occasion. Present ethnographic and historical data indicate that the record of women as leaders of indigenous churches has been precarious and short-lived. However, case study material drawn from the Maranke Apostles indicates that participation in their own subgroupings leads women to have a sense of efficacy and to use their collective interactions to redefine their position in the religious community. The next step in such research is to begin to compare information about household structure, the economic autonomy of women, and childrearing practices with traditional ideals. This comparative information also becomes the basis for assessing the sources of their leadership and self-assertiveness in other contexts.

Studies of the relationship of ritual expression to women's positions in the family and in other associational subgroupings are strangely absent from the literature on indigenous African churches. Primary research on the Apostles and other related groups, however, points to the critical relationship between ceremonial leadership and the opportunities that women have for various forms of association outside of these events. The utopian ideals of many of the religious movements founded by women have often failed in their inability to delineate redefinitions of authority and of family, and in their assumption that the establishment of major leadership roles for some women would affect the rank and file adepts. Neither privileged nor exceptional charismatic leadership nor its counterpart in familial organization (monogamy) have assured women of political leadership in indigenous churches. Further insight into the relationships among family, subgroup, and ritual interactions is necessary to render the concept of charismatic leadership, so central to religious movements, a viable concept for explaining the participation of women in these churches. We may understand charismatic leadership in its initial form to be found in the privileged and ephemeral position of women as leaders in the holy communities. This discussion has suggested that the difficulties that women have had in redefining family structure and collective action have contributed to the existing imbalance between ephemeral leadership often in a ceremonial context, and the pervasive experience of women's adepthood in indigenous African churches.

NOTES

1. This spectrum includes contemporary developments within traditional cults and secret societies as well as movements such as the Jamaa in Zaire and the Balokole in Uganda that have remained within the Catholic and Anglican churches, respectively.

2. The distinction between leadership and adepthood is made by Breidenbach in his treatment of a West African Harrist church. Breidenbach,

Paul S., "The Woman on the Beach and the Man in the Bush: Leadership and Adepthood in the Twelve Apostles Movement of Ghana," in Bennetta Jules-Rosette, ed., *The New Religions of Africa: Priests and Priestesses in African Cults and Churches*, forthcoming. Adepthood is defined as rank and file participation in a group as opposed to political or spiritual leadership.

3. Cf. Weber, Max, *The Theory of Social and Economic Organization* (New York: Free Press, 1947), pp. 328, 358-369.

4. *Ibid.*, pp. 363-370. Weber defines "charisma" as the "quality of an individual personality by virtue of which he is set apart from ordinary men and treated as endowed with supernatural, superhuman, or at least specifically exceptional powers or qualities." For Apostles, there is a charismatic element in all leadership. All church members feel as though they have been directly and divinely ordained to fulfill a special mission. However, a distinction is made between ceremonial leadership based exclusively on a spiritual or miraculous gift or power and political leadership that involves organized and formal decision-making validated by authority of office as well as by a charismatic element. The former are referred to by Apostles as *bipedi* ("gifts") and the latter as *mianza* ("ranks").

5. See Bellman, Beryl L., *Village of Curers and Assassins: On the Production of Kpelle Cosmological Categories.* (The Hague: Mouton, 1975), p. 486, and personal communication.

6. Hoffer, Carol P., "Madam Yoko: Ruler of the Kpa Mende Confederacy," in Michelle Rosaldo and Louise Lamphere, eds., *Women in Culture and Society.* (Stanford: Stanford University Press, 1974): 172-187. Madam Yoko, an exceptional woman who consolidated several Mende kingdoms, was similar to other exceptional women in the traditional African case in taking on the role of a ritual male. The relationship of clientship is described by several researchers on the Kpelle. See, e.g., Gibbs, James L., "The Kpelle of Liberia," in James L. Gibbs, ed., *Peoples of Africa,* (New York: Holt, Rinehart and Winston, 1965), pp. 210-211. Bellman, *op. cit.*, pp. 186.

7. Barrett, David B., *Schism and Renewal in Africa: An Analysis of Six Thousand Contemporary Religious Movements.* (Nairobi: Oxford University Press, 1968), pp. 47-48. Barrett distinguishes nativistic and syncretic movements from revivals within "orthodox" mission churches.

8. This is the case in an overall sense for Islam as well, where reformist movements have attempted to redefine the traditional place of Muslim women. See Quimby, Lucy, "Sex Roles and the Modernization of a Muslim Community," in Jules-Rosette, ed., *op. cit.*

9. Cf. Oosthuizen, G. C., *Post-Christianity in Africa,* (Grand Rapids: Eerdmans, 1968), esp. pp. 179-194. He emphasizes the importance of the acceptance of polygamy and of purification rites as social and ritual themes of independency.

10. Vansina, Jan, *Kingdoms of the Savanna,* (Madison: Wisconsin, 1968), p. 154. Doutreloux, André, "Prophétisme et Culture," in Fortes, Meyer and

G. Dieterlin, eds., *African Systems of Thought.* (London: International African Institute, 1965), p. 225. Barrett, op. cit., pp. 52 and 148. Andersson, Efraim, *Messianic Popular Movements in the Lower Congo,* (Uppsala: Almqvist and Wiksells, 1958), pp. 244-255.

11. Andersson, op. cit., p. 244; Barrett, op. cit., p. 52.

12. Cf. Doutreloux, op. cit., pp. 230-237. Banda-Mwaka, Justin, "Le Kimbanguisme en tant que Mouvement Prépolitque chez les Kongo," *Bulletin Trimestriel du CEPSI: Problèmes Sociaux Ziarois,* Nos. 92-93. Heimer, Haldor E., "The Church Suited to Home Needs," in Parsons, R.T., ed., *Windows on Africa: A Symposium,* (Leiden: E. J. Brill, 1971), pp. 21-37.

13. Paulme, Denise, "Une Religion Syncrétique en Cote D'Ivoire: Culture Le Déimatiste," *Cahiers D'Etudes Africaines* 1 (1962), pp. 5-90. Barrett, op. cit., p. 55. Walker, Sheila S., "The Message as the Medium: Harrist Churches in the Ivory Coast," in Bond, George, Sheila Walker and Walton Johnson, eds., *Prophets and Sects in Black Africa,* forthcoming.

14. William Wade Harris, a Grebo from Liberia, converted large numbers of people in the Ivory Coast and the Gold Coast (Ghana) to Christianity in 1913-1914. Preaching against witchcraft and idolatry, he baptized converts and encouraged them to join mission churches where they existed. Subsequently, a number of Harris' converts established independent churches espousing variants of the principles he had taught, including the Déima cult discussed here. Walker points out that the Harrist churches at increasing distances from urban centers included more traditional practices. Walker, op. cit., pp. 61-62.

15. Martin, Marie-Louise, "The Mai Chaza Church in Rhodesia," in Barrett, David B., ed., *African Initiatives in Religion,* (Nairobi: East Africa Publishing House, 1971), p. 118. In the case of polygamous unions, only the first wife enjoys church privileges.

16. Personal observation, Umtali, Rhodesia, July 1974.

17. Cf. Perrin Jassy, M.-F., "Women in the African Independent Churches," *Risk* 7, 2 (1971): 48. Sr. Mary Aquina, O.P., "The People of the Spirit: An Independent Church in Rhodesia," *Africa* 37 (1967):206. They argue that ritual positions may ultimately imply political subordination.

18. Perrin Jassy, op. cit., pp. 47-49. Perrin Jassy, M.-F., *La Communauté de Base dans les Eglises Africaines,* (Bandundu: Centre des Études Ethnologiques), Série II, 3 (1970), pp. 80-82. Barrett, 1968, op. cit.

19. Perrin Jassy, 1970, op. cit., p. 81.

20. See Kileff, Clive and Margaret Kileff, "The Masowe Vapostori of Seki," in Jules-Rosette, ed., op. cit. Kileff, Margaret, "The Apostolic Sabbath Church of God: Organization, Ritual, and Belief," unpublished ms., 1974, pp. 55-56.

21. Detailed information on Maranke women's conversion experiences including abstracted interview material is discussed in Jules-Rosette, Bennetta, *African Apostles,* (Ithaca: Cornell University Press, 1975), pp. 68-71.

22. More conclusive comparative data on membership and conversion will be collected in a study of Maranke and Masowe Apostles in the Marrapodi community, 1975.

23. Mayer describes incapsulation as the process by which urban migrants maintain unbroken contact with their rural home while abstaining from unnecessary contact with other urban groups. Mayer, Philip, *Townsmen or Tribesmen,* (Cape Town: Oxford University Press, 1961), p. 90.

24. This contrasts with Taylor and Lehmann's conclusion that many in Northern Rhodesian Christian churches seemed to fear the individualization, emotional strain, and responsibilities implied in monogamous urban marriage. This conclusion may very well be an artifact of the observer's preconceptions since substantiating data are not presented. Taylor, J.V. and Dorothea A. Lehmann, *Christians of the Copperbelt,* (London: SCM Press, 1961), pp. 116-117.

REFERENCES

Andersson, Efraim *Messianic Popular Movements in the Lower Congo.* Uppsala: Almqvist & Wiksells, 1958.

Aquina, Sister Mary, O.P. "The People of the Spirit: An Independent Church in Rhodesia," *Africa* 37:203, 219, 1967.

"Zionists in Rhodesia," *Africa* 39, (1969) 2:113-137.

Banda-Mwaka, Justin "Le Kimbanguisme en tant que Mouvement Prépolitique chez les Kongo," *Bulletin Trimestriel du CEPSI: Problèmes Sociaux Zairois,* Nos. 92-93.

Barrett, David B. *Schism and Renewal in Africa: A Study of Six Thousand Contemporary Religious Movements.* Nairobi: Oxford University Press, 1968.

Bellman, Beryl L. *Village of Curers and Assassins: On the Production of Kpelle Cosmological Categories.* The Hague: Mouton, 1975.

Breidenbach, Paul S. "The Woman on the Beach and the Man in the Bush: Leadership and Adepthood in the Twelve Apostles Movement of Ghana." Jules-Rosette, Bennetta, ed., *The New Religions of Africa,* forthcoming.

Doutreloux, A. "Prophétisme et Culture." Fortes, Meyer and G. Dieterlin, eds., *African Systems of Thought.* London: International African Institute, 1965.

Fernandez, James L. "African Religious Movements: Types and Dynamics," *Journal of Modern African Studies* 2, 4 (December 1964): 531-549.

Gibbs, James L. "The Kpelle of Liberia." Gibbs, James L., ed., *Peoples of Africa.* New York: Holt, Rinehart and Winston, 1965.

Heimer, Haldor E. "The Church Suited to Home Needs." Parsons, Robert T., ed., *Windows on Africa: A Symposium*. Leiden: E. J. Brill, 1971.

Hoffer, Carol P. "Madam Yoko: Ruler of the Kpa Mende Confederacy." Rosaldo, Michelle and Louise Lamphere, eds., *Women in Culture and Society*. Stanford: Stanford University Press, 1974.

Jules-Rosette, Bennetta *African Apostles: Ritual and Conversion in the Church of John Maranke*. Ithaca: Cornell University Press, 1975.

Kileff, Clive and Margaret Kileff "The Seki Mapostori." Jules-Rosette, Bennetta, ed., *The New Religions of Africa: Priests and Priestesses in African Cults and Churches*, forthcoming.

Kileff, Margaret "The Apostolic Sabbath Church of God: Organization, Ritual and Belief." Unpublished ms., University of Tennessee, Chattanooga, 1974.

Lanzas, A. and G. Bernard "Les Fidèles d'une Nouvelle Eglise au Congo," *Genève-Afrique: Acta Africana* 5, (1966) 2:189-216.

Martin, Marie-Louise "The Mai Chaza Church in Rhodesia." Barrett, David B., ed., *African Initiatives in Religion*. Nairobi: East Africa Publishing House, 1971.

Mayer, Philip *Townsmen or Tribesmen*. Cape Town: Oxford University Press, 1961.

Murphree, Marshall W. *Christianity and the Shona*. London: The Athlone Press, 1969.

Oosthuizen, O.C. *Post-Christianity in Africa*. Grand Rapids: Eerdmans, 1968.

Paulme, Denise "Une Religion Syncrétique en Cote D'Ivoire: Le Culte Déimatiste," *Cahiers D'Etudes Africaines* 1: (1962) 5-90.

Perrin Jassy, Marie-France *La Communauté de Base dans les Eglises Africaines*. 1970, Bandundu: Centre des Etudes Ethnologiques, Série II, 3.

"Women in the African Independent Churches," *Risk* 7, 3: 46-49.

Quimby, Lucy "Sex Roles and Modernization in a Muslim Community." Jules-Rosette, Bennetta, ed., *The New Religions of Africa: Priests and Priestesses in African Cults and Churches*, forthcoming.

Sundkler, B. G. M. *Bantu Prophets in South Africa*. London: International African Institute, 1961.

Taylor, J. V and Dorothea A. Lehmann *Christians of the Copperbelt*. London: SCM Press, 1961.

Vansina, Jan *Kingdoms of the Savanna*. Madison: University of Wisconsin Press, 1968.

Walker, Sheila S. "The Message as the Medium: Harrist Churches in the Ivory Coast." Bond, George, Sheila S. Walker, and Walton Johnson, eds., *Prophets and Sects in Black Africa*, forthcoming.

Weber, Max *The Theory of Social and Economic Organization*. New York: The Free Press, 1947.

Matourkou expert (right) giving instructions to a woman farmer on the proper use of a plow. Photo: United Nations/Ray Witlin, No. 128048. (1974)

9
Definitions of Women and Development: An African Perspective

Achola O. Pala

In this brief paper, I do not propose to engage in a discussion of what development is or what an African perspective means. Rather, I wish to draw attention to points which I consider to be central to an understanding of the contemporary position of African women. It is reasonable to say that in Africa today the position of both women and men can be largely described as an interplay between two parameters. The first, which we may call dependency, comprises economic and political relationships through which our peoples have found themselves increasingly involved with metropolitan Europe (e.g., England, France, Germany, Belgium, Spain, and Portugal) and the United States of America, especially since the sixteenth and seventeenth centuries, starting with the slave trade and colonialism and continuing up to contemporary neocolonial links. The second embraces indigenous African socioeconomic norms (e.g., in food production, family ideology, property rights, and perceptions of respect and human dignity), insofar as these continue to regulate social behavior.

In other words, the position of women in contemporary Africa is to be considered at every level of analysis as an outcome of structural and conceptual mechanisms by which African societies have continued to respond to and resist the global processes of economic exploitation and cultural domination. I am suggesting that the problems facing African women today, irrespective of their national and social class affiliations, are inextricably bound up in the wider struggle by African people to free themselves from poverty and ideological domination in both intra- and international spheres.

Neither research on African development potential and problems nor specific emphasis on issues relating to the participation of African women in local economies is new. The British colonial government, for instance, commissioned and/or supported a number of studies specifically to investigate the role of women in African societies, in order to formulate policies which would "integrate" women more effectively into the colonial development. Even a quick perusal of local newspapers in a given colonial period will reveal a "concern" by the colonial government, backed by women's associations (usually made up of wives and sisters of colonial administrators and missionaries), for the education and training of African women. More recently, in the last two decades, African women's national organizations have taken up the cry for equal opportunities for women in such matters as employment and training. In every instance, it will be found that research or social protest launched on behalf of or by women themselves is invariably motivated by economic and political considerations rather than feminism per se. In some instances, the issue of women's rights is used as a means of social control; in others, it serves to consolidate the political position of individual men and women. In all cases, it is a reliable indicator of ideological alignments within a particular national or international situation.

It cannot be stated too often that up to this time research on African problems has been greatly influenced by intellectual trends from outside the continent. Like the educational systems inherited from the colonial days, the research industry has continued to use the African environment as a testing ground for ideas and hypotheses the locus of which is to be found in Paris, London, New York, or Amsterdam. For this reason, the primary orientation to development problems tends to be created on the basis of what happens to be politically and/or intellectually significant in the metropoles. At one time, it may be family planning; at another, environment; at yet another, human rights and women's social conditions. At one time, there is funding for a particular type of study; at another time, money for yet another research topic. Such continual redefinition of research priorities means that African scholars are forced into certain forms of intellectual endeavors that are peripheral to the development of their societies. Such a redefinition of research problems and programs concerning Africa sometimes manifests itself in the emphasis of research orientations which have little to offer African women. I have visited villages where, at a time when the village women are asking for better health facilities and lower infant-mortality rates, they are presented with questionnaires on family planning. In some instances, when women would like to have piped water in the village, they may be at the same time faced with a researcher interested in investigating power and powerlessness in the household. In yet another situation, when women are asking for access to agricultural credit, a researcher on the scene may be conducting a study on female circumcision.

There is no denying that certain statistical relationships can be established between such variables as fertility, power, initiation rites, and women's overall standing in the household/community. What I am trying to emphasize, however, is that a statistical relationship per se, which can be established as an academic exercise, does not necessarily constitute relevant information or a priority from the point of view of those who are made the research subjects. In essence, research efforts which seek to enhance the participation of women in contemporary Africa, whether or not they emanate from the continent, should be formulated in relation to the socioeconomic realities which African women confront today. Furthermore, as we stand between the corridors of international intellectual corporations and national ethnic class divisions, the struggle which is being waged by women at various levels for equity in access to land or educational opportunities, better nutritional standards, or lowered infant-mortality rates is by no means separate or different from efforts made at the level of analysis to understand the nature of real or putative problems facing African women today.

Two further points may illustrate some of the analytical mileage to be gained when the two basic parameters outlined above are brought to bear on understanding African women. First, in considering the issue of the impact on women of colonial and/or neocolonial socioeconomic processes, it is well to bear in mind that, although such processes have enclaved women in the reserves and exploited their labor while withdrawing men to work in wage-earning jobs, in reality wages alone cannot constitute an argument that men have benefited from those systems of oppression. In fact peoples who are dominated by a repressive regime, whether they are men or women, share a similar subordinate structural position vis-à-vis the dominant culture. What we must look for, then, is not how African women lost their development opportunity during colonial or contemporary neocolonial periods (since our men have also suffered the same loss) but, rather, the differential impact of such socioeconomic conditions on men and women.

In this respect, I am reminded of men in our villages who were once recruited as plantation workers or infantry soldiers to fight in colonial wars. They left their villages thinking that they would earn money or make some other fortune from earning wages in work or benefits from the army. Meanwhile, their wives worked on the land to keep the family on its feet at home. Now these men (some of them at least) are retired at home with no benefits, having spent their youth feeding the industrial and military machines of their days. In actuality they are no better off than their wives, who had to till the land to feed their children.

The alienation experienced by low-paid African (Senegalese) dockworkers and their womenfolk at the hands of French colonials is also well documented by Sembene Ousmane in his novel *God's Bits of Wood*. In another novel, *Mine Boy*, Peter Abrams vividly depicts the situation of Ma Leah, a strong African woman in the slums of Johannesburg who earns a living by brewing and selling illicit liquor. She tries to evade the police but is finally arrested and jailed. In the same story her "daughter" Eliza, who is well educated, is estranged from the slum community in which she grew up. Yet she is excluded from the community of others (white people) who have comparable educational experience. Meanwhile Xuma, a man from the rural hinterland, arrives in Johannesburg to look for work. He gets a job and even becomes a leader of his co-workers in the mines. However, he is haunted by the idea of his friend who is dying of tuberculosis, having spent all his youth in the service of the mining industry. The three—Ma Leah, Eliza, Xuma—are all earning wages, but their position as Africans in a discriminatory job market remains in reality the same.

The second point I want to consider here is a problem with the notion of "integration of women in development," an expression developed by the United Nations and largely adopted by international aid agencies. One may well ask, "Integrating women into what development?" Historically, African women have been active in the provisioning of their families. This is a role which they play today, although they are being constricted in their efforts to feed their families by multinational corporations in food processing and agribusiness as well as by national land reform and crop programs. These women are well "integrated" into the dependent national economies. While it is possible to anticipate some structural changes through the implementation of some of the UN recommendations for special women's programs and women's bureaus or commissions, it is also likely that such institutional arrangements may serve in some instances to restrict rather than enhance the participation of women in their societies. Member states that pursue a program of development that negates equity can only be paying lip service to the issue when they agree to establish a women's bureau or commission. Such concepts as "integration of women in development" therefore require close scrutiny, in view of the fact that the majority of African peoples still operate within dependent economies. In such circumstances local participation tends to be characterized by what is sometimes referred to as "resistance to change," "apathy," or "indifference." Whenever a people have to use much of their creative energy for resistance, it means they are set back one step each time they approach a problem. The majority of Africans (men and women) find themselves in this situation. Thus questions of autonomy and self-determination still remain critical to an understanding of the problems surrounding female participation in contemporary Africa.

In ending this brief statement, I wish to reiterate what I consider to be central in understanding the position of African women today.

a) Any analysis must embrace the relationship between the international and national economic systems and women's position, including expectations of women in society and the contradictions associated with and arising from these expectations at the international, national, and domestic level.

b) African scholars, and especially women, must bring their knowledge to bear on presenting an African perspective on prospects and problems for women in local societies.

c) Scholars and persons engaged in development-research planning and implementation should pay attention to development priorities as local communities see them. This means an effort to bring these priorities to the attention of national governments and research groups and to encourage participation by local communities in identifying issues which they consider primary in their daily lives. In this way, there need not be an artificial boundary between practical and academic research, or between policy and theoretical research, on the role of women in development.

I would close by recalling a peasant woman in rural Kenya, who said the following when I asked her what development means to her: "During the anticolonial campaigns we were told that development would mean better living conditions. Several years have gone by, and all we see are people coming from the capital to write about us. For me the hoe and the water pot which served my grandmother still remain my source of livelihood. When I work on the land and fetch water from the river, I know I can eat. But this development which you talk about has yet to be seen in this village.

10

The Black Woman in South Africa: An Azanian Profile

Elizabeth Thaele Rivkin

INTRODUCTION

In focusing on the women of Azania,* the intent is not to pit women against men. Such action is counterproductive because it is divisive. Toni Cade, celebrated African-American writer, states the position taken here most eloquently:

> I have always, I think, opposed stereotypic definitions of "masculine" and "feminine," not only because I thought it was a lot of merchandizing nonsense, but rather because I found the either/or implicit in those definitions antithetical to what I was all about-the whole person . . . that the usual notions of sexual differentiations in roles is an obstacle to political consciousness . . .

> (The Black Women, p. 101)

To reemphasize, we are opposed to activities which obscure the identity of the real enemy.

The objective is to reaffirm the conviction that Azanian women are indispensible participants in the struggle by virtue of their status and roles in existing society and blossoming opposition. We will, therefore, focus on three areas:

---

*Azania is commonly known as South Africa. Here it is used in referring to the rightful heirs the African people.

1. conditions which have dictated the present status of the women of Azania;
2. their present conditions; and
3. the nature of their resistance to oppression.

First, we will concentrate on cultural traditions of the Azanian people. Second, the distortion of identity which takes place in economic relations will be traced to the white minority regime. Third, examples of the heroic spirit of Azanian women will be described and commented on to remind us of the calibre of these women lest we are deluded into thinking of them as merely passive. The concluding remarks are brief as these concern conditions for liberation which are in the hands of those who are facing death so that we may all be free. It would, therefore, be presumptuous to prescribe strategies for liberation.

I IN RETROSPECT

It was not until the colonial system introduced its shameful practices of oppression and exploitation that the role of African women in African society became distorted in its focus and content, resulting in the insane disqualification which our free countries must liquidate thoroughly.

—Sekou Toure

A realistic appraisal of the conditions of women in Azania would favor the remarks made by Sekou Toure. The equality of men and women in traditional societies was not absolute. Given social circumstances, however, optimum conditions existed. The predominance of women made polygamy natural; the grouping of women together as a united labor force, spawned the grouping of men and children with sets of duties and responsibilities. From the life style created by this type of social organization grew the customs and laws which controlled the life of the individual, family and community.

A. The Organization of Family

Communal life took a physical form—circles within circles— sometimes called a "kraal." Each wife headed her family and lived in her own house. Distinction was made between the first two wives and the others. The first wife was the principal one, in whose house all business was transacted; her house was easily recognized by its size and central position in the circle. The second wife was known as the left-hand wife. Her house was located to the left of the principal house and was also distinguishable by size. In the outer circle, beyond the homes of the other wives, were bachelors' quarters.[1] Where monogamy was the way of life, egalitarian marriages were the norm. Women still grouped together in friendship and rivalry, and so did men. Agriculture was a family responsibility. Moreover, men proposed laws which women could veto if these were discriminatory. Women, in short, took an active part in the politics of the community.

Tradition, respect for elders, courtesy, duties, responsibilities, and games and dancing were the primary means of socialization. The family and community shared these responsibilities. The most intimate and personal experiences, however, took place in the individual family unit headed by the mother. The father was only marginally involved though more closely with the older boys. As the need for land grew, younger families would leave and relocate in the vicinity of the parent group.[2] (Closeness to the parent group was important because ancestral graves and the bond of kinship required frequent visits.) These customs cemented attachment to the group as opposed to the individual family.

Sex Role Differentiation

The group's precedence over the individual pervaded even common courtesy. For example, Mazizi Kunene, in *Zulu Poems* (p. 12) makes the following comment:

> ...(W)hen a Zulu greets, he says (even if he is alone) 'sawubona' meaning 'we see you,' or more accurately, 'I on behalf of my family or community pay our respects to you.' He may even say 'sanibona' meaning 'I on behalf of my family pay our respects to you and your family.'

Group consciousness was also reflected in the organization of roles. Women had their tasks as did men and children.

The guiding principles in allocating roles reflected physical considerations in providing for societal needs. These needs can be categorized as survival and protection. As childbearers, women were more suited to be the guardians of survival. Their duties and responsibilities were extended to the cultivation of the soil because their mobility was somewhat restricted. The men, in contrast, were the protectors, and their role demanded physical prowess. They were expected to be warriors, hunters and performers of hard labor. Because the man was subjected to considerable danger, he received social rewards in the form of privileged status and praise in song and legends. Men's marginal involvement in the day-to-day activities of the family also seemed to equip him with the necessary detachment to intervene when friction arose among the wives and children. Thus, he performed additional functions as disciplinarian and arbitrator. Women and children were not, however, left to the mercy of his possible capriciousness. Ill-treatment of women and children were cause for divorce. The injured family would return to the home of the wife's parents or oldest brother. Such a drastic measure would bring with it a decline in the social prestige of the male. Social laws were thus geared to encourage cooperation among various segments of society and women enjoyed considerable autonomy.

African societies also placed singular importance on mother-right. From this grew power and a number of privileges. For example, among the Lovedu of Azania, the controlling figure was the Rain-Queen in whom political and religious power were combined. Women played roles of importance as "Queen Mother" or "Queen Sister" who acted as advisors to the king and were, in some cases, the real decision-makers. In some instances, nations were headed by women.[3]

With the advent of colonialism, social relations came under attack. Where the community had been a source of power, an alien force replaced it. The central focus, now, is not the well-being of the community, but its exploitation for the purpose of economic domination.

In this economic environment, social, religious, constitutional and political privileges and rights disappear, while exploitation is intensified. Men are torn away from the family as migrant laborers and women and children now are forced to fulfill the roles of men in addition to their own.

Another phenomena emerges: women are demoted. Despite the increase in their responsibility, their work begins to be viewed as inferior, because men receive greater monetary rewards on the employment market. Since women's work is traditional, traditional society is similarly devaluated.[4]

II THE DISPOSSESSED

The contradictions in the lives of men, women, and children in a family unit is a result of industrial capitalism. The capitalist system thrives on keeping part of the family hostage, while enslaving the rest for its labor. The events which occur in Azania are, thus, only unique in the intensity of the exploitation which persists. South Africa has the only system which purposefully and systematically makes civil liberty meaningless in order to maintain a privileged minority. Even Rhodesia does not come close to the savagery practiced in South Africa.

When examining the suffering of the women of Azania, the source of these practices can be traced directly to the apartheid policy which attempts to maintain numerous areas of cheap labor camps referred to as "Homelands" or "Bantustans." On these reserves, women, children, and the chronically ill are kept hostages, while the able-bodied men are forced to seek employment in the cities. Where Azanians enacted their lives in one environment, they are now required to live dual lives. In the "homeland" environment children are expected to ripen as the next wave of cheap labor while the adults await death, and in the urban environment called "white areas," Azanians are valued for their usefulness as cheap laborers to be expelled once their usefulness is over.

A. Societal Dislocation

The "Homelands" are areas which were designated as African reserves in 1913, after the conquest of African nations by European colonizers. By 1932, an Economic Commission chaired by J.E. Holloway reported overcrowded conditions. The population of South Africa was then said to number four and a half million. Today, the population has increased to seven and a half million and an equal number are told that South Africa is their homeland. Government spokesmen complain that oppposition to this policy is a result of distortion of the facts. Apparently, the Homelands policy is in keeping with "the wording and spirit of the United Nations Charter."[5] However, Henrik Verwood, the architect of "apartheid" as separate development, has proved such a claim to be hypocritical. In speaking on the establishment of the Homeland policy in the so-called South African parliament he commented:

Now the Hon. Senator wants to know whether the series of self-governing areas would be sovereign. The answer is obvious ... How could small scattered states arise? The areas will be economically dependent on South Africa. If they would only take a look at the map, they would see that it is a completely impossible and impracticable interpretation of self-government in their own areas.[6]

In 1959, he retracted these words. The facts and the map, however, remain the same. The social consequences for Azanain women are tragic. Two of the major effects discussed here are poverty and the fragmentation of family life.

Even though Azanians form almost three quarters of the total population, only 2 percent of the Gross Domestic Product is utilized by them.[7] Their poverty in terms of economic status is summed up in the following table which shows the discrepancy in wages between Africans and other racial groups.

TABLE 1: MONTHLY WAGES (LAST QUARTER OF 1970)

	Whites (R)*	Coloreds (R)	Indians (R)	Africans (R)
Mining	360	75	98	18
Manufacture	307	73	77	52
Construction	325	109	150	49
Electricity	369	76	—	55
Bank & Build. Socs.	298	80	106	66
Government	282	114	114	44
Administration	224	59	73	35
Local Authorities	293	85	60	45
S.A. Railways	295	70	53	52

*R = Rand = $1.40
(S.A. Dialogue, p. 408)

The differences between the wages of unskilled and skilled labor is usually 30 percent in most Western countries. In South Africa it is more than 400 percent, with Africans located at the bottom of the wage scale for all levels of employment[8]

Yet, South Africa has the highest per capita income in Africa and competes favorably with other industrialized nations, with regard to the standard of living of white South Africa. Azanian women, however, face multiple problems which have their origin in poverty. Malnutrition is acute. Its toll is especially great among women and children. For example, white women have 24 and Azanian women 128 infant deaths out of every 1000 live births.[9] These figures do not include miscarriages due to improper diets nor do they include children who died before the age of five due to lack of medical attention or to starvation. As medical services are miserably inadequate and poverty far greater in the rural areas, the extent of deprivation which haunts women in the so call "homelands" is immeasurable.

The callousness of officials is not limited to economic exploitation. It seeps into the very fabric of family life. As mentioned earlier, women have been left to carry out the role of father and mother because the men have had to leave home to find employment in the cities. The man is not permitted to take his family with him. If he marries in the city he can only do so under stipulated conditions. The following remarks of the deputy minister of Bantu Administration illustrate the latter point and gives an indication of the indifference of officials to the plight of Azanian men and women:

> A Bantu woman who qualifies to be in an urban area wishes to marry a man employed there but not yet qualified (he is not born there, has not been employed for ten years by one employer or for fifteen years by different employers). The couple may marry. If the man ceases to work in the area, he has no longer a right to remain there. If that Bantu male cannot obtain employment he will have to go, but that is something which the Bantu woman knew from the first day; the Bantu male himself knew it; they entered into this union with their eyes open. They both knew that if he lost his employment then the last vestige of justification for his presence here would disappear. If he has to leave, therefore, she will have to accompany him.[10]

What is usually regarded as the most sacred ties by the vast majority of societies—marriage and family—are treated as inconsequential. The lack of humane interest and the monstrous effect of policy on the lives of Azanians is evident. These man-made afflictions are treated as if they were immutable with the only recourse open to Azanian women that of adaptation to them.

The viciousness of the South African government's laws is further dramatized in its effect on parent-child relationships. In 1965, the following case was reported:

> Mr. Joseph Dyantiyi, a resident of Hermanus since 1942, was married and has six children between the ages seven and sixteen years. Sometime after his wife died he wished to remarry, to a woman working in Cape Town, but they were refused permission to set up house together and he was ordered to move into bachelor accommodations and to send his children to the Transkei where he had no land rights or close relatives to care for the children...[11]

Women and children are thus taught that the man cannot fulfill his traditional responsibility, that of protecting them against the enemy. They have to depend on themselves. Yet, the communal spirit of their culture has taught them to be generous in their relations with others. Consequently, despite the political and economic impotence of the man, it is recognized that he executes his duties to the best of his ability. Desertion is low, husbands continue to support their families even though they are only able to send one-fifth of their wages home. Women carry on with the traditional responsibility of providing for the family, and the homecoming of the husband-father is greeted with fanfare as great as that of a warrior returning from the field of battle. For the short period that he is home, he is king of his household and the children know that the boss is home. The responses of wife and children may not meet with the approval of antisexists, but these responses are certainly a requirement for the mental and psychological health of the family, especially the men.

The laws of South Africa apply directly to women, as in a case similar to that of Mr. Joseph Dyantiyi. As reported:

> Mrs. Rebecca Motale, born in Cape Town and with three children, lost her right to remain there with her parents when she married a Stellenbosch man, and was refused permission to join him. She was convicted for being in Cape Town unlawfully. The case was, unsuccessfully, taken on appeal and meanwhile, according to her counsel, she disappeared to live in the bush.[12]

The mother can no longer return to her family with her children at the demise of her husband. No provision is made for her, other than banishment to a strange land—her supposed homeland—where she had no land rights, has no friends, and, in all probability, does not know the language spoken there. The dread with which she faces the prospects offered to her by the government is underscored by her willingness to face the hardships of the wilderness where she must fend for herself and her children like a hunted animal. Thus, the support that was once afforded by the extended family and which has become even more necessary for survival, is outlawed by the South African government.

African society has been deliberately fragmented in order to enslave the people of Azania. Normal relations between men and women and parents and their children have been replaced by an economic system which has as its foundation the welfare of colonial whites. Homelands are concentration camps from which men emerge with the permission of white authorities whose only interest is in meeting the employment needs of white society. When these are met, and when a worker is no longer able-bodied, he and his family become rejects whose only alternative is starvation. The African woman is thus trapped in a situation in which all her energies are geared toward the maintenance of her family in the face of starvation, amongst others who are in a similar predicament.

III TOWARD REVOLUTION

Thus far we have dealt with the realities miscreated by the South African government in contrast with traditional society. What has surfaced is the absence of legal protection and the barriers against positive assertion by the Azanian peoplehood. But while human beings are creatures of social reality, we are also capable of creating our own.

Violence of government has placed constraints on the extent to which Azanians are free to create their own social reality. The repugnance of the people to the use of violence as a means of eradicating the barriers which have resulted in social regression have urged them to use nonviolent tactics in opposing the South African government. Therefore, organized political action, under the leadership of the African National Congress, was waged according to the dictates of a democractic society. The ANC formulated grievances in petitions, and action took the form of negotiations and demonstrations. As an integral part of the movement, the women formed a Woman's League which participated in these strategies and quite often spearheaded them. But, democratic action presupposes the responsiveness and openness of government to the voice of the people. The South African government is disqualified on both counts. It is, therefore, not surprising that the tactics of nonviolence failed. To substantiate and illustrate the nature of the struggle against oppression the response that it evoked from the government, and the lesson that it taught a peace-loving people, we will draw on a number of incidents which marked the decades of the 1950s and 1960s.

The opposition of the women relates to the harsh pass-laws of the South African government. The pass restricts the movement of the individual who carries it. He or she is not allowed to seek employment in a place of their choice, and is restricted in his or her right to live with spouses or visit relatives. The individual can be stopped at any hour of the day or woken up at any hour of the night by a demand from the police to produce the pass. Failure to comply results in imprisonment. Even if the pass has been left at home by accident, an immediate arrest is made and no allowances made for women or men to arrange for the care of their children. It is, therefore, understandable why the women have resisted carrying this pernicious document.[13]

In July 1913, women staged the first demonstration against a proposed law requiring them to carry passes. Their opposition was so final and intense that it was not until 1952 that the government dared to pass a law stipulating that African women would from then on carry a pass. The women once more refused to comply. In 1955 and 1956, close to 40,000 women took part in demonstration held in 30 different places on 38 separate occasions.

In July 1957, under the leadership of the ANC (African National Congress) the Women's League and the Federation of South African Women, the resistance reached a peak. Unity and determination on the part of women were matched with police brutality, and retaliatory sentences. But, despite the arrest of 600 women and the serving of jail sentences by 120 of them, they remained undaunted. After eight weeks in jail, they returned to a massive crowd of friends. That same year, August 9 marked the anniversary of the great Pretoria demonstration. Over 7,000 women across the Union once more declared their determination to resist. In one small town, Zeerust, when 35 were arrested, 235 more came forward and demanded that they too be arrested. At the end of that year, despite stiff year-long sentences, they remained resolved in their opposition.[14] (Sachs, pp. 302-303)

Another area in which women were roused to active opposition is recounted by Leo Kuper in his diary. Here the issue was not the pass-laws, but blatant attempts by the "gestapo" police to destroy the only avenue of economic enterprise open to most women: that of brewing and selling beer. (Beer brewed according to a traditional recipe is one of the favorite beverages of African men. Unlike alcoholic beverages of the West, it is nutritious and free of any artifical ingredients.) The opposition of the women was in response to the shattering of their stills at a time when they were also plagued by an unusually high unemployment rate as well as other social considerations. Kuper made the following entrees:

> June 18, 1959, *Natal Daily News:* "Large numbers" of African women demonstrate outside Cato Manor, Dalton Road, and Victoria Street beer halls. These three beer halls closed. Three thousand women baton charged, by several hundred police armed with Sten guns, rifles, and submachine guns, after a parley with the Director of Bantu Administration. Women say they will picket all beer halls in Durban and Pinetown tomorrow. Women smash beer containers and spill 1,000 gallons of beer at Victoria Street, warning men not to patronize the beer halls. Two hundred women pelt male drinkers at Dalton Road Beer Hall with mugs and hit them with sticks. Tear gas used against crowd at Dalton Road. Mr. Bourquin says that the disturbances are not solely a retaliation for the destruction of Cato Manor liquor stills. Natal employers agree that an immediate improvement in the lot of unskilled African labor is required.[15]

The women were not merely fighting for the privilege of brewing their own beer. The grievances went much deeper. Official beer halls were draining the community of its economic resources. Husbands were patronizing the establishment and unemployed friends with the wages that were meant to feed their families. They were victims of bandits along the way and they were spending time away from the family.[16]

The result of the women's rebellion against the system is summed up by the next entry concerning the day following resistance:

> June 19, 1959, *Rand Daily Mail:* Fifteen thousand Africans camp in hills, singing anthems and chanting, surrounding the area where

earlier police opened fire on 5,000 African women and again on crowds of advancing Africans ... Women shouting to men "Don't be cowards. Kill them (the police). 17

A year later in mid-June 1960, the country is in a state of emergency.

The Durban incidents described are only the tip of the iceberg of oppression. One cannot fully appreciate the frustration, helplessness, and anger which pervades the life of the women of Azania. The words of the African chairman of the Locations Combined Advisory Boards of Durdan, and one participant in the rebellion convey some insight into the nature of such protests:

> The African women of Natal have demonstrated that the suffering endured by many families cannot be described in constitutional words. It is the voice of oppressed people who have no other means of voicing their grievances before the governments of the land ... I do not blame them. I lay the blame at the door of the multiplicity of the laws and their regulations, which are harshly administered by men who do not show sympathy. Men and women in urban areas and rural areas suffer and feel the same.

> One of the demonstrators illustrated the point more vividly: In destroying a dipping tank, the people had written a letter which the government would read.[18]

Women have consistently fought on issues which they felt were in their province. They have fought at the side of their men as well. It is, however, clear that the South African regime has no intention of hearing their pleas or grievances.

Organized resistance is often met with police violence. We only need to look at the following confrontations which occurred in the course of one year in Azania:

February 26, 1959	Lady Selbourne, Pretoria, protest against the issuing of passes to women - police open fire on demonstrators.
August 15, 1959	Maritzburg, Natal, women protest restrictions on the earning power of their husbands - police open fire.
November 11, 1959	Paarl, Cape, demonstration against the banning of trade union leaders - police open fire.

December 11, 1959	Windhoek, South West Africa, Herero tribesmen protest against relocation in a new township - police open fire.
March 21, 1960	Sharpeville, Natal, protest - police open fire; Langa, Cape, protest - police open fire.
March 28, 1960	Johannesburg, Transvaal, Day of Mourning - police open fire.[19]

The way legitimate complaints are handled is to shoot into unarmed crowds of women and children. Recently, we witnessed the same approach being used on school children demonstrating against the compulsory use of the Afrikaan's language in school.

An incident after incident was reported, we were told of police firing on crowds. It is, therefore, understandable that the frustrations of Azanian people have reached the point of violence. But, the contest is often uneven—police guns against sticks and stones.

Lately, we have heard arguments which assert that the South African government is changing. One of the most prominent white politicians, Helen B. Suzman, leader of the small, but resilient Progressive Party, has taken the lead in popularizing this notion. She attributes her optimism to the observed changes in the economic sector. The high demand for skilled labor has apparently given "economic muscle to blacks" making a "decided bent in the industrial color bar."[20] Another source, Dick Richard, editor of *Die Vaderland*, the leading oracle of the government and watchdog of the status quo, states the reasons why the government *should* change. According to him, blacks could easily be influenced by the "unuru ideals" of black Africa, if the government does not move away from discrimination.[21] The advice, however, is meaningless, because at the bottom line he cautions that the end of discrimination "should not endanger the policy of separate development." We have discussed at length how separate development is interpreted. If a new direction by the illegitimate government is being taken, it should be tested against four measures:

1. Has the power structure reordered its priorities?
2. Is there a link between the economic and policial powers aiming at the redistribution of the wealth and resources of the country?
3. Does the previously dominated group agree that the changes lead to their liberation?[22]

4. Does the previously dominated group participate fully in the making of national decisions?

Fundamental change transforms earlier patterns of domination into a system which permits the optimum conditions for the development of all the members of the society. Less than this invites opposition, with weapons if need be.

CONCLUSION

The oppressive conditions surrounding Azanian woman in the twentieth century have not evolved from traditional society. They are inventions of minds shaped by the profiteering endemic in Europe. These types of minds are still attempting to dominate the world. Consequently, the injustices in Azania are largely ignored, while Kissinger and his ilk scuttle all over Africa putting up a smoke screen pretending to be the messengers of peace and justice.

Polarized forces are pitched in battle and none of us can claim to be neutral. If we assert that we are for a new order, yet contribute to the exploitation of women, we are deceiving ourselves. We would have, in reality, joined the ranks of the oppressors. There must be a careful evaluation, therefore, of the implications and consequences of our actions on all people: women, men, children of every race. Claiming ignorance will not suffice, blaming tradition in passé. There is room only for those who have reached true consciousness, because history will not be turned back.

NOTES

1. Selby B. Ngcobo, "The Bantu People", *The South African Way of Life*, (ed. G.H. Calpin, William Heinemann Ltd., 1953), pp. 62.

2. Ibid, pp. 63-66 (see also A.T. Bryant, *The Zulu People Before the White Man Came*, (New York: Negro University Press, 1st printing 1948, reprint 1970).

3. Walter Rodney, *How Europe Underdeveloped Africa*, (Dar es Salaam: Tanzania Publishing House, 1972), pp. 248.

4. *Ibid.*

5. C.P. Mulder, "The Rationale of Separate Development" in *South African Dialogue*, (Nic. Rhodie, ed. Phil: Westminster Press, 1972), pp. 49.

6. G. Jacobs, "Hazards of the Homeland Policy" ibid., pp. 155.

7. G.M.E. Leistner, "Non-Whites in the South African Economy," Ibid., p. 289.

8. Arthur Curry, "The Frustration of Being Colored," p. 408.

9. Ibid. p. 29.

10. *Apartheid: Its Effects on Education, Science, Culture and Information,* (UNESCO, 3rd printing 1969), pp. 132.

11. Ibid., pp. 133.

12. Ibid., pp. 133.

13. Albie Sachs, *Anatomy of Apartheid* (London: Collet's Publishing Company, 1965) pp. 302-303.

14. Ibid.

15. Leo Kuper, *An African Bourgeoisie: Race, Class and Politics in South Africa,* (New Haven: Yale University Press, 1965), pp. 10.

16. Ibid. pp. 19.

17. Ibid. pp. 10.

18. Ibid. pp. 19.

19. L. E. Neame, *The History of Apartheid,* (London: Pall Mall Press, 1963), pp. 163-164.

20. Interview with Helen B. Suzman, *Intellect,* (April 1975, No. 103), p. 418.

21. Reported in the *Rand Daily Mail,* (November 29, 1975).

22. Congress J. Mbata, "Profile of Change," *Contemporary Changes in South Africa,* Leonard Thompson and Jeffrey Butler, eds., (Berkeley: University of California Press, 1975), pp. 202.

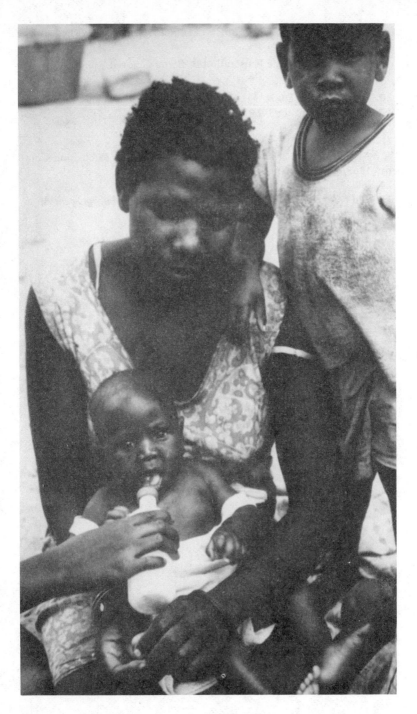

A Bantu family in South Africa. Photo: United Nations/J. Frank, No. 133702.
(1975)

11
The Role of Women in the Struggle Against Apartheid in South Africa[1]

Richard E. Lapchick

This article examines and analyzes the role played by women in the struggle against the vicious apartheid laws in South Africa, and the struggle for the liberation of the black people of South Africa from racial oppression by the white minority.

On account of the gravity of the oppression experienced by both men and women under apartheid, women's struggle for equality with men in South Africa historically has been subordinated to the wider struggle for national liberation. Thus the main goal for African women in South Africa has been to achieve national liberation: the essential prerequisite for any real change in the social status of women in general has been that they work with men in their common struggle against political oppression. The two are seen as complementary, and the participation of women is seen as a way of ensuring that women's liberation will accompany national liberation.

Women in South Africa have emerged since the turn of the century as primary catalysts for protest and as challengers to the apartheid regime in South Africa itself. With all the disabling and devastating effects of apartheid on the status of women, these most oppressed of the oppressed have never lost sight of the fact that meaningful change for women cannot come through reform but only with the total destruction of the apartheid system. Thus the common exploitation and oppression of men and women on the basis of color has led to a combined fight against the system instead of a battle of women against men for "women's rights." While women desire their personal liberation, they see it as part of the total liberation movement. Although there is no doubt that the overt leadership has been dominated by men, the seemingly unacknowledged and informal segment of society controlled by women has been the key to many of the most significant mass movements in modern South African history. It is only in the very recent past that the crucial role played by women in raising basic issues, organizing, and involving the masses has become more widely recognized.

Even before the contemporary era began to unfold, the Zulu elder Mkabi became a heroine to the South African peoples when she took her own life in 1879 rather than face the prospect of the warrior hero Cetshwayo becoming a fugitive. Her example, in different ways, has been courageously repeated over the course of the next one hundred years.

WOMEN IN THE TRADE UNIONS

While South African women have become involved to some degree in all kinds of organizations from church groups to liberation movements, in many ways it was the trade union movements that became the spawning ground for women organizers. It was also in the trade unions that women first rose to positions of importance in South Africa. Trade union actions such as strikes also served to politicize some women.

Ironically, in the 1920s African women could belong to registered unions since they did not carry passes, a provision of South African labor laws that did exclude men. For negotiating purposes under the 1924 Industrial Conciliation Act, Africans were not even considered as "employees." The South African industrial trade unions became increasingly black in their membership, while craft unions, because of the system of job reservation which maintains the skilled worker positions for whites only, remained white.

According to Bettie du Toit, one of the historic figures in this movement, the initial emphasis was on workers' rights but progressively shifted racial equality. This occurred despite the fact that many of the early organizers were white like Ms. du Toit. Ms. du Toit said that:

It was easier for us to organize African women than men. First the African women trusted the white women while the men were suspicious. Then, the women's legal position was better because they could join the registered unions. But most importantly, they better understood the need for unions, as they were more concerned with providing for the basic necessities for themselves and their families.[2]

The organizing of women began in the 1920s, principally in the laundry, clothing, mattress, furniture, and baking industries. Several black national federations were formed and dissolved in the 1920s. The one that endured in spite of the new labor legislation of the 1920s[3] was the Non-European Trade Union Federation which was formed in 1928.

Three women emerged in the 1930s as decisive figures in the women's labor movement and remained active for four decades until the apartheid government totally restricted them through arrests and bannings. Bettie du Toit started by organizing colored and African women garment workers; Ray Alexander organized African, Indian, and colored workers in several trades; and Johanna Cornelius, who became president of the Garment Workers Union in 1935, organized the first general strike of garment workers against wage cuts in 1932. By 1932 both du Toit and Cornelius had been arrested for organizing labor activities. Theirs were the first of many arrests for women in trade unions.

During the 1930s women trade unionists were in the leadership of the opposition toward growing Afrikaner nationalism and apartheid in the unions. Their positions were that racial divisions should not split a union. They sought free compulsory education for all races, an end to job reservations by race, and training for all races.[4] Women were both being organized and being trained to organize and lead.

As the economy developed in the 1930s and 1940s, there was a growth of capital accumulation and increased demand for labor. Women were rapidly becoming urbanized to fill this need. These demographic changes, coupled with the crippling labor legislation that would follow the assumption of power by the National Party in 1948, made the 1940s the peak period for women organizing other women and black industrial workers. African women organizers valiantly but vainly defied the increasing spread of Afrikaner nationalism, soon to engulf the nation.

Ms. du Toit maintained that the direction of those opposing unions was clear. Union activists were being labelled "communist" and women union activists were being labelled "immoral" and "communist." When du Toit went to Huguenot to organize a non-racial branch of the Textile Workers Industrial Union, the Dutch Reformed Church campaigned to have her thought of as promiscuous and "a terrible viper" in their midst: "I was completely ostracized by the community, including the women I helped organize. When I got on a bus, it would empty out."[5] As labor strikes increased, so did the arrests. However, these actions did lead to important, if only temporary, victories. Agreements were made in 1944 providing for equal pay for equal work which was unheard of for women in secondary industries. In some industries forty-hour work weeks were instituted with two-week paid vacations, as were paid public holidays, extra pay for night work, sick funds and other concessions.[6]

Clearly, however, Afrikaner nationalism was becoming in overwhelming force. Foreign capital investment also grew dramatically in this period. In 1933, 65 percent of the workers in the textile industry were white. In 1950, whites were only 16[7] percent Foreign capital, which accounted for most of the new investment in the textile industry by the end of World War II, was relying on cheap African labor for its huge profit margins.

The National Party enacted labor legislation that crippled efforts to organize Africans.[8] Even though strikes by Africans were then illegal, the women still led strikes. The government began to dismantle the hard-won influence of women in the trade unions by bannings and house arrests. Bettie du Toit and Ray Alexander were among the first prohibited from union activity in 1953.

Again, the women would not cease. By the 1960s, one half of the African unions had women as their secretaries general. By 1974, fifteen unions with white, Asian, and colored members had women as secretaries general while the same was true of nine of the twenty-three unregistered African trade unions. In spite of likely repercussions, there were 374 strikes in 1974 involving some 57,656 African workers-841 of whom, including many women, were arrested, according to the Black Women's Federation.[9] Women have maintained their roles of leadership. The trade union movement has historically helped to inspire women in many other areas. But the main impact was that the unions provided a training ground for female political leaders. Female factory workers learned new methods of organizing and were exposed to the principles of nonracial worker solidarity.

THE EARLY ROLE OF WOMEN IN OTHER ORGANIZATIONS

From the founding of the African National Congress (ANC) Bantu Women's League under Charlotte Maxeke in 1913, women have been active in other organizations, especially those emanating from the urban areas.

Although they are now acknowledged as important historical figures, few of the women attained major positions of power in these organizations. An exception was the trade unions, as was the Communist Party of South Africa, the only political party that as far back as 1920 opposed segregation. In CPSA, which was banned in 1950, had several women in both its Central Executive Committee and in its Political Bureau. Such women as Mary Wolton, Cissie cool, Hilda Watts (Bernstein), Ray Alexander, Ruth First, and Betty Radford Sacks were active not only in the CPSA but in many other organizations.

Indian women, perhaps by tradition the most restricted of all South African women, emerged into politics during the Indian Passive Resistance Campaign of 1940. Women also helped lead the Alexandra bus boycott when 15,000 men and women walked 18 miles per day for nine days in 1943 and seven weeks in 1944 to protest an increase in the bus fare.[10]

Women were also active in the Campaign of Defiance Against Unjust Laws during which many were arrested in 1952. They also helped to organize the Congress of Democrats, a white organization in alliance with the ANC and the Colored People's Congress, and, consequently, many women were among the 156 defendants in the infamous Treason Trial which lasted from 1956 to 1961.

However, the lack of a broad-based women's organization made the participation of women sporadic. An additional problem was that almost all activity was urban-based with almost no contact with women in the reserves.*

---

*The reserves are the areas set aside by the white government for the African people. The areas make up approximately 13 percent of the total land of South Africa and are generally mineral-poor and not suitable for agriculture, and thus have become reserves of cheap labor for white society.

THE FEDERATION OF SOUTH AFRICAN WOMEN

With these organizational problems being magnified by the domination of the National Party and its rapid expansion of apartheid legislation, the time was right for the formation of the Federation of South African Women in 1954. Its members, said to represent some 230,000 womem, were drawn largely from the Congress Alliance, but especially from the ANC Women's League.[11] The FSAW had two primary aims: 1) to work for majority rule and end the policy of apartheid and 2) to build a multiracial women's organization that would work also for the rights and freedom of women.

The creation of the FSAW marked a tremendous period of expansion of the political involvement of women. This was especially true of black women. Ida Mtwana of the ANC Women's League (ANCWL) became the first president. Trade unionist Ray Alexander was its first secretary. Within a year Alexander had been banned and Mtwana resigned. The new leadership, although constantly threatened by the government, led South African women into one of their most vigorous periods. Lilian Ngoyi, president of the ANCWL, became president with Helen Joseph as secretary. They were a strong team together until Ngoyi herself was banned in 1961. The FSAW, along with its constituent members participated in, or conducted some of the most important political efforts of the decade.

Bantu education campaign

The Bantu educational system was one that was intended to inculcate a servile attitude in the African people. It taught girls to clean, wash, cook, and do all the domestic duties they might perform for their masters. Boys were trained not to expect more from the regime than the little it was prepared to give to African men. In addition to the ideological component, the facilities afforded Africans were very poor, classes were overcrowded, and the teachers, few of whom held university degrees, had to teach two shifts each.

In December 1954, the FSAW campaigned for a boycott of government controlled schools. The women organized on a house-to-house basis. However, when the state announced that all children out of school on a certain date would be expelled, the boycott collapsed. The women formed the National Education Movement. Francis Baard, a defendant in the Treason Trial and union leader with the Food and Canning Workers Union, described the efforts:

We protested against it. We even took our children out of school to be outside in the Veld - that's where they attended school. And the teachers there were arrested - one was my daughter - for being a teacher of the children outside. We called those schools cultural clubs.[12]

That people still had to fight the "Bantu Education" system more than twenty years later was partially the cause of the Soweto uprisings in 1976.

Bus boycott campaign

In December 1956, the Public Utility Transportation Company (PUTCO) which transported some 25,000 Africans each day from the townships of Alexandra, Sophiatown, and Lady Shelbourne, announced a one penny fare increase.

On 7 January 1957 Africans began a bus boycott by walking up to nine miles each way, some leaving their homes at 3:00 A.M. Within three weeks, the 25,000 Africans from these towns had been joined by 20,000 other Africans in sympathy. The boycott was organized mainly by women and was led by Florence Mposho, then the secretary of the ANCWL in Alexandra.

The response of the state was quick and severe. Mass raids resulted in 6,606 Africans being arrested and another 7,860 subpoenaed. A rally of 5,000 people in Lady Shelbourne was attacked by two police baton charges resulting in 17 Africans being hospitalized. The government announced legislation that would result in a permanent end for bus services to the African towns. But the Africans continued to resist and after five very trying months, the Native Transportation Amendment Act No. 52 of 1957 rolled back the fare increase.[13] It was a stunning victory.

Cato Manor uprising

Cato Manor, near Durban, became the site of large-scale protests against "Bantu authorities." When the municipality attempted to end all illegal liquor stills, it ignited the fire that had been smoldering because of the abject poverty of the people there. Beer brewing had been an important source of income for African women. Under the law, African men had to drink in municipal beerhalls.

In June 1959, 2,000 women marched to express their grievances. Others entered a beerhall and destroyed the beer. They organized a beer boycott which led to wide-scale uprisings all over Natal. Symbols of Bantu authorities were destroyed by the women. During 1959, an estimated 20,000 women in Natal protested and more than 1,000 were convicted in the courts.[14] Violence erupted in January 1960 when twenty-six police raided Cato Manor to search for illegal liquor. The people began stoning police after they had arrested thirty-two residents. Police opened fire. The crowd attacked and eventually killed four white and five African policemen while injuring six others. One African civilian was killed.

In an incident unrelated to Cato Manor but indicative of the esteem people had developed for their African women leaders, violence also erupted when authorities announced that on 9 November 1959 Elizabeth Mafeking, the vicepresident of the ANCWL and president of the African Food and Canning Workers Union, was to be banished from Paarl to a remote area. The mother of eleven children, she secretly fled to Basutoland (now Lesotho) on 8 November. With the escape unknown to her supporters, 3,000 people assembled early in the morning outside her house. Stones were thrown at passing cars and police opened fire injuring twelve. Sixty-four were arrested for public violence.

The anti-pass campaign

It is the example of courage and determination displayed by South African women in their struggle to refuse to take the restrictive passes that has best epitomized their overall participation in the struggle to eradicate apartheid.

The government attempted to get women to take passes as early as 1913 but the resistance at the time was so fierce that it was not attempted again until the National Party came to power. Charlotte Maxeke, a founding member of the ANC in 1912 and head of the Bantu Women's League, led the women in the Orange Free State to stop carrying passes in 1913. In Bloemfontein some 600 women brought their passes in a bag to the major's office, and informed the deputy mayor that they would not carry them anymore. Maxeke mounted another campaign in Johannesburg in 1919 while Ms. T. Mapikela and others organized efforts in the Orange Free State from 1920 to 1924.[15] The government finally gave up and this became one of the most significant antiapartheid victories of the era.

However, the situation had dramatically changed in 1952 when the Native Abolition of Passes and Coordination of Documents Act was enacted. The National Party was in power and apartheid legislation was being hastily designed. Unlike the earlier period, a large number of women had moved to the urban areas to seek employment and keep their families together. For the National Party, this fact was the·sign of a permanent urban labor force and, therefore, a serious threat to the apartheid structures. The 1952 Act was intended to permit only the necessary labor for industrial and domestic work into urban areas. Passes were to be extended to women. However, as a result of success of the earlier campaigns, the government did not announce until October 1955 that passes would be issued to women in January 1956.

Lilian Ngoyi described why women resisted so fiercely:

> We women have seen the treatment our men have—when they leave home in the morning you are not sure if they will come back. If the husband is to be arrested and the mother, what about the child?[16]

Helen Joseph, a white activist who was secretary of the FSAW further explained:

> The women lived it. The whole system was part of the life they lived. They realized it was going to be very much worse if it was extended to themselves because it would be the mother who would be taken away from the child. What they saw was in fact what had happened. It was a direct attack on their home life and their family life and this is what sparked it off in such a dynamic way because they knew the danger of passes as only the black woman can know. Because they lived it.[17]

The women understood that influx control could destroy the increasing unity and stability in the urban areas that family life represented. Therefore, they became activated as they never had been before to stop this from happening. The women saw and dramatically responded to the attempt to destroy the family which many believed to be one of the few stable parts of the lives of Africans in this very abnormal apartheid society. The resistance of the women was so dogged that the government waited eleven years from the passage of the Act in 1952 until making it mandatory for women to carry the passes.

Government officials tried to divide the African men from their protesting women by, at first, dealing only with the men. When African women resisted, the secretary of Bantu Affairs refused to speak to the "masses of African women" and their "so-called leaders" and told officials only to speak to their men, to recognized Bantu authorities and tribal chiefs. He said:

> Recognition of women demonstrators on the lines that have found favor among whites, where women have a status altogether different from that of the Bantu women, can at this stage only have harmful and dangerous effects which could undermine the entire community structure.[18]

It is impossible to adequately discuss all the heroic actions of women and is therefore necessary to highlight only a few of the most important.[19]

The women hastily organized a demonstration for October 1955 as soon as the announcement was made that they must carry passes. The women in the Black Sash organization staged an all-white protest. Their effort was quickly put in perspective when 2,000 African women rallied in Pretoria. The government had banned the meeting, cancelled the buses that had been hired, and set up road blocks to prevent the women from coming, leaving the trains, which were expensive, as the only alternative. Not knowing what the results would be, Helen Joseph left to pick up FSAW president Ngoyi before 6:00 A.M. She described the scene:

> I saw the train come over the top of the embankment and out of every window of the train there were women's heads and they were waving and shouting and singing, singing the freedom songs and I knew that it was going to succeed. I knew then that nothing could stop them.[20]

The passes were issued first in the Orange Free State in the town of Winburg in March 1956. Many women were arrested when they burned their passes. At this time it was not mandatory to carry a pass, but it was illegal to destroy a pass if one had a pass.

By far the most well-known effort was organized for 9 August 1956 by FSAW. More than 20,000 women came to the Union Buildings in Pretoria. They had to walk in groups of two or three since marches had been banned in Pretoria. They tried to see the prime minister, who refused, so they placed petitions with more than 100,000 signatures in his office. Bettie du Toit described the scene:

> The women said it was almost eerie. They stood in complete silence while the petitions were delivered. Then they sang freedom songs,

ending with the famous line to Strijdom: 'Now you have touched the women, you have struck a rock, you have dislodged a boulder, you will be crushed.'[21]

Frances Baard said what it meant to the women:

We were proud that we were there. We were disappointed he wouldn't see us but ... we left our message, and he must have heard how many people were there ... he must have hidden himself in the offices when he saw us ... he knew there were a lot of people.[22]

The almost spiritual and serene quality of these demonstrations was, however, not the norm. More typical was the case of Lichtenburg in the Western Transvaal. When government officials arrived to register women in November 1956, more than 1,000 women met them to protest. When the police made a baton charge, the women threw stones in retaliation. The police opened fire and two Africans were killed.[23]

In May 1957, the strategy of the government was still to issue passes first in the villages. Thus, women in Johannesburg were asked to carry only "permits of identification," which the police bagan to demand. On 12 May, some 2,000 Africans attended an antipermit meeting in Sophiatown. They requested an interview with the mayor and on 16 May more than 20,000 met to send off a seven-person deputation from Sophiatown. Six thousand people escorted them to city hall where they met with the mayor who agreed to suspend police action and issue exemption certificates for women.[24] It was a victory.

In Nelspruit in the eastern Transvaal, women attacked the car of the magistrate when he announced passes would be distributed. When five women were arrested, 300 women marched to demand their release. Police made a baton charge and then opened fire. Four were hurt. The women organized a strike that was 95 percent effective on the following day. Police fired on crowds again and eight Africans were wounded. When the police conducted extensive raids they arrested 140. The women were forced to accept the passes.[25]

On the day that passes were to be distributed in Sanderton in southeastern Transvaal, all 914 women who went to protest to the mayor were arrested for taking part in an illegal procession.

But the resistance of the women was undaunted. In July 1957 in Gopane Village in the Baphurutse Reserve, some women burned their passes. When 35 women were arrested, 233 more volunteered to be arrested. When officials arrived in Motswedi and Braklaagte to register the women,the villages were deserted. In Pieterburg in the northern Transvaal, 2,000 women stoned officials who came to register them in June. When they returned in July, 3,000 women greeted them, forcing officials to withdraw again.[26]

The spontaneous and sustained resistance in Zeerust was a sign of the new level of tensions surrounding the passes. Chief Abraham Moiloa refused to aid officials in their attempts to get women to accept passes. In April 1957, Moiloa was given fourteen days to leave for another area. When officials arrived, only a few women accepted. Other women collected and destroyed most of the passes issued. When the men and women attempted to kill the new pro-government chief and his three bodyguards, police arrived and many were arrested. Five were convicted of attempted murder.

People became more militant against those who cooperated with the officials. A church was set on fire and a school was boycotted because teachers accepted passes. Many passes were burned in spite of a heavy police presence. When a hearing was set up to investigate the unrest, several hundred women who tried to attend were turned back at a roadblock by forty police backed by eight planes flying low over the women. Some women were injured and reportedly had to go to a hospital in Bechuanaland because the police would not allow them into Zeerust.

Progovernment chiefs allowed their bodyguards to harass and beat up women and men opposed to the passes. When men working as migrants returned over Christmas holidays they beat up the chiefs and their bodyguards and killed one of the senior chief's bodyguards. On 25 January 1958 five Africans were shot by a policeman who was being stoned by the crowd. Ultimately, up to 2,000 women and children fled Zeerust for Bechuanaland rather than take the passes.[27]

Officials began to push the campaign in October 1957 when they registered women in Johannesburg. While many did accept the passes as impossible to avoid, many thousands protested during the week of 21-28 October 1957. More than 2,000 were arrested. Helen Joseph recalled the situation:

Their attitudes was they're not going to do it (accept passes). That's when the first mass arrests took place . . . Within the space of a week there were 2,000 women in jail. It was incredible (they) left their children, left their husbands, left their homes, went to jail and simply would not pay the fines.

The men felt that they couldn't cope with the home situation anymore. All they had to do was to go up to the jail and pay the fine. And if you're in jail and your fine is paid, you're put out. The women were very angry but they couldn't do anything about it. And then the decision was taken by the leadership that this particular aspect of the campaign must be called of which was in fact correct, because it was weakening at the perimeters with the men pulling their own wives out.[28]

Although the will to resist the passes had not changed, the reality of government coercion forced more and more women to take the passes. Resistance and demonstrations did continue but it was reported that by March 1960, 3,020,281 or about 75 percent of the adult women, had accepted passes. Winnie Mandela, one of the leading South African women who has herself been severely restricted by the regime for almost seventeen years, explained reasons why women were forced to accept passes in addition to the physical punishment mentioned above. She said:

We have to carry passes which we abhor because we cannot have houses without them, we cannot work without them, we are endorsed out of towns without them, we cannot register births without them, we are not even expected to die without them.[29]

THE SHARPEVILLE MASSACRE AND ITS AFTERMATH

In December of 1959 the Pan Africanist Congress of Azania, which had been formed in 1959 as a second major African nationalist organization in South Africa, announced it would launch "decisive and final positive action" against the pass laws under the slogan of "no bail, no defense, no fine." The ANC was also planning a major campaign against the passes with varying tactics. ANC events were to comence on 31 March 1960. The antipass campaigns were now focusing on men as well as women.

Mr. Robert Sobukwe, president of the PAC announced that his organization's campaign would begin on 21 March. Members were requested not to bring their passes and to surrender themselves for arrest at the nearest police station. When released from jail the campaigners would again offer themselves for arrest.

PAC members had been instructed to act strictly in a spirit of nonviolence. If ordered by the police to disperse, Mr. Sobukwe said, they should do so quietly and with discipline.

On the morning of 21 March, tens of thousands of Africans gathered in locations around the country. In Sharpeville, up to 20,000 came to the police stations in a tense atmosphere. Police opened fire and 67 Africans were killed and 186 wounded, including 40 women and 8 children. More than 80 percent had been shot in the back while fleeing.

What has come to be known as the Sharpeville Massacre marked the beginning of an even more repressive era. A state of emergency was declared. The ANC and the PAC were both banned. Massive arrests were made under new restrictive legislation while women led hunger strikes to protest conditions in the jail, and it became virtually impossible to organize. A stay-at-home demonstration planned for the last three days of May 1961 did not succeed after the police arrested upwards of 18,000 Africans in lage scale raids.[30]

Proclamation 268 and Government Notice 1722 of 26 October 1962 made it obligatory for African women to carry passes as of 1 February 1963. In October 1963 the Black Sash, which had campaigned hard against the passes and other repressive legislation, opened its membership to all races.

By the time it was obligatory for African women to carry passes, the Federation of South African Women had effectively ceased to exist although it was never dissolved. The government had attaked FSAW's leadership. As stated above, its first secretary, Ray Alexander, was banned almost immediately after FSAW's formation. Lilian Ngoyi and Helen Joseph, president and secretary, respectively, since 1955 were both defendants in the Treason Trial. Ngoyi was placed under severe bans and restrictions in 1961. Joseph became the first South African to be placed under "house arrest" in 1962 under the new law passed in 1962. Both Ngoyi and Joseph were kept under these orders until 1973.

It is clear that the government feared the organizational talents of the women since they restricted so many of them during this period. The fact that it took the government eleven years to put its 1952 pass legislation into effect is another indication of the power of the women.

Former ANC president and Nobel Peace Prize winner Albert Luthuli later wrote about the women's actions:

Among us Africans, the weight of resistance has been greatly
increased in the last few years by the emergence of our women. It
may even be true that, had the women hung back, resistance would
still have been faltering and uncertain. . . .

The demonstration made a great impact, and gave strong impetus-
. . . Furthermore, women of all races have had far less hesitation than
men in making common cause about things basic to them.[31]

Helen Joseph concluded that:

Many people see the Pass Campaign as a failure. I see it as an
incredible success in what it achieved . . . in what it was responsible
for - the fact that thousands of women resisted authority and went to
jail.[32]

When asked what the legacy of that time is for now, she answered:

A legacy of self-confidence, of hope because I'm sure you realize that
not one of the people you speak to has any doubt whatsoever about
what the ultimate future's going to be. I think we inherited a legacy of
hope and defiance and passed it on.[33]

Subsequent events in Soweto, Crossroads, Majeng, and many
other places indicate that the legacy was, indeed, passed on to
future generations.

THE BLACK CONSCIOUSNESS MOVEMENT

A period of intense repression followed the Sharpeville Massacre
and the declaration of the state of emergency. With the ANC and
PAC banned, the possibilities of African trade union organizing
weakened and the Federation of South African Women dissolved in
all but name after most of its leaders were banned in 1963. A period
of ostensible political inactivity became inevitable. While the level of
the armed struggle for men and women in Zimbabwe and Namibia,
neighboring countries with similar political, economic, and military
control by the white majority rapidly expanded during this period,
the South African regime precluded this in South Africa by building
its powerful police and military state with an increase in military
spending of 4,230 percent from the time of Sharpeville to the
1978/1979 budget.[34]

On the surface, women turned toward activities to ease the
burdens of the deprivations created by apartheid. Thus, the African

Self-Help Association, formed in 1964, established numerous day-care centers and children's feeding programs.

However, during this time, the ANC and PAC began to develop an underground inside South Africa, as well as operations in exile. The roots of what has become known as the Black Consciousness Movement (BCM) developed inside South Africa also. A new, dynamic generation of youthful leaders grew up during this period to complement the experience of those involved for so very long.

Although many people outside South Africa think of Steve Biko as the only important BCM figure, there have been many others, both men and women. Mapetla Mohapi, like Biko, died in police custody in August 1976. His wife, Nohle Mohapi, has been severely restricted and detained. Barney and Dimza Pityana, former leaders in SASO, the South African Students' Organization, an important BCM organization, now live in exile. Among the important women leaders are Dr. Maphela Ramphele, who ran a Black Consciousness self-help clinic in King Williamstown, and Thenjie Mtintso, a journalist. Ramphele has been banished to a remote area in the Northern Transvaal, and Mtintso, arrested and banned several times, is in exile. Others are Thoko Mpumlwana, the former editor of the BCM program publication *Black Review*, and Nikiwe Deborah Matshoba, former literary director of SASO, who have both been detained and are now under banning orders. The Black Peoples Convention (BPC) had a woman, Winnifred Kgware, as its first president.

Thenjie Mtintso described what Black Conscoiusness means:

> Black Consciousness has the outstanding feature of teaching the black man.... It has got this effect of psychological freedom which we have not had for decades. Black Consciousness says to the black men, "whatever you have been doing so far, you have been trying to emulate whites. You have lost your values. You have been uprooted. Now go back to your roots and from there you can emerge as a man in your own right. Black Consciousness goes on to black solidarity and black power."[35]

This is not to say that Black Consciousness is antiwhite, but it does call for new strategies. Mtintso discussed what this means:

> Whatever we do in this country, be it on the economic, social or political level, it has to be by blacks for blacks, period. It doesn't matter how well-meaning white people may be...they can never deliver me from the hands of the Nationalist...whatever they do,

they must try to work within their own community and concentrate on liberating their counterparts. I'll be doing the same thing in the black community.[36]

Helen Joseph, one of the crucial white leaders opposing apartheid for decades, believes that in the present context, whites must be content with a supportive role and accept what some interpret as an apparent rejection of their full participation. She said, "There isn't the same opportunity now. Don't forget that the whites that identified themselves with the struggle of the people for justice were very few."[37] Others, such as Winnie Mandela, disagree that whites are rejected as participants in the liberation struggle:

> Black Consciousness means to develop the awareness in people, to develop their pride, and it does not confine itself to blacks only. Black people include all the oppressed peoples of this country whatever the shade of their skin. All those who are prepared to honor what we are fighting for...are included in this concept.[36]

Without the passes themselves as an issue, others emerged or resurfaced and drew women back into the political world. An African woman, who asked to remain anonymous, described her own evolution:

> I lived in a women's hostel where most of the women had children. Many could barely sleep worrying about where their children were staying—with strangers, or old grannies—paying out most of their money so their children could survive. Still they could not see them. This experience turned me around....
>
> If the government had set out to create a society that would consume itself, it couldn't have done better. It has destroyed our family life, left the homelands fatherless with mothers struggling to help the remains of their family survive. Either the women must go mad or revolt.[39]

BLACK WOMEN'S FEDERATION

In December 1975, 210 delegates representing forty-one organizations gathered in Durban to found the Black Women's Federation (BWF).

The BWF had roots similar to the Federation of South African Women which, as has been described, was multiracial and very powerful until 1963 when most leaders were banned. The 1975 organization had the same objectives but allowed only black membership because it was based on opposition to the legislation governing blacks.

Fatima Meer, the prominent sociologist at Natal University, became the first president. Ms. Meer discussed its purposes:

> Mainly...to galvanize black women, to bring them together and consolidate grievances and create opportunities for them to do something, to help themselves and to help the general South Africa situation to move towards change.[40]

She credited the Black Consciousness Movement with:

> having infused into the black person that even if the official structure does not use him, does not place him in places of decision-making...he himself has the ability to do this, to manage his own government.[41]

The BWF worked both in urban and rural areas—something that its predecessor did not do. It attempted to teach women to realize their own potential and to increase their awareness and level of education. It formed literacy, nutrition, and health classes. It was starting to establish small cottage industries. It was preparing to work in the areas of housing, trade unions, rural development, and the legal disabilities of black women.

The government acted swiftly to crush the BWF. Within a year, seven leaders were detained. Fatima Meer was banned. Winnie Mandela and Sally Motlana, the vicepresident of the South African Council of Churches, were both detained. Ms. Deborah Mabiletsa, who became president when Mrs. Meer was banned, reflected:

> While our leader is banned let us not be afraid. We are all leaders, let us ask ourselves what each can contribute.

> The ban is not directed at Mrs. Meer alone, but to everyone of us. You or me might be next, today or tomorrow[42]

In fact, the entire organization was banned in October 1977.

SOWETO UPRISINGS

South African women have become articulate spokespeople about the June 1976 Soweto uprisings during which South African youths put their lives on the line to protest Bantu Education, which their parents had been fighting against for more than two decades. The BCM only served to increase the awareness of youth of the hated "Bantu laws." At least 600 children were killed by the South African police when they demonstrated in the streets.

Sikose Mji, a BCM member, described her initiation into the uprisings:

> One morning I decided I also had to participate, I also had a part to play—and I joined the crowd...there had been already lots of killings, and the children were playing in the streets, when suddenly a police van passed, a young seven-year old child raised his fist and said to the plice: 'POWER' - whereupon the policeman got off the van and aimed at the child and shot at him directly.... When the police started to shoot that is when students picked up stones, hit back, and took dustbin lids to protect themselves,...[43]

Nkosazana Dlamini, the former vicepresident of SASO, discussed the reaction of parents and their role after the killings:

> Even initially, during the peaceful demonstrations, parents supported the pupils.... But what really thrust the parents into action was the brutal police killings. The police had always been ruthless with peaceful demonstrators, but nobody expected the cold-blooded murder of young children. So besides their solidarity with young people they were angered—and their hatred and rejection of the whole system came to the surface. They were completely with the students in their militancy. Even the workers' strikes were very successful.[44]

The Western press portrayed a South African resistance divided by age, in addition to race, culture and sex. Fatima Meer said that "the outside world seems to think there is some kind of conflict between the younger and older generation. Meanwhile, there is no such conflict at all. They're all one in their rejection of the system.[45]

Meer also felt that the Soweto uprisings had a special significance for black women which was similar to their reaction to the introduction of passes for women:

> And when they see their children die, their feelings are more intense. They become more activated...their role is no different from other black South Africans or even white South Africans who have the welfare of their country at heart, have to play. But from history, I would say the black women will play it far more actively, she will be more involved.[46]

Ms. Gladys Tsolo, a PAC activist, affirmed this viewpoint:

> ...Once the kids had committed themselves, the parents felt that they had to become involved themselves. The women became specially active ... The women were always on the scene because of their great social activism.[47]

Soweto is now a symbolic rallying cry of South African blacks when they discuss resistance. It does not, however, symbolize young against old or women versus men. Thenjie Mtintso said, "If you were to ask the enlightened black woman what her priorities are, she wouldn't say women's liberation. She would say freedom, freedom."[48]

THE WOMEN OF CROSSROADS

Just as Soweto has come to symbolize black resistance to "Bantu laws," so Crossroads has come to symbolize resistance to the policy of forced migration. Crossroads is a so-called "squater camp" in the Cape Town area.

While the women in Crossroads fiercely defended their homes, most have valiantly tried but failed. A group was moved from Majeng to Vaslboschoek, some eighty kilometers away, in 1975 after a two year legal battle. In February 1975, ten women marched the eighty kilometers back to Majeng. They were arrested for trespassing in their own homes. They refused to pay the fines imposed and remained in jail.[49] In March, police arrested twenty-seven more women on their way back to Majeng.[50] These women did not regain their homes.

The government announced in 1977 that the camp would be demolished and the 20,000 residents would be sent to the Transkei. While this has been a consistent technique of the regime to prevent the formation of a stable urban population, the determination of the women in Crossroads proved formidable. They organized the Crossroads Women's Movement. Contrary to the government's propaganda that Crossroads is a transient camp, the average length of time that heads of households have lived there is 18.2 years while that for spouses is 11.7 years. Even so, because of the very complicated and restrictive legislation that keeps urban families apart, less than 10 percent of the spouses are legally in Crossroads.[51] This, of course, serves to increase their vulnerability to the police. It is the women who risk most through harrassment and arrest by the police. But it is also the women who have no future outside Crossroads, away from their husbands and families. For them it is Crossroads or nothing.

In spite of their legal problems, the rallying cry of the women has been, "we are not moving." In June 1978, more than 200 women demonstrated at the Bantu Affairs Administration Board. Seven spokspeople expressed their grievances to the officials. They were all called in by the police ten days later. The police began conducting sweeping raids, arresting women and children in their homes and when they went to the wells for water. The women developed several strategies according to Regina Ntongana, one of their leaders:

> The women in the movement sat in parked cars near the wells for months and months until Crossroads was saved. As long as they were watching, the police didn't arrest people. I don't know why. Perhaps they are a little ashamed of what they're doing and don't like to be watched.[52]

Ms. Ntongana added that:

> We have fought so hard for the little progress we've made here. They used to come at all hours of the night and raid us. We women would warn each other and grab a blanket and sit together in the open field. There would be hundreds of us. They couldn't arrest all of us, and it was some protection. The babies and the men would stay in the shacks, except for the very little babies on their mother's backs. And sometimes, you would go to the well for water during the day and when you got back home, your shack was demolished. That happened to my family twice in other camps.[53]

In July, a multiracial crowd of between 4,000 and 5,000 people participated in a 2-1/2-hour prayer service for the preservation of the camp despite a police warning that the meeting was illegal.

The police expanded their raids in September. Eight hundred were arrested, and three people were shot—one of whom died. When the first lot of bulldozers arrived, the women sat down. Three people were killed. The women continued to protest. They sought and received international support.

> We are hurt. Three-month-old babies, and eleven-year-old children are in jail—pregnant women, and sick people. In jail, little babies are being fed on nothing but water all day long. Babies are crying. One man asked for some food for the children, and he got beaten up.[54]

Alexander Luke of the Crossroads Women's Committee summed up the spirit of the women:

> And when they came to demolish Crossroads, what will the women do? We are not going to move here in Crossroads. We are giong to stay. And build our houses again. They can take guns and shoot us.... We are not prepared to move. We don't want to move.[55]

Finally, in December 1978, the government, by then under massive international pressure which was rallied by the Crossroads community announced it would not force the residents to leave the Cape Town area. It appeared to be a remarkable victory for the women, although the authorities seem to be hedging on their position.

OTHER WOMEN'S ORGANIZATIONS

As has been demonstrated throughout this report, South African authorities have exhibited their fear of women organizing against apartheid by their fierce actions in attempting to silence the women's leaders of the most important federations, trade unions and liberation movement.

Over the past twenty-five years many more moderate women's groups have entered the sphere of race relations. As has already been mentioned, the Black Sash has been the best known and most active of these. Formed in 1955, it is now a multiracial group opposed to discrimination on the basis of race. It has protested the introduction of most of the major apartheid legislation, but has been especially concerned with influx control and the migrant labor system. Security legislation has severely limited the types of public protest Black Sash has generally employed in the past.

An individual woman whose views and actions have closely paralleled those of Black Sash in Helen Suzman. Ms. Suzman, a member of the Progressive Federal Party, has for decades been a lonely dissenting parliamentarian voting against apartheid legislation and challenging government repression.

Two groups were formed after international attention focused on women through the International Women's Year in 1975. Women for Peace was established in 1976 as a multiracial group seeking a "dialogue" among racial groups. Mrs. Bridget Oppenheimer, its cochairperson, called it a "totally nonpolitical organization."[56] A group of Afrikaans-speaking women formed Kontak in

1976 to promote contact with women of other racial groups, especially colored women. While both groups have received extensive publicity inside and outside South Africa, neither has entered the political sphere. An insight into the philosophy of the members of Kontak was given by one of its members, Gabriela Malan, when she justified the apartheid policy of separate development:

> I see this whole policy of separate development as an excellent policy. But now you find people moving out of the rural areas, coming to the big cities to work and you have to accommodate them. The best would be to do what they do in Japan—to move people with bullet trains into the white working areas by day and to take them back to their tribal homelands at night. I don't see why this country can't do it . . . we've got the money . . . this would be the ideal thing.[57]

In fact, the South African regime has attempted to use the women's issue in its international propaganda campaign. To mark the IWY, South Africa held a "World Convention of Eminent Women" in December 1975. The prime minister's wife, Tini Vorster, opened the meeting with the theme of "peace, goodwill, and equality for women." Not only did it not seriously address the racial issue, but its programs listed—without their permission—many of the world's best known women as participants, including then Prime Ministers Gandhi of India and Bandaranaike of Sri Lanka. Fatima Meer had challenged South Africans on the opening of the IWY:

> If South African women commemorate the year of women simply in terms of the disabilities of women alone, they will have completely overlooked the fact that over 90 percent of our women suffer disabilities not simply on account of their sex but principally on account of their colour.[58]

The situation inside South Africa reflects Meer's Apprehension.

In 1978, the Federal Council of the National Party published a propaganda booklet titled "Women—Our Silent Soldiers." It instructed white women to carefully monitor their servants by searching their rooms and belongings and observing their lifestyles, that is, to become unpaid spies for the government. It concluded with:

> None of us need have a guilt complex toward the people of a different skin color, because it is none other than the National Party which has

created opportunities for the colored, the Indian and the black man and has fostered a feeling of self-esteem and consciousness of identity among them.[59]

THE CONTINUING STRUGGLE OF WOMEN IN SOUTH AFRICA

In spite of the banning, detentions, arrests, killings, and harasment, the women inside heroically sustain their resistance. Fatima Meer's home was attacked by gunmen in December 1977.[60] Amina Desai, now aged fifty-nine, served five years under the Terrorism Act.[61]

Mavis Magulane was badly beaten while being detained for thirteen months without charge. She had a hole in her scalp through which her skull was visible and which took eight months to heal. A mother of six, she was arrested while attending her husband's trial in September 1976. He was sentenced to fifteen years.[62]

Winnie Mandela was charged with breaking her banning order in January 1978. Four white women were convicted of "obstructing the course of justice" by refusing to discuss their visits to Mandela. Helen Joseph, now seventy-four received only four months because of her heart condition. Illona Kleinschmidt, Jackie Bosman, and Barbara White were sentenced to one year in prison. They knew that if they made statements to police they would have to later testify against Winnie Mandela under South African law. Winnie Mandela was convicted in February 1978 of receiving visitors without permission and attending a social gathering.[63]

After fifteen consecutive years of bannings and house arrests, sixty-year-old Albertina Sisulu was given a new two-year banning order in August 1979.[64]

Thus, the regime has not reduced the repression against the women leaders. But neither have the women reduced their resistance.

THE AFRICAN NATIONAL CONGRESS AND THE PAN AFRICANIST CONGRESS OF AZANIA IN EXILE

While both the ANC and PAC maintain underground operations inside South Africa, many of their members are in exile as a result of their being banned as organizations. Women are very active in both the ANC and PAC.

Many of the women mentioned in the historical account of the women's role in fighting apartheid were related to the ANC. This is partially due to the fact that the PAC was established in 1959 after many of the important campaigns had taken place.

However, since its formation, women have played key roles in the PAC. Elizabeth Sibeko, who along with Gertrude Mathutha is a member of the PAC's Central Committee, explained this:

Many of these liberation forces are women who play important roles in the liberation struggle. In the PAC of Azania we have a lot of women, especially young activists who have themselves played a key role in our struggle for liberation.... Many of the women members of the PAC both inside and outside of Azania have been in the forefront of the struggle.... These women have been harassed by the police and even detained themselves. Ms. Urbaniah Mothopeng, the sixty-four-year-old wife of Zeth Mothopeng of the PAC Bethal eighteen trials...was arrested in August 1977 together with her husband...for furthering the aims and objectives of the PAC. Ms. Mothopeng was beaten up in jail and detained for a year leaving a blind son home in Soweto. Ms. Mark Shinner was harassed by the police along with the wives of the other Bethal eighteen members. There are countless names of PAC women activists who have played a leading role in the struggle whose names I cannot reveal for fear of reprisals.[65]

The ANC Women's Section now operates in exile under the leadership of Florence Mphosho, who had herself been extremely active inside South African before being banned.

Both the ANC and PAC have been infused with many youthful members who left South Africa after Soweto. Women from both liberation movements are being given extensive training to perform functions at all levels. They do a great deal of the organizing in the refugee camps where they perform health, welfare, and educational work.

Women from the liberation movements also travel extensively internationally to educate people of other nations about apartheid and about their plight as women under apartheid.

Women along with men, reenter South Africa with grave risk, in order to carry out missions for the liberation movements. While the level of the armed struggle is not as advanced as those of Namibia or Zimbabwe, there is no doubt that ANC and PAC women are being prepared for armed combat.

Elizabeth Sibeko said that "the activity of women during the fight for freedom is the only way to ensure their full participation when we have true majority control.[66] Dulcie September, leader of the branch of the ANC Women's Section of the United Kingdom and Europe, declared that "we women have always been active and leaders. But we are not fighting our men but the apartheid regime. We are now one with the men and with the youth. We will be one with them after liberation and we will have achieved a status for women we never would have thought possible twenty years ago."[67]

There is little doubt that those inside South Africa who strongly oppose the regime are supporters—whether overtly or covertly— of the liberation movements. Even people in the Black Consciousness Movement, whom the Western press frequently portray as rivals of the liberation movements, do not themselves think this way. Sikose Mji affirms this:

> While the Black Consciousness Movement within South Africa and the liberation movement are separate movements, the two movements came about when there was a vacuum created by the absence of the liberation movement within the country. Something really had to keep people going.... The Black Consciousness Movement could never have replaced the liberation movement and when the black consciousness movement was formed we were very aware of its shortcomings and the fact that it didn't really go far enough.[68]

Internationally, the ANC and PAC are widely recognized as the organizations representing the true opinions of freedom-loving South Africans. They are boldly preparing for their country's liberation and, at the same time, laying the ground-work for a new society. Women are now playing key roles in these combined processes.

CONCLUSIONS

As in most societies, there is no doubt that the top leadership positions in organization in South Africa opposing apartheid and racism have been held by men. However, women have frequently been the ones to raise the primary issues and to organize and involve the people around those issues.

In almost all cases, women were first brought into the struggle when they saw the attempt by the government to destroy their family structure and with it the basic fabric of their respective societies. Thus, in South Africa, women reacted most vigorously to the introduction of passes in the 1950s and the consequential restrictions on families; to the mass killings of their children two decades later in Soweto; and to the attempt to destroy urban family life as epitomized by Crossroads.

The involvement of women took different forms. Women were very active in trade unions and in women's federations. Participation in political parties was not meaningful since African voting rights were virtually nonexistent. Active women most frequently operate through the respective liberation movements. The Black Consciousness Movement in South Africa has been a major centre of activity in the 1970s.

That the women have had a significant impact in South Africa is beyond question. Women have participated in ever-increasing numbers both inside South Africa and in exile, always with escalating risks to themselves individually and to the groups they represent. The level of risk is reflected by how severe government repression against the women has been. In South Africa one can hardly think of a prominent organizer who has not been detained, baned, or imprisoned. By eliminating the leadership, the authorities destroyed the Federation of South African Women. When this tactic did not work with the Black women's Federation, it banned the entire group. The authorities have fully appreciated the power of the women and responded accordingly.

The African men have gradually moved toward accepting the women as equal participants in the struggle although this appears less true than in Zimbabwe, Namibia, Angola and Mozambique where the women functioned as armed combatants in their liberation struggles. While women have by no means reached parity with men in leadership roles, great progress toward this has been achieved. Among other reasons for this are increased education, the equalizing effects of their common oppression on racial grounds, and the example of other nation's experiences. Finally, as women have had to take on many of the roles that had been exclusively male roles when husbands left as migrant laborers, the patriarchal society has begun to be broken down.[69]

The ability of the women's movement to reach all segments of society has been less encouraging. The activities have been centred in urban areas to the exclusion of the rural areas.

According to those in the struggle, there is little gap between young and old, at least in their objectives. White women have been prominent in the struggle in South Africa, even if their numbers were few. Events important to the women have seemed to transcend educational or economic backgrounds.

It is not easy to judge to what degree the women were able to meet their short-term objectives. In South Africa, the women won the early antipass campaign, did achieve a roll-back of bus fares and did apparently save Crossroads. They did not end "Bantu Education," and have had to accept passes even though they withstood the final imposition for eleven years. However, in the light of all the odds against them in these major campaigns, it would have to be concluded that, on balance, the women did make an effective contribution to the struggle for liberation.

It is certain that the women of South Africa have increasingly attracted the attention and solidarity of women and men internationally. The fact that the 980 World Conference of the UN Decade for Women had a major agenda item on this very topic is a very important indication. The importance of such solidarity was expressed by Winnie Mandela:

> Over the past fifteen years, when I was confined and restricted . . . I got my inspiration from the very knowledge . . . that the struggle is an international struggle for the dignity of man and . . . just that knowledge alone that we belong to a family of man in a society where we have been completely rejected by a minority. . . . this alone sustains you.[70]

No rational person can doubt that the same forces of history that have swept out the racist regimes in the north must also engulf South Africa. The questions that remain are how it will happen and when it will happen. Winnie Mandela gives us an indication of how it will happen:

> It is only when all black groups join hands and speak with one voice that we shall be a bargaining force which will decide its own destiny. . . . We know what we want. . . . We are not asking for majority rule; it is our right, we shall have it at any cost. We are aware that the road before us is uphill, but we shall fight to the bitter end for justice. . . . [71]

The women have historically had a major role to play in this. It is critical that they be afforded all the assistance they deem necessary both to win the fight and then to reconstruct their societies.

While death has taken Lilian Ngoyi from her people, her spirit and that of other South African women lives on today. Lilian Ngoyi, who lived most of her later years under banning, proudly told the world in the few months that she was unrestricted:

> You can tell my friends all over the world that this girl is still her old self, if not more mature after all the experiences. I am looking forward to the day when my children will share in the wealth of our lovely South Africa.[72]

NOTES

1. This article is adapted from research done by the author on behalf of the 1980 World Conference of the United Nations Decade for Women. The research resulted in a World Conference report on "The role of women in the struggle for liberation in Zimbabwe, Namibia and South Africa."

2. Richard Lapchick, Interview with Bettie du Toit, London, April 1979.

3. The Industrial Conciliation Act of 1924 (mentioned in the text); the Wage Act of 1925 which protected white workers by granting higher wages to "white job" categories; and the Apprenticeship Act of 1922 which banned blacks from apprenticeship due to their lack of education.

4. Lapchick, *op. cit.*

5. *Ibid.*

6. Bettie du Toit, *Ukubamba Amadolo: Workers Struggle in the South African Textile Industry*, London, Onyz Press, 1978.

7. *Ibid.* By 1974, the figure had dropped to 9 percent white.

8. The Industrial Legislation Commission (1950) enforced *apartheid* by law in the trade unions; the Suppression of Communism Act allowed fifty-six trade union activists to be banned by 1955. The Industrial Legislation Bill (1956) made job reservations the law.

9. Black Women's Federation, *Conference Report* - 1975.

10. Hilda Watts Bernstein, *For their Triumph and for their Tears, Women in Apartheid South Africa*, London: International Defence and Aid Fund for Southern Africa 1975.

11. The Congress Alliance was made up of the African National Congress, the Indian Congress, the Coloured Peoples Congress, the Congress of Democrats, as well as many of the progressive trade unions.

12. Deborah Mav, Interview with Francis Baard, January 1979, transcript of interviews for film *Amandla*.

13. Muriel Horrell, *A Survey of Race Relations in South Africa, 1955-57.*

14. Nancy Van Vuuren, *Women Against Apartheid: The Fight for Freedom in South Africa*, Palo Alto, 1979.

15. *Ibid.*

16. Mary Benson, "Struggle for a Birthright," in Bernstein, *op. cit.*

17. Deborah May, Interview with Helen Joseph, January 1979, transcript of interview for film *Amandla*.

18. Hansard, Vol. 7, Col 1656-1666.

19. A fact sheet prepared by the FSAW simply listing actions for 1957-58 took seven pages to complete, in "Federation of South African Women," a paper presented by Cheryll Walker to Conference on History of Opposition in South Africa, January 1978.

20. May, Joseph Interview, *op. cit.*

21. Lapchick, *op. cit.*

22. May, Baard Interview, *op. cit.*

23. Muriel Horrell, *A Survey of Race Relations in South Africa, 1956-57.*

24. *Ibid.*

25. *Ibid.*

26. *Ibid.*

27. Rev. Charles Hooper, *A Brief Authority*, London: Collins, 1960.

28. May, Joseph Interview, *op. cit.*

29. Winnie Mandela, from a speech to Soweto residents in June 1976, as reprinted in *Winnie Mandela: Profile in Courage and Defiance*, UN Centre against *Apartheid*, Notes and Documents Series, No. 1/78 (February 1978).

30. Muriel Horrell, *A Survey of Race Relations in South Africa, 1961.*

31. Albert Luthuli, *Let my People Go: An Autobiography*, London: Collins, 1962.

32. May, Joseph Interview, *op. cit.*

33. *Ibid.*

34. *Rand Daily Mail*, Johannesburg, 30 March 1978.

35. June Goodwin, from the manuscript of her forthcoming book due to be published in 1980.

36. *Ibid.*

37. May, Joseph Interview, *op. cit.*

38. Winnie Mandela, from an Interview with the South African News Agency, March 1976, in *Profile, op. cit.*

39. Goodwin, *op. cit.*

40. Black Women's Federation, *Conference Report of December 1975.*

41. *Ibid.*

42. *Ibid.*

43. Sikose Mji, Testimony on Repression in South Africa.

44. Nkosazana Dlamini, "Interview", in *Southern Africa*, March 1977.

45. Almust Hielscher, Interview with Fatima Meer, in draft of report prepared by Ruth Weiss and Peter Chappel for UNESCO.

46. Hielscher, *op. cit.*

47. Gladys Tsolo, unpublished interview, 1 November 1978.

48. Goodwin, *op. cit.*

49. *Rand Daily Mail*, Johannesburg, 15 February 1976.

50. *Ibid.*, 9 March 1976.

51. Horrell, et. al., *A Survey of Race Relations in South Africa, 1978.*

52. Shelby Howatt, Interview with Regina Ntgonana, Crossroads, June 1979 (for future publication).

53. *Ibid.*

54. Women's Committee Statement of 15 September 1978, in "We will not move: the Struggle for Crossroads," by the National Union of South Africa Students.

55. Deborah May, Interview with Alexandre Luke, January 1979, from transcript of interviews for the film *AMANDLA.*

56. *Sunday Times*, Johannesburg, 7 November 1976.

57. Goodwin, *op. cit.*

58. Report of the Women's Teach-In, Durban, 15 February 1975.

59. Federal Council of the National Party, "Women-Our Silent Soldiers," August 1978.

60. *Rand Daily Mail*, Johannesburg, 13 December 1977.

61. *Citizen*, Pretoria, 6 January 1978.

62. *Post*, Transvaal, 18 January 1978.

63. Post, Transvaal, 18 January 1978, *International Herald Tribune*, Paris, 24 January 1978, and the *Rand Daily Mail*, 10 February 1978.

64. *Post*, Transvaal, 1 August 1979.

65. Elizabeth Sibeko, Speech to the Second Meeting of the Preparatory Committee of the World Conference for the UN Decade for Women, at UN Headquarters, New York, 3 September 1979.

66. Richard Lapchick, Interview with Elizabeth Sibeko, New York, 4 September 1979.

67. Richard Lapchick, Interview with Dulcie September, London, 18 April 1979.

68. Sikose Mji, Interview, in *Southern Africa*, December 1976.

69. Silisi, H. "How African Women Cope with Migrant Labour in South Africa," *Signs*, Vol. 3, No. 1, pp. 167-177.

70. Winnie Mandela, *Profile, op. cit.*

71. Mandela,*op. cit.*

72. Bernstein, *op. cit.*

Child of migrant workers in care of grandmother in North Carolina. Photo: United Nations/S. Rotner, No. 141 925. (1978)

Part II:
UNITED STATES OF AMERICA

Photo: Rudolph R. Robinson.

The United States of America

INTRODUCTORY SUMMARY

The section of the black woman in the United States presents a number of contributions which deal with the black woman in historical perspective, the myth of the black matriarchy, the impact of racism and sexism, and the image of the black woman in literature. Ladner's chapter gives a history of black womanhood from its African roots through slavery, and discusses the importance of the family unit, the close bond between the mother and her children, and the multiplicity of factors that acted to mold the black family. Above all, she stresses the need to understand the political context of racism and poverty that influence black families all over the world.

During slavery various forms of resistance were practiced by slaves. Female slave resistance was directed against her sexual oppression. Hine and Wittenstein analyze the economic implications of such acts as sexual abstinence, abortion, infanticide, and feigning pregnancy as rejections of the vital economic role of black women as reproducers of the exploitative slave system.

Perkin's chapter discusses the important role played by women in improving the conditions of their race during the antebellum period. Activities included self-help through mutual aid and benevolent societies, and efforts to abolish slavery. Discrimination even existed in anti-slavery societies from which blacks, with few exceptions, were barred. She also discusses the concept of racial obligation which was very much linked to the concept of racial 'uplift'.

The controversial thesis of the black matriarchy has been extensively discussed since the publication of Moynihan's report, *The Negro Family: The Case for National Action*. The chapter by Staples dispels this myth as a divisive tool for facilitating white domination. He points out the danger of such a myth in emasculating black males by depicting them as ineffective husbands and fathers who are mere caricatures of men.

The lifelong conditions of poverty and racism have resulted in, among other things, the chronic unemployment of black males. Stack examines survival strategies for black women in urban areas, particularly the interplay between the two main factors, namely, the maximization of relationships within the domestic network, and dependency on the precarious social welfare system.

Victimization by the criminal justice system is one of the most destructive ways in which racism and poverty affect black families. Additionally, the criminal justice system can be viewed as sexist or, according to French, "separate but masculine." The chapter by French focuses on the abuse of female inmates who are often poor, undereducated and black. The criminal justice system also denies the black female the extra legal protection associated with female status.

The implication of the feminist movement for the black women in America has been a controversial topic mainly because of the complexity posed by issues of racism. The institutionalization of racism has been so effectively executed in the United States that it even permeated the women's liberation movement for almost a century. Terborg-Penn examines the black female experience in the history of reform movements in the United States, particularly the Women's Movement from 1830 to 1920. She shows how institutionalized discrimination against black women by white women traditionally has led to the development of racially separate groups that address themselves to race.

In view of the oppressive conditions under racism black women, in addition to developing survival strategies through social networks, have used music for cathartic purposes. Jackson's chapter is an examination of black women's involvement in music, and a demonstration that black women are in fact the essential bearers of certain musical traditions.

Rushing contrasts the images of white consciousness with that presented in Afro-American poetry. Naturalness and beauty are also images used, but Rushing feels that in recent years moral, intellectual, and political stances have become more critical than physical beauty. According to Rushing, the main attraction of the images of the black woman in Afro-American poetry lies in the fact that they at once express the agony of life and the possibility of conquering it through sheer toughness of spirit.

1
Racism and Tradition: Black Womanhood in Historical Perspective

Joyce A. Ladner

Black womanhood has become a popular topic of discussion during the past decade, when social analysts, policy makers, community leaders, and others became concerned about the so-called plight of the black family and sought to intervene in this institution in an effort to "uplift" it from its alleged decay and disorganization. This focus on the black family and its women began decades ago when E. Franklin Frazier asserted in *The Negro Family in the United States* that the family is matriarchal and disorganized as a result of having inherited the legacy of slavery, and as a result of the mass migration to the cities which causes further disruption. In 1939 Frazier wrote the following:

> when one undertakes to envisage the probable course of develop-
> ment of the Negro family in the future, it appears that the travail of
> civilization is not yet ended. First it appears that the family which
> evolved within the isolated world of the Negro folks will become
> increasingly disorganized. Modern means of communication will
> break down the isolation of the world of black folk, and, as long as the
> bankrupt system of southern agriculture exists, Negro families will
> continue to seek a living in the towns and cities of the country. They
> will crowd the slum areas of southern cities or make their way to
> northern cities where their family life will become disrupted and
> their poverty will force them to depend upon charity.... the ordeal of
> civilization will be less severe if there is a general improvement in the
> standard of living and racial barriers to employment are broken
> down. Moreover, the chances for normal family life will be increased

if large-scale modern housing facilities are made available for the masses of the Negro population in the cities. Nevertheless, those families which possess some heritage of family life and traditions and education will resist the destructive forces of urban life more successfully than the illiterate Negro folk and in either case their family life will adapt itself to the secular and rational organization of urban life.[1]

During subsequent periods, analyses of various aspects of the black family life were conducted, including the works of Charles S. Johnson (*Growing Up in the Black Belt*), Allison Davis and John Dollard (*Children of Bondage*), St. Clair Drake and Horace R. Cayton (*Black Metropolis*), Hylan Lewis (*Black ways of Kent*) and others. All of these works generally followed the Frazierian thesis by tactily comparing the black family to that of the white middle class, and thereby emphasizing its weaknesses, instead of attempting to understand the nature of its strengths—strengths which emerged and withstood formidable odds against oppression.

All of the classic studies which have investigated black life and culture have focused on the attitudes and behavior of blacks. None have dealt with the structural effects of oppression, or with specific ways to change the social system so that it no longer produces its devastating effects on black people. Because of this faulty conceptualization of the nature of the real problem—oppression as the source—the attitudes and behavior of blacks became the object of considerable stigmatization because they did not conform to the American status quo. The strong resilience and modes of adaptation which black people developed to combat the forces of poverty and racism, produced by neocolonialism, were *never* recognized as important areas of intellectual inquiry. Indeed, many students of black life and culture so emphasized the "pathological" that the positive features were virtually unknown. Thus, the dominant trend of thought came to be that which purports that blacks do not value family life. Martin Luther King once voiced strong sentiments to the contrary when he said: "... for no other group in American life is the matter of family life more important than to the Negro. Our very survival is bound up in it.... no one in all history had to fight against so many physical and psychological horrors to have a family life."[2]

The work of black sociologist Andrew Billingsley is the first comprehensive study of the black family that attempts to assess its strengths instead of concentrating on its weaknesses. His volume, *Black Families in White America*, also places the family in a historical perspective as it relates to the African background, slavery in the Americas, etc.[3]

The black woman is again emerging as an important figure within the family and community, to be investigated and reinterpreted in light of the foregoing discussion.

Because there has been much controversy and concern over the black woman, and since there are a great number of misconceptions and myths about who she is, what her functions are, and what her relationship to the black man in fact is, it is necessary that one understand some of the historical background that has shaped her into the entity she has become. It is important to realize that most of the analyses concerned with black women (largely the poor) are ahistorical and do not attempt to place them in the context of the African background, through slavery and into the modern era. Indeed, scholars generally assume that blacks were stripped of their heritage during slavery. (This will be discussed more fully below).

It would seem impossible to understand what the black woman is today without having a perspective on what her forebears were, especially as this relates to the roles, functions and responsibilities she has traditionally held within the family unit. This, of course, will involve her relationship to her husband, children, and the extended family. Only by understanding these broader sociohistorical factors can we properly interpret her role today.

There are basically three periods relating to the black woman included in this analysis: (1). the African background; (2). slavery; and (3). the modern era. In discussing the black woman from a historical perspective, it is important to know that there is no monolithic concept of *the* black woman, but that there are many models of black womanhood. However, here is a common denominator, a common strand of history, that characterizes all black women: *oppression*.[4] Even though many black women today consider themselves middle-class and often are socialized in a tradition similar to that of middle class white women, the common ancestry and oppressive conditions under which all black people have had to live to varying degrees provide the strong similarities and commonalities. Therefore, this chapter will broadly focus on the black woman, taking into consideration the differences and similarities that have been mentioned.

THE AFRICAN BACKGROUND

Before Africans were brought to American shores, they had developed highly complex civilizations along the West Coast, the area where a considerable amount of slave trading occurred. Tribal customs and laws for marriage and the family, property rights, wealth, political institutions and religion revolved around distinct patterns of culture which had evolved out of the history of the African people. Family patterns were viable entities unto themselves and were not influenced by, nor modeled after, the Western tradition of the monogamous unit; and strong protective attitudes toward kinsmen, including the extended family, likewise had their legitimate origin within African societies and were highly functional for African people. John Hope Franklin states that, "At the basis even of economic and political life in Africa was the family, with its inestimable influence over its individual members."[5] The family was extended in form, and acted as a political, economic, and religious unit. All of these institutional functions and arrangements took place within the broader extended family presided over by the patriarch. Another writer has noted that, "Although there were various types of states, the fundamental unit politically . . . was the family. . . . It was a kinship group numbering in the hundreds, but called a family because it was made up of the living descendants of a common ancestor. The dominant figure in this extended community was the patriarch, who exercised a variety of functions. . . . "[6]

A striking feature of precolonial African society was the importance that was attached to the family unit. The extended family was highly structured, with clearly designated roles for its male and female members. Marriage was always considered a ritual that occurred not between two individuals alone, but between all the members of the two extended families. It was a highly sacred ritual that involved bride price and othe exchanges of property. Often marriages were arranged by parents of the bride and groom but sometimes by the two consenting partners. The emphasis was placed upon the binding together of two individuals who represented different families, and upon the mutual duties and obligations they were to carry out for each other. The elderly were highly regarded if African society. The patriarch of the extended family, who was sometimes considered a chief, was usually an elderly man.

Since the families lived in tribes, most of the functions now considered extrafamilial were also carried out within the broader extended unit. These included providing for the family's food, clothing, shelter, recreation, religious instruction, and education. The family, through the tribe, also engaged in warfare against other hostile tribes. As a social system, the extended family was complete and autonomous. This independence perhaps encouraged the development of close ties between family members and a high regard for the sanctity of the family.

Notably, the roles of women in precolonial Africa were very important ones and quite different from the understood duties and obligations of women in Western society. Two of the important roles of the African woman perpetuated during slavery and continued until today are: (1). her economic function; and (2). the close bond she had with her children. Politically, women were very important to the administration of tribal affairs. Since lineage was often matrilineal (descent traced through the female), "Queen Mothers" and "Queen Sisters" assumed highly significant duties in the tribe. For example: "Each major official had a female counterpart known as his 'mother', who took precedence over him at court and supervised his work. When officials reported to the King, groups of women were present, whose duty was to remember what had happened."[7]

In attempting to explain the origin of the important roles played by women in precolonial African society, one historian has noted:

> There is a recurring theme in many African legends and mythology of a woman who is the founder or the mother of the tribe who is either a queen or the daughter of a king. She is an aristocratic lady who is involved in politics. For example, the creation myths of the Hausa people in Northern Nigeria or of Niger or Chad begin with a woman who goes out and founds a kingdom. She is the Black Moses who is leading her people into the promised land which is an area near the water where communication is relatively free. She settles down and establishes the traditions of the people.[8]

It is clear that the roles of women in precolonial West African societies were very different from those of women in Western society. Their positions of economic and political power could also be observed in the family.

One of the ways in which the role of women can be observed is in their relationship to children. The Queen Mother or Queen Sister among the Ashanti, who traced descent matrilineally, placed the woman in the highest order because of her role as procreator: "Like a mother's control of her children, a queen mother's authority depends on moral rather than legal sanctions and her position is a symbol of the decisive function of motherhood in the social system."[9] Furthermore, "as Ashanti often point out, a person's status, rank and fundamental rights stem from his mother, and that is why she is the most important person in his life."[10]

The relationship between mother and child was important in all of West Africa. Although there were clearly defined roles for adult men and women, with the male taking a strong role as the patriarch, there were still vital functions that the mother fulfilled for the children and which were reserved only for her. Thus, "the Ashanti regard the bond between mother and child as the keystone of all social relations."[11] Even in the societies where descent was patrilineal or double, there was a high regard for the mother's function as child bearer and perpetuator of the ancestral heritage. This emanates from the value that is attached to the childbearing powers of women. Barren women are pitied, if not outcasts, even today in much of Africa. Barrenness is often considered a legitimate reason for a man to seek a divorce from his wife. Similarly, women who bear great numbers of children are accorded high status.[12] This emphasis upon the woman's role does not underestimate the importance of the male as provider, disciplinarian, and teacher. The strong patriarchal figure was of utmost importance to the child's rearing, but the day-to-day contact was primarily with the mother.

Another area of importance with regard to women's roles in African society was their economic function as traders in the villages. Meier and Rudwick note that "Women played an important role in the administration of political and economic affairs. . . . They were the chief traders in the village."[13] Even in contemporary West African society, women still fulfill the important economic function as traders. Marie Perinbaum states: "The West African market woman is an institution in West Africa. She is the small capitalist, or the entrepreneur, and is sometimes one of the major cash winners of the family. She is also the one who brings in the consumer goods."[14] Melville Herskovits also describes the prominent role that women played as traders in the market, and indicates that some of them became independently wealthy as a result of their endeavors.[15]

These are the traditions and life-styles to which Africans were accustomed. As products of highly complex civilizations, with a high regard for the family—both living and dead—they must have been totally unprepared for the barbaric conditions to which they would be subjected in the New World. From the early seventeenth century to the mid-nineteenth century when slavery ended, approximately forty million Africans were brought to the United States. Historians note that slavery in the United States assumed the most cruel and harsh form, and was designed systematically to dehumanize its captives. All the highly developed institutions which were an integral part of African society were crushed (from their original form) and slaves had to fight to preserve whatever remnants of their civilization they could.

In this cursory view of the black woman's relationship to the African past one can observe that she was part of a cultural tradition that was very different from that which she was to enter in the New World. Thus, "The Negro who came to the New World varied widely in physical type and ways of life, but there were many common patterns of culture. Whatever the type of state, the varied groups all operated under orderly governments, with established legal codes, and under well-organized social systems. The individual might find it necessary to submerge his will into the collective will, but he shared a deep sense of group indentity, a feeling of belonging."[16] The degradation a woman suffered in slavery had total effects on all aspects of her life—her identity as a woman and as an African, her relationship and roles with regard to her husband and family.

SLAVERY

When Africans were sold into slavery they were introduced to an alien culture and an attempt was made to force them to adopt the way of life of Western society. The highly organized social order from which they emerged was considered "barbarous" and "uncivilized" because of the inability of Europeans to understand and appreciate the cultural differences which set them apart from the Africans. Because of the fact that slavery was engaged in for economic reasons, Africans became property and were thus denied the rights of human beings. They were not publicly allowed to practice their native religions, speak their native languages, nor engage in the numerous other cultural traditions which were characteristic of African society. Obviously the effects were devastating on the family, which, in fact, could not be recognized as the one they had been part of in Africa, notably in its structure. Legal marriage was denied, allowing for the emergence of the ephemeral quality of male-female liaisons. Men were denied the right to fulfill the long-standing tradition of patriarch over the extended family, and women, in effect, became the backbone of the family. Parents were denied the right to exercise authority over their children, an important aspect of African culture. Especially absent was the function of the economic provider, disciplinarian, and teacher, strong characteristics of the African male.

Of considerable importance is the emphasis slaveholders placed upon the legal contract between slave and master as well as the various informal sanctions of slavery. Quarles notes, "All slaves were inculcated with the idea that the whites ruled from God and that to question this divine right-white theory was to incur the wrath of heaven, if not to call for a more immediate sign of displeasure here below."[17] Numerous legal restrictions were enacted to prohibit the slave from exercising his rights as a free person. In spite of these restrictions, there were many outward signs of rebellion against the mores of the slave masters. The structure and processes of slave family life have not been adequately documented because of the scarcity of information recorded by slaves. Yet there are some data concerning the family and, particularly important for the purposes of this analysis, the role of women in slave society.

Most of the accounts of the relationships between slaves and their regard for each other are to be taken from slave narratives and autobiographies of ex-slaves such as Frederick Douglass, Nat Turner, and Sojourner Truth. These provide information about the role women in particular played within the family and society. It must be noted that these frequently differ from the analyses and portraits some historians have given. One of the positions that has been advanced by social scientists is that slaves rarely developed strong familial bonds with each other because of the disruptive nature of their family and community life. This position runs counter to the firsthand accounts given by slaves. For it will be observed that the family during slavery, with all its modifications, was a strong unit in that parents were able oftentimes to impart certain values and cultural ethos to their offspring. It appears that whenever it was economically feasible for this family pattern to emerge, parents sought to exert this responsibility. The family was also extended in form whenever it was economically feasible.

Nat Turner, the revolutionary, provides information about his relationship with his parents and grandmother. In his own *Confessions*, he speaks of the religious instruction he received from his grandmother, to whom he was closely attached, and of the encouragement he received from his mother and father to become a prophet. He states: "My father and mother strengthened me in this my first impression, saying in my presence, I was intended for some great purpose, which they had always thought from certain marks on my head and breast."[18]

Frederck Douglass, the noted abolitionist, in the *Life and Times of Frederick Douglass* describes the close relationship he had with his grandmother, who cared for him in the absence of his mother. Douglass states: "If my poor, dear old grandmother now lives, she lives to remember and mourn of the the loss of children, the loss of grandchildren and the loss of great-grandchildren... My poor old grandmother, the devoted mother of 12 children is left alone...."[19] On one occasion he remembers his own mother, who had been sold to another plantation, slipping into their home in the night to see him: "I was grander upon my mother's knee than a king upon his throne.... I dropped off to sleep, and waked in the morning to find my mother gone.... My mother had walked twelve miles to see me, and had the same distance to travel again before the morning sunrise."[20]

Sojourner Truth, the prophet and leader, who referred to slaves as Africans, provides a vivid account of the trauma her mother suffered when she was separated from her children. She recounts: "I can remember when I was a little, young girl, how my old mammy would sit out of doors in the evenings and look up at the stars and groan, and I would say, 'Mammy, who makes you groan so?' And she would say, 'I am groaning to think of my poor children; they do not know where I be and I don't know where they be. I look up at the stars and they look up at the stars!' "[21] When Sojourner's five-year-old son was taken and she was told that he was to be sold into the Deep South (although she was a slave in New York State), she made the statement that she felt as "tall as the world and mighty as the nation," indicating that she had the faith that she and her son would some day be reunited.

Numerous slave narratives provide dramatic accounts of the events surrounding the forced separation between parents and children. The following is one such example.

My brothers and sisters were bid off first, d one by one, while my mother, paralyzed with grief held me by the hand. Her turn came and she was bought by Issac Riley of Montgomery County. Then I was offered.... My mother, half distracted with the thought of parting forever from all her children, pushed through the crowd while the bidding for me was going on, to the spot where Riley was standing. She fell at his feet, and clung to his knees, entreating him in tones that a mother could only command, to buy her baby as well as herself, and spare to her one, at least, of her little ones.... This man disengaged himself from her with ... violent blows and kicks.... I must have been between five and six years old.22

Even when separation was apparent, and fathers and mothers found themselves unable to prevent it, there was evident a profound feeling that the family would one day be reunited. Slaves also tried to instill within their children who were being separated from them a sense of morality: "I was about twelve or fourteen years old when I was sold.... On the day I left home, everything was sad among the slaves. My mother and father sung and prayed over me and told me how to get along in the world."23 This strong bond also transcended actual separation, for when families were not reunited, memories and grief about kinsmen remained strong.

Solomon Northup, who spent twelve years as a slave, recalls one such experience.

On my arrival at Bayou Boeuf, I had the pleasure of meeting Eliza, whom I had not seen for several months.... She had grown feeble and emaciated, and was still mourning for her children. She asked me if I had forgotten them, and a great many times inquired if I still remembered how handsome little Emily was—how much Randall loved her—and wondered if they were living still, and where the darlings could then be. She had sunk beneath the weight of an excessive grief. Her drooping form and hollow cheeks too plainly indicated that she had well nigh reached the end of her weary road.24

Northup's account of Eliza's grief demonstrate the mortal psychological wounds she suffered as a result of being separated from her children. It appears that she would almost rather have been dead than to have given them up.

Indeed, some accounts show that mothers chose death for themselves and their children rather than experience the humiliation and torture of slavery, separation, and the total denial of their humanity. There is much in the oral history of slavery that speaks about the vast number of captives who jumped overboard en route to the Western Hemisphere, preferring to die rather than become slaves. It is said that others threw their newborn infants overboard for the same reason. After arriving on the mainland, women sometimes killed their children rather than allow them to grow up in slavery. This highest form of rebellion can be observed in the following oral historical account, taken from a slave narrative.

> My mother told me that he [slave master] owned a woman who was the mother of seven children, and when her babies would get about a year or two of age he'd sell them and it would break her heart. She never got to keep them. When her fourth baby was born and was about two months old, she just studied all the time about how she would have to give it up, and one day she said, "I just decided I'm not going to let ol' master sell this baby; he just ain't going to do it." She got up and give it something out of a bottle and pretty soon it was dead.[25]

This example shows the total commitment this mother had to fighting a system which violated what must have been her most sacred principles.

All of these are some of the symbols of the strong bonds that existed between parents and children (notably between mother and child) during slavery and the strong attachment all the family had for each other. Contrary to popular myth, black parents had a tremendous capacity to express grief when separated from their children. One must also recognize the fact that, because of the inability of slaves to marry legally and have sustained unions, mothers were more often left with the ongoing care of the children, for whatever period they were able to do so. This also meant that they served the vital economic function of providers for their families in the absence of a sustained husband-father figure. Staples notes that "only the mother-child bond continually resisted the disruptive effect of economic interests that dictated the sale of fathers away from their families."[26] The institution of slavery only acted to reinforce the close bond that had already existed between mother and child in African society. It could be argued that this strong attachment, although very positive, in many respects probably would not have developed if Africans had been allowed the basic freedoms and liberties of the Europeans who had settled on this continent. This was a necessary adaptation to the system, and without doubt acted to reinforce the subjugation of men to women. It is clear that within the cultural context of the dominant society, slave women were forced to assume the basic duties and responsibilities toward their families men assumed in the white world. The impact this had on black men is immeasurable, and remnants of this effect can be found today, especially since many of the fundamental conditions are unchanged.

> Historians have adequately documented the numerous rebellions/ revolts staged by slaves against the social system. The most widely known form of rebellion was the slave revolt but there were a variety of other ways that slaves expressed their indignation, such as the day-to-day feigning of illness or acting "stupid" (recalcitrance). There is little evidence that slaves were a docile, happy lot without hesitation gave up their African heritage and contented themselves to adapting to whatever life-styles their masters dictated.

The question is often raised as to what the black man's role was in defending his family against all the ravages and mass assaults of the slave system. It seems to be generally assumed that the men did very little, and most often nothing, to defend their mothers, wives, and children. But there are numerous historical accounts of black men lashing out against slavery because of its inhuman effects upon their families. One notable example is David Walker's *Appeal*, given in 1829:

> Now, I ask you, had you not rather be killed than be a slave to a tyrant, who takes the life of your *mother, wife, and dear little children?* Look upon your *mother, wife, and children,* and answer God Almighty; and believe this, that it is no more harm for you to kill a man, who is trying to kill you, than it is for you to take a drink of water when thirsty; in fact, the man who will stand still and let another murder him, is worse than an infidel, and, if he has common sense, ought not to be pitied.[27] [Emphasis added.]

One could imagine that Walker voiced the sentiments of the hundreds of thousands of black men who found themselves unable to protect their mothers, wives, and children from the barbarous slave system. Some accounts can be found of black men who attempted to uphold the system of marriage by defending their wives against the attacks of white men. The following is one such account of a man who described the harsh experiences of his father, who had attempted to defend his mother:

His right ear had been cut off close to his head, and he had received a hundred lashes on his back. He had beaten the overseer for a brutal assault on my mother, and this was his punishment. Furious at such treatment, my father became a different man, and was so morose, disobedient, and intractable, that Mr. N. decided to sell him. He accordingly parted with him, not long after, to his son who lived in Alabama; and neither mother nor I ever heard from him again.[28]

This severe punishment is a reflection of the problems black men encountered when trying to exercise their rights and obligations to their families. They were harshly dealt with, sometimes unto death, when doing so. Almost any compassion expressed by slaves toward each other was dealt with severely. The following account was taken from a slave narrative: "They whipped my father 'cause he looked at a slave they killed and cried."[29]

Slave masters, through their demands for absolute obedience, and reinforced by harsh slave laws, attempted to crush every symbol of humanity, affection, and compassion within slaves. There were, of course, exceptions among some slaveholders who attempted to develop a more humane system.

If slaves revolted against the Western political and cultural system in the ways indicated, there is strong reason to believe that in the process of revolting they attempted to preserve some of their African traditions. One could argue that slave revolts (minor and major) were evidence of a two-pronged attack: (1). against the cruelty of slavery; and (2). against the denial to blacks of the right to practice their past cultural traditions, etc. Indeed, both are closely related. This is not to underestimate the effects slavery had in the attempts to crush every single remembrance of Africa, because the impact was obviously devastating. But one could argue that the oppression forced some of the native traditions underground. It is also clear that individual slaves had a strong reaction to slavery and the denial of Africans in this country the ability to relate to the native customs. Sojourner Truth's reference to blacks as Africans is a notable example. It is most clear, however, that slavery forged many distinct adaptations and acted to create a unique set of behavior patterns, attitudes, and values—a black culture—that are more American than African. Yet it would be in error to say that all of the African heritage was destroyed during slavery, because we have observed certain conditions that encouraged the perpetuation of African traditions related to the family. Immediately we can recognize the effects oppression had and subsequent adaptations it caused in the sharp change in status of black men, who were strong patriarchs in African society and mere subhumans in America, with none of the rights and privileges of American household heads. There are numerous other changes that affected the roles of men and women, such as the inability to marry legally and have children within the Western societal framework, and the undue hardships women experienced in being forced very often to accept total responsibility for their families.

A multiplicity of factors—notably slavery—acted to mold the black family. It is too simple an explanation to attribute all of the behavior characteristics of the family during slavery to either Africanisms or to the series of adaptations that blacks were forced to make to the social system. On this point, Herskovits states:

> Slavery did not cause the "maternal" family; but it tended to continue certain elements in the cultural endowment brought to the New World by the Negroes. The feeling between mother and child was reinforced when the father was sold away from the rest of the family; where he was not, he continued life in a way that tended to consolidate the obligations assumed by him in the integrated societies of Africa as these obligations were shaped to fit the monogamic, paternalistic pattern of the white masters.

The economic, political, and social institutions to which Africans had to relate during slavery provided the opportunity for the survival of many of the African traditions. The woman continued to play important functions within the family with regard to the welfare of children, as well as in the economic sphere. This allowed for the strengthening of her role as an independent figure within the family; in the New World her role as an economic provider only assumed a different form. However, the demands in slave society were more acute than those she had experienced in Africa because of the mandatory status that was applied: "That the plantation system did not differentiate between the sexes in exploiting slave labor, tended again, to reinforce the tradition of the part played by women in the tribal economics."[30] As already stated, had there not been a continuing need for black women to continue to fulfill these functions their roles would probably have been little different from those of most white women, whose statuses were economically secure.

Today a popular debate revolves around whether or not American blacks possess a distinct cultural heritage that is a hybrid of the culture developed during slavery and certain remnants of African culture that were preserved. E. Franklin Frazier argues in *The Negro Family in the United States* that slavery and the Middle Passage destroyed all remnants of African culture:

> Probably never before in history has a people been so nearly completely stripped of its social heritage as the Negroes who were brought to America. Other conquered races have continued to worship their household gods within the intimate circle of their kinsmen. But American slavery destroyed household gods and dissolved the bonds of sympathy and affection between men of the same blood and household. Old men and women might have brooded over memories of their African homeland, but they could not change the world about them. Through force of circumstances, they had to acquire a new language, adopt new habits of labor, and take over, however imperfectly, the folkways of the American environment. Their children, who knew only the American environment, soon forgot the few memories that had been passed on to them and developed motivations and modes of behavior in harmony with the New World. Their children's children have often recalled with skepticism the fragments of stories concerning Africa which have been preserved in their families. But, of the habits and customs, as well as the hopes and fears that characterized the life of their forebearers in Africa, nothing remains.[31]

In his perceptive analysis, Melville Herskovits disputes Frazier in *The Myth of the Negro Past* and argues that many "Africanisms" survived slavery and are to be observed in contemporary black lifestyles, including the family, religion, music, dance, and the arts. The debate continues today among scholars such as Nathan Glazer and Daniel P. Moynihan, who assert that, "It is not possible for Negroes to view themselves as other ethnic groups viewed themselves because . . . the Negro is only an American and nothing else. He has no values and culture to guard and protect."[32] Some black intellectuals have argued that blacks in American society are an African people, and that few of the continuities between Africa and America have been broken.[33] Others propose that black culture is authentic. Charles Keil, whose study of black blues singers demonstrates the distinctiveness of the "soul ideology" and its peculiarity to the black experience, is one of the chief proponents of this thesis: "Like it or not, ... a Negro culture exists, and its existence ought to be recognized by all concerned, no matter what their policy or proposed solutions to the Ameican dilemmas."[34] Robert Blauner asserts that the peculiar historical experiences of blacks allowed for the development of a distinctive Negro lower-class life-style, although compared to the cultures of other ethnic minorities it is relatively weak.[35] It is very easy to concentrate on the thesis that blacks were denied their heritage, because that idea allows for the perpetuation of various myths regarding the inferiority of black people. Herskovits states: "The myth of the Negro past in one of the principal supports of race prejudice in this country. Unrecognized in its efficacy, it rationalizes discrimination in everyday contact between Negroes and whites, influences the shaping of policy where Negroes are concerned, and affects the trends of research by scholars whose theoretical approach, methods, and systems of thought presented to students are in harmony with it."[36]

It seems more difficult to recognize the unique heritage of blacks because most of the current historical documentations present a stereotyped portrait of the servile slave personality, as well as the "disorganized" family structure. One is forced to perceive black people today in a more positive manner if recognition is given to the rich cultural tradition from which blacks emerged. Such an analysis would put black people close to the same context in which the European immigrants to this country have been placed—immigrants who have been allowed to be assimilated into the mainstream of the society, and whose cultural heritages are highly respected.

Much of the heritage of slavery was passed on to blacks in the modern era. The basic economic inequities and racial discrimination in all walks of life prevented the majority of the black population from entering the mainstream and competing in an open society. Therefore, some of the problems black women faced during slavery, notably those of providing the economic sustenance for the family in the absence of a strong male provider, the maintenance of the extended family and the close ties between mother and children, are also characteristics today.

So black people had no choice but to develop their own distinctive culture with some elements from the old and some from the new and many innovative adaptations. It was necessary to develop this black culture in order to survive, to communicate, and to give meaning to life. For culture is the very way of life of a people.

The debate over the retention of Africanisms and the controversy over whether either a total black social system or a black subculture exists has only relative importance. There are both sharp discontinuities and strong uniformities between Africa and the New World (the United States and the Caribbean), and the principal factor among these should be an understanding of the political context of the black family all over the world. The black families in Africa, the Caribbean, and the United States have all been strongly influenced by the effects of neocolonialism, and thus have suffered similar problems emanating from racism and poverty.

Numerous studies have been conducted on the black family in the Caribbean and all of them provide a considerable amount of information about the way in which the continuities between Africa and this part of the New World have been maintained, although these assumptions are only implicit in most of these investigations.[37] One can recognize the similarities that exist between the Caribbean society and the broader black community in the United States, although the interpretations that researchers have provided vary widely. Blake argues, for example, that lower-class family relations are merely deviations from the traditional Western social system instead of being representative of a distinct culture. This position was challenged by Braithwaite, Rodman, and others who assert that this seemingly disorganized culture is a normal and legitimate one for its adherents.

It is generally recognized that the institution of slavery was less severe in this part of the New World than in the United States, a fact which accounted for, among other things, a higher retention of African culture. Melville Herskovits's pioneering efforts in studying the continuities are perhaps still considered the foremost work in this field, although other scholars have challenged many of Herskovits's assumptions. Hannerz says:

> Noting the strong bond between mother and children in black American households, and the weak and marginal relationship of the husband and father to this household nucleus, Herskovits related this to West African polygyny where he held that the male naturally was somewhat peripheral to each group of mother and children. West

African women are also traditionally rather independent economically, a fact which could contribute to keeping the husband-wife relationship rather weak. West Africans had an idea of the conjugal relationship as relatively weak, and when taken into slavery in the Americas they brought this idea along.[38]

A position that is somewhat different from both Herskovits's and from E. Franklin Frazier's "culturally stripped" thesis is held by M. G. Smith, who maintains that in the West Indies many of the cultural adaptations to the slave system which devloped are still transmitted because of their functional value, and other family forms that are closer to the dominant society have developed out of the contemporary social context because certain conditions have been conducive to their emergence.[39]

An understanding of the Caribbean family structure provides the broader perspective that is needed to interpret the common sociohistorical experiences of blacks in the Americas. Such an analysis also generates a proper political context in which to analyze and propose solutions to the problems of the black family in all of the New World.

NOTES

1. E. Franklin Frazier, *The Negro Family in the United States* (Chicago: University of Chicago Press, 1966), 367-68.

2. Address delivered at Abbott House, Westchester County, N.Y., October 29, 1965.

3. Andrew Billingsley, *Black Families in White America* (Englewood Cliffs, N.J.: Prentice-Hall, (1968).

4. African women were not shaped by oppression and it was only after they came to the New World that they had these experiences.

5. John Hope Franklin, *From Slavery to Freedom* (New York: Knopf, 1956), 28.

6. Benjamin Quarles, *The Negro in the Making of America* (London: Collier-MacMillan, 1964), 16-17.

7. August Meier and Elliott Rudwick, *From Plantation to Ghetto* (New York: Hill and Wang, 1966), 14.

8. Marie Perinbaum, lecture delivered at Spelman College, Atlanta, Ga., 1969.

9. Meyer Fortes, "Kinship and Marriage among the Ashanti," in *African Systems of Kinship and Marriage,* ed. A. R. Radcliffe-Brown and Daryll Ford (New York: Oxford University Press, 1950).

10. R. S. Rattray, *Ashanti* (London: Oxford University Press, 1923).

11. Fortes, "Kinship and Marriage among the Ashanti," 262.

12. Clark D. Moore and Ann Dunbar, *Africa Yesterday and Today* (New York: Bantam, 1968), 33.

13. Meier and Rudwick, *From Plantation to Ghetto*, 14.

14. Perinbaum, Spelman College lecture.

15. Melville Herskovits, *The Myth of the Negro Past* (Boston: Beacon Press, 1958), 62.

16. Quarles, *The Negro in the Making of America*, 18-19.

17. *Ibid.*, 71.

18. "The Text of the *Confessions of Nat Turner*, as reported by Thomas R. Gray, 1831," reprinted in John Henrik Clarke, ed., *The Confessions of Nat Turner: Ten Black Writers Respond* (Boston: Beacon Press, 1968), 93-118.

19. Benjamin Quarles, ed., *Narrative of the Life of Frederick Douglass, an American Slave, Written by Himself* (Cambridge, Mass.: Harvard University Press, 1960), 35-36.

20. *Ibid.*

21. Taken from W. E. B. Du Bois, "The Damnation of Women," *Darkwater* (New York: Schocken, 1969), 179.

22. Josiah Henson, *Father Henson's Story of His Own Life* (New York: Corinth, 1962), 12-13.

23. *God Struck Me Dead: Religious Conversion Experiences and Autobiographies of Negro Ex-Slaves* (Nashville, Tenn.: Fisk University Social Sciences Institute, 1945), 161-63.

24. Solomon Northup, *Twelve Years a Slave* (Baton Rouge: Louisiana State University Press, 1968), 77.

25. Lou Smith and B. A. Botkin, eds., *Lay My Burden Down: A Folk History of Slavery* (Chicago: University of Chicago Press, 1945), 40.

26. Robert Staples, "The Myth of the Black Matriarchy," *Black Scholar* (January-February 1970), 10.

27. Reprinted in Floyd Barbour, *The Black Power Revolt* (Boston: Porter Sargent, 1968), 25.

28. Frazier, *The Negro Family in the United States*, 53.

29. Roberta Manson, quoted in Julius Lester, *To Be a Slave* (New York: Dial Press, 1968), 33.

30. Herskovits, *The Myth of the Negro Past*, 181.

31. Frazier, *The Negro Family in the United States*, 15.

32. Nathan Glazer and Daniel Moynihan, *Beyond the Melting Pot* (Cambridge, Mass.: M.I.T. Press, 1963), 53.

33. abd-L Hakimu Ibn Alkalimat, "The Ideology of Black Social Science," *Black Scholar* (December 1969), 28-35.

34. Charles Keil, *Urban Blues* (Chicago: University of Chicago Press, 1966), 191-92.

35. Robert Blauner, "Negro Culture: Myth or Reality," *Black Experience: The Transformation of Activism* (New Brunswick, N.J.: Trans-action, 1970).

36. Herskovits, *The Myth of the Negro Past*, 1.

37. All of the following scholars have provided penetrating insights into the family structure of West Indians: Edith Clarke, *My Mother Who Fathered Me* (London: George Allen and Unwin, 1957); R. T. Smith, *The Negro Family in British Guiana* (New York: Grove Press, 1956); M. G. Smith, *The Plural Society in the British West Indies* (Berkeley: University of California Press, 1965); Judith Blake, *Family Structure in Jamaica* (New York: Free Press, 1961); William Goode, "Illegitimacy in the Caribbean Social Structure," *American Sociological Review* XXV (February 1960), 21-30; Hyman Rodman, "Marital Relationships in a Trinidad Village," *Marriage and Family Living* XXIII (May 1969), 170; Rodman, "Lower-class Attitudes toward 'Deviant' Family Patterns, a Cross Cultural Study," *Journal of Marriage and the Family* (May 1969), 315-21; Rodman, "The Lower Class Value Stretch," *Social Forces* XLII (December 1963), 205-15; Lloyd Braithwaite, "Sociology and Demographic Research in the Caribbean," *Social and Economic Studies* VI (Jamaica: University College of the West Indies); and F. M. Henriquez, *Family and Colour in Jamaica* (London: Eyre and Spottiswoode, 1953).

38. Ulf Hannerz, *Soulside: Inquiries into Ghetto Culture and Community* (New York: Columbia University Press, 1969), 72.

39. See *ibid.*, 71-76, for a full discussion of the various schools of thought on the black family in the New World.

2

Female Slave Resistance: The Economics of Sex

Darlene Hine and Kate Wittenstein

The question of the extent and nature of black resistance to slavery has been the subject of a number of recent historical studies.[1] These works, concentrating as they do on the examination of black male resistance to the slave system, have demonstrated that such resistance was carried on both overtly in the form of slave rebellions and covertly in indirect attacks on the system through resistance to the whip, feigning of illness, conscious laziness, and other means of avoiding work and impeding production. None of these studies, however, has considered in depth the forms of black female resistance to slavery, although they have suggested a methodology for attempting such an investigation. This paper is concerned with uncovering the means through which female slaves expressed their political and economic opposition to the slave system. What behavior patterns did enslaved black women adopt to protect themselves and their children and to undermine the system which oppressed and exploited them?

Unlike male slaves, female slaves suffered a dual form of oppression. In addition to the economic exploitation which they experienced along with black males, females under slavery were oppressed sexually as well. Sexual oppression and exploitation refer not only to the obvious and well-documented fact of forced sexual intercourse with white masters, but also to those forms of exploitation resulting from the very existence of their female biological systems. For example, the female slave in the role of the mammy was regularly required to nurse white babies in addition to, and often instead of, her own children. In his *Roll, Jordan, Roll: The World the Slaves Made*, Eugene Genovese acknowledges the uniquely difficult position in which this practice placed the mammy:

> More than any other slave, she had absorbed the paternalist ethos and accepted her place in a system of reciprocal obligations defined from above. In so doing, she developed pride, resourcefulness, and a high sense of responsiblity to white and black people alike.... She did not reject her people in order to identify with stronger whites, but she did place herself in a relationship to her own people that reinforced the paternalist social order.[2]

While Genovese gives evidence of the mammy's manipulation of her favored position, the pivotal question of how it must have felt to be forced to nurse and raise her future oppressors remains unexamined.

Another major aspect of the sexual oppression of black women under slavery took the form of the white master's consciously constructed view of black female sexuality. This construct, which was designed by the white master to justify his own sexual passion toward her, also blamed the female slave for the sexual exploitation which she experienced. Winthrop Jordan comments in his *White Over Black: American Attitudes Toward the Negro 1550-1812* that white men

> ... by calling the Negro woman passionate ... were offering the best possible justifications for their own passions. Not only did the Negro woman's warmth constitute a logical explanation for the white man's infidelity, but, much more important, it helped shift responsiblity from himself to her. If she was *that* lascivious—well, a man could scarcely be blamed for succumbing against overwhelming odds.[3]

It is clear from several slave narratives that the female slave was well aware of the image of her sexuality which was fostered among the white male population. In her narrative *Incidents in the Life of a Slave Girl*, Linda Brent offers a revealing observation on the effect of this image on the female slave: "If God has bestowed beauty upon her, it will prove her greatest curse. That which commands admiration in the white woman only hastens the degradation of the female slave."[4] In his article "New Orleans: The Mistress of the Slave Trade," Frederic Bancroft documents Brent's observation and shows how this image of black female sexuality gave rise to a section of the slave trade specifically designed to profit from the sale of attractive black women, or as they were known at the time, "fancy girls."[5] Bancroft points out that slave traders frequently took pride in the numbers of such women they had for sale, and on the high prices commanded by their physical appearance. Often, these women sold for prices which far exceeded that which planters were willing to pay for a field laborer. In 1857, for example, the *Memphis Eagle and Enquirer* ran an editorial in which it was observed that "a slave woman is advertized to be sold in St. Louis who is so surpassingly beautiful that $5000 has already been offered for her, at private sale, and refused."[6]

How, then, did the female slave resist both the economic and sexual oppressions which were a part of her daily life? Three intimately related forms of resistance peculiar to the female slave emerge from the narratives. The first method can be called sexual abstinence. This ranged from refusing or attempting to avoid sexual intercourse with the white master to a strong wish to delay marriage to a male slave while hope remained that marriage and childbirth could occur in a free state. Elizabeth Keckley who, toward the end of her life became a seamstress for Mrs. Abraham Lincoln, discusses this form of resistance in her narrative *Behind the Scenes: Thirty Years a Slave and Four Years in the White House.* Her story is typical in outlining the extent and duration of her attempt to avoid the designs of her licentious master. She recalls that she was "regarded as fair-looking for one of my race,"[7] and that as a result of her appearance her master pursued her for four years:

> I do not care to dwell upon this subject, for it is fraught with pain. Suffice it to say, that he persecuted me for four years, and I—I—became a mother. The child of which he was the father was the only child I ever brought into the world. If my poor boy ever suffered any humiliating pangs on account of birth, he could not blame his mother, for God knows that she did not wish to give him life; he must blame the edicts of that society which deemed it no crime to undermine the virtue of girls in my then position.[8]

Presumably, Mrs. Keckley found this experience so upsetting that she could not bring herself to have another child, not even after she had gained her freedom.

Similarly, Linda Brent described her prolonged attempts to avoid sexual relations with her master, Dr. Flint. She recalls that she was able to use the presence of her grandmother on the plantation to avoid her master's advances because "though she had been a slave, Dr. Flint was afraid of her. He dreaded her scorching rebukes. Moreover, she was known and patronized by many people; and he did not wish to have his villainy made public."[9]

Ellen Craft along with her future husband, William, escaped slavery in a most ingenious fashion. Mrs. Craft was so reluctant to have children while she remained in slavery that she and William agreed to delay their marriage until they reached the North. In their narrative *Running a Thousand Miles for Freedom*, William Craft perceptively explains his wife's motivations:

> My wife was torn from her mother's embrace in childhood, and taken to a distant party of the country. She had seen so many other children separated from their parents in this cruel manner, that the mere thought of her ever becoming a mother of a child, to linger out a miserable existence under the wretched system of American slavery, appeared to fill her very soul with horror; and as she had taken what I felt to be an important view of her condition, I did not, at first, press the marriage, but agreed to assist her in trying to devise some plan by which we might escape from our unhappy condition, and then be married.[10]

A second method of female resistance to slavery, in general, and to sexual exploitation, in particular, took the form of abortion. Because abortion appears to have been less common than sexual abstinence, it seems fair to assume that destruction of the fetus exacted a higher psychological toll than did abstinence. In his recent study of the black family, Herbert Gutman observes that the conscious decision on the part of the slave woman to terminate her pregnancy was one act that was totally beyond the control of the master of the plantation. Gutman offers evidence of several southern physicians who commented upon abortion and the use of contraceptive methods among the slave population:

> The Hancock County, Georgia, physician E. M. Pendleton reported in 1849 that among his patients 'abortion and miscarriage' occured more frequently among slave than white free women. The cause was either 'slave labor (exposure, violent exercise, & c.') or 'as the planters believe, that the blacks are possessed of a secret by which they

destroy the fetus at an early stage of gestation. All county practitioners,' he added, 'are aware of the frequent complaints of planters'
about the 'unnatural tendency in the African female population to
destroy her offspring. Whole families of women . . . fail to have any
children.[11]

Gutman also recounts a situation in which a planter had kept
between four and six slave women "of the proper age to breed" for
twenty-five years and that "only two children had been born on the
place at full term." It was later discovered that the slaves had
concocted a medicine with which they were able to terminate their
unwanted pregnancies.[12] Gutman found evidence as well of a master who claimed that an older female slave had discovered a remedy
for pregnancies and had been "instrumental in all . . . abortions on
his place."[13]

This last instance suggests that even those women who did not
resist slavery through actually having an abortion themselves, resisted even more covertly by aiding those who desired them. It is
therefore possible that a sort of female conspiracy existed on the
southern plantation which requires further study. In an interesting
twist to the apparently chronic problem of unwanted and forced
pregnancies, there is evidence that female slaves recognizing the
importance of their role of procreation to the maintenance of the
slave system, often feigned pregnancy as a method of receiving
lighter work loads. The limited success of this kind of ploy would
also require the aid of other female slaves on the plantation—a
midwife, for example, who might testify to the master that one of
his female slaves was indeed pregnant.

In their illuminating article "Day to Day Resistance to Slavery,"
Raymond and Alice Bauer note that "pretending to be pregnant was
a type of escape in a class by itself, since the fraud must inevitably
have been discovered."[14] The following contemporary report is
contained in their article:

> I will tell you of a most comical account Mr. _____ has given of the
> prolonged and still protracted pseudo-pregnancy of a woman called
> Markie, who for many more months than are generally required for
> the process of continuing the human species, pretended to be what
> the Germans pathetically and poetically call 'in good hope' and con-
> tinued to reap increased rations as the reward of her expectation, till
> she finally had to disappoint the estate and receive a flogging.[15]

Apparently, the increased allotment of food and the possibility of lighter work was enough inducement for this woman to risk the punishment which she must have known would follow. In this case, the slave woman was perceptive enough of the importance of her procreative function for the maintenance of the slave system to manipulate to her own advantage the precise function for which she was most valued by the master.

Possibly the most pyschologically devastating means for undermining the slave system which the slave parent had at his or her disposal was infanticide. The frequency with which this occured is by no means clear. Several historians have contended that infanticide was quite rare and Genovese writes that "slave abortions, much less infanticide, did not become a major problem for the slave holders of an ordinary form or 'resistance' for the slaves. Infanticide occured, but so far as the detected cases reveal anything, only in some special circumstances."[16] The subject of infanticide under slavery is clearly in need of further study, but for our purposes it is important to note that the relatively small number of documented cases of infanticide is not as significant as the fact that it occured at all as possibly the ultimate statement, with the exception of suicide, of opposition to both sexual and economic exploitation which was available to the slave. Raymond and Alice Bauer reveal how both infanticide and suicide were combined in the following account:

> Not only were slaves known to take the lives of their masters or overseers, but they were now and then charged with the murder of their own children, sometimes to prevent them growing up in bondage. In Covington, a father and mother, shut up in a slave baracoon and doomed to the southern market, 'when there was no eye to pity them and no arm to save,' did by mutual agreement 'send the souls of their children to heaven rather than have them descend to the hell of slavery,' then both parents committed suicide.[17]

Genovese notes one instance in which "the white citizens of Virginia petitioned in 1882 to spare a slave condemned to death for killing her infant. The child's father was a respectable white man, and the woman insisted that she would not have killed a child of her own color."[18] There are numerous instances in which slave women simply preferred to end their children's lives rather than allow the children to grow up enslaved. When Genovese writes that "for the most part, however, the slaves recognized infantcide as murder.

They loved their children too much to do away with them; courageously, they resolved to raise them as best they could, and entrusted
their fate to God,"[19] he does not appear to be acknowledging the
motivations for infantcide offered repeatedly by the slave parents
themselves. Far from viewing such actions as murder, and therefore indicative of a lack of love, slave parents who took their children's lives may have done so out of a higher form of love and a clear
understanding of the living death that awaited their children under
slavery. Since this is the explanation that is offered most frequently
in the narratives, there does not seem to be any evidence, at this
time, not to accept the slaves' statements as reflective of their true
motivations.

It is also possible that there were other motivations behind infanticide. It may have occured as a response to rape or forced pregnancy and it was an act which, along with sexual abstinence and
abortion, had economic implications as well. The narratives reveal
that slave children were sometimes used as pawns in a power
struggle between plantation owners and their slaves. Owners used
the sale or the threat of sale of slave children as a means for
manipulating their recalcitrant or troublesome slaves, and the
slaves in turn used their children to manipulate the behavior of
their masters. There is one documented instance, for example, in
which a particularly rebellious female slave, Fannie, was told that
she would have to be sold following an incident in which she
physically attacked her mistress. To increase the harshness of the
punishment, she was informed by her master that her infant would
remain on the plantation: One of her older daughters recalls her
mother's response:

> At this, Ma took the baby by its feet, a foot in each hand, and with the
> Baby's head swinging downward, she vowed to smash its brains out
> before she'd leave it. Tears were streaming down her face, It was
> seldom that Ma cried and everyone knew that she meant every word.
> Ma took her baby with her....[20]

In this instance the threat of infantcide on the part of the slave
mother was transformed into an effective means for gaining power
over the planter and control over at least a part of her life. Thus, it
seems that there were complex motivations involved in both infantcide and the threat of infantcide.

In attempting to evaluate the consequences for the slave system of these acts of resistance, Genovese's definition of paternalism is most helpful. He writes that "Paternalism in any historical setting defines relations of superordination and subordination. Its strength as a prevailing ethos increases as the members of the community accept—or feel compelled to accept—these relations as legitimate."[21] As was pointed out above, slave women were expected to serve a dual function in this system and therefore suffered a dual oppression. They constituted an important and necessary part of the work force and they were, through their childbearing function, the one group most responsible for the size and indeed the maintenance of the slave labor pool. Therefore, when they resisted sexual exploitation through such means as sexual abstention, abortion and infantcide, they were, at the same time, rejecting their vital economic function as breeders. This, of course, became especially important after 1808 when it was no longer legal to import slaves into the United States from Africa.

The slave woman's resistance to sexual, and therefore to economic exploitation, posed a potentially severe threat to paternalism itself, for implicit in such action was the slave woman's refusal to accept her designated responsibilities within the slave system as legitimate. This acceptance of mutual responsiblity on the part of both the slaves and the masters was, as Genovese points out, at the heart of the maintenance of the paternalistic world view. The female slave, through her sexual resistance, attacked the very assumptions upon which the slave order was constructed and maintained.

Resistance to sexual exploitation, therefore, had major political and economic implications. A woman who elected not to have children or, to put it another way, to engage in sexual abstinence, abortion, or infantcide, negated through individual or group action her role in the maintenance of the slave pool. To the extent that in so doing she redefined her role in the system, she introduced a unit of psychological heterogeniety into a world view which depended, for its survival, on homogeniety at least with respect to the assumptions of its ideology.

The examples quoted above strongly indicate that the slave woman's decision to participate in these particular forms of resistance was made consciously and with full awareness of the potential political and economic ramifications involved. In rejecting her role in the economic advancement of the slave system, she could reduce the numbers of slaves available for the slave trade and undermine her master's effort to profit from exploiting her sexually. Since the master had a dual stake in the female slave as worker and as breeder, the woman who engaged in these activities impeded the economic advantage of the sale and transfer of her child accruing to the master through the slave taders. The planters were the only beneficiaries of the increase in the numbers of slaves: $1,500 for a good, strong buck; $1,200 for a hardworking, childbearing wench, with no large-scale investment necessary to insure future profit. The master could, presumably, simply sit back and wait for the children to be born. If there was no black male available, he could engage in the procreative process himself. The result was the same, made conveniently so, by laws which stipulated that the child inherited the condition of the mother.

In his *Once a Slave: The Slaves' View of Slavery* Stanley Feldstein notes that, in his narrative, Frederick Douglass makes explicit the importance of breeding slaves even for the less wealthy planters:

> ...Frederick Douglass told of the case of a master who was financially able to purchase only one slave. Therefore, he bought her as a 'breeder,' and then hired a married man to live with her for one year. Every night he would place the man and woman together in a room, at the end of the year, the woman gave birth to twins. The children were regarded by the master as an important addition to his wealth, and his joy was such that the breeder was kept in the finest of material comfort in the hope that she would continue providing good fortune to the master and his family.[22]

Perhaps the most revealing example of the female slaves' awareness of the sexual and economic nexus inherent in her dual role in the slave system is offered by Jane Black in her narrative *Memoirs of Margaret Jane Blake*. She comments that many slave women resisted pregnancy because they did not want their children to grow up in a state of bondange and that if "all the bond women had been of the same mind, how soon the institution could have vanished from the face of the earth, and all the misery belonging to it, been lifted from the hearts of the holders of slaves."[23]

One of the more striking aspects of the subject of female slave resistance is its complex nature. The decision to resist in the three ways which have been outlined involved sexual, emotional, economic, and political concerns. The examination of the strategies which were developed by the female slave to resist sexual and economic exploitation represents a legitimate and necessary field of inquiry if we are to understand slave resistance in general. In connection with this, it is important to note that we need to know much more about the role which the male slave played in helping the slave woman to resist both sexual and economic exploitation. The dynamics of female slave behavior cannot be fully understood if examined in a vacuum.

Instances of sexual abstinence, abortion, and infantcide are important for the same reasons that we study the three major slave rebellions of the nineteenth century. Like the rebellions, the important point with respect to these modes of female resistance is not the infrequency with which they occured, if indeed they were infrequent, but the fact that these methods were used at all. Through a closer examination of the responses of black women to slavery, we can gain further insight into the interaction of males and females of both races on the southern plantation.

NOTES

1. See, for example, Herbert Aptheker, *American Negro Slave Revolts* (New York: International Publishers, 1963); Eugene Genovese, *Roll, Jordan, Roll: The World The Slaves Made* (New York: Random House, 1972); Herbert Gutman, *The Black Family in Slavery and Freedom, 1750-1925*; Gerald Mullin, *Flight and Rebellion* (New York: Oxford University Press, 1972); and Peter Wood. *Black Majority* (New York: W. W. Norton and Co. Inc., 1974).

2. Genovese, pp. 360-361.

3. Winthrop Jordan, *White Over Black: American Attitudes Toward the Negro, 1550-1812* (Baltimore: Penguin Books Inc., 1969), pp. 151.

4. Linda Brent. *Incidents in the Life of a Slave Girl* (New York: Harcourt Brace Jovanovich, Inc., 1973), p. 27.

5. Frederic Bancroft, "New Orleans: The Mistress of the Slave Trade," in Irwin Unger and David Reimers (eds.). *The Slavery Experience in the United States* (New York: Holt, Rinehart and Winston, Inc., 1970), pp. 77.

6. Quoted in Bancroft, p. 77.

7. Elizabeth Keckley, *Behind the Scenes: Thirty Years a Slave and Four Years in the White House* (New York: Arno Press and the New York Times, 1968), pp. 38-39.

8. Keckley, p. 39.

9. Brent, p. 28.

10. William and Ellen Craft, "Running a Thousand Miles for Freedom," in Arna Bontemps ed., *Great Slave Narratives* (Boston: Beacon Press, 1969), pp. 285.

11. Gutman, pp. 80-81.

12. Gutman, p. 81.

13. Gutman, pp. 81-82.

14. Raymond and Alice Bauer, "Day to Day Resistance to Slavery," in Unger and Reimers. p. 186.

15. Bauer, p. 186.

16. Genovese, p. 497.

17. Bauer, p. 190.

18. Genovese, p. 497.

19. Genovese, p. 497.

20. Quoted in Gerda Lerner ed., *Black Women in White America* (New York: Vintage Books, 1973), p. 38.

21. Genovese, p. 6.

22. Stanley Feldstein, *Once a Slave: The Slaves' View of Slavery* (New York: William Morrow and Co., Inc., 1970), p. 90.

23. Quoted in Feldstein, p. 90.

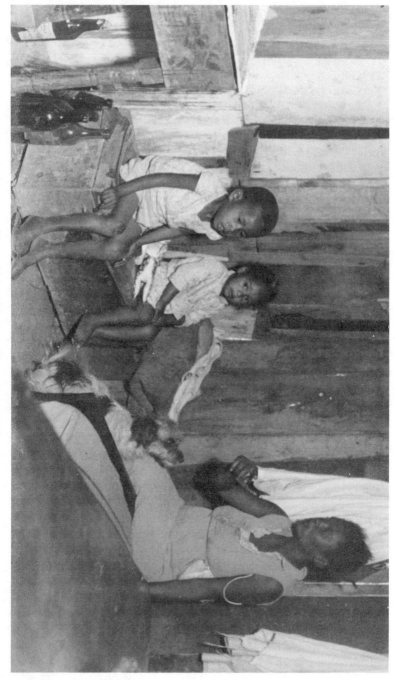

Photo: United Nations, No. 47974. (1955)

3
Discrimination Against Afro-American Women in the Woman's Movement, 1830-1920

Rosalyn Terborg-Penn

Discrimination against Afro-American women reformers was the rule rather than the exception within the woman's rights movement from the 1830s to 1920. Although white feminists Susan B. Anthony, Lucy Stone, and some others encouraged black women to join the struggle against sexism during the nineteenth century, antebellum reformers who were involved with women's abolitionist groups as well as woman's rights organizations actively discriminated against blacks. The late-nineteenth-century woman's club movement and the woman suffrage movement of the early twentieth century were also characterized by discriminatory policies and contained individuals who discriminated against black women.[1]

The pheonomenon of disrimination against blacks in reform movements is fairly well known in United States history. However, the prevailing historiography as well as the popular view of the feminist movements of the nineteenth and twentieth centuries is that white women welcomed black women into the cause.[2] Influenced by the rhetoric of female solidarity expressed by white feminists, recent histories of the woman's rights movement in the United States have concluded that because of disinterest, only a very few black women responded to the call.[3] When, however, one looks behind the rhetoric to examine the actual experiences of black women who attempted to join the organizations of white feminists, it becomes clear that the recent assumptions by historians need to be revised. In addition, when the neglected subject of black woman's rights organizations is studied, the need for further revision of the historical record becomes more apparent.

Not all Afro-American women sought to join racially integrated organizations. Some organized separate racial groups in response to common problems and to a common sense of identity. The trend became more pronounced during the late nineteenth century and the early twentieth century, when black men and black women organized self-help groups, which sought to combat racial discrimination and to express racial identity and solidarity on a national as well as on local levels.

The twin phenomena of antiblack discrimination in white women's organizations and the propensity of black women to form their own organizations raises several questions about the black female experience in the history of reform movements in the United States. Did most Afro-American women seek the security of their own organizations as a result of discrimination against them by white women, or did race consciousness stimulate the development of racially separate women's groups? Are there data sufficient to evaluate the role of black women in the woman's movement in historical materials left by white feminists and their organizations, or are there gaps in the data which have distorted the existing historical interpretations? A look at some of the incidents in which black women were either discriminated against directly by white contemporaries or discriminated against indirectly by historians who have neglected them in studies of the movement provides some clues to answers to these questions.

Discrimination against black women in abolitionist societies organized by white women appears ironic when one considers that white women complained of discrimination by men. Although some black women formed their own societies or joined successfully with black men in such groups, others attempted to participate in racially integrated women's groups. The signers of the Female Anti-Slavery Society of Philadelphia, in 1833, included four Afro-American women: Sarah Mapps Douglass, the principal of the Institute for Colored Youth, and the three daughters of abolitionist James Forten, Sr.—Sarah, Margaretta, and Harriet, the wife of abolitionist and feminist supporter Robert Purvis. The same year, the Boston Female Anti-Slavery Society organized, with Susan Paul among the black members.

These Afro-American women attended the first two national female antislavery conventions, where the issue of receiving black delegates was raised. The first convention was held in New York in 1837, and there it was finally decided that "colored" members could be admitted. Sarah Douglass and Sarah Forten were among the delegates. Forten circulated her poem calling upon women to abandon their race prejudice and to join as "sisters" as well as Christians in their common cause. The body met again in Philadelphia in 1838, where once again the plea to abandon race prejudice among white female reformers was heard from the delegates. Significantly, the same Afro-American women's names are listed in attendance at the national female antislavery conventions. Although the Forten sisters, Susan Paul, Sarah Douglass, and her mother Grace appear to have been outstanding leaders among female abolitionists, the paucity of black women in attendance is apparent despite the fact that several black female societies could be found throughout the North and West.[4]

Abhorrence of slavery was no guarantee that white reformers would accept the Afro-American on equal terms. In 1835, for example, Afro-American women began attending the Massachusetts Female Anti-Slavery Society at Fall River, causing such a controversy among the white members that dissolution of the group nearly resulted. Furthermore, Sarah Douglass, an active member of the Quakers, a group known for their participation in the antislavery cause, expressed her feeling of alienation from white church members because they discriminated against her. In 1837, she wrote fellow Quaker and feminist Sarah Grimké and explained how she and the other black members of the congregation were segregated from the white members on a special bench reserved for "people of color." Degree of skin color was also a factor in determining the acceptability of blacks by whites. Light-skinned Afro-American women appear to have been preferred in white female groups. Benjamin Quarles notes comments made to this effect by a member of the Boston Female Anti-Slavery Society about the fair-skinned Susan Paul.[5] Because of this antiblack prejudice, Afro-American women may have avoided participation in groups like the National Convention of Female Anti-Slavery Societies.

From the writings of the black antislavery advocates it appears, however, that white women accepted black men more readily than black women in their reform circles. Frederick Douglass, William C. Nell, and Charles Lenox Remond, all feminist supporters as well as abolitionists, have made note of the support they received from white female abolitionists. Historian Louis Filler notes that when black reformers turned to the women's rights issue, few black women were prominent in the movement; the best known woman's rights advocates among blacks were men.[6] Among the Afro-American men active in the mid-nineteenth-century feminist movement were Frederick Douglass, Charles Remond, James Forten, Sr., James Forten, Jr., Robert Purvis, Charles Purvis, William Whipper, William J. Whipper, C. Nell, James McCune Smith, Jermain Loguen, Henry Highland Garnet, and George T. Downing.

Historian Eleanor Flexner, a pioneer in the scholarly study of the woman's movement in the United States, acknowledges the work of black abolitionists Frances Ellen Watkins Harper, Sarah Remond, and Sojourner Truth.[7] Although the names of Afro-American men more than double those of Afro-American women who have been noted as associated with woman's rights during the antebellum period, more black women were equally involved in the movement. Mary Ann Shadd Cary, Harriet Purvis, and Margaretta Forten participated also during the antebellum years. By the 1860s and the 1870s, Hattie Purvis, Josephine St. Pierre Ruffin, Caroline Remond Putman, Louisa Rollin, Lottie Rollin, and K. Rollin were among the ranks of female suffragists. The names of these women can be found in the *History of Woman Suffrage.*

Sojourner Truth was one of the few black women noted by historians to have frequented women's rights conventions. She, however, was not always welcomed. Her narrative reveals that the white women at the Akron, Ohio, Woman's Rights Convention in 1851 beseeched the chairman to forbid her to speak before the group. They felt she would ruin the movement by giving the public the impression that their cause was "mixed with abolition and niggers." In 1858, at an antislavery meeting in northern Indiana, members of the group demanded that she submit her breasts to inspection by the "ladies" present to prove that she was not a man in disguise. The "ladies" did not come to her defense, whereupon Sojourner rebuked them all and bared her breasts to the entire group.[8]

The alliance between abolitionists and feminists was further damaged during the post-Civil War years when male abolitionists argued that reformers should concentrate more upon gaining the franchise for black men first, then work toward female suffrage. Some of Frederick Douglass's strongest female supporters, like Susan B. Anthony and Elizabeth Cady Stanton, rebuked him because he failed to support their efforts to have the Fifteenth Amendment include women. Douglass argued in 1866, at the meeting of the American Equal Rights Association held at Albany, that the ballot was "desirable" for women, but "vital" for black men. At the meeting in New York held in 1868, Douglass reaffirmed his position in these emotional terms:

> I have always championed woman's right to vote; but it will be seen that the present claim for the negro is one of the most "urgent" necessity. The assertion of the right of women to vote meets nothing but ridicule; there is no deep seated malignity in the hearts of the people against her; but name the right of the negro to vote, all hell is turned loose and the Ku-klux and Regulators hunt and slay the unoffending black man.[9]

Douglass's effort to keep the white women from abandoning the black suffrage issue failed. A majority of the feminists withdrew from the Equal Rights Association, whose chief aim was universal suffrage, and formed the National Woman Suffrage Association, which was entirely divorced from the black suffrage issue. Despite this rebuff, Douglass and other black feminists remained active in the woman's movement. Douglass reestablished his relationship with Stanton and Anthony immediately thereafter. On the other hand, white suffragists held Douglass's position against him and blacks in general as late as the woman's suffrage campaign of the twentieth century in spite of the fact that men like Robert Purvis had publicly renounced the Douglass position at the woman's rights meeting of 1870 in the District of Columbia. Furthermore, although Frances Harper had supported the Douglass position, she continued her participation in the suffrage movement and affiliated with the American Woman Suffrage Association.[10]

During the last quarter of the nineteenth century, the woman's club movement demonstrated, through the formation of woman's clubs on a national level, the desire of American woman to assert their independence in the drive for reform. For the most part, these clubs developed along racially separate lines. Perhaps one reason for this development lay in the unique needs of black women during this period. White women had no need to vindicate their dignity in the midst of national cries that they were wanton, immoral, and socially inferior. White women did not have the severe problems of racial discrimination, which compounded the black woman's plight in employment and education. Moreover, race consciousness was evident among Afro-Americans in general as civil rights organizations, business groups, and self-help societies emerged with names signifying race.

Another reason, however, for the development of racially separate women's groups was the exclusion of black women from most white female clubs. Despite the differences between the two groups, there were some common causes and attempts at unity on local levels. Black women were involved in temperance work, suffrage groups, and club work. Nevertheless, the experiences of Frances Ellen Watkins Harper, Josephine St. Pierre Ruffin, Mary Church Terrell, and Ida B. Wells-Barnett indicate the pervasiveness of white female prejudice and discrimination against black females in woman's groups.

Afro-American participation in the temperance movement dated back to the 1830s. Roslyn Cleagle, in her study of the colored temperance movement from 1830 to 1860, concluded that black women joined with white women to form temperance groups because they were discriminated against by men and that blacks formed their own associations of men and women because they were discriminated against by whites. Despite Cleagle's assumption that black and white women worked together without discrimination prior to the Civil War, the experiences of black women in the antislavery organizations as well as the policies of the Woman's Christian Temperance Union (WCTU) indicate that the opposite was true. Moreover, Cleagle neglects to explain why so many Afro-American women formed their own organizations if the New England Colored Temperance Society was the only men's club that discriminated against black women desiring membership. In addition, it should be noted that although white feminist Amelia Bloomer protested discriminatory policies against Afro-American men and women during the antebellum temperance movement, the policies of the WCTU, founded in 1874, encouraged separate black and white local unions.[11]

Frances Harper, the black pioneer in the WCTU, spoke highly of the movement, encouraging blacks to join the segregated local unions because she believed alcohol was one of the root causes of disruption among black families. Her reports during the late 1880s indicate, however, that prejudice was prevalent not only among southern locals, but among northern and western clubs as well. Convinced that temperance was essential to black people, Harper admitted that she was nevertheless reluctant to approach the local Philadelphia union although she had spoken on behalf of temperance many times in the past. With respect to the Philadelphia union, she noted:

> For years I knew little of its proceedings, and was not sure that colored comradeship was very desirable, but having attended a local union in Philadelphia, I was asked to join and acceded to the request, and was made city and afterwards state superintendent of work among colored people. Since then, for several years I have held the position of the National Superintendent of work among the colored people of the north.[12]

When Harper was appointed to the national office, no other black women held positions on the executive committee or on the board of superintendents. However, the race question was an issue which concerned her because "some of the members of different unions have met the question in a liberal and Christian manner, others have not seemed . . . to make the distinction between Christian affiliation and social equality." In 1889, Harper published a summary of reports from the black state superintendents throughout the nation. The attitudes which prevailed among black women reflected race identity on the one hand and the issue of discrimination against black women by white women on the other.[13]

Throughout the 1890s, Josephine St. Pierre Ruffin, a younger contemporary of Harper, challenged white women to unite with blacks for the benefit of humanity. Her words went unheeded. She was discriminated against personally when attending the Milwaukee convention of the General Federation of Women's Clubs in 1900. Very fair in color, Ruffin was mistaken for a white woman by the female delegates until they discovered that she was not only representing the predominantly white New England Federation of Woman's Clubs but also the black Woman's Era Club. Her credentials were discredited, and the women attempted to bar her from the convention. After much protest on her part, Ruffin was recognized as a delegate from the white group, while her credentials from the black group were rejected. Disillusioned by the incident, the

Woman's Era Club made an official statement which included the view "that colored women should confine themselves to their clubs and the large field of work open to them there."[14]

At the same convention of the General Federation of Women's Clubs, Mary Church Terrell, president of the National Association of Colored Women, was refused permission to bring the group greetings on behalf of her association because the southern clubs objected, threatening resignation. Despite this rebuff, Mary Church Terrell was invited to speak before other white groups during the early years of the twentieth century. At the Minneapolis Convention of Women in 1900 she addressed the group not only about the needs of black women but also about the prejudice and lack of sympathy on the part of white women. She indicated them for not extending a helping hand to blacks whose aims were similar to their own. The same year Terrell made a similar speech at the National American Woman Suffrage Association meeting in Washington.[15]

Ida B. Wells-Barnett, another nationally known black club leader, noted the attempt of Fannie Barrier Williams, a black woman, to join the Chicago Woman's Club in 1894. The all-white group split over the controversy created by those who wanted a black member and those who did not. After fourteen months of controversy, Williams was admitted. At the turn of the century, Wells-Bernett noted that the issue was still significant in Illinois when the State Federation of Women's Clubs membership made it impossible for black clubs to become members. Nonetheless, black women's clubs were so numerous that by the second decade of the century a large federation of colored women's clubs was active in black communities throughout Illinois. In 1914, Wells-Barnett helped to organize the Alpha Suffrage Club of black women, who were influential later in electing black Congressman Oscar De Priest.[16]

The experiences of Harper, Ruffin, Terrell, Williams, and Wells-Barnett were not unique. Fannie Barrier Williams, chronicler of the club movement among Afro-American women, assessed the attitudes of both black and white women during the early twentieth century. Of the attitude of white women's clubs she said:

> While many colored women in the Northern states have been welcomed as members to white women's clubs as individuals, the question of their admission in some instances has given rise to some of the

fiercest controversy over the colored question that has been witnessed in this country for many years.[17]

As for the attitude of Afro-American women in the controversy,
she said:

> The colored women have kept themselves serene while this color-
> line controversy has been raging around them. They have taken a
> keen and intelligent interest in all that has been said for and against
> them, but through it all they have lost neither their patience nor their
> hope in the ultimate triumph of right principles.[18]

During this same period, the woman suffrage campaign gained
momentum. As historian Aileen Kraditor has observed, white
supremacy was an influential factor in the strategy of the suffragists as the need developed for southern support for a woman
suffrage amendment. As early as the 1890s, Susan B. Anthony
realized the potential to the woman suffrage cause in wooing
southern white women. She chose expedience over loyalty and
justice when she asked veteran feminist supporter Frederick Douglass not to attend the National American Woman Suffrage Association convention scheduled in Atlanta. Anthony explained to Ida B.
Wells-Bernett that Douglass's presence on the stage with the
honored guests would have offended the southern hosts. Wells-
Barnett, however, admonished Anthony for giving in to racial
prejudice despite the potential setbacks to the woman suffrage
cause.[19]

During the National American Woman Suffrage Association
(NAWSA) meeting of 1903 in New Orleans, the *Times Democrat*
assailed the association because of its negative attitude on the
question of black women and the suffrage for them. In a prepared
statement signed by Susan B. Anthony, Carrie C. Catt, Anna Howard Shaw, Kate N. Gordon, Alice Stone Blackwell, Harriet Taylor
Upton, Laura Clay, and Mary Coggeshall, the board of officers of
the NAWSA endorsed the organization's states' rights position,
which was tantamount to an endorsement of white supremacy in
most states, particularly in the South. During the convention week,
Susan B. Anthony visited the black Phillis Wheatley Club in New
Orleans. In presenting flowers to Anthony on the occasion, Syl-
vamie Williams, president of the club, indicated that black women
were painfully aware of their position among white suffragists. She

compared black women to flowers "trodden under foot," stating: "When women like you, Miss Anthony, come to see us and speak to us it helps us believe in the Fatherhood of God and the brotherhood of Man, and at least for the time being in the sympathy of women."[20]

Although those national suffrage leaders who courted black support spoke in terms of equal suffrage among the races while in black circles, their public actions and statements to the mainstream society were often contradictory. Alice Paul, organizer of the suffrage parade in front of the White House in 1913, had professed her sympathy for black woman's suffrage. Before the parade, however, the leaders asked Ida B. Wells-Barnett, who was representing the Chicago suffrage club of black women, not to march with the white Chicago delegation. The rationale was fear of offending white southern women. In 1919, Mary Church Terrell confided her feelings about Alice Paul to Walter White of the NAACP. Both questioned Paul's loyalty to black women, concluding that if she and other white suffragist leaders could get the amendment through without enfranchising black women they would.[21]

Why this suspicion among black leaders on the eve of the passage of the Nineteenth Amendment? In the past, nearly all the major white suffrage leaders had compromised their support of black woman suffrage. Despite endorsement of black suffrage, Anna Howard Shaw had been accused of refusing to allow a black female delegate at the Louisville suffrage convention in 1911 to make an antidiscrimination resolution. As president of the NAWSA from 1910 to 1915, she avoided offending the states' rights position of the South, which rejected universal female suffrage because black women would be included.[22]

Aileen Kraditor observed the strength of the states' rights arguments among southern white suffragists when she contrasted the positions of Laura Clay of Kentucky and Kate Gordon of Louisiana. Kraditor noted their 1910 positions:

Kentucky, with a small Negro minority, could, according to Miss Clay, afford to give the Negro full security in his voting rights, provided women were enfranchised. Her views on the question of Negro suffrage were moderation itself contrasted to those of Miss Gordon, who lived in a state with a very large Negro population. To her, woman suffrage should, if possible, be accompanied by a "whites only" clause, and she showed considerable ingenuity in her endeavors to make such a clause constitutional.[23]

By 1919, however, Laura Clay had amended her position. She proposed, at the Jubilee convention of the NAWSA, "that certain sections be amended with particular reference to those parts that would permit the enfranchisement of Negro women in the South."[24]

Although southern white suffragists remained somewhat consistent in their position on race and suffrage, throughout the period, northern white suffragists continued to maintain ambivalent positions. Jeannette Rankin of Montana, the first female elected to the United States Congress, courted black support for the suffrage amendment among black women at Howard University, in May 1917. A few months later, in October 1917, she took the white side in a labor dispute among black and white women working at the Bureau of Engraving in the District of Columbia when the white women protested against working with blacks. As a result, in his column in the *New York Age*, suffrage supporter James Weldon Johnson questioned Rankin's loyalty to black women.[25]

Carrie Chapman Catt, president of the NAWSA in 1919, was supported by Ida Husted Harper, editor of the *History of Woman Suffrage*, when she discouraged the black Northeastern Federation of Women's Clubs representing nine states from applying for membership in the national suffrage body. Both women felt the black group would offend the white southern organizations and hamper passage of the amendment. Both Catt and Harper had argued in favor of black female suffrage in the past.[26]

Despite white resistance, most black leaders, both men and women, supported woman's suffrage because they hoped that black women could help uplift the standards of the race through exercising the franchise. The vote was believed to be the panacea to race problems. When white groups rejected black members, blacks formed their own groups as they had done in the cases of the abolitionist, temperance, and woman's club movements.

The failure of white female reformers to include the activities of black women in their records of the woman's movement has led some historians to assume that Afro-Americans did not participate or were merely objects of discrimination. Historian Louis Filler contends that the paucity of black women in the antebellum woman's movement was not because they were not welcomed by white reformers but was due to the fact that black women regarded the antislavery movement as the more urgent cause. Filler's position rests upon a shaky foundation, however, for historian Benjamin Quarles finds that the black female abolitionists believed in equal suffrage not only between the races but between the sexes. If Quarles is correct, one must find other reasons why black women did not join woman's rights groups.[27]

Eleanor Flexner's interpretation of the black female reformer and her relationship to feminism is similar to that of Louis Filler. She believes that black women considered antislavery work more imperative than woman's rights. To date, the role of the black female reformer during the antebellum period has not been examined thoroughly. For this reason, the Filler and Flexner conclusions appear to be premature. For example, Flexner mentions the abolitionist and journalist Mary Ann Shadd Cary, but neglects to include her among the black feminist supporters of the day. During the post-Civil War years, Cary lived in the District of Columbia, where she not only supported and attended woman's suffrage activities, but advocated women's cooperatives, women's newspapers, and temperance. Throughout the 1870s, she attended meetings of the National Woman Suffrage Association and, in 1878, she marked twenty years of service to the woman's rights cause.[28] Although Cary's reform activities extended from the 1850s until her death in 1893, she received little recognition by the contemporary leadership of the woman's movement during the nineteenth century and by historians of today.

The Cary case is not an isolated one. In 1870, several blacks in South Carolina organized the racially integrated South Carolina Woman's Rights Association under the auspices of the American Woman Suffrage Association. Among the Afro-American women were the wives of black congressmen Robert C. De Large and Alonzo Ransier. K. Rollin served as the secretary for the group, and her sister Lottie represented the body at the American Woman Suffrage Association convention held in New York City in 1872. Despite these activities, when the history of the woman's movement in South Carolina was written for the *History of Woman Suffrage* in 1900, Virginia D. Young, president of the South Carolina Woman Suffrage Association, dated the start of the movement as

1890, the year her organization was founded. No mention was made of the group founded twenty years earlier.[29]

Furthermore, in the *History of Woman Suffrage*, volume six, editor Ida Husted Harper included only passing reference to the role of black women in the movement from 1900 and 1920. The historical fallacy has been perpetuated by feminists in the 1960s and 1970s as well. In repeating what history has taught them, they have assumed that black women heretofore have been uninterested in woman's rights issues. In describing the current participation of black women in the feminist struggle as a recent development or in describing black women merely as objects of discrimination in the woman's movement or in neglecting the participation of black women entirely, these feminist writers grossly distort reality.[30]

The black feminist movement in the United States during the mid-1970s is a continuation of a trend that began over 150 years ago. Institutionalized discrimination against black women by white women has traditionally led to the development of racially separate groups that address themselves to race-determined problems as well as to the common plight of women in America. At the same time, Afro-American women, motivated by sense of racial solidarity and a special identity arising out of the uniqueness of the black experience, have tended to identify in their own way with the larger social movements in American society.

NOTES

1. For white feminists who encouraged black women, see Susan B. Anthony and Ida Husted Harper, eds., *History of Woman Suffrage, 1883-1900* (New York: Arno Press and the *New York Times*, 1969), pp. 395, 398-99; Josephine St. Pierre Ruffin, "Trust Women," *The Crisis* 10 (August 1915): 188.

2. Louis Filler, *The Crusade Against Slavery, 1830-1860* (New York: Harper and Row, 1960), p. 179; Eleanor Flexner, *Century of Struggle: The Woman's Rights Movement in the United States* (Cambridge, Mass.: Belknap Press of Harvard University Press, 1959; paperback edition, New York: Atheneum, 1973), pp. 43-44, 89-90; June Sochen, *Herstory: A Woman's View of American History* (New York: Alfred Publishing Co., 1974), pp. 130-134, 390-92.

3. Flexner, *Century of Struggle* p. 144; Miriam Schneir, ed., *Feminism: The Essential Historical Writings* (New York: Vintage Books, 1972), p. xiv; Robert L. Allen and Pamela P. Allen, *Reluctant Reformers: Racism and Social Reform Move-*

ments in the United States (Washington, D.C.: Howard University Press, 1974), pp. 145-46, 156.

4. William C. Nell, *Colored Patriots of the American Revolution* (Boston: Robert F. Wallcut, 1855), p. 351; J. W. Gibson and W. H. Crogman, *Progress of a Race, Or the Remarkable Advancement of the Colored American* (Naperville, Ill.: J. L. Nichols and Co., 1902, 1912), pp. 181-82; Benjamin Quarles, *Black Abolitionists* (New York: Oxford University Press, 1969), pp. 26-30.

5. Gerda Lerner, ed., *Black Women in White America: A Documentary History* (New York: Pantheon Books, 1972), pp. 362-65; Quarles, *Black Abolitionists* pp. 48-49.

6. Filler, *The Crusade against Slavery*, p. 179.

7. Flexner, *Century of Struggle*, pp. 89-90, 97-98.

8. Sojourner Truth, *Narrative of Sojourner Truth: A Bondswoman of Olden Time* (Chicago: Thompson Publishing Co., Inc. Ebony Classics, 1970), pp. 102-4, 107-8.

9. Elizabeth Cady Stanton, Susan B. Anthony, and Matilda J. Gage, eds., *History of Woman Suffrage, 1861-1876* (New York: Arno Press and the *New York Times*, 1969), pp. 310-11.

10. Stanton, et al., *History of Woman Suffrage, 1861-1876*, p. 849; Elizabeth Cady Stanton, Susan B. Anthony, and Matilda J. Gage, eds., *History of Woman Suffrage, 1876-1885* (New York: Arno Press and the *New York Times*, 1969), pp. 346-47, 358.

11. Roslyn Cleagle, "The Colored Temperance Movement: 1830-1860" (Washington, D.C.: unpublished M.A. thesis, Department of History, Howard University, 1969), pp. 63, 64-65, 67-69.

12. Frances W. Harper, "The Woman's Christian Temperance Union and the Colored Woman," *A.M.E. Church Review* 4 (1888): 314.

13. Frances W. Harper, "National Woman's Christian Temperance Union," *A.M.E. Church Review* 5 (1889): 242-45.

14. Gibson, *Progess of a Race*, pp. 216-20.

15. Rayford W. Logan, *The Negro in the United States* (Princeton: Van Nostrand, 1957), p. 52; *Minneapolis Journal*, November 1900, Mary Church Terrell Papers, Manuscript Division, Library of Congress, Washington, D.C.; Anthony, *History of Woman Suffrage*, pp. 358-59.

16. Ida B. Wells-Barnett, *Crusade for Justice: The Autobiography of Ida B. Wells-Barnett* ed. Alfreda Duster (University of Chicago Press, 1970), pp. 345, 346-47.

17. Gibson, *Progress of a Race*, p. 216.

18. Ibid., p. 226.

19. Aileen Kraditor, *The Ideas of the Woman Suffrage Movement, 1890-1920* (Garden City, N.Y.: Anchor Books, Doubleday and Co., Inc., 1971), pp. 213-14; Wells-Barnett, *Crusade for Justice*, pp. 229-30.

20. Ida Husted Harper, ed., *History of Woman Suffrage, 1900-1920* (New York: Arno Press and the *New York Times*, 1969), pp. 55, 59, 60, n.1.

21. Kraditor, *Ideas of Woman Suffrage* pp. 167-68; Walter White to Mary Church Terrell, 14 March 1919, Mary Church Terrell Papers, no. 3.

22. Anna H. Shaw, "Votes for All," *The Crisis* 15 (November 1917): 19; *The Crisis* 4 (June 1912): 76-77.

23. Kraditor, *Ideas of Woman Suffrage*, p. 144.

24. *The Crisis* 17 (June 1919): 103.

25. *The New York Age* 10 May 1917, 11 October 1917.

26. Ida Harper to Mary Church Terrell, 18 March 1919, Mary Church Terrell Papers, no. 3; Carrie C. Catt, "Votes for All," *The Crisis* 15 (November 1917): 20-21.

27. Filler *Crusade against Slavery*, p. 179; Quarles *Black Abolitionists*, p. 179.

28. Statement of Purpose, Colored Women's Progressive Franchise Association, Biography; D. Bethune Duffie to Hon. I. M. Howard, 29 July 1870, Correspondence, Cary, MAS, 1 September 1874, Mary Ann Shadd Cary Papers, Moorland-Spingarn Research Center, Howard University, Washington, D.C.; Flexner, *Century of Struggle*, pp. 89-90, 97-98.

29. Stanton, *History of Woman Suffrage 1876-1885*, p. 828; Anthony, *History of Woman Suffrage, 1883-1900*, p. 922.

30. See Anthony, *History of Woman Suffrage, 1883-1900*; Anne F. and Andrew M. Scott, *One Half the People: The Fight for Woman Suffrage* (Philadelphia: J. B. Lippincott, 1975); Celestine Ware, *Woman Power* (New York: Tower Public Affairs Books, 1970); Schneir, *Feminism*. For additional sources see a general assessment of the historiography on blacks in the twentieth-century suffrage movement in Rosalyn Terborg-Penn, "The Historical Treatment of the Afro-American in the Woman's Suffrage Movement, 1900-1920: A Bibliographical Essay," *A Current Bibliography on African Affairs* 7 (Summer 1974): 245-59. For a discussion of the stereotyped images of black women, see Mae C. King, "The Politics of Sexual Stereotypes," *Black Scholar* 4 (March-April 1973): 12-23.

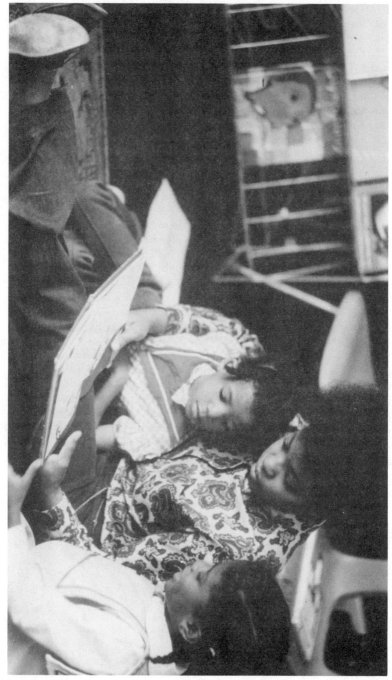

Day care center, Washington, D.C. Photo: United Nations/W. A. Graham, No. 140 155.

4

Black Women and Racial "Uplift" Prior to Emancipation*

Linda Perkins

The efforts of whites, both male and female in the abolitionist and antislavery movement have been well documented. And, while numerous studies and biographies provide some information concerning black male involvement in the pre-Civil War era, with the exception of Harriet Tubman and Sojourner Truth, little is known of the important role that black women played in improving the condition of their race during the antebellum period.[1]

In view of the dual oppression of blacks and females, an assessment of black women's efforts in the early and mid-nineteenth century sheds light not only on their significance to the race but also reveals the difference in the perception of a woman's "place" and role within the black community from that of the larger American society.

This essay examines the role of the black female prior to emancipation and highlights some of her activities in the "uplift" (as it was then termed) of the black race. Particular focus shall be given to the attention placed upon self-help, aiding improverished members of the race in the North, as well as the ardent efforts made by black women to abolish slavery. Throughout the nineteenth century, the threads that held together the organizational as well as individual pursuits of black women were those of "duty" and "obligation" to the race. The concept of racial obligation was intimately linked with the concept of racial "uplift" and "elevation".

Although slavery had been legally abolished in the North by the 1830s, racism remained. In the aftermath of Northern slavery, free

*The author would like to thank the National Institute of Education for support given during the preparation of this article.

blacks were subjected to severe economic, occupational, and educational restrictions. Particularly destitute were black women, who outnumbered black men and were often widowed or single with dependent children. A report at the beginning of the nineteenth century illustrated the occupational caste into which most blacks were placed. It noted that while some black men in the North were employed as mechanics or mariners, most were day laborers. Black women, the report continued, "generally, both married and single, wash clothes for a livelihood."[2]

Northern blacks often voiced the opinion that the activities of white abolitionists were more theoretical than practical and tended to stress merely the abolition of Southern slavery while overlooking the dire needs of Northern blacks. Further, many blacks complained of the prejudice and condescension they experienced in their associations with the white abolitionists. One black stated, "whatever they [white abolitionists] do for us savors of pity, and is done at arm's length," while another commented that white abolitionists were only interested in the emancipation of blacks and not their "elevation."[3]

Thus, in an attempt to "elevate" themselves economically, educationally politically, and socially, blacks formed societies and organizations to work towards that end. The 1827 premier issue of the first black newspaper, Freedom's Journal, stated its purpose, reflecting the attitude of many blacks of the North: "we wish to plead our own cause. Too long have others spoken for us."[4]

Pooling their financial resources, blacks organized mutual aid and benevolent organizations as early as the 1780s. The African Union Society of Newport, Rhode Island was the first such organization to appear in 1780. Consisting of both black men and women, the group formed "to promote the welfare of the colored community ... by helping apprentice Negroes, and by assisting members in the time of distress." Similar societies such as the African Society of Boston and the Friendly Society of St. Thomas in Philadelphia also appeared by the 1790s with the focus of their beneficence being widows and orphaned children.[5]

By the 1820s, Philadelphia maintained the largest population of blacks in the North, two-thirds of which were female. This statistical imbalance within the black community resulted in a proliferation of mutual aid societies to assist women. By 1838, two-thirds of the 100 black mutual aid societies of the city with memberships totaling 7,600 were female. In addition, the poor black women in these societies provided two-thirds of the $20,000 raised by the groups in 1838 to help support themselves as well as others. Paying normally 12 1/2 cents a month or $1.00 quarterly to organizations such as the Dorcas Society, the Sisterly Union, the United Daughters of Wilberforce, or the African Female Union could provide a poor black woman assurance that she would be taken care of if she became ill, would receive a decent burial when she died, and that her children would be provided for by the funds from the societies. Because the societies had various foci, many women joined several of the groups. The Dorcas Society, for example, provided clothing and funds for the sick or infirm of any age while membership in the Daughters of Absalom was restricted to women over forty-five years of age.[6]

The above societies were testimonies to the ability of blacks to aid themselves. Throughout the pre-Civil War years, self-reliance was stressed. At a black national convention in 1848, the body stated, "to be dependent, is to be degraded,". Thus, as Benjamin Quarles noted in hist study of black abolitionists, the formation of black mutual socieites demonstrated that "a Negro family, no matter how poor, was determined that no town hearse would ever drive to its door." The predominatly Quaker Pennsylvania Abolition Society also commented upon the significance of the mutual aid societies in 1837 stating the groups had "a powerful influence in preventing pauperism and crime."[7]

As antislavery activities increased in the 1830s, black women, despite their poverty, were among the forerunners in such endeavors. When William Lloyd Garrison, famed abolitionist and editor of *The Liberator*, lectured in Salem, Massachusetts during the fall of 1832, and commented that there were no black antislavery socieites, a letter to the editor appeared in the paper shortly thereafter informing him that there was indeed such a society formed by "females of color" in February of that year. The letter enclosed a copy of the constitution of the Female Anti-Slavery Society of Salem, the first such organization by American women. In common with all black organizations formed during this period, the women stated that their purpose was to work for "mutual improvement" and "to promote the welfare of our color". Also, the writer informed the readers that there was still another black female organization established for over fifteen years—the Colored Female Religious and Moral Society of Salem formed in 1818. In a subsequent issue of *The Liberator*, a copy of the organization's constitution was also published. Although the group termed itself "religious and moral," the constitution revealed that the group was also an educational and benvolent organization. Membership was open to any female agreeing to conform to the bylaws of the constitution and pay the annual 52 cents dues. The group resolved to keep "a charitable watch over one another; to aid the sick and destitute members, and to meet weekly to study history, read interesting and useful books, and write and converse upon the sufferings of our enslaved sisters," and requested that "any plan that may be suggested for their melioration" would be welcomed.[8]

Predominantly white female antislavery societies such as the Boston Female Anti-Slavery Society and Philadelphia Female Anti-Slavery Society were subsequently formed in the 1830s and received greater prominence because of the membership of leading personalities such as Maria Weston Chapman and Lucretia Mott. Although blacks were with few exceptions barred from membership in the white antislavery societies, the Salem Female Anti-Slavery Society and the Colored Female Religious and Moral Society which were organized prior to the establishment of their white counterparts, indicated black women's desire to control and head their own socieites as well as demonstrate self-help. The above two black societies along with many others during and after the antebellum period raised money and supported a range of abolitionsts' activities.[9]

While many Northern black women were active participants on the underground railroad, the most famed being Harriet Tubman, Southern black women such as Ellen Craft and Anna Murray Douglass, wife of Frederick Douglass, aided in the escape of slaves and participated in slave revolts. Organizing with black men, the women of the race established and held positions on vigilance committees that aided runaway slaves by providing food, clothing, and money as well as finding employment for them. For example, two of the seven black directors of the New England Freedom Association whose function was to "extend a helping hand to all who may bid adieu to whips and chains" were females. Similarly, four of the nine members of the black vigilance committee of Cleveland were also women.[10]

Cooperative efforts between black females and males were common during the early nineteenth century. The disenfranchisement and oppression of all blacks left little room for male chauvisnism. Because the institution of slavery forced black women into work situations alongside the black male, having to endure the same punishments and hardships, sex role differentiation was minimized to a large extent within the slave community. Thomas Webber in his study of education of the slave quarters found this aspect of the slave community the most startling. He wrote, "one is struck by the absence of the familiar theme of male superiority and by the lack of evidence to support the view that the quarters was a female-dominated society." Although the traditional sex roles of cooking for females and hunting for men were prevalent,. It was not uncommon to find slave narratives depicting men as sewing, caring for children, or cooking. By the same token, women were frequently found as preachers, doctors, conjurors, storytellers, champion cotton pickers and respected leaders within the slave community. Since liberation of the race was the immediate goal of blacks, the men attached great importance to the females' roles in this effort. While sexism was not completely absent from the black community, black men became some of the earliest advocates of women's rights. In 1869 when black men formed the Colored National Labor Union, they admitted black women and elected a female to the executive committee of the group. The body voted to uphold equal rights for women and further stated that they were "profiting by the mistakes heretofore made by our white fellow citizens in omitting women."[11] Even by the turn of the century, John Daniels in his study of blacks in Boston observed that "with the Negroes there is a closer approximation to equality between the sexes than is yet the case among those of the other race." He concluded that this was due to the economic condition of blacks and further commented, thus,

> they [black women] have made a relatively greater economic contribution within their race than have white women in theirs, and so they have attained a place of relatively greater importance in the social order of their own community. Negro women manifest a marked independence, coupled with a sober realization of the extent to which the welfare of the race is in their hands. Negro men recog-

nize and respect their position. The women take and are given a very important share in race affairs.[12]

The reality that a free black woman and later her emancipated sister would often become the primary, supplemental, or sole breadwinner, resulted in black men speaking out for women's economic and educational improvement as well as their own. Black abolitionist Martin Delaney wrote in 1852 of the menial occupations of black women and how black men lamented that the women were forced to perform "the drudgery and menial offices of other men's wives and daughters." And, while white females were found employed in more than a hundred industrial occupations during the first half of the nineteenth century, prejudice by this group barred black women from similar occupations—the same prejudice by that barred black men from jobs. Thus, race and not sex solidarity was the priority among blacks.[13]

And, while white females were found employed in more than a hundred industrial occupations during the first half of the nineteenth century, prejudice by this group barred black women from similar occupations—the same prejudice by that barred black men from jobs. Thus, race and not sex solidarity was the priority among blacks.[13]

Although a few white female abolitionists such as Abby Kelly Foster, Lucretia Mott, and the Grimke sisters were staunch advocates of social as well as political equality for blacks, they held a minority opinion even among abolitionists. For example, members of the Female Anti-Slavery Society of Fall River, Massachusetts vehemently opposed black female membership and threatened to dissolve when the issue was raised. The women argued that if admitted, black women would be perceived as being "on an equality with ourselves."[14] This view was no different than that of their male counterparts. In fact, many of the white female abolitionists were the nonworking daughters, wives, and sisters of prominent men and involved themselves in the antislavery movement because of the availability of leisure time rather than a great sympathy to the cause. Making this observation, in 1839 abolitionist Hannah Smith wrote Abby Kelly of her apparent displeasure with many of the white female anti-slavery workers:

> . . . they [white females] appeared to join [antislavery societies] more because their husbands were abolitionists than they themselves felt

interested, and hardly seemed to understand the principles of the cause they were advocating—Indeed, I do not know of one anti-slavery women of the right stamp in Connecticut of sufficient infor-mation and energy to organize a Society or manage its concerns.[15]

In contrast, black female antislavery activites included poor working women as well as the middle class. Many had been former slaves and were intimately linked to the abolitionist as well as other self-help activities not as a social outlet or to please a husband, but out of a lifetime commitment to not only emancipate but "elevate" the race.

Continuing their separate activities, black women frequently received praise for their endeavors from abolitionist newspapers. When the Colored Female Produce Society was established in early 1831 for the purpose of boycotting slave made products, the *Genius of Universal Emancipation* reported that: "their [black women's] promptness and numbers are a reproach to the inactive carelessness of their white sisters and we sincerely hope they will persevere undiscouraged in the noble course they have commenced."[16]

Of the many contributions made by black women during the antebellum period, their role in education was one of their most salient. Since the intellectual inferiority of the race was the primary justification for slavery, central to their mission of "uplift", blacks sought as a central goal in their mission of uplift to improve their education to help dispel the widespread myth of the dull black intellect. In the 1829 *Appeal* of the militant David Walker, he told the members of his race:

> I would crawl on my hands and knees through mud and mire, to sit at the feet of a learned man, where I would sit and humbly supplicate him to instill into me, that which devils nor tyrants could remove, only with my life—for coloured people to acquire learning in this country, make tyrants quake and tremble on their sandy founda-tion...the bare name of educating the coloured people, scares our cruel oppressor almost to death.[17]

The need for the education of the race was again voiced at a black national conference in 1832 with the body resolving that "if we [black people] ever expect to see the influence of prejudice decrease and ourselves respected, it must be by the blessings of an enlight-ened education."[18] This emphasis upon education was directed to the black female as well as the male.

As in other activities during the period, black women were among the earliest educators of the race. In 1793, Caterine Ferguson purchased her freedom and opened "Katy Ferguson's School for the Poor" in New York City for both black and white pupils. In the same year "the Committee for Improving the Condition of Free Blacks in Pennsylvania" opened a school and recommended "a well qualified" black female teacher.[19]

And, while the dangers of education for women were constantly being debated in the larger society, and articles proliferated regarding a "womens sphere" and the "cult of true womanood"—all stressing the servility and submissiveness expected of females— blacks encouraged the women of their race to become educated to aid in race improvement. In the black newspaper *The Weekly Advocate*, an 1837 article entitled "To the Females of Colour" urged black women to seek an education for the benefit of the race. The article stated, "In any enterprise for the improvement of our people, either moral or mental, our hands would be palsied without woman's influence." Thus, the article continued, "let our beloved female friends, then, rouse up, and exert all their power, in encouraging, and sustaining this effort (education) which we have made to disabuse the public mind of the misrepresentations made of our character; and to show to the world, that there is virtue among us, though concealed; talent, though buried; intelligence, though overlooked."[20]

Prior to and after the Civil War, it was not uncommon for black families to relocate in areas where their daughters could receive a better education or to send their daughters away to be educated. For example, when Blanche V. Harris was denied admission to a white female seminary int he State of Michigan where she lived in the 1850s, her entire family moved to Oberlin, Ohio where she and her four brothers and sisters could receive an education. She graduated from the Ladies' Department of Oberlin College in 1860 as a sister did ten years later. Similarly, the parents of Mary Jane Patterson, who in 1862 became the first black female to earn a college degree in America, also moved to Oberlin from North Carolina in the 1850s to educate their children. Four of the Patterson children graduated from Oberlin College (three were female).[21]

Furthermore, as arguments in the larger society continued regarding coeducation, black females were included in schools for males from the beginning. An advertisement such as "the B.F. Hughes School for Coloured Children of Both Sexes" found in an 1827 issue of the *Freedom's Journal* was typical.[22]

The largest black literary society of New York, the Pheonix, organized in 1833 provided lectures, evening schools, and a high school that was available to both male and female students and employed both black men and women as teachers. When a Philadelphia Quaker, Richard Humphreys, bequeathed $10,000 for the establishment of a trade school for blacks in that city, a group of black men approached the Quaker Managers and persuaded them to establish instead a school of "higher learning" that taught "literary subjects" to females as well as males. The men agreed and the Institute for Colored Youth of Philadelphia was opened in 1852 and became one of the leading educational institution for blacks during the nineteenth century. The Institute always maintained an all-black faculty that included the most educated black men and women of the times. Sarah Mapp Douglass, a black Quaker and abolitionist who had been trained in physiology at the University of Pennyslvania, was Principal of the Preparatory Department of the school and in 1865, Fanny Jackson Coppin and Mary Jane Patterson, the first two black women to receive college degrees in the nation, were appointed Principal and Assistant Principal, respectively.[23]

Literary and educational societies for the expressed purpose of mental improvement came into being during the early nineteenth century. Philadelphia was the leader in such organizations. In 1831, three years after the first black male literary society was established, a group of black women formed the Female Literary Association of Philadelphia. This group viewed their efforts not only as a means of self-improvement but also as a means of race improvement. In the preamble of the group's constitution, the women stated, "it therefore becomes a duty incumbent upon us as women, as daughters of a despised race, to use our utmost endeavors to enlighten the understanding, to cultivate the talents entrusted to our keeping, that by so doing, we may in a great measure, break down the strong barrier of prejudice, and raise ourselves to an equality with those of our fellow beings, who differ from us in complexion." Upon election into the organization, a $1.50 annual fee was required. Poems, essays, and short stories were submitted unsigned to be critiqued by the group. To counteract charges against the intellectual capabilities of blacks, *The Liberator* often published samples of the women's literary works. After visiting a meeting of the organization, William Lloyd Garrison reported, "if the traducers of the colored race could be acquainted with the moral worth, just refinement, and large intelligence of this association, their mouths would hereafter be dumb."[24]

One year after the formation of the Philadelphia association, the Afri-American Female Intelligence Society was established in Boston "to associate for the diffusion of knowledge, the suppression of vice and immorality, and for cherishing such virtues as will render us happy and useful to society." An initial fee of twenty-five cents was required to join the organization and 12 1/2 cents was charged thereafter. The funds were used for the purchasing of books and newspapers and for the renting of a room for their meetings. Regular attendance was strictly enforced with a fine imposed for absenteeism. Although educational in purpose, the organization also had a charitable component providing one dollar a week to any member of one year's standing who became ill. Despite the year's qualification for aid, the group agreed to aid any number "in case of unforeseen and afflictive event," stating "it shall be the duty of the Society to aim them as far as in their power . . . " This was the first such society among blacks in Boston.[25]

A black female, Maria W. Stewart, lecturing before the Afric-American Society became the first American female to speak in public in 1832. Less than six weeks of education in her background, the deeply religious Stewart had been inspired by the words of David Walker in his *Appeal* and urged black women to improve their education and aid in the struggle for racial "uplift." She told the women: "Oh, daughters of Africa, awake! arise!, show forth the world that yea are endowed with noble and exalted faculties . . . let us promote ourselves and improve our own talents." She expressed the importance of higher education and academies for black women and suggested that the women pool their resources to establish a high school. Informing her audience that "knowledge is power", she also told them to establish businesses and become economically independent. "Don't say I can't, but I will" was her challenge to her fellow sisters. Giving four lectures in Boston in 1832-33, Stewart continued to impress upon blacks their duty and obligation to the race. In the 1830s she moved to New York City, was educated through membership in the black female literary societies of the city, and subsequently became a teacher.[26]

Not only was Maria Stewart's public speaking viewed as radical, but the message that she provided her mixed audience, during an age when women, like children, were expected to be seen and not heard, was viewed as being quite "promiscuous". Yet, she paved the way for many other black women who would take the public platform to plead for the rights of their race.

The literary societies established by blacks prior to the Civil War performed great services with their communities in the education of their race by providing lectures, libraries, and reading rooms as well as instruction. In 1849, over half of the black population of Philadelphia belonged to one of the 106 literary organizations of the city. And, by the 1840s, the Ohio Ladies Education Society, formed by black women in 1837, was reported to have done "more towards the establishment of schools for the education of colored people at this time in Ohio than any other organized group."[27]

While most of the literary associations greatly aided adults in obtaining or increasing their literacy, the black communities during the antebellum period frequently voiced concerned regarding the lack of educational institutions available to their female youth. *The Colored American*, a black newspaper of the 1830s appealed to white females to admit black females into their seminaries, and when these appeals went unheard, again in 1839 wrote that there was only one seminary available for black females to attend. The article stated, "the culture of the black female's minds require more care and attention, and it should not be neglected."[28]

Though there were scattered opportunities for black females to receive a common school education in the North prior to the Civil War, a secondary education was far more difficult to obtain. Thus, the founding in 1829 of the St. Frances Academy for Colored Girls in Baltimore, a boarding school, was an important event for the race. The institution was established by a group of black nuns (the Oblate Order) who had migrated to Baltimore from Santo Domingo. Most of the women had been educated in France and were of financial means. Elizabeth Lange, who became the First Superior of the Order and head of the school, had operated a free school for poor black children in her home prior to the opening of the St. Frances and conducted her classes in French and Spanish. Because the St. Frances Academy was the only institution that was available to black females that offered courses above primary level, the school was well known. Black females from across the nation and Canada were sent there to study. To perserve their native language, the Sisters conducted classes at the Academy on alternate days completely in French. By 1865, the school was coed and known simply as the St. Frances Academy.[29]

The Institute for Colored Youth in Philadelphia, established in 1852 by Quakers as the first classical high school for blacks (both male and female), produced, along with the St. Frances Academy, some of the first formally trained black female teachers in the North prior to emancipation.

Although opportunities for the education of blacks were located overwhelmingly in the North prior to the Civil War, many clandestine schools existed in the South during this period. For example, numerous such schools were reported in Savannah, Georgia. Julian Froumountaine, a black woman from Santo Domingo, openly conducted a free school for blacks in Savannah as early as 1819 and continued secretly after the 1930s when education of blacks in the South became illegal. Another black woman, known only as Miss Dea Veaux, opened an underground school in 1838 and operated it for over twenty-five years without the knowledge of local whites. Susan King Taylor, who served in the Union Army during the Civil War as a nurse and teacher, was educated in several of the "secret" schools of Savannah and in her *Reminiscences* recalled the methods devised by the black pupils to deceive the unsuspecting whites as they went to school. Similar schools were in other areas of the South. In Natchez, Mississippi, Milla Granson became literate through the teachings of her master's children and taught hundreds of slaves to read and write in what they termed her "midnight" school because the classes were held after midnight. These educational activities reveal not only the importance that blacks placed upon education but indicated the risk that black women took to ensure that members of their race obtained it.[30]

Oberlin College in Ohio gained notoriety in 1833 when it announced that it would admit blacks and women on an equal basis with white men and became the only collegiate institution available to black women prior to the Civil War. By 1865, 140 black women had attended the College. But it was not until the 1860s that the first baccalaureate degrees were received by black women—three by the end of the Civil War. This small group of Oberlin trained black women along with those trained in other Northern high schools would contribute greatly to the formal schooling of blacks after emancipation.

One such example is Fanny Jackson Coppin. Born a slave in 1837 in the District of Columbia, her freedom was purchased by an aunt who earned only 6 dollars a month but saved until she had the necessary $125 for Fanny's manumission (by the time she was twelve). She was sent to New Bedford, Massachusetts and later to Newport, Rhode Island to live with relatives where they believed her educational opportunities would be greater. Surrounded by the mutual aid and other self-help groups, as a young girl Fanny decided her life's goal was "to get an education and teach my people." While working as a domestic in Newport, her employers allowed her to hire a tutor for one hour, three days a week. She later attended the segregated schools of Newport and by 1859 had completed the normal course at the Rhode Island State Normal School. By this time, Fanny's life's goal had expanded to meet the challenge of the antebellum Senator John C. Calhoun who stated that if he could find a black who could conjugate a Greek verb, he would change his opinion regarding the inferior intellect of blacks. Thus, deciding to continue her education, she learned of a college in Ohio whose cirriculum was the same as Harvard's and that admitted women as well as blacks. With financial assistance from her relatives and a scholarship from Bishop Daniel Payne of the African Methodist Episcopal Church, she enrolled in Oberlin College in 1860.

Recalling her days at Oberlin, Fanny Jackson stated that although Oberlin in theory offered the "gentleman's course" (as the collegiate department was termed) to females, in practise they did not encourage it. But it was the belief in racial inferiority and not sexism that most concerned her while pursuing her studies. Remembering her Oberlin days, she stated that when she rose to recite in her classes she felt as if she carried the weight of the entire African race on her shoulders for if she failed, it would have been attributed to the fact that she was black. Far from failing, she distinguished herself as an outstanding student at the College and became involved in all fascets of campus life. However, when the freedmen began pouring into Oberlin during the Civil War years, despite her studies, Fanny established a free evening school to teach them. This experience had a profound effect upon her as she witnessed black elderly working men struggling to learn simple words. She remarked, "I rejoiced that even then I could enter measurably upon the course of life which I had long ago chosen."[31]

Another black female of the North, Charlotte Forten, was also eager to help her race through education. Born free in 1837, Charlotte was the granddaughter of the wealthy John Forten and grew up in material comfort in Philadelphia. She spent her days as other affluent females did by reading classics and poetry and attending lectures and concerts. Despite the Forten's wealth, they had suffered discrimination as blacks and the entire family was actively involved in antislavery and abolitionist organizations. Charlotte studied with a private tutor as a girl because her family refused to send her to the segregated schools of Philadelphia. As an adolescent she was sent to Salem, Massachusetts to attend the integrated schools there. While in Salem, Charlotte submerged herself in the various abolitionist activities of the black women and became a member of the Female Anti-Slavery Society of Salem. These activities impressed upon her the role that black women could have in race improvement and in her journal of 1854, Charlotte wrote that she would improve her intellect to enable her "to do much towards changing the condition of my oppressed and suffering people." Deciding to become a teacher, by 1856 she had completed the normal course at Salem Normal School. Afterwards, she was appointed the first black teacher in the Salem Public Schools where she taught for two years, resigning due to poor health.

The Civil War years brought Charlotte, like Fanny Jackson, her first opportunity to teach her race. When the call came for teachers to take part in the social experiment at Port Royal, South Carolina in 1861, Charlotte enthusiastically volunteered to teach the contrabands. Arriving on St. Helena Island in October of 1861, she chronicled in detail the successes of the black pupils in her diary. While on the island she published articles in various magazines testifying to the great progress being made and the eagerness of the students of all ages to learn. She returned North in May, 1864 because of ill-health, and as Ms. Forten's biographer, Ray Billington, commented, her greatest reward in leaving "was the knowledge that the social experiment was successfull . . . and that Negroes were as capable of progress as whites."[32]

Working in the Sea Islands during the same period as Charlotte Forten was Susan King Taylor. With a background vastly different from Forten's, Taylor was born a slave in the Georgia Sea Island and grew up in Savannah where she was educated in several of the clandestine schools of the city. When only fourteen years old, she volunteered to teach in one of the freedmen schools on St. Simon Island. While there she joined the first black military regiment, Company E, serving as a laundress and nurse in the day and a teacher at night. Remaining on the island for over four years, she taught most of the men in the Company to read and write, never receiving pay the entire time. Her only compensation was to view a once illiterate slave read from a primer or Bible. In her *Reminiscences* published in 1902 Taylor stated that she was simply happy to know that her efforts had been successful and that her services had been appreciated. She did note, however, concern that by the turn of the century little attention or credit had been given to the great sacrifices and courageous acts that black women had made during the War. She noted that black women had assisted the Union Army, even at the price of death. She wrote,

> There are many people who do not know what some of the colored women did during the war. There were hundreds of them who assisted the Union soldiers by hiding them and helping them to escape. Many were punished for taking food to the prison stockades ... Others assisted in various ways the Union army. These things should be kept in history before the people. There has never been a greater war in the United States than the one in 1861, where so many lives were lost, not men alone but noble women as well.[33]

As the Civil War came to an end, black women for over half a century had sought to "uplift" themselves and the race. And, although as Susan King Taylor noted, history has overlooked their efforts, their contributions have been vast and noteworthy. Mindfully aware of their poverty, they pooled their resources to aid one another financially; with educational resources limited to them, they educated themselves as well as others; spiritually they supported each other and prayed together for a better day for black people; abhorring the insitution of slavery, they banded together to initiate and support abolitionist causes, and aided, in untold ways, to ensure the victory of the Union Army.

The early involvement of black women in the struggle for racial equality was not barred by geographical, class, educational, or age boundaries as the above examples of Coppin, Forten, and Taylor exhibit. Poor black women, throughout the pre-Civil War era, literally gave the widow's mite to support the "uplift" of their race.

And, after emancipation was finally obtained by 1865, black women were left with the arduous task of seeking elevation not only with their men but for their men. Continuing in the footsteps of their mothers and gradmothers, black women's efforts during and after Reconstruction would result in DuBois characterizing their work as the "finest chapter" in the history of black women.[34]

In assessing the role of blacks in the pre-Civil War period, it is imperative, as Susan King Taylor commented, that the efforts of black women are "kept in history before the people."[35]

NOTES

1. Standard works on white abolitionists are Alice D. Adams, *The Neglected Period of Anti-Slavery in America, 1808-31* (Boston, 1908); Louis Filler, *The Crusade Against Slavery, 1830-60* (New York, 1960); Alma Lutz, *Crusade For Freedom: Women of the Anti-Slavery Movement* (Boston: Beacon Press, 1968); Blanche G. Hersh, *The Slavery of Sex: Feminists-Abolitionists in America,* (Urbana: University of Illinois Press, 1978); Gerda Lerner, *The Grimke Sisters From South Carolina: Pioneers for Woman's Rights and Abolition,* (New York: Schocken Books, 1975); for information regarding black abolition: Herbert Aptheker, *The Negro in the Abolitionist Movement,* (New York, 1941); Frederick Douglass, *My Bondage and My Freedom* (New York, 1855); Leon F. Litwack, *North of Slavery: The Negro in the Free States, 1790-1860;* Jane H. and William H. Pease, *They Who Would Be Free: Blacks' Search for Freedom, 1830-1861,* (New York: Atheneum, 1974): for an excellent description of black male and female abolitionists' activities see Benjamin Quarles, *Black Abolitionists* (London: Oxford University Press, 1969).

2. Litwack, *North of Slavery,* p. 14; *Minutes of the Committee for Improving the Condition of Free Blacks,* Pennsylvania Abolition Society, 1790-1803, Historical Society of Pennsylvania, p. 112.

3. *Douglass's Paper,* April 13, 1855; quoted in Angelina Emily Grimke to Abby Kelley, April 15, 1837 in *Abby Kelley Foster Papers,* American Antiquarian Society.

4. *Freedom's Journal,* March 16, 1827.

5. Quoted in Irving H. Bartlett, *From Slave to Citizen: The Story of the Negro in Rhode Island* (Providence, Rhode Island, 1954), p. 35; Dorthorty Porter (ed.), *Early Negro Writings, 1760-1837* (Boston: Beacon Press, 1971), pp. 5-78.

6. Edward Needles, *An Historical Memoir of the Pennsylvania Society for Promoting the Abolition of Slavery,* (Philadelphia, 1848), p. 86; *Facts on Beneficial Societies,*

1823-1838 in Minutes of Pennyslvania Abolition Society, Historical Society of Pennsylvania.

7. *North Star*, September 22, 1848; Quarles, *Black Abolitionists*, p. 100; Needles, *An Historical Memoir*, p. 96.

8. *The Liberator*, November 17, 1832; February 16, 1833.

9. See for example Lutz's, *Crusade for Freedom*, Ira V. Brown's "Cradle of Feminism: The Philadelphia Female Anti-Slavery Society, 1833-1840" in *the Pennsylvania Magazine of History and Biography*, vol. CII. number 2, April 1978, pp. 143-166; Quarles, *Black Abolitionists*, p. 20.

10. For Ellen Craft's role in the escape of her husband and herself from slavery see William Craft's "Running a Thousand Miles for Freedom, or the Escape of William and Ellen Craft from Slavery", reprinted from the 1860 edition in Arna Bontemps (ed.), *Great Slave Narratives*, (Boston: Beacon Press); for Anna Murray's role in aiding Douglass escape see Sylvia Lyons Render's, "Afro-American Women: the Outstanding and the Obscure" in *The Quarterly Journal of the Library of Congress*, vol. 32, no. 4, October, 1975, pp. 306-321; quoted in Quarles, *Black Abolitionists*, p. 153.

11. Thomas Webber, *Deep Like the Rivers: Education in the Slave Quarter Community, 1831-1865* (New York: W. W. Norton and Company, 1978), p. 149; *Proceedings of the Colored National Labor Convention Held in Washington, D.C. on December, 6, 7, 8, 9, 10, 1869*, (Washington, D.C., 1870).

12. John Daniels, *In Freedom's Birthplace: A Study of the Boston Negroes* (reprint of the 1914 edition, New York: Arno Press, 1969), pp. 212-13.

13. Martin R. Delaney, *The Condition, Elevation, Emigration and Destiny of the Colored People of the United States* (Philadelphia, 1852), pp. 41-45; Eleanor Flexner, *Century of Struggle: The Women's Right Movement in the United States*, (Cambridge, Massachusetts: The Belknap Press of Harvard University, 1976), p. 52.

14. quoted in Litwack's, *North of Slavery*, p. 221.

15. Hannah H. Smith to Abby Kelley, July 25, 1839 in *Abby Kelley Foster Papers*, American Antiquarian Society.

16. *The Genuius of Universal Emancipation*, August, 1831, p. 57.

17. *David Walker's Appeal to the Coloured Citizens of the World* (reprint of the 1828 edition, New York: Hill and Wang, 1965), pp. 31-32.

18. *Minutes and Proceedings of the Second Annual Convention for the Improvement of the Free People of Color in these United States*, (Philadelphia, 1832), p. 34.

19. Gerda Lerner, (ed.), *Black Women in White America: A Documentary History, (New York: Vintage Books, 1973), p. 76;* Needles, *An Historical Memoir*, p. 43.

20. *The Weekly Advocate*, January 7, 1837.

21. Ellen Henle and Marlene Merrill, "Antebellum Black Coeds at Oberlin College," *Women's Studies Newsletter*, VII, number 2, (Spring, 1979), p. 10.

22. *Freedom's Journal*, March 23, 1827.

23. *The Colored American*, January 14, 1837; see Linda Marie Perkins', "Quaker Beneficence and Black Control: The Institute for Colored Youth, 1852-1903" in Vincent P. Franklin and James D. Anderson, (eds.) *New Perspectives in Black Educational History*, (Boston: G. K. Hall, 1978), pp. 19-43.

24. *The Liberator*, December 3, 1831; November 17, 1832.

25. *Genius of Universal Emancipation*, March, 1832, pp. 162-163.

26. *The Liberator*, November 17, 1832; April 27, 1833.

27. Leslie H. Fishel, Jr. "The North and the Negro, 1865-1900: A Study in Race Discrimination"(Ph. D. dissertation, Harvard University, 1953). p. 49; Dorothy B. Porter, "The Organized Educational Activities of Negro Literary Societies, 1828-1846", *The Journal of Negro Education*, volume 5, October, 1936, pp. 555-576.

28. *The Colored American*, March 18, 1837; November 23, 1839.

29. Grace H. Sherwood, *The Oblates' Hundred and One Years*, (New York: The MacMillian Company, 1931), pp. 5, 29, 34, passim.

30. Henry Allen Bullock, *A History of Negro Education in the South from 1619 to the Present*, (New York: Praeger Publishers, 1970), p. 25; J.W. Alvord, Bureau of Refugees, Freedmen and Abandoned Lands, *Fifth Semi-Annual Report on Schools for Freedmen* (Washington, D.C., 1868); pp. 29-30; W.E.B. DuBois, *The Negro Common School*, (Atlanta: University Press, 1901), p. 21; Susan King Taylor, *Reminiscences of My Life in Camp*, (reprint of 1902 edition, New York: Arno Press, 1969), pp. 7, 11; Laura S. Haviland, *A Woman's Life-Work: Labors and Experiences of Laura S. Haviland*, fourth edition, (Chicago: Publishing Association of Friends, 1889), pp. 300-311.

31. Fanny Jackson Coppin, *Reminiscences of School Life and Hints on Teaching*, (Philadelphia: AME Book Concern, 1913), passim.

32. Charlotte Forten, *Journal of Charlotte Forten*, (New York: The Dryden Press, 1953), passim.

33. Taylor, *Reminiscences*, p. 67.

34. W.E.B. DuBois, *Darkwater*, (New York: Harcourt, Brace & Howe, 1920, p. 178.

35. Taylor *Reminiscences*, p. 67.

5

The Myth of the
Black Matriarchy

Robert Staples

In dealing with the question of the role of the black woman in the
black struggle one must ultimately encounter the assertion that the
black community is organized along matriarchal lines, that the
domineering black female has been placed in a superordinate position in the family by the historical vicissitudes of slavery, and that
her ascendency to power has resulted in the psychological castration of the black male and produced a host of other negative results
that include low educational achievement, personality disorders,
juvenile delinquency etc. One of the solutions to the "Negro" question we hear is that black males divest themselves of this female
control of black society and reorganize it along patriarchal lines
which will eventually solve the problem created by black female
dominance.

And one can easily understand how the typical black female
would react when told that the problem of black liberation lies on
her shoulders, that by renouncing her control over the black male,
their other common problems such as inadequate education,
chronic unemployment and other pathologies will dissipate into a
dim memory.

The myth of a black matriarchy is a cruel hoax.

It is adding insult to injury to black liberation. For the black
female, her objective reality is a society where she is economically
exploited because she is both female and black; she must face the
inevitable situation of a shortage of black males because they have

been taken out of circulation by America's neo-colonialist wars, railroaded into prisons, or killed off early by the effects of ghetto living conditions. To label her a matriarch is a classical example of what Malcolm X called making the victim the criminal.[1]

To explode this myth of a black female matriarchy, one must understand the historical role of the black woman and the development of that role as it was influenced by the political and economic organization of American society. Like most myths, the one of a black matriarchy contains some elements of truth. Black women have not been passive objects who were satisfied with watching their menfolk make history. If they had been contented to accept the passive role ascribed to the female gender, then the travail of the past four centuries might have found the black race just as extinct as the dinosaur. It is a poor tribute to their historical deeds to characterize them as "sapphires," an opprobrious term that belies their real contribution to the black struggle.

Referring to black women as matriarchs is not only in contradistinction to the empirical reality of their status but also is replete with historical and semantic inaccuracies. It was in the study by J.J. Bachofen[2] that the term matriarchy was first employed. He was attempting to present a case for the high position of women in ancient society. His conclusion was that since free sexual relations had prevailed during that time and the fathers of the children were unknown, that this gave women their leading status in the period he called "mother-right."

A matriarchy is a society in which some, if not all, of the legal powers relating to the ordering and governing of the family-power over property, over inheritance, over marriage, over-the-house—are lodged in women rather than men.[3] If one accepts this formal definition, the consensus of most historians is that "men reign dominant in all societies; no matriarchy (i.e., a society ruled by women) is known to exist."[4]

From a historical perspective, the black woman has always occupied a highly esteemed place in black culture. The African woman who first reached the shores of the American continent was already part and parcel of the fabric of history. She was descended from women who had birthed some of the great militarists of antiquity and from whose number had come some of the most famous queens to set upon the thrones of ancient Egypt and Ethiopia. Her exploits and beauty were remembered by Semitic writers and fused into Greek mythology.[5]

Despite her important historical role, there is little doubt about the respective authority patterns in the black family of the pre-slave period of African civilization. There, the family organization was patriarchal in character and was a stable and secure institution. E. Franklin Frazier described the African patriarchal family this way:

> His wife and children gathered around him, and served him with as much respect as the best drilled domestics serve their masters; and if it was a fete day or Sunday, his sons-in-law and daughters did not fail to be present, and bring him some small gifts. They formed a circle about him, and conversed with him while he was eating. When he had finished, his pipe was brought to him, and then he bade them eat. They paid him their reverences, and passed into another room, where they all ate together with their mother.[6]

The ordeal of slavery wrought many changes in the family life of Afro-Americans, including the male and female roles. Family life of the African model was an impossibility when the slave's existence had to be devoted primarily to the cultivation and manufacturer of tobacco and cotton. The buying and selling of slaves involved the splitting up of families, while the maintenance of discipline on the plantation prevented the husband and father from protecting his wife and children against his white masters and other more favored slaves. The financial value set on slave children and the rewards given to successful motherhood in cash, kind, and promotion from field slave to house slave gave an especially high status to the mother, a status which the father could only enjoy if placed in a position akin to a stud animal, this leading to a breaking of family ties and the degradation of family life still further.

Under the conditions of slavery, the American black father was forcefully deprived of the responsibilities and privileges of father-hood. The black family's desire to remain together was subordinated to the economic interests of the slave-owning class. Only the mother-child bond continually resisted the disruptive effect of economic interests that dictated the sale of fathers away from their families. Not only did the practice of selling away fathers leave the black mother as the prime authority in the household but whenever the black male was present, he was not allowed to play the normal masculine role in American culture. Davie reports that:

In the plantation domestic establishment, the woman's role was more important than that of her husband. The cabin was hers and rations of corn and salt pork were issued to her. She cooked the meals, tended the vegetable patch, and often raised chickens to supplement the rations. If there was a surplus to sell, the money was hers. She made the clothes and reared the children. If the family received any special favors it was generally through her efforts.[7]

Just as in the society at large, power relationships in the family are aligned along economic lines. The power base of the patriarchal family is, in large part, based on the economic dependence of the female member. In the black slave family, the black woman was independent of the black male for support and assumed a type of leadership in her family life not found in the patriarchal family. At the same time, white society continued to deny black males the opportunity to obtain the economic wherewithal to assume leadership in the family constellation.

The reasons for this suppression of the black male are found in both the economic imperatives of slavery and the sexual value system of white America. In the early period of colonial America, the white family was strongly patriarchal and many of the income and property rights enjoyed by women and children were those 'given' to them by the husband or father. White women had primarily a chattel status, particularly in the Southern part of the country. They were expected to remain chaste until marriage while white southern males were permitted, or often encouraged, to sow their wild oats before, during and after marriage.[8]

A double standard of sexual behavior allowing premarital sex for men while denying it to women, always poses the problem of what females will provide the source of sexual gratification for bachelor males. There is adequate historical evidence that black slave women were forced into various sexual associations with white males because of their captive status. That physical compulsion was necessary to secure compliance on the part of black women is documented by Frazier, in relating this young man's story:

> Approximately a century and a quarter ago, a group of slaves were picking cotton on a plantation near where Troy, Alabama, is now located. Among them was a Negro woman, who despite her position, carried herself like a queen and was tall and stately. The overseer (who was the plantation owner's son) sent her to the house on some

errand. It was necessary to pass through a wooded pasture to reach
the house and the overseer intercepted her in the woods and forced
her to put her head between the rails in an old stake and rider fence,
and there in that position my great-great-grandfather was conceived.[9]

Thus, the double-standard of premarital sexual behavior allowed
the Southern white woman to remain "pure" and the bodies of the
captive female slaves became the objects of their ruler's sexual
passion. Consequently, black males had to be suppressed to prevent
them from daring to defend the black woman's honor. For those
black males who would not accept their suppression passively, the
consequences were severe. As one person reports the story of his
father's defense of his mother:

> His right ear had been cut off close to his head, and he had received a
> hundred lashes on his back. He had beaten the overseer for a brutal
> assault on my mother, and this was his punishment. Furious at such
> treatment, my father became a different man, and was so morose,
> disobedient, and intractable, that Mr. N. decided to sell him. He
> accordingly parted with him, not long after, to his son, who lived in
> Alabama; and neither mother nor I ever heard from him again.[10]

During the period of slavery, the physical resistance of black
males to the rape of their women was met with all the brutal
punishment white society could muster. That they were not totally
successful in their efforts to crush the black man is evidenced in the
heroic deeds of Denmark Vesey, Nat Turner, Frederick Douglass,
David Walker and others. The acts of these black males are sometimes played down in favor of the efforts of Harriet Tubman,
Sojourner Truth and other black females in securing the slave's
freedom. Such favoritism can be expected of a racist society bent on
perpetuating the myth of a black female matriarchy, with males
pictured as ineffective husbands and fathers who are mere caricatures of real men. The literary castration of the black male is
illustrated by the best selling novel, *The Confessions of Nat Turner*,[11]
which generated much heat and little light, in terms of understanding one of the most important black revolutionists of his time.

The cultural stereotype of the domineering black woman belies
the existence of the masses of black women who constituted a
defenseless group against the onslaught of white racism in its most
virulent sexual and economic manifestations. The black women are

still involuntarily subjected to the white male's lust is reflected revelations in the revelations of a white employer to John Howard Griffin, as reported in his book, *Black Like Me*:

> He told me how all of the white men in the region crave colored girls. He said he hired a lot of them both for housework and in his business. "And I guarantee you, I've had it in every one of them before they ever get on the payroll."
> "Surely some refuse," I suggested cautiously.
> "Not if they want to eat—or feed their kids," he snorted. "If they don't put out, they don't get the job."[12]

Black women have frequently been slandered by the cultural folklore that the only free people in the South were the white man and the black woman. While there have been a few black women who have gained material rewards and status through the dispensation of their sexual favors to white men, the massive indictment of all black women for the acts of a few only creates unnecessary intra-group antagonisms and impedes the struggle for black self-determination.

Many proponents of the black matriarchy philosophy assert that the black female gained ascendancy in black society through her economic support of the family. Although the unemployment rate of black males is disproportionately higher than that of white males, only a very small minority of black families with both parents present are dependent on the mother for their maintenance. It is a rather curious use of logic to assume that black females, who in 1960 earned an annual wage of $2,372 a year as compared to the annual wage of $3,410 for white women and $3,789 for black men,[13] have an economic advantage over any group in this society.

However, what semblance of black female dominance that is found in our society can be traced to the persistent rate of high unemployment among black males which prevents them from becoming the major economic support of their family. The economic causes of female dominance are manifest. For instance, the percentage of black women in the labor market declines as the percentage of black males employed in manufacturing and mechanical industries is increasing. The effect of higher black male employment is the male's added responsibility for his family's support; the authority of the wife declines and that of the husband increases.

Many black men have not been permitted to become the kings of their castles. If black women wanted to work, there was always employment for them—even during depressions. Sometimes it was even a higher kind of work than that available to black men. Historically, black males have suffred from irregularity of employment more than any other segment of the American proletariat. Thus, they have been placed in a weak economic position which prevents them from becoming steady providers for their families. Any inordinate power that black women possess, they owe to white America's racist employment barriers. The net effect of this phenomenon is, in reality, not black female dominance but greater economic deprivation for families deprived of the father's income.

The myth of a black matriarchy was strengthened by the Moynihan Report released in 1965.[14] Moynihan's central thesis was that the black family was crumbling and that a major part of the blame lay with the black matriarchy extant in the black community. Some of the evidence cited would lack credibility to all but a group bent on making the victim responsible for the crimes of the criminal. Such sources of proof as the higher educational level of black females vis-a-vis black males conveniently overlook the alternative posibility—that many black males are forced to terminate their formal education early in order to help support their family. Instead, they cite the wholly unsupported statement by a "Negro" expert that, "Historically, in the matriarchal society, mothers made sure that if one of their children had a chance for higher education the daughter was the one to pursue it."[15] In a society where men are expected to have a greater amount of education and earn a higher income, it is difficult to imagine black women celebrating the fact that over 60 percent of the college degrees awarded American blacks are received by women. The end result of this disparity, according to one study, is that almost 50 percent of black female college graduates are married to men employed at a lower socioeconomic than their wives.[16]

Moreover, according to Moynihan and his cohorts, the black matriarchy is responsible for the low educational achievement of black males. In marshalling this arsenal of evidence, Moynihan was apparently unable to find any likelihood that the racist educational system, with its concomitant racist teachers, bore any responsibility for the failure of black males to reach acceptable educational levels by white standards. In the criminalization of the victim, countervailing evidence is dismissed out of hand. The fact that black schools are more likely to be housed in inadequate buildings, with inferior facilities, staffed by inexperienced and racist teachers and over-crowded,[17] only confuses the issue, especially when there is a matriarchal structure that is more handily blamed.

According to the "experts" on the black family, the black male is harshly exploited by the black matriarchy. Many black mothers, they report, express an open preference for girls.[18] This charge is confirmed by a white psychologist, described by a major magazine as devoid of any racism, who states that black males have an inordinate hatred for their mothers.[19] Although there are research studies that reveal no sex-role preference on the part of black mothers,[20] it appears that the practitioners of white social science have not been content with pitting husband against wife but also wish to turn sons against mothers, brothers against sisters. The evidence for these assumptions is not only flimsy, but in some cases also non-existent. If the research is similar to other psychological studies, they have probably used a sample of ten blacks, who on the verge of a psychotic breakup, wandered into their mental clinic.

These charges of black men hating their mothers must be very puzzling to the black mothers aware of them. They would be puzzled because they realize that if a preference is shown for any sex-role in the black family, it would more likely be expressed in favor of the male child. The problems of raising a black male child in a racist society have been great. Many black mothers out of fear—real or fancied—repressed the aggressive tendencies of their sons in order to save them from the white man's chopping block. For to act as a man in a society which feared his masculinity, the black male was subject to the force of brutal white retaliation. The black mother had to constantly live with the realization that her son might be killed for exercising the prerogatives of manhood. For those black mothers who exorcised their son's aggressive drives out of concern for their safety, hatred seems to be an inappropriate, and most improbable, response.

In addition to the host of pathologies putatively generated by the black matriarchy, the familiar theory of a relationship between fatherless homes and juvenile delinquency is brought up again. While there is nothing inherently wrong with a woman heading a family, the problem arises when she tries to compete in a society which promotes, expects and rewards male leadership. Consequently, she is unable to bring to her family the share of the social and economic rewards received by father-headed households. It is this very factor that probably accounts for any discernible correlation between motherheaded households and juvenile delinquency. The children in a fatherless home are frequently relegated to the lowest living standards in our society. The problems facing husbandless women with children are compounded by the inequities in American society based on sex role ascriptions.

It is impossible to state that the black woman is just like the women of other races. Her history is different from that of the prototypical white woman and her present-day behavioral patterns have evolved out of her historical experiences. In general, she is more aggressive and independent than white women. There are studies that show that black females are more nonconforming than white females as early as age ten. The reason for her greater self-reliance is that it has been a necessary trait in order for her and her children to survive in a racist and hostile society. Moreover, the society has permitted her more self-assertion than the white female.

Among male chauvinists, aggressiveness per se may be considered an undesirable trait in women and should be restricted to the male species. But this is all part of the age-old myth about the inherent nature of woman as a passive creature. more often than no, it has served as a subterfuge for the exploitation of women for the psychological and material gain of the male species Black women lose nothing by their greater tenacity. That tenacity has, historically, been a source of strength in the black community. While white women have entered the history books for making flags and engaging in social work, black women have participated in the total black liberation struggle.

While recognizing these differences, the question before us now is how much power do black women really have and how is it exercised? Power is commonly defined as the ability to dominate men, to compel their action even against their wishes.[21]

The black woman has often been characterized as a more powerful figure in the family because she participates more in making decisions about what kind of car to buy, where to go on a vacation, etc.[22] In certain cases, she is the only one to make major decisions. A closer inspection of her decision-making powers often reveals that she does not make decisions counter to her husband's wishes, but renders them because he fails to do so. The reason he defers to her in certain decisions is simply because she is better equipped to make them. Usually, she has more formal education than her mate and in matters relating to the white society, she knows her way around better. She is more familiar with the machinations of white bureaucracies since contacts with the white world have been more available to black women than to black men.

Making decisions that black men cannot, or will not, make is a poor measure of the power a black woman has in the family. The chances are good that no decisions are made which he actively opposes. The power of black women is much like American democracy—it is more apparent than real. Power alignments are frequently based on the alternatives a individual has in a situation where there is a conflict of interests. It is here where the black male achieves the upper level of the power dimension.

Whenever a black man and black woman find themselves in objective and irremediable conflict, the best solution is to find another mate. The objective reality of black women is that black men are scarcer than hen's teeth. For a variety of reasons, there is an extremely low sex ratio in the black community, especially during the marriageable years—eighteen to forty-five years.[23] This means that black women must compete for a relatively scarce commodity when they look forward to marriage. They are buyers in a seller's market. Black women, like all women, have their affectional and sexual needs. Many a black male's shortcomings must be tolerated for the sake of affection and companionship. In a sense, many black women have to take love on male terms.

The low sex ratio hardly allows black women to exercise any meaningful control over black men. In fact, as one black woman states:

> As long as she is confined to an area in which she must compete fiercely for a mate, she remains the object of sexual exploitation and the victim of all the social evils which such exploitation involves.
>
> In the Negro population, the excess of girls is greatest in the fifteen-to-forty-four age group which covers the college years and the age when most marriages occur . . . the explosive social implica-

tions of an excess of more than half a million Negro girls and women over fourteen years of age are obvious.... How much of the tensions and conflicts traditionally associated with the matriarchal framework of Negro society are in reality due to this imbalance and the pressures it generates.[24]

Another index of the matriarchy is simply the percentage of female-headed households in the black community. The Moynihan theory of the black matriarchy derives from his findings that 25 percent of all black families have a female head. This "proof" of a matriarchal family structure brings up many interesting questions, not excluding the important one: over whom do these women have control? Logically, the only power they have is to face a super-exploitation by the system of white racism that bi-parental black families do not encounter to the same degree.

The matriarchal myth is not always applied to only black families. A number of social scientists claim that suburban white families are matriarchal. They point out that the commuting father's disappearance during the day leaves the mother in charge of the home and children. As a result, the father's power is reduced in these areas, and he is relegated to enacting the "feminine" role of handyman.[25] This observation has prompted one person to suggest that exhorting black slum dwellers to emulate the presumably more stable white middle-class, restore father to his rightful place, and build a more durable family life will subsequently expose them to the threat of the suburban matriarchy.[26]

Any profound analysis of the black matriarchy proposition should reveal its fallacious underpinnings. Recognition of this fact raises the crucial question as to why white society continues to impose this myth on the consciousness of black people. This writer submits that it has been functional for the white ruling class, through its ideological apparatus, to create internal antagonisms in the black community between black men and black women to divide them and to ward off effective attacks on the external system of white racism. It is a mere manifestation of the divide-and-conquer strategy, used by most ruling classes through the annals of man, to continue the exploitation of an oppressed group.

In the colonial period of Algeria, the same situation existed wherein the colonists attempted to use the female population to continue their colonial rule. Fanon reports the the colonial administration devised a political doctrine for destroying the structure of Algerian society. By encouraging Algerian women to break the bonds of male domination in their society—setting male against female—the colonialists hoped to dilute the Algerian capacity for resistance. According to Fanon, it was:

> ...the woman who was given the historic mission of shaking up the Algerian man. Converting the woman, winning her over to the foreign values, wrenching her free from her status, was at the same time achieving a real power over the man and attaining a practical, effective means of destructing Algerian culture.[27]

In contemporary America, a female liberation movement is beginning to gain impetus.[28] This movement is presently dominated by white women seeking to break out of the centuries-old bondage imposed upon them by the male chauvinists of the ruling class. Whether black women should participate in such a movement is questionable. Hatred of a social curse which is part and parcel of an exploitative society that discriminates not only against blacks but also women should not be confused with hatred of men. The adversary is not one sex or the other—it is the racist, capitalist system which needs, breeds and preys upon oppressions of all types.

Any movement that augments the sex-role antagonisms extant in the black community will only sow the seed of disunity and hinder the liberation struggle. Whether black women will participate in a female liberation movement is, of course, up to them. One, however, must be cognizant of the need to avoid a diffusion of energy devoted to the liberation struggle lest it dilute the over-all effectiveness of the movement. Black women cannot be free *qua* women until all blacks attain their liberation.

The role of the black woman in the black liberation struggle is an important one and cannot be forgotten. From her womb have come the revolutionary warriors of our time.[29] The revolutionary vanguard has a male leadership but the black woman has stepped beside her man engaged in struggle and given him her total faith and committment. She has thrust herself into the life or death struggle to destroy the last vestige of racism and exploitation in the American social structure. In the process of continuing her life-long fight against racist oppression, the myth of her matriarchal nature will soon join the death agony of America's racist empire. Until that time arrives, the black woman should be revered and celebrated—

not only for her historical deeds in the building of African civilization, in the struggle to maintain the black peoples of America as a viable entity—but for her contemporary role in enabling black people to forge ahead in their efforts to achieve a black nationhood.

NOTES

1. George Breitman, *Malcolm X Speaks*. New York: Merit Publishers, 1965.

2. J. J. Bachofen, *Das Mutterrecht*, Stuttgart, 1861.

3. Margaret Mead, *Male and Female*, New York: William Morrow and Company, 1949, p. 301.

4. William Goode, *The Family*, Englewood Cliffs, New Jersey, 1964, p. 14.

5. John Hope Franklin, *From Slavery to Freedom*, New York: Random House, 1947.

6. E. Franklin Frazier, *The Negro Family in the United States*, Chicago: University of Chicago Press, 1939, p. 7.

7. Maurice Davie, *Negroes in American Society* New York: McGraw-Hill, 1949, p. 207.

8. Arthur W. Calhoun, *A Social History of the American Family*, New York: Barnes and Noble, 1919.

9. E. F. Frazier, op. cit., p. 53.

10. *Ibid.*, p. 48.

11. William Styron, *The Confession of Nat Turner*, New York: Random House, 1967.

12. John Howard Griffin, *Black Like Me*, New York: Signet, 1963.

13. *United States Census of Population Report*, 1960.

14. *The Negro Family: The Case for National Action*, United States Department of Labor, 1965.

15. Whitney Young, *To Be Equal*, New York: McGraw-Hill, 1964, p. 25.

16. Jean Noble, *The Negro Woman College Graduate*, New York: Columbia University Press, 1956, p. 64.

17. *Equality of Educational Opportunity*, United States Department of Health, Education and Welfare, Office of Education, 1966.

18. Thomas F. Pettigrew, *A Profile of the Negro American*, Princeton, New Jersey: D. Van Nostrand, 1964, p. 16.

19. The particular psychologist in question, Herbert Hendin, was quoted in *Newsweek*, November 17, 1966, pp. 119-120.

20. Robert Bell, *The One-Parent Mother in the Negro Lower Class*, Unpublished paper represented to the Eastern Sociological Society, 1965.

21. Henry P. Fairchild, *Dictionary of Sociology and Related Sciences*, Totowa, New Jersey: Littlefield, Adams and Co., 1965, p. 227.

22. Robert Blood and Donald Wolfe, *Husbands and Wives*, Illinois: The Free Press of Glencoe, 1960.

23. In New York City, for instance, there are only 75 black men for every 100 black women in about this same age range.

24. Pauli Murray, *The Negro Woman in the Quest for Equality*, paper presented at Leadership Conference, National Council of Negro Women. (Washington, D.C., November, 1963), pp. 11-12, 12-13.

25. Ernest W. Burgess and Harvey J. Locke, *The Family*, New York: American Book Co., 1960, p. 112.

26. Eric Josephson, "The Matriarchy: Myth and Reality." *The Family Coordinator*, 1969, pp. 18, 268-276.

27. Frantz Fanon, *A Dying Colonialism*, tr. by Haakon Chevalier, New York: Grove Press, 1967, p. 39.

28. See Evelyn Reed, *Problems of Women's Liberation*, New York: Merit Publishers, 1969, for one white radical's approach to the matriarchal origin of society question.

29. It is interesting to note that, despite unfounded rumors, about the emasculation of the black male, the thrust of the black liberation struggle has been provided almost exclusively by a black male leadership. In selecting leaders of black organizations, black females inevitably defer to some competent black male, an act which shows how much they really prefer the dominating position they supposedly have in black society.

6

Sex Roles and Survival Strategies in an Urban Black Community

Carol B. Stack

The power and authority ascribed to women in the Black ghettos of America, women whose families are locked into lifelong conditions of poverty and welfare, have their roots in the inexorable unemployment of Black males and the ensuing control of economic resources by females. These social-economic conditions have given rise to special features in the organization of family and kin networks in Black communities, features not unlike the patterns of domestic authority that emerge in matrilineal societies, or in cultures where men are away from home in wage labor (Gonzalez, 1969, 1970). The poor in Black urban communities have evolved, as the basic unit of their society, a core of kinsmen and non-kin who cooperate on a daily basis and who live near one another or co-reside. This core, or nucleus, has been characterized as the basis of the consanguineal household (Gonzalez, 1965) and of matrifocality (Tanner, this volume; Abrahams, 1963; Moynihan, 1965; Rainwater, 1966).

The concept of "matrifocality," however, has been criticized as inaccurate and inadequate. Recent studies (Ladner, 1971; Smith, 1970; Stack, 1970; Valentine, 1970) show convincingly that many of the negative features attributed to matrifocal families—that they are fatherless, unstable, and produce offspring that are "illegitimate" in the eyes of the folk culture—are not general characteristics of low-income Black families in urban America. Rather than imposing widely accepted definitions of the family, the nuclear family, or the matrifocal family on the ways in which the urban poor describe and order their world, we must seek a more appropriate theoretical framework. Elsewhere I have proposed an analysis based on the notion of a domestic network (Stack, 1974). In this view, the basis of familial structure and cooperation is not the nuclear family of the middle class, but an extended cluster of kinsmen related chiefly through children but also through marriage and friendship, who align to provide domestic functions. This cluster, or domestic network, is diffused over several kin-based households, and fluctuations in individual household composition do not significantly affect cooperative arrangements.

In this paper I shall analyze the domestic network and the relationships within it from a woman's perspective—from the perspective that the women in this study provided and from my own interpretations of the domestic and social scene. Many previous studies of the Black family (e.g. Liebow, 1967, and Hannerz, 1969) have taken a male perspective, emphasizing the street-corner life of Black men and viewing men as peripheral to familial concerns. Though correctly stressing the economic difficulties that Black males face in a racist society, these and other studies (Moynihan, 1965; Bernard, 1966) have fostered a stereotype of Black families as fatherless and subject to a domineering woman's matriarchal rule. From such simplistic accounts it is all too easy to come to blame juvenile deliquency, divorce, illegitimacy, and other social ills on the Black family, while ignoring the oppressive reality of our political and economic system and the adaptive resiliency and strength that Black families have shown.

My analysis will draw on life-history material as well as on personal comments from women in The Flats, the poorest section of a Black community in the Midwestern city of Jackson Harbor.* I shall view women as strategists—active agents who use resources to achieve goals and cope with the problems of everyday life. This framework has several advantages. First, because the focus is on women rather than men, women's views of family relations, often ignored or slighted, are given prominence. Second, since households form around women because of their role in child care, ties between women (including paternal aunts, cousins, etc.) often constitute the core of a network; data from women's lives, then, crucially illuminate the continuity in these networks. Finally, the life-history material, taken chiefly from women, also demonstrates the positive role that a man plays in Black family life, both as the father of a woman's children and as a contributor of valuable resources to her network and to the network of his own kin.

I shall begin by analyzing the history of residential arrangements during one woman's life, and the residential arrangements of this woman's kin network at two points in time, demonstrating that although household composition changes, members are selected or self-selected largely from a single network that has continuity over time. Women and men, in response to joblessness, the possibility of welfare payments, the breakup of relationships, or the whims of a landlord, may move often. But the very calamities and crises that contribute to the constant shifts in residence tend to bring men, women, and children back into the households of close kin. Newly formed households are successive recombinations of the same domestic network of adults and children, quite often in the same dwellings. Residence histories, then, are an important reflection of the strategy of relying on and strengthening the domestic kin network, and also reveal the adpativeness of households with "elastic boundaries." (It may be worth noting that middle-class whites are beginning to perceive certain values, for their own lives, in such households.)

In the remainder of the paper, the importance of maximizing network strength will be reemphazied and additional strategies will be isolated by examining two sets of relationships within kin networks—those between mothers and fathers and those between fathers and children. Women's own accounts of their situations show how they have developed a strong sense of independence from men, evolved social controls against the formation of conjugal relationships, and limited the role of the husband-father within the mother's domestic group. All of these strategies serve to strengthen the domestic network, often at the expense of any particular male-female tie. Kin regard any marriage as a risk to the woman and her children, and the loss of either male or female kin as a threat to the durability of the kin network. These two factors continually augment each other and dictate, as well, the range of socially accepted relationships between fathers and children.

RESIDENCE AND THE DOMESTIC NETWORK

In The Flats, the material and cultural support needed to sustain and socialize community members is provided by cooperating kinsmen. The individual can draw upon a broad domestic web of kin and friends—some who reside together, others who do not. Residents in The Flats characterize household composition according to where people sleep, eat, and spend their time. Those who eat together may be considered part of a domestic unit. But an individual may eat in one household, sleep in mother, contribute resources and services to yet another, and consider himself or herself a member of all three households. Children may fall asleep and remain through the night wherever the late-evening visiting patterns of the adult females take them, and they may remain in these households and share meals perhaps a week at a time. As R. T. Smith suggests in an article on Afro-American kinship (1970), it is sometimes difficult "to determine just which household a given individual belongs to at any particular moment." These facts of ghetto life, are of course, often disguised in the statistical reports of census takers, who record simply sleeping arrangement.

Households in The Flats, then, have shifting memberships, but they maintain for the most part a steady state of three generations of kin: males and females beyond child-bearing age; a middle generation of mothers raising their own children or children of close kin; and the children. This observation is supported in a recent study by Ladner (1971: 60), who writes, "Many children normally grow up in a three-generation household and they absorb the influences of a grandmother and grandfather as well as a mother and father." A survey of eighty-three residence changes among welfare families, whereby adult females who are heads of their own households merged households with other kin, shows that the majority of moves created three-generation households. Consequently, it is difficult to pinpoint structural beginning or end to household cycles in poor Black urban communities (Buchler and Selby, 1968; Fortes, 1958; Otterbein, 1970). But it is clear that authority patterns within a kin network change with birth and death; with the death of the oldest member in a household, the next generation assumes authority.

Residence changes themselves are brought on by many factors, most related to the economic conditions in which poor families live. Women who have children have access to welfare, and thus more economic security than women who do not, and more than all men. Welfare regulations encourage mothers to set up separate households, and women actively seek independence, privacy, and improvement in their lives. But these ventures do not last long. Life histories of adults show that the attempts by women to set up separate households with their children are short-lived; houses are condemned; landlords evict tenants; and needs for services among kin arise. Household composition also expands or contracts with the loss of a job, the death of a relative, the beginning or end of a sexual partnership, or the end of a friendship. But fluctuations in household composition rarely affect the exchanges and daily dependencies of participants. The following chronology of residence changes made by Ruby Banks graphically illuminates these points:

AGE	HOUSEHOLD COMPOSITION AND CONTEXT OF HOUSEHOLD FORMATION
Birth	Ruby lived with her mother, Magnolia, and her maternal grandparents.
4	To be eligible for welfare, Ruby and Magnolia were required to move out of Ruby's grandparents' house. They moved into a separate residence two houses away, but ate all meals at the grandparents' house.
5	Ruby and Magnolia returned to the grandparents' house and Magnolia gave birth to a son. Magnolia worked and the grandmother cared for her children.
6	Ruby's maternal grandparents separated. Magnolia remained living with her father and her (now) two sons. Ruby and her grandmother moved up the street and lived with her maternal aunt Augusta and maternal uncle. Ruby's grandmother took care of Ruby and her brothers, and Magnolia worked and cooked and cleaned for her father.
7-16	The household was now composed of Ruby, her grandmother, her grandmother's new husband, Augusta and her boyfriend, and Ruby's maternal uncle. At age sixteen Ruby gave birth to a daughter.
17	Ruby's grandmother died and Ruby had a second child, by Otis, the younger brother of Ruby's best friend, Willa Mae. Ruby remained living with Augusta, Augusta's boyfriend, Ruby's maternal uncle, and her daughters.
18	Ruby fought with Augusta and she and Otis moved into an apartment with her two daughters. Ruby's first daughter's father died. Otis stayed with Ruby and her daughters in the apartment.
19	Ruby broke up with Otis. Ruby and her two daughters joined Magnolia, Magnolia's "husband," and her ten half-siblings. Ruby had a miscarriage.
19½	Ruby left town and moved out of state with her new boyfriend, Earl. She left her daughters with Magnolia and remained out of state for a year. Magnolia then insisted she return home and take care of her children.

20½   Ruby and her daughters moved into a large house rented by Augusta and her mother's brother. It was located next door to Magnolia's house, where Ruby and her children ate. Ruby cleaned for her aunt and uncle, and gave birth to another child, by Otis, who had returned to the household.

21   Ruby and Otis broke up once again. She found a house and moved there with her daughters, Augusta, and Augusta's boyfriend. Ruby did the cleaning, and Augusta cooked. Ruby and Magnolia, who now lived across town, shared child care, and Ruby's cousin's daughter stayed with Ruby.

21½   Augusta and her boyfriend have moved out because they were all fighting, and the two of them wanted to get away from the noise of the children. Ruby has a new boyfriend.

Ruby'a residential changes, and the residences of her own children and kin, reveal that the same factors contributing to the high frequency of moving also bring men, women, and children back into the households of close kin. That one can repeatedly do so is a great source of security and dependence for those living in poverty.

A look in detail at the domestic network of Ruby's parents, Magnolia and Calvin Waters, illustrates the complexity of the typical network and also shows kin constructs at work both on the recruitment of individuals to the network and in the changing composition of households within the network, or less than three months:

HOUSE-HOLD	DOMESTIC ARRANGEMENTS, APRIL 1969	DOMESTIC ARRANGEMENTS, JUNE 1969
1	Magnolia, her husband Calvin, their eight children (4-18).	Unchanged.
2	Magnolia's sister Augusta, Augusta's boyfriend, Ruby, Ruby's children, Ruby's boyfriend Otis.	Augusta and boyfriend have moved to #3 after a quarrel with Ruby. Ruby and Otis remain in #2.
3	Billy (Augusta's closest friend), Billy's children, Lazar (Magnolia's sister Carrie's husband, living in the basement), Carrie (from time to time—she is an alcoholic).	Augusta and boyfriend have moved to a small, one-room apartment upstairs from Billy.
4	Magnolia's sister Lydia, Lydia's daughters Georgia and Lottie, Lydia's boyfriend, Lottie's daughter.	Lottie and her daughter have moved to an apartment down the street, joining Lottie's girl friend and child.

		Georgia has moved in with her boyfriend. Lydia's son has moved back into Lydia's home #4.
5	Ruby's friend Willa Mae, her husband and son, her sister, and her brother James (father of Ruby's daughter).	James has moved in with his girl friend, who lives with her sister; James keeps most of his clothes in in household #5. James's brother has returned from the army and moved into #5.
6	Eloise (Magnolia's first son's father's sister), her	Unchanged.
	husband, their four young	
	children, their daughter and her son, Eloise's friend Jessie's brother's daughter and her child.	
7	Violet (wife of Calvin's closest friend Cecil, now dead several years), her two sons, her daughter Odessa, annd Odessas's four children.	Odessa's son Raymond has fathered Clover's baby. Clover and baby have joined household #7.

These examples do indeed indicate the important role of the Black woman in the domestic structure. But the cooperation between male and female siblings who share the same household or live near one another has been underestimated by those who have isolated the femaleheaded household as the most significant domestic unit among the urban Black poor. The close cooperation of adult siblings arises from the residential patterns typical of young adults (Stack, 1970). Owing to poverty, young women with or without children do not perceive any choice but to remain living at home with their mothers or other adult female relatives. Even when young women are collecting welfare for their children, they say that their resources go further when they share food and exchange goods and services daily. Likewise, the jobless man, or the man working at a part-time or seasonal job, often remains living at home with his mother—or, if she is dead, with his sisters and brothers. This pattern continues long after such a man becomes a father and establishes a series of sexual partnerships with women, who are in turn living with their own kin or friends or are alone with their children. A result of this pattern is the striking fact that households almost always have men around: male relatives, affines, and boyfriends. These men are often intermittent members of the households, boarders, or friends who come and go—men who usually eat, and sometimes sleep, in these households. Children have constant and close contact with these men, and especially in the case of male relatives, these relationships last over the years. The most predictable residential pattern in The Flats is that individuals reside in the households of their natal kin, or the households of those who raised them, long into their adult years.

Welfare workers, researchers, and landlords in Black ghetto communities have long known that the residence patterns of the poor change frequently and that females play a dominant domestic role. Wis much less understood is the relationship between household composition and domestic organization in these communities. Household boundaries are elastic, and no one model of a household, such as the nuclear family, extended family, or matrifocal family, is the norm. What is crucial and enduring is the strength of ties within a kin network; the maintenance of a strong network in turn has consequences for the relationships between the members themselves, as demonstrated in the following discussion or relationships between mothers and fathers and between fathers and their children.

MOTHERS AND FATHERS

Notwithstanding the emptiness and hopelessness of the job experience in the Black community, men and women fall in love and wager buoyant new relationships against the inexorable forces of poverty and racism. At the same time, in dealing with everyday life, Black women and men have developed a number of attitudes and strategies that appear to mitigate against the formation of long-term relationships. Even when a man and woman set up temporary housekeeping arrangements, they both maintain primary social ties with their kin. If other members of a kin network view a particular relationship as a drain on the network's resources, they will act in various and subtle ways to break up the relationship. This is what happened in the life of Julia Ambrose, another resident of The Flats.

When I first met Julia, she was living with her baby, her cousin Teresa, and Teresa's "old man." After several fierce battles with Teresa over the bills, and because of Teresa's hostility toward Julia's boyfriends, Julia decided to move out. She told me she was head over heels in love with Elliot, her child's father, and they had decided to live together.

For several months Julia and Elliot shared a small apartment, and their relationship was strong. Elliot was very proud of his baby. On weekends he would spend an entire day carrying the baby around to his sister's home, where he would show it to his friends on the street. Julia, exhilarated by her independence in having her own place, took great care of the house and her baby. She told me, "Before Elliot came home from work I would have his dinner fixed and the house and kid clean. When he came home he would take his shower and then I'd bring his food to the bed. I'd put the kid to sleep and then get into bed with him. It was fine. We would get in a little piece and then go to sleep. In the morning we'd do the same thing."

After five months, Elliot was laid off from his job at a factory that hires seasonal help. He couldn't find another job, except part-time work for a cab company. Elliot began spending more time away from the house with his friends at the local tavern, and less time with Julia and the baby. Julia finally had to get back "on aid" and Elliot put more of his things back to his sister's home so the social worker wouldn't know he was staying with Julia. Julia noticed changes in Elliot. "If you start necking and doing the same thing that you've been doing with your man, and he don't want it, you know for sure that he is messing with someone else, or don't want you anymore. Maybe Elliot didn't want me in the first place, but maybe he did 'cause he chased me a lot. He wanted me and he didn't want me. I really loved him, but I'm not in love with him now. My feelings just changed. I'm not in love with no man, really. Just out for what I can get from them."

Julia and Elliot stayed together, but she began to hear rumors about him. Her cousin, a woman who had often expressed jealousy toward Julia, followed Elliot in a car and told her that Elliot parked late at night outside the apartment house of his previous girl friend. Julia told me that her cousin was "nothing but a gossip, a newspaper who carried news back and forth," and that her cousin was envious of her having an "old man." Nevertheless, Julia believed the gossip.

After hearing other rumors and gossip about Elliot, Julia said, "I still really liked him, but I wasn't going to let him get the upper hand on me. After I found out that he was messing with someone else, I said to myself. I was doing it too, so what's the help in making a fuss. But after that, I made him pay for being with me!

"I was getting a check every month for rent from welfare and I would take the money and buy me clothes. I bought my own wardrobe and I gave my mother money for keeping the baby while I was working. I worked here and there while I was on aid and they were paying my rent. I didn't really need Elliot, but that was extra money for me. When he asked me what happened to my check I told him I got off and couldn't get back on. My mother knew. She didn't care what I did so long as I didn't let Elliot make an ass out of me. The point is a woman has to have her own pride. She can't let a man rule her. You can't let a man kick you in the tail and tell you what to do. Anytime I can make an ass out of a man, I'm going to do it. If he's done the same to me, then I'll quit him and leave him alone."

After Elliot lost his job, and kin continued to bring gossip to Julia about how he was playing around with other women, Julia became embittered toward Elliot and was anxious to hurt him. There had been a young Black man making deliveries for a local store who would pass her house every day, and flirt with her. Charles would slow down his truck and honk for Julia when he passed the house. Soon she started running out to talk to him in his truck and decided to "go" with him. Charles liked Julia and brought nice things for her child.

"I put Elliot in a trick," Julia told me soon after she stopped going with Charles. "I knew that Elliot didn't care nothing for me, so I made him jealous. He was nice to the kids, both of them, but he didn't do nothing to show me he was still in love with me. Me and Elliot fought a lot. One night Charles and me went to a motel room and stayed there all night. Mama had the babies. She got mad. But I was trying to hurt Elliot. When I got home, me and Elliot got into it. He called me all kinds of names. I said he might as well leave. But Elliot said he wasn't going nowhere. So he stayed and we'd sleep together, but we didn't do nothing. Then one night something happened. I got pregnant again by Elliot. After I got pregnant, me and Charles quit, and I moved in with a girl friend for a while. Elliot chased after me and we started going back together, but we stayed separate. In my sixth month I moved back in my mother's home with her husband and the kids."

Many young women like Julia feel strongly that they cannot let a man make a fool out of them, and they react quickly and boldly to rumor, gossip, and talk that hurts them. The power that gossip and information have in constraining the duration of sexual relationships is an important cultural phenomenon. But the most important single factor affecting interpersonal relationships between men and women in The Flats is unemployment. The futility of the job experience for street-corner men in the Black community is sensitively portrayed by Elliot Liebow in *Tally's Corner*. As Liebow (1967:63) writes, "The job fails the man and the man fails the job." Liebow's discussion (p. 142) of men and jobs leads directly to his analysis of the street-corner male's exploitive relationships with women: "Men not only present themselves as economic exploiters of women but they expect other men to do the same." Ghetto-specific male roles that men try to live up to at home and on the street, and their alleged round-the-clock involvement in peer groups, are interpreted in *Soulside* (Hannerz 1969) as a threat to marital stability.

Losing a job, then, or being unemployed month after month debilitates one's self-importance and independence and, for men, necessitates sacrificing a role in the economic support of their families. Faced with these familiar patterns in the behavior and status of men, women call upon life experiences in The Flats to guide them. When a man loses his job, that is the time he is most likely to being "messing around."

And so that no man appears to have made a fool of them, women respond with vengeance, out of pride and self-defense. Another young woman in The Flats, Ivy Rodgers, told me about the time she left her two children in The Flats with her mother and took off for Indiana with Jimmy River, a young man she had fallen in love with "the first sight I seen." Jimmy asked Ivy to go to Gary, Indiana, where his family lived. "I just left the kids with my mama. I didn't even tell her I was going. My checks kept coming so she had food for the kids, but I didn't know he let his people tell him what to do. While he was in Gary, Jimmy started messing with another woman. He said he wasn't but I caught him. I quit him, but when he told me he wasn't messing, I loved him so much I took him back. Then I got to thinking about it. I had slipped somewhere. I had let myself go. Seems like I forgot that I wasn't going to let Jimmy or any man make an ass out of me. But he sure was doing it. I told Jimmy that if he loved me, he would go and see my people, take them things, and tell them we were getting married. Jimmy didn't want to go back to The Flats, but I tricked him and told him I really wanted to visit. I picked out my ring and Jimmy paid thirty dollars on it and I had him buy my outfit that we was getting married in. He went along with it. What's so funny was when we come here and he said to me, 'You ready to go back?' and I told him, 'No, I'm not going back. I never will marry you.' "

Forms of social control in the larger society also work against successful marriages in The Flats. In fact, couples rarely chance marriage unless a man has a job; often the job is temporary, low-paying, and insecure, and the worker is arbitrarily laid off whenever he is not needed. Women come to realize that welfare benefits and ties within kin networks provide greater security for them and their children. In addition, caretaker agencies such as public welfare are insensitive to individual attempts for social mobility. A woman may be immediately cut off the welfare rolls when a husband returns home from prison or the army, or if she gets married. Unless there is either a significant change in employment opportunities for the urban poor or a livable guaranteed miminum income, it is unlikely that urban low-income Blacks will form lasting conjugal units.

Marriage and its accompanying expectations of a home, a job, and a family built around the husband and wife have come to stand for an individual's desire to break out of poverty. It implies the willingness of an individual to remove himself from the daily obligations of his kin network. People in The Flats recognize that one cannot simultaneously meet kin expectations and the expectations of a spouse. Cooperating kinsmen continually attempt to draw new people into their personal network; but at the same time they fear the loss of a central, resourceful member in the network. The following passages are taken from the detailed residence life history of Ruby Banks. Details of her story were substantiated by discussions with her mother, her aunt, her daughter's father, and her sister.

"Me and Otis could be married, but they all ruined that. Aunt Augusta told Magnolia that he was no good. Magnolia was the fault of it, too. They don't want to see me married! Magnolia knows that it be money getting away from her. I couldn't spend the time with her and the kids and be giving her the money that I do now. I'd have my husband to look after. I couldn't go where she want me to go. I couldn't come every time she call me, like if Calvin took sick or the kids took sick, or if she took sick. That's all the running I do now. I couldn't do that. You think a man would put up with as many times as I go over her house in a cab, giving half my money to her all the time? That's the reason they don't want me married. You think a man would let Aunt Augusta come into the house and take food out of the icebox from his kids? They thought that way ever since I came up.

"They broke me and Otis up. They kept telling me that he didn't want me, and that he didn't want the responsibility. I put him out and I cried all night long. And I really did love him. But Aunt Augusta and others kept fussing and arguing so I went and quit him. I would have got married a long time ago to my first baby's daddy, but Aunt Augusta was the cause of that, telling Magnolia that he was too old for me. She's been jealous of me since the day I was born.

"Three years after Otis I met Earl. Earl said he was going to help pay for the utilities. He was going to get me some curtains and pay on my couch. While Earl was working he was so good to me and my children that Magnolia and them started worrying all over again. They sure don't want me married. The same thing that happened to Otis happened to many of my boyfriends. And I ain't had that many men. I'm tired of them bothering me with their problems when I'm trying to solve my own problems. They tell me that Earl's doing this and that, seeing some girl.

"They look for trouble to tell me every single day. If I ever marry, I ain't listening to what nobody say. I just listen to what he say. You have to get along the best way you know how, and forget about your people. If I got married they would talk, like they are doing now, saying, 'he ain't no good, he's been creeping on you. I told you once not to marry him. You'll end up right back on aid.' If I ever get married, I'm leaving town!"

Ruby's account reveals the strong conflict between kin-based domestic units and lasting ties between husbands and wives. When a mother in The Flats has a relationship with an economically nonproductive man, the relationship saps the resources of others in her domestic network. Participants in the network act to break up such relationships, to maintain kin-based household groupings over the life cycle, in order to maximize potential resources and the services they hope to exchange. Similarly, a man's participation is expected in his kin network, and it is understood that he should not dissipate his services and finances to a sexual or marital relationship. These forms of social control made Ruby afraid to take the risks necessary to break out of the cycle of poverty. Instead, she chose the security and stability of her kin group. Ruby, recognizing that to make a marriage last she would have to move far away from her kin, exclaimed, "If I ever get married, I'm leaving town!" While this study was in progress, Ruby did get married, and she left the state with her husband and her youngest child that very evening.

FATHERS AND CHILDREN

People in The Flats show pride in all their kin, and particularly new babies born into their kinship networks. Mothers encourage sons to have babies, and even more important, men coax their "old ladies" to have their babies. The value placed on children, the love, attention, and affection children receive from women and men, and the web of social relationships spun from the birth of a child are all basic to the high birthrate among the poor.

The pride that kinsmen take in the children of their sons and brothers is seen best in the pleasure that the mothers and sisters of these men express. Such pride was apparent during a visit I made to Alberta Cox's home. She introduced me to her nineteen-year-old son Nate and added immediately, "He's a daddy and his baby is four months old." Then she pointed to her twenty-two-year-old son Mac and said, "He's a daddy three times over." Mac smiled and said, "I'm no daddy," and his friend in the kitchen said, "Maybe going on four times, Mac." Alberta said, "Yes you are. Admit it boy!" At that point Mac's grandmother rolled back in her rocker and said, "I'm a grandmother many times over, and it make me proud." A friend of Alberta's told me later that Alberta wants her sons to have babies because she thinks it will make them more responsible. Although she usually dislikes the women her sons go with, claiming they are "no-good trash," Alberta accepts the babies and asks to care for them whenever she has a chance.

Although Blacks, like most Americans, acquire kin through their mothers and fathers, the economic insecurity of the Black male and the availability of welfare to the mother-child unit make it very difficult for an unemployed Black husand-father to compete with a woman's kin for authority and control over her children. As we have seen, women seek to be independent, but also, in order to meet everyday needs, they act to strengthen their ties with their kin and within their domestic network. Though these two strategies, especially in the context of male joblessness, may lead to the breakup of a young couple, a father will maintain his ties with his children. The husband-father role may be limited, but, contrary to the stereotype of Black family life, it is not only viable but culturally significant.

Very few young couples enter into a legal marriage in The Flats, but a father and his kin can sustain a continuing relationship with the father's children if the father has acknowledged paternity, if his kin have activated their claims on the child, and if the mother has drawn these people into her personal network. Widely popularized and highly misleading statistics on female-headed households have contributed to the assumption that Black children derive nothing of sociological importance from their fathers. To the contrary, in my recent study of domestic life among the poor in a Black community in the Midwest (Stack, 1972), I found that 70 percent of the fathers of 1,000 children on welfare recognized their children and provided them with kinship affiliations. But because many of these men have little or no access to steady and productive employment, out of the 699 who acknowledged paternity, only 84 (12 percent) gave any substantial financial support to their children. People in The Flats believe a father should help his child, but they know that the mother cannot count on his help. Community expectations of fathers do not generally include the father's *duties* in relation to a child; they do, however, assume the responsibilities of the father's kin. Kinship through males in The Flats is reckoned through a chain of acknowledged genitors, but social fatherhood is shared by the genitor with his kin, and with the mother's husband or with her boyfriends.

Although the authority of a father over his genealogical children or his wife's other children is limited, neither the father's interest in his child nor the desire of his kin to help raise the child strains the stability of the domestic network. Otis's kin were drawn into Ruby's personal network through his claims on her children, and through the long, close friendship between Ruby and Otis's sister, Willa Mae. Like many fathers in The Flats, Otis maintained close contact with his children, and provided goods and care for them even when he and Ruby were not on speaking terms. One time when Otis and Ruby separated, Otis stayed in a room in Ruby's uncle's house next door to Ruby's mother's house. At that time, Ruby's chidren were being kept by Magnolia each day while Ruby went to school to finish working toward her high school diploma. Otis was out of work, and he stayed with Ruby's uncle over six months helping Magnolia care for his children. Otis's kin were proud of the daddy he was, and at times suggested they should take over the raising of Otis and Ruby's children. Ruby and other mothers know well that those people you count on to share in the care and nurturing of your children are also those who are rightfully in a position to judge and check upon how you carry out the duties of a mother. Shared responsibilities of motherhood in The Flats imply both a help and a check on how one assumes the parental role.

Fathers like Otis, dedicated to maintaining ties with their children, learn that the relationship they create with their child's mother largely determines the role they may assume in their child's life. Jealousy between men makes it extremely difficult for fathers to spend time with their children if the mother has a boyfriend, but as Otis said to me, "When Ruby doesn't have any old man then she starts calling on me, asking for help, and telling me to do something for my kids." Between such times, when a man or a woman does not have an ongoing sexual relationship, some mothers call upon the fathers of their children and temporarily "choke" these men with their personal needs and the needs of the children. At these times, men and women reinforce their fragile but continuing relationship, and find themselves empathetic friends who can be helpful to one another.

A mother generally regards her children's father as a friend of the family whom she can recruit for help, rather than as a father failing his parental duties. Although fathers voluntarily help out with their children, many fathers cannot be depended upon as a steady source of help. Claudia Williams talked to me about Harold, the father of her two children. "Some days he be coming over at night saying, 'I'll see to the babies and you can lay down and rest, honey,' treating me real nice. Then maybe I don't even see him for two or three months. There's no sense nagging Harold. I just treat him as some kind of friend even if he is the father of my babies." Since Claudia gave birth to Harold's children, both of them have been involved in other relationships. When either of them is involved with someone else, this effectively cuts Harold off from his children. Claudia says, "My kids don't need their daddy's help, but if he helps out then I help him out, too. My kids are well behaved, and I know they make Harold's kinfolk proud."

CONCLUSIONS

The view of Black women as represented in their own words and life histories coincides with that presented by Joyce Ladner: "One of the chief characteristics defining the Black woman is her [realistic approach] to her [own] resources. Instead of becoming resigned to her fate, she has always sought creative solutions to her problems. The ability to utilize her existing resources and yet maintain a forthright determination to struggle against the racist society in whatever overt and subtle ways necessary is one of her major attributes" (Ladner, 1971:276-77).

I have particularly emphasized those strategies that women can employ to maximize their independence, acquire and maintain domestic authority, limit (but positively evaluate) the role of husband and father, and strengthen ties with kin. The last of these—maximizing relationships in the domestic network—helps to account for patterns of Black family life among the urban poor more adequately than the concepts of nuclear or matrifocal family. When economic resources are greatly limited, people need help from as many others as possible. This requires expanding their kin networks—increasing the number of people they hope to be able to count on. On the one hand, female members of a network may act to break up a relationship that has become a drain on their resources. On the other, a man is expected to contribute to his kin network, and it is assumed that he should not dissipate his services and finances to a marital relationship. At the same time, a woman will continue to seek aid from the man who has fathered her children, thus building up her own network's resources. She also expects something of his kin, especially his mother and sisters. Women continually activate these lines to bring kin and friends into the network of exchange and obligation. Most often, the biological father's female relatives are also poor and also try to expand their network and increase the number of people they can depend on.

Clearly, economic pressures among cooperating kinsmen in the Black community work against the loss of either males or females—through marriage or other long-term relationships—from the kin network. The kin-based cooperative network represents the collective adaptations to poverty of the men, women, and children within the Black community. Loyalties and dependencies toward kinsmen offset the ordeal of unemployment and racism. To cope with the everyday demands of ghetto life, these networks have evolved patterns of co-residence; elastic household boundaries; lifelong, if intermittent, bonds to three-generation households; social constraints on the role of the husband-father within the mother's domestic group; and the domestic authority of women.

REFERENCES

Abrahams, Roger. 1963. Deep Down in the Jungle. Hatboro, Pa.

Bernard, Jessie. 1966. Marriage and Family Among Negros. Englewood Cliffs, N.J.

Buchler, Ira R., and Henry A. Selby. 1968. Kinship and Social Organization: An Introduction to Theory and Method. New York.

Fortes, Meyer, 1958. "Introduction," in Jack Goody, ed., The Development Cycle in Domestic Groups. Cambridge, Eng.

Gonzalez, Nancie. 1965. "The Consanguineal Household and Matrifocality." American Anthropologist, 67: 1541-49.

———— 1969. Black Carib Household Structure: A Study of Migration and Modernization. Seattle: University of Washington Press.

———— 1970. "Toward a Definition of Matrifocality," in N. E. Whitten and J. F. Szwed, eds., Afro-American Anthropology: Contemporary Perspectives. New York.

Hannerz, Ulf. 1969. Soulside: Inquiries into Ghetto Culture and Community. New York.

Ladner, Joyce, 1971. Tomorrow's Tomorrow: The Black Woman. Garden City, N.Y.

Liebow, Elliot. 1967. Tally's Corner. Boston.

Moynihan, Daniel Patrick. 1965. The Negro Family: The Case for National Action. Prepared for the Office of Policy Planning and Research of the Department of Labor, Washington, D.C.

Otterbein, Keith F. 1970. "The Developmental Cycle of the Andros Household: A Diachronic Analysis," American Anthropologist, 72: 1412-19.

Rainwater, Lee. 1966. "Crucible of Identity: The Negro Lower-Class Family," Daedalus, 95 (2): 172-216.

Smith, Raymond. 1970. "The Nuclear Family in Afro-American Kinship," Journal of Comparative Family Studies, 1 (1): 55-70.

Stack, Carol B. 1970. "The Kindred of Viola Jackson: Residence and Family Organization of an Urban Black American Family," in N. E. Whitten and

J. F. Szwed, eds., Afro-American Anthropology: Contemporary Perspectives. New York.

———— 1972. "Black Kindreds: Parenthood and Personal Kindreds Among Blacks Supported by Welfare," *Journal of Comparative Family Studies*, 3 (2): 194-206.

———— 1974. All Our Kin: Strategies for Survival in a Black Community. New York.

Valentine, Charles 1970. "Blackston: Progress Report on a Community Study in Urban Afro-America." Mimeo. Washington University, St. Louis.

United States of America

7
The Incarcerated Black Female: The Case of Social Double Jeopardy

Laurence French

Our society has long adhered to a double standard of justice, one for male offenders and yet another for females. And while females have certainly been discriminated against in many social situations, they have traditionally been spared the pains of imprisonment. In fact, female offenders have normally been subjected to a judicial policy of "reverse discrimination" resulting in fewer women being arrested, convicted or incarcerated. The reason for this is attributed to the protective attitude men, especially those possessing social power, have for women. Accordingly, western cultures have been reluctant to submit females to the same corrective measures applied to males. Some contend that men suffer from a self-deception concerning women, an attitude which is internalized during the socialization process and is used to rationalize the subordinate role females are assigned in our social order. Hence, males are hesitant to credit females with such "masculine" actions such as crime. It also follows that many males are hesitant to admit that they have been victimized by a female criminal, thus contributing to the image that females are less criminal than males.

This system survived with little controversy mainly due to the small female prison populations. But recently, a number of spectacular events have drawn considerable attention not only to the issue of female criminality, but to her treatment while institutionalized as well. This study focuses on both the emerging phenomenon of increased female criminality and the long-awaited investigation into the treatment of female offenders. Particular attention is given to the state of North Carolina which has been involved in many of these current controversies.

NATURE OF THE PROBLEM

Two factors contributed to this phenomenon. The riots and protests of the 1960s provided the catalyst for increased female participation in aggressive and rebellious behavior. This and the resulting Women's Liberation Movement led to increased awareness of the female's plight in our society. The nation saw middle and upper class females being beaten violently at the 1968 Chicago convention riot, as well as viewing women being gassed and harassed at subsequent protests and rallies up to and including the 1971 May Day demonstration in Washington, D.C. The Kent State and Jackson State incidents probably best illustrated the decline of the sexual double standard regarding the administering of justice when male legal controls agents (police, national guard) fired indiscriminately into student populations consisting of both sexes.

Many feel that the female's increased consciousness has contributed to the rise in female criminality. This coupled with increased severity in criminal adjudication has led to the current situation. According to the FBI "Crime Index," female offenders in 1974 accounted for 21% of the nationwide total. Over time (1960-1974), they registered an 108.8% increase over their male counterparts whose increase was 23.7%. Moreover, female offenders have also accounted for a proportionately higher amount of arrests for general crimes, resulting in an 81% increase in the federal prison population within the past five years. Yet, while female criminality has apparently increased markedly over the past fifteen years, it still comes nowhere near that for their male counterparts. Although the feminist movement may have contributed in part to this phenomenon, a more positive outcome of the movement has been the increased public attention drawn toward the poor institutional environment long suffered by the incarcerated female. Few cared about the female inmate, mainly because of the small numbers involved and the race and social class of these persons. Then, as now, most are poor Blacks.

The cases of Marie Hill and Joann Little best reflect the plight of the poor Black female before the law. Both are from North Carolina, the state with the most people on death row and the second highest incarceration rate (207/100,000). Marie had the dubious distinction of being the youngest person to sit on North Carolina's death row. When 17 in 1968, she was convicted of the murder of a white grocer, William E. Strum, whose body was found in the back room of his store in Rocky Mount. According to the Commission for Racial Justice (December 1974), Marie was arrested and forced to write a confession without benefit of legel counsel. Later she pleaded "not guilty" to the charges. Marie's background, being Black, poor, and having a juvenile record, weighted heavily against her, while Strum's reputation as a gambling house operator and molester of young girls apparently was of little consequence to the prosecutor, jury, or judge. Today Marie is serving a life sentence although she continues to voice her innocence. Even this judicial turnaround came about only after the U.S. Supreme Court reviewed the case and sent it back to North Carolina for reconsideration.

Joann Little's cause gained national attention forcing the state of North Carolina to give her a fairer trial than usually is offered poor Black defendants. Ms. Little was being held in the Beaufort County jail awaiting an appeal on a breaking and entering and larceny conviction. She was in her third month at the temporary holding facility when in August 1974 she was charged with the ice pick slaying of the 62-year-old white jailer, Clarence Alligood. Ms. Little freely conceded to an alteration with Mr. Alligood which arose when the jailer forced her to perform an unnatural oral sex act. The ice pick belonged to the county and was found in the jailer's hand. Alligood was found in Ms. Little's cell on the bunk unclothed from the waist down. He had emitted seminal fluid shortly prior to his death. Ms. Little was successful in her self-defense trial, but only after a change of venue and with the aid of civil rights groups.

Examples abound of female inmate abuse at the hands of the primarily male criminal justice system. North Carolina has been plagued with other female correctional issues including other inmates being sexually molested, complaints about compulsory pelvic examinations, and even a riot at the correctional center for women (Women's Prison). On June 15, 1975, a third of the inmates (150) at the women's prison went on strike over the institution's living, working, and treatment conditions. Most notable of these complaints was the compulsory eight-hour work shift in the hot laundry, sewing shop, and the lack of effective treatment programs and poor health service facilities. Within the next four days, 19 inmates and 16 guards were slightly injured. Instead of viewing the inmate complaints as viable, the North Carolina Secretary of Corrections, David Jones, placed the blame on "outside agitators": "I think the cause was outside activists, liberals, radicals, and my favorite words, fools, because I think they are all the same" (Ashville Citizen, June 26, 1975). Concerning the inmates grievances, Jones said he was not sympathetic with the inmates' complaint concerning the laundry heat which reaches 120 degrees in the summer. He replied that construction workers and others "in the free world" have to work in 120 degree temperatures to make a living. Of course, he failed to mention these people in the "free world" are paid for their labors.

What makes a female inmate more susceptible to these abuses? The main factor is sexual discrimination, better known as "sexploitation." The criminal justice system, including law enforcement, the judiciary, and corrections is dominated by male practitioners and, as a result, a masculine philosophy. Thus, our dual prison system ends up being "separate but masculine." Furthermore, women's prisons are less specialized than are male facilites, forcing together inmates with a wide array of offenses and backgrounds, often placing first offenders in the same population with hard-core criminals. The current situation was precluded by a precedent over a century old. In the 1860s reform for women offenders stressed sexual morality and sobriety. Treatment involved teaching female inmates their appropriate social role—housekeeping, laundry, cooking, and the like. Most female institutions went a step further, exploiting their inmates by providing a cheap labor force to do institutional laundry, sewing, and other housekeeping tasks. Hence, while most male inmates face the problem of too little to do, their female counterparts are often overworked. The most crucial consequence of the female penal philosophy is that it tends to reinforce the female's inferior and dependent role in society, thereby further weakening their self-resolve and self-respect, making them all the more susceptible to continual exploitation both within the institution and on the outside, once released.

This precarious situation places the female inmate at a tremendous disadvantage. Due to their conditioning to be dependent upon males and to compete for male recognition, the female inmate finds it hard to adjust to the unisexual institutional evnironment. Once adapted to the institutional setting, female inmates tend to generate more intense subcultural relationships than do male inmates. Yet, by the same token, they seem more capable of transferring their dependency from females, a condition determined by the artificial unisexual institution population, to males, once released. The point illustrated here is that most of the problems facing female inmates, whether in jail or prison populations, is brought about mostly by social-structural situations and not by anything inherent in females themselves.

Given the tendency of our society not to punish most female offenders, a look at those who eventually are incarcerated indicates a racial bias. Granted, this racial bias extends to male offenders as well. However, when considering the inverse relationship which exists between female criminal adjudication and the discriminatory racial factor, a situation of social double jeopardy emerges. That is, the Black female is denied the extra-legal protection associated with the female status on the one hand, while at the same time being disproportionately subjected to harsher penal sanctions on the other. Being Black only serves to exacerbate the female's already dependent social role while tending to intensify her sense of negative self-worth. The additional and common factor of being poor only makes matters worse.

CHARACTERISTICS OF A FEMALE PRISON POPULATION

Given North Carolina's unique involvement in a multitude of correctional issues (female riots, jail sexploitation, and high incarceration and death row populations), it seems best suited for an exploratory investigation such as this. A brief description of the North Carolina adult correctional system shows that it consists of 77 facilities: one maximum security unit, Central Prison; three closed custody units, including the Correctional Center for Women (Women's Prison); 23 medium security units; the fifty minimum custody facilities. Because of this unusual arrangement, North Carolina has a two-year maximum penalty for misdemeanor sentences, twice that of the national average. The state system has over ten thousand inmates at any given time. This is from a state with a population of slightly over five million people. In comparison,

New York State, with a population of over 18 million people, has only 12,000 inmates institutionalized in its 12 correctional facilities.

The uniqueness of the North Carolina criminal justice system does not rest solely with its correctional system. Still on the law books, although unenforceable, is Statute GS 14-181, miscegenation, a felony. In addition, judges can declare escaped convicts "outlaws," which in effect allows any citizen to pursue these persons and present them to the court, dead or alive. Another current North Carolina criminal justice controversy concerns capital punishment. From 1868 to April 1974, North Carolina had four capital offenses: first degree murder, forcible rape, first degree arson, and first degree burglary. In April 1974, the General Assembly modified capital offenses to include only first degree homicide and first degree rape. Reviewing North Carolina's capital punishment record starting in 1910 when the state took over the task of executing condemned criminals, 706 persons received the death sentence while 362, or slightly more than half, were actually executed. Of those executed, 282 were Black males, 73 white males, 5 Indian males, and 2 Black females. Today, two-thirds of the 108 persons condemned to die in the state are Black, four are Indian, while there are two females: an Indian and a Black.

It is from this correctional and criminal justice environment that this profile is generated. The profile is of the entire women's prison 1972 population. They in turn are compared with the incarcerated population of the state's male maximum security unit—Central Prison.

Four social variables are examined: criminal offense, race, education, and occupation.

(1). *Type of criminal offense.* Crimes were classified according to personal, property, and victimless offenses. Tables 1a, 1b, and 1c indicate a significant difference between male and female offenders. Most males (59%) were incarcerated for serious personal offenses in comparison to 39% of the female population. Both sex groups had a little over one-third of their members incarcerated for property offenses, while the female population had a considerably higher victimless offense rate with 22%. Most of these victimless offenses were drug-related. Victimless offenses only accounted for 6% of the male population. Black females had a higher personal and victimless offense rate than did their white counterparts. When using the FBI seven-offense Crime Index for comparison, the difference still remains statistically significant at the .001 level (Tables 2a and 2b). The male population had a far greater proportion of "violent crimes" (murder, rape, assult, and robbery), with 83% in comparison to 64% for the female population.

TABLE 1a
TYPE OF OFFENSE—WOMEN'S PRISON

Offense:	Personal	Property	Non-Victim	N
WHITE	33	50	16	99
	33%	51%	16%	
BLACK	82	64	47	193
	43%	33%	24%	
TOTAL	115	114	63	292
	39%	39%	22%	

*percentages calculated by rows

TABLE 1b
TYPE OF OFFENSE—CENTRAL PRISON

Offense:	Personal	Property	Non-Victim	N
WHITE	201	144	26	371
	54%	39%	07%	
BLACK	273	136	26	435
	63%	31%	06%	
TOTAL	474	280	52	806
	59%	35%	06%	

*percentages calculated by rows

TABLE 1c
TYPE OF OFFENSE—BY SEX (COMPOSITE)

Offense:	Personal	Property	Non-Victim	N
WOMEN'S PRISON	115	114	63	292
	39%	39%	22%	
CENTRAL PRISON	474	280	52	806
	59%	35%	06%	
TOTAL	589	394	115	1,098

X^2 = 64.59/sig. at .001 level
*percentages calculated by rows

TABLE 2a
CRIME INDEX OFFENSES—BY SEX

	Women's Prison			Central Prison			Total
	White	Black	N	White	Black	N	N
MURDER	11	14	25	58	86	144	169
RAPE	0	0	0	32	39	45	60
AGGRAVATED ASSAULT	3	12	15	15	30	45	60
ROBBERY	3	5	8	62	69	131	139
BURGLARY	0	0	0	15	8	23	23
GRAND LARCENY	11	14	25	17	25	42	67
AUTO THEFT	1	1	2	6	11	17	19
TOTAL	29	46	75	205	268	473	548

TABLE 2b
CRIME INDEX COMPOSITE

	Violent Crimes	Property Crimes	N
WOMEN'S PRISON	48 64%	27 36%	75
CENTRAL PRISON	391 83%	82 17%	473
TOTAL	439	109	548

X^2 = 13.005/sig. at .001 level
*percentage calculated by rows

(2). *Racial distribution*. Both the women's prison and Central Prison populations were compared with their statewide race/sex distribution (Tables 3a and 3b), while Table 3c provides a comparison between the two institutions. It becomes readily apparent that an inverse relationship exists between racial affiliation and incarceration. Whites who represent the vast majority of North Carolinians (76% of the females and 77% of the males) are underrepresented in these prison populations (34% of the women's prison and 45% of

TABLE 3a
RACE DISTRIBUTION—WOMEN'S PRISON

RACE:	WHITE	BLACK	N
WOMEN'S PRISON	99 34%	193 66%	292
N.C. FEMALE POPULATION*	2,128,000 76%	672,000 24%	2,800,000

*estimated population
**percentages by rows

TABLE 3b
RACE DISTRIBUTION—CENTRAL PRISON

RACE:	WHITE	BLACK	N
CENTRAL PRISON	363 45%	443 55%	806
N.C. MALE POPULATION	2,079,000 77%	621,000 23%	2,700,000

*estimated population
**percentages by rows

TABLE 3c
RACE DISTRIBUTION—BY SEX (COMPOSITE)

RACE:	WHITE	BLACK	N
WOMEN'S PRISON	99 34%	193 66%	292
CENTRAL PRISON	363 45%	443 55%	806
TOTAL	462 42%	636 58%	1,098

X^2 = 10.45/sig. at .001 level
*percentages calculated by rows

Central Prison). Over half of Central Prison's inmates (55%) and two-thirds of those at Women's Prison were Black.

(3). Occupation. Here Hollingshead's seven-category scale was used in Tables 4a, 4b, and 4c. When dichotomizing Hollinghead's scale into "acceptable" (categories 1-4) and "unacceptable" (categories 5-7)

TABLE 4a
CIVILIAN OCCUPATION—WOMEN'S PRISON

INDEX:	1	2	3	4	5	6	7	N
BLACKS	0	0	0	0	17 9%	56 29%	118 62%	191
WHITES	0	0	0	0	16 16%	21 22%	61 62%	98
TOTAL	0	0	0	0	33 11%	77 27%	179 62%	289

*percentages calculated by rows.

TABLE 4b
CIVILIAN OCCUPATION—CENTRAL PRISON

INDEX	1	2	3	4	5	6	7	N
BLACKS	5 1%	10 2%	14 3%	20 5%	91 21%	121 28%	173 40%	434
WHITES	4 1%	7 2%	9 2%	15 4%	154 42%	89 24%	94 25%	372
TOTAL	9 1%	17 2%	23 3%	35 5%	245 30%	210 26%	267 33%	806

*percentages calculated by rows

TABLE 4c
CIVILIAN OCCUPATION—BY SEX (COMPOSITE)

INDEX:	1	2	3	4	5	6	7	N
WOMEN's PRISON	0	0	0	0	33 11%	77 27%	179 62%	289
CENTRAL PRISON	9 1%	17 2%	23 3%	35 5%	245 30%	210 26%	267 33%	806
TOTAL	9 1%	17 2%	23 2%	35 3%	278 25%	287 26%	446 41%	1,095

X^2 = 31.37/sig. at .001 level
(comparisons made between categories 1-4 and 5-7).
*percentages calculated by rows

occupations, we notice that all female offenders fell within the unacceptable occupational category as did 90% of the male offenders. And when controlling on race, a greater proportion of Blacks were from the lower occupational categories than were whites.

(4). Education. Tables 5a, 5b and 5c indicate the educational levels reached by the inmates at these two institutions. Both populations had a large proportion of inmates with less than a high school education (82% of the women's prison and 78% of Central Prison). And a closer look shows that Blacks again were more undereducated than their white counterparts.

TABLE 5a
EDUCATION—WOMEN'S PRISON

EDUCATIONAL LEVEL	less than 8th	completed 8th	>8th <12th	completed 12th	12 +	N
BLACKS	46	19	95	21	10	191
	24%	10%	50%	11%	5%	
WHITES	19	11	47	12	9	98
	20%	11%	48%	12%	9%	
TOTAL	65	30	142	33	19	289
	23%	10%	49%	11%	07%	

*precentages calculated by rows

TABLE 5b
EDUCATION—CENTRAL PLAN

EDUCATIONAL LEVEL	less than 8th	completed 8th	>8th <12th	completed 12th	12 +	N
BLACKS	138	46	153	70	27	434
	32%	11%	35%	16%	06%	
WHITES	92	77	120	60	23	372
	25%	21%	32%	16%	06%	
TOTAL	230	123	273	130	50	806
	29%	15%	34%	16%	06%	

*percentages calculated by rows

TABLE 5c
EDUCATION—BY SEX (COMPOSITE)

EDUCATIONAL LEVEL	less than 8th	completed 8th	>8th <12th	completed 12th	12 +	N
WOMNEN'S PRISON	65 23%	30 10%	142 49%	33 11%	19 07%	289
CENTRAL PRISON	230 29%	123 15%	273 34%	130 16%	50 06%	806
TOTAL	295 27%	153 14%	415 38%	163 15%	69 06%	1,095

$X^2 + 2,146$/not significant (comparison made between less than H.S. versus H.S. or +)
*percentages calculated by rows

DISCUSSION

The social profile bears out the fact that most incarcerated inmates are from the lower class. The social indices portray North Carolina's serious male and female offenders as being Black, poorly educated, and with few job opportunities. The criminal offenses for which these people are imprisoned are of little consequence when it is realized that over 100,000 serious offenses (Index Crimes) were recorded in North Carolina in 1972 alone, a figure nearly ten times the total incarceration rate for the entire state correctional system. Moreover, most of those incarcerated are for crimes other than "Index" offenses. Yet, when female/male comparisons were made, significant differences surfaced between the two populations. The female population had a higher proportion of Blacks than did the male population. Also, the females, especially the Black females, had poorer educational and occupational backgrounds. Furthermore, a greater proportion of Black females were instutionalized for victimless crimes, notably drug-related offenses. Given this profile, it is not difficult to ascertain that the Black female offender surely suffers from social double jeopardy in North Carolina, a state which is usually overprotective of their acceptable" female population. this is substantiated by the state's sexual distribution of its total prison population—97% males/03% females. This compares with the national average distribution of 85% males/15% females.

Clearly, the female offender, especially the poor and nonwhite offender, is discriminated against according to our existing extralegal judicial double standard. While most females may benefit from this condescending judicial practice, it places considerable psychological and physiological strain on those females who are incarcerated. The challenge for the future is better female facilities and a new feminist awareness among criminal justice practitioners. Certainly, the first objective at hand should be to renovate our traditional "separate but masculine" system of judicial practice. This would help resolve a number of problems afflicting our judicial system from the handling of rape cases, jail sexploitation, female penal institution exploitation, and the mainly ineffective rehabilitation, resocialization, and reintegration programs for female offenders.

The original version of this article appeared under the title, "The Incarcerated Black Female: The Case of Social Double Jeopardy," by Laurence French published in *Journal of Black Studies*, Vol. 8, No. 3 (March 1978): pp. 321-335 and is reprinted herewith by permission of the publisher, Sage Publications, Inc.

Photo: United Nations/Kay Muldoon, No. 120,998. (1970)

8

Black Women and Music: A Survey From Africa to the New World

Irene V. Jackson

The invisibility of women in studies of music of African and African-derived societies has led to this preliminary study about the musical activities of Black women from Africa to the New World. The very marginal attention usually given to this unfortunately neglected topic suggests that women are somehow on the periphery of musical activities, and hence, implies that women are not actually essential bearers of musical traditions. However, it can be demonstrated that women are bearers of certain musical activities, and hence, implies that women are not actually essential bearers of musical traditions and are active music-makers in Black societies.

To begin, it must be recognized that womanhood is power: as bringer of life, woman is highly valued for her natural bond with the life force. Whatever a woman does, what she is and what she is valued for, becomes projected into some kind of image or symbol. Homage is paid to Queen Oya among the Yoruba as the spirit of the River Niger. Oya is the faithful wife of Shango, who becomes the River Niger upon Shango's death. Oya is water, a symbol of fertility. Yemaya, goddess of rivers and springs, is the sea itself; she is orisha of fertility. In Africa, Yemaya is mother of all orisha, the Prime Mother of all things; her colors are blue and white like the waves of the sea, and her dance is the dance of waves, characterized by large, slow and dignified movements.[1]

The same regard for woman's power existed even within the institution of slavery in the New World, which tended to develop a community where leaders were regarded as such because of their physical strength, wisdom and mystical power. On a Georgia plantation, a female slave, Sinda, prophesied the end of the world, and for a while no threat or punishment could get the slaves back to work. In another instance, a Louisiana planter noted angrily that Big Lucy, a slave, was the leader who corrupted every young Black in her power.[2] Such authority of women over life and death can thus provide one index of their involvement in music making. This notion is revealed by examining music associated with the primary events of the life cycle or the *rite de passage*.

In African and African-derived societies, where women have the responsiblity of instructing girls about womanhood create and perform music for puberty rituals. This music is created by women out of a feminine purpose: this is women's music. Dancing, instrumental music and songs generally accompany puberty rites. Here—in the puberty ritual—African girls are taught the pelvic dance celebrating the glory of their womanood. The pelvic dance survives in New World Black society and is known as the *chica* or *calenda*. The mastery of the *chica* or *calenda* depends on the degree to which the female dancer is able to move her hips and the lower part of her back.[3]

In addition to dances, certain musical instruments have come to be associated with these rites: drums, rattles, xylophones, horns and musical bows. The Bavenda girls, for example, have an orchestra comprised of different instruments to accompany the ritual dance, *phala-phala*.[4]

Among the Venda, women play drums as a part of *domba*, the last of a series of initiation schools to prepare girls for marriage.[5] The music and dance of the *domba* initiation school symbolize sexual intercourse, growth of the fetus and childbirth. Within girls' puberty rites, women are drummers in many African societies. On the other hand, in many traditional African societies, women are not permitted to play the drum, and in some instances, women are not even allowed to touch or even look at a drum.

The use of musical instruments, the drum in particular, in girls' puberty rites deserves more attention than the present survey can allow. It is interesting to note, however, that, among the Umbundu of Angola, the word for "drum" and "milking" is the same, the drum thereby representing the feminine principle.[6] Sachs, in *The History of Musical Instruments* (1940), raises the question of the ritual use of the drum, pointing out that if the drum were used by adult women, it would be beaten with hands and not sticks. Sachs argues that a player's sex determines the kind of instrument played, a man's instrument the form of the male organ, a woman's instrument a female organ.

Sachs also observes that the manner in which a drum is played relates to its user and maintains that the "friction" drum is the characteristic instrument at boys' and girls' initiations in Africa.[7] The "friction" drum resembles a "struck" drum, but the "friction" drum is played in a manner involving a to and fro movement which Sachs believed symbolized cohabitation.[8]

Another variety of the "rubbed" drum is used in the initiation rites of the Ba-ila maidens of South Africa: " . . . the maternal aunt holds between her legs a large earthenware pot covered with a piece of dressed skin. In one hand she grasps loosely a reed standing upright on its skin; the other hand she dips into water and draws up and down along the reed."[9]

In addition to the musical instruments played in the puberty rituals, the songs that are sung at initiation rites are created by women, sung by women and passed on to the next generation of women. Among the Bundu of Sierra Leone one of the most power-ful of women's secret societies, called "Soko," controls puberty rites. These women know the secrets of life of which music is one.[10] Where girls prepare for womanhood under the guidance of women they train in feminine musical traditions. This is music performed and created by women for a woman's puposes and needs.

The marriage ritual involves women in music making from Black Africa and New World Black societies. The Umbunda of central Angola have numerous bride songs which are sung to the bride by the girls and women of her husband's village.[11] During a Jamaican maroon wedding, one scholar observed elderly dames and young girls taking hands, dancing and singing the length of the grounds.[12] A pygmy wedding has been described in the following manner:

> When a girl to be married, the clan of the fiancé comes to her village to take her away.... The mother-in-law places in the bride's arms the latest born baby of the village. The bride says nothing. Silently she gives the baby back and turns away. At this, all of the bridesmaids begin to sing and the bride bursts into tears. Her bridesmaids keep on singing the whole night through.[13]

Among the Wolof there is a special category of songs known as *cheit* songs which are sung for brides whose husbands are already married. The words of one such *cheit* song are: "Bride, there will be sweet food where you sleep,/ And the drums will play until dawn...."[14]

Empirical evidence is readily available to demonstrate that women are musicmakers at the wedding ceremonies of Black Americans in the United States. Generally their wedding music is performed by the bride, her bridesmaids, female relations and special women singers.

Another *rite de passage*, childbirth, is sometimes accompanied by musical activity. Sophie Drinker in her study, *Women and Music* (1948), reported that among the Fans (people of Cameroon and Gabon), a special enchantress hides in the bushes near the place where the birth is to occur and chants an elaborate melody for hours—even the pregnant woman sings.[15] The practice of singing through childbirth is referred to as "wailing." Drinker describes the wail of Nubian women as beginning on a high note and dropping the voices by thirds to a twelfth below the original note. The wail created out of the birth experience becomes the song of death, death being a kind of rebirth of new life marking the beginning of another existence.

The authority of women over life and death is also evident in the degree to which women are involved in funeral rites. The participation of women in matters surrounding death insures the "rebirth" of the deceased. When a Basonga chief has been dead for three months, the oldest woman of the tribe is called upon to dance the womb dance which imitates every movement of generation and childbirth in order that the chief's soul might be delivered.[16] In Dahomey the oldest woman of the family watches the dead body with the widow, and it his her responsibility to compose burial songs.[17] Additional roles that women have in the funeral ritual are wailing and singing laments.[18]

The Grebo women of Liberia have developed the wail into a long and elaborate composition which must be performed by the mourner, who is the high ranking official, lawyer and historian of the tribe. At the Grebo funeral this person, a woman, presides while a chorus of women wail for hours. This high ranking female official chants the virtues of the deceased and sings the names of their ancestors. No funeral of a man of property could be conducted without her.[19]

In New World Black societies the funeral wail is also an important aspect of the funeral cermony. In an account of a Southern rural funeral in the United States, Puckett, in *Folk Beliefs of the Southern Negro* (1926), observed that a widow's wailing was so melancholy as to leave the listener with the false, romanticized impression that married life was a turtle-dove, rather than cat and dog, affair. Puckett maintains that mourning is an essential feature of the funeral, and to be done well the mourn must be given in spontaneous song. The women—not the men, are always the mourners.[20]

Paul Oliver, in *The Meaning of the Blues* (1970), points out that during the wake, which sometimes lasts for two or three days and nights, the women moan the blues through the long hours.[21] The "blues" to which Oliver refers are the lamentations or wails sung in the florid style. Undoubtedly, they were spontaneous creations. One Black woman, Ma Eileen Shedrick, who lived during the nineteenth century in the Southern United States, was known in her community as the "Death Angel." She was always called upon to sing at the deathbed of a sinner to make the passage over hell easier.[22]

In addition to vocal performances on the occasion of death, women sometimes use musical instruments in connection with burials. Often these instruments are ritually bound and are therefore used only in the ceremonial context. The women occupy the front portion of the house of the deceased, weeping lamenting and scraping the ground with calabashes reserved for this occasion.[23] In a study of Jamaican folk life, Martha Beckwith notes that a Jamaican burial practice involves the shaking of rattles by women.[24]

Other examples of musical roles assigned to women at funeral ceremonies occur in certain Afro-Hispanic communities in South America. Women singers called *cantadoras* sing *arrullos* (spirituals) and *alavados* (dirges) to dismiss the ghost of the deceased person from the world of the living. These women singers construct their own musical instruments used only for funerals.[25]

Women, then are called upon to perform music in the face of death. The *cantadoras* are called on to perform a public duty for the spiritual reassurance of all. Drinker contends that the dirge, elaborated on by women out of the childbirth wail, and from their faith that all life is one, becomes woman's most important and distinctive contribution to music.[26] Though Drinker has somewhat overstated the case by arguing that the dirge or wail is woman's most important contribution to music, it is apparent, however, that the dirge or wail is a woman's business.

The institution of slavery in the United States tended to develop women as leaders whose authority extended into the larger life of the community. There were several roles to which the majority of slave women were assigned, house or fieldworker or breeder. Music played such an important part in slavery that specific kinds of music came to be associated with the activities of slave women.

It was generally as house slave or "mammy" that the Black woman was able to have the greatest impact on white American culture. The "mammy" became an integral part of early America, and her cradle songs or lullabies are a significant aspect of American song tradition. Lullabies comprise the single most important part of Black feminine song tradition and constitute a notable portion of women's work songs. The influence of the lullaby on the course of American music has been overlooked in most sources concerned with American and Afro-American music since many writers tended to be as naive as this author who said: " . . . there were but few cradle songs among the Negroes of slavery days, for the reason, I presume, that under the institution of slavery Negro mothers had little or no time to devote to their children and therefore the maternal instinct was seldom expressed in lullabies. . . . "[27]

Since lullabies are composed not only by mothers, but by any woman responsible for the care of children, a real understanding of the slave community in the United States would reveal that the care of infants was generally assigned to older women who could no longer go to the field to work. The Black nurse or "mammy" "raised and reared" children, both Black and white. Her cradle songs are celebrated and remembered: " . . . sometimes she would sing to us, low crooning songs in words of some strange language. I think now it must have been some remembered sounds of her own far-away childhood, near Africa's sunny fountains."[28] Or: "the best recollection I have of this [Afro-American] music is one evening when a Negress was singing her baby to sleep in her cabin above our tents. . . . Her songs to me were impossible to copy, weird intervals and strange rhythm; peculiarly beautiful. . . . "[29] One field collector, who happens to have been a woman, describes the lullabies of Black women as having: " . . . a crooning sweetness about them, a tenderness as manifest in the tones as in the words. . . . One discerns in them something more than ordinary mother-love . . . a racial mother heart which can take in not only its own babies, but those of another, dominant race as well."[30] The texts of these lullabies were taken from several sources, mainly from Afro-American and African lore. In some instances lullaby texts were identified as variants of English ballads.[31] The singing style, however, was distinctively Afro-American. In referring to the beauty of the spirituals, one writer has advised that: "The best way to experience the beauty of the spirituals is to be cradled by an old Mauma, who sits at evening in a squeaky rocking chair by an open fireplace and sings the baby to sleep. . . . The long mysterious shadows on the wall seem but parts of the old melodies that mightily mark the stations to dreamland."[32] One ex-slave from Georgia remembered: " ' rocka-bye-baby in the trees tops' as the onliest song I heard my mama sing to get the babies to sleep."[33]

In addition to lullabies with lyrics that lull and coax babies to sleep, some lullabies of slave women contained hidden meaning and functioned as freedom and protest songs:

De moonlight, a shinin' star,
De big owl hootin' in de tree;
O, bye, my baby, ain't you gwinter sleep,
A-rockin' on my knee?
By my honey baby,
A-Rockin' on my knee,
Baby done gone to sleep,
Owl hush hootin' in de tree.

She gone to sleep, honey baby sleep,
A-rockin' on my, a-rockin' on my knee.[34]

The lullabies of Afro-American women kept the African past alive. W.E.B. Du Bois, in *The Souls of Black Folk* (1903), speaks of this tradition which is passed down from African mothers to their Afro-American daughters. "My grandfather's grandmother was seized by an evil Dutch trader two centuries ago; and coming to the valley of the Hudson and Housatonic, black, little and lithe, she shivered and shrank in the harsh north winds, looked longingly at the hills, and often crooned a ... melody to the child between her knees."[35] One scholar, Hugh Tracey, claims to have traced "within a reasonable margin" of possible error the melody of a lullaby heard in Charleston, South Carolina, to a Bantu East African source.[36]

In addition to lullabies created and sung by Black women, there are songs associated with specific kinds of woman's work. These songs can be said to rise out of the patterns and rhythms of a woman's work. The rhythmic possibilities of the washboard in the hands of a washerwoman are nearly unlimited. The following is an example of a "rubbing song" collected by Scarborough in Louisiana: A very little Negress down on the bayou/ Washing shirts, Oh, Mama,/ Oh, lady, the washer woman.[37]

Aside from washboards, Afro-American women used "Battlin' blocks" and "Battlin' sticks" to wash clothes. The clothes taken from the water were put on a block and beaten with a stick, and the pounding sticks became musical instruments that accompanied washing songs.

Scarborough also includes the following as a favorite among Black women during the time when spinning was done at home by hand: Spin ladies, spin all day/ Sheep, Skill corn,/ Rain rattles up a horn. . . .[38]

Songs often accompany food preparation. The sound of pounding, produced when women pound mullet, corn, rice, yam, or any other carbohydrate solid, serves as musical accompaniment for songs the women sang to hasten and lighten their tasks.[39]

An ex-slave reported to Scarborough that songs sung by Black women churning butter had to be sung effectively so that the cream would not be hoodooed into not making butter. The churning songs of these Black women, in effect, become songs of invocation. They believe that the butter will never come unless some special means, in this instance effective songs, are used to lift the evil charm.[40] Drinker writes that among one Bantu tribe women hold high positions and assume responsibility for the spiritual life of the tribe. In this tribe there are numerous songs for the preparation of a particular beverage called *ponibe*. This beverage can be seen as the life force of this tribe; it is the responsibility of women to perform a kind of ritual act: to prepare the beverage or food for consumption by song offerings.[41]

In terms of the labor force, Black women in the slave community in the United States were on an equal par with men. Accounts reveal that babies of slave women were often born in the field, that these women worked the fields sometimes with babies strapped to their backs, and that women sang while working.

The counterparts of the Black women who worked in the field were those women designated as "house slaves." Puckett contends that these female house slaves were the chief bearers of European beliefs,[42] and I might add, African beliefs. Black female house slaves were not closely associated with the household life of Southern planters; they were agents of cultural exchange and catalysts for a new cultural synthesis. A wealth of folklore surrounds the activities of these Black female house servants; many songs are the results of sewing, cooking, childcare, washing and household activities in which these women are the principal engagers.

An entire tradition of street cries or calls resulted from the labors of hucksters, an activity in which Black women participated. Beginning in the nineteenth century, for example, Black women sold blueberries and potato cakes on the streets of New Orleans. One cry used by these women was:

Black-ber-ries, fresh an' fine,
I got black-berries, lady, Fresh from de vine,
I got black-berries lady, Three glass fo' a
dime,
I got black-beries, I got black-berries,
black-berries.[43]

A street cry of the Creole women of New Orleans who sold hot potato cakes made from sweet potatoes was: Bel pam pa-tat, Bel pam pa-tat,/ Madam, ou-lay-ou le bel pam pa-tat, pam pa-tat.[44] Such are reminiscent of the field hollers sung by slaves.

There were also songs of Afro-American women who functioned as folk doctors, or "doctoresses" as they were called. Their songs were used for healing and lifting fixes, conjures or hoodoos. Folk medicine in Afro-American culture seems to be within the feminine province.[45] In some traditional African societies women often organized into divination and healing groups and sung chants as an aspect of the ritual. An important contribution by Black women in the United States to folk medicine was in the area of midwifery. The midwife, or "granny," as she is known in the Black tradition, was a source of both folklore and folksongs. Beginning in the 1920s, trained nurses were sent to rural Black communities to instruct the midwives about up-to-date procedures. Midwives were required to be licensed. This song, sung to the tune of "Glory, Glory Halle-lujah," describes the practices and reflects the impact that the nurses had on the midwives:

Chorus: Glory, glory hallelujah,
         Glory, glory hallelujah
         As we go marching on.

Versus: We aim to be good midwives of the State,
         We try hard to be up to date,
         To be on time to meeting and never be late,
         As we go marching on.

         We tell the mothers they should breath fresh air.
         We show them what they need to prepare,
         We teach them what their baby should wear,
         As we go marching on.

         We tell them plenty of water to drink,
         About good food we tell them to think,
         We say when tired, take a sleep a wink,
         As we go marching on.

         We put on water in a great big pot,
         We know of this we must have a lot,
         We boil it all, use some cool, some hot,
         As we go marching on.

         We put drops in the baby's eyes,
         Whether the mother laughs or cries,
         The State for us the eye drops buys,
         As we go marching on.

         We report births and deaths and all,
         When anything is wrong, we the doctor call,
         We hope we never from grace may fall,
         As we go marching on.

         We wear clean dress, clean cap, clean gown,
         We have clean homes, clean yards, clean town.
         We'll make our country of good renown,
         As we go marching on.

> Our county midwives are the best in the State,
> They try hard to be up to date,
> Are on time to meetings and never are late,
> As we go marching on.[46]

Two women who lived during the nineteenth century, Marie Leveau of New Orleans, Louisiana, and Aunt Caroline Dye of Newport News, Virginia, were practitioners of voodoo and root work. The activities of such women folk doctors are also celebrated in the lyrics of some blues:

> Yes, I went out on the mountain looked
> over in Jerusalem,
> Well, I see them hoodo women, ooh Lord,
> makin' up in their low-down tents.... [47]

Other work often becomes to occasion for music making. Quilting, for example, was frequently accompanied by dancing, yet it should be noted that the importance of this activity varied from one slave area to another. In the narrative of an ex-slave, Mary Wright of Kentucky, the following account of a quilting is provided: "...den weums [women] quilt awhile den a big dinner war spread out den after dinner we'd quilt in de evening, den supper and a big dance dat night, wid de banjo a humming 'n us niggers a dancing. ..."[48]

From the musical activities thus far examined, Black women have been seen primarily as singers. This is partly the case since much of Black music makes extensive use of the drum for accompaniment. In an examination of African music, Francis Bebey points out: "Because the drum is, in certain circumstances, equated with a man...women must consequently treat it with the same respect that they show towards their menfolk. No woman would dream of beating her husband in public (even though she may occasionally do so in private!), nor may she beat the drum in the village square. In some African societies, women are not permitted to touch a drum under any circumstance."[49] Bebey also mentions that in some African societies where the Islamic faith has been adopted, certain types of drums may be played by women. Further, the spread of Christianity in Black Africa, as well as the "Africanization" of the Catholic Mass and Protestant church music, has given rise to "sights that some Africans find profoundly shocking; for example, women playing tom-toms or xylophones in church."[50]

In contrast, the literature describes many uses of rattles (or gourd or calabash) among Black women. Sachs sees the rattle as a woman's instrument, with the rattle itself symbolizing the womb. In some East African tribes many hundreds of women occasionally stand together and shake gourd rattles as if their life depended upon it.[51]

The rattle is played by Black women in drum ensembles in most African and New World Black societies. The fact that the calabash persists as a woman's instrument suggests a strong continuation of tradition. An observer of nineteenth century Black life in New Orleans, Benjamin Latrobe, has provided one of the richest descriptions of musical activity of slaves in that city. From his journal published in 1905, we are informed that " ... a calabash with a round hole in it, the hold studded with brass nails, was beaten by a woman with short sticks."[52]

Drinker reports that among the Bush-women of Surinam, women entertain one another by dancing the "Lokucurra," a flute dance, while playing their flutes.[53] Women use "tappers" as musical instruments during worship activities of the Eshu cult (Yoruba). When not used as instruments by women, "tappers" made of ivory, wood or metal are used by the diviner for tapping the divination board.[54]

Laura Bolton, in the Music Hunter (1969), describes how women in Angola use just their bodies as an instrument to accompany dance: "The women, as they sing, place their right hands in their left armpit and bring the left upper arm down sharply against the hand, producing a smacking sound. At the same time, their cupped left hand beats a fast rhythm against their lips, making a bubbling sound."[55]

There are many kinds of taboos concerning women's relationship to music making. Folklore studies of United States Blacks conducted by Puckett point out that Black women are discouraged from whistling. The following couplet, collected by Puckett, gives evidence of this: De whis'lin woman, and de crowin' hen,/ Nevah comes to no good en'.[56]

And in Surinam, where women are the principal singers, they do not play drums; these women believe that if they break this taboo their breasts will grow to the ground.[57] In Brazil among the Carajas, there is a complete barrier between women and music; women do not sing at all, not even lullabies.[58]

Women are also often involved with music making in recreational activities. For example, the females of Taureg participate in a musical pastime, as described here by Bolton: "Girls and women sit in two rows facing each other, legs straight and interlocked. A cloth ball is bounced from one end of the line to the other by rhythmic motions of the legs."[59]

Dance, often a recreational activity and not always ritually bound, provides another index to the musical activities of Black women. One genre of slave dancing in the United States in known as the "water dance." Two accounts of the "water dance" are found in slave narratives. An ex-slave from Virginia, Betty Jones, remembered that she "set a glass of water on [her] haid [head] an- de boys would bet on it."[60] Hannah Crasson, an ex-slave who lived near Raleigh, North Carolina, told the following about her aunt: "One of the slaves, my aint [aunt] she wuz a royal slave. She could dance all over de place wid a tumbler of water on her head, widout spilling it."[61]

The practice of carrying burdens on the head is common in African and African-derived cultures. For the most part, women are the ones who employ this method for carrying burdens. The evidence suggests, then, that these recreational "water dances" were chiefly within a feminine province.

The *tamborito*, an African-derived Panamanian dance, is essentially women's music. In its present form the song accompanying the *tamborito* is usually sung by a woman soloist, followed by a chorus singing the refrain.[62]

A curious dance activity, restricted to a certain segment of the Black population in early America, was the quadroon ball of Louisiana. A quadroon is one-fourth Black, often the offspring of a mulatto mother and white father. The Duke of Saxe-Weimar Eisenach, who traveled in America in 1825 and 1826, describes the quadroon women as: " ... almost entirely white; from their skin, no one could detect their origin ... the strongest prejudice reigns against them on account of their black blood. ... "[63] Quadroon balls were held so that white men could secure their concubines. A European traveler to America in the 1850s describes the dancing at quadroon balls this way: "...their movements are the most easy and graceful that I have ever seen....I never saw more perfect dancing on any stage."[64] Although the dancing was primarily European, and the ball itself a parody of white culture, the participants were, however, partly of African ancestry.

Among the slaves in the United States, a pheonomenon referred to as "the shout" existed. The shout is one manifestation of spirit possession. One description of the ring shout indicates that most of the shouters appeared to be women who had an unique style of movement. In field research among the Georgia Sea Islanders, one collector gives the following account of a shout performed by two women, Edith and Gertrude: "Edith gives a stylized, angular performance as though copying the poses of the figures in Egyptian decorations...or the pause Gertrude makes with head and shoulders bowed slightly forward, arms held close to her body, elbows bent in a supplicating gesture."[65]

In contemporary Afro-American society, a religious dance, referred to as "shouting" or "gettin' happy," had its origin in the ring shout during slavery, and women are usually the most active shouters.

The final area of women's music-making activities involves women's use of music for cathartic purposes. In Dutch Guiana, or what is now known as Surinam, an established form of social criticism is maintained through poetic-musical composition. The fact that this society gives it the name *lobi singi* endows this women's music with importance. This *lobi singi* is a socially recognized form of ridicule most often directed against a woman who has taken a man away from another woman. Examples of the songs sung in the course of a *lobi singi* are:

What can an ant do
With a cow's head?
Ha! Ha!
She must eat the meat,
And leave the bones
Ha! Ha!

The injured woman might reply:

You are handsomer than I
You are fatter than I

But I am sweeter than you.
Ha! Ha!
That is why, my treasure,
My treasure, cannot bear,
To leave a sweet rose
To come to the house of a crab.
Ha! Ha![66]

Herskovits in an article, "Freudian Mechanisms in Negro Psychology" (1954), provides the following description of the *lobi singi*.: "In ritualized form it is a ceremony of recrimination which takes preparation and must be carefully staged. The performance is located in the compound of the offender, and the injured woman arrives with friends and the music. The players arrange themselves before the house; the music to one side.... The songs are all of a leader-chorus type, and ending phrase is sung with a few dancing steps, accompanied by a disdainful lifting of voluminous skirts of the women as the steps are executed, the exclamation "Ha! Ha!" is heard." There is a twofold purpose to the lobi singi: to make the wronged woman feel better and to castigate the offender, and second, to provide release through public confession for the girl who desires to restore her respectable place in the community. The following is another example of a song sung at a *lobi singi*, given by a young woman for herself:

If I were a rich man
I would buy a large farm
And what would I plant?
I would plant experience in it
So that when I went out
Experience would be a perfume
    for my body.
Ha! Ha![67]

In the United States during the 1920s, a tradition called "the blues" developed. The so-called "classic blues" singers were women. The blues became love songs and often provided opportunity for a woman to express superiority over another; thus, blues have a cathartic function. Often female blues singers speak about the sexual prowess of their man, as the following lyrics indicate: "He shakes my ashes, freezes my griddle,/ Churns my butter, strokes my pillow,/ My man is just a handy man...."[68]

In tracing African retentions in the blues tradition, one scholar discusses the *griots* or *gewels* as corresponding in function to the blues singer in the United States.[69] Although Oliver only mentions in passing that there are female *griots*, more recent research indicates that often women *griots* provide the memory bank for large geneologies. In the context of women's activities, *gewel* women are especially proficient dancers and composers of wedding and insult poems.[70]

The religious counterpart to the classic blues is gospel music which provides a cathartic function similar to the blues. Gospel, a Black feminine musical tradition, found its roots in the urban Black folk church, an institution which is largely sustained and supported by women. The spread of gospel singing has resulted primarily from the efforts of women, and even today many singing groups in Black folk churches are comprised largely of women.

A rather rapid and cursory survey of various modes of music making among Black women demonstrates that their power—their traditional power as women who have authority over literal and symbolic life and death—extends to an importance that scholars have not previously recognized. Black women, whether African or members of African derived societies, are frequently the principal musical forces in various *rites de passage*, including the rites of childbirth, initiation, marriage, and death. In African societies, the New World slave communities, and contemporary urban areas, Black women create, encourage and sustain musical traditions, and in so doing provide significant links between the ceremonial, ritual, artistic, and social foundations of Black culture.

NOTES

1. Janheinz, Jahn, *Muntu* (New York: Grove Press, 1961), p. 65.

2. *Southern Cultivator*, IX, 1851, p. 206, in Kenneth Stampp, *The Peculiar Institution* (New York: Alfred A. Knopf, 1956), p. 333.

3. Jahn, p. 8.

4. Sophie Drinker, *Music and Women* (New York: Coward-McCann, Inc., 1948), p. 31.

5. John Blacking, *How Musical is Man* (University of Washington Press, 1973), p. 79.

6. Laura Bolton, *The Music Hunter* (New York: Doubleday and Co., Inc., 1969), p. 130.

7. Curt Sachs, *History of Musical Instruments* (New York: W. W. Norton and Co., 1940), p. 40.

8. Sachs, p. 40.

9. Sachs, p. 40.

10. Drinker, p. 31; Roslyn A. Walker, *African Women/African Art* (New York: The African-American Institute, 1976), p. w5.

11. Bolton, p. 195.

12. Bolton, p. 195.

13. Drinker, p. 32.

14. David W. Ames, "Wolof Co-Operative Work Groups," in *Continuity and Change in African Cultures*, ed. William Bascom and M. J. Herskovits (Chicago: University of Chicago Press, 1958), pp. 224-37.

15. Drinker, p. 25.

16. Drinker, p. 38.

17. Drinker, p. 39.

18. J. H. Niketia, *The Music of Africa* (New York: W. W. Norton and Co., 1974), p. 38.

19. Drinker, p. 38.

20. Newbell M. Puckett, *Folk Beliefs of the Southern Negro* (University of North Carolina Press, 1926), p. 90.

21. Paul Oliver, *The Meaning of Blues* (New York, Macmillan Co., 1960), p. 304.

22. R. Emmett Kennedy, *Mellows: A Chronicle of Unknown Singers* (New York: A and C Boni, 1925), pp. 61-2.

23. M. Palau, *Les Dogon* (Paris: Presses Universitares de France, 1957), p. 105.

24. Martha Beckwith, *Black Roadways* (University of North Carolina Press, 1929), p. 79.

25. Norman E. Whitten, Jr., *Afro-Hispanic Music from Western Columbia and Ecuador*, Ethnic Folkways, Liner notes, FE 4376.

26. Drinker, p. 41.

27. Harris Barrett, "Negro Folksongs," *Southern Workman*, 41 (1912), pp. 238-45.

28. Henrietta Daingerfield, "Our Mammy," *Southern Workman*, 30 (1901), pp. 559-601.

29. Charles Peabody, "Notes of Negro Music," *Southern Workman*, 33 (1904), pp. 305-09.

30. Dorothy Scarborough, *On the Trail for Negro Folksongs* (Cambridge: Harvard University Press, 1925), p. 159.

31. Jeanette Murphy, *Southern Thoughts for Negro Thinkers* (New York: Bandanna Publishing Co., 1904), p. 63.

32. Marion A. Haskell, "Negro Spirituals," *The Century Magazine* 36 (1899), pp. 557-8.

33. Federal Writer's Project of the Works Project Administration for the State of Georgia, *Georgia Narratives*, part 4, p. 9, interview with Jasper Battle.

35. W. E. B. DuBois, *The Souls of Black Folk* (1903; rpt. New York: The New American Library, 1969), p. 207.

36. Hugh Tracey, "Tina's Lullaby," *Journal of the African Music Society*, 2 (1961), pp. 99-101.

37. Scarborough, p. 212.

38. Scarborough, p. 215.

39. Walker, p. 48.

40. Scarborough, p. 215.

41. Drinker, p. 56.

42. Puckett, p. 312.

43. Kennedy, p. 22.

44. Kennedy, p. 21.

45. Puckett, p. 385.

46. Marie Campbell, *Folks Do Get Born* (New York: Rinehart and Co., 1946), p. 89.

47. Paul Oliver, *The Meaning of the Blues* (New York: Macmillan Company, 1960), p. 166.

48. Federal Writers' Project, *Slave Narratives*, VII, p. 62.

49. Francis Bebey, *African Music: A People's Art*, trans. Josephine Bennett (New York: Lawrence Hill and Co., 1975), p. 14-16.

50. Bebey, p. 16.

51. Sachs, p. 28.

52. Benjamin H. B. Latrobe, *Journal of Latrobe* (New York, 1905), n.p., in Eileen Southern, *Readings in Black American Music* (New York: W. W. Norton and Co., 1971), p. 51.

53. Drinker, p. 51.

54. Walker, p. 24.

55. Bolton, p. 78.

56. Puckett, p. 183.

57. Drinker, p. 57.

58. Drinker, p. 57.

59. Bolton, p. 78.

60. Virginia Writers' Project, *Negro in Virginia*, pp. 92-3.

61. Federal Writers' Project, *Slave Narratives*, XI, Part I, p. 191.

62. John Storm Roberts, *Black Music of Two Worlds* (New York: Praeger Publishers, 1972), p. 89; See also Nicholas Slonimsky, *Music of Latin America* (New York: Da Capo Press, 1972), p. 259.

63. Duke of Saxe-Weimar Eisenach, *Travels Through North America During the Years 1825 and 1826* (Philadelphia: Carey, Lea and Carey, 1828), II, p. 61, in Lynne Emery, *Black Dance* (Palo Alto: National Press Books), pp. 149-54.

64. Edward Sullivan, *Rambles and Scrambles in North America*, 2nd ed. (London: Richard Bentley, 1853), p. 211, in Emery, *Black Dance*, pp. 152-53.

65. Lydia Parrish, *Slave Songs of the George Sea Islands* (New York: Creative Age Press, Inc., 1942), p. 55.

66. Melville J. Herskovits, *The New World Negro* (Indiana University Press, 1966), p. 140.

67. Herskovits, p. 140

68. Victoria Spivey, *My Handy Man*, Okeh Records, 8615.

69. Paul Oliver, *Savannah Syncopators* (New York: Stein and Day, 1970), p. 69.

70. Judith Irvine, "Cast and Community in a Wolof Village," Diss. University of Pennsylvania 1974, p. 69.

Photo: Reginald L. Jackson

9

Images of Black Women In Afro-American Poetry

Andrea Benton Rushing

first
a woman should
be
a woman *first*,
but
if she's *black*, really black
and a woman
that's special, that's real special.[1]

"The Negro," Richard Wright said, "is America's metaphor." In a way, black women function as metaphors for salient aspects of the black experience in this strange and terrible land. The symbolism which surrounds them creates a paradox: images of black women in Afro-American poetry are both varied and narrow. They afford a greater range of types than the two-stop Mammy-Sapphire syndrome of films, but, except on rare occasions, they fail to portray the multifaceted nature of the black woman in America. Although audience, the author's sex, and the prevailing literary conventions are all contributing factors, the main reason we do not see the richness and variety of black women reflected in Afro-American poetry is that women often symbolize aspects of black life that are valued by the race. As Dunbar says:

The women of a race should be its pride;
We glory in the strength our mothers had,

We glory that this strength was not denied
   To labor bravely, nobly, and be glad.[2]

That usually unconscious symbolic thrust has been something of a straitjacket. It is not so much that there are, in Waring Cuney's words, "No Images," but rather that the images only rarely reflect the full reality.

The most prevalent image of black women in Afro-American poetry is the image of mother. We find it in early poetry like Frances Harper's "Eliza Harris" and "The Slave Auction," in Helene Johnson's "The Mother's Rock," in John Wesley Holloway's "Black Mammies," and in Jessie Fauset's "Oriflamme." We also find it in recent poetry like Ed Sprigg's "my beige mom." Almost all the images of mother revolve around her strength under stress. This is in contrast to African literature, where, according to Wilfred Cartey, the West Indian Africanist, mother and the earth of Africa are one symbol, and mother is the cushion from troubled and chaotic conditions who manifests affection, possessiveness, and shrewd practicality: an emblem of strength and support.[3] Cartey cites the Guinean author Camara Laye: "She was Mother. She belonged to me. With her everything was always all right."[4] It is rare to find an Afro-American mother likened to the earth; this may be because we are not still a peasant people or because, after the agonies of slavery and Reconstruction, we are too bitter about the land to use it as a nurturing metaphor. In the Afro-American tradition, mother is not a cushion but the impetus and example for perseverance in a hostile world. (There are, though, suffering mothers like the one portrayed in Sterling Brown's "Maumee Ruth," where the dying woman has lost her children to the city, cocaine, and gin.) Langston Hughes's "Mother to Son," with its brilliant staircase metaphor, is the best-known example of this.

The most extensive treatment of mother in black poetry comes from master poet Gwendolyn Brooks, whose gallery includes Emmett Till's strongly passive mother; Mrs. Sallie Smith, the "prudent patridge"[5] mother of nine; Mrs. Martin, who disowns her son when he makes Rosa Brown pregnant; and Jessie Mitchell's vindictive yellow mother, who, ill, comforts herself comparing her "exquisite yellow youth"[6] to the hard fate she predicts for her black daughter. Two of Brooks's most memorable figures are the dazed and doomed speaker of "the mother," recalling the children her abortions deprived her of, and the figure in "What shall I give my children who are poor?" lamenting her inability to give her children access to rich life. Other mothers include the tough one in Betty Gates's "Mamma Settles the Dropout Problem":

Umgoing up side yo head
Wit my big fiss
An' when I swings
I don aim to miss[7]

and the boldly eccentric mother in Lucille Clifton's "Admonitions":

children
when they ask you
why is your mama so funny
say
she is a poet
she don't have no sense.[8]

Often, as in poems like Sterling Brown's "When the Saints Go Ma'chin In" and Owen Dodson's "Black Mother Praying," a poet combines mother and religion to express deep emotion. This is effective because both are still points in the turning world of black experience both in Africa and in the diaspora, so combining them provides emotional resonance.

Afro-American attitudes toward mother are extremely complex, but in almost all the mother poems, mother is above criticism, the almost perfect symbol of black struggle, suffering, and endurance. Reading about her, we know where Sterling Brown's strong men come from, for she says:

You must keep going
You can't stop there; World will
waive; will be
facetious, angry. You can't stop there
You have to keep on going.[9]

Black women singers are our culture heroes. More durable than movie stars, the giants among them endure and symbolize both transcendent beauty and deeply experienced pain. The images of black women singers alternate between expressing what they share with other black people and what makes them extraordinary. The African proverb says, "The spirit will not descend without a song,"[10] and black women singers (there is no comparable body of poems by male singers) express, manage, modulate the pain we sustain. Treatment of this subject goes back as far as Dunbar's "When Malindy Sings" and comes right up to Don Lee's dedication in *We Walk the Way of the New World*: "To those who helped create a New Consciousness ... Miriam Makeba, Nina Simone: two internationally known black women entertainers that are consistently black and relevant, can u name me two brothers/blackmen that are as ..."[11]

Dunbar establishes the humble Malindy as a symbol by deflecting from details of her appearance and personality and emphasizing her naturalness (as opposed to Miss Lucy's studied art), which is in concord with and even surpasses nature, so that birds are awed by her singing. She is also a bridge, a conduit making the transcendent immanent in the lives of singers. Langston Hughes in "Jazzonia" and Claude McKay in "The Harlem Dancer" illustrate the Negro Renaissance use of black women entertainers. The significance is apparent in three lines of McKay's poem:

> Grown lovelier for passing through a storm
> ....
> But looking at her falsely-smiling face,
> I knew her self was not in that strange place.[12]

Two all-important poems about black women singers are "Ma Rainey" and "Poem to Aretha." The first contrasts Ma Rainey's little and low appearance with her ability to articulate her listeners' experience. Sterling Brown stresses the nexus of shared life between the singer, a priestess, and those she sings for:

> O Ma Rainey
> Sing yo' song;
> Now you's back
> Whah you belong,
> Git way inside us,
> Keep us strong...
> O Ma Rainey
> Li'l and low;
> Sing us 'bout de hard luck
> Round our do';
> Sing us 'but de lonesome road
> We mus' go...

Dere wasn't much more de fellow say:
She jes' gits hold of us dataway[13]

Another important poem about a woman singer begins linking the singing Aretha to mother images, moves through the pedestrian in her life, refers back to Dinah Washington and Billie Holiday; then Giovanni gives Aretha a scepter of blackness making her the impetus for steps toward and essence of black life and art:

the blacks songs started coming from the singers on stage and the dancers in the streets.

Finally, she ascribes political potential to Aretha's songs:

aretha was the riot was the leader if she had said "come let's do it" it would have been done.[14]

Although very early Afro-American poetry (like Phillis Wheatley's), under the influence of neoclassical models that stressed elegance and formality, shunned self-revelation[15] and cherished the universal rather than the racial, Afro-American poetry is replete with examples of our attempts to translate the beauty of black women into language. In the face of the mass of cultural support for the beauty of white women, black poets move to create the uncreated consciousness of their race. An early poem like Holloway's "Miss Melerlee" pictures a black woman:

Sof' brown cheek, an' smilin' face,
An' willowy form chuck full o' grace—
. . . .
Pearly teef, an' shinin' hair,
An' silky arm so plump and bare![16]

Later Gwendolyn Bennett's "To a Dark Girl" links black women to their historical antecedents by mentioning "old forgotten queens" and suggesting that "something of the shackled slave/sobs in the rhythm of your talk."[17] Langston Hughes also reflects a history-tuned sense of black women in "When Sue Wears Red" with references to "ancient cameo/Turned brown by the ages" and "A queen from some time-dead Egyptian night."[18]

Gwendolyn Brooks, writing before the 1960s black-is-beautiful wave, provides a window on our perverse preoccupation with color, hair, noses, and lips. A woman asks for an upsweep with humpteen baby curls:

> Got Madam C. J. Walker's first
> Got Poro Grower next
> Ain't none of 'em worked with me...
> But I ain't vexed
>
> Long hair's out of style anyhow, ain't it?[19]

In "the ballad of chocolate Mabbie," a seven-year-old girl's boy friend prefers "a lemon-hued lynx/with sand-waves loving her brow."[20] Annie Allen's husband takes up with a "maple banshee" and thinks of his wife:

> Not that woman! (Not that room!
> Not that dusted demi-gloom!)
> Nothing limpid, nothing meek
> But a gorgeous and gold shriek[21]

And, in an extremely unusual poem, Pearl Mae Lee sings a crazed song after her lover is lynched for making love with a white woman who cries rape to cover her acquiescence:

> At school, your girls were the bright little girls.
> You couldn't abide dark meat.
> Yellow was for to look at
> Black for the famished to eat...
>
> You grew up with bright skins on the brain
> And me in your black folk's bed.[22]

Contemporary Afro-American poetry often glories in details of black beauty. Ishmael Reed mentions "juicy Ethiopian art/Lips,"[23] Michael Harper uses "nutmeg reflection"[24] and "raisin skin."[25] Emmett Till's mother's face has the "tint of pulled taffy."[26] Mrs. Sallie Smith is a "low-brown butterball,"[27] Dougherty Long has a gingerbread mama "all sweet and brown" valued above collard greens, candied yams, and new watermelon[28] Black breasts against a windowpane are blackbirds for Lucille Clifton;[29] Carolyn Rodgers refers to ashy skin and nappy hair;[30] Dudley Randall likens lips to cherries in their curve, grapes in their fullness, and blackberries in their sweetness[31] Hoagland starts with "honeystain," compares breasts to "african gourds" and "american pumpkins," and calls his woman "night interpreted";[32] and he pulls out all stops in the rash of food imagery in "love Child—a black aesthetic": "sweet baked apple dappled cinnamon speckled," "nutmeg freckled peach brandy and amber wine woman," african pepper pot, coffee flowing with cream, brown sugar, cocoa, candied yams, sweet-potato pie, raisins, blackberry pie, and honey love syrup.[33]

Note that the audience for black poetry has historically been white and distanced from black standards, and the poetry reflects that in the shift from the general descriptions of early poetry to the specificity of the poetry, for a changed audience, for the 1960s and 1970s. Also, black women can look so many different ways, there is so much intraracial variation, that poetry cannot show an "ideal." Finally, much recent poetry, despite the interest in the physical represented by black-is-beautiful, considers moral, intellectual, and political stances more critical than physical beauty.

In 1918, when William Stanley Braithwaite wrote an introduction to Georgia Douglas Johnson's *The Heart of a Woman*, he emphasized the short time (less than fifty years) that women had spoken or acted with a sense of freedom; he went on to say:

> Sadness is a kind of felicity with woman, paradoxical as it may seem; and it is so because through this inexplicable felicity *they* touched, intuitionally caress reality ... Mrs. Johnson creates just that reality of woman's heart and experience with astonishing raptures. It is a kind of privilege to know so much about the secrets of woman's nature, a privilege all the more to be cherished when given, as in these poems, with exquisite utterance, with such lyric sensibility.[34]

Du Bois wrote the foreword to Johnson's 1922 *Bronze*. He starts by mentioning her blackness, which Braithwaite had omitted and which the poet herself had downplayed in her earlier volume. "Her work is simple, sometimes trite, but it is singularly sincere and true, and as a revelation of the soul struggle of the women of a race, it is invaluable."[35] In his 1970 introduction to June Jordan's *Some Changes* Julius Lester wrote:

> June Jordan is a black poet, a black woman poet. That's a devastating combination. To be black and to be a woman. To be a double outsider, to be twice oppressed, to be more than invisible. That's a triple vision. June Jordan is faithful to the three primary aspects of her being.[36]

In recent years the image of black women in Afro-American poetry has become more autobiographical (more in keeping with the assertive mood of the race than with the confessional trends in Euro-American poetry). It is as if the younger women poets see themselves as similes of their sisters. Poems in this category include Mari Evans's "To Mother and Steve" with its search for love and struggle against the thrall of drugs. Her "into blackness softly" is like both Audre Lorde's "Naturally" and Johari Amini's "Identity (For Don L. Lee)" in registering the poet's new black consciousness. Carolyn Rodger's "Me, In Kulu Se & Karma" is autobiographical, as is Nikki Giovanni's "Nikki-Rosa." Sonia Sanchez's "poem for my father," "poem for etheridge," and "why I don't get high on shit" are all autobiographical, and the whole section "In these Dissenting-... Surrounding Ground and Autobiography" in *Revolutionary Petunias* is autobiographical.

White women, are, as part of their new consciousness, fighting sterotypes. No student of this movement. I use Mary Ellmann's categories (formlessness, passivity, instability, confinement, piety, materiality, spirituality, irrationality, compliancy, the shrew, and the witch)[37] as a gauge. Few of these seem appropriate to Afro-American images of black women because they are rarely seen as weak or frivolous or incompetent. As Faulkner said of Dilsey, black women in Afro-American poetry have "endured." They have had, given their economic and political powerlessness, and their social status, no other choice. Passivity, for example, is inapplicable. Except for examples like Emmett Till's mother (but it may just be that we cannot see the "chaos" in her "red prairie"),[38] the women are action-oriented: aggressiveness is part of the matriarch stereotype black women labor under. Passivity had a certain vogue under the 1960s influence of Muslim ideology, which elevated black men—often at the expense of black women:

    blackwoman:
    is an
    in and out
    rightsideup
    action-image
    of her man...
    in other
    (blacker) words:
    she's together
    if

he
bes[39]

though Kay Lindsey says:

> ...But now that the revolution needs numbers
> Mothers got a new position
> Five steps behind manhood.

> And I thought sittin' in the back of the bus
> Went out with Martin Luther King.[40]

All the examples of irrationality I found in my survey of Afro-American poetry were in the blues tradition of loving a man who doesn't love you; but who *does* love wisely? Compliancy doesn't apply: black women are not portrayed as compliant to their men, their children, or their white employers. Ellman's spirituality means refining or ennobling the man who loves one;[41] for black women it means strengthening, centering black men, being keepers of the flame of black culture (as seen in the coalescence of women and the integrity of Africa in the poetry of the 1960s).

Molly Means, "Chile of the devil, the dark, and witch,"[42] who changes a young bride into a howling dog, is the only explicit witch my research revealed—though Saint Louis woman, who enchants a man with diamond rings, power, and store-bought hair,[43] is perhaps an urbane, urban witch.

The most common stereotypes of black women are tragic mulatto, hot-blooded exotic whore, and matriarch.[44] I found no examples of tragic mulatto in the poetry. I found several street women (Gwendolyn Brooks's Sadie, Countee Cullen's "Black Magdelens," and Fenton Johnson's "The Scarlet Woman"), but none of them were exotic. Sapphire is another stereotype in black life, but she is nowhere visible in formal Afro-American poetry, where the relations between black women and black men are usually tender, desperate, or tragic, but never angry, domineering or aggressive. The strong black mammy, "bad-talking, ball-busting, strong enough to sustain her family and herself through the hardest conditions,"[45] does exist in the literature, but she is humanized by being scaled down as Gwendolyn Brooks does Mrs. Sallie Smith, Emmett Till's mother, Mrs. Small, and Big Bessie, who "throws" her son into the street. Washington says:

To outsiders, she is the one-dimensional Rock of Gibralter—strong
of back, long of arm, invincible. But to those writers whose perceptions are shaped by their own black womanhood, who can take us
into the dark recesses of the soul, she is an individual—profound,
tragic, mysterious, sacred, and unfathomable—strong in many ways,
but not all.[46]

While this may be true of fiction, few of the images in Afro-
American poetry reveal the complexity she describes.

The epic (heroic, archetypal) is an aspect of many of the images of
black women in Afro-American poetry, though few poems, and
most of them are recent, have only this thread:

> and the breath of your life
> sustains us . . .
> the female in the middle passage,
> you endure
> we endured through you[47]

and

> i am a blk/woo OOMAN
> my face
>   my brown
>   bamboo/colored
> black/berry/face
> will spread itself over
> this western hemisphere and
> be remembered
>   be sunnnnnNNGG
> for i will be called
>   QUEEN
> walk/move in
>   blk/queenly ways.
> and the world
>   shaken by
> by blkness
>   will channnnnNNGGGEEE
> colors. and be
> reborn.
>   blk.again.[48]

and

I
am a black woman
tall as a cypress
strong
beyond all definition still
defying place
and time
and circumstance
  assailed
    impervious
      indestructible
Look
  on me and be
renewed.[49]

Usually, however, the heroic is a strand in a poem about a mother or a singer. Consider Helene Johnson's "The Mother's Rock" or Imamu Baraka's "leroy," where the mother is seen as the transmitter and interpreter of "our life from our ancestors/and knowledge, and the strong nigger feeling," with Baraka picturing his mother with "black angels straining above her head,"[50] a bridge between old and new blues. Mari Evans handles the epic this way:

and the old women gathered
and sang His praises
standing
resolutely together
like supply sergeants who
have seen
everything
and are still
Regular Army: It
was firece and
not melodic and
although we ran
the sound of it
stayed in our ears...[51]

Robert Hayden's "Runagate, Runagate" provides a magnificent example of the epic black woman:

  Rises from their anguish and their power,
    Hariet Tubman

woman of earth, whipscarred,
a summoning, a shining

Mean to be free
....
and fear starts a-murbling, Never make it,
we'll never make it. *Hush that now,*
and she's turned upon us, levelled pistol
glinting in the moonlight;
Dead folks can't jaybird-talk, she says;
you keep on going now or die, she says.

Wanted ... Harriet Tubman   alias The General
alias Moses   Stealer   of Slaves

In league with Garrison   Alcott   Emerson
Garrettt   Douglass   Thoreau   John Brown

Armed and known to be Dangerous

Wanted   Reward   Dead or Alive
....
Mean mean mean to be free.[52]

Images of black women in Afro-American poetry come very close
to what Ellison said about the blues: "Their attraction lies in this,
that they at once express the agony of life and the possibility of
conquering it through sheer toughness of spirit."[53] The limitation is
that the intensely symbolic nature of the images has often limited
both the range of women we see and the ways in which they are
presented. We need, now, poems to reflect our myriad realities.

NOTES

1. Don L. Lee, *We Walk the Way of the New World* (Detroit: Broadside,
1970), p. 39.
2. Paul Laurence Dunbar, *The Complete Poems* (New York: Dodd, Mead,
1913), p. 214.
3. Wilfred Cartey, *Whispers from a Continent* (New York: Vintage, 1969),
pp. 3-4.
4. Ibid., p. 38.
5. Gwendolyn Brooks, *The World of Gwendolyn Brooks* (New York: Random House, 1971), p. 377.

6. Ibid., p. 329.

7. Betty Gates, "Mamma Settles the Dropout Problem," *Understanding the New Black Poetry* (New York: William Morrow, 1973), p. 309.

8. Lucille Clifton, "Admonitions," *The Black Poets* (New York: Bantam, 1971), p. 251.

9. Brooks, p. 381.

10. LeRoi Jones, *Blues People*, (New York: William Morrow, 1963), p. 41.

11. Lee, p. 5.

12. Claude McKay, "The Harlem Dancer," *The Book of American Negro Poetry* (New York: Harcourt, Bruce & World, 1959), p. 170.

13. Sterling Brown, "Ma Rainey," *Southern Road* (Boston: Beacon, 1974), pp. 63-64.

14. Nikki Giovanni, "Poem for Aretha," *Black Poets*, p. 329.

15. Robert Hayden, ed., *Kaleidoscope* (New York: Harcourt, Bruce & World, 1967), p. xx.

16. John Wesley Holloway, "Miss Melerlee," *Book of American Negro Poetry*, pp. 134-35.

17. Gwendolyn Bennett, "To a Dark Girl," *Book of American Negro Poetry*, p. 243.

18. Langston Hughes, "When Sue Wears Red," *Understanding the New Black Poetry*, p. 126.

19. Brooks, p. 37.

20. Ibid., p. 14.

21. Ibid., p. 88.

22. Ibid., p. 45.

23. Ishmael Reed, "To a Daughter of Isaiah," *Chattanooga* (New York: Random House, 1972), p. 35.

24. Michael Harper, "Echoes: One," *Dear John, Dear Coltrane* (University of Pittsburgh Press, 1970), p. 24.

25. Ibid., p. 69.

26. Brooks, p. 324.

27. Ibid., p. 377.

28. Dougherty Long, "Ginger Bread Mamma," *Black Poets*, p. 310.

29. Lucille Clifton, "If I Stand in My Window," *Black Poets*, p. 251.

30. Carolyn Rodgers, "Me, in Kulu Se & Karma," *Understanding the New Black Poetry*, p. 345.

31. Dudley Randall, "Blackberry Sweet," *The New Black Poetry* (New York: International Publishers, 1969), p. 103.

32. Everett Hoagland, "The Anti-Semanticist," *Black Poets*, pp. 314-15.

33. Ibid., p. 312.

34. Georgia Douglas Johnson, *The Heart of a Woman* (Freeport, N.Y.: Books for Libraries Press, 1971), p. xx.

35. Georgia Douglas Johnson, *Bronze* (Boston: B. J. Brimmer, 1922), p. 7.

36. June Jordan, *Some Changes* (New York: E.P. Dutton, 1971), p. ix.

37. Mary Ellmann, *Thinking about Women* (New York: Harcourt, Brace & World, 1968), p. 55.

38. Brooks, p. 324.

39. Don L. Lee, "blackwoman:" *Don't Cry, Scream* (Detroit: Broadside, 1969), p. 51.

40. Kay Lindsey, "Poem," *The Black Woman* (New York: New American Library, 1970), p. 17.

41. Ellmann, p. 102.

42. Margaret Walker, "Molly Means," *Book of Negro Folklore* (New York: Dodd, Mead, 1958), p. 545.

43. W. C. Handy, "St. Louis Blues," *The Negro Caravan* (New York: Arno, 1969), p. 473.

44. Mary Helen Washington, "Black Women Image Makers," *Black World*, 23 (August, 1974): 10.

45. Ibid. p. 11.

46. Ibid. p. 13.

47. Larry Neal. "For Our Women," *Black Fire* (New York: William Morrow, 1968), p. 311.

48. Sonia Sanchez, *We a BaddDDD People* (Detroit: Broadside, 1970), p. 6.

49. Mari Evans, *I Am a Black Woman* (New York: William Morrow, 1970), p. 12.

50. Imamu Amiri Baraka, "leroy," *Black Poets*, pp. 215-16.

51. Mari Evans, "... And the Old Women Gathered (The Gospel Singers)," *New Negro Poets: U.S.A.* (Bloomginton: University of Indiana Press, 1964), p. 79.

52. Robert Hayden, "Runagate, Runagate," *Understanding the New Black Poetry*, pp. 158-9.

53. Ralph Ellison, *Shadow and Act* (New York: Vintage, 1972), p. 94.

Part III: CARIBBEAN

Jamaican youngsters in Hope Gardens, Kingston, Jamaica. Photo: United Nations, No. 86286. (1963)

Caribbean

INTRODUCTORY SUMMARY

Much of the literature on the Caribbean woman has emerged through analyses of family and household structure and organization. A number of the contributions in this section present various aspects of the role of the Caribbean woman in society. Among other topics discussed are women's economic role and survival strategies, the centrality of the mother, and the image of women in the literature.

Solien Gonzalez' chapter sets out a framework for the definition of the 'family' and 'household', insisting that some distinction between the two is necessary in analyzing Caribbean society. This is because many individuals belong to both a family and a household, but the two units may not coincide. Consequently members of the nuclear family may reside in different households.

Justus presents a critique of the various explanations of West Indian matrifocality as being essentially structural in focussing on the interaction of the family and the larger society. She argues that these presentations lack the perspective of the family as "a system of interacting roles and statuses." Furthermore they lack an understanding of the West Indian woman's role in her society, especially in the significance of group solidarity and sharing.

Fresh insight into the situation of rebel slave communities is given by Bilby and Steady in a discussion of the important role of women in the survival of Maroon communities, with special reference to Moore Town. Since Maroon communities were constantly under attack, men had to be released for combat. Women therefore formed the main core of Maroon society. Although the key protagonists in the military struggles of the Maroons may have been men, the key protagonists of regeneration, and biological and social action were women. An analysis of the myth of Nanny, the Maroon ancestor and supernatural specialist, seems to bear this out as does the position of women in the economic, political and religious life of Moore Town today.

Barbados is one of the most stratified societies in the Caribbean. Sutton and Makiesky-Barrow examine the dynamics of social inequality and sexual status in this Caribbean country. They examine access to resources in the kinship system and in the economy by both men and women, and the cultural ideology as it relates to the sexes, and conclude that women have a great deal of autonomy and independence in Barbados society.

The chapter by Mintz is a study of Haiti and Jamaica, two Afro-Caribbean societies where women's independent economic activities in trade are highly valued and form part of a cultural tradition which endows women with equal economic status. In concluding his analysis he makes the following important statement: "The fact is that West Africa and Afro-Caribbean societies have been able in some contexts to achieve sexual equality still quite unheard of in Western societies, for all their vaunting of individual freedom."

Moses examines the middle-class basis for sexism in Montserrat, and relates it in part to inherited English law and imposed Victorian morality. She points out the discrepancy between an ideology that socializes men and women to believe that men are superior, and the reality of male unemployment, and the dependence of female kin.

Latortue's contribution, the last chapter in this section, looks at black women in Haitian society and literature. She shows the sharp contrasts between the life experiences of the elite and the working class and their varying degrees of oppression. The images presented in literature also reveal this contrast, so that the working class women are seen as earthy and expressive, while the elite appear more sophisticated and reserved.

1
Household and Family in the Caribbean: Some Definitions and Concepts

Nancie Solien Gonzalez

In recent years much attention has been directed toward the family system observed in Afro-American communities. Typical features of this system include the high percentage of "non-legal" or "irregular" conjugal unions, legal marriage being typical only of the upper classes and well-to-do. The separation rate is high and children almost invariably remain with the mother. Women occupy a prominent position in this sytem; some writers even describe certain household groups, as being "matrifocal" (15), "mother-headed" (4), "matriarchal" (8), "maternal" (8), etc. Such designations have served to emphasize the fact that many domestic groups in these societies include no male in the role of husband-father. In spite of minor differences, especially in regard to quantitative data on the types of families found in any given community, it is apparent that the situation is fundamentally the same in such widespread areas as Jamaica, Trinidad, British Guiana, Haiti, Brazil, the southern United States, and the Caribbean coast of Central America.

The specific object of investigation in many of these societies has been the family (1, 7, 11, 14, 15). There has been a tendency to identify the family with the household, a procedure which, as we shall see, has some precedent in anthropological usage. However, the situation in these societies differs so much from those described in other parts of the world, that great difficulty often arises when one tries to apply the classical concepts of "family" and "household" in Afro-America. Unfortunately, too often the writer merely glosses over the conceptual difficulty, using the terms interchangeably without defining them, and as a result there is much confusion in the literature.

It is the purpose of this paper to examine various definitions and usages of the terms "family" and "household" in order to determine their usefulness in analyzing Afro-American society.

Few writers have distinguished between family and household on either a theoretical or a descriptive level. Empirically the two are quite often identical, especially when one is dealing with the nuclear family. There is general agreement in the literature that within a household one finds a family of one type or another. Thus, Murdock includes common residence, along with economic co-operation and reproduction, as defining characteristics of the family (12, p. 1).

Radcliffe-Brown, after defining his term, "the elementary family," as a father, a mother, and their children, says that this unit "usually provides the basis for the formation of domestic groups of persons living together in intimate daily life" (13, p. 5). He goes on to give several examples of such domestic groups, each of which could be classified as an extended family.

Lowie defines the family as "the association" that corresponds to the institution of marriage, recognizing that the character of the interpersonal relations among the members is of more importance than the actual membership. He notes that a household may include persons unrelated by kinship ties who are excluded from the family, yet presumably to him too the family forms the core of the household (10, pp. 215-16).

Linton distinguishes between what he calls "conjugal" and "consanguine" families. His definition of each implies common residence of spouses and their offspring, the primary difference between the two types being that in the consanguine family the inmarrying spouses are relatively unimportant (9, pp. 159-63).

It is apparent that most anthropologists think of a family as a coresidential group within which there is at least one conjugal pair plus at least some of the offspring of this pair. Various extensions of this unit may occur typically in different societies, such extensions being based upon kinship ties (consanguineal and/or affinal) between other persons and one member of the original conjugal pair. Conversely, the household generally refers to a group of persons who live together and co-operate in at least some if not all domestic affairs. A family unit of some type is generally assumed to be the nucleus of the household, though there may also be present some unrelated persons.

Outside of the Afro-American area there have been a few other societies described in which the above concepts do not prove useful. Notable examples include the Nayars in South Malabar and Cochin in which the household unit traditionally contained as regular members only matri-lineal kin. Gough states that "the simplest traditional dwelling-group is therefore a sibling group, together with the children and maternal grandchildren of the women" (6, p. 85).

The Ashanti also exhibit a pattern of duo-locality, in which husbands and wives, especially during the early years of marriage, do not reside together. Fortes describes three types of domestic unit: (a) households grouped around a husband and wife; (b) households grouped around an effective minimal matrilineage, or part of it; and (c) households made up of combinations of the two previous types (2, p. 69). Type (b), containing no conjugal pair, would not be equivalent to a family.

Henriques says in regard to Jamaica, "...the best method of classifying family groupings appears to be the adoption of the term domestic group as the unit of family structure in the island" (7). Yet he also notes, "In Jamaica the domestic group is the residential unit which constitutes a household. The domestic group may, but does not always, consist of the elementary biological family." On the other hand, he says, "Family groupings can be divided into those with a conjugal and those with a consanguineous basis" (p. 105).

R. T. Smith (16, p. 67), states that "...most writers are agreed that the main functioning family unit in the Caribbean is a household group". He then defines the household as "...a group of people occupying a single dwelling and sharing a common food supply". His data, as well as those of many other writers show that very often the household group contains no conjugal pair. He does not further define the family, but instead uses the term interchangeably with household group.

Obviously, these usages do not correspond to the definitions ordinarily used by anthropologists. As we have seen, in spite of minor differences in phraseology, most writers insist upon some form of marriage as the basis of the family. A household, on the other hand, is primarily a residential unit, and although it *may* and usually does include some sort of family as its core, the definition does not insist upon this as a criterion.

Goody (5, p. 56) takes this view when he says " ... the use of the blanket term 'family' to indicate groups which are specifically defined by residence and descent as well as those defined by the existence of the marriage bond may be adequate for Euro-American systems in which there is considerable overlap, but it can be highly confusing in terms of other societies".

Fortes too, has pointed out that in many cases it is useful to distinguish analytically between the elementary family and the domestic group. He notes that the actual composition of the two may be identical, but that the reproductive functions of the group may be separated from the householding and housekeeping functions. He differentiates the two units on the basis of the types of bonds obtaining among the members. An elementary family is constituted solely by the bonds of marriage, filiation, and siblingship, while the household or domestic group may include persons bound together by various kinds of jural and affective bonds other than these (3).

One aspect of the problem in the Caribbean has been well phrased by Clarke, who says:

> The anthropologist in search of the family *sees* [italics hers] first the house ... Within that house, be it hut or cottage, is contained, for some part of the day or night, part of the group which he is about to study.

> But what part of it? Will he find the majority of these households to contain parents and their children, or mothers only with their daughters and their daughters' children; or a man and woman with some only of their offspring? Or, instead, will he find a heterogeneous collection of kin, brought together by some new pattern of association, based on a system of relationships fundamentally different from that found in other societies elsewhere? (1, p. 28).

In fact, all of these situations may be found within most Caribbean communities today. Clarke suggests a typology in which she distinguishes between "family" households and "consanguineous" households. The latter may be one of three types: (a) denuded family households in which there is only one parent, plus children, grandchildren, or other lineal relatives of the parent; (b) sibling households in which adult brothers and sisters live under one roof; and (c) single person households (common only in towns on which people travel to obtain wage-labour during part of the year) (1).

It is my view that some distinction between family and household such as that made by Clarke is not only useful but necessary in dealing with Caribbean society. It seems to me that the fact that some households contain no family as ordinarily defined by anthropologists is one of the most important characteristics of Caribbean society. Elsewhere I have stressed the consanguineal nature of these households as a key to their understanding (17).

It is, of course, perfectly legitimate to view the society in terms of household units as long as the investigator distinguishes these from families. Presumably, the universe may be completely divided with a classification like Clarke's, for all persons would belong to one or another type of household. Does this mean then, that some persons are members of families and others are not? Undoubtedly, this is sometimes the case, but I suggest that in order fully to understand Afro-American society it is necessary to view it in terms of household units on the one hand, and family units on the other. I would maintain that many, if not most, individuals belong to both a family and to a household. At times the two units coincide, but quite often they do not.

In order to illustrate this point I shall draw upon my fieldwork of a year's duration among the Black Carib of Livingston, Guatemala—a group of people whose culture is similar enough to other Afro-American groups to warrant classifying them together (18). The nuclear family unit among the Carib may be scattered in several different households. For example, the husband-father may be living with his own mother, one or more children may be with their maternal relatives or with non-Caribs, while the mother may be working and "living in" as a maid in one of the port towns. Some may then assert that under such circumstances this no longer constitutes a family unit. However, if the nature of the personal interrelationships among the group members is considered, it may be seen that there exists a pattern of affective and economic solidarity among them. It is true that many such groups are extremely brittle and unstable, but they do exist for varying lengths of time. And for their duration the members think of themselves as a unit; when questioned as to their family connections they will immediately name and locate their primary relatives. Furthermore, there is some economic co-operation among them, the man generally contributing a part of his wages (or money from sale of cash crops) to the woman and the children. The woman too, if working, may give money to the man, and certainly sends clothing and money to the household(s) in which her children are living.

Another common arrangement is that in which the husband maintains a single-person household in one town, leaving his wife and children living together in another. The latter would appear to be Clarke's denuded family household. However, I think it is important to recognize that within this type of household one may find either of two fundamentally different relationship patterns. The man, though living elsewhere, may make frequent trips to visit his wife and children, contributing a large part of his wages toward their support. They consider that he "lives" with them, though he may not actually have resided there for a number of years. The man will return to his family immediately in times of crisis, or when important decisions must be made. He also returns whenever possible to assist the woman in clearing fields, to make repairs on the house, etc. He remains a highly important influence in the socialization of his children. I would call this group a non-localized family.

On the other hand, the single parent (most often the mother, although occasionally one finds a father alone with his children) may be completely unattached to any individual who might be called a spouse. She may receive a small amount of economic assistance from the father or fathers of her children, but for the most part she is dependent upon herself and her consanguineal relatives in maintaining and socializing her children. This situation, which on the surface appears identical to that described above, is obviously entirely different. Although Clarke's term, the "denuded family", is somewhat descriptive of the situation, it is nevertheless ambiguous since it may refer to either set of relationships described above. I would not call this unit a family at all; consisting only of a mother and her children, it is on a lower level of organization than a family which must include a conjugal relationship and what Fortes would call patri-filiation (3).

Another interesting and pertinent example is that of the Israeli *kibbutz*. Here we find a situation in which married couples co-reside, but their children live elsewhere. Although Spiro (19), following Murdock's definition of marriage (12), states that the relationship between these couples does not constitute marriage, it seems clear from his data that the society itself recognizes the relationship as such. He points out that these couples are eventually united in accordance with the marriage laws of the state. Furthermore, he goes on to state that the family does not exist within the *kibbutz* system, unless one wishes to consider the *kibbutz* itself as a large extended family. Again, Spiro has followed Murdock's definition of the family in arriving at this conclusion.

However, Spiro makes it clear that within the *kibbutz* there does exist a group which could, by another definition, be termed a nuclear family. He says: "The social group in the *kibbutz* that includes adults of both sexes and their children, although character- ized by reproduction, is not characterized by common residence or by economic co-operation" (*19*, p. 840). He goes on to show that this group is characterized by psychological intimacy, affection, and joint recreational activities. Although the children's physical and mental development for the most part is supervised by persons outside this family unit, Spiro notes that, 'Parents are of crucial importance in the *psychological* development of the child" (italics his). "They serve as the objects of his most important identifications, and they provide him with a certain security and love that he obtains from no one else" (*19*, p. 844). In view of the strength of the affective bonds among this group, which includes their own recog- nition of themselves as a separate, cohesive, and enduring unit, I suggest that the family as an institution *does* exist within the *kibbutz*. If one wishes to liken the entire *kibbutz* to an extended family, then why not consider these smaller units of mother, father, and chil- dren as nuclear families?

In conclusion, I propose that the family be defined as a group of people bound together by that complex set of relationships known as kinship ties, between at least two of whom there exists a conjugal relationship. The conjugal pair, plus their offspring, forms the nuclear family. Other types of family may be defined as extensions of the nuclear type, each being identified by the nature of the relationship between the conjugal pair (or one member of that pair) and other members.

The household, on the other hand, implies common residence, economic co-operation, and socialization of children. Although the members of the household may be bound by kinship relationships, no particular type of tie is necessarily characteristic. In any given society a particular family may or may not form a household. Conversely, a household may or may not contain a family. Although it is probably useful to make an analytical distinction between the two concepts in all cases, the investigator must be particularly careful to examine the structure and functioning of both types of units in those societies in which their membership does not coincide.

REFERENCES

1. Clarke, Edith. 1957 *My Mother Who Fathered Me*. London.
2. Fortes, Meyer. 1949 "Time and Social Structure: An Ashanti Case Study," in *Social Structure: Studies Presented to A. R. Radcliffe-Brown*, Meyer Fortes, ed. Oxford.
3. Fortes, Meyer. 1945 Introduction to *The Devlopmental Cycle in Domestic Groups*, Jack Goody, ed. Cambridge Papers in Social Anthropology, No. 1.
4. Frazier, E. Franklin. 1939 *The Negro Family in the United States*. Chicago.
5. Goody, Jack. 1958 "The Fission of Domestic Groups among the Lodagaba," in *The Developmental Cycle in Domestic Groups*, Jack Goody, ed. Cambridge Papers in Social Anthropology, No. 1.
6. Gough, E. Kathleen. 1952 "A Comparison of Incest Prohibitions and the Rules of Exogamy in Three Matrilineal Groups of the Malabar Coast," *International Archives of Ethnography*, XLVI, No. 1, pp. 82-105.
7. Henriques, Fernando M. 1953 *Family and Colour in Jamaica*. London.
8. Herskovits, Melville J. 1958 *The Myth of the Negro Past*. Beacon Edition, Boston.
9. Linton, Ralph. 1936 *The Study of Man*. New York.
10. Lowie, Robert H. 1950 *Social Organization*. London.
11. Matthews, Dom Basil. 1953 "Crisis of the West Indian Family," *Caribbean Affairs*, Vol. 9. University College of the West Indies.
12. Murdock, George P. 1949 *Social Structure* New York.
13. Radcliffe-Brown, A. R. 1950 Introduction to *African Systems of Kinship and Marriage*, A. R. Radcliffe-Brown and Daryll Forde, eds. London.
14. Simey, T.S. 1946 *Welfare and Planning in the West Indies*. Oxford.
15. Smith, Raymond T. 1956 *The Negro Family in British Guiana*. London.
16. Smith, Raymond T. 1957 "The Family in the Caribbean," in *Caribbean Studies: A Symposium*, Vera Rubin, ed. University College of the West Indies, Jamaica.
17. Solien, Nancie L. 1958 "The Consanguineal Household Among the Black Carib of Central America." Ph.D. dissertation, University of Michigan.

18. Solien, Nancie L. 1959 "West Indian Characteristics of the Black Carib," *Southwestern Journal of Anthropology*, Vol. 15, No. 3, pp. 300-7.
19. Spiro, Melford E. 1954 "Is the Family Universal?", *American Anthropologist*, Vol. 56, No. 5, pp. 839-46.

A street scene on Fredrick Street, Port-of-Spanin, Trinidad. Photo: United Nations, No. 84890. (1963)

2

Women's Role in West Indian Society

Joyce Bennett Justus

INTRODUCTION

As an ethnographer and an insider* I find the literature on the West
Indian family both intriguing and frustrating. It is intriguing
because social scientists have, for more than a quarter of a century,
tried to understand family and kinship in the Caribbean. The literature is extensive, the differing points of view equally persuasive and
equally well-documented. The literature frustrates me since, as an
insider, I am left with the feeling that perhaps the most important
aspects of the West Indian family and kinship are still essentially
unexplained. This essay attempts to reexamine the available data
and to raise questons, some of which were not the concern of the
social scientists who carried out the initial research. As such, it may
be said that this essay does injustice to what is among the finest
body of social science research on the family. Yet since my concerns
are structural[1] as well as cultural, it is my hope that the answers I
propose will shed further light on the relationship between behavior as observed and the values from which it emanates.

My approach differs from the studies from which I have derived
my data[2] in another basic manner: I assume that theoretical stances
and cultural biases have affected all kinship studies, especially as
they have influenced discussions on the West Indian family. My
convictions are strengthened by the intensity of the debate and the
length of time over which it has been carried. As an ethnographer
and an insider I, too, have theoretical stances and cultural biases,

*See note, p. 448

431

but I hope that my biases as an insider will serve to temper my biases as an ethnographer. Kinship itself is based on cultural constructs which are deep and rarely examined. It is concerned with aspects of individual behaviors which are intimate, a situation which further compounds the problem of bias.

A careful review of the literature on the West Indian family reveals a preoccupation with the high frequencies of mother-child households, illegitimacy, and father absenteeism. Another question which arises out of the first set of concerns and is also hotly debated is whether marriage is the norm for all segments of West Indian society? Answers to both these questions emerge within discussions of the structural conditions of West Indian society; socioeconomic differentiation, and the role of race and class in the formation of the society at large. Problems often debated include lack of upward mobility, high unemployment and underemployment rates, relationships among unemployed males, male migration in search of employment, and father absenteeism. The answers that have been offered ignore the fact that two quite different questions are being asked. First is the question of the structural conditions of the poor. This problem is generally the reason given for high the frequency of illegitimacy, mother-child households, and father absenteeism. Second is the question which underlies all of these concerns and is often not asked explicitly: do the poor share the same values as the middle and upper classes? Often the structural answer to the first question becomes the basis for commenting on the value orientation of the middle and lower classes.

In response to the question of whether marriage is the norm for all segments of West Indian society, these studies have suggested that the observed differences in behavior between the upper-middle and lower classes are the result of different beliefs and values (the conflict model), or conversely, that there are no grounds for arguing that these differences in behavior originate in different shared understandings (the consensus model). In both cases, these are mere speculations about behavior, and in neither case are the speculations justified. My approach is essentially one which attempts to look at the family as a system of interacting roles and statuses. I suggest that such an approach will better provide the type of data from which to draw inferences about value orientations of each segment of West Indian society.

A DIFFERENT APPROACH[3]

This new approach focuses on the family itself as a system of interactions among members, with each member fulfilling a position or status with a number of roles, supported and constrained by the reference group and the structure of society. What this approach does that others do not is allow for considerations such as the formations of gender personality, gender identity, the acquisition of sex roles, and the cultural constraints of each of these developments.

Little is known of Caribbean socialization. Very few culture and personality studies of the West Indian family have been undertaken. Studies which include discussions of socialization present data in the context of other concerns, and such data are included in studies of other aspects of Caribbean social organization (e.g., interpersonal relations, conflict). Furthermore, the majority of the studies of the West Indian family have been concerned exclusively with lower class families. Only recently has the middle class become the focus of investigation, and even among this emergent body of literature there has been very little written on socialization. Still, I propose here a model to account for the centrality of the female and the marginality of the male in the Caribbean family, and for the solidarity among females regardless of social class distinctions.

The Development of Gender Personality

According to psychoanalytic theory, personality development is the result of the internalization and organization of the nature and quality of the social relationships that the child experiences. Different male and female experiences lead to differences in the way masculine and feminine psyches resolve certain relational issues (Chodorow: 1974: 46). A child's earliest experience is usually one of identity with and attachment to a single mother. Children, in their first few years, are preoccupied with issues of separation and individuation. These experiences include breaking or attenuating primary identification with the mother and beginning to develop a sense of self. The pre-Oedipal experience is likely to differ for boys and girls. The experience of mothering for a woman involves double identification (Klein and Riviere, 1937). A woman identifies with her own mother through her identification with her child, and thus experiences herself as a cared-for child. The particular nature of the double identification of a woman is bound up with her relationship with her own mother. Given that she was a female child, a woman's identification with her female child might be stronger than her identification with a male child, and mothers tend to treat children of different sexes in different ways. There is anthropological evidence which suggests that this is in fact the case. Minturn and Hitchcock (1963), writing on Rajput mothers, suggest that they are likely to like girl babies better after they are born, Minturn, Hitchcock, and Harper (1969), writing on Havik Brahmins of South India, suggest that mothers treat daughters with greater affection and leniency than sons. Levy reports[4] that his data on Nepal about Hindu mothers provide additional support for this argument. My own data on Dominican mothers indicates that they prefer their daughters, feel closer to them, and come to rely upon them earlier. They also expressed greater anxiety for their daughters than for their sons. In the words of one informant:

> boys are o.k. . . . but the girls . . . I worry for them . . . maybe life treats them hard . . . maybe they don't get good jobs . . . no good husbands . . . you understand . . . life can be real hard for a woman- . . . still . . prefer my girl children . . . they are always more attentive to the parents . . .

In all cases it can be argued that mothers' anxiety stems from the concern for the future plight of their daughters. Rajput and Havik Brahmin mothers treat daughters more leniently than their sons in anticipation of the difficult times ahead when their daughters will become young brides in the households of their husbands. Dominican mothers treat their daughters more strictly in anticipation of the fact that their daughters will have to carry the burden of responsibility not only for themselves but perhaps also for their own children *and* their mothers. In other words, mothers are preparing their daughters to assume responsibility for the three-generation household when the mothers are no longer able to care for themselves. From the time of the daughters' birth, mothers in these cultures identify with them by reexperiencing their own past, and develop a particular attachment to their daughters because of this. Mothers experience their daughters' life achievements, frustrations, and disappointments as if they were their own.

Mothers' reactions to their sons are quite different. Cultural evidence suggest that mothers treat sons differently, emphasizing their sons' masculinity in opposition to their own femininity. One way the mother does this is by pushing her son toward differentiation and the assuming of male roles. Sometimes the mother does this prematurely. This is particularly true in families in which the fathers are absent totally. Mothers in this type of household often express great anxiety about their sons becoming "real men," mothers are concerned about their sons' over-identification with females, and the other effects that being constantly surrounded by females will have on their development.

For boys then, the quality of the pre-Oedipal relationship to their mothers is quite different than for girls. Even before development of gender identity, gender-related personality differentiation begins. In most societies, women's lives tend to be private and domestic, while men's tend to be more public and social (Rosaldo: 1974). Given this dichotomy, we can assume that for boys and girls there will be differences in the devlopment of gender identification mediated by the fact that boys must, in the process of devloping a masculine gender identity, replace their primacy identification with the mother with an identification with the father and other adult males. Since the father's work and social life take him away from home, boys identify with aspects of a role not clearly defined, the performance of which is not clearly defined; the performance of which is not observed in totality. Dominican mothers are keenly aware of this. They often speak of the need for boys to be around the father more, in order to get to know him as a man. As one informant put it:

> my son should spend more time with his father ... father is a good man ... good provider ... could teach him many things ... I would prefer the boy children to be with the father more ... down the beach with him and the other fishermen ... go to sea ... to go to the bar ... (in response to question as to when she would consider him to be old enough) when he bigger ... 6 maybe ... depend on how he grow ... he kind of frail ...

Here we see the mother's basic dilemma: she *wants* her son to be around males more, but still is unsure of his ability to take care of himself. This kind of ambivalence persists throughout the son's life, a point I return to later in this essay.

Fathers are often inaccessible to sons. In the lower class this is often explained by the fathers' economic marginality, which keeps them permanently outside of the household, or, at best, only imperfect participants in it. Boys must identify with a father whose value within the household is often defined in economic terms, and who leaves the household when he is unable to assume the functions of father. For lower class boys, the identification becomes a "positional identification with aspects of father's not so clearly defined male role." (Chodorow, 1974:49) The middle-class father is not much more accessible. Here work and social activities take him away from home during most of the child's waking hours, and although he may be a more permanent member of the household, the father rarely is involved with son to the extent that the mother is. The middle-class male's culturally defined role does not permit him to be involved in child care. Sons rarely see fathers performing male roles. The father is either the authority of last resort when mothers are unable to cope, or a person with whom the child has ritualized interactions. Middle-class sons, like lower class sons, have little experience with their fathers' personality, values, and behavioral traits.

A girl's situation is quite different. Although men are also important to their primary object world, the relationship between men and female children is an emotional one. That men and fathers are absent from the home during most of their waking hours has a very different effect on the life of girls. Girls develop a genuine relationship with mother, and their identification with mother's general traits, character, and values. Gender and gender role identification are mediated by and dependent upon real, affective relations. Girls are surrounded by their mothers and other women and as a result learn to be feminine gradually.

West Indian mothers not only convey to their daughters a sense of feminine gender identity, but surround both boys and girls with women who share in caring for them. The infant is exposed to a series of females from birth onward: mother, mother's mother, mother's sister, mother's other female kin, mother's female friends, older respected women in the community, and mother's female employees. For the woman who works, (and there are many working mothers both among the middle and lower classes) this cadre of women assumes child-care responsibilities: in the lower class in exchange for gifts and services, in the middle and upper classes in exchange for wages. For boys, this means that the necessity to negate feminine traits is overemphasized; men become men and exhibit their manliness in a variety of culturally approved ways. Fathers and mothers are concerned that sons develop appropriately. However, gender identification for girls does not involve the negation of the feminine, and therefore, for girls, the presence of many women can be seen as enhancing the development of gender personality.

That this discussion has been general, and has drawn heavily from areas outside of the Caribbean, is a result of a virtual absence of data on the subject in the Caribbean. I argue that this does not invalidate the conclusions that I present. It is in the area of conscious sex role learning that the social context and specific cultural understandings become important. The remainder of this paper is concerned less with the general question of the development of gender personality and identity, and more with the specifics of sex role learning in its cultural context.

Sex Role Learning and its Cultural Context

Role learning and social interaction build upon and largely reinforce the unconscious development discussed above. In the West Indies a girl is usually with her mother and other female relatives in interpersonal situations that facilitate early and continuous role learning and emphasize the mother-daughter identification. The major aim of socialization is the repression of agression and independence (Cohen, 1953; Kerr, 1953). Children are closely watched, confined to the immediate vicinity of the home, and rarely play with children other than siblings until they enter school or are at least five years old. For the middle-class child, there is more likelihood of exposure to the children in his or her neighborhood, due perhaps to the fact that, although relatives and siblings are preferred playmates, the middle-class child is less likely to live with or near relatives than is the lower class child.

At the age of five male-female socialization patterns diverge sharply and females begin role training, while boys are permitted, and expected, to continue to be "babies" and are allowed to play. Girls are confined to the home environment, and learn woman's work, first by imitating their mothers or mother surrogates, and later through deliberate instruction from them. They are rewarded for tasks done well, and are punsihed for failure to at least approximate the ideal. The system of punishments and rewards serves to reinforce learning, and thus assures that the female child develops in an "orderly" and "appropriate" manner.

Formal education begins at six years of age, and for many children it marks the first experience outside the home and the first opportunity to interact freely with age-mates. Primary education is coeducational, but custom dictates that boys and girls are segregated within the classroom. Play is usually unisex, and encouraged by teachers and parents to be so. At this time, children are also introduced to church. Since few young men attend church, especially lower class young men, children accompany their mother to church. Girls often accompany their mother to church-affiliated women's groups whose primary aim is to train women and girls to be Christian women and mothers. Education past the primary level is available to few. The larger segment of the population completes primary school only. Admission to secondary school is by competition examinate (the so-called eleven-plus examination, and, as a result, mothers are very concerned that their children do well. Although it is interpreted in different ways by each social class, the general pattern throughout the region is that girls receive more education than boys: more girls complete secondary school; and there are more women than men in teacher-training colleges. More jobs regarded as female employment (nursing, elementary school teaching) have educational prerequisites. Moreover, there are more employment opportunities for men without secondary educational prerequisites (the Police and Army, for example) which are relatively prestigious, and farm work and agricultural labor traditionally have less social stigma attached to them than do corresponding levels of employment for women. (Justus, 1971) Mothers interpret education as expanding life options for their daughters. They are concerned that their daughters obtain as much education as possible and go to great lengths to see that they do, often derpriving themselves and postponing their own gratification. During this period, great care is exercised to protect daughters from forming relationships with men, as this is seen as potentially detrimental to the achievement of their full potential, and as diverting their attention away from what should be their primary concern.

Adolescence formally begins with the completion of schooling. This is a time of greater freedom and greater responsibility. For those who do not attend secondary school, this occurs at fifteen years of age—few complete secondary school before seventeen years. The rural male adolescent begins farm working on his father's farm with him (if he owns land), or working on someone else's farm as a paid laborer in order to buy his clothing and the like. For a while, he remains under the loose control and supervision of his parents, but this is minimal and he is often free to leave the household whenever he chooses, provided he is out of school. (Cohen, Clarke) The urban male also goes to work, contributes to the family, becomes more involved in peer group activities and spends more and more time away from home. For both rural and urban males, the economic motive is paramount, and the ability to earn enough money to purchase clothing and attend local clubs, bars, movies, and the like, is a sign of true independence and emergent adult status. Since adolescent unemployment is high, this is a time of much difficulty for many young men. Many urban young men are unemployed and an even larger proportion is under-employed. As a result, adolescence is prolonged, and hostility among this group of young men prevalent (Wedenoja, 1976). Mothers are concerned to keep their daughters away from these "no good, bad manners young men."

Female adolescents remain firmly under the control of their mothers since mother realizes that the ultimate success of her daughter—in marriage, in employment, or other areas—may in actuality determine *both* of their futures. This is the period of greatest mother/daughter conflict: the daughter no longer is content to remain home with the mother and the mother's kin and is anxious to spend more time with her peers, while the mother is determined to keep daughter off the street. However, role training has been such that women are integrated socially and fully competent adults at the age of fifteen. Despite the potentially hostile situation, daughters have their mothers to turn to for advice, to observe constantly in interaction with men, and as a constant reminder of the difficulties she, herself, will have to face and of the options she, herself, has to exercise to ensure that she will be successful.

Both boys and girls have been socialized in a situation in which males have been evaluated in terms of their ability to achieve the cultural ideal of what a husband/father should be. The main relationships to which they have been exposed are colored by the ability of the male to provide for the family. In many cases, this has been a deciding factor, a major determinant of whether or not the man will be actually present in the household. Paternal absences have been explained by referring to the necessity for men to make a living whether this entails short absences, absences for more extended periods, or termination of membership within the household. The father has also been presented as the person from whom the family derives its status. He is the main arbiter in the event of intersibling rivalry, intrafamilial or community conflicts and the ultimate disciplinarian. Father, and by extension males, are not only the major authority in the household, but also the major participants in community affairs.

As previously mentioned, the educational system presents females with the opportunity for interaction with other females, and although familial relationships are preferred, friendships developed during school years often persist throughout adult life. Many females remain in their natal villages, surrounded by many persons with whom they attended elementary school, and with whom they have attended church. Others migrate to urban centers, often for the purpose of attending secondary school, and subsequently to remain for employment. Others complete school in the rural areas and migrate to the urban centers in search of employment. Often, friendships developed during early adolescence persist throughout adult life and serve as a basis for adult female social interaction. Indeed, as one informant stated:

> she had been my friend since third standard—brighter than me you know . . . went to teacher college and all them things . . . now she in big time job . . . but she still don't forget me you know . . . send present for me and the children dem at Christmas . . . birthday . . . she help me with the children all the while . . .

and another:

> I still keep up with all the girls I was in sixth form with . . . one is in England . . . one in Canada . . . another in New York . . . One in Kuala Lumpur . . . we still exchange letters and presents . . . they send presents for me and my children. I send presents for them and their children . . . Two of my best friends here are from that group and we see each other all the time . . .

Thus, bonds developed in adolescence often persist into adult life.

One of my informants was 38 years of age, the other 42. One was lower class, the other an upper-middle class professional. Yet both continued to exchange gifts with friends of bygone days. One woman had fared less well than her former schoolmate, and, as a result, was the recipient of her gifts (the friend had not married and had no children of her own). Both of the women interviewed had developed new friendships based on place of residence, or place of employment, or both. Many had friends among daughters of friends of their own mothers, and they continued to exchange gifts not only with members of their own generation, but also with the members of their mother's generation. Many of these women associated in a network of god-parent relationships.

The church has traditionally been one of the few places where any form of nonfamilial interaction takes place. For lower class families it is often the only place for such interaction, and continues to be so throughout adult life. For the church, established denominations as well as Protestant sects, Christian marriage is the ideal; illegitimacy is discouraged, and, after the birth of the first child out of wedlock, women are no longer allowed to attend church until they form a stable union (legal or nonlegal). Marriage, then, is an ideal shared by all, regardless of social class, and is a prerequisite for full church membership. Church memberships *and* marriage are marks of respectability, a status to which all members of society aspire. Without both, leadership in community affairs is not legitimized, and competent and able persons must achieve both before being accorded adult status, leadership positions, or respect.

Two important facts emerge from this discussion: for women, adult status, physically and psychologically, is attainable at a relatively early age as the result of developments which have their roots in gender identity and social role learning. Girls are not given an idealized impression of womanhood. On the contrary, they are face to face with female kin and other adult females in school and in church as well as in the home, and participate in a family within which father's role and social position is defined in economic terms. Boys are not socialized to assume responsibility, and the achievement of adult status for males is not the natural culmination of social role learning: rather, it depends on a proven ability to accumulate the wealth needed to support a family. Since for both males and females the ability to establish an independent residential unit is a true mark of adult status, adolescence is prolonged for men who cannot provide for a woman, and hence establish a permanent household which will prove to the world that they have indeed achieved adult status. The church, with its influence on females, marriage, and legitimacy, presents to women a view of man as a provider upon whose shoulders the decision to marry, rests and upon whom her ultimate fate depends. Men, therefore, are evaluated by women in terms of their ability to fulfill a culture-wide definition of what a husband should be; women are evaluated by men in terms of their abilities to be good mothers; good help-mates; and respectable in the eyes of their husbands' peers.

Mating, Marriage, and the Family

The onset of adulthood also presents different options for males and females. For males, post adolescence is a period of relative instability. Peer groups are of considerable importance, and sixteen to twenty-one-year-olds stick together in something like a "juvenile cluster," usually apart from the older males but deferring to them whenever they come into contact. Many remain in the family of orientation. Few obtain employment away from home. Those who do tend to be the better-educated, and as a result, the more likely to become economically independent early. Seasonal migration is less significant than it used to be, e.g., Solien (1960). Now most males who leave home do so because they have obtained work elsewhere, and although they return home to visit, and perhaps still regard themselves as members of the family of orientation, they rarely, if ever, return to their natal villages to set up permanent households. As they leave the family of orientation, males participate increasingly in community discussions, village affairs. Full male status, then, is based on a combination of age, economic security, and independence from the family of orientation. This presents fewer problems for upper- and middle-class men. For them, the means for establishing economic independence is more easily attainable. Since the same criteria for adult status apply to upper- and middle-class men they tend to marry earlier. In doing so, they seize upon the culturally approved means for informing the world that they are indeed adults, that adolescence is over, and that they are ready to assume responsibility, not only for themselves, but for their families as well. Many become active members in community and religious affairs *after* marriage, thereby further validating the onset of adulthood.

Women remain in the family of orientation, where they are protected and supervised by the mother and, if he is present, the father. They enter the labor force but return home to the family of orientation. If employment takes them away from direct parental supervision, they are placed under the care and guidance of the mother's kin, or a close female friend of the mother. Much care is exercised in selecting the home within which a daughter should be placed. In the absence of family, kin, or a close friend (and this is very rare indeed), or if family or friends are not viewed as likely to be able to exercise sufficient control or supervision, attempts will be made to identify appropriate role models: older, respected women in the community, whether married or single, whose reputation and respectibility is such that mothers (and fathers) feel confident that daughters will receive proper supervision (e.g., school teachers, social workers, clergy) will be chosen. For women, full adult status is achieved by either the birth of the first child or by marriage. For the upper and middle classes, marriage usually occurs, at the latest, before the delivery of the first child and pregnancy is sufficient cause for marriage, whereas pregnancy and childbirth precede marriage and pregnancy is not a sufficient cause for marriage among the lower class.

First sexual experiences and pregnancy often occur when both men and women are in the postadolescent stage, and heralds adulthood for women; it also signals the time for marriage for middle- and upper-class men and women. Lower class parents are not expected to marry, but with the birth of each succeeding child, and if the union looks otherwise stable, expectations are that it will eventually be legalized when the economic position of the male is more clearly defined (Davenport, 1961). One reason for this is that the females are under constant pressure from the church or other middle- and upper-class institutions (e.g., the Child Welfare Association) to marry. Mothers continuously remind daughters that a nonlegal union is inherently unstable and that men cannot be compelled to support them or their children, but that once legal marriage has taken place, the man is head of the household and is obligated to support the family. The wife is his dependent and legally entitled to a share of whatever he owns. Perhaps the stress placed by women on the economic functions of the husband can be seen as contributing to the situation wherein men mate and have children, but remain in their family of orientation, though often peripheral to it. Many men live most of the time with the mother of their children or one of the mothers of their children, but still identify with their family of orientation as long as their ability to totally provide for their own family is held in doubt. Indeed, Rodman (1971) suggests that it is this culture-wide definition of what is involved in legal marriage which contributes to the high frequencies of nonlegal unions, since men see women as expecting less prior to legal marriage. In other words, women in consensual unions are less likely to make demands on men, since they see men as not obligated to support them, and, as a result, are more likely to be happy with whatever is given them. Illegitimacy, therefore, becomes acceptable for the lower class, whereas for the middle and upper classes there are no culturally approved explanations for failing to marry prior to the birth of the first child. Furthermore, middle- and upper-class females, protected by their parents in every way conceivable, may desire to establish their independence in a manner similar to their lower class sisters, but must remain in their family of orientation until marriage. Marriage, for the middle-class woman is the only culturally approved reason for establishing independence and formally severing connections with the family or orientation. These females remain "daughters" until marriage or until, after the death of one parent, the remaining parent becomes the dependent member of the adult daughter's household (Moses, 1975).

Socialization data throws further light on the significance of the economic marginality of men. Male adult status involves an ability to provide for a family and economic marginality, in effect, deprives males of becoming adults. Furthermore, this inability to provide for a family, at even some acceptable minimal level, prevents men from establishing permanent unions without the benefit of legal mariage, since, as Davenport suggests, there is the expectation that stable consensual unions will evolve into marriage (Davenport, 1961).

Women also evaluate men in terms of their ability to provide for a family and are less likely to enter into permanent unions with men who are unable to perform economic functions, status defining functions, or both. Finally, women are enmeshed in a network of relationships with other women which are not only supportive but culturally approved. Women spend time with other women, and together they are involved in activities, many of which begin in early childhood and persist through adolescence and into adult life. (child-minding or child-keeping is but one) Since women tend to obtain more schooling than do men, they have increased chances of obtaining employment. In the case of extreme marginality, women are more likely to be able to find some employment, especially in the service sector of the economy, and can somehow manage. They look to other women for assistance when men are unwilling or unable to support them, perhaps because of their even more marginal position in the economy. If they enter into liaisons with men who are unable to marry and children result, these children define their mothers' adult status. The economic marginality data and the socialization data suggest a rationale for men remaining in the family of orientation, mating, and not settng up permanent households. These data also suggest reasons for the sense of solidarity among females regardless of social class, and the far greater limitations that social class position places upon the upper- and middle-class female.

CONCLUSIONS

In examining West Indian culture as ethnographer and as an insider, I chose to look at one institution about which considerable controversy exists, and which is of central significance for understanding West Indian culture and society. Existing social science research, essentially structural, has focused on the interaction between the family and the larger society. I argue that this is only a partial approach if the concern is the true nature of the West Indian family. Lacking in these presentations is any real understanding of the role of the West Indian woman in her society and the significance of group solidarity and sharing among women.

I present an alternative model by which to evaluate West Indian matrifocality. Essentially interactional, it focuses on the family itself as a system of interacting members. It proceeds by examining the development of gender identity, gender personality, and social role learning among men and women. It recognizes the significance of socioeconomic factors in defining what is acceptable, and what adaptive strategies are appropriate. As such it does justice to the flexibility of the institution of the family, and to the ability of women to evaluate the varying life options open to them. It also throws light on the much-debated question of the central position of the West Indian woman in her society: the apparent paradox of the woman as economically dependent yet capable of supporting herself and her family for long periods of time. This alternative model does more to capture the total complexity of the situation and contributes to explaining why the resourceful woman is the cultural ideal. It further highlights the importance of examining the range of alternatives available to both men and women of all social classes without losing the significance of the reality of the current economic situation in the region.

In summary, there is evidence that males and females learn gender identification differently. They experience similar interpersonal environments, but these have different effects upon their development. Differences in masculinity, the denial of an attachment of relationship, "the repression and devaluation of femininity on both psychological and cultural levels" (Chodorow, 1974: 51), the absence of a satisfactory affective relationship with father, femininity as the generalized personal identification, and the gradual learning to be feminine, are established in the early stages of development and are the foundations upon which role training and purposive socialization are constructed.

The structural approach has done much to bring to our attention the reality of the West Indian experience. Countless numbers of men *and* women are in a marginal position in relation to the political economy and are unable to adequately provide for each other and for their offspring. The lower their position in the socioeconomic hierarchy the more extreme the manifestations: unemployment is highest among the lowest strata, and within these strata, highest among males. Females are unemployed or underemployed, but there are more avenues open to them in the informal sector, and they are thus better able to support themselves and their offspring. Among the middle classes it takes two salaries to adequately support a family and to ensure that succeeding generations are at least not downwardly mobile.

The interactional approach, with its emphasis on role behavior and gender identity formation, brings into focus the reasons for the centrality of women in West Indian society. Women are socialized to be resourceful. Each succeeding generation learns from the preceding what it takes to survive in an environment often unfavorable to women. Women turn to other women for advice and counsel, perhaps initially for help with child-bearing and child-rearing, later through identification in infancy, and finally through peer group exposure which begins in childhood and persists throughout adolescence and into adulthood. Young women are constantly exposed to the resourceful woman who may or may not be biological kin. Gift exchanges, sharing of work, child-minding, and child-keeping, also serve to further strengthen these ties. In the evening of life, parents, and especially mothers, look to daughters to provide for them physically and financially when they are no longer able to provide for themselves. As one aged informant poignantly put it:

"I proud of me son... but me daughter... that is me life... without her I would die for hungry... no one to care for me in me old age... "

But if women learn from women, men learn from other men. Although the development of male gender personality and identity is more disjunctive than it is for females, development proceeds nonetheless. During adolescence, free from the controls of the family, the focus of male activity becomes the club and the bar. Here young men come to grips with the reality of their situation, the fact that without economic independence they cannot establish their own household and assume an active role in community affairs. It is here, for example, that men become aware of their plight; exposed to the successful returnee, they learn that leaving one's family of orientation, one's village and country, may indeed be the only way of breaking out of the cycle of poverty (Manning, 1973).

Finally, I suggest that the strong position of the female in West Indian society should be seen not as a form of deviance resulting from economic marginality, but as both an adaptive strategy and a value in itself, resulting from a dynamic interplay of forces which have their origins in gender identity and personality, and of which economics, important though it may be, is but one of many. If we accept this position, we can then hypothesize that with changes in the economic position of large segments of the West Indian society, marriage may indeed precede mating and childbirth and illegitimacy may decline, but the society will continue to be matrifocal, since women and women's roles may remain "structurally central" (Tanner, 1974), and relationships among women continue to be highly prized.

NOTES

1. Structural as opposed to interactional, i.e., the jural rules governing the interaction, the environmental constraints upon action.
2. Clarke (1957)
   Davenport (1961)
   Foner (1973)
   Rodman (1971)
   M. G. Smith (1962) (1965)
   R. T. Smith (1956) (1963)
   Solein (1960)
   Moses (1975)
3. I am grateful to Roy D'Andrade for helping to clarify my thinking on this section.
4. This section owes much to the stimulation received from reading Chodorow (1974) and Tanner (1974), and to discussions with my colleagues Luker, Hecht and Blumberg.
5. Personal communication.

---

*As a West Indian woman, born into a middle class matrifocal family I experienced female solidarity firsthand. Furthermore, I was a social caseworker with a female adult caseload for four years (1959-63) and carried out field research in Dominica, West Indies (1968-69). Sylvia Wynter, Yolande Moses, Joyce Wade, Inez Stephens, Verna Steward and Sheila Washington contributed much to sharpening my recognition of the position of the middle-class female. To them I owe much.

BIBLIOGRAPHY

Blumberg, R. L. with M. P. Garcia "The Political Economy of the Mother/ Child Family: A Cross-Societal View" *in* L. Lemtero-Otero, ed., *Beyond the Nuclear Family Model: Contemporary Family Sociology in a Cross-Cultural Perspective*. London: Sage Publishing. 1976.

Braithwaite, L. "Social Stratification in Trinidad: A Preliminary Analysis" *in* Social and Economic Studies, Volume 2, Nos. 2 & 3 October, 1953.

Chodorow, N. "Family Structure and Feminine Personality" *in Woman, Culture and Society*, M. Rosaldo and L. Lamphere, eds., Palo Alto: Stanford University Press, 1974.

Clarke, E. *My Mother Who Fathered Me: A Study of the Family in Three Selected Communities in Jamaica*. London: Allen & Unwin, 1957.

Cohen, Y. *A Study in Interpersonal Relations in a Jamaican Community*, Ph. D. Thesis. Xerox facsimile, Ann Arbor: University Microfilms, 1953.

Cumper, G. *The Economy of the West Indies* Institute of Social and Economic Studies, University College of the West Indies. United Printers, 1960.

Davenport, W. J. "The Family System of Jamaica" in *Social and Economic Studies* 10, 1961.

Foner, N. *Status and Power in Rural Jamaica: A Study of Educational and Political Change*. New York: Teachers' College Press, 1973.

Frazier, E. F. *The Negro Family in the United States*. Chicago: University of Chicago Press, 1939.

Goode, W. "Illegitimacy, Anomie, and Cultural Penetration" *in* W. J. Goode, ed., *Readings on the Family and Society*. Englewood Cliffs: Prentice-Hall, 1964.

Harper, E. B. "Fear and the Status of Women" in *Southwestern Journal of Anthropology*, Volume 25: 1969 pp. 81-95.

Herskovits, M. J. *The Myth of the Negro Past*. New York: Harper, 1941.

Justus, J. B. Unpublished Ph.D Dissertation. University of California at Los Angeles, 1971.

Kerr, M. *Personality and Conflict in Jamaica*. Liverpool: University Press, 1953.

Klein, M. and J. Riviere *Love, Hate and Reparation*. New York, 1964.

Manning, F. E. *Black Clubs in Bermuda: Ethnography of a Play World*. Ithaca: Cornell University Press, 1973.

Minturn, L. and J. T. Hitchcock "The Rajputs of Khalapur, India" in B. Whiting, ed., *Six Cultures: Studies in Child-Rearing*. New York.

Moses, Y. "What price education: The working women of Montserrat" in *Council on Anthropology and Education Quarterly*, Volume 6 (1975), pp. 13-16.

Munroe, T. *The Politics of Constitutional Decolonization*. Surrey, England: Unwin Brothers, 1972.

Rodman, H. *Lower Class Families: The Culture of Poverty in Negro Trinidad.* New York: Oxford University Press, 1971.

Rosaldo, M. Z. "Woman, Culture, and Society: A Theoretical Overview" in *Woman, Culture, and Society*, M. Rosaldo and L. Lamphere, eds., Palo Alto: Stanford University Press, 1974.

Smith, M. G. *The Plural Society in the British West Indies.* Berkeley: University of California Press, 1965.

Smith, R. T. *The Negro Family in British Guiana.* London: Routledge & Kegan Paul, 1956.

Solien, N. "Household and Family in the Caribbean: Some Definitions and Concepts" in *Social and Economic Studies* 9. March, 1960.

Tanner, N. "Matrifocality in Indonesia and Africa and Among Black Americans" in *Woman, Culture and Society*, M. Rosaldo and L. Lamphere, eds., Palo Alto: Stanford University Press, 1974.

Wedenoja, W. Unpublished manuscript, 1976.

3

Black Women and Survival: A Maroon Case

Kenneth Bilby and Filomina Chioma Steady

To a certain extent it can now be accepted that subsistent and precarious economic conditions are correlated with matrifocal forms of social organization.[1] In this paper we propose that precarious conditions related to military exigencies can have similar implications. In particular, we suggest that the persistence of matrifocal institutions and the positive valuation of women may represent strategies of adaptation in societies under constant threat of economic or military extinction. The role of women in the survival of a particular group—the Maroons of Jamaica—is examined.

In the New World, resistance to slavery was a widespread condition which involved both men and women[2] and took several forms, the most spectacular of which was marronage. Maroonage, or flight from slavery, was quite widespread and became a major problem for all the great European slavocracies. Throughout the Americas, from Brazil to Haiti, from Cuba to the United States, slaves rebelled against the plantation system to which they were bound by fleeing and setting up alternative and independent ways of life.[3]

These runaway slaves became known as maroons, and in many cases they were able to band together and set up separate communities apart from the plantations. Wherever geographical conditions permitted some isolation—such as in the vast stretches of unsettled forests in Brazil and the Guianas or the inland mountain wildernesses of the larger Caribbean islands—they were able to lead a life of relative seclusion. Many long term, viable maroon enclaves were

451

created between the 16th and 18th centuries but only a few of the more inaccessible and resilent communities were able to survive the repeated assaults of the colonial powers against whom they had rebelled.

Only a few of the maroon communities have survived to the present. These can be found in Suriname, French Guiana and Jamaica. Many maroons became dispersed over time. Some of the Jamaican Maroons were sent off to Freetown, Sierra Leone along with repatriated slaves in the late 18th century, through the efforts of the British government. These Maroons became part of the blended group of ex-slaves whose descendants are today collectively known as Creoles.[4] In both the Guianas and Jamaica the major maroon groups signed treaties of peace during the 18th century with the colonial governments. These treaties granted them freedom, recognized their sovereignty as semi-autonomous polities, and in effect, guaranteed their continuing existence as communities apart—though not totally divorced—from the larger society.

This paper briefly treats one aspect of life—the valuation of women and their contribution to Maroon survival. Although similar features appear to be evident among the Maroon descendants of Freetown, Sierra Leone and may be applicable to other maroon groups, our case illustration will be restricted to Moore Town, a Maroon community in the island of Jamaica. Moore Town, located in the Blue Mountains on the eastern side of the island, is the primary settlement of the group known as the Windward Maroons, and is the largest Maroon community in Jamaica. The Moore Town Maroons are descendants of African and Creole[5] slaves who escaped the Jamaican plantations during the 17th and 18th centuries and fled to the mountainous interior. In actual fact, Moore Town developed as an outgrowth of an earlier community named Nanny Town. When Nanny Town was captured by British forces in the 1730s, a large number of Maroon survivors retreated to a new location and founded New Nanny Town, which was later renamed Moore Town.[6]

One of the dominant cultural themes in a maroon society such as that at Moore Town is bound to be survival. The Jamaican Maroons were surrounded by a hostile and powerful slavocracy and were constantly under threat of attack from outside. It therefore became necessary for them to evolve some sort of military organization. It might even be said that in real terms the maroon societies themselves came into being as a result of successful military alliances between fragmentary bands of runaways. When viewing a society with such a strong military tradition, one may be tempted to assume that the key protagonists in the struggle for survival were males, and that the society itself was fundamentally male-oriented. Correspondingly, one might also assume that, in contrast, the society placed a low valuation on women, who were likely to be perceived as mere accessories in the battle for survival. Adoption of this reasoning is bound to produce an image of a harsh, patriarchal, militaristic society in which women would be relegated to the lowest echelon and accorded little respect.

One colonial historian from Jamaica, writing in 1796, was of this persuasion:

> ... the Maroons, like all other savage nations, regarded their wives as so many beasts of burthen; and felt no more concern at the loss of one of them, than a white planter would have felt at the loss of a bullock... this spirit of brutality which the Maroons always displayed towards their wives, extended in some degree to their children. The paternal authority was at all times most harshly exerted; but more especially towards the females... Nothing can more strikingly demonstrate the forlorn and abject condition of the young women among the Maroons, than the circumstances which every gentleman, who has visited them on festive occasions, or for the gratification of curiosity, knows to be true; the offering their own daughters, by the first men among them, to their visitors; and bringing the poor girls forward, with or without their consent, for the purpose of prostitution.[7]

This passage, written several decades after the "pacification" of the Jamaican Maroons, betrays an obvious colonial bias which colors the interpretation and renders its validity questionable. The very use of concepts such as "savage nation" reveals the writer's ethnocentrism, which borders on racism. The author of the above passage, an eighteenth century white planter, was a well known detractor of the Maroons.

On the other hand, if one examines the available information with a measure of detachment, a considerably different and more complex picture of Maroon women will emerge. Information on the pre-treaty Maroon groups is rather scarce, but one may extrapolate on certain basic points from the little that is known.

Firstly, it is known that a predominant number of the fugitive slaves who became Maroons, particularly from the late seventeenth century onward, came from the region of Africa known then as the Gold Coast. The Akan-speaking peoples, particularly the Ashanti and the Fanti, were most strongly represented. Significantly, the societies of the Akan are matrilineal. They are composed of a number of matrilineal clans which are in turn divided up into matrilineages. The members of a clan are believed to be related through descent from a mythical common ancestress. While the presence of matrilineal descent does not indicate direct political control by women, it does often correspond to a higher status for women than in patrilineal societies and a positive valuation of women, through whom important social relationships are traced. Among the Akan, although the affairs of the lineage are formally dominated by men, women do in fact sometimes wield considerable influence, and attain a high degree of prestige.

We recognize that other factors influencing Maroon social organization could have produced an independent devlopment which would reflect some of the aspects of matrifocality peculiar to the Caribbean experience.[8] However, it is still reasonable to surmise that this matrilineal aspect of Akan society may have left its mark on the early Maroons. One would not expect any actual kinship system in itself to have been transplanted intact from Africa to Jamaica, especially since the Maroons included not only Akan individuals, but also a smaller number of persons from several unrelated ethnic groups, as well as a substantial number of Creoles. But it is quite possible that certain general elements of Akan kinship, perhaps certain corollary values, contributed to Maroon culture. We are suggesting that the exigencies of survival are likely to reinforce values and institutions more compatible with survival, such as a high valuation of women and matrifocality.

Maroon societies were often faced with the problem of reproducing new members. Among the Windward Maroons, especially during their early history, there was a serious shortage of women. This was partially the result of an imbalance of male and female slaves on the plantations from which the Maroons escaped; it was further aggravated by the fact that a larger number of men than women successfully escaped the estates. The shortage of women in Maroon settlements led to a situation in which women were highly valued. Maroons organized many raids on the plantations, sometimes for the specific purpose of capturing female slaves to be incorporated into their communities. Oral traditions in Moore Town today make reference to a separate "Woman Town" where women, children, and valuables were secluded for protection during times of threat.[9]

Most likely, the Maroon leaders were aware of the threats of schisms occurring within the community over competition between males for the few available women. But from a more basic perspective, the attempts of the early Maroons to increase their female population reflect their emerging consciousness of themselves as a *society*, as opposed to a temporary aggregate of individuals. Over a period of time the overriding issue of survival must have shifted in emphasis from the individual (the initial act of marronage, after all, was in most cases a bid for survival on the individual level) to the nascent *body politic*. Clearly, a key consideration of the early Maroon groups must have been how to reproduce, if not increase, their numbers, not only for reasons of military security, but also to ensure their physical and social continuity. It is obvious enough that this enterprise required a sufficient number of females of child-bearing age. Thus, from a purely practical viewpoint, women were highly valued among the Maroons.

Women contributed also in more direct economic activities as cultivators. The Maroons could not depend solely on hunting wild boar (for which they were famous), nor on plantation foraging, for their subsistence. To supplement these, they practiced a form of swidden horticulture in which women played an important, perhaps central, role.

Maroon women shared in the everyday struggle for survival in more ways than one and their contribution had more fundamental and far reaching implications. Women as a group represented the most stable single element in the somewhat loose, shifting federation which made up Windward Maroon society. In a very real sense, they may be seen as the main source of stability and continuity within the group. Owing to the military nature of the society, women and children came to comprise a stable core tied to the village and the land immediately around it, while the men were formed into a sort of transient integument, a peripheral military force occupied almost full-time with the protection of that core, and with offensive maneuvers against the white settlements on the lowland plains. Men came and went; some never returned. The women, however, remained with the children, though always prepared for emergency evacuation and combative activities if necessary.[10] They were the true denizens of the Maroon settlements.

Maroon society was internally differentiated, being made up of heterogeneous congeries of individuals from diverse ethnic backgrounds banded together to enhance the chances of survival in a hostile environment. As previously noted, the Maroons were composed of individuals from many different African ethnic groups, possessing different cultural and linguistic backgrounds—as well as a number of Creoles. This ethnic diversity was bound to create tensions within the society, and indeed, at times loomed as a major threat to Maroon unity and stability.[11] The divisive potential characteristic of ethnic plurality was substantially reduced with the eventual emergence of a *Creole* majority, that is, a majority of individuals born in Jamaica rather than Africa. It was only with these new generations of Maroon Creoles, those *born* into a condition of marronage, that Maroon society became firmly anchored; for the first time there existed a solid foundation of individuals inalienably tied to their land. For them, Jamaica was the only country, the only land they had ever known. As a result, the internal ethnic divisions of their foreparents faded into the background and "creolization" became the main process in the creation of a new Afro-Jamaican culture shared by all Maroons.[12]

The early socialization of this new creole element was perhaps primarily in the hands of women. It might in fact be said that the cultural process of creolization itself, so essential to the success of Maroon society, transpired largely within the context of child-rearing. The developing creole culture, the result of a blending and adaptation of the diverse cultural past to contemporary conditions, most likely was propagated in large part by women. Early enculturation was the responsibility of women, perhaps more so than in most societies, owing to the ephemeral male presence in the Maroon settlements, where the true "settlers," as previously noted, were women.

It is well to reemphasize here the most salient point at hand: that concerning *stability*. In view of all that has been said above, we may postulate that, in a fundamental sense, the Windward Maroons were organized as a "matrifocal" society. It would seem that the most basic unit of social organization among them—apart from their military organization—must have consisted of some sort of matrifocal family: one or more women, living together with their offspring from one or more men (the Maroons were polygynous, to some extent). We cannot speculate far beyond this. But it would appear that this matrifocal principle operated on a general level among the Maroons in such a way as to support their social survival, offering them a basis for social stability, while freeing the adult males for crucial military activity. Males, individually or in groups, spent much of the time roving the woodlands, hunting, scouting, and fighting. At other times they were out raiding the lowland plantations. All of these activities involved a high level of risk, and many individuals were killed in the process. But for those who survived, there was always the matrifocal village, the only place to which they could retreat for stability and a sense of security.

More fundamentally, in this matrifocal principle may be found the key to continuity in Maroon society. While males for the most part held the positions of political/military power, their presence was relatively transitory; females and their offspring were the enduring segment of Maroon society, through which the developing creole culture, and most importantly, Maroon identity, were passed on from one generation to the next. Hence, although the key protagonists in the military struggles of the Maroons may have been men, the key protagonists of *regeneration*, biological and social, were women.

The present-day Maroons of Moore Town retain an interesting body of oral history. In nearly all the legendary heroics recounted, one monolithic figure stands out with such brilliance as to obscure all the rest. Not surprisingly, this person is a woman. Nanny, or "Grandy Nanny," as she is known to the Maroons, is the culture heroine of Moore Town.[13] Nanny's significance goes beyond that of a mere mortal leader. To the Maroons, she is a mythical original ancestress, from whom all present-day Maroons are descended.

The myth states that two sisters were captured as slaves in Africa and transported overseas to Jamaica in the distant past. Once in Jamaica, one of the sisters, Nanny, rebelled and fled to the mountains, from where she waged a fierce guerilla war against *bakra* (the

British); the other sister, named Sekesu, was unable to withstand the rigors of war and remained a slave on one of the plantations. The children of Nanny grew up to become the Maroons who fought for and finally achieved their freedom from *bakra*, while those of Sekesu grew up as slaves on the plantations, unable to fight, and attaining their freedom at a much later date, only after *bakra* saw fit to grant it.[14]

Today the Moore Town Maroons, in keeping with this myth, see themselves as Nanny's *yoyo*—meaning Nanny's progeny. This is very much in accord with the Akan tradition from which many of the early Maroons came. As previously mentioned, Akan society is matrilineal, being based upon matrilineal clans whose members believe themselves to be related through descent from a mythical common ancestress. It is therefore of particular interest that the Moore Town Maroons, even though not matrilineal, refer to themselves as a single "family" or "clan," and claim that all Maroons are related by blood, whether or not such relationships are traceable, by virtue of being Nanny's *yoyo*.[15] We shall return to this matter at a later point.

In the various Maroon legends recounting Nanny's great deeds of the past, there is one dominant theme: the supernatural. Nanny was a supernatural manipulator par excellence. Her great mystical power was derived from her close contact with and intimate knowledge of the spirit world, the realm of the departed ancestors. In this role, as mediator between the living and the dead, Nanny symbolizes the continuity of Maroon society through time and space.

Today Maroon storytellers overwhelmingly attribute the great historical victories of the Maroons to Grandy Nanny's phenomenal supernatural powers. The tales they recite underscore the importance of Nanny, and by symbolic extension, the female contribution, to the survival of the Maroons. For instance, when *bakra* destroyed the provision grounds of the Maroons, forcing them to the brink of starvation, it was Nanny who received a message from the spirit world urging her not to give up the fight; along with the message, she received a handful of seeds, with instructions to plant them. In less than a day these supernaturally-endowed seeds brought forth a lavish crop of full grown pumpkins, which saved the Maroons in their time of crisis. What myth could better symbolize the vital role of women in ensuring regeneration and continuity to a fledgling society struggling for survival?

Other stories detail Nanny's confrontations with *bakra*, once again emphasizing her supernatural cunning. It is said that Nanny kept a magical cauldron along the approach to the Maroon village. The hugh vessel, whose contents boiled continuously without need of a fire underneath, attracted *bakra* and other unwelcome outsiders to the edge for a curious look. No sooner would the unfortnuate victim glance down than he would be pulled into the seething mess to disappear forever.

Another story, perhaps the most commonly told of all, relates how Nanny, upon meeting a large *bakra* force, stooped down and tauntingly presented her rump toward their guns; as they fired on her, she proceeded to shock them by catching between her buttocks a full round of lead shot, rendering them inactive.

The Maroons today regard Nanny not only as a ritual specialist, but as an actual military leader. They recount the story of how, when *bakra* first sued for peace, she refused to accept the terms. A short while later, the story goes, when *bakra* approached her a second time she accepted. Her topmost captain was strongly opposed to peace with the traditional enemy, and tried in vain to reverse Nanny's decision. When she refused to budge, the captain, in protest, dove into a nearby river and disappeared forever. This story highlights the fact that extreme militarism was potentially counter-productive to survival. At the time of the treaty, the Maroons were in fact becoming hard-pressed by the advances of the British, and a continuing state of war could have spelled eventual defeat. It is significant that the mover for peace (and as a result, long-term stability), at least in legend, was a woman.

Although the foregoing stories about Nanny are examples of legend and should not be seen as actual history, there is no doubt that an important personage named Nanny really existed.[16] It is believed that her ethnic background was Akan and that she was born in Africa. There are references to her in the contemporary British literature as a powerful obeah-woman, or sorceress. It is evident that in her status as a supernatural specialist she exercised strong sanctions, and these undoubtedly shaded into the political sphere. Whether or not she ever actually joined in combat is uncertain, but there is no doubt that she wielded great authority, military and otherwise, as a result of her ritual status. Although the actual military officers among the Windward Maroons appear to have all been males, "it was Nanny who had the greatest, most enduring authority, while headmen came and went."[17]

Nanny's influence among the Maroons was so great that the largest community of the Windward Maroons, Nanny Town, was named after her. As noted before, Nanny Town was destroyed by British forces in the 1730s; Nanny's followers established a new settlement soon afterward at Moore Town. Although Nanny was clearly an exceptional woman, there are indications that she was not the only woman of influence among the Maroons. Two of the minor settlements in the Nanny Town complex were also given women's names—Molly and Diana.[18] And other powerful women are remembered in oral tradition, such as Mama Juba, like Nanny a great "Science-woman"—as Maroons refer to those well-versed in the supernatural arts.

Today, as in the past, women play an important part in Maroon life. A great many changes have come to Moore Town since the time of the treaty. The Maroons have settled into a peaceful, agrarian way of life; there are few hints of the militarism which once pervaded their society. Farming continues to form the basis of subsistence; the technique used is still slash-and-burn. The community has long been integrated with the cash economy of the island through trade in bananas, which are cultivated as a primary cash crop. In recent years, Moore Town has also become integrated with the national political system, although some vestige of autonomy is preserved in the traditional Maroon jural institution called the "committee"—a village council, headed by an elected community leader called the "Colonel." Thus, while Moore Town in many respects has come to resemble other rural Jamaican communities, it has also maintained some distinctiveness as a Maroon community.

The remainder of this paper shall be devoted to an examination of the continuing significance of women in several facets of life in present-day Moore Town. As mentioned earlier, the Maroons of Moore Town do *not* possess a system of matrilineal descent. Their actual kinship organization varies little from that found in rural villages throughout Jamaica. Descent is traced bilaterally to a depth of at most two or three generations; the kinship terminology used in Moore Town is for all intents and purposes the standard English one. However, there is a matrifocal element in social organization and it is possible that there may have been an earlier matrilineal principle in operation in Moore Town.

Perhaps it might be of help to digress here with a passage by Richard Price concerning the Saramaka maroons of Suriname (who *do* possess a matrilineal descent system):

> Matriliny pervades every aspect of Saramaka descent ideology. Women, it is said, are like hearthstones, men like axe handles. Once placed in a house, a set of clay hearthstones may never be moved; they endure. But an axe handle is made to travel, and once worn out from use, it is discarded on the spot; it leaves no traces.[19]

Like their Suriname counterparts, the Moore Town Maroons also possess a descent "ideology" which, though less explicit, displays a matrilineal streak. In response to probing questions, several Moore Town informants stated that one's personality traits are inherited primarily from the mother, whose side is really the strongest. Here, people will sometimes cite Nanny as an example of the strength of the female principle. On the other hand, a dictum commonly recited by males is "me tata get me" (my father begot me). This is interpreted to mean that it is the father's "seed" that generates the individual child; but it is also pointed out that, while the father is largely responsible for bringing the child into the world, it is the mother who "makes families." In other words, although the father is seen as the more important in terms of biological contribution, it is the mother who generates social ties—including the primary social unit, the family.

The myth of the "two sisters" also points to the possible influence of an antecedent matrilineal ideology—perhaps derived, at least in part, from Akan culture. The Moore Town Maroons, as noted, see themselves as Nanny's *yoyo*, her "children." The usage is metaphorical, and there is no attempt to trace actual relationships. But Nanny is sometimes spoken of as the "mother" of her people, and it is through her that all Maroons acquire a sort of broad, fictive kin relationship with all other Maroons. Thus, all of those "in the blood"—that is, born of one or more Maroon parents—are automatically members of the "clan." By virtue of birth, they are *yoyo* themselves. Intcrestingly enough, this metaphor of motherhood is sometimes extended, when propitious, to encompass non-Maroon Jamaicans of African descent. On such occasions Maroons will refer to these people as "children" of Sekesu, Nanny's mythical sister, and will invoke a fictive relationship between them by asserting that Maroons and other Afro-Jamaicans are, after all, "two sister pickney" (two sisters' children)—in other words, first cousins.

An important feature of the present-day social organization of Moore Town is the matrifocal family, in one form or another. Family organization in Moore Town is highly variable, and several common patterns coexist. The ideal is the monogamous conjugal family, sanctioned by church marriage. But the reality is a good deal more complex; only a brief sketch can be offered here.

As is the pattern in the rest of Jamaica, common-law marriage, or cohabitation, is the most common union between men and women, and church marriage tends to take place, if at all, relatively late in life. The conjugal family—a man, a woman, and their children—does in fact often occur; but just as common is a type of matrifocal trend which has particular significance in the context of large-scale out-migration, a persistent feature of Moore Town life since at least the beginning of this century. This migratory drift outward has consisted primarily of younger males in search of temporary employment on the outside. Often such persons find positions as temporary wage laborers on large estates, and their employment may last as briefly as one season or as long as several years. One result has been a continuum of shifting matrifocal family arrangements in Moore Town, ranging from a woman and her children by one or more men on the one hand, to an older woman and her grandchildren on the other. Men make periodic appearances in these households, but women constitute the most stable element. It would appear that the matrifocal principle which operated in earlier days as an adaptive mechanism for survival continues to carry some significance in the present Maroon situation, lending stability and continuity to an otherwise fragmentary social situation. This is a matter which deserves further investigation.

Women in Moore Town tend to enjoy a certain degree of economic independence. Even in the case of conjugal families, the woman may act as the true "head" of the household; the man will contribute a portion of his income to the family, but it is usually the woman who manages the money and administers household affairs. Today banana is a primary cash crop and both men and women participate in this trade. A woman can therefore command a substantial income of her own. In many cases, women hold and cultivate their own plots of land, the yield from these accruing to themselves. In addition, some women further contribute to the support of their families by working one or two days a week as "higglers" in nearby market towns. (The higgler is a type of entrepreneur common to rural Jamaica, who buys produce from others for eventual resale in the market place.) In this way, women often play a vital role in economic survival.

It is not only possible, but common, for women to achieve a high status in Moore Town, particularly in the context of traditional Maroon affairs. Nearly one third of the Maroon council (the "committee") are women. In fact, probably the single most influential bloc within the council is made up of six women elders, whose opinions weigh heavily in the final decisions of this body.

In the traditional ritual arena, women continue to exert considerable influence. One of the strongest binding forces in the history of Moore Town has been the *Kromanti* dance.[20] In the past, the great crises of the Maroons were dealt with in the context of this ritual. Nowadays it is infrequently practiced and is used primarily for the purpose of healing spirit-caused illnesses. The central figure in the *Kromanti* dance is known as the *fete-man*. An expert dancer and medicinal herbalist, the *fete-man* becomes possessed by an ancestral Maroon spirit in the course of the ceremony, and in this state effects a ritual cure. The continuity of Maroon society across the generations has been reinforced by this tradition, which serves to maintain close contact between present day Maroons and their ancestors.

Some of the greatest ritual practitioners among the Maroons have been *fete-women*. In fact, the greatest of all, Grandy Nanny, was a woman. A few elderly and respected *fete-women* continue to be capable of dancing *Kromanti* on occasions of crisis, and the skills of these *fete-women* are no less valued than those of their male counterparts. At any rate, whether the central figure of any particular *Kromanti* dance is male or female, the female presence is integral. Women form the nucleus of the back-up chorus in the songs of invocation used to call the ancestral spirits. The singers are sometimes organized under a leading woman called the *governess*.

It is especially noteworthy that both *fete-men* and *fete-women* can be possessed by either male or female ancestral spirits. It is not uncommon for a male dancer to become possessed by the spirit of a female ancestor. When this occurs, the dancer's head is tied with a piece of cloth in female fashion, as opposed to the usual male style. Female spirits are seen as being every bit as powerful as male spirits. The ultimate criterion of a spirit's efficacy rests in the amount of ritual power acquired by that individual when he or she was a living person. Since Moore Town has produced many great *fete-women* in the past, there is no paucity of powerful female spirits who may be invoked for aid in the context of *Kromanti* dance. Thus traditional ceremonial life in Moore Town is as much the province of females as of males. This should be no surprise, given the primacy of females throughout Maroon history in the renewal and continuity of the society.

Today, the importance of traditional Maroon culture in Moore Town is rapidly waning. There is a clear split between the generations. For a variety of complex reasons, younger Maroons have lost touch with the traditions of their parents. Having entered an era of full-fledged participation in the larger Jamaican society, Moore Town is experiencing fundamental social changes. The eventual outcome of these changes can only be conjectured, but it is certain that strategies for survival—primarily an economic problem in these times—will take new forms to suit new conditions.

Whatever the outcome, the matrifocal principle will continue to be symbolically embodied in the legendary person of Nanny. Even among the least traditional of Maroon youths today, among those who profess a complete lack of interest in "Maroon things," the memory of Nanny persists, larger than life.[21] In the future, when the ways of the past have been long forgotten, a single thread of the Maroon heritage will almost certainly survive, and this is the saga of Nanny. It is *she* who, in the end, will endure.

Both authors have conducted research among Maroon descendants in different areas. Bilby spent twelve months during 1977-78 engaged in field work in Moore Town. The data concerning present-day Moore Town, including current oral traditions, were collected during this stay which was made possible by a Fellowship from the Organization of American States, No. 58755-PRA. Steady has conducted research among Maroon descendants in Freetown, Sierra Leone as part of her study of Freetown Creole Society. She has done extensive research on women's changing roles in

Africa and cross-culturally, in addition to teaching and writing on the subject. The idea of Nanny as a central figure in Maroon society and the role of women in ensuring Maroon survival evolved during several discussions between the authors and culminated in this paper.

NOTES

1. From the ethnographic record, matrilineal forms of organization tend to be characteristic of horticultural societies where food production is at subsistence levels. Matrifocality has been studied as an adaptive response to poverty—i.e. survival (e.g. Blumberg and Garcia 1976).

Engels views the matriarchate within an evolutionary framework in seeking to explain the relationship between the development of private property and the patriarch family and its replacement of the matriarchal clan. For a recent re-examination of the matriarchate within a neo-Marxist framework and a review of the literature on the matriarchate, see Fluehr-Lobban 1979.

2. See Mathurin 1975.

3. For a comprehensive treatment of Maroon societies throughout the New World see Price 1973.

4. Steady 1973 includes a study of the Creoles of Sierra Leone. For a history of this group see Fyfe 1962.

5. "Creole" here refers to slaves born in Jamaica as opposed to Africa.

6. Information on Maroon history is drawn from the following sources: Edward 1796, Dallas 1803, Kopytoff 1973, Campbell 1977.

7. Edwards 1796,. xxx-xxxii.

8. See Solien 1960.

9. Braithwaite 1977, p. 12, notes that written records also refer to a "Woman's Town" among the Windward Maroons.

10. See Braithwaite 1977, p. 11.

11. For a detailed discussion of ethnic-based tensions among the early Maroons, see Kopytoff 1976.

12. An interesting theoretical examination of this process, with reference to the Caribbean in general, may be found in Mintz and Price 1976. Of particular interest, because of its focus on the Jamaican Maroons, is Kopytoff 1976.

13. For a recent account of Nanny and the oral traditions surrounding her, see Tuelon 1973.

14. A fragment of this myth has been recorded previously in Dalby 1971, pp. 49-50.

15. Leann Martin, in her unpublished Ph.D. dissertation (1973), mentions this perception by Maroons of themselves as a "family" or "clan."

However, she apparently did not encounter the common tradition which attributes "motherhood" of the "clan" to Nanny. (The word *yoyo* belongs to the secret Kromanti language, and refers to Nanny's progeny or "children." It is also used as a synonym for "Maroon.")

16. Braithwaite 1977 proves the actual existence of Nanny.
17. Kopytoff 1978, p. 301.
18. Ibid., p. 300.
19. Price, *Saramaka Social Structure*, 1973, pp. 45-46.
20. For an examination of traditional Maroon ritual, see Bilby 1979.
21. A monument commemorating Nanny was recently built in the center of Moore Town after she was declared a National Heroine by the government of Jamaica.

BIBLIOGRAPHY

Bilby, Kenneth M. "Partisan Spirits: Ritual Interaction and Maroon Identity in Eastern Jamaica." Unpublished M.A. Thesis, Wesleyan University, 1979.

Blumberg, R. L. and M. P. Garcia. "The Political Economy of the Mother/Child Family: A cross-societal view" in L. Lemtero-Otero, ed., *Beyond the Nuclear Family Model: Contemporary Family Sociology in a cross-cultural Perspective*. London, Sage Publishing, 1976.

Braithwaite, Edward K. *Wars of Respect: Nanny and Sam Sharpe*. Kingston, Agency for Public Information, 1977.

Campbell, Mavis. "Marronage in Jamaica: Its Origin in the Seventeenth Century" in Vera Rubin and Arthur Tuden, eds., *Comparative Perspectives on Slavery in New World Planatation Societies*. New York, New York Academy of Sciences, 1977.

Dalby, David. "Ashanti Survivals in the Language and Traditions of the Windward Maroons of Jamaica." *African Language Studies* XII, 1971, pp. 31-51.

Dallas, Robert Charles. *History of the Maroons, vols. I and II*, London, T. N. Longman and O. Rees, 1803.

Edwards, Bryan. *Observations on the disposition, character, manners, and habits of life of the Maroon Negroes of the Island of Jamaica*. London, John Stockdale 1796.

Engels, Frederick. *The Origin of the Family, Private Property and the State*. New York, Pathfinder Press, 1972.

Fluehr-Lobban, Carolyn. "A Marxist Reappraisal of the Matriarchate." *Current Anthropology* XX, 1979, pp. 341-348.

Fyfe, Christopher. *A History of Sierra Leone*. London, Oxford, 1962.

Kopytoff, Barbara, "The Incomplete Polities: An Ethnohistorical Account of the Jamaica Maroons." Unpublished Ph.D. Dissertation, University of Pennsylvania, 1973.

_____ . "The Development of Jamaican Maroon Ethnicity." *Caribbean Quarterley* XXII, 1976, pp. 33-50.

_____ . "The Early Political Development of Jamaican Maroon Societies." *William and Mary Quarterly* XXXV, 1978, pp. 287-307.

Martin, Leann. "Maroon Identity: Processes of Persistence in Moore Town." Unpublished Ph.D. Dissertation, University of California, Riverside,   1973.

Mathurin, Lucille. *The Rebel Woman in the British West Indies during Slavery.* Kingston, African-Caribbean Publications, 1975.

Mintz, Sidney W. and Richard Price. *An Anthropological Approach to the Afro-American Past: A Caribbean Perspective.* Philadelphia, Institute for the Study of Human Issues, 1976.

Price, Richard, ed. *Maroon Societies: Rebel Slave Communities in the Americas.* New York, Anchor/Doubleday, 1973.

_____ . *Saramaka Social Structure: Analysis of a "Bush Negro" Society.* Rio Piedras, Puerto Rico, University of Puerto Rico, 1973.

Solien, Nancie L. "Household and Family in the Caribbean." *Social and Economic Studies* IX, 1960, 101-106.

Steady, Filomina. "The Structure and Function of Women's Voluntary Associations in an African City: A Study of the Associative process among women in Freetown." Unpublished D. Phil. Dissertation, Oxford University, 1973.

Tuelon, Allen "Nanny—Maroon Chieftainess." *Caribbean Quarterly* XIX, 1973, pp. 20-27.

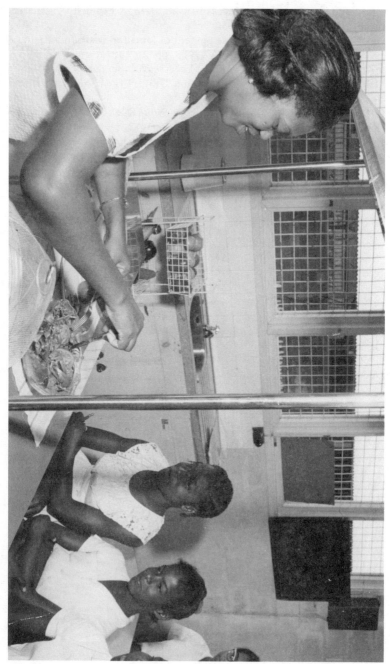

A cooking demonstration by the Ministry of Education, Trinidad. Photo: United Nations, No. 100,093. (1967)

4

Social Inequality and Sexual Status in Barbados

Constance Sutton and Susan Makiesky-Barrow

We are only beginning to develop an adequate theoretical paradigm for understanding sexual stratification. But recent studies directed at the issue of sexual equality and inequality have begun to shift the focus of analysis away from the search for universals in the nature of sex roles and tasks and toward an examination of how the structuring of sex-role differences is related to other structures of inequality. In the light of the growing documentation of the relation between an increase in inequalities among social groups and an increase in sexual inequality, the Afro-Creole societies of the Caribbean raise an intriguing set of issues and paradoxes. These societies have experienced two of the most extreme forms of exploitation and inequality known in human societies—slavery and colonialism; yet the Afro-Caribbean is notable for the absence of marked sexual inequalities. In this paper we shall relate our own observations of the positions, roles, and interactions of women and men in one Afro-Caribbean community to some more general considerations about the relationship between sexual stratification and societal inequality.

In considering the structure of sex roles in an Afro-Caribbean society, we are dealing with a colonial capitalist system that has had very difficult consequences for sexual stratification than was the case in Europe, where capitalism first developed, or in other colonial societies of the Third World, where capitalism was imposed on very different cultural and socioeconomic systems. In the Caribbean, the baseline for capitalist development was the slave plantation. Not only was the slave plantation one of the starkest systems of exploitation for profit ever devised, but it was a prototype of industrial economic regimentation, separating productive activity from other aspects of social life, even before such economic practices were fully established in Europe. However, in its impact on the structuring of sex roles, the slave plantation differed from other forms of capitalist economic organization (Fogel and Engerman 1974). It was perhaps the only such system that did not for the mass of the population strongly favor male economic participation at the expense of women, who elsewhere were relegated to a domestic sphere of activity and became increasingly dependent on men to support them economically and to "represent" them within the larger system. On the slave plantation, both sexes were equally involved in the "public" world of work, and both were equally exploited. Moreover, slavery and colonialism combined to divide the slave population so sharply from the dominant social groups that they were prevented from an easy identification with or adoption of the dominant group's structure and ideology of male dominance and control. In fact, their exclusion from the dominant cultural tradition fostered, in the "shadow of the plantation," the development of a distinct though not easily visible set of counterstructures and counterconcepts.

The society we examine is Barbados, a small sugar-producing island in the English-speaking West Indies. We focus on one rural community as we observed it during two different periods of fieldwork, in the late 1950s and the early 1970s. In the account that follows, we discuss both the historical background and the contemporary community in terms of the following issues: (1) participation of the sexes in familial and nondomestic realms of activity; (2) the relative autonomy of women and men and the bases by which they acquire status and presitge; (3) the significance attached to motherhood and its influence on women's economic dependence and independence; (4) the cultural conceptions of sex roles and identities; (5) the effects of recent changes on the balance of power between the sexes.

HISTORICAL BACKGROUND

On the 250,000 people living in Barbados today, 95 percent are the descendants of Africans brought as slaves to work on the islands sugar plantations during the first 200 years of its history as a British colony. Emancipation in 1838 interfered with neither sugar production nor colonial rule; not until 1966 did political independence and a measure of economic diversification produce significant departures from the patterns established by 350 years of sugar and colonialism. These recent changes have expanded the opportunities available to the large mass of black Barbadians and have permitted increased socioeconomic mobility. But despite a softening of the sharp divisions between classes and races, and despite the decline of the sugar estate as the key institution of the society, contemporary life on the island continues to reflect its history as a sugar-producing colonial plantation society, one in which the power of the white planter-merchant class was exercised by men, the primary status of the women of this class being that of wife and mother.

This tradition of male dominance among the Barbadian planter-merchant class was an extension of the tradition of patriarchy brought from Britain. However, a very different set of sex-role definitions was imposed on the slave population. The Slave woman was not a ward of her father, husband, or brother and did not derive her status from her position as wife and mother; nor were her activities centered primarily on domestic and family life. Instead, her status, like that of the slave man, was determined in the first instance by her position within the plantation community. Differences in the rights and privileges of slaves were based on differences in occupational status within the plantation, and the slave woman's position was not mediated by the men of her group. She was her own economic provider and was not shielded from the harsh realities that existed in the public world of work. Moreover, laboring in the fields alongside the men, slave women were forced to deal with organizational structures of power and authority, and thus they acquired a knowledge of how the system worked and a consciousness of their oppressed and victimized position within it.

Recent work (Genovese 1976; Gutman 1976; Mathurin 1974) has begun to examine the sexual division of labor on the slave plantation and to consider its implications. While the studies are of slave communities elsewhere in the West Indies and the United States, some of their general findings can be applied to Barbados, where the slave plantations were similarly organized. One important finding of this recent research is that neither sex was particularly favored. Although it is premature to make definitive statements about the particulars of male and female activities and hardships, certain facts have begun to emerge: women and men were both distributed between house tasks and field labor; women, like men, operated in positions of authority, such as "drivers," and in such a capacity served as articulators with the dominant group, and, to some extent, as protectors of the slave community; severe punishments, including flogging and death, were equally imposed on women and men, though for a pregnant woman, the death sentence would be postponed until after she had given birth. While male and female tasks may have differed somewhat on the plantation, considerations of age and health were more important than sex in assigning work (Mathurin 1975, p. 5). And the hardships faced by the masses of women who labored in the fields and bore and reared children were certainly no less than those experienced by men.

Slave women, like men, surely used whatever weapons were available, including sex, in the struggle to resist degradation and to make a better life for themselves. Occasionally sexual liaisons between masters and slave women developed into enduring close relationships, but more often a woman's sexuality was a source of particular exploitation and vulnerability, as the accounts of sexual assaults on slave women by white men attest (Davis 1971). Others have seen the sexual relations between masters and slaves as a source of privilege for slave women. According to Wilson, "from early on, black women were treated differently from black men and were more readily and firmly attached to the alien society of the whites" (1973, p. 193). But recent research gives little support to theories of differential treatment of women and men or of women's greater attachment to or collaboration with the power structure. Instead, there is increasing documentation that women were as active as men in resistng oppression, and they played an important role in acts of rebellion (Davis 1971; Mathurin 1975).

Slavery then was a leveler of sex differences, promoting, in Angela Davis's words, a "deformed equality." Aspects of the sexual equality imposod on slaves, however, were not incongruent with patterns of sexual autonomy that had been part of their African cultural roots. Slaves brought with them traditions and cultural orientations, derived from their West African background, which defined sex roles in complementary and relatively equal terms and gave women considerable public respect and independence. Nor were the women who worked on the slave plantations unaccustomed to agricultural work or to providing for themselves and their children. For in contrast to the European pattern of conjugal pooling of economic resources with the husband as the organizer and manager of productive activites, the sexual division of labor in many West African societies involved a separation of the economic resources of husbands and wives and a greater sharing with consanguineal kin. Women and men carried on their own economic activites, and a woman was frequently the chief provider for herself and her children, though the husband contributed. Analyses emphasizing the inability of the black man to fill his role as the chief source of economic support for his family have missed the significant fact that the West African man was not viewed as the primary economic provider. Nor was the exercise of authority of women in the slave community without precedent; for in West Africa, where public life was not identified as a male domain, women occupied formal political and ritual positions in their societies.

This is to say that the slaves did not create *de novo* a set of responses to their loss of freedom. And as recent historical research on slave social life indicates (Genovese 1976; Gutman 1976), West African patterns of family, kinship, and friendship ties, once believed to have been destroyed by slavery, in fact provided cultural models that shaped the development of those aspects of slave culture outside the control of the plantation. We will mention only a few significant examples: the forging of strong extended family ties; the centrality of the mother-child and sibling bonds; the importance ascribed to the role of mother in contrast to the role of wife; a positive view of sexuality and its identification with creativity and potency rather than with temptation and sinfulness; exogamous tendencies in the selection of conjugal partners; the application of kin terms to friends and public figures; respect for the powers of the elderly.

It was in the slave quarters that family and community life develpoed. Although the slave quarters did not fully escape the control of the plantation system, this more private "domestic" domain[1] was the one realm of plantation life that afforded slaves a measure of autonomy. Here slaves worked long hours on their own plots of land and developed a social life separate from the regimentation of the plantation. Here they garnered resources for resisting planter power and ideology and struggled to protect and expand their sphere of autonomous activities. While much of the literature on sex roles views the domestic sphere as an area of confinement that is associated with women and their dependent status, for the slave population, the domestic arena was the one area of life that for both sexes was associated with human freedom and autonomy. Under the extreme conditions of slavery, it acquired a very special meaning.

The slave plantation, then, provides a baseline for examining sex roles in contemporary Barbadian society. It established the sharp, racially based distinction between slave and free, separated the central public institutions of economy and polity from the arena of slave community and family life, and determined the relative position of the sexes within the two domains.

Emancipation, which occurred in 1838, produced no dramatic changes in Barbados' socioeconomic structure. Most of the freed population was compelled to remain on the sugar estates, as land was too scarce to permit the growth of a significant class of peasant proprietors. Working for wages, the ex-slaves became, instead, one of the earliest agricultural proletariats known. The occupational stratification established during slavery continued with only some expansion of nonplantation employment. Skilled trades provided opportunities primarily to men, while jobs as midwives and seamstresses, though few in number, offered some parallel positions for women. Both sexes moved into such nonplantation jobs as hawking, shopkeeping, and schoolteaching. Though undoubtedly women, like men, sought to move away from plantation employment whenever circumstances allowed, there is little evidence that they withdrew in any substantial numbers from the wage economy, as occurred elsewhere in the West Indies after emancipation.

CONTEMPORARY BARBADOS

The island, then, has had a long history of female participation in the labor force, and in contemporary cross-cultural comparsions it ranks, along with other Afro-Caribbean societies, as one of the countries with the highest rates of female employment. In 1966 in Barbados, 49 percent of the adult female population was employed. And in contrast to industrial societies, this figure rises to 63 percent for women in the childbearing years of nineteen to thirty-nine

(Census Research Program 1973, pp. 194-97). (Eighty-six percent of adult males in Barbados are in the labor force.) Of the 93,200 persons in the total island labor force, 43 percent are women (Barbados Statistical Service 1966). As these figures indicate, female employment is unusually high; moreover, the systematic channeling of women into low-income "female" occupations which occurs in industrial labor markets is not so marked in Barbados, where there is a rather similar distribution of women and men in occupational categories (see Table 13. 1).

The educational system also shows an absence of marked sex differentials—roughly equal proportions of males and females achieve different levels of education. The 1970 census indicates that approximately 15 percent of each sex has acquired secondary-school certificates that permit entry into white-collar occupations (Barbados Statistical Service 1974). This contrasts sharply with the sex differentials in educational achievements found in other developing countries. Barbados' literacy rate has been estimated at 98

TABLE 13.1
OCCUPATIONAL DISTRIBUTION OF
BARBADIAN WOMEN AND MEN IN 1970 (IN PERCENT)

Major Occupational Group	Male	Female	Total
Professional and technical workers	9.0	9.0	9.0
Administrative, executive, and managerial workers	2.0	.3	1.3
Clerical and related workers	6.0	13.0	9.0
Workers in transport and communication	2.0	.3	1.3
Sales worker (including shop proprietors and assistants, hawkers)	6.0	13.0	9.0
Service workers (including domestic, hotel, protective services)	11.0	32.0	19.0
Farm managers, supervisors, and farmers	1.2	.2	.7
Other agricultural workers	14.0	14.0	14.0
Production and related workers (including artisans, seamstresses, manufacturing workers)	38.0	12.0	28.0
Laborers not elsewhere classified	6.0	2.0	4.4
Other	4.8	4.2	4.3
Total			
100.0100.0	100.0		

Source: Based on Barbados Statistical Service (1974), p. 8-11, Tables 4 and 5.

percent, one of the highest in the world, and education has been highly valued as the main route to socioeconomic mobility. Moreover, it is valued as much for women as it is for men.

However, despite these similarities, there are some important structural inequalities in the occupational position and earnings of the sexes. We do not have figures that compare male and female incomes throughout Barbados, but smaller samples indicate a gap between their earnings. Those who control the Barbadian economy have operated with the western assumption that women have fewer economic responsibilites as providers. This bias, which has not been challenged by the (male) trade-union leaders, has been noted in a study of workers in manufacturing industries introduced into Barbados as part of a ten-year-old program of industrial development (Stoffle 1972). The management of these industries, which are primarily foreign-owned, have justified a low wage structure in terms of the preponderance of female employees. Although hiring policies favor women workers, the wage structure effectively discriminates against them. These differences may not be sufficient to erode women's interest in economic independence or to promote the kind of economic dependency that has characterized women in the West, but it fosters economic inequalities between the sexes.

Women's access to resources is further limited by the direction of recent economic developments. Although low-status argicultural jobs have been equally available to women and men, women for the most part have been excluded from the middle-level categories of skilled laborers, including artisans of various sorts. With economic diversification, these jobs have grown increasingly important as a way out of plantation labor, thus giving women fewer opportunities than men to improve their socioeconomic status. Differentials in the economic position and income of the sexes exist at various class levels, but they are most pronounced at the highest levels of the occupational pyramid, particularly at the level of management, an arena still dominated by whites.

Black Barbadian women thus face greater economic discrimination than the men of their group; but it is in politics that sexual inequality is most marked. Until recently, the political arena was totally under the control of men of the planter-merchant class. The majority of black Barbadians were excluded from any form of political participation until property qualifications were lowered in the 1940s and universal suffrage was introduced in 1950.[2] While both sexes now participate as voters, the centers of governmental decision making continue to be controlled by men. A very recent increase in the number of women seeking positions of political leadership at the national level suggests that the black Barbadians who have replaced the white political elites may not have fully adopted their assumption that political leadership should be reserved for men. At present, however, it constitutes an area in which women have lagged behind.

This overall national picture indicates a number of areas of sexual inequality. Now let us look at the organization and conceptualization of sex roles at the community level and how this relates to these national patterns and structures.

THE STATUS OF WOMEN AND MEN AT THE COMMUNITY LEVEL

Access to Resources

Endeavor, a pseudonym for the community we studied, was originally a slave settlement. With time it encompassed a growing number of individuals who found the means to purchase small plots of land and a way to earn a livelihood outside the confines of the plantation; and today, less than one-third of Endeavor's adult population continues to work on the sugar estates that surround the community or for the nearby factory where cane is processed. Recent changes have reduced ties to the plantation and caused its influence on community life to recede into the background. People in Endeavor now participate directly in the economic and political institutions of the island, though most occupy a subordinate position in these structures.

While they may refer to Endeavor as a place of "poor black people," Endeavor's residents are not unmindful of differences in wealth and status that exist within the community. Nor are they unaware that over the past two decades expanded educational opportunities, shifts in employment patterns, and an increase in emigration and in remittances from relatives abroad have provided greater possibilities for socioeconomic mobility. This has altered the occupational structure and social hierarchy of the community, though not its basic contours (see Makiesky-Barrow 1976). Status differences are important in structuring social interaction in Endeavor, despite the fact that in certain contexts people regard themselves as a community of social equals.

These differences are based, in part, on the criteria that are used to determine stratification at the national level—occupation, income, and education. Both women and men are ranked in these terms and both occupy varied positions in the community social hierarchy. The position a woman acquires often results from her own achievements rather than from those of her spouse, and women tend to be individually ranked even if they are married. Although both sexes speak critically of status ranking and its negative role in the social life of the community, status mobility is in fact of major concern. Women as well as men are preoccupied with finding a way of "rising a notch above" within the social hierarchy, and both look to the occupational system as the means of doing so.

We begin our examination of the status of the sexes with a look at their participation on the economy, their roles in the occupational structure, and their independent access to economic and social resources valued by the community. During the two periods of our fieldwork, between 40 and 50 percent of the women in the community were gainfully employed outside the household, and this figure rose to 59 percent for women between the ages of twenty and forty.[3] These levels of participation, which are similar to those at the parish and national levels, indicate both the economic importance of women in the work force and the fact that they, like men, work during the prime years of their adult lives. The distribution of the sexes in specific occupational categories during the two time periods is similar to that at the parish level, as shown in Table 13.2. Agricultural labor on the sugar estates remains the largest single occupation for both sexes, though the proportion of the population employed in agriculture has declined from one-third to one-quarter in the past decade. Even more dramatic is the withdrawal of women from this type of labor: in ten years, the percentage of women who are agricultural laborers dropped from 46.5 to 28. This decline has been facilitated by the availability of other forms of employment, including low-paying unskilled jobs in the new industrial parks, and, for younger women entering the labor force with secondary education, white-collar jobs. The magnitude of the withdrawal should not come as a surprise, for agricultural labor retains the stigma of slavery and women plantation workers are even further discriminated against by male-female differentials in wages and task assignments. Thus, while labor has been a source of independent income for a large number of women, it has not served to equalize access to economic resources. But neither have the sex differentials in wages and tasks been sufficient to undermine the sense of common status and common cause that exists between women and men who are agricultural laborers.

TABLE 13.2
OCCUPATIONAL DISTRIBUTION OF WOMEN AND MEN IN PARISH LABOR FORCE, 1960 AND 1970 (IN PERCENT)

Occupational Category	1960			1970		
	Male	Female	Total	Male	Female	Total
Professional and clerical workers	4.0	6.5	5.0	7.5	17.0	11.0
Workers in transport and communication	2.0	.5	1.0	2.0	.5	1.0
Sales workers (including shop proprietors and assistants, hawkers)	3.5	14.0	7.5	2.5	10.0	5.5
Service workers (including domestic, hotel, and protective services)	3.0	22.0	10.5	4.0	25.0	12.0
Agricultural workers	33.0	46.5	38.0	22.0	28.0	24.0
Production and related workers (including artisans, seamstresses, manufacturing workers)	43.0	10.0	30.5	52.0	14.0	38.0
Laborers not elsewhere classified	4.5	.5	2.5	6.0	3.0	5.5
Other workers	7.0	—	5.0	4.0	2.5	3.0
Total	100.0	100.0	100.0	100.0	100.0	100.0

Source: Based on Makiesky-Barrow (1976), pp. 108-9, Table 3.

Other occupations pertinent to community members are somewhat more differentiated by sex: artisans and skilled sugar factory workers are mainly men; domestic servants are nearly all female; and market vendors, called hawkers in Barbados, are predominately female. Neither in terms of income earned nor related social status do the latter two occupations match those of skilled production workers. But at the top of the community occupational hierarchy, sex typing is virtually absent. Both women and men are engaged in shopkeeping, one of the most remunerative occupations in Endeavor, and both women and men are found in the high-status white-collar and professional jobs, mainly as teachers, nurses, clerk-accountants, medical assistants, and other positions in the civil service. In fact, women exceed men in this category. Together with successful shopkeepers, these women and men are sometimes referred to as the community's "poor greats"—that is, the "greats" among the poor; and it is worth noting that in the late 1950s two of the four reputedly wealthiest community members were women shopkeepers, while eight women and five men were schoolteachers. In the recent past, the community's "poor greats" played an important role as cultural brokers between community members and the wider society. Although social change has reduced the significance of this brokerage role, the women and men in the top positions of the community hierarchy are still highly regarded and often turned to for advice and assistance by other members of the community.

Thus not only do both sexes occupy prestigious occupational statuses, but women, as well as men, aspire to and acquire other socially valued resources: land, houses, and education. Owning land is for Barbadians a primary goal in life, partly because of the security and potential income it provides, but also because it remains a primary symbol of independence from planatation control. No customary or legal principles bar women from inheriting or purchasing land, and many women own plots of land of varying size. Of the household heads who own land, 43·percent are women, 57 percent men. More men than women acquire their own plots of land through purchase, while women landowners more often acquire their land through inheritance. Perhaps more to the point, in the late 1950s only one-third of the adults in Endeavor had managed to acquire land. This, however, was not the case with respect to house ownership, also an important goal in establishing adult status in the community and one that in most cases precedes acquiring land. House ownerhsip is furthermore associated with a complex concept of household headship, which is identified with ideas about personal independence and the right to impose one's will. Houseowners assert their freedom from outside control in phrases such as "I don't bow down before any person," and "Nobody can tell me what to do!" Although household heads often claim "I boss here," the aspect of authority associated with the concept of headship is more subtle and indirect. It resides in the assumption that the head of a house has a right to know about and take part in decisions affecting other members of the household, as well as to receive special consideration for his or her needs and desires. Household headship is not strongly linked with sex differences: both in the late 1950s and the early 1970s, 43 percent of the households in Endeavor were owned and headed by women (Sutton 1969; Makiesky-Barrow 1976).

While land and house ownership are associated with the important value of personal autonomy, education is viewed as the prime means of acquiring social prestige. Here sexual equality is most evident, for both sexes are actively encouraged to achieve. While parents often find it a struggle to pay the costs of keeping several children in school, their decision to give one child more schooling than another is based on the academic promise of the child, not its sex. Nor do they hesitate to express an equal pride in the educational attainments of their female and male children. Moreover, parents actively encourage young girls as well as boys to prepare themselves to earn a good living. A job or career for a woman is never spoken of as an alternative to marriage or maternity. Although it is realized that a woman's household and childcare responsibilities might necessitate her withdrawal from work for short periods, the "dual career" conflict experienced by women in industrial societies is not marked. This reflects not only different expectations and assumptions about a woman's economic and social roles but also the presence of a family and kinship system that acts as a support for women of all ages. It is a system in which strong ties between consanguineally related kin serve to distribute the chores and responsibilities of rearing children. Moreover, child fostering, whether for shorter or longer periods, is an approved practice and may in fact serve to strengthen ties of kinship and friendship. To the extent that these supports are available to employed mothers, they constitute a most valuable resource for reducing role conflict.

What then can be said in summary about the position of women in the occupational heirarchy and their available economic resources? First, it is clear that the tradition of women's active involvement in the economy has persisted through time. Second, in

Endeavor women have access to those occupations that carry prestige and rank high in the community's social hierarchy. Moreover, the nature of women's distribution within the occupational categories precludes the development of any systematic link between gender differences and social status. Third, while women's economic activities and patterns of land and house acquisition indicate that they have somewhat less control over resources than men, these differences are not sufficient to give men any decisive control over the distribution of resources to women and children.

In addition, the economic imbalance between the sexes tends to be somewhat reduced by women's greater access to resources beyond those they derive from employment. Most women are likely to receive varying amounts of economic support over the course of their lives from men related to them as spouse, lover, or father of their children. Moreover, women tend to be the main recipients of the economic assistance that adult children, especially sons, are expected to and do give to parents. Women expressed the expectation of such support from children in comments like, "Never mind they humbug you in the early, they crown you in the late." And, as the figures on labor-force participation indicate, the rates of female employment are highest for the age groups bearing and rearing children and begin to decline for women over forty, who usually have adult children. (This pattern is an interesting reversal of a pheonomenon in the United States which has received recent attention, namely, the entry of women into the labor market as a response to the "empty-nest syndrome.")

Household and Kinship Relations

While the above considerations do not imply that there is economic parity between the sexes, they do indicate the absence of female economic dependency. The significance of this point requires further comment. In previous studies of family life in Barbados as well as other Afro-Caribbean societies, the relatively high proportion of women in the economy has been attributed either to the absence of a male provider or to his inability to fulfill his role (Greenfield 1966). This interpretation is predicated on the western assumption that women take on major economic roles only when circumstances prevent men from doing so. But in Endeavor, the economic roles of women and men are conceptualized differently.

Providing for children and household is regarded as a joint, though not necessarily equally shared, responsibility of men and women. Women, like men, take pride in and are applauded for successfully providing for their children.[4] Women are expected not only to contribute to their own and their children's support but also to acquire and build separate economic resources, control their own earnings, and use them as they see fit. Men readily accept the idea of their wives working; in fact, a man might boast about his wife's position and earnings. A woman, like a man, is not expected to disclose her assets to her spouse, though some may do so. These cultural expectations and assumptions about women's and men's economic activities qualify analyses of sex roles that are based on a notion that providing economic support is a predominantly male activity.

As other studies of Afro-American and Afro-Caribbean peoples have shown, family and kinship relations are important dimensions of the social world of both women and men. In Endeavor, people use kinship idioms to express close social relationships, as in the claim that in the community, "all o' we family." But more significant is the density of actual kinship connections among community residents. In 1958, 66 percent of 883 senior household members had close family relatives living in the community, often in an adjacent or nearby household, along with a large number of more distantly related kin. These ties serve to reinforce the social relations based on contiguity, providing what people refer to as a "backprop"—a source of assistance and support. Women are active in maintaining these extended kinship networks; and although the system is in principle bilateral, kinship connections through women figure more prominently in defining the sets of people considered to be "family" to each other. The strong sense of family based on these connections counterbalances the relative instability of conjugal unions. Moreover, these family ties, in addition to women's economic activities, account for the relative independence women maintain within their conjugal relationships.

A large part of the literature on the West Indian family is devoted to the variability of conjugal relationships and the related complexity in the composition of domestic groups. The several accepted forms of conjugality are referred to, in this literature, as visiting relationships, consensual or common-law unions, and legal marriage. In Endeavor, children are the expected outcome of each type of union, but children may serve either to bring a man and woman closer together of to "race a man away," and are not considered by a man or woman as sufficient reason for staying together. The concept of biological parenthood is nevertheless emphasized and the principle of bilateral affiliation recognized. Parental responsibility, however, tends to be shared among a number of relatives, more often on the mother's side, though there is nothing to prevent the family members of a biological father from taking on responsibility for children he has sired, and in many cases they do. There is then wide latitude in the roles biological parents may adopt and an accepted interchangeability of persons who assume responsibility for childrearing. Most variable, though, is the role a biological father plays in relation to his own children, which ranges from no contact and no support to extensive economic support and an affectionate and enduring relationship.

The variability in the social roles assumed by biological fathers is related to the variation in types of conjugal relationships, each of which entails different definitions of conjugal and parental rights and responsibilites. Consensual unions and legal marriage involve coresidence and joint responsibility for the children produced in the union, but separate responsibility for the children a man or woman may have had from previous unions. By contrast, a man has limited rights over the children produced in a visiting relationship. In this least stable form of conjugality, the couple live separately, refer to each other as girlfriend and boyfriend, and have limited obligations to or rights over each other.

While legal marriage carries prestige, it is not necessarily seen by either women or men, as a preferred form of living together. People in Endeavor frequently commented that "good living is better than bad marriage," a view also expressed in one woman's assertion that "plenty people living a sweet life and from the moment they get married is a different thing." Most men and women spend some part of their lives in a coresidential relationship, either with one or a series of different partners. And while some relationships develop into lifelong unions, permanence is not a strongly held expectation in entering any of the three forms of conjugality. The tendency is to move through the three types of unions sequentially, but beyond the visiting relationship, the order is not fixed. In Endeavor in the late 1950s, 20 percent of women between the ages of fifteen and twenty-four were living in visiting unions, 15 percent were living in consensual unions, and 15 percent were legally married. Forty-two percent of Endeavor women in this age category were already mothers. Between the ages of twenty-five and thirty-nine, consensual unions among women rose to 20 percent and legal marriages to 50 percent; 90 percent of the women had borne children. After forty, 70 percent of women in Endeavor were or had been married and only 2 percent were living in consensual unions, while a larger but hard to determine number of women who had been in legal or consensual unions were maintaining a visiting relationship with a different partner.

Conjugal instability and a relatively frequent changing of sexual partners are features of West Indian family life that have been attributed to a number of different factors—poverty, selective male migration, the legacy of slavery. But in Endeavor, the formation and breakup of unions is more related to the fact that a conjugal union is not the ony or essential context for either economic support or childrearing. Consequently, compatibility emerges as a much more important criterion in forming and maintaining conjugal relationships.

People in Endeavor believe compatibility can only be assessed after a couple have had sufficient opportunity to observe each other's character and test each other's responses to situations that arise in an ongoing relationship. Time is needed to determine whether "minds and spirits meet"—time to know whether a couple can "live lovin'." Compatibility cannot be deduced from the qualities that attract a couple initially and lead them to form a visiting relationship. The guarded attitude that women and men express about the outcomes of their sexual and coresidential unions is reflected in descriptions of the formation of relationships as a process of "trying one's luck." As one woman stated: "I feal a certain amount of 'outdoor livin' is a good thing. I feel I could now get married because I know what would make me happy. But you first got to check a man out and got to know what you lookin' for."

The behavior of women and men in conjugal relationships is guided by cultural assumptions about such unions and the roles appropriate to each sex. We have already noted that a couple's economic resources and social interests are only partially merged.

Nor is the conjugal tie expected to take priority over all other social ties or become the most intimate and emotionally intense of all social relationships, as is the case where the nuclear family forms the key unit for procreation, economic support, childrearing, and status placement. Instead, women and men assume that conjugality implies some joing responsibility for economic and childrearing responsibilities, a continued sexual interest in each other, and a mutual willingness to keep affairs between them a private matter rather than the subject of community gossip.

Women are expected to take the major responsibility for childrearing, cooking, and keeping the household clean.[5] Men cook and perform other domestic tasks when their spouses are not available to do so, but generally the sexual division of tasks allocates to men the responsibility for house building and maintaining physical structures. Men express their expectations of their conjugal partners in the following terms: a woman should not criticize her man in public (though she may do so in moderation privately); she should be a good manager of household finances and of economic resources generally, and, by extension, should try to see that her man does not spend his money foolishly (though it is recognized that meeting this expectation too zealously may create tension and conflict between a couple); she should not desert her man when he faces periods of hardship; she should cook for him, launder his clothes, and look after his general physical needs; she should treat her spouse's friends cordially and adhere to the norms of sociality that operate within the community. Finally, she should not shame her man by getting into roadside agruments, appearing unkempt or untidy, or "running around" with other men.

Women express a complementary set of expectations: a man should help with household finances and childrearing expenses; he should not divert an unreasonable amount of his income to other social obligations, to other women, or for drinking with his male friends; he should treat the children of a woman's previous unions well; he should be considerate, affectionate, and remain sexually interested in his spouse and be willing to assist her if she faces physical or verbal assault. A husband or male partner is not cast in the role of special protector and guardian of his spouse. Women are regarded neither as jural minors nor as wards of male partners who represent their interests in the wider society. Rather a woman is expected, in most situations, to represent herself, and men speak with admiration of a woman who "knows how to look out for herself."

While these are generally stated cultural expectations regarding conjugal relationships, they are not taken for granted. Each couple has to work out for themselves what they imply concretely, and each of these expectations thus becomes the subject of individually negotiated agreements on what constitute satisfactory terms for maintaining a conjugal relationship. In one woman's words: "From the start we set it clear: You mustn't hold back me and I mustn't hold back you. No man going to do me that. You lay down your terms and he lay down his, and if you don't agree, shift! Pull out!" Separation occurs when a couple "can't agree."

A particularly pervasive source of male-female conflicts is the issue of sexual fidelity. The cultural expectation that both sexes will remain sexually interesting and active makes both men and women jealously watchful for any sign of their partner's interest in outside affairs, and the issue of sexual infidelity generates a level of distrust and sex antagonism that is absent from other areas of male-female interaction. It is an area not only of conflict but of sexual inequality. For while sexual activity is viewed as equally pleasurable to women and men, women have fewer opportunities for initiating and maintaining outside affairs and are more likely than men to tolerate their spouse's infidelities. The double standard reflects the fact that a man's ability to control his partner's sexual life is an essential part of his masculine identity, whereas for a woman learning to live with a man's outside affairs does not pose a comparable threat to her feminine identity. This asymmetry favoring men produces tensions in the relations between the sexes and can lead to the dissolution of a relationship.

The relatively frequent shifting of conjugal partners creates complexities in the organization of domestic groups. While conjugal couples are the usual nucleus of household units, women who are not coresiding with a man are frequently houehold heads. Moreover, domestic units generally incorporate a variety of kin other than nuclear family members. These aspects of domestic and kinship oranization have been cited as indices of "matrifocality," defined in terms of the prominence of women as the focus of consanguineal kin groups and the priority of consanguineal over conjugal ties. The importance of consanguineal kin has been seen as a source of conflicting loyalties, which produces marital conflicts and conjugal instability. In our view, however, conjugal instability is related to the autonomy of the sexes more generally. For in Afro-Caribbean societies, women are not enclosed in discrete, bounded domestic units that are linked to the wider system through male economic and status-defining roles; nor are they submerged within kin groups. Rather, there is an overlap in the spheres of domestic, family, and community life that makes setting off the domestic from nondomestic domains inappropriate and particularly misleading for understanding sex roles and ideologies. In Endeavor, women's important roles in the family and kinship system are neither fully distinct from nor at odds with their participation in community life.

Community Relations

Now as under slavery, the community constitutes a major arena of social life for rural residents—one in which they receive recognition and reputations that are only partially dependent on their larger societal roles. It is here that the structures and cultural values of the dominant system intersect with the Afro-Creole patterns. To the extent that the national economic and political structures favor men, this is reflected in locally based branches of national economic and political institutions. Thus, the local political and trade-union activists in Endeavor are disproportionately male, as are the officers of the local branch of the national credit union system. But there are no community-wide administrative institutions that permit the imposition of male leadership on the community as a whole, and in the locally generated social patterns, a different set of assumptions about male and female roles operates.

The community provides a context for an active life of economic cooperation, entertainments, religious activity, and socializing. In these areas, both women and men are active participants—sometimes jointly, sometimes separately, but virtually always as individuals rather than as conjugal pairs.

There are a number of locally based economic institutions for saving or raising funds, and women and men are equally involved in them. Both sexes organize and participate in rotating credit as sociations, known as "meeting turns," and both act as "bankers" in such associations, with responsibility for collecting and distributing monies. Husbands and wives often participate in different "meetings," with each individual maintaining full claim to the savings he or she thus amasses.

Both sexes, separately or together, also organize as money-making events dances, known as "brams," and picnic excursions. Brams are usually sponsored by one or two individuals who seek to make a profit on entrance fees and the sale of food and liquor. Both sexes attend in approximately equal numbers; couples may arrive together, but more commonly they come alone or in same-sex groups. Like brams and excursions, social clubs provide a context in which women and men socialize together. Positions of leadership in these clubs tend to be given to better-educated, high-status people, with no discernible preponderance of one or the other sex.

As in other Afro-Caribbean communities, religion is an important focus of activity in Endeavor. Most of the community's residents are Anglican, and baptism, marriage, and funeral ceremonies are usually performed at one of the parish's several Anglican churches. But more important in local social life are the dozen or so "meeting halls" that house a range of Protestant fundamentalist groups. While the largest hall in Endeavor has an active membership numbering around 100, and the smaller ones have only a dozen or so "brothers" and "sisters" in their congregations, the halls are more important in community life than the numbers of active members indicate, and nonmembers sometimes attend meetings and participate in hall activities.

In most halls women participate more actively and in greater numbers than men, but both women and men attend and offer "testimony" at hall meetings; both also take on leadership roles as singing leaders and preachers. While men more often establish a new hall and install themselves as pastors, this is not an exclusively male prerogative. Coresidential couples may be active members of different halls; for in this as in other areas of activity, both sexes are expected to behave autonomously.

Despite the numerous areas of overlapping activity, the social lives of women and men are markedly independent of each other In activities involving both sexes, they participate as individuals, and the presence of a spouse is often merely coincidental. Other aspects of community activity involve greater separation of women and men. This is particularly pronounced in patterns of informal socializing, which are focused on same-sex friendships. There are small groups of five to ten men, similar in age and socioeconomic status, who meet in the rumshops and on the streetcorners to talk and drink run or tour together to dances or other social events. In addition to socializing together, clique members provide for each other reciprocal assistance and support. Studies of male cliques have added an important dimension to understanding Afro-Caribbean social life and values and have served to counteract the stereotype of male powerlessness and peripherality created by the emphasis in many earlier studies on domestic units. But less attention has been given to women's patterns of informal socializing outside the household.

In Endeavor, women are both highly mobile and highly sociable, though after late adolescence their social lives tend to be less group-centered than those of men. Working women have a range of contacts and experiences similar to men's, and a recent study of women factory workers notes that female cliques similar to the all-male peer groups have emerged among coworkers (Stoffle 1972, p. 190). women who are not employed make frequent daytime visits to neighbors, to one of the general shops, or to friends elsewhere in the district, and thus maintain a flow of information and contact among women. Most women have one or two close friends with whom they exchange confidences, and maintain relations characterized by the exchange of favors, gossip, and goods and services with a broader circle of women. These social networks are often wide-ranging and may include friends in other districts. They rarely constitute relatively bounded groups like men's cliques, and they appear to be less homogeneous in terms of social status. Women's social networks have tended to be ignored in discussions of sex roles in the West Indies, partly because they are more dispersed and therefore less visible than men's groups, but also because assumptions that women's social lives revolve around family and kinship have diverted investigators from studying these networks.

In addition to these contexts for same-sex socializing, there is considerable informal cross-sex contact among community member. Although friendship between a woman and a man may raise the suspicion of a sexual relationship, there are nevertheless many such friendships. And the "public" nature of community life—in the yards, roads, and shops of the district—means that women and men frequently encounter one another in a range of contexts and are familiar with one another's activities through elaborate networks of community gossip which include both sexes. While community social life is characterized by considerable autonomy of the sexes and a separation of some activities, this does not preclude either extensive cross-sex interaction or their joint knowledge of spheres of life that in other societies are often segregated into separate male and female domains.

Thus, we see that the importance of women in the domains of kinship and domestic life does not conflict with either economic participation or active involvement in nondomestic realms of community social life. The structure of kin relations not only provides a woman with important social ties beyond her own household, but also distributes domestic tasks and responsibilities so as to permit women to be active in a range of nondomestic contexts. The woman who confines her activities to the household is, in Endeavor, ridiculed for "always drawing up in the house" by women and men alike.

In sum, the relatively independent access women and men have to resources in the kinship system and in the economy provides a basis for considerable autonomy and promotes their relatively independent achievement of status and prestige within the community. While the status of a spouse is not irrelevant to the position of either women or men in the socioeconomic hierarchy, it is not often the sole or even the primary determinant. Moreover, men do not "represent" the domestic group in the wider society or link domestic and juropolitical domains. While there are some spheres in the community that favor male participation and leadership, there are no community-wide administrative institutions that either permit the imposition of the dominant culture's forms of male leadership and authority on the community as a whole, or through which men (or women) "represent" the community to the wider system.

CULTURAL CONCEPTS OF
SEX ROLES AND IDENTITIES

We earlier suggested that there was a congruity between aspects of the allocation of sex roles that emerged in the plantation context and aspects of West African sex-role traditions. The Afro-Creole culture of lower-class black West Indians involves a complex interaction of European-derived norms and values, and the assumptions and ideologies that emerged from the experience of Africans on the slave plantations. While people in Endeavor share the general dualism of this cultural orientation, their attitudes and concepts expressed about appropriate sex-role behavior, sexuality, and the characteristics and abilities of women and men depart significantly, though not uniformly, from the assumptions prevalent in western societies.

This is particularly evident in attitudes toward sex and sexuality. Both men and women regard sex as pleasurable, desirable, and necessary for health and general well-being, and they discuss, separately and together, how to improve sexual performance and pleasure. Stylized sexual banter between women and men occurs in public and private settings and is enjoyed by both sexes.

Some observers of male peer groups have emphasized the importance men give to sexual prowess and the conquest of women (Freilich 1968). However, such descriptions omit the important fact that the West Indian men's preoccupation with sexual activities, is unlike machismo, very profemale. A man's reputation as a lover is not based on "conquest" of the "inaccessible" woman but on his success in sexual performance, in knowing the techniques that give a woman sexual pleasure. The West Indian notion of masculinity has built into it, then, the concept of satisfying the woman, and this performance-oriented approach to sex and sexuality is supported by the active interest and expectations of women.

Both sexes are aware of and sometimes voice the dominant culture's traditional European concepts of male and female characteristics and abilities. However, rather different definitions of masculinity and femininity guide interpersonal behavior within the community. Unlike the dominant ideology in which gender is the basis for an opposition of roles, values, and personal traits, this system of rules and meanings makes few distinctions between male and female abilities and attributes. Sex and sensuality, which symbolize creativity and "power" (in the sense of effectiveness, not dominance), are equally valued in men and women. Nor is sensuality thought to interfere with effectiveness in public roles; for both sexes, it is believed to enhance abilities to think and act decisively.

A woman's procreative powers, rather than disqualifying her from societal prestige and esteem, command considerable respect,[6] and motherhood is a basis of support in later years. But motherhood also has important symbolic meanings: bearing a child is the major *rite de passage* from girlhood to womanhood, and it constitutes the more salient element of adult female identity. Marriage, if it occurs at all, often comes later and marks a transition from one stage of adult relationships and responsibilities to another; it does not play an essential role in defining womanhood. A childless woman is pitied and occasionally derided with such epithets as "mule." Female sterility is attributed to insufficient "nature"—i.e., vaginal secretions—and thus implicitly linked to frigidity. Sexuality and procreative power are perceived to be positively associated.

Childbirth itself is viewed as a cleansing process, and while a woman's children from previous unions may occasionally be a source of conflict with a man, they constitute evidence of a womanly "cleanliness" that more often enhances than diminishes her attractiveness as a mate. The act of childbirth not only cleanses the body; it also demonstrates a woman's capacity to endure pain. Women discuss their own and other's performances during delivery, and special prestige attaches to the woman who can "stand up hands on hips, and drop her child like so." Children express the specialness of the mother-child tie in terms that acknowledge the strength required of women in childbirth, as in the frequently heard comment, "After all, she is the one who bear the pain to have me."

Despite the cultural elaboration of motherhood, and the fact that women are the ones who speak about "making a baby," men's roles in procreation are not ignored. While they are not conceptualized as the major agents of procreation, they are believed to partake of the experience of pregnancy; when conception has occurred, it is believed that they will physically experience some of the early symptoms of pregnancy. A number of women and men told us that frequently a man knew of his woman's pregnancy before being told because he experienced the symptoms. We also heard men dispute allegations of paternity on the grounds that they did not experience the pregnancy symptoms.

Thus the distinct qualities of masculine and feminine sexual and reproductive abilities are not viewed by either sex as a basis for different male and female social capacities. And unlike the self-limiting, negative sexual indentities that Euro-American women have had to struggle with, female identity in Endeavor is associated with highly valued cultural attributes. Because women are assumed to be bright, strong, and competent, nothing in the definitions of appropriate sex-role behavior systematically excludes them from areas of economic and social achievement open to men.

CHANGING CONDITIONS

Historically, the sharp division in Barbados between dominant and subordinate groups not only excluded black men and women from participating in the island's political institutions but also prevented a fuller imposition and assimilation of the ideologies and norms of the dominant group. From the beginning, then, family and community life among the majority black population have operated in accordance with principles that have remained distinct from, though not unaffected by, those of the colonial elite. With recent changes in island political and economic structures, however— particularly the enfranchisement of the working class and the ascendance of middle-class blacks—the socially inherited cleavage between those in control and those controlled is no longer so marked.

Politics is one of the new areas of achievement open to the black population of Barbados. The absence of local political institutions and the colonial tradition of island politics have precluded the development of definitions of appropriate behavior for women and men in this sphere. In 1971 and again in 1975, only one woman was among the 24 members elected to the Barbados House of Assembly, and women seeking public office were at a disadvantage in the campaigning techniques of canvassing and buying drinks in the rumshops. However, female candidates and speakers at political rallies were well received; and many women in Endeavor are knowledgeable and interested in island politics, following closely the issues of general concern in the community, discussing with one another and with men the pros and cons of governmental policy, and often expressing enthusiastic partisanship in their political allegiances.

Emigration is another phenomenon that has expanded considerably in recent years. Both women and men seek to go abroad to England, Canada, or the United States, and for the same reasons— primarily financial but also for the "experience." The relative proportions of male to female emigrants have been determined more

by the nature of job opportunities in these countries than by
women's marital status or domestic roles. A woman with children
may leave them with relatives until she can send for them to join
her abroad. Like male emigrants, she has obligations and responsibilities to support or assist relatives at home through remittances.

The ultimate impact of this expansion of economic and political
options for black women and men in Barbados is not yet clear.
Whether present political and economic changes will contribute to a
decline in women's autonomy and status, or whether Barbadian
women will respond to the new situation in the light of their
historical experience and cultural assumptions, remains an open
question. To the extent that a different set of cultural assumptions
influences societal arrangements, there is reason to believe that
women and men in Barbados will avoid the development of the
sexual stratification that has accompanied capitalist economic and
political development in the West.

CONCLUSION

In this paper we have focused on an Afro-Caribbean society in
which women are both more autonomous and more highly regarding than in western industrial societies. This is particularly interested because Barbados shares with western industrial nations a
capitalist economy with a well-developed labor market and a pronounced division between "domestic" and "public" spheres of activity. These conditions have been identified as the source of women's
loss of autonomy and public esteem and of their dependent roles
within the family. We have sought to identify the conditions that
have prevented West Indian societies from replicating the western
pattern of sexual stratification.

Two factors emerge as critical in accounting for the relative
equality and autonomy of the sexes. First, the sexual division of
labor on the slave plantation produced few differences in the "public" economic participation of women and men; and second, the
social cleavage between free whites and enslaved blacks minimized
the imposition of the dominant class ideologies and permitted the
slaves a degree of autonomy in retaining and developing distinct
cultural patterns and concepts about sex roles and attributes. We
have examined the contemporary legacy of these differences in the
sexual division of labor and cultural ideologies. We found the

women's independent income-producing activities, combined with their positions within the kinship system, provide a basis for their autonomy and self-esteem and for maintaining a relatively equal balance of power between the sexes. Moreover, they operate with a cultural ideology that attributes to women and men a similar set of positively valued characteristics and abilities and that identifies parenthood and sex as two highly valued experiences.

At a more general level, our analysis suggests that for women as well as men a wide network of social relations and supports provides an important basis for independence and autonomy. In contrast to the western concept of individual autonomy and equality, which implies a shedding of social attachments, the Afro-Caribbean and black American concept of autonomy is linked to a strong sense of interpersonal connectedness—an involvement in the lives of others. The status of the sexes in Barbados, therefore, rests on their relatively independent access to the resources of the kinship system and the economy and on an ideology that minimizes sexual differences and emphasizes the effectiveness of the individual regardless of gender.

NOTES

1. The distinction between "domestic" (private, familial, informal system) and "public" (juropolitical, formal, external system) has been applied both to roles and to spheres of activity. The terms have been widely used and variously defined in recent studies of sex roles, sometimes as an analytic distinction and sometimes as an analytic distinction and sometimes as a presumed difference "out there" in society. "Domestic domain" typically refers to the internal affairs of a small social unit, usually the household or extended family, and has been regarded as the locus of female activity. The "public domain" is the term used most frequently in referring to all aspects of social life occurring outside the "domestic domain," especially those activities and networks of social ties that link one domestic unit to another. The public domain is allegedly where men and societal power are located. Although we do not accept its universal applicability or its universal identification with a sex dichotomy, it is a useful distinction in the analysis of particular societies. On the slave plantation it was, rather, the sharp cleavage between the slave community and the wider society that formed the boundary between internally and externally oriented spheres of activity. We have therefore treated the community and family together as constituting a more relevant domain of "internal relations" than the

more narrowly defined domestic shere.

2. This pattern was evidently established early. Handler (1974; p. 215) indicates that among both the white elite class and the free colored population prior to emancipation, the absence of women from political activity was notably similar.

3. These and subsequent statistics are based on a personal census of Endeavor taken in 1958 by C. Sutton and on material drawn from the 1960 and 1970 Commonwealth Caribbean Population Censuses.

4. A similar phenomenon was reported in a study on self-esteem among black American women: "76 percent of the employed women referred to themselves as successful mothers based on being 'a good provider'" (Myers 1975; p. 247).

5. Cooking is an especially important aspect of a woman's relationship to a man. In male-female exchanges, there is a symbolic association between the giving and receiving of sex and food.

6. The cultural meanings assigned to pregnancy and childbirth, and the social power thought to reside in the role of mother, throw an interesting sidelight on the argument that these activities and roles are responsibile for an alleged universal cultural devaluation of women (Ortner 1974). This devaluation is attributed to a universal identification of women with nature and men with culture. In this culture/nature dichotomy, "cultural" activities are more highly regarded than those defined as "natural" and are thus the source of male ideological dominance. Not only were we unable to find such a linkage at either the conscious or unconscious symbolic level, but people in Endeavor explicitly and consistently reverse the allegedly universal superiority of culture over nature. What is identified as "natural" is more highly regarded, while "culture" is linked to artifice, hypocrisy, and the exploitation by the dominant group. Moreover, the nature/culture dichotomy was not symbolically coded in sex-linked terms.

REFERENCES

Barbados, Statistical Service, 1966. *Labour Force Survey, April*. St. Michael, Barbados.

———— 1974. *Commonwealth Caribbean Population Census, 1970. Barbados Preliminary Bulletin, Education*. St. Michael, Barbados.

Census Research Program. 1973. *Commonwealth Caribbean Population Census*, 4 (4): *Economic Activity, Barbados, 1970*. Jamaica: University of the West Indies.

Davis, Angela. 1971. "Reflections on the Black Woman's Role in the Community of Slaves." *Black Scholar* 3:3-15.

Fogel, Robert and Stanley L. Engerman. 1974. *Time on the Cross: The Economics of American Negro Slavery*. Boston: Little, Brown.

Freilich, Morris. 1968. "Sex, Secrets, and Systems. "In S. Gerber, ed., *The Family in the Caribbean*, pp. 47-62. Rio Piedras, Puerto Rico: Institute of Caribbean Studies.

Genovese, Eugene. 1976. *Roll Jordan Roll: The World the Slaves Made*. New York: Vintage.

Greenfield, Sidney. 1966. *English Rustics in Black Skin*. New Haven: College and University Press.

Gutman, Herbert. 1976. *The Black Family in Slavery and Freedom, 1750-1925*. New York: Pantheon.

Handler, Jerome. 1974. *The Unappropriated People: Freedmen in the Slave Society of Barbados*. Baltimore: Johns Hopkins Press.

Makiesky-Barrow, Susan. 1976. "Class, Culture, and Politics in a Barbadian Community." Ph.D. dissertation, Brandeis University.

Mathurin, Lucille. 1974. "A Historical Study of Women in Jamaica from 1655 to 1844." Ph.D. dissertation, University of the West Indies (Mona, Jamaica).

_____ 1975. *The Rebel Woman in the British West Indies*. Kingston, Jamaica: The Institute of Jamaica.

Myers, Lena W. 1975. "Black Women and Self-Esteem." In M. Millman and R. M.

Kanter, eds., *Another Voice: Feminist Perspectives on Social Life and Social Science*, pp. 240-50. New York: Doubleday Anchor.

Ortner, Sherry B. 1974. "Is Female to Male as Nature Is to Culture?" In M. Z. Rosaldo and L. Lamphere, eds., *Woman, Culture, and Society*, pp. 67-88. Stanford:

Stanford University Press.

Stoffle, Richard W. 1972. "Industrial Employment and Inter-Spouse Conflict: Barbados, West Indies." Ph.D. dissertation, University of Kentucky.

Sutton, Constance, 1969. "The Scene of the Action: A Wildcat Strike in Barbados." Ph.D. dissertation, Columbia University.

Wilson, Peter J. 1971.

"Caribbean Crews: Peer Groups and Male Society." *Caribbean Studies* 10; 18-34.

_____ 1973. *Crab Antics: The Social Anthropology of English-Speaking Negro Societies of the Caribbean*. New Haven: Yale University Press.

5

Female Status, the Family, and Male Dominance in the West Indian Community

Yolanda T. Moses

This chapter is a contribution to the study of the relationship between female economic contributions to the family and female status using data from the small, predominantly black island of Montserrat[1] in the British West Indies. Writers have argued that substantial economic contributions from women need not result in higher status, especially if existing cultural traditions define their activities as less prestigious than those of men.[2] My data support this claim. The status of employed women has less to do with economic contributions per se than with the presence or absence of males in the household and the degree to which women have internalized and perpetuate ideologies of male dominance, "a situation in which men have highly preferential access, although not always exclusive rights, to those activities to which society accords the highest value, and permits a measure of control over others."[3] Historically, such an ideology comes from British traditions, officially reflected in the law on Montserrat,[4] in which women are perceived as subordinate to men. Though laws have been modified in recent years to provide a more egalitarian view, older values are still inseparable from institutions and individual male-female role relations.

Montserrat also provides a chance to look at the status of women across class lines within the same society. The West Indies were, and are, a society based on class distinctions. Most work on the family or household in the West Indies has centered on the working class and especially the matrifocal family,[5] but I investigated middle-class and elite women as well as variants of the working-class family. The anthropological literature has noted that the middle-class family is patriarchal and that women are subordinate to men.[6] Working-class families, on the other hand, are thought to be female centered and men in the role of husband-father marginal.[7]

Looking at decision-making powers of employed working-class women within their own class context and then comparing them to the decision-making powers of the middle-class women, I have tried to provide more detailed structural-functional descriptions of female power.

My method was to analyze archival information such as surveys, government records, and interviews with government specialists (i.e., lawyers, educators, and administrators) and to use participant observation and comprehensive in-depth interviews with my sample of women and their families. I chose to do an intensive study of a small number of women for two reasons. First, there is a history of community surveys for the Caribbean area that have focused on household structure but not on the internal dynamics of these households, on male-female relations, or on information regarding people's attitudes and feelings about their roles.[8] The second and perhaps most important reason is that the nature of the data collected depended on the kind of rapport established with my informants. The interviews were conducted with employed women, that is, those who work for wages or a salary, married and single, with and without children and their partners where available (see table 1 for breakdown).

MONEY, RESPONSIBILITY, POWER, AND IDEOLOGY

Domestic relationships often reveal much about sex roles in a society. For most married women at both economic levels, the husband is considered the head of the household and ultimate authority figure, even for those who make as much money as their husbands. One said, "In any *normal* family, there has to be a head. Somebody has to have final word and authority. I was always taught it was the man's place to be the head." In one case, where the husband was away from the island for several years and the wife was contributing about half of the income to the household, she would wait as much as two or three weeks to make decisions concerning routine purchases until she had gotten his permission by mail.

However, single women at both social and economic levels present a more varied picture of what "head of the household" means. Where there is no male present in the role of husband-father, the final authority figure in decision making is often determined by age, usually the deciding factor where female siblings and their children live with the mother. Two junior household members said, "My mother is the head. My sister and me live with my mother. We live in her house. She takes care of all the children [five] while we work.

TABLE 1
A. BREAKDOWN OF SAMPLE BY MARITAL STATUS AND PRESENCE/ABSENCE OF CHILDREN

Marital Status	With Children	Without Children	Total
Married	11	0	11
Divorced/separated	4	1	5
Widowed	2	2	4
Single (never been married)	10	15	25
Total	27	18	45

B. WOMEN WITH CHILDREN BY MARITAL STATUS AND EMPLOYMENT RANKING

Marital Status	Skilled*	Unskilled	Total
Married	11	0	11
Single †	4	6	10
Divorced	1	1	2
Separated	0	2	2
Widowed	0	2	2
Total	16	11	27

*Skilled women have training past primary level: including secondary (high) school, technical training, university training. Their jobs include teachers, nurses, social workers, clerical assistants, and beauticians. Unskilled women have six years or less of education and are employed in jobs such as domestic, store clerk, and farmer. On Montserrat skilled occupations are usually associated with middle-class status and unskilled occupations with working-class status.

† Single included only women who have never been married.

She don't mind; she says she is too old to work anyway. She also tells us what food to buy, we bring it home to her and she cooks it." "We live in the house that my aunt gave to my sister. My mother watches the children while we work. We make the money. My mother spends it. She buys the food, and sometimes the clothes when we have money. She is a good mother. She loves children."

Skilled single women, whose education and income offset the age authority of a mother, can also be household heads. "I am considered the head of the household because I am the only person working. My mother is too old. She tells me to make most decisions since it is my money I am spending. She is really grateful that I support her. I always ask her what she wants to do even though I know the final decision is mine." Some households are egalitarian; decisions are made jointly, and the person who is available carries them out. This kind of household is usually composed of skilled siblings with roughly the same income. A sister, who had an egalitarian arrangement with her brother, said, "I took this apartment in Plymouth near my job. But I was not able to afford it by myself. My brother also had a job in Plymouth, so we decided to live together. We share expenses. We buy food together and he sometimes even looks after the baby when I go out. It is really nice having him here and we get along well. The only thing is I wish he would help cook more."

Owning property in the form of houses or land is a part of the local status structure. Many people who leave the island and go to Britain or the United States to work have their relatives buy land and have houses built on the island for them.[9] Most skilled married women confirm this, as they owned houses jointly with their husbands, but few of them decided or helped to decide to buy the house or have the house built. In most instances it was the husband's decision, made before he married. The women were all basically happy with the outcome. As one woman stated: "George already had the land before we got married. So we built here. Before the house was built we lived with his mother. I like the location and the neighbors. I like living a little away from the town, not too far, but just far enough." The wives of middle-class husbands derive satisfaction because houses symbolize middle-class status for both of them, and who makes the decision to buy or build one seems irrelevant. Skilled single women, on the other hand, usually fall into the category of renters, because it is too expensive to try to buy property or build a house as a single person. Married couples are pooling two incomes, while the single person is supporting herself and children, if any, on one salary. Most unskilled women do own property: small one- or two-room houses that have been in the family for at least two generations, inherited from a member of the family who has either left the island or died. Owning a home holds the same kind of value and prestige for unskilled women as it does for the skilled ones, but they seem to be more dependent on help from kin on the island or wherever they may live to secure their houses.

Skilled married women, except in one case, make less than one-half of the total household income. Though this group receives remittances, they give financial support to other relatives who are in need. Indeed, over a third of these couples have relatives living with them, while two-thirds of them give financial support to relatives who do not live in the household but on the island. I found among the husbands a deep sense of duty. "I take care of this old lady, she is not really related to me, but she was a good friend of my grandparents who raised me. I have known her for a long time. She has no one left to look after her, so I do. She must be about ninety years old now I guess. I take care of her because there is no one else to do it. I have an uncle who is a carpenter, he does a lot of odd jobs for me. I know that sometimes he doesn't do good work, but he *is* my uncle, and that's why I hire him." Because there is very little formalized support given to the needy, the care of the aged is still done mainly by the relatives.[10] Most middle-class people on Montserrat still have a strong sense of family duty, in part because they are what I call "the new middle class." That is, the majority are from working-class backgrounds but through education and income have become more affluent.

The consequences of this help to avoid a conflict between a Victorian British notion of sex roles (i.e., a woman's place is in the home) and the reality of the middle-class woman working outside the home. Ideally, though the male is to be provider and decision maker for the family, income from all sources is still needed. So, the working-class norm, that women must work to make a living, is still part of the value system of the middle class. This value will probably remain even after the middle class on Montserrat becomes firmly entrenched, because money will be needed from all working members in a household in order to maintain the new middle-class life-style. Moreover, women do not compete in traditionally male areas in the labor market, and they continue their role as nurturer in the home. Nor do the majority of men do increased housework or routine childcare activities as a result of their wives' employment. So, for the middle-class women, while education may confer social mobility, a good job, more income, and better housing when compared to working-class women, vis-à-vis her partner she is still considered and considers herself subordinate to him. Plus, she is expected by society to marry, raise children, and be faithful to her husband, while he still enjoys the sexual and social double standards of the society.

Indeed, middle-class women internalize and manifest a male dominance ideology to a greater degree than the working-class women for several reasons. First, middle-class men are able to live up to their roles set forth by the ideology, that is, they are able to provide the major economic support for their families. Second, they are physically present in the household to make decisions and to see that women play their complementary roles in maintaining and perpetuating this ideology through early childhood socialization patterns as well as by acting as role models for their female children.

Single and divorced skilled women, in contrast to married skilled women, do not give much familial support. Instead, they must rely on friends and relatives to help them. One said, "My father gives me from $15.00 t0 $20.00 a week because I am always short of money. He comes to town about once a week and that's when I see him. My older brothers and sisters send him money from Canada, and I get it from him. The man who owns this building is a friend of my father, so he too keeps an eye on me. The people next door bring me vegetables because I don't have space or the time for a garden with my job and my baby."

The income of unskilled women is appreciably less than for all skilled women. One wonders how the little money is stretched to take care of the basic needs of its members. Yet, in the unskilled group, the women must provide 50 percent and more of the total household income. Among single women, remittances from relatives working abroad and the pooling of resources help ends meet. One informant who lives with her mother, her sisters, and their children said, "My cousins help us sometimes you know. But they don't have much. The children's grandmother she takes care of them sometime. I take them over to see my mother-in-law on Sunday." (She calls the mother of her children's father mother-in-law even though they are not married and she does not know where he is.) Single women who live alone with their children, separated, divorced, and widowed women also depend on their friends and relatives. One domestic said: "I get $25.00 a week from one of my daughters and $30.00 a week from the other. With the little money I make, my mother and me are able to get by. We have a garden, and my married sister here on Montserrat sometimes 'gives [to] the old lady.' "

Skilled married women usually make the routine purchases of small items such as food, dishes, appliances, and tools for the kitchen. But men decide on the larger, less frequently purchased items, such as radios, record players, or automobiles. Only in the area of buying furniture do women make major decisions. Most are quite satisfied with the arrangement. They frequently justify the husband's decision making in these areas by saying he is more "knowledgeable" about mechanical gadgets: "Lord, I don't know anything about record players. That's my husband's interest. So I let him buy whatever he wants. We did decide to buy the furniture together. I guess he really didn't care too much as long as it was nice." There is little conflict over these areas of involvement since both men and women have clear-cut ideas about what should be their areas of interest and expertise. Even single skilled women seek the help of "knowledgeable" males before they make the major purchase of a car.

Most skilled women feel that their working contributes very little to their decision-making power but rather to a good understanding between them and their partners: "I only make a little money. It surely doesn't decide what we do. My salary is too small. We decide together what is to be done." Another woman said, "I feel I could still help make decisions even if I wasn't working, my husband and I have a good understanding." Though the majority feel their economic contributions have little effect on their decision-making power, several also feel it is a definite advantage to work since that way they can buy what they want when they want. According to a head teacher of a primary school, "Well, I know I could buy something even if he didn't want me to. I can be very stubborn about things like that. This way, I don't have to depend upon him for everything."

Most skilled single women, in contrast, see themselves in the role of decision maker by necessity: "If I didn't work, I would be very dependent on other people. I don't like that idea." Yet a single woman who does live with her parents feels that her income from her occupation contributes nothing to her power in the household because her father is there and she is considered a daughter and not an adult: "I pay for rent at my father's house. He makes the big decisions in our family. Sometimes, he will ask my mother but not me."

Among the unskilled women in general, decision making about the purchase of goods is done on a much smaller scale. Working is necessary for survival. Basics, like food and clothing, are priorities. Luxury items usually come in the form of gifts from boyfriends or remittances from relatives.

As decision-making areas are grouped along sex lines, so are notions of what is "women's work" and what is "men's work" among middle-class families. Both women and men consider housework unsuitable for males. The cultural traditions of Montserrat dictate that women do housework. If they work outside of the home, in addition, that is fine, but they still must do the housework or have it done. Women and others (maids, helpers, or female relatives) overwhelmingly do cooking, cleaning, shopping, washing, and ironing. Husbands usually do repairs, yardwork, and gardening (see Table 2). In the two instances where gardening is the wives' task, the husbands are away from the island. In the two cases of the "wife and others" that included husbands and wives, couples like to garden and take turns doing it.

How do these women work and take care of a household? It is usually done smoothly and with little conflict of roles because middle-class couples can afford domestic help. This frees them from household chores to become employed, and men are not required to "help out." Men, in turn, have thier duties, which do not overlap with their wives'. Single skilled women either can afford to hire help or have a relative help for free. If their children are large enough, they, too, can do chores.

TABLE 2
MARRIED SKILLED WOMEN: HOUSEHOLD TASKS BY SEX AND TYPE OF TASK (N = 11)

Tasks	Husband	Wife	Children	Other	Wife with Others
Cooking	....	3	....	....	8
Cleaning	....	2	....	7	2
Shopping	....	5	....	....	6
Washing	....	2	....	8	1
Ironing	....	2	....	9	....
Repairs	6	1	....	4	....
Lawn (yardwork)	6	.....	....	3	2
Gardening	6	2	....	1	2

Unskilled women depend on friends and relatives for getting household tasks done. They cannot hire domestics (see Table 3). Few of these women have repairs made, and when they do they are done by males—either a relative, a boyfriend, or, on rare occasions, a hired man. Repairs are expensive, and since the income level of the unskilled women is far below that of the skilled women, they are not considered a priority. Only roughly half of the women have yardwork to do. Having a lawn assumes that one has both spare time and money to plant grass and shrubs. Unlike the skilled women, the unskilled women usually do their own gardening. Vegetable gardening is an essential part of many unskilled women's subsistence. So, if a male is not present, gardening cannot not go undone the way repairs can.

Male children are not enlisted to ease the burden of the working unskilled woman. While talking to informants, I found that they themselves discourage male participation at an early age, cultivating a kind of relationship in which the boys are made to feel like pampered strangers in the household, catered to by mothers and sisters. The girls are trained to be hard workers, both inside and outside the home—responsible, dependable, tolerant, adept in domestic skills, and loyal to their kin group. Consequently, when the males grow up they will expect a similar kind of treatment from their wives or girlfriends, who will be trained to give it to them. A Monserration woman sums up the dichotomy of sex roles:

TABLE 3
ALL UNSKILLED WOMEN BY HOUSEHOLD TASKS, PERFORMANCE OF TASK BY SEX, AND RELATIONSHIP TO INFORMANT (N=11)

Tasks	Informant	Relative		Children		Friend		Informant and Relatives		Other
		F	M	F	M	F	M	F	M	
Cooking	5	2	....	..	..	..		4	..	.....
Cleaning	5	1	....	..	..	..		4	..	.....
Shopping	5	1	....	..	..	1		4	..	.....
Washing...........	6	....	....	..	..	..		4	..	.....
Ironing	5	....	....	..	..	..		5	..	.....
Repair............	0	....	1	..	..	..		..	..	1
Lawn (yardwork)	2	....	1	1	..	..		..	..	1
Gardening........	4	....	....	..	..	..		2	..	1

Women do run the households. West Indian men don't like to do any work at all either. A lot of West Indian men like to drink. Those that do work to support their families usually do not make enough to support their drinking habits and their families. So women have to go to work too. Some of them who have no education or who can't get jobs as domestics go out and plant a garden or do farming to make ends meet. Not only do these women work all day, but they come home and cook for their families too. They have to do it to keep the family going. Women are used to supporting themselves, so they do it when the men are here and when the men are gone as well. They tell their daughters not to depend on men, but on themselves. They should tell the sons to have responsibilites, but they don't. It is the women who become responsible.

A vocal male nationalist also commented on the enormous responsibilities that women have: "Men here are basically lazy—they have it too easy. There is no stress placed upon production among men. So they do a nominal amount of work. As a result, women have worked out a system wherein they have to provide for children twenty-four hours a day. For men, this is not so. After work he comes home and relaxes." Another informant has a teen-age daughter and a son in his early twenties. The daughter has a job as a clerk in a store in Plymouth, the capital town of Montserrat; the son is a "sweet man"[11] and does little work: "My son used to help me build the room on my house, but he is a 'sweet man' now. He don't have no money, but he won't work. When he comes home he gets his guitar and he sits and plays. I tell him that I want him to give me money to buy food and things—and he gets mad and moves out; but I don't care."

In the cycle of socializing children, both male and female, we can observe the actual perpetuation of the conflict between the ideal and actual sex roles that children will take on as adults. Girls are taught strategies to insure their survival and maintenance whether males are present or not. Boys, on the other hand, are treated as guests. The main reason women say they do this is that it assures a mother her son's economic and emotional loyalty in her old age. Ideally, mothers believe their sons will have a good "position" (job) in life and that they will dote on an aged mother who may have no man of her own to depend on. Sisters do it because they say they need to have a man around to help them. But, due to the lack of economic alternatives these working-class men will have to face in life, they are not being socialized by their mothers to survive. Girls are actually being better equipped to survive, although it is still ideally believed and valued that men should be economically superior at providing and at decision making.

This kind of sex role training does in fact influence courtship and conjugal ties. Working-class women know they cannot always depend on males in the role of husband-father for economic and emotional support, so they take what they can get from their conflicted situation. They may form a series of "friending" relationships with men for sex, presents, and status. While a man may not be able to provide for a woman economically, her status in her circle of friends is enhanced if she can "hold a man" and keep him satisfied sexually.

Marriage is perceived by the majoirty of working-class women in my study as undesirable because it restricts their alternatives. If they married, they would have to be economically dependent upon and loyal to *one* man. While this may work for middle-class married women whose husbands have more steady jobs and incomes to help support a family, it would be a "dead end" for most young working-class women. They would not be able to form "friending" relationships with other men nor would they be able to expect a great deal of assistance from their kin groups.

Ideally, working-class women have the same value for males as middle-class women. They believe that men should take care of women and their children. But, in reality, working-class males in Montserrat have a difficult time finding employment. The alternative is, of course, migration to find jobs. Most of the men who migrate are forced to leave their families behind. Some of them send remittances to their families;[12] some do not. In their mates' absence, women must work. And, because there is no male present in the role of husband-father, she usually makes the decisions as head of the household. Whether men are absent or sporadically employed, women tend to form and to maintain very strong bonds with their kin (usually female) as a source of reassurance as well as a ready source for financial assistance. This strong pull toward the kin group tends to make conjugal bonds weaker.[13] I am not suggesting that women do not form love relationships and sexual relationships with men but rather that these relationships are generally shorter and less binding than ties with their kin group. As a result, while the majority of women in the working class may ideally consider themselves subordinate to men (i.e., they may believe men are supposed to take care of them and make decisions for them), in reality, it is not true.

Here a tension between ideology and reality occurs. Both men and women are socialized to belive that men are superior, but one man cannot provide for a family because he has little or no political and economic control and no access to centers of power. A man may even be dependent upon his female kin for support. Working-class women can and do take care of themselves economically. (The frustration that stems from lack of access to political and economic power is also reported for working-class black males in the United States by Liebow and Hannerz, and from other areas of the West Indies by Wilson and Dirks.)[14] An argument that working-class women are not bound by the same social restrictions as middle-class women and therefore there is little sex role conflict between women and men at this level is not borne out completely. There is, in fact, conflict for several reasons: (1) both males and females are aware of the cultural ideal for the role of the male as provider and protector, but since males cannot live up to this expectation, women must assume this responsibility; (2) due to migration of the male labor force, both historical and contemporary, males are not often physically present to assume their roles and women have to take over; (3) last, and probably the most important, women are actually perpetuating the ideology that males should provide economically for their mothers and sisters while they are not preparing them to do so. Instead of teaching them responsibility, indpendence, and flexibility, the way they teach their girls, they are smothering them with attention. While they (mothers) are socializing females to take care of themselves, the males with whom they are to interact and ideally depend on as husband-fathers have not been taught those things. A cycle goes on. Both men and women learn contradictory ideal sex roles that they cannot fulfill.

IMPLICATIONS FOR FUTURE RESEARCH

Some other approaches to the study of female economic contribution and decision making should now be undertaken. For example, studies of women's roles in politics and community affairs would tell us to what extent, cross-culturally, women participate in official and unofficial policymaking. Studies of kinship relationships and networks provide natural settings in which to study female status, as it is often through the kin group that women develop and maintain a sense of solidarity, continuity, and status.[15] The study of friendships would be another fruitful area of inquiry. With whom women associate is important, because it is one way of determining the degree of alternatives that women have in a culture and the degree to which the sexes are segregated socially.[16] But perhaps most important, the investigation of female status through religion and other symbolic systems such as myth and ritual provides insight into how and why ideologies such as male dominance are started, internalized, and perpetuated.

NOTES

1. Research, conducted over a thirteen-month period with forty-five employed women and their families, was sponsored by a fellowship from the Ford Foundation.

2. Beverly Chinas, *The Isthmus Zapotecs: Women's Roles in Cultural Context* (New York: Holt, Rinehart & Winston, 1973), p. 99; Phyllis Kaberry, *Women of the Grass Fields: A Study of the Economic Position of Women in Bambenda, British Cameroons* (London: Her Majesty's Stationery Office 1952), p. 300; Peggy Sunday, "Toward a Theory of the Status of Women," *American Anthropologist*

75 (October 1973): 1682-1700. For a study of the United States, see Lois Hoffman, "Parental Power Relations and the Division of Household Tasks," in *The Employed Mother in America* (Chicago: Rand McNally & Co., 1963).

3. Ernestine Friedl, *Women and Men: An Anthropologist's View* (New York: Holt, Rinehart & Winston, 1975), p. 7.

4. See Laws of Montserrat (Montserrat: Government of Montserrat, 1962).

5. For more information on family studies in the Caribbean, see M. G. Smith, *West Indian Family Structure* (Seattle: University of Washington Press, 1962); R. T. Smith, "Culture and Social Structure in the Caribbean: Some Recent Work on Family Kinship Studies," in *Black Society in the New World*, ed. Richard Frucht (New York: Random House, 1971), pp. 251-72; and Sidney Mintz and William Davenport, "Working Papers in Caribbean Social Organization," *Social and Economic Studies* vol. 10, no. 4 (1961).

6. Lloyd Braithewaite, "Social Stratification in Trinidad," *Social and Economic Studies*, vol. 2 and 3, nos. 2 and 3 (1953); and M. G. Smith, "The Plural Framework of Jamaican Society," in *Slaves, Free Men and Citizens*, ed. Lambros Comitas and David Lowenthal (Camden City, N.J.: Doubleday & Co., Anchor Books, 1972), pp. 174-93.

7. Judith Blake, *Family Structure in Jamaica* (New York: Free Press, 1961); Stuart Philpott, *West Indian Migration: the Montserrat Case* (New York: Athlone Free Press, 1973); and Nancy J. Pollock, "Women and the Division of Labor: A Jamaican Example," *American Anthropologist* 74, no. 2 (1972): 689-92.

8. Interview with the chief statistical officer for Montserrat, Richard Douthwaite, March 1973.

9. Richard Frucht ("A Caribbean Social Type: Neither 'Peasant' nor 'Proletarian,'" in *Black Society in the New World*) reports similar activity for the nearby island of Nevis. See also Nancy Foner (*Status and Power of Rural Jamaica* [New York: Teachers College Press, 1972], p. 211) for a study of such values in a rural Jamaican village.

10. A social security system was started on the island in 1972, but it is still in its infancy and does not provide adequate support for the aged yet.

11. "Sweet man" refers to men who are lovers, men who love a lot of women and move on to the next: a kind of "ladies' man."

12. See Philpott (n. 7 above).

13. For data on black women in the United States, see Joyce Aschenbrenner, *Lifelines: Black Families in Chicago* (New York: Holt, Rinehart & Winston, 1975); and Carol B. Stack "Sex Role and Survival Strategies in an Urban Black Community," in *Women, Culture and Society*, ed. Michelle Zimbalist Rosaldo and Louise Lamphere (Stanford, Calif: Stanford University Press, 1974), pp. 113-28. For data on Navajo women, see Louise Lamphere, "Strategies Cooperation and Conflict among Women in Domestic Groups"

in ibid., pp. 97-112. See Chinas (n. 2 above) on women in Mexico. See also Nancie Solien Gonzalez, "Toward a Definition of Matrifocality," in *Afro-American Anthropology*, ed. Norman Whitten and John Szwed (New York: Free Press, 1970), pp. 231-43; Michael Young and Peter Willmont, *Family and Kinship in East London* (New York: Penguin Books, Pelican Books, 1962).

14. Elliot Liebow, *Talley's Corner* (Boston: Little, Brown & Co., 1967); Ulf Hannerz, *Soulside: Enquiries into Ghetto Culture and Community* (New York: Columbia University Press, 1969); Peter Wilson, "Caribbean Crews: Peer Groups and Male Society," *Caribbean Studies* 10, nos. 3-4 (1971): 18-34; and Robert Dirks, "Networks, Groups and Adaptation in an Afro-Caribbean Community," *Man* 7, no. 4 (1972): 568-85.

15. Elizabeth Bott, *Family and Social Network*, 2d ed. (New York: Free Press, 1972); Gonzalez; Yolanda Murphy and Robert Murphy, *Women of the Forest* (New York: Columbia University Press, 1974); Stack (n. 13 above); Joyce A. Ladner, *Tomorrow's Tomorrow: The Black Woman* (New York: Doubleday & Co., 1971); and Aschenbrenner (n. 13 above).

16. See Bott.

A Maroon woman of Moore Town, Jamaica working on her farm. Photo:
Kenneth Bilby.

6

Economic Role and Cultural Tradition

Sidney W. Mintz*

The importance of women in the markets of the Guinea Coast has long been recognized, and it needs but a review of the literature of precolonial and colonial times, and no more than brief first-hand observation of the postcolonial scene, to establish their continued functioning in this capacity. The energy these women expend in carrying out these functions and the organized activity their work entails express the importance of their effort, both for themselves and for the economy as a whole...

There can be little question but that the power of economic motivation traditionally found in these societies accounts largely for the favorable economic position held by these women. In much, if not all the Guinea Coast countries of West Africa, a woman's earnings belong to her. During the late colonial and postcolonial period, in countries such as Nigeria and Ghana, for example, this fact had significant ramifications into noneconomic spheres. Support for the nationalist movements that were the instruments of political independence came in considerable measure from the donations of the marketwomen. It is also plain that their traditionally sanctioned economic position made it possible for them to adapt to innovations that were in the nature of continuities. Thus they seem easily to have grasped how credit, in the banking sense, could be a factor of importance in extending the scope of their dealings, after European currencies became the universal medium in effectuating exchanges. The extent of their adaptation in this case becomes apparent when we examine the relations between these women and the large European commercial enterprises, wherein some marketers are reported as

*See note, p. 532

having monthly credit ratings with these companies running into hundreds and even thousands of pounds sterling...

Should the new markets of eastern and southern Africa develop lines of sex division in buying and selling comparable to those which characterize the markets of the western and central parts of the continent, it seems likely that not only the economic position of women but their place in the social order in general may undergo change... With the growth of the African commercial sector, social implications of the persistence of these patterns of sex division of labor in the distributive process, or ways in which they may be strengthened, have implications that go far beyond the field of economics (Herskovits 1962:x-xiii).

In an earlier paper (Mintz 1971), I suggested that the relationship between economic sex-role differentiation and status has special implications in situations where change is rapid—that is, in those contexts in which "modernization" has involved a deeper penetration of local economies by world economic forces. In such cases, so-called "Western" norms may be superimposed upon traditional patterns of the division of labor along sexual lines, with serious consequences for the relationships between men and women. Thus in West Africa, contrary to Herskovits' optimistic view cited above, for instance, the growth of the market economy may actually reduce the prerogatives available to females, even where commercial activities have traditionally rested in the hands of women, and even when such activities may increase in absolute terms. In general, deeper penetration of local economies by powerful external forces may be expected to stimulate economic activity outside the retail sector even more than within that sector—so that markets for labor, land, and capital generally grow far more in relative importance than does the retail sector itself. Moreover, the opportunities for gain within the retail sector are likely to attract men, even into lines of commerce formerly monopolized by women (Katzin 1964). Hence "modernization" of the Western sort may lead to significant retrogressive changes in the status of women, even if the ideological apparatus of Western society pays constant lipservice to civil equality, the rights of individuals, "free enterprise" and other familiar ideals associated with the early history of European capitalism. The egalitarian ideology itself was produced, in the case of the West, by social and economic processes very different from those which mark the precontact histories of non-European societies.

Hence there is a possibility of serious discontinuity in certain contact situations involving the imposition of Western values, and this problem has probably not received as much serious attention as it may, in fact, deserve.

In my earlier paper, the bulk of cases relating sex role to economic activity were drawn from West Africa and from the non-Hispanic Caribbean—areas in which Africans (and in the Antilles, those of African origin) are numerically dominant. The positive local valuation of female economic activities in such regions cannot be attributed solely to local ecology or contemporary economic conditions as such, or to mere accident. Instead, we discover that the value placed on independent economic activity by women has a long and sturdy tradition behind it, and that this value is consonant with other aspects of the role of women, as well as with their positions in the social structures of the societies of which they are members. Boserup's statistics (1970:87-92), while admittedly imprecise, reveal the correlation between African (and Afro-American) women on the one hand, and trade on the other, in striking fashion. Thus, for instance, for three African states, Boserup offers us the following:

	All women in trade and commerce as percentage of:		Women trading on own account as percentage of all women in trade and commerce
	All adult women	Total labor force in trade and commerce	
Sierra Leone	3	47	75
Liberia	1	35	78
Ghana	15	80	94

The figures for the Caribbean are even less complete, but one may usefully contrast two such statistics provided by Boserup:

Puerto Rico	1	18	17
Jamaica*	6	65	unavailable

*urban areas only.

It is quite certain that, were the figures available, they would be even more striking in the case of such countries as Sénégal and Nigeria in West Africa, and Haiti in the case of the Caribbean. Puerto Rico, however, stands out in this array, since its statistics run wholly counter to the other cases; it has been included here just for this reason. To a substantial extent, the importance of women in trade is correlated with the region in question (as in West Africa and parts of Southeast Asia) and, presumably, with local values that encourage or facilitate this form of economic participation. In the Caribbean region—wholly colonized from abroad during the period 1492 to present—the correlation appears to be with a particular cultural tradition imported from elsewhere. Thus in Jamaica, Haiti, and many of the Lesser Antilles, where the population is predominantly of African origin, independent trading activities by women are important and highly valued. In the Hispanic Caribbean, however, (where, among other things, persons of African origin are less numerous), such activities are scarcely noticeable.

Boserup has sought to explain these differences:

> In Latin America, different cultural patterns are reflected in opposing attitudes to female participation in trade. In some countries with a predominantly Negro or Indian population, more women than men are in trade, while women account for less than 10 percent of the labor force in trade in countries on the Atlantic coast where Arab influence, transmitted through the Spanish upper class, has penetrated more deeply (Boserup 1970:91).

The difficulty with this argument is that it does not deal with the persisting importance of women in trade in West Africa, even in areas of considerable Moslem influence, as Boserup herself acknowledges (*ibid.*: 92). Thus, for instance, Le Cour Grandmaison (1969) has not only demonstrated that Moslem women play a vital role in the local trade of Dakar, but also that the Islamic prescription making the husband responsible for the support of his family serves to *reinforce*, rather than to reduce, the rights of women to use as they will their own marketing profits. While "Arab" ideology might be thought to "explain" why more women do not market in parts of Hispanic America, such reasoning fails utterly to handle what appear to be West African "exceptions." This argument may be pushed further since, in some African instances, even the seclusion of Moslem women has interdicted neither their trading activities nor their rights to their profits. A good example is provided by Hill (1969:308):

> Despite their virtual incarceration for the first 35 years of their married lives, the women of the *gari* [town] enjoy a considerable degree of economic independence—thus having somewhat more in common with their sisters in southern forest country than might be

supposed. Just as the economic relationship between fathers and sons (and between brothers) often involves cash transactions identical to those between non-kin, so it is between husbands and wives: thus, to take two examples, fathers pay their married sons in *gandu* [a form of economic cooperation between fathers and their married sons] for evening work on the farms, this being outside the range of their customary duties, and a husband will pay his wife at (or near) the standard rate for "threshing" groundnuts, her obligations being confined to domestic duties, mainly cooking. Just as fathers are apt to sell their farms to their sons, so a wife who makes groundnut oil for sale will pay her husband the proper "market price" for any groundnuts she buys from him. Although, of course, husbands and wives are apt to help each other in numerous different ways, a wife's economic autonomy is often sufficient to insulate her from her husband's poverty—as shown by the example of prominent house-traders whose husbands are notably poverty-stricken.

Appeals to one or another "cultural tradition" do not explain entirely the differential distribution of female trade, and its attached values. Continuities in certain traditions appear to be marked as well by serious discontinuities—discontinuities that cannot be handled as mere exceptions to some general rule. In the case of the Caribbean region, such discontinuities are historical as well as geographical, for those African traditions transmitted to the New World by the slaves passed through the crucible of plantation slavery, with corresponding reorganizations of both the behavior and the attached values of the slaves themselves (Mintz and Price 1976). This is by no means to say that African traditions were abandoned or forgotten in the New World; but they were inevitably subject to considerable change in the new situations in which the slaves found themselves.

In Jamaica and Haiti (Saint Domingue), the leading slave colonies of the Antilles, slaves were early enabled (or compelled) to produce much of their own subsistence on the peripheral lands of the plantations; and in both colonies, the slaves soon became purveyors of their surplus products in local marketplaces (for Jamaica, see Mintz and Hall 1960; for Haiti, see Mintz 1964). During the slavery periods in these two societies, however, there is no evidence that women predominated in marketing—in fact, the evidence suggests that men, or whole families, engaged in local market trade, while still enslaved. But in both of these societies, the end of slavery (by revolution in one case, and by emancipation in the other) led to an emergence of a class of predominantly female traders.

I hypothesize that freedom signified an opportunity for many male exslaves to acquire land in sufficient quantity so that they could devote themselves full-time to agricultural production. In other words, female domination of the marketplace trade may have been correlated in these cases with a new division of labor made possible by increased access to land. Such an hypothesis, however, does not "explain" the presence of female traders, any more than "Arab influence" can be used to "explain" their absence. Even where males are taken up with agricultural production, it does not follow automatically that women will become traders. Boserup writes: "Thus, in Southeast Asia we seem to have a basically 'female trade pattern' but, owing perhaps to Arab and Chinese influence, there is a belt of male trade running from North India and Pakistan through Malaysia to Western Indonesia. Within this belt, only one-tenth of the traders are women, as against one-half outside this belt" (Boserup 1970:91). "Arab and Chinese influence" or no, in this subregion male domination of agriculture does not lead inevitably to female domination of trade. Boserup reasons that "those regions where women dominate the food trade of rural and urban markets are usually the regions which are characterized by female farming traditions" (ibid.). This may be the case in West Africa—it is difficult to generalize—but it is emphatically not the case in the Afro-Caribbean, where trade by females seems better correlated with *male*-dominated agriculture.[1]

Thus, if one wishes to seek to analyze the trading patterns of Afro-Caribbean females by contrasts within and outside the region, it becomes clear that "values" as such are an inadequate explanation of these patterns, even while they undoubtedly played a part in the emergence of contemporary norms for the sexual division of labor. From the cultural perspective, we are dealing with situations in which the society at large—or, at least, substantial segments of it—acknowledges an equal economic status for women in local, culturally-prescribed terms. Métraux (1951:147) tells us that some Haitian farmers are left at such a loss by thier marketer wives' absence that they "fast stoically for two or three days" until their spouses return from market. In general, our own findings, partly supported by the work of others (e.g., Métraux 1951:120-126,

146-147), indicate that Haitian men are not prepared to insist that their wives forsake *any* trading activity at all, merely in order to fulfill their domestic obligations. For Africa, Le Cour Grandmaison and Hill both describe women whose commercial activities are far more successful than those of their husbands, and quite independent of them; Le Cour Grandmaison offers one instance of a highly successful *dakaroise* who employs her husband on salary (1969:150). Marshall, writing of the Yoruba of Awe, Nigeria, gives lively instances of trade relationships between husband and wife that are in no way confused with (nor substituted for) the noncommercial aspects of the relationship (Marshall 1964:187-188).

In all of these instances, in fact, we are dealing with societies concerning which, for our purposes, it probably makes more sense to think of the rights of individuals, in terms of age, sex, kinship group, and other bases of social assortment, than to limit ourselves to the category of the rights of men or women. The Haitian *habitant* who fasts while his wife is at market (or who cooks his own food) plainly does not perceive this situation as one in which his status as an adult, husband, father, male, or otherwise is at stake. To put it differently, cultural prescriptions do not permit the male individual to interpret his temporary inconvenience as a status deprivation; women are *supposed* to market, and men to fend for themselves meanwhile. Similarly, the husband employed by the *dakaroise* Awa G. presumably does not perceive her economic success as his failure, at least not in terms of male-female differences. Such examples may be easily multiplied; we draw a final case from the commentary of an American visitor, "J.B.," to the Republic of Haiti in 1854. The writer was invited to the baptism of a house owned by one of the leading women merchants of Port-au-Prince, and he has described the relationship between the hostess, called "Elsiné," and her consort, "Emilien," in a revealing fashion:

> Elsiné—I name her first because she was the head of the house—was a wide-awake, intelligent, amiable and well-conditioned black woman, about forty years of age; Emilien, her faithful consort, was not near as intelligent, nor quite as fat, nor quite as tall, nor quite as dignified as Elsiné ... His whole heart was evidently in the gaiety of the occasion, and his whole dependence for his enjoyment of it, seemed to repose upon the administrative talents of his better half. Their relations to each other and to the public, though not peculiar

here, need a brief explanation, to be intelligible to American readers. She is the capitalist of the concern, owns all the property, and does all the business. He has no more to do with the direction of affairs, in or out of the house, than if he were her child. She is worth from fifteen to twenty thousand dollars, all of which she has made as a dealer in provisions.

Elsiné began her commercial career in the market without any money; by gradual accumulations she got some capital ahead, and now buys from the commission merchants in large quantities, and sells on credit to retail dealers—mostly to girls whom she has trained, and upon whose business she keeps a careful eye. Her monthly purchases, I understand, average about $8,000 a month, and though neither she nor her husband can read or write a line, she has an unlimited credit—that is, any merchant in Port au Prince would be glad to trust her all they could induce her to buy ... Besides this house, she owns all the other houses on the block, and is building all the time. When I was informed of all these evidences of female enterprise and success, I very naturally inquired what might be her husband's function, and why he was such a silent partner in the connubial firm. The reply which I received revealed to me a glimpse of one of the 'peculiar institutions' of the country. Elsiné and her companion-at-arms are not married, but in conformity with the practice of the country, sanctioned by law, they are *placéed*,, as it is termed. This is a temporary marriage, determinable at the will of the parties, and the offspring from which, inherit as heirs-at-law. I mention the usage now, to explain what appear to me a strange inversion of the ordinary relations of husband and wife. They have been *placéed,* a long time, but have never married, because she thought Emilien made a much better lover than husband; in other words, she did not think him competent to manage her business, and she did not care, therefore, to place herself or her property irretrievably in his power. Emilien appeared perfectly conscious of his inferiority, and as contented with the narrow sphere of connubial duty assigned him, as a prince-consort to the mightiest Queen in Christendom (J.B. 1854).[2]

We cite this lengthy passage, in part because it reveals nearly as much about the cultural values of the observer as it does about those of the observed. That the male should have no say in the economic affairs of the female is perceived by this Westerner as "a strange inversion of the ordinary relations of husband and wife"; the male is depicted as "conscious of his inferiority," and yet proud and contented. But it should be perfectly apparent that the male's "inferiority" in this instance is, at worst, far less demonstrable than that of most females in Western society who, in their "ordinary" family relations, may neither participate in their husbands' businesses nor engage in their own. That "J.B." should read as "a strange inversion" what is, in fact, a much more equal relationship than that typical of his own society is not surprising, given the dominant tone of male-female relationships in the West.

These various cases point up some special valuation of female economic roles and particularly an acknowledged right of the female to economic *independence* are of special interest because they implicate no corresponding loss of status for the male. They reveal that Western conceptions of male "integrity," "dignity," "pride," and "worth" are much more deeply imbedded in notions of male economic dominance than may be generally widely recognized. They also suggest that the supplantation of such non-Western values by Western values may, in some cases, eventuate in a regressive social direction for women—or, at any rate, for some women.

The point here is, first of all, whether a given society regards a substantial and publicly recognized economic contribution by the female spouse as "normal," "natural," desirable, and appropriate; and secondly, whether the rewards of that economic contribution are regarded as properly accruing to the woman herself, rather than to some other member of her group, as an individual or as an executor of group wealth. Both of these points plainly have to do with local conceptions of the kinship group, especially with its internal organization of statuses and roles, and the accompanying values. The particular composition of such kinship groups must be analyzed according to our understanding of their *internal* allocations of authority, resources, and prerogatives, especially the charter of rights and duties as applying to men and women. A very brief comparison of two Caribbean cases, the first Hispano-Caribbean and the second Afro-Caribbean, may help me to enumerate certain differences.

The first case is that of Puerto Rico, the data based on the research of Eric Wolf (1956) in a peasant community in the interior. The field work was completed thirty years ago, and the details cannot be generalized in any sense to Puerto Rican rural society at large; yet the case provides a striking contrast to the non-Hispanic Caribbean. Wolf notes that the keystone of peasant productivity is the low cost of labor within the family. The economic tasks of the family are carried out by family members; the family is an indivisible unit, economically, and there are no payments of cash among family members for work done. If a dependent child is paid for work done outside the family, the money must go to his father. The father, as family head, disposes of all of the family resources; in fact, he is in a position to sell the labor of his dependent children, or to dispose of their labor within the traditional labor exchanges of the peasant community. Among the peasants of whom Wolf writes, he discusses with special care that subgroup consisting of smallholders who cultivate ten *cuerdas* (approximately 4 hectares) or less. Such small-scale peasants cultivate tobacco and coffee for sale, as well as many subsistence crops, but hardly anything to be sold locally. In other words, these peasants produce one or two cash crops for sale to the world market, and much of their own food, but do not participate significantly in any system of local sale of commodities. They depend above all upon family labor; more and more, local outmigration has made it difficult to employ others, at the same time that many of them must seek wage payments elsewhere themselves, in order to supplement their own limited productivity. Family labor is hence heavily engaged in production on the limited land available, with the father as executive. On one *cuerda* (ca. 4/10 hectares) of tobacco land, Wolf determined that a male might invest as much as thirty-eight to thirty-nine days of labor; yet at the same time his wife might invest between forty-eight to fifty-four days of labor. In other words, the family commitment of effort, as managed by the father-husband, varies for each family member, and the quantity of work of the wife-member is fixed by her spouse according to his estimate of what is required.

In this milieu, the economic rights and privileges of the wife-mother are intimately tied to the status and role of the husband-father as head of the family enterprise. We take account of a situation in which there is what we would call one single structure of risk, and one center only of authority. The wife must prepare all of her husband's meals, even though they do not eat together. When they go elsewhere together, the wife follows behind her husband. Of course the wife may not attend festivals or dances by herself, or other than in the company of her husband. Wolf's description is precise: "Her status is tied to that of her husband. Her standing is judged according to the possessions which he owns and the treatment he accords her...A woman does not acquire any rights to assert herself directly in her own behalf until she is beyond the child-bearing period" (1956:223). It may be worth adding to this description that the husband has the right to insist that his wife *bathe him* weekly, and that she wash his feet daily! To which one may say that the differences between this situation and that typical of peasant Haiti are absolutely staggering.

In the Haitian situation, the husband-father's control of family labor is much less sweeping, at least today. The fundamental expression of this difference lies in the woman's wholly recognized entitlement to independent trading activity. "African usage," writes Herskovits (1973:258), "has here been reinforced by the historical fact of Haitian political instability. The fact that the proceeds from trading belong to the woman who does the trading, and that in consequence women are encountered who, though married, command independent means and exercise full control over their resources, is a carry-over of African tradition and, as in Africa, this gives women a position in the economic world quite foreign to conventional European practice." While we may ponder with some doubt Herskovits' description of "reinforced" African usage, the fact is that a sexual division of labor that acknowledges and validates women's independent roles in commerce typifies Haitian peasant life, and comparable expressions of female economic independence occur even in urban bourgeois segments of the Haitian population.

Peasant wives and *placées* can and do carry out agricultural tasks; a very complete list of tasks by sex is provided by Métraux (1951:89-91), and women are not by definition exempted from most agricultural labor, even hoeing. But, in fact, the husband's claims on his wife's or *placée's* labor are powerfully qualified by her own enterprises, and most Haitian peasant women vastly prefer trade to agricultural work. We lack adequate detail on the division of authority along sexual lines among Haitian peasants. Simpson (1942:662) claims that "the husband's caprices have the force of law in the peasant family. His wife or *placée* must give him unquestioning obedience." Our own impressions are radically different, particularly insofar as the sphere of economic activity is concerned. It is of some interest, then, that Simpson goes on to say: "However, because of the knowledge which she has gained in her trading contacts with the villages and towns, the woman is more practical than the man, and she acts as the treasurer of the family" (*ibid.*)— hardly convincing evidence of the crushing authority of the male. "A peasant will often say he has no money in the house", adds Simpson, "when the truth is that he does not wish to do business without his wife or *placée.*" These and similar comments suggest that the male-female division of authority is much more complex among Haitian peasants than among Puerto Rican peasants—or, at least, that male authority is substantially more qualfied in the case of peasant Haiti.

The cultural origins of the majority of Haitian rural folk are in large measure African, as we have already suggested, while those of the majority of Puerto Ricans are predominantly Hispanic. Of course elements from many other traditions enter into the contemporary cultures of both groups: Amerindian in the case of Puerto Rico, for instance (and to some degree in the case of Haiti as well), African in the case of Puerto Rico (though to a much lesser degree than in Haiti). It needs to be recalled that the western third of Santo Domingo (French Saint Domingue) only became a French colony in 1697, and received its strongest impulse to growth in the ensuing century, during which time perhaps 850,000 African slaves were imported (Curtain 1969:79), while the European population remained relatively small.

The Revolution, begining in 1791, eliminated the bulk of non-Africans, and the subsequent century of virtual isolation facilitated the consolidation of a culture that was in good measure African in origin. In Puerto Rico, on the other hand, though African slaves were present almost from the moment of Spanish domination, the numbers of slaves always remained very small relative to the population of European freemen (many of whom were part Indian in origin). Moreover, Puerto Rico remained Spanish from the Conquest until the North American occupation in 1899; during almost exactly four hundred years of continuous Spanish rule, it acquired a cultural character that might fairly be described as much more European (Hispanic) than anything else. Thus one could perhaps argue that, with regard to the economic role of women, at least, such differences find their origins in a difference between the values of West African and Southern European cultures, without taking account of immediate economic, ecological and other factors. This is, indeed, the way Herskovits has appeared to argue, for instance, in the quotation cited earlier, and as Boserup has argued in discussing "Arab" and "Chinese" influences upon the sexual division of labor. In our opinion, such a view does not explain enough. Within Puerto Rico itself, for instance, data on rural proletarian groups (cf. Mintz 1953, 1956) reveal sharp contrasts with the Puerto Rican peasant materials collected by Wolf, and these contrasts do not lend themselves to explanation in terms of different ancestral values. Rather, they seem to suggest that specific local conditions have had their differentiating effects upon traditional patterns of behavior.

In other words, it seems to us necessary to distinguish between those characteristics of a particular situation that express the acceptable limits of variability of behavior at one point in time, and the values, beliefs and attitudes of the local population—an ideological assemblage, so to speak, ultimately attributable to forces in the past. The Puerto Rican peasant woman who dutifully washes the feet of her husband does not do so *because* he completely controls the labor resources and wealth of the family—rather, the economic domination of the husband furnishes the context within which this custom is permitted to survive. Again, the Haitian peasant husband does not make his own dinner *because* his wife is the independent head of her own enterprise—rather, that economic independence furnishes the context within which he finds it expectable and acceptable to be required to do so.

Thus there is not, in my view, some single simple formula according to which one can resolve the problem of the association of a particular value or item of behavior with a particular society or social group. Generally speaking, we are still unable confidently to assign a precise estimate of importance to specific contemporary economic conditions, on the one hand, or to specific historical traditions, on the other, in attempting to "explain" the presence or absence of some mode of behavior. Instead, we are required to state as fully as we can the conditions imposed by ecological, economic and other factors, within which family structures, models of intrafamilial authority, and notions of status and role, of obligations and rights, of values, take on their characteristic forms. In each specific instance a set of values and attitudes is expressed in behavior, but particular conditions may serve to facilitate that expression, or to hamper or modify it. We have only a vague idea of the ways older values maintain themselves in the face of new pressures, when change does (or does not) occur.[3]

Hence, we are left with the important problem of determining as best we can why Haitian rural women enjoy so wide a field of economic maneuver while their Puerto Rican sisters are correspondingly deprived of all significant access to economic independence. Though various economic factors undoubtedly played a crucial role in the evolution of Haitian marketing, and probably in determining its absence in Puerto Rico, I remain unconvinced that these factors fully account for the preeminence of women in Haitian commerce. At the same time, I suspect any *direct* reference to West Africa for the explanation of the Haitian case, not only because the slaves were drawn from many different African societies and because slavery itself intervened between the African past and the postrevolutionary present, but also because we lack evidence that women played a paramount role in Haitian marketing during the period of slavery itself.

Cultural traditions do not merely reassert themselves unmodified after long intervals; and one may reasonably doubt whether any Haitian freemen in 1804 carried about in their heads an ideal image of women as marketers. Herskovits (1937) and others (Leyburn 1941) have suggested that women emerged as marketers after the Haitian revolution because the periodic warring and forced conscription typical of Haitian life after 1804 made rural men wary of towns, so that women perforce became the intermediaries. Yet women also became the intermediaries in Jamaica after Emancipation (1838), when internal peace was undisturbed. Ottenberg, writing of the Nigerian Afikpo Ibo, tells us that *men* are the principal marketers in that society precisely because of the previous absence of internal peace! Neither the Jamaican nor the Ibo case, in other words, can be wholly explained by this argument. In both Haiti and Jamaica, however, it was only after the end of slavery that rural males were able to acquire their own land, as I have already indicated, and this doubtless had something to do with the emerging pattern of female marketing. This assertion, however, fails to "explain" the pattern; as we have seen, there are of course many places in the modern world where men have land but women do *not* market, Puerto Rico being only one of them.

Can one go any further than this in attempting to clarify the Haitian case? I believe so, but only by invoking a general principle for which there is no specific evidence as yet in the case of Haiti. The real question, perhaps, is not that of the tasks men and women may do, but the psychological significance of this division, in terms of the comparative status of members of the other sex. As I have sought to explain, it is not so much a matter of what men or women can do—but rather of what they do do without endangering the social status of their opposite numbers. Haitian peasant males are plainly not diminished, but elevated, by their wives' economic success. In contrast, it seems quite likely that Puerto Rican peasant males are diminished by an *independent* economic activity on the part of their wives—the question of success or failure cannot even rise to the surface. What, then, in the history of Haitian (and Jamaican) peasant life might explain the thoroughgoing acceptance of independent economic roles for women, other than simply the acquisition of more land by the men, and the harking back to a "tradition" separated from the aftermath of slavery by a century or more of radically different life conditions?

I think that the answer is of a culture-historical order—that is, that one may explain the present by reference to some aspect of the past—but not in terms of culturally defined male-female differences as such. The emergence of women as marketers in Jamaica and Haiti presumably did not represent a radical change in the relative statuses of men and women, though the success of women as marketers may eventually have contributed to a relative improvement of feminine status. I find it difficult not to suppose that the ease with which Jamaican and Haitian market women were able to dominate trading activities was related to their spouses' views of themselves (according to local conceptions of masculine status), and not only to their views of their wives. In the Afro-Caribbean as in West Africa, the social manipulation of those values enabling women to function in independent economic fashion apparently represented no problem to the effective functioning of traditional kinship groups or sex-based status attributions. And while it may be argued that, in the West African case, this was possible because of far-flung kinship networks limiting the primary family to a very minor role, such an argument (if it had any merit at all) certainly would not make sense for the Afro-Caribbean. The central question, we believe, continues to be not whether the kin group can function when women's economic activities have grown as important as men's—the answer is, of course, "yes"—but whether men can accept women's independent participation in a different risk structure without feeling threatened *as men*. Obviously there is expressed in this view the now-familiar association between female submission to male economic domination on the one hand, and the view of women as property on the other. Such an association should be of more than passing interest when we reflect that, in Haitian and Jamaican societies, slaves of both sexes were viewed as property by their masters, and won the right to independent economic activity as slaves only because such activity was ultimately profitable to the masters, as well as to the slaves themselves. We are very far from understanding the "personalities" of Haitian and Jamaican slave men and women on the eve of freedom. Yet it would not surprise us to discover that regard for *individual* prerogatives in these groups was at least as strong as that for the prerogatives of males as against females—given the fact that slavery itself had not always made it possible for male slaves to assert "paterfamilial" domination over female slaves.

Hence, I am seeking to suggest that it may have been partly in the experience of slavery itself that Jamaican and Haitian males found the capacity to tolerate female autonomy, while Jamaican and Haitian females were finding the capacity to exercise that autonomy—eventually in ways remarkably consistent with those of their West African sisters. Such a view is not intended to slight the force of the African past in the lives of Caribbean peoples of African origin; but it does raise a question about assertions of uninterrupted continuities with that past, surviving unchanged through slavery, as if cultural traditions were not responsive even to radically changed life conditions. My suggestion does not, of course, explain why marketing by women develops in some societies and not in others; nor does it assign differential weight to the variables that probably affect such emergence. From a historical point of view, it might be useful to amass whatever commentary is available for these two societies, on relations between male and female slaves, and for the free rural peoples of these societies thereafter. We are quite unable at present to specify any steps by which female marketing gradually became the rule in these societies, or to relate such steps to prevailing attitudes about male and female roles. Thus the case continues to rest largely on surmise and assumption, rather than on hard data, either ethnographic or historical.

To sum up, the various West African patterns of sexual division of labor were probably profoundly modified under slavery in the Caribbean region. However, in situations where slaves were compelled or permitted to grow their own subsistence, as in Jamaica and Saint-Domingue, slave family groups of some kind apparently engaged in this practice, and slave family units also participated in the marketing of agricultural surpluses. While some of the related tasks may indeed have been restricted to one or the other sex, our descriptions indicate that men and women both cultivated and marketed. After freedom, however, female-dominated marketing rapidly developed in these Afro-Caribbean societies, in marked contrast to the Hispanic Caribbean (Puerto Rico, Cuba, and Santo Domingo). The emergence of such female-dominated marketing was probably related, on the one hand, to the acquisition of larger amounts of agricultural land by the freemen, requiring their fuller commitment to agricultural labor.

But acquisition of more land by males could not be expected to result in female domination of trade, if such domination were to run counter to male values and male prestige notions in the society in question. In other words, we hypothesize that independent economic activity by females in these societies was not only concordant with new agricultural conditions, but also not discordant with existing male-female relationships. Posed this way, our "explanation" becomes no less "historical" on the one hand, and no less "functional" on the other. Nor do we discount the possible significance of cultural continuities with the African past, though our view of such continuities may share little with older conceptions of this kind. The massing of historical data on male and female attitudes among slaves (and, later, freemen) in these societies of the sort recounted by "J.B.," could conceivably allow us to sharpen our assertions or to set them aside if they do not, in fact, explain adequately.

In the absence of more information, it may appear that we leave off not far from where we began. And yet this exercise may not be entirely in vain. The fact is that West African and Afro-Caribbean societies have been able, in some contexts, to achieve sexual equality still quite unheard-of in Western societies, for all of their vaunting of individual freeedom. The independence and authority exercised by a West African or Haitian market woman in regard to her uses of her own capital, or in regard to the economic influence of her husband, has few parallels in the Western world, where individual prerogatives are commonly seen as flowing from individual *male* wealth, embedded in a nuclear family organization. With histories radically different from those of the Caribbean and West Africa, Europe and America have busily exported doctrines of equality rooted in their own past—their own primary-family, monogamous, male-property past. Meanwhile, West Africa and the Afro-Caribbean, influenced so profoundly and for so long by European power and domination, have demonstrated a version of equality in some population sectors that European societies, with their quite basic view of *women as property*, neither understand nor accept.

The day may yet come when the contribution of black women to the perpetuation of their respective societies will be recognized; it is still far off. Further off still, perhaps, is the recognition that African and Afro-American societies have contributed a good deal more to a vision of individual equality transcending sexual chauvinism than has the West itself.

*Thanks go to Melle Françoise Morin and to Jacqueline W. Mintz for helpful criticisms of an earlier draft of this paper.

NOTES

1. I have dealt with this matter at somewhat greater length in Mintz and Price, 1976.

2. The writer is grateful to Prof. Joseph Boromé for calling his attention to this unusual report.

3. It would be useful to compare the development of marketing institutions and the roles of men and women in these institutions throughout Afro-America. Such an exercise might help us to assess somewhat more precisely the importance of antecedent values in affecting the ways new institutions develop, in this case. Among the factors that would enter into this comparison would be: African traditions of female marketing; African traditions of economic autonomy for spouses; the role of slavery in levelling and homogenizing the sexual division of labor; the allocation of marketing roles, if any, under slavery; the Spanish pattern of male dominance in economic life as in all else; the role of internal strife in affecting the sexual division of labor; and, finally, ideal role-models for slave men and

women in each society. Needless to add, a complete picture of these factors will probably never be possible; but assembling the relevant data might prove useful and revealing, nonetheless.

REFERENCES:

Boserup, E. *Women's Role in Economic Development*. London: Geo. Allen and Unwin, 1970.

Curtin, Philip. *The Atlantic Slave Trade*. Madison: University of Wisconsin Press, 1969.

Herskovits, M. J. "Preface" to Bohannan, P. and G. Dalton (eds.), *Markets in Africa*. Evanston: Northwestern University Press, 1962 pp. vii-xvi.

Hill P. "Hidden Trade in Hausaland." *Man*, (1969) 4:392-409.

J. B. "Notes of a Tour in Haiti." *The Evening Post*, Vol. LIII (Friday, 19 May 1854), p. 1.

Katzin, M. "The Role of the Small Entrepreneur." in Herskovits, M., and M. Harwitz (eds.), *Economic Transition in Africa*. Evanston: Northwestern University Press, 1964. pp. 179-198.

Le Cour Grandmaison C. "Activités économiques des femmes dakaroises." *Africa*, XXXIX: (1969) 138-52.

Leyburn, James A. *The Haitian People*. New Haven: Yale University Press, 1941.

Marshall, G. A. "Women Trade and the Yoruba Family." Ph.D. Dissertation, Columbia University, 1964.

Metraux, A. *Making a Living in the Marbial Valley (Haiti)*. UNESCO Occasional Papers in Education 10. Paris, 1951.

Mintz, Sidney W. "The Folk-Urban Continuum, and the Rural Proletarian Community." *American Journal of Sociology* 59 (1953) 2:136-143.

——— "Cañamelar: The Subculture of a Rural Sugar Plantation Proletariat." in Steward, J.H., *et al.*, *The People of Puerto Rico*. Urbana: University of Illinois Press, 1956. pp. 314-317.

——— "The Employment of Capital by Haitian Market Women" in Firth, R. and Yamey, B (eds.), *Capital, Saving and Credit in Peasant Society*. Chicago: Aldine Publishing Co., 1964. pp. 256-86.

——— "Men, Women and Trade," *Comparative Studies in Society and History*, 13 (1971) 2:247-269.

Mintz, S. W. and D. Hall "The Origins of the Jamaican Internal Marketing Pattern." *Yale University Publications in Anthropology*, 57, 1960.

Mintz, S. W. and Rice. Price. *An Anthropological Approach to the Afro-American Past: A Caribbean Perspective*. Philadelphia: ISHI Occasional Papers in Social Change, 2, 1977.

Ottenberg, Phoebe. "The Changing Economic Position of Women among the Afikpo Ibo." in Bascom, W., and M. Herskovits (eds.), *Continuity and*

Change in African Cultures. Chicago: University of Chicago Press, 1959.
Simpson, George E. "Sexual and Familial Institutions in Haiti." *American Anthropologist* 44 (1942) 4:655-674.
Wolf, Eric R. "San José: Subcultures of a Traditional Coffee Municipality." in Steward, J. H., et al., *The People of Puerto Rico.* Urbana: University of Illinois Press, 1956, pp. 171-264.

7

The Black Woman in Haitian Society and Literature

Régine Latortue

I HISTORICAL BACKGROUND: THE HAITIAN WOMAN IN SOCIETY

Before launching into discussion of the black woman in Haitian literature, it is necessary to examine the structure of Haitian society. It is clear that women of different classes and social strata have different problems and concerns which are reflected in literature accordingly. When social gaps are as wide as they are in Haiti, there is definitely a certain level of specificity which needs to be defined. Thus, we will find the modern upper-class woman more affected by the feminist movement than the rural, peasant woman who does not perceive her oppression as stemming from her sex, but, rather, from her class. A theory which has been put forward, and which was repeatedly rehashed at a conference on "Women and Development",[1] proposes that in the so-called underdeveloped or Third World countries, the higher a woman stands on the social ladder, the more oppressed she finds herself as a woman. In the lower classes, women are oppressed certainly, but not necessarily as women. They are oppressed by other factors.

Today, the Haitian population numbers roughly five million and falls primarily into two classes: the elite or upper class, which represents less than 10 percent of the population,[2] and the mass or working class, which comprises the peasants and the urban proletariat. There is also a middle-class minority composed of the various shopkeepers and tradesmen of the towns, who ally themselves with the elite, though they are regarded by the latter as socially inferior.

Women of the Working class

Let us now take a closer look at the way of life led by women of various classes. The differences are striking, and there is really no indication that the gaps will ever be filled.

In Haiti, working-class women represent more than half of the country's total population.[3] Jean Price-Mars, the eminent Haitian ethnologist, notes that in 1917, in the department of the North[4] alone, there were twice as many women as men.[5] Yet, at that time, women had practically no legal or political rights. The judicial system of Haiti was still operating under the old-fashioned *Code Civil* established by Napoléon Bonaparte in 1825, which had no relevance to the Haitian reality. It was not until 1944 that changes were made, giving some legal rights to the married working woman, and still today the role that women are allowed to play in performing their civic and political duties, is minimal[6].

The peasant woman has an especially hard burden to bear. As Price-Mars so rightly points out, in a country where technology is still a foreign concept, where cultivation of the land is still conducted at a very fundamental level, and where the ordinary peasant cannot afford a pair of sturdy horses or cows to till his soil, the peasant's woman is his best instrument of work, his most valuable one: his "beast of burden," so to speak. Of course, the peasant—the man, the master,—takes it upon himself to do what he considers to be the most difficult part of the job: the clearing of the land:[7] work which he does with the help of his neighbors. All the men join to form a *coumbite*,[8] and work together accompanied by songs and drumming. Even then the women, do not remain idle. They must prepare huge meals to satisfy the appetite of the working men.

Other than clearing the land, the rest of the work is considered to be solely the woman's concern: sowing, harvesting, transporting the produce to the market, and finally selling it. She must also clean the hut, wash, iron, cook, shop, and feed and care for her children who are often quite numerous. Consequently, it is not difficult to assess the amount of work which falls to the Haitian peasant woman, whose resignation and placid attitude toward life has often been criticized. Her contributions provide the peasant man with a security which he could hardly find without her. It is equally easy to understand why the peasant man often accommodates himself with more than one woman. This would assure him, if he has more than one plantation, one working woman on each plantation.

The problems facing the peasant and rural women are even more acute when one takes into consideration that the arable land in Haiti is progressively becoming barren, due to erosion, and to the fact that no effective measures are being taken to stop the erosion and irrigate the soil. As mentioned earlier, technology and its benefits are still quite foreign to Haiti, and the land is cultivated according to old-fashioned methods which accelerate its deterioration. Moreover, the rural population suffers from malnutrition and is almost completely without medical services. There is approximately one doctor available per 44,000 inhabitants in the rural areas as opposed to one doctor per 6,000 in the cities.[9]

At first sight, in the cities the situation seems a little less appalling—a fact which has prompted a heavy migration of rural women to cities. The cities are totally unprepared for this influx. The migration pattern is directed primarily toward the capital, Port-au-Prince, and women who are lured to the city, out of hope or despair, find that the situation in Port-au-Prince does not offer many more advantages than in the rural areas. In the city, the women become part of the urban proletariat, and this change, which some economists insist on calling "development," is not much more satisfying. However, the city does offer certain fringe benefits such as education—tradition maintains that the earnings of the working-class woman must go to the care of her children—and better medical care. The city is unable to accommodate all the working-class women who often fall prey—especially the young ones—to a life of prostitution, unless they are lucky enough to make a happy "plaçage."[10] "Plaçage" is very often the rule for the working-class woman, and it frees men from their legal responsibilities toward their children, so that the care of the children becomes solely woman's business.

In the cities then, rural women usually become factory-workers or the servants of the elite. In the elite class, which is influenced by the former colonizers' way of life, marriage is the norm. Husbands (government officials, businessmen, doctors, lawyers, teachers and so forth) leave the business of the running of the household entirely to their wives. Daily contact with the servants or "bonnes" is confined primarily to the upper-class woman. The "bonnes" are expected to clean the house, take care of the laundry, shop, cook, and care for the children of the household, for an average salary of ten dollars per month. In addition, the servants still have to perform these same services for their own family. Sometimes they are provided with lodging, in the servants' quarters, which present a striking contrast to the employer's house. A live-in arrangement is a convenience for both employer and employee. The employee does not have to worry about finding her own lodging and commuting to work, and the employer benefits from round-the clock availability.

The working-class woman is perhaps able to earn a better living in the cities than in the rural areas. However, in this exchange, there can be a loss of self-pride. At least as a peasant she had the illusion of working for herself, an illusion which can no longer be maintained in the urban situation. The upper-class woman, who daily orders and closely supervises her "bonne's" work, thus becomes the concrete, visible symbol of the servant's oppression. This explains why there is no strong, honest feeling of solidarity among Haitian women per se—a fact which is deplored by many leading women anthropologists and economists. The working-class woman is oppressed by men and women of the elite *and* by men of her own class.

The Bourgeoise: Women of the elite

The *bourgeoise*, or upper-class woman in Haiti, generally does not have to worry about her daily bread. But she is oppressed by a series of rules and social traditions which are extremely difficult to break.

As a young girl, she is strictly kept in check by her parents, and receives an education which rarely helps to broaden her horizons. The educational system of Haiti does not allow one to question, but simply to memorize, the teachings of acknowledged scholars. Memorization is stressed more than comprehension, and the emphasis is on form rather than substance or content. A student is not encouraged to think or to take up individual projects.

A single girl living alone is a rarity. Such a situation, if it should arise, would create a scandal and cause the certain loss of reputation. So the young *bourgeoise* remains home until marriage. Upon marrying, she falls under the guardianship of her husband which can often be more constraining than that of her parents. Once divorced or widowed, the upper-class woman becomes a victim of public opinion and must be extremely careful not to jeopardize her reputation.

The legal system of Haiti is flagrantly favourable to men. The *Code Civil* of 1934, which has undergone certain amendments, plainly states that a wife owes obedience to her husband and that he owes her protection. Adultery, in the case of the woman, is punishable no matter where it has been committed. When the husband is the party at fault however, it is only punishable when it has taken place in the conjugal home. Furthermore, for her crime, the woman can be imprisoned for a period of three months to two years; the man has only to pay a fine of twenty to eighty dollars.[11] It is only lately that the working upper-class woman has acquired legal rights and even so, a third of her salary must go to the running of the household, leaving the remaining two-thirds to be used as she deems appropriate.[12]

In effect, the role and status of the *bourgeoise* is hardly more than that of a "superior domestic." She represents a symbol of his achievement to the husband who can afford to adorn her and buy her jewelry. This explains why she is the symbol of oppression to the working-class woman. Moreover, the upper-class woman is usually totally unaware of her own state of oppression. Price-Mars sums up her situation very well when he explains that:

> La femme, heureuse d'être un objet de luxe et de plaisir, vivant dans un milieu où l'étalage des vêtements riches, des carosses de prix, des demeures cossues donnent non seulement l'étiage de la valeur sociale, mais l'étiage de toutes les valeurs humaines, la femme, dans notre bourgeoisie, a rétréci lentement son horizon au point que l'idéal du bonheur, pour elle, se résume tout simplement *à partaître, rien qu'à paraître.*[13]

> (The woman in our bourgeoisie, happy to be an object of luxury and pleasure living in a milieu where the display of expensive clothes, costly cars and rich dwellings dictates not only the level of social status, but also the measure of all human values, has progressively narrowed her horizon, to the point that the ideal of happiness, for her, is solely epitomized *in the act of displaying herself, in strictly showing herself off*.)[14]

Unfortunately, this condition is still more often the case than not. Yet, technically, today all the careers which are open to men are also open to women. Women do not suffer from discrimination as far as education is concerned. Women can attend the same schools as men, and they do. But after graduation, the whole situation changes. Women who engage in professional pursuits are rare. The reason, of course, is the age-old oppression from which all women suffer in the higher echelon of the social system in Haiti. The lack of confidence in women displayed by men has resulted in women's adoption of the same mentality. Women lack confidence in themselves and do not exert the aggressiveness which is necessary in order to survive in the "man's world." The pattern is slowly changing, in Haiti as it is everywhere else, but in Haiti the process is slower. Today, for instance, one finds more women doctors, lawyers, teachers, more women holding public office—though for public office, they are constrained principally to the rural areas. The upper-class women even seem to have acquired a monopoly in the realm of small businesses: local food stores, sewing shops, bakeries, etc.

There has always, however, been a number of concerned women in the elite—particularly those who have travelled and been educated abroad. These elite women have made considerable contributions to the improvement of the lot of the working-class woman, and in the general areas of women's social, cultural, and political development. Unfortunately, they have not yet succeeded in altering the social structure of Haiti in any significant way.

As early as 1934, an organization called the "Ligue Féminine d'Actions Sociales," was founded which devotes itself to the political and social amelioration of the feminine condition in Haiti. This organization has branches in all the major cities of Haiti, and merged in 1952 with the International Alliance of Women in order to unite its efforts with those of all the women of the world who fight for the same causes. This organization has attempted to diminish the rate of illiteracy (Haiti is 90% illiterate) by creating several centers which offer evening instruction for wokring-class women. Another organization "Ligue de Protection de l'Enfance," founded in 1939, has tried to care for abandoned children or those abused by unfit parents, and has succeeded in the adoption of several laws helping to protect such children. Moreover, there exist a number of feminist organizations for young girls which aim at diminishing prostitution. Although several professional organizations for women have recently emerged, the aforementioned associations which devote themselves to social work, most of them directed and staffed by women, have been more helpful. The most important of these is the "Foundation Madame Paul E. Magloire," founded in 1950 by the wife of the then President of Haiti. In 1975, the "First National Seminar for Responsible Women" was organized. This seminar resulted in the creation of a feminist magazine, *Femina*, which is published and edited by Ms. Marie-Carmel Lafontant, who was also president of the Delegation of Haitian Women to the International Women's Conference held in Mexico in 1975.

II THE IMAGE OF THE BLACK WOMAN IN EARLY HAITIAN LITERATURE 1804-1915

Traditionally, the educated women of the elite have preferred to devote their artistic talents to the areas of music, dance, painting, and the decorative arts. In nineteenth century writings, the only female writer ever mentioned is Virginie Sampeur, whose poems figure in most reputable anthologies.[15] It was not until the twentieth century was well under way that women began to make serious contributions to the field of literature. Consequently, the image of the black woman represented in Haitian literature has been shaped and formed by men.

All Haitian literary scholars agree that the birth of Haitian literature dates back to the period immediately following independence in 1804. It is ironic, however, that the only writer who is remembered before that period was a woman: Anacaona, the Indian[16] queen who was tricked and savagely killed by the Spaniards at the end of the fifteenth century. She was a renowned poet and musician, and has inspired numerous works of art throughout the years. Unfortunately, there remains no written account of her work.

From 1804 to 1915, most of Haitian literature reflects a strong influence of the various literary schools of France. As Edgar La Selve points out,[17] hardly a French literary movement exists that is not echoed in Haiti; these imitations, though some works remain outstanding, generally do not surpass or even equal the quality of the original French writers. It was not until 1915 that indigenous innovations in style and form were attempted. Nevertheless, many writers of that period did express various aspects of Haitian reality in their works.

The Haitian writer of the nineteenth century hardly praises his country without also celebrating the beauty of the Haitian women.[18] When the Haitian woman appears in literature she is at first described in abstract terms, since the traditional attributes for beauty have been reserved exclusively to fit the white woman, and specifically, in this case, the French woman. In general, she is seen as a sex symbol, described with tropical and botanical metaphors, and by means of food images. The most famous example of that style is Emile Roumer's "Marabout de mon coeur":

Marabout de mon coeur aux seins de mandarine,
tu m'es plus savoureux que crabe en aubergine.
Tu es un afiba dedans mon calalou,
le doumboueil de mon pois, mon thé de z'herbe à clou.
Tu es le boeuf salé dont mon coeur est la couane,
l'acassan au sirop qui coule dans ma gargane.
Tu es un plat fumant, diondion avec du riz,
des akras croustillants et des thazars bien frits
Ma fringale d'amour te suit on que tu ailles;
ta fesse est un boumba charge de victuailles."[19]

(High yellow of my heart, with breasts like tangerines,
You taste better to me than eggplant stuffed with crab.
You are the tripe in my pepper-pot,
The dumplings in my peas, my tea of aromatic herbs.
You are the cornbeef whose customhouse is my heart,
My mush with syrup that trickles down the throat.
You are a steaming dish, mushroom cooked with rice.
Crisp potato fries and little fish fried brown
My hankering for love follows you wherever you go;
Your bum is a gorgeous basket brimming with fruits and meat."[20]

In this literature which covers a period from 1804 to 1915, the Haitian woman is seen as a product of the earth, a sexual object created for man's pleasure or pain, a very intimate part of the surrounding flora and fauna, which form the frame for the thinking man. It is even assumed that, more than her male counterpart, she has an instinctive knowledge of and an essential communion with nature that is not accessible to man. But she is never seen as his equal. Even in revolutionary literature, she becomes the symbol of oppression, the victim of injustice, but she is never shown as a person who can participate and fight in the struggle for liberation.[21]

III THE IMAGE OF THE BLACK WOMAN IN CONTEMPORARY LITERATURE

By contemporary literature, we mean the period starting roughly from 1915, the date of the beginning of the occupation of Haiti by the American Marines,[22] to the present. It is not our intention to delve into a lengthy explanation of the historical factors, causes, and results of the occupation. Let us say simply that at the beginning of the twentieth century, Haiti was politically in a chaotic state of affairs, and the United States government deemed it necessary to intervene. The United States justified its actions by arguing that "utter collapse of self-government and the resulting state of anarchy in a country of such strategic interests would vitiate hemispheric security." The intervention was imperative to "forestall any attempt by a European power to take advantage of the chaotic conditions in Haiti to gain a foothold in the Western hemisphere."[23] It should be noted that, with the outbreak of war in Europe, any such European intervention was unlikely to occur.

The Americans landed in Haiti on July 28, 1915, encountering little oppoisition from the Haitians, who were in no position to offer effective military resistance. Since the occupation had been imposed and was a *fait accompli*, and since the Haitians realized that their political system was unstable, they hoped that the Americans would present a viable solution to their numerous problems. They were to be sadly deceived.

The original humanitarian goal of the American government might have been sincere, but the form and the tactlessness with which it decided to conduct its business raised many questions. The higher offices among the American Marines were filled by conservative Southerners, very much imbued with their own racial prejudices, and lacking any understanding of Haitian customs. More liberal Americans, thinking it their duty to convert the Haitians' view of life to a more pragmatic outlook, made a total mockery of the latter's ancestral traditions and cultural values. The outcome of this encounter was a Haitian mistrust of American values and a reaffirmation of Haitian culture.

Referring specifically to the Haitian as a prime example, Gordon K. Lewis has defined the West Indian as a cultural schizophrenic.[24] Mr. Lewis makes a common mistake in thinking of Haitians as the 10 percent who form the elite. The Haitians, instead, are composed primarily of the 90 percent of illiterates who belong to the working class and who are oppressed into supporting the elite's sophisticated way of life. The Haitians of the working class have always kept very close ties with ancestral Africa. This is evidenced in the social customs and the rich folklore of the country such as the form of communal work (the *coumbite*), the polygamous nature of the unions, and the devotion to *Vaudou*. The individual of the elite, however, is often culturally ambivalent torn between the Western elements which direct his life and the indigenous culture of his country that he feels through his close proximity to the masses.

The American occupation provided the necessary crisis of consciousness to remedy this state of affairs, reviving the Haitians' dormant patriotism, and forcing them to take a closer look at their own culture. The instigator of this national reaffirmation movement was Jean Price-Mars (1876-1961).

When Price-Mars returned to Haiti in 1917, after studying medicine in Paris, he found the whole nation in a general state of depression. By that time, two years after the beginning of the occupation, the Haitians were completely demoralized from having had their mores and culture ridiculed by the occupants. Having successfully defeated the resistance movement, the United States had by then made it perfectly clear that military superiority rested on its side. The leader of the Resistance of the *Cacos*, Général Charlemagne Péralte, was killed, along with most of the members of the *Cacos*. Communication with France had been broken since the beginning of the First World War. Military domination of Haitians by the United States stretched to include other fields, as well; that is, the Americans also viewed themselves as intellectually and culturally superior. The masses generally tired of the disorders and the excesses of the Haitian government, accepted this new mode of oppression with a distressing apathy. The commercial class, resigned and seduced by the material promises of the Americans held a rather tolerant attitude toward the occupants. The younger generation, disappointed by its elders and completely disoriented, no longer knew where to turn for guidance, and was undergoing the heaviest consciousness crisis. Extremely concerned over this situation, and aware of the necessity to overcome it for the future of the nation, Price-Mars undertook an effort to uplift the national spirit and to effect the resurgence of national consciousness.

African Links

In a series of ethnological studies gathered under the title of *Ainsi parla l'Oncle* and published in 1928, Price-Mars offers the results of his scientific research. He re-creates the grandeur of African civilizations of earlier times, presents the brilliant organization of their political systems, the richness of their artistic talents, and finally traces the links between their way of life and the contemporary Haitian way of life. Prince-Mars heavily criticizes the elite for their failure at bridging the gaps existing between themselves and the masses, and for their inability to effectively lead the masses. Price-Mars is, moreover, appalled at the bourgeois writers and artists, who claimed not to find material worthy of inspiration in the Haitian condition for their works.

Accordingly, Price-Mars reviews the literature of Haiti in an effort to determine which works are truly representative of Haitian literature, and which works cannot in fact be properly considered to be Haitian literature. He sets up criteria by which he determines the degree of "hai'tienneté" in the literature of the people, and suggests guidelines destined to lead the young writers of the day toward a truer rendition of Haitian life. Having rehabilitated *Vaudou* as a religion,[25] Price-Mars exhorts writers to exploit the treasure of their folkloric heritage, and to make use of the vernacular (créole) as a more effective means of expressing the modes of speech particular to the Haitian people. He cites as examples Afro-American writers such as William Burghart DuBois, Booker T. Washington, Langston Hughes, and others who have used their local language successfully and have developed their own black literature. Price-Mars thus founded the Indigenist school in Haiti, which was an artistic and sensitive application of his theories by writers who shared his ideas. This school was to later lead to the movement of Negritude, which picks up most of the themes and characteristics of Indigenism.[26]

He cites as examples Afro-American writers such as William Burghart DuBois, Booker T. Washington, Langston Hughes, and others who have used their local language successfully and have developed their own black literature. Price-Mars thus founded the Indigenist school in Haiti, which was an artistic and sensitive application of his theories by writers who shared his ideas. This school was to later lead to the movement of Negritude, which picks up most of the themes and characteristics of Indigenism.[26]

IV FOUR CONTEMPORARY HAITIAN WORKS

In the final section of our study, we have chosen to concentrate on some selective works of the contemporary period which reflect the changes that the Indigenist school has effected in the portrayal of the Haitian woman in literature. We will examine four works, the first authored by a man, and the other three by women.

Masters of the Dew

Jacques Roumain's Masters of the Dew[27] was published posthumously in 1944, just a few months after the author's death. Roumain led an extremely active life. Along with Carl Brouard he was, co-founder of the Revue Indigène in 1927, and in 1934, he organized the Haitian Communist Party, for which he was imprisoned and then exiled. Upon his return to Haiti, he created the Haitian Bureau of Ethnology. Roumain was inspired all his life by the vision of a united Haitian people and saw Marxism as the only hope of the masses.

In Roumain, we find a more positive and realistic image of the black woman, and of her role and importance in Haitian life. On the surface, Masters of the Dew appears to be a simple novel: it is the story of a man bringing his community together. The novel reflects a pronounced Marxist viewpoint. It deals exclusively with the peasant's life, and offers an excellent presentation of that life, in the true tradition of the Indigenist school. But it is the sensitive characterization of the women which makes this novel a chef-d'oeuvre.

After living in Cuba as a cane-cutter for a number of years, Manuel, the protagonist, returns home to Haiti, only to find his once prosperous community of Fonds-Rouge in a state of dire poverty. The community's poverty had been caused by a violent argument which had occurred a few years earlier between two prominent members of the community. In the course of that argument, blood had been shed. As a result, the coumbites, which had once united the community into one big family, had ended, and there had now emerged two rival factions. Consequently, the land no longer produced anything to sell at the market, which ordinarily provided the revenue upon which the peasant lived. The neglected land was also being impoverished by the continuous felling of trees that the peasants sold at the market in order to continue living, and this resulted naturally in drought. Erosion naturally had resulted, and with no rain in sight, the peasants were in a desperate plight. A spirit of resignation reigned, reminiscent of the period of the American occupation.

This acceptance of misery and the rationalization backing it are challenged only by Manuel, who searches incessantly for water until he finally finds a spring far up in the mountains. Despite the fact that he and his wife, Annaise, belong to opposing sides, Manuel attempts through her mediation to convince the peasants that the water could be irrigated down to Fonds-Rouge with the help of all the members of the small village. Before he can attain his goal, however, Manuel is killed by Gervilen, a villain formerly rejected by Annaise. As he is dying, Manuel refuses to divulge the identity of his assassin so as to prevent the same sort of animosity from reoccurring and splitting the community once more into two factions. The *coumbite*, once again, reunites the peasants in their struggle for daily survival.

There is a definite change in the portrayal of women in Roumain's novel. Although statements relating woman with nature abound in the book, the woman is no longer described in terms of natural symbols. Rather, nature is described in terms of feminine attributes: "Behind the house, a round hill, whose skimpy bushes hugged the earth, resembled the head of a Negro girl, with hair like grains of pepper"[28] ... "The earth is like a good woman: if you mistreat her, she revolts."

The other main characters of the book, besides Manuel, are the two women closest to him: his mother Délira, and his lover Annaise. Both women are strong peasant women, described by the author in simple terms, and with a gentleness which betrays his sympathy for and understanding of the suffering which the peasant woman encounters daily. Délira's difficult life is described realistically, with no direct criticism of the peasant man's indifference or unawareness of a certain basic injustice: that's just the way life is:

> Every Saturday, Délira would load two burros with charcoal and go to the city. She would return at nightfall with a few wretched provisions and a bit of change. Then she'd sit in her hut, broken down under the weight of an immense fatigue. Bienaimé [her husband] would demand his tobacco and would never find it strong enough.[29]

Annaise is also described in simple terms as she goes about the business of performing her daily chores. We no longer find the woman exclusively represented as a sex object: "He [Manuel] saw that she had lovely white teeth ... ands very fine black skin ... She was wearing a blue dress gathered at the waist by a foulard. Carrying a wicker basket, she walked quickly, her robust hips moving in cadence with her long stride."[30] The accent is more on the strength of these women than their sex appeal. And though there is no implicit criticism of the men, it is evident that salvation can only come from the female, as the author eventually shows.

Roumain takes care to imply that Manuel, the hero, is unusually open-minded and different from his compatriots because he lived in Cuba for several years, suffered with his black brothers there at the cane plantations, and finally actively participated in the *huelga* (strike) organized by them. It was there that he began to understand the true meaning of brotherhood, and he learned that "cooperation is the friendship of the poor." The realization of this ideal, the actual act of bringing the community together again, is accomplished by the women. Manuel is able to communicate with his mother and make her accept his new ideas, whereas these same ideas completely antagonize his father who will no longer speak to his son. Annaise is the instrumental factor in reinstating the *coumbite*. While Manuel searches for the spring and plans the irrigation canals, she works behind the scenes, talking first to the women of her own family, and then to the other women of her clan. Délira undertakes the same task with the rival faction. They implant the idea in the peasant women's minds that life would resume its normal pace if everyone worked together once water was found. In turn, these women talk to their men, and finally bring them around to the idea. Moreover, after Manuel's death, Annaise is the only person who knows the location of the spring, the only force that can restore life to the dying village. She is also the giver of life in the physical sense: Manuel continues to live on through the child she carries at the end of the novel.

The emphasis placed on the mental strength of the women in *Masters of the Dew* is a rarity in contemporary literature written by men. Even after the death of Manuel, who has inspired such profound love in Annaise and Délira, these women do not allow themselves to grieve since they know that there are more important matters to attend to. The women's strength and their endurance of the suffering necessary for their survival, is expressed sensitively by the author when Délira sings at the funeral:

> She sang after the fashion of black women. Life has taught black women to sing as though they are choking back a sob, and it's a song

that ends always with a beginning because it is in the image of misery.
And does the circle of misery ever end?

Marie Chauvet, Amour, Colere et Folie

With Marie Chauvet, we move toward a more profound examination of the feminine condition in the highest echelon of the social
stratification. Marie Chauvet, was an acknowledged "romancière."
She received the "Prix de l'Alliance Française" in 1935 for her first
novel, Fille d'Haiti, and the "Grand Prix France-Antilles" for her
third novel, Fonds des Nègres, in 1960. The three novels published in
one volume in 1968, Amour, colère et folie,[31] are considered her
masterpiece.

Marie Chauvet exposes brilliantly and subtly the utter powerlessness of women, and the impossibility of them controlling their
own lives no matter how capable or motivated they are because the
system does not allow it. She shows how they are forced to redirect
and rechannel their energies in ways which prove fruitless due to
their inherent frustration.

The political events surrounding Amour, colère et folie are reminiscent of the terror-stricken climate of the Duvalier regime. The
atmosphere is tense, the violence blatant, and a certain common
fear and frustration, inspired by the vacillations of the government,
can be felt between the lines. We will concern ourselves here only
with Amour.

Amour is a complex novel which offers us an in-depth study of a
thirty-nine year-old "vieille fille" (spinster), Claire, who is still a
virgin and who will in all probability remain so. Claire lives with her
two younger sisters, Eugénie and Annette, managing their home.
She has fallen in love with Eugénie's French husband, Jean-Luze,
who also lives with them. Claire is a bitter woman, prepared to live
at almost any cost the life of which she has been robbed, and the
youth she has wasted. She was first as a victim of a set of stern
prejudices and moral codes, and then of the hang-ups and the
inhibititions she acquired. Traumatized by the fact that she is very
dark-skined, unlike her two sisters, who, like their deceased parents, are of a very light complexion, Claire has never been able to
trust anyone's love. She has never thought herself attractive, suffered from feelings of extreme insecuirty, and never married despite a marriage proposal from a man she loved. She comes to realize

that her emotional complexes are perhaps without grounds, and that her problems may have been of her own making. Nevertheless, she is incapable of giving up the prestige her situation assures, or jeopardizing her image of respectability, and so is obliged to search for this happiness at home.

At the beginning of the novel, when Claire becomes aware that Annette, her youngest sister, also is attracted to Jean-Luze, she decides to help provoke a love affair between them, and to live vicariously through Annette's happiness. Claire multiplies opportunities for intimate tête-à-têtes between Annette and Jean-Luze, keeping her other sister Eugénie, Jean-Luze's wife, occupied meanwhile. Though Jean-Luze finds it difficult to resist Annette's dazzling beauty and sex appeal, he regains his strength after succombing once to her charms, and becomes the prototype of the loving husband. Claire, annoyed and disappointed by Annette's failure, gives up on her younger sister and decides upon another course of action: working strictly on her own this time. Desperately in need of an illusion in her life, she needs to feel that she is alive before it is too late. But it is already too late.

Jean-Luze now has to be kept away from his wife during her second pregnancy in order not to fatigue the fragile Eugénie whose health was considerably worsened by her first pregnancy. He consequently spends much time with Claire, playing with his son in her room, and sleeping there with the child. She becomes the victim of a fantasy, imagining that Jean-Luze would love her if Eugénie did not exist. Claire feels that she is more his intellectual equal than his wife; they talk politics openly, and Jean-Luze confides in her about his past. In fact, she almost forgets Eugénie's existence, so strong is her illusion that she is Jean-Luze's real wife and the mother of his son. But this illusion is swiftly destroyed at the expiration of Eugénie's term of pregnancy, when Jean-Luze, unaware of Claire as a woman, can once more shower his attention upon his wife, there by lessening his guilt over his previous near infidelity.

Claire experiences an uncontrollable anger at being once more robbed of her illusions. The author offers us an intimate view of her private moments, as she pitifully caresses a doll she keeps as a surrogate child, as she is driven wild by sexually vivid dreams, and avidly devours the pornographic postcards that she once ordered from France which have taught her all that she will ever know about the act of love. Claire decides to murder her sister Eugénie, to make it look like a suicide, and then live in everlasting bliss with Jean-Luze who will undoubtedly need her to look after his children. At the moment of action, however, she finds that she cannot execute the plan; she cannot murder her own sister. And out of utter frustration, she decides to take her own lfie.

Just at that moment she sights Calédu, the Chief of Police, terrorizer of the community, who had taken to killing the people who annoyed him, and was in the habit of arresting the upper-class women who had snubbed him, and "castrating" them. Calédu and Claire have shared a mutual hatred for each other. Calédu is cornered by a horde of famished beggars, and is driven accidentally to her house. She swiftly opens the door, and plunges the knife meant to kill herself into his back. Calédu struggles back to the street and dies. In performing that one act, Claire has released her inner frustrations and has finally reached a state of peace and satisfaction. She has, somehow, defied the set life prepared for her.

The striking portrait of Claire is unforgettable and her frustration is shared by the reader. Claire wants to revolt against the role assigned to her by her family and by society of the trustworthy older sister, proper and discreet, the perfect confidant, relegated to the role of governess of the house, and treated with due respect. It is inconceivable to anyone around her that she might have other needs: that she might not appreciate the honor of leading the Procession of the Virgin Mary, an honor which is awarded to her every year. At thirty-nine, she is an old maid, and cannot hope to escape from the behaviour pattern to which society expects her to conform. She does, however, have the unique opportunity to perform an act which reconciles her with herself.

Marie-Therese Colimon: Fils de Misere

The next novel is also the portrait of a woman, her inner feelings, joys and tribulations, but the setting of Fils de Misere is more modern and the story concerns the lower echelon of society. Marie-Thérèse Colimon's Files de misère[32] was awarded the "Prix France-Haiti." The author founded a home for young rural girls, was president of the "Ligue Féminine d'Actions Sociales" for eleven years, and is currently Chairperson of the Haitian Branch of the "Organization Mondiale pour l'Education Pré-scolaire."

Fils de misère offers a realistic representation of contemporary urban proletarian life. The political atmosphere is not as tense as in the Chauvet novel, and the primary concern is once more that of achieving a better economic status. As President Jean-Claude Duvalier recently stated: "The political revolution is over. We are now engaged in an economic revolution."[33]

Lamercie, the protagonist, would perhaps experience the same feelings of frustration as *Amour*'s heroine, Claire, but fortunately, she is not bound by the moral codes of the upper class. In the gift of motherhood she has found a reason for living. Having once lost a child at the young age of seventeen she has been anxious to become pregnant again, and is determined to take care of the new baby that God has given her. The difference in attitudes towards sexual mores between the elite and the working class is admirably drawn by the author. When Lamercie goes to visit her "protectrice" in order to ask the latter to be her child's godmother, the author writes:

> Un jour, sa protectrice l'avait vue arriver le ventre proéminent. Malgré tout le respect que Lamercie éprouvait pour la vieille demoiselle son état ne semblait lui procurer aucune honte. An contraire, son allure n'était pas dénuée d'une provocante fierté. Habituée, résignée, Mlle. Régulier n'avait pas laissé éclater sa déception a philosophie, rompue aux choses haitiennes, avait su contenir l'éclat de ses paroles réprobatrices et de sa vaine indignation. Elle n'avait pas demandé qui en était le père. C'était inutile, elle le savait. Ayant joué son rôle d'instrument reporductif, il n'avait plus aucun compete à rendre, celui-là, et nul ne lui tiendrait rigueur. Que pouvait-elle, pauvre catéchiste, au milieu d'un ordre de choses accepté, établi depuis longtemps? C'était l'affaire du bon Dieu qui réservait les unions consacrées par le mariage à un petit nombre d'élus. D'ailleurs, que répondre à ces assertions d'une absolue logique qu'elle avait si souvent entendues: "Manzé Rezia! pitite, ce bon Dié qui baille li, oun femme bon Dié pa baille pitite, ce rinmin bon Dié pas rinimin li."[34] On décelait dans de telles répliques et dans le comportement de ces femmes . . . une telle ignorance du vice et de la perversité, une mentalité tellement fruste et simple considérant l'enfant comme la fin naturelle de leur condition de femme que toute confite en dévotions qu'elle fut, et toute imbibée de chasteté candide, Mlle. Rézia, confondue, s'inclinnait.[35]

(One day, her protectress has seen her arrive with her stomach jutting out. In spite of the respect Lamercy felt for the old lady, her state did not seem to inspire in her any shame. Quite the contrary! Her bearing was not devoid of a provocative pride. Accustomed to it all, resigned, Mlle. Régulier had not shown her deception... Her philosophy, adapted to the Haitian ways, had enabled her to control the extent of her reproachful words and of her useless indignation. She did not ask who the father was. She knew it was pointless. Having played his role of reproductive instrument, he was no longer accountable for anything, and no one would think of blaming him. What could she, poor catechist, do in the midst of an accepted order of things, established for so long? It was the affair of the good Lord who restricted unions consecrated by marriage to a chosen few. Besides, what could she answer to these affirmations of such absolute logic that she had so often heard: "Manzé Rézia, it is God who gives children. Sterility is a sign of divine malediction." One felt in such statements, and in the comportment of these women... such an ignorance of the notion of vice or perversity, such an unpolished and simple mentality, considering children as the natural end of the feminine condition, that, as steeped in piety and as saturated with candid chastity as she was, Mlle. Rézia, confounded, yielded.)[36]

Mlle Rézia Régulier plays the role assigned to women of her class and condition. (The role against which Claire had tried to revolt in *Amour*.) Strict and rigid in her attire, and unmarried, she attends church by six o'clock every morning so that she can flower the altar. Not content to simply belong to charitable organizations, she takes the poor unmarried girls of the community, in hand tries to instill in them the importance of Christianity and education, baptizes their children, and uses her influence to better the women's lives in any way she can.

Lamercie had tried to benefit from her protectress's advice. She had enrolled in an evening course. But one hour of classes per night, taught by a distracted poorly-paid young student, was not enough to fill the gaps left by thirty years without instruction. Discouraged at not being able to retain anything, Lamercie had given up classes. She is, however, determined to send her son, Ti-tonton, to school, and when Mlle. Régulier makes arrangements to enroll him, she cannot contain her maternal pride.

Lamercie supports her son and herself by working as a domestic for Mme. Ledestin, a prosperous *bourgeoise*. She earns eight dollars per month, a salary which barely permits her to survive. The contrast between the situation of these two women is obvious. Lamarcie cannot understand the nature of Mme. Ledestin's dissatisfaction at minor things, the fact that her husband does not quite understand her, for instance, when Mme. Ledestin has such a beautiful house and her children are always well-fed, well-dressed, and doing well in school. Unfortunately, Mme. Ledestin, who has already mothered quite a few children, has once more become pregnant. She becomes irritated over the least little detail, which makes Lamercie nervous and unable to perform her tasks properly, so that Mme. Ledestin fires her.

Momentarily broken down by the lose of her job, and unable to find another one, Lamercie regains her strength and courage at the prospect of having to send her son to someone's house as a "resté-avec."[37] She decides to go into business on her own; she prepares food, and establishes herself at a strategic corner in Port-au-Prince, selling the food to other members of the working-class. Soon, her business flourishes, and she begins to think Ti-tonton's future is assured. But there is another set-back in store for her. She falls ill from exhaustion, and takes a long time recovering. Meanwhile, her son at home suffers from hunger, and when she can again function, she realizes that she can no longer hope to resume her business. Her competitors have taken over her corner; she has still not completely recovered from her sickness and is neither physically nor mentally well. In a wild moment, she is driven to stealing a chicken in the market in order to feed her son. Sent to prison, she is fortunately released through Mlle. Régulier's intervention. But Lamercie's spirit is broken. Inspired still by her concern over her son's welfare, she decides upon another course; she goes back to her former employer, Mme. Ledestin, offering to do her excess laundry and that of her friends; and she is able once more to eke out a meagre living.

The story is a very factual account of the life of the woman of the proletariat, the tribulations she encounters daily and the small consolations that make it somehow worthwhile. Lamercie's only consolation and driving force is her son; she is determined that he will have a better life than hers. When Ti-tonton graduates from grade school and receives his "certificat d'études primaries," she is so proud that she feels that everyone must share her joy, and she pays to have his achievement announced on the radio. Unfortunately, Lamercie also becomes victim of the system. Ti-tonton has just entered high school. Having heard that the government had sent troops to his school to stifle a students' demonstration, Lamercie, along with a number of other worried mothers, rushes down to the school, only to be killed by the officer in charge who had a petty grudge against her. And who will question the murder of a proletarian, in such an overpopulated city; who would even think of bringing charges against the officer? At this lowest echelon of the social ladder, there is really not much hope for the woman struggling alone.[38]

Nadine Macloire: Le Sexe Mythique

The last work we will look at is Nadine Magloire's *Le sexe mythique*,[39] published in 1975. It is a witty short story which has scandalized the reading public, because of its contraditions to the normal social pattern one is expected to follow in Hiati.

The protagonist, Annie, is a modern, liberated single woman, who faces a slight dilemma which she resolves at the end of the story. She has already openly defied social norms by choosing to live alone in a small apartment, remaining unmarried by choice, and maintaining her financial security by teaching mathematics in two schools. Her desire and need of independence is, even today, quite unusual in Haiti: often a bourgeois woman is unsatisfied until she has made a successful match. The few upper-class women who choose not to marry or not to remain married, and feel comfortable in this state, are usually those who have studied and lived abroad for a number of years.

Annie gets involved in an adulterous situation with Frank, the husband of her best friend. Their relationship is satisfying, both intellectually and physically, in the moments that the two lovers spend alone. However, Frank must spend a good deal of time at home with his wife and children, and cannot take Annie out to fulfill her social obligations. To resolve her loneliness and the feelings of frustration and resentment which this situation triggers, Annie starts another relationship with a cultured single young man, Yves, whom she has met at a diplomatic party. But Annie is eventually bored by his company: Yves is quite adept at recounting the opinions of renowned masters, but does not seem to hold any ideas or convictions of his own. She also becomes annoyed at his pompousness and highly condescending attitude toward women, and he fails to satisfy her as a lover. She must decide whether to continue this relationship and submit to the constant little humiliations a woman must undergo in order to keep such a pretentious man. Finally, she decides to give him up, but realizes that she must have other affairs in order to be fulfilled, since Frank cannot possibly meet all her needs. Anxious to keep things on an open and honest level between them, she would like to inform him of her feelings. As she is about to tell him, she realizes that Frank would never be able to accept such a blow to his ego, and that her other affairs must be kept clandestine. She remains quiet; if these are the rules of the game, she is ready and able to play.

Certain critics have labelled the work as blatant pornography and others have claimed it is not worthy of literary comment. The truth is that the reading public has difficulty dealing with the frankness of the author and her open criticism of Haitian women for their passivity in submitting to a code of rules dictated by men. Nadine Magloire ends her story by judging the Haitian *bourgeoise* quite harshly, saying that: "Les femmes haitiennes n'atteignent jamais la maturité mentale. Toute leur vie elles demeurent des mineures en tutelle."[40]

CONCLUSION

In this essay we have tried to show that in Haiti, women belong to two main classes in which they lead strikingly different lives and experience varying degrees of oppression. In the literature of the nineteenth and early twentieth centuries, the image of the Haitian woman as represented by the "littérateurs" was that of a sexual object—earthy and expressive in the case of the working-class woman, more sophisticated and reserved in the instance of the upper-class woman. This image has undergone considerable transformations in more contemporary literature, where the woman is viewed as a person rather than an object. But the image presented by Jacques Roumain appears to be more idealized than that of the women authors who offer a deeper insight and a more realistic picture of the feminine condition today. The women authors show that women in Haiti are still very much socially oppressed, and cannot easily step out of the traditional social structure. Lamercie (Colimon, *Fils de misère*) is more oppressed by her social condition as a proletarian than by the men she encounters, or by concern over society's judgement of her acts. Claire (Chauvet, *Amour*), as an upper-class woman, is oppressed precisely by the judgement of a society which has a pronounced double standard toward men and women, and she cannot shake off that oppression without loss of her social status. Annie (Magloire, *Le sexe mythique*) presents the image of the more liberated woman of the foreseeable future in her display of the freedom necessary to reject the unjust rules set up by the ruling class of men, freedom which would enable the woman to lead a fulfilling life. With hope, Haitian women will ponder carefully over the message offered at the end of the Magloire work examined, and will make a real attempt at self-determination in conducting their own lives.

NOTES

1. *Conference on Women and Devlopment*, Wellesley University, Wellesley, Massachussets, June 2-6, 1976.

2. James Leyburn (*The Haitian People*, Yale U. Press, New Haven, 1945) defines the elite as the 3 percent of the Haitian population which does not work with its hands.

3. Jean Price-mars, *La vocation de l'élite*, Imprimerie Edmond Chenet, Port-au-Prince, 1919, p. 99.

4. Haiti is divided into five departments or states.

5. Price-Mars, *op. cit.*, p. 110.

6. For more information on the legal working rights of women and men in Haiti, consult François Latortue's *Le droit du travail en Haiti*, Les Presses Libres, Port-au-Prince, 1961.

7. In some regions, women participate also however. Dr. Madeleine Sylvain Bouchereau, *Haiti et ses femmes*, Les Presses Libres, Port-au-Price, 1957, p. 163.

8. Coumbite: a collective agricultural effort in which neighbouring farmers help each other at times such as harvest.

9. François Latortue, "Haiti et sa main d'oeuvre: perspectives d'avenir," *Culture et développement en Haiti*, Editions Leméac, Ottawa, 1972, p. 49.

10. Plaçage: to live in concubinage; common-law marriage.

11. Bouchereau, *op. cit.*, pp. 103-105.

12. Amendment of the *Civil Code*: "Lou du 11 janvier 1944." Ertha Pascal-Trouillot, "Droits et privilèges de la femme dans la législation civile et sociale d'Haiti," *Conjonction*, #124, August 1974, p. 13.

13. Price-Mars, *op. cit.*, p. 103. Italics in original.

14. Translated by the present writer.

15. Bouchereau, *op. cit.*, p. 169. Mme. Bouchereau also offers an impres-

sive bibliography of works written by women up to 1957, and an array of the achievements of Haitian women in other fields.

16. Haiti was originally inhabited by Arawak Indians, before the arrival of Christrophe Colomb, whose men exterminated the Indians—one million by 1514. That invaluable labor force was later replaced with African slaves.

17. Cited by Manuel Pompilus, *Manuel illustré d'histoire de la littérature haitienne*, Editions Henri Deschamps, Port-au-Prince, 1961, in his introduction.

18. Léon-François Hoffman, "Image de la femme dans la poésie haitienne," *Présence Africaine*, #34-35, 1970-61, pp. 183-206.

19. Cited by Naomi M. Garret, *The Renaissance of Haitian Poetry*, Présence Africaine, Paris, 1963, p. 135.

20. Translated by C. R. Coulthard, *Race and Colour in Caribbean Literature* University of London Press, London, 1966, p. 95.

21. Hoffman, *op. cit.*

22. The American Occupation of Haiti lasted until 1934.

23. Garret, *op. cit.*, p. 56, referring to Ludwell Lee Montague's *Haiti and The United States, 1714-1938*, Durnham, N. C., 1940.

24. Gordon K. Lewis, *The Growth of the Modern West Indies*, Monthly Review Press, New York, 1968, p. 392.

25. *Vaudou* is a religion deserving the same status as others, since it is founded upon the belief in the existence of spiritual or supernatural beings, and possesses a theology, a set of morals, an ecclesiastic hierarchical body, temples, ceremonies and rites: in brief, it comprises the general stock of all known religions. See Jean Price-Mars, *Ainsi parla l'Oncle*, Imprimerie de Campiègne, Port-au-Prince, 1928.

26. An essential distinction must be made however between these two movements, Indigenism being strictly a nationalist movement whereas Negritude grew to encompass all black writers of French expression, its political dimension being expressed in the notion of Pan-Africanism. That Negritude started in Haiti is evidenced by various leading writers and critics of the movement; for example:

—Aime Césaire, who first coined the word in *Return to my Native Land* in 1939, speaking of: "Haiti where Negritude stood up for the first time."
—Professor C. R. Coulthard: "The concept of Negritude grew out of the Haitian situation." *Race and Colour in Caribbean Literature.*
—C. L. R. James: "In 1915, the ceaseless battering from foreign pens was reenforced by the bayonets of the American Marines. Haiti had to find a rallying point. They looked for it where it can only be found, at home, more precisely in their own backyard. They discovered what is known today as Negritude." *The Black Jacobins* (p. 394).

27. Jacques Roumain, *Masters of the Dew (Gouverneurs de la rosée)*, translated by Langston Hughes and Mercer Cook in 1947, Macmillan Company, New

York, 1971. This book has been translated into seventeen languages, and was recently made into a movie, in Haiti, which was aired in France and in Haiti in 1976.

28. *Ibid.*, p. 24.
29. *Ibid.*, p. 72.
30. *Ibid.*, p. 36.
31. Marie Chauvet, *Amour, colère et folie*, Editios Gallimard, Paris, 1968.
32. Marie-Thérèse Colimon, *Fils de misère*, Editions Caraibes, Port-au-Prince, Editions de l'école, Paris, 1974.
33. Kyle Ahrold, "Interview with Jean-Claude Duvalier," *Essence*, January 19/26, 1976, p. 19.
34. créole
35. Colimon, *op. cit.*, pp. 23-24.
36. Translated by present writer.
37. resté-avec: child or adolescent placed as a servant by his parents, who receives no wages, but is housed, clothed and fed by his employers.
38. All the women's names in this novel are significant: Lamercie: Mercy: Melle. Régulier: Ms. Regular; Mme. Ledestin: Mrs. Destiny.
39. Nadine Magloire, *Le sexe mythique*, Editions du Verseau, Port-au-Prince 1975.
40. *Ibid.*, p. 58. "Haitian women never attain mental maturity. All their lives, they remain like minors under guardianship." Translated by present writer.

BIBLIOGRAPHY

Chauvet, Marie. *Amour, colère et folie*, Editions Gallimard, Paris, 1968.
Colimon, Marie-Thérèse. *Fils de misère*, Editions Caraibes, Port-au-Prince, Editions de l'école, Paris, 1974.
Magloire, Nadine. *Le sexe mythique*, Editions du Verseau, Port-au-Prince, 1975.
Roumain, Jacques. *Masters of the Dew*, Macmillan Company, New York, 1971.

SECONDARY AND CRITICAL SOURCES

Ahrold, Kyle. "Interview with Jean-Claude Duvalier," *Essence*, January 19/26, 1976, pp. 19-20.
Bouchereau, Madeleine Sylvain. *Haiti et ses femmes*, Les Presses Libres, Port-au-Prince, 1957.
Coulthard, C. R. *Race and Color in Caribbean Literature*, University of London Press, 1966.
Garret, Naomi M. *The Renaissance of Haitian Poetry*, Présence Africaine, Paris, 1963.
Hoffman, Léon-François. "Image de la femme dans la poésie haitienne," *Présence Africaine*, # 34-35, 1960-61, pp. 183-206.

Latortue, François. "Haiti et sa main d'oeuvre: perspectives d'avenir," *Culture et développement en Haiti*, Editions Leméac, Ottawa, 1972.

———. *Le droit du travail en Haiti*, Les Presses Libres, Port-au-Prince, 1961.

Lewis, Gordon K. *The Growth of the Modern West Indies*, Monthly Review Press, New York, 1968.

Leyburn, James. *The Haitian People*, Yale University Press, New Haven, 1945.

Pascal-Trouillot, Ertha. "Droits et privilèges de la femme dans la législation civile et sociale d'Haiti," *Conjonction*, #124, August 1974, pp. 9-12.

Pompilus, Manuel. *Manuel Illustré d'histoire de la littérature haîtinne*, Editions Henri Deschamps, Port-au-Prince, 1961.

Price-Mars, Jean. *Ainsi parla l'Oncle*, Imprimerie de Compeìgne, Port-au-Prince, 1928.

———. *La vocation de l'élite*, Imprimerie Edmond Chenet, Port-au-Prince, 1919.

Sylvain, Jeane G. "Notes sur la famille haitienne," *Conjunction*, #124, August 1974, pp. 22-33.

Part IV: SOUTH AMERICA

Carnival, Rio de Janeiro, Brazil.

South America

INTRODUCTORY SUMMARY

This section on the black woman in South America is the shortest in the volume mainly because of the difficulty of finding papers in English on this subject. The three contributions included here deal with black women in Guatemala, Colombia and Brazil. Blacks in South America share a common history of slavery with blacks in the New World, and Brazil was one of the last countries to end slavery. Sections of Brazil such as Bahia have a large black population which still has a strong cultural identity with Africa.

Solien Gonzalez' article considers the black Carib culture of Guatemala as a variant of West Indian negro culture rather than American Indian culture, although she recognizes other cultural influences. She discusses family organization, the economic activities of both men and women, and the multicultural aspects of their religious beliefs and ritual.

Rubbo examines the deleterious effects of commercialized agriculture on black women peasants in rural Colombia. On account of changes in relations of production, women are being turned into a cheap labor force with increasing dependency on men, and at the same time women retain sole responsibility for the children. According to Rubbo, this new dependency on men induces competition between women, and creates tensions that have to be resolved through the use of sorcery and love magic. Rubbo also observes that the women may choose not to marry for fear of domination by males.

Nunes' chapter is a critique of the images of women of color in Brazilian literature. The racial diversity of Brazilian society creates a racial hierarchy in which the lighter color and a higher social class tend to be predominant at the apex of the social pyramid. The writings of three men and one woman are examined in the light of various aspects such as race, class, sexuality, attitudes towards men and reactions to women of color. Nunes feels that the male authors usually focus on the sexual aspects of women's lives and were obsessed by the theme of the woman of color as a sex object. The *mulata* woman (of mixed blood) is symbolized as the most desirable, and in some ways is a symbol of Brazil itself in that she represents a synthesis of various elements. However, according to Nunes, there is always an aura of immorality about her and she is, in the final analysis, a victim of sexual and other forms of exploitation, like all women of color in Brazilian society.

1

West Indian Characteristics of the Black Carib[1]

Nancie Solien Gonzalez

Since the year 1797 there has been living on the Caribbean coast of Central America a group of people known as "Black Carib." They are the descendants of the Red Caribs who occupied the Lesser Antilles at the time of Columbus, and of Africans brought to the New World during the seventeenth and eighteenth centuries. Taylor has outlined the history of this group in detail up to the time of their arrival on the Central American mainland.[2] These people, originally having landed at Trujillo, Honduras, have now spread up and down the coast and live in a series of towns and villages from Stann Creek, British Honduras, to the Black River in Honduras.

Studies of Black Carib culture in the past have stressed its similarity to the Tropical Forest type of culture of their Red Carib ancestors. In fact, in Taylor's opinion, "It is in its imponderable aspects that the culture of the Black Carib differs most from that of their Indian forbears in the Lesser Antilles, so as to constitute, as it were, a Negro cake composed of Amerindian ingredients."[3]

The present writer conducted field work among the Black Carib from July 1956 to July 1957. Livingston, Guatemala, was the community studied most intensively, but survey trips of one month each were made in British Honduras and the Republic of Honduras. During this study many striking similarities between the culture of the Black Caribs and that of their Negro neighbors were noted. Especially were there resemblances to the British Honduran Creole culture.[4] This finding led to a comparative study of materials published on West Indian Negro cultures. The purpose of this paper is to suggest that the culture of the Black Carib, though differing in many ways from that of other New World Negroes, nevertheless should be considered as a variant of West Indian Negro culture. It will also demonstrate that the most probable sources of the West Indian traits in Carib culture were the non-Carib Negro groups living on the coastline of Central America during the nineteenth century. In other words, the evidence indicates that the Black Carib were more similar, both racially and culturally, to the Red Carib upon their arrival on the mainland than they are at the present time.

The groups with which the Black Carib have been compared here are the rural Creole of British Honduras, the Haitians and Trinidadians as reported by Herskovits, and Jamaica as studied by Beckwith and Henriques.[5] In addition, historical accounts of the customs of slaves during the eighteenth and nineteenth centuries in the various West Indian islands have been drawn upon freely.

In the realms of economics and social organization there are great similiarities throughout the Caribbean, including the Black Carib area. Wage labor, whether on plantations, road-building gangs, loading bananas, etc., has high prestige value, and is generally sought by most men, even though the work is often of a periodic or seasonal nature. Among the Black Carib horticulture has been traditionally women's work, the men assisting with clearing and burning, but in recent years many men have become small farmers. They grow crops different from those of the women, and usually sell the greater portion of their yield. The most important of these crops are rice, beans, coconuts (for copra), and formerly, bananas. All of these are products which enter into the national economies of the countries in which the Caribs live.

Women, on the other hand, grow cassava, sugarcane, plantains, yams, and various other roots, primarily for home consumption or local sale. Here, as elsewhere in the West Indies, the woman has exclusive right to her own earnings.

Fishing, formerly one of the main bases of the Carib economy, is still important, but now tends to be done either by specialists or by other men at irregular times when they have nothing else to do or when the fish are said to be plentiful and biting. Women do not fish, but they play an important role in distribution, since they preserve the fish by salting and drying, after which they carry them to market.

Home industries, especially dressmaking done by women and tailoring by men, contribute greatly to the domestic economy. Both sexes, but especially men, tend to dress in fashions copied from certain segments of the Negro populatiion in the United States. Many Carib men have traveled to New Orleans, New York, San Francisco, and other United States ports while working on steamships. From these places they have brought back articles of clothing which have then been copied by their less fortunate brethren. For everyday wear, however, the women still use a one-piece smock-like dress over which is worn a full gathered skirt. On their heads they invariably wear a cotton cloth knotted at the nape of the neck and/or a widebrimmed straw hat. All of these clothes, except the straw hats, are made locally and follow patterns which bear a close resemblance to those worn in other parts of the Caribbean. They are quite different from the clothing worn by mestizo peasants in Central America.

Basketmaking, woodworking, and canoe-building are all men's specialty occupations. Basketry items still manufactured include the water-tight *pataki*, or travel-basket, also made by the Creoles of British Honduras. Presses and sifters used in processing the bitter manioc into cassava cakes are obviously of Tropical Forest origin, but it is interesting to note that certain West Indian Negroes also adopted this equipment.[6] Beckwith noted the manufacture of fish-traps in Jamaica which she likened to those of the Tropical Forest Carib illustrated by Roth.[7] The Black Carib still make these fish-traps today. Woodworkers make mortars and pestles for grinding plantains and husking rice, as well as various bowls and troughs, all of which have their counterparts among the Creole of British Honduras.

The manufacture of dug-out canoes has now also become specialists' work, the methods employed and the finished products being undistinguishable from the industry among the Creoles, and similar to those described by Beckwith.[8]

The present-day family form among the Black Carib shows all the characteristic traits noted by investigators in other areas in the West Indies. Within the household consanguineal ties are far more important than affinal. Marital relationships are unstable and primarily consensual, though in later years couples may be joined in legal marriage as a means of gaining presitge within the community. A strong emphasis on the maternal kin, continued association of the children with the mother after divorce or separation, plus adoption of children for economic reasons, generally by some member of the mother's kindred, are all common features of this organization.

Another institution prominent throughout the Negro Caribbean is that known as the "caretaker" system.[9] In this, a young child is sent to live with a family of higher social position and greater means, exchanging its services for food, shelter, education, and other advantages which its own family could not provide. In most cases, if not all, the host family is non-Carib and non-Negro.

Carib religious beliefs and rituals stem from at least three general traditions—the African, the European, and the American Indian. This statement, of course, can be made concerning most or nearly all peoples living in Latin America today. However, the religion of any local group usually shows a predominance of one of these traditions over the others. Among the Carib there is no good reason to doubt that the African is the most important. There is great emphasis on the importance of the family ancestors, although Taylor believes that the cult which surrounds this may have been as typical of the Island Arawaks as of Africa.[10] However, Coelho has recently pointed out resemblances between Black Carib rituals and those of Negroes in Brazil.[11]

Customs surrounding death correspond almost exactly to those described in Jamaica, Trinidad, and British Honduras.[12] As soon as the death is announced relatives and friends begin to gather at the home of the deceased. Wailing begins then and continues throughout the first night wake. At this and again on the ninth night after death, the friends and relatives keep vigil by praying, singing, dancing, playing games such as checkers, forfeits, and bingo, and listening to stories of the Anansi type. Refreshments are served several times during the night, gifts of food, rum, and coffee having been brought by the guests.

Christianity, among the Black Carib universally Roman Catholicism, has had a great effect on ritual and custom, though these still retain a flavor of non-Christian sources. For example, masses for the dead are as important as elsewhere in Catholic America, but they are given at irregular intervals and usually in response to dreams in which the dead ancestors request such rites.

The belief in and practice of obeah, or black magic, are of vital concern to most Black Caribs today. Significant also is the fact that the term "obeah" itself is in general usage among them. Most deaths are attributed to the magic of obeah-men, whose services have been purchased by some enemy of the deceased. In addition to causing death, magic may have an effect on the course of a love affair, the well-being of one's crops, one's animals etc.

There is also a belief in spirits, both of the dead and those of the "bush." Although such beliefs are so widespread both in Africa and in the New World that it is impossible to trace their exact provenience, there are a number of parallels between Carib culture and other West Indian cultures. For example, the Black Caribs paint an indigo cross (using household bluing) on the forehead of infants to ward off evil spirits. Beckwith reports the identical custom in Jamaica.[13] Although fear of the evil eye is undoubtedly European in origin, the Caribs have a preventive measure not generally found among the mestizo peoples of Latin America. A charm consisting of a closed fist with the thumb inserted between the index and middle fingers is worn, commonly incorporated into a bracelet. Pierson notes the same charm worn for the same purpose among Negroes in Brazil.[14]

It is in the realms of folk-lore, music, and dancing that the most specific resemblances to the West Indies may be seen. Thus, as Taylor has mentioned, the proverbs, riddles, and folk-tales nearly all have themes identical to those recorded in Trinidad, Gaudaloupe, Martinique, and elsewhere.[15] Folk-tales are now generally told only at wakes by men who specialize in this art.

Music is an integral part of their life, and one encounters a number of types of songs and dance, each appropriate for a different occasion. Work songs are sung by women as they coöperate in grinding cassava or working in the fields, while other songs are used with drums as accompaniment in various dances. All of these songs have in common the element that they are comments on current happenings, although many of them are so old that the people no longer remember the events for which they were composed. They serve as moral instruction, as a form of social control, and as a means of broadcasting the latest events.

One of the most popular dances is that called *punta*. This is performed primarily at wakes, and appears to be very similar to the "plays" described by early writers among the slaves.[16] It is still danced in other parts of the Caribbean, though to the writer's knowledge it carries the name *punta* only among the Caribs and the Creoles of British Honduras. One couple occupies the center of a ring of onlookers who aid the drummers' accompaniment with singing and handclapping. The man and woman alternately pursue each other about the floor, at times attempting to get as close as possible to the other without actually touching. During the dance the feet move rapidly in a kind of sideways shuffle, the hips shimmy, and the arms are held alternately outstretched over the head, akimbo, or extended backwards. Occasionally a partner will drop out, leaving the other circling alone about the floor until some other person from the audience enters the circle. Often too, one person, usually a woman, will dance alone with no attempt to draw a partner out onto the floor. Although the word *punta* generally refers to the above complex of singing, dancing, and drumming, the Caribs also think of it as applying to the rhythm involved and to the *kind* of song sung in accompaniment to it. The themes are often derisive or critical, never naming the subject, but making his or her identity entirely clear. Herskovits notes that in Haiti women who share the same mate may sing derisive songs against each other, and that these songs are referred to as "point."[17] Conzemius believed it likely that the Caribs had adopted certain dance elements from Haiti.[18]

During the Christmas season there are a number of dances using costumes and masks held in the streets. Some of these have not yet been identified or linked by this writer to customs elsewhere, but most of them are suggestive of dances described in the Caribbean. The Caribs themselves have no knowledge of their origin or meaning. The first group to appear, about 24 December, are called *warîn*. This consists of a number of men dressed in costumes made of dried plantain leaves, with masks of papier-mâché or wire-screening material. They dance in various houses or yards to the accompaniment of drums, receiving small amounts of money, a drink of rum or wine, and perhaps a bit of food in return. This type of costume has been described by Crowley as one of the traditional masques of the Trinidadian carnival.[19] The type of behavior involved in this dance complex will readily be recognized as typical of many Negro groups in the Caribbean both during the days of slavery and at the present time.

On Christmas Day, and again on 1 January, another male dance group appears dressed in short full skirts, blouses with yokes and long full sleeves, flesh-colored stockings, masks, and elaborate headdresses built up something like a crown decorated with feathers and ribbons. Colored ribbons are also attached to the dress and stream out on all sides when the body is in motion. The dance has two names—one is *wanáragua*, which merely means "mask," according to Taylor.[20] The other name, and the one more commonly used, is "John Canoe." This is the name of a character widely portrayed in masked dances in Jamaica. In the 1830s the dance was described as follows: " . . . rapid crossings of the legs . . . terminating in a sudden stoppage."[21] Although hardly a complete description, this is also true of the dance as performed by the the Black Caribs today.

Throughout the Christmas season there appear from time to time other performers, whom the Caribs call *pia manádi*. These characters always go about in pairs, one dressed as a man, the other as a woman with pillows placed to emphasize the secondary sexual characteristics. These two are thought of as clowns. The most important aspect of their performance is verbal, consisting of repartee designed to amuse. It is always somewhat lewd, and the accompanying actions are often obscene. At times they beat each other with sticks. Part of the Carnival in Trinidad today involves a similar character called Pierrot Grenade, though it would be pushing the similarity too far to say the two are identical.[22]

Regardless of where the Black Caribs live today, they form a separate ethnic group which some social scientists might choose to call a caste. They tend to be endogamous, and though they mix freely with other people on many levels of daily intercourse, they usually prefer to return to their own group for the more intimate functions of life, including recreation, marriage, birth, and death.

In spite of the outcast status which they tend to hold today, it should not necessarily be assumed that the Black Caribs have been placed in such a position throughout their residence on the Central American shore. References to the Black Caribs during the first century after their arrival there make frequent mention of their friendly relations with other ethnic groups—in particular with other Negro groups.

The history of Negro occupation of the coast of Honduras goes back to the early sixteenth century when slaves were imported to work in the silver mines. In 1641 a slave ship direct from Africa was lost near Cape Gracias a Dios; the passengers escaped and settled on the coast all the way from the San Juan River to Trujillo.[23] In 1795 a group of Negroes from Santo Domingo was transported to Trujillo after the revolt in their country made it dangerous for them to remain there.[24] These references show that when the Black Caribs arrived on the mainland in 1797 it was already inhabited by numerous Negroes from various areas. In later years, especially during the first half of the twentieth century, thousands of Negroes came from all over the West Indies to work in the banana industry.[25]

It is this writer's opinion that economic competition, among other factors, contributed toward forming the present-day situation in which the Black Caribs are set apart as being "different," and therefore "inferior" to other Negro groups of the area.

Another early contact which the Black Caribs made with Negroes was in British Honduras. As early as 1802, only five years after their arrival on the mainland, we know that they were making frequent trips to that colony for the purpose of smuggling British goods to Honduras.[26] Some of them remained for longer periods to work in the mahogany plantations along with the Negroes who resided in British Honduras. In 1832 large numbers of Black Caribs left Honduras to settle permanently in the British colony after they had coöperated in an unsuccessful attempt by the Royalists to overthrow the Republican government in Honduras.

Several Black Carib genealogies were collected by the writer along the northern coast of Honduras, as well as in Livingston, Guatemala, which indicate non-Carib ancestors two to three generations back—usually Negroes from Haiti, Jamaica, or British Honduras. In Livingston they claim that their village was founded by a group of Black Caribs from Trujillo led by a Haitian. Although many of the details of this story are fantastic and show its myth-like character, it is not altogether improbable since we know that there was a group of Negroes from Haiti living in Trujillo when the Caribs arrrived there (see above).

In summary, an analysis of Black Carib culture combined with the evidence available concerning the group's recent history indicates that during the past 160 years they have become more similar culturally and racially to other Negro groups in the Caribbean than they were at the time of their deportation from the island of St. Vincent in the Lesser Antilles. Since the culture traits were adopted piecemeal from a variety of different Negro groups, their total culture resembles no one New World African pattern, but rather presents a configuration unique to the Black Carib. Nevertheless, this pattern should be considered as a variant of Afro American, rather than American Indian culture.

Because they have since become a more isolated in-group, if not to say a caste, these people have retained many traits which have changed or disappeared among their neighbors—traits which have generally been assumed to be strictly "Carib" by both Caribs and non-Caribs today.

NOTES

1. Materials from this article have been presented in two papers—one read at the Annual Meeting of the American Anthropological Association, December 1957, and the other at the International Congress of Americanists, July 1958. I wish to thank the Henry L. and Grace Doherty Foundation and the University of Michigan for grants which made the field work among the Black Carib possible.

2. Douglas M. Taylor, *The Black Carib of British Honduras* (New York, 1951), pp. 15-27.

3. *Idem*, p. 143. Also see Eduard Conzemius, "Ethnographical Notes on the Black Carib (Garif)" (*American Anthropologist*, vol. 30, pp. 183-205, 1928).

4. The term "Creole" as used here with respect to British Honduras refers to any person born in the Colony of Negro or mixed-Negro blood. This is the meaning currently attached to the term in the Colony itself. Although no studies of British Honduran culture have been published, the writer's own observations there indicate that it is similar in many ways to the cultures of other Negro groups in the Caribbean, especially in areas which are or have been British colonies. On the other hand, it does seem to exhibit many distinctive characteristics and would form an excellent field for study.

5. Melville J. Herskovits, *Life in a Haitian Valley* (New York, 1937); Melville J. Herskovits and Frances S. Herskovits, *Trinidad Village* (New York, 1947); Martha Warren Beckwith, *Black Roadways* (Chapel Hill, 1929); Fer-

nando M. Henriques, *Family and Colour in Jamaica* (London, 1953).

6. Charles Kingsley, *At Last: A Christmas in the West Indies* (London, 1887).

7. Beckwith, *op. cit.*, p. 30.

8. *Ibid.*

9. Herskovits and Herskovits, *op. cit.*, p. 290.

10. Taylor, *op. cit.*, pp. 140-42.

11. Ruy Galvao de Andrade Coelho, "The Black Carib of Honduras: A Study in Acculturation" (Ph.D. dissertation, Northwestern University, 1955).

12. Beckwith, *op. cit.*, pp. 78-84; Herskovits and Herskovits, *op. cit.*, pp. 134-41; *The Honduras Almanack* (Belize, 1830), p. 17.

13. *Idem*, p. 57.

14. Donald Pierson, *Negroes in Brazil* (Chicago, 1942), p. 257.

15. Taylor, *op. cit.*, p. 152.

16. James M. Phillippo, *Jamaica: Its Past and Present State* (Philadelphia, 1843), p. 93.

17. Herskovits, *op cit.*, p. 115.

18. Conzemius, *op. cit.*, p. 192.

19. Daniel J. Crowley, "The Traditional Masques of Carnival" (*Caribbean Quarterly*, vol. 4, 1954, p. 198).

20. Taylor, *op. cit.*, p. 7.

21. P. M. Sherlock, "West Indian Society a Century Ago" (*Caribbean Quarterly*, vol. 2, 1954, p. 47).

22. See Andrew T. Carr, "Pierrot Grenade" (*Caribbean Quarterly*, vol. 4, 1954, p. 281).

23. *Comisión de Las Islas del Cisne* (Teguicigalpa, 1926), p. 18.

24. Jacques Houdaille, "Negroes Franceses en America Central a fines del Siglo XVIII" (*Antropologia e Historia de Guatemala*, vol. 6, 1954, p. 65).

25. For information on this see Malcolm J. Proudfoot, *Population Movements in the Caribbean* (Port-of-Spain, 1950).

26. See John Alder Burdon, ed., *Archives of British Honduras.* (London, 1934), vol. 2 pp. 57, 60. Also Antonio R. Vallejo, *Primer Anuario Estadistico Correspondiente al Año de 1889* (Tegucigalpa, 1893), p. 123.

2

The Spread of Capitalism in Rural Colombia: Effects on Poor Women

Anna Rubbo

This essay will focus on peasant and lower-class urban women in the rapidly modernizing Puerto Tejada region of the Cauca Valley, western Colombia. As the process of rural proletarianization gathers momentum in this region, it appears that sex roles are not only altered in rather fundamental ways, but that possibly the new sex roles facilitate the docility of the work force that the new economy requires. One of the main conclusions drawn from this study is that, with the transition from a peasant to a rural proletarian community, the position of women has deteriorated both in the absolute sense and in relation to men, and that this deterioration has counterprogressive or even counter-revolutionary consequences.

By peasant I mean a person who has more or less secure control over the use of an area of land. In this region such areas are usually quite small, but in all cases they provide a significant part of the household income. By and large all people residing outside the town are classified as "peasants" in the above sense, while most people living in the town are landless. The peasants live in dispersed settlements within five miles of the township.

In tracing the recent history of this group of black peasants, the ecological effects of commercialized agriculture will be touched on, as will the social disruption of rural society. The focus of the discussion will be on the position of women in peasant and in plantation modes of production, and the ways in which patterns of social organization are affected by the change from one mode to the other. The role of sorcery in mediating these new relationships between men and women will also be discussed, and some comparisons will be made with middle-class women to differentiate class values in regard to gender.

THE REGION AND ITS HISTORY

According to nineteenth-century travelers, the Cauca Valley was a paradise of flora and fauna. Simon Bolivar, the famous South American liberator, called it a Garden of Eden. But that once-varied ecology has now been replaced by large scale monocropping, predominantly sugarcane. Rice, soya, corn, and a variety of beans are also grown commercially, and lower quality areas are devoted to cattle raising. This relatively seasonless, equatorial valley is approximately 90 miles long by 10 miles wide and nestles between the central and western *cordilleras* ("chains") of the Colombian Andes. The change in ecology from past to present is dramatic, and the remaining peasant farms are reminders of that past: a "jungle" of bamboo, coffee and cocoa trees, plantians, bananas, fruits, and plants for thatching and making twine, etc. The peasants call the monotonously regular green desert of cane *el monstruo verde* ("the green monster")—the god of the landlords.

The majority of the population are blacks, descendants of slaves brought to work the gold mines for the Spanish in the sixteenth and seventeenth centuries. Following abolition in 1852, they refused to work as day laborers on the haciendas, instead squatting on adjacent land. They cleared the thick jungle and began farming alongside communities of runaway slaves who had been growing contraband tobacco since the late eighteenth century. These "new" peasants grew corn, plantains, fruits, and sugarcane for domestic consumption, and were basically self-sufficient until the early twentieth century. In the 1920s coffee was introduced and quickly became an important cash crop along with cocoa.

Farm work is (and always has been) constant but does not require daily or full-time input. Coffee and cocoa are perennials, and they produce for most of the year. Each has two peak crop seasons annually, but are balanced so that while one is rising the other is falling, and total farm production is fairly constant. Twice a year the undergrowth beneath the coffee, cocoa, and plantians must be cleared, but in a farm with adequate shade trees and a mixture of tree types, the sun barely penetrates to allow much weed growth. Given the nature of the work, the crops, and the overall ecology, it was easy for women to own, manage, and work a farm as well as raise children, thus giving an economic base to female independence. There is no clear-cut sexual division of productive labor as far as the crops are concerned. In this culture women are as adept as men at handling the basic technology, but men rarely partake in domestic chores. Hence, women do both "women's" and "men's" work, while men do only "men's" work.

With the construction of a railway to the Pacific Ocean port of Beunaventura in 1914, the valley was opened up to foreign markets, and foreign investment occurred at an unprecedented rate. Subsequently, sugar production (all on large estates) rose dramatically, and this was due in part to the appropriation of peasant plots. Production in the Puerto Tejada region increased from 2,000 metric tons in 1938 to over 90,000 in 1969. But it was not until the Violencia that plantations made significant inroads into the Puerto Tejada area of the valley. The Violencia was a ten-year war (1948-1958), ostensibly between the Liberal and Conservative parties. It was not only a war between political parties, but in some ways, a frustrated social revolution in which an estimated 200,000 people lost their lives. But in addition, rich speculators capitalized on the fear of people and bought land cheaply. The plantations introduced aerial spraying of pesticides, and local people tell the story of how the airplanes sprayed peasant farms, killing shade trees vital for healthy coffee and cocoa. Furthermore, farms were flooded intentionally by the plantations as the latter acquired control of water canals. Some peasants had their crops stolen or destroyed, while others had their access blocked as the plantations acquired the surrounding land. The people describe the Violencia as a many-headed beast, not the least threatening part of it being the land-hungry plantations.

However, there was another factor. Since the expansion of the sugarcane plantations there have always been local peasants and plantation workers willing to collaborate with the plantation owners, some working as brokers persuading their neighbors to sell, others reporting back any signs of unrest or subversion, either within the work force or outside of it. Curiously, it is often said that women do not report on their fellow female workers. Apart from state law enforcement, there is an extensive network to combat "subversion"—from the workers who "sing" to the bosses, to the local parapolice organization, Defense Civil (Civil Defense), and the sugar growers' organization, Asocaña.

The plantation owners, cattle ranchers, and absentee aristocratic families who own the land today view the people with varying degrees of racism and fear (although racism as a national character- istic is always denied), and plantation owners move in convoys with armed guards supplied by the state. The foremen and administra- tive staff drive powerful jeeps and stay close to their two-way radios. To these people, the work force is an unhappy necessity and they would prefer a mechanized sugar industry if it were politically and economically possible. As long as that is not possible, certain steps are taken to minimize the troublesome factors of a recalci- trant work force, the *sindicatos patronales* (owner-controlled trade unions), and the *contratista* system being the most significant steps.

The latter is a system whereby the plantations contract a set piece of work to a local contractor, who in turn subcontacts to local workers. This type of "casual" worker has no right to form trade unions or to receive social service benefits. It is crucial to realize that women, especially townswomen, are being drawn increasingly into this *contratista* system, as the contractors consider them to be less trouble than men, and can hire them at lower wages.

The changes necessitated by modern capitalist enterprises are difficult ones, and clearly result in both social atomization and individual alienation. Witness the men who work from 6:00 a.m. to 5:00 p.m. in the canefields five and a half days a week, and then spend most of Saturday afternoon waiting for pay; or the women who must leave their young children while they work an eight-hour day far from home. Emerging leaders are frequently co-opted, and self-interest nearly always supersedes collective interest. As one local put it: "The problem with Colombia is that there is too much imperialism, egoism, and poverty."

Most of the plantation workers live in the township. With the coming of the sugarcane plantations, the town itself has changed from being a service and market center into a rural slum, little more than a barracks and dormitory of landless sugarcane workers. In the 1960s the flood of black immigrants from the Pacific coast added to the number of locally dispossessed peasants. The town's population more than doubled in the thirteen years between 1951 and 1964, with the immigrants constituting 26 percent of the population. By 1964 most of the land was in sugarcane, and only one-fifth of the area's population lived in the countryside. In a short space of time, the majority of the people changed from semisubsistence farmers to landless rural proletarians (DANE [Departamento Administrativo Nacional de Estadistica], 1954, 1964).

Although Puerto Tejada is the richest municipality in the department of Cauca in terms of material output, it is one of the poorest in services. There is neither sewerage nor clean drinking water. Production taxes go to the national government, and no local taxes are exacted from the plantations. Use of the roads, for instance, is vital to the plantations, but the roads are maintained at local expense. The plantations do not feed profits back into the town, and workers have little power to demand better working conditions or a more responsible involvement of plantations in urban improvement. For instance, the major source of drinking water, the Palo River, is dangerously contaminated with fecal bacteria. One of the sugar mills, located upstream from the town, draws water from the river to clean its machinery and pigpens, and then returns the water to the river. Not surprisingly, the incidence of intestinal parasites is widespread. Periodically the impurity of the water is protested, but to date the situation has not changed. People of the upper and middle classes bring their drinking water from nearby Cali or have their own purification plants.

HOUSEHOLD SOCIAL STRUCTURES AND WOMEN—GENERAL CONSIDERATIONS

Some general remarks can be made about women in the region with reference to their lifestyles and the attitudes of women toward men (and vice versa), although there are variations according to location, age, civil status, and so on.

Domestic work is "women's work." This includes marketing (all buying and much of the selling), cooking, cleaning, washing, mending, fetching water, chopping wood, and caring for the children in general. Women often do "men's work" as well, as agricultural day laborers and peasants. Men, however, rarely do "women's" work.

In their relationships with men, women are frequently subjected to male jealously and possessiveness, which apply in descending degrees to legal wives, free-union wives, daughters, and lovers.

Men, although they cause women to be jealous, do not accept any claims on their freedom of movement, nor do they modify their behavior on account of female pressures. For the men it is considered customary and "correct" to come and go as they please, to go drinking and dancing, and to have a concubine or "woman in the *calle* [street]." Women's activities in public places are curtailed, and subject to much malicious gossip. Women cannot go to the cinema, bars, or cafes alone, or even with female friends. Men often demand that women leave the house only for a specific destination and that they must be accompanied by a child or friend. Women can stroll in the plaza at dusk, if accompanied, and are free to go to church alone. Women's most social meeting places are the marketplace and the riverbank where they wash several times a week. However, if a man is ambitious he will forbid his wife to wash in the river, in which case she will be forced to do it in the isolation of her own backyard or, money permitting, hire a washer-woman.

These restrictions apply generally more to townswomen than rural women, more to officially married women than to those living in free unions, more to whites than to blacks, and more to women of higher than lower class.

If we look at the social structure of households—either statically or over time—we see that the restrictions imposed by men must be weakened in many cases, since households headed by women are quite common, as are free unions in comparison with official (i.e., church) marriages.

Fluidity and flux are the keynotes in the social organization of this culture. The outstanding characteristics of household structure are the high degree of those headed by women, and of extended, rather than nuclear, units. The latter, in fact, account for less than half the households, whether they are in the town or the countryside. Serial polygamy is very common, as are "visiting" or extraresidential liaisons between women and men. Inheritance is partible, shared equally between males and females, and offspring from all the deceased's sexual unions are entitled to share. Blood ties are considered to be far more important than marriage or affinal ties, and of those blood ties the mother-child bond is the most important of all. These patterns of residence, mating, and inheritance lead to an extremely diffuse series of social networks in which it is possible for any individual to claim kinship with a vast number of people. On the other hand, such claims are bound to be ambiguous and conflicting and are by no means necessarily binding.

TABLE 1
COMPARISON OF HOUSEHOLD STRUCTURES BETWEEN RURAL AND TOWN AREAS IN 1973 (AS PERCENTAGES OF ALL HOUSEHOLDS)

Household type	Rural household (N = 36)	Town household (N = 35)
Simple nuclear	32	45
Extended	32	26
Denuded nuclear:		
headed by women	8	6
headed by men	2	0
Denuded extended:		
headed by women	24	23
headed by men	2	0
	100%	100%

TABLE 2
COMPARISON OF AFFINAL STATUSES BETWEEN RURAL AND TOWN SAMPLES IN 1971 (AS PERCENTAGES OF HOUSEHOLD CHIEFS)

	Rural sample (N = 36)	Town sample N = 35)
Church married	18	14
Free union (co-resident)	50	49
Visting union	9	18
No spouse	23	19
	100%	100%

We now turn to some of the differences between the town and the countryside seen in Table 1. In the town the nuclear type of household is much more common than in the countryside (45 percent of all households as against 32 percent). There is also a marked increase in the proportion of sexual unions that are visiting or extra-residential (18 percent as compared with 9 percent). Households headed by women form roughly the same proportion in both areas.

It would appear that these two major differnces are a result of basic differences in the modes of production that are associated with each locality. Whereas peasant women invariably have an economic base in their land, the townswomen do not have land and are forced to unite with those who have some economic security, fragile as that might be—the male plantation workers. As a general rule townswomen depend on male wage-earners to a far higher degree than do peasant women, and this would seem to account for most of the differences between their mating and residential patterns.

Although the nuclear type of household is more common in town than in the countryside, the rate of marriage (church or consensual) is not more frequent, as seen in Table 2. Rather, there are fewer church marriages in the town than in the countryside. This apparently contradictory phenomenon needs explanation. It appears that in the past (including the slave past) church marriage was considered customary, but statistics show that the rate has continually fallen over the past forty years. Some informants say this is due to landlessness. As one young married peasant male expressed it: "Parents made one marry. But now young people have nothing to look forward to in the future. They have no land" Furthermore, divorce is impossible, and with women becoming more dependent on men, the restrictions and obligations of church marriage are not all that enticing. By contrast, peasant women, with their relative economic independence, have not felt the same "negative" pressures that marriage can exert upon lower-class townswomen.

The latter quite consciously regard marriage as a silly or even bad thing to do, and in this way they are joined by the male folk. Women say, for example, that marriage "spoils a relationship," "gives the spouse too much control," "is not necessary now since a 'natural child' [i.e., a bastard] has the same rights as a 'legitimate' one," and that marriage "is worse than living in a free union if [as is highly likely], the marriage breaks up and one is forced into sin [living with another man out of wedlock, or just the fact of separation itself]." A common saying is that marriage brings seven years of bad luck, and most persons, of either sex, energetically regard marriage as a severe restriction on one's liberty.

Peasant Women

Peasant women have the possibility of leading a life relatively free from the restraints imposed by men and by the system of wage labor. Because of partible inheritance they can own land, and it is not uncommon, for example, to find instances of a nuclear family with the women as the sole landowner. In such cases the restrictions on women described above apply with much less force, if they apply at all. Men in this situation are sometimes maintained as cheap labor and are occasionally considered to be untrustworthy and unreliable in providing for offspring. A common saying goes: *"Se pican y se van"* ("they sting and they leave," or, they get you pregnant and go). In extended families (often headed by women due to the widowhood of the mother), the mother frequently decides to exclude men from the household, with her daughters' approval. It is not expected that the daughters will remain childless. Rather, each will be a welcome addition to the family.

In the practice of traditional agriculture (the cultivation of coffee, cocoa, plantains, etc.), the work can be, and often is, done by women. During harvest, extra labor from kin and neighbors can always be found if necessary, but the peasant ecology and crop types are such that not only is there year-round production with harvesting every two weeks, but a few hands can generally cope. Labor input and income vary little over the annual cycle. It appears that traditionally there was reciprocation of labor during harvests, but now every job and exchange is mediated by money. In a situation where men and women have various mates, and have children by each mate, it is usual to find wives working for husbands for cash, sons working for mothers for cash, mothers working for sons for cash, and so on. The mediation of the cash nexus is not necessarily the same, and need not imply the unbiquity of the profit motive. To the contrary, these peasants orient themselves to certain subsistence goals, as defined by the culture, and the prevalence of cash transactions testifies to the fact that even the peasantry depend on store-bought goods for a significant part of their daily consumption.

Let us sketch out a typical day for a woman from an extended, woman-headed household. She rises at 6:30 a.m. and over a wood fire makes breakfast of deep-fried plantains and sweet black coffee, with corn cakes or bread occasionally substituted for plantains. Her very young children stay with her mother; others go to school or work. Work may be helping the mother, or working on neighboring commercial farms or as casual day laborers. By the time children are three or four years old they can do a variety of tasks, such as helping in the house, running messages, and caring for younger brothers and sisters. They are disciplined but not passive, and are brought up to be honest and trustworthy.

At 7:30 the woman will go to work picking coffee, cocoa, fruits, or plantains, or weeding around the trees. If she is close to home she will come home at 11:00 for lunch, then leave again until her return at 3:30. At 4:00 she will begin making the evening meal of soup, rice, and perhaps meat or beans, although these latter are rare. At 5:30 dinner will be over and the family will sit talking by candlelight, or listen to the *novelas* (serialized dramas) on the transistor radio (if they have one). It is not necessary to farm every day, and two or three days a week will be allocated to washing, marketing, sewing or mending, visiting, etc. Sunday is a festive day, a day for fine clothes, dancing, drinking, visiting, and marketing.

If a woman likes agricultural life and has sufficient land (three to four acres), she will pass her working life in this way. If not, she may turn to higgling—wholesaling and retailing agricultural products from neighboring peasant holdings in various local markets. If she does not have sufficient land to support her family, she or a teen-age daughter may go to the nearby big city to work as maids, but they are not likely to stay long. They will say the work "bores" them, a boredom arising out of a master-slave relationship, low wages, and virtual imprisonment in the employer's house (except for a half-day off every week or two weeks). Generally a maid is an object for abuse from the master, mistress, and their offspring.

The peasant woman can lose her independence if her landholding produces too little, or alternatively when agricultural methods and crops start to change. Such a transformation is now frequently given an impetus by government agencies like the agricultural extension agency, ICA, which tries to persuade peasants to cut down their perennial coffee and cocoa trees and replace them with seasonal "green revolution" crops such as corn, soybeans, tomatoes, etc. The decision to cut down the trees is usually made after a struggle between the older women and the young men in the house. The women are adamantly against such a change, realizing that although the aging and sometimes diseased trees do not produce much, they always produce something. It is a form of agriculture the women understand, and a landscape they love. But when the chaotic-looking jungle of plants and trees is replaced by open fields full of the same plants, tractors driven by men are required to plough the ground, and fertilizers are necessary to enrich the soil. Pesticides become essential to keep the insect population under control, and delicate plants such as tomatoes need constant care and spraying. The new agriculture requires much greater capital and labor inputs than did the traditional agriculture, and the financing organizations usually prefer to do business with men than with women. Likewise, ICA is an all-male organization and conducts all its dealings with the male peasants, even when the women may be substantial landowners.

The struggle tends to be won increasingly by the young men as the old women die, and the hope of making a lot of money quickly becomes irresistible. Although credit to the small farmer is limited and interest rates are high, many peasants with small landholdings are turning to these seasonal crops. What the young men do not realize is that the risks are high and that a bad season can ruin the small farmer. An example (and not an isolated one) is the case of Elberto. He borrowed the equivalent of $800 to plant tomatoes. One month before harvesting. Some exceptionally heavy rains washed the plants away. Now Elberto cannot pay the penalty interests imposed on the loan, let alone the loan itself. It is probable that ultimately his land will be confiscated and made available to one of the plantations.

It would seem that the old women are right, and that to cut down the coffee and cocoa trees is to court disaster. A critical time is coming, due to the fact that there has not been any systematic tree replanting over the years. Now that the trees are old, production is dropping and people have no savings to fall back on.

Lower-Class Townswomen

The life of the townswomen is very different from that of the peasants. Many peasant women will say town life is much better because you do not have to fetch water and chop wood, there is more company, and there are more things happening (*ambiente*). But living in town is expensive, and "free" farm products such as water, fuel, a house, etc., have to be paid for, thus accentuating the need for a paying job. However, there are few jobs for women, especially in the town, and they tend to go to the lower middle class rather than to the lower class: i.e., jobs as shop assistants or waitresses. Some women make a living selling baked goods, drinks, and food on the two weekly market days. Others station themselves daily outside the prison, the bus station, dance halls, or in the *zona de tolerancia*. Women with capital often buy a sewing machine, and dressmaking can be a relatively lucrative profession. Lower-class women without capital tend to become prostitutes, and little stigma is attached to this by persons of the same class. As one woman explained, *"Vendo mis carnes para mis hijos"* ("I sell my flesh for my children"). Alternatively, some of these women work in agriculture, sometimes combining both prostitution and agricultural work according to what is offered. The majority of jobs for townswomen are found in the fields, as casual day laborers rather than permanent, affiliated workers with health and retirement benefits. It is extremely important to point out that contractors prefer to employ women because they are thought to be *más mansa* (more docile) than the men, and will work for lower wages. They are *más mansa* because they frequently have numerous children to feed, often with minimal help (or none at all) from the father of the children. These are the women from the extended or female-headed families experiencing the difficulties of the proletarian role.

The work these women do is tiring and often extremely harmful to their health, as in the common case where they must apply powerful organo-phosphorous pesticides by hand, plant by plant, from a small container. They work in the cane and soybean fields sowing and weeding, and in the cornfields sowing weeding, fumigating, and harvesting. The bean crops are harvested mechanically, but the harvesters fail to pick up the whole crop. What remains (the *requisa*) is harvested by gleaners who give half to the owner and keep the other half for themselves. Many poor families rely heavily on the *requisa* to augment their incomes. From this activity has grown the derogatory use of the word *iguaza* (a small duck that digs in the earth) to describe the female lumpenproletariat. Their earnings barely suffice for basic necessities. Emergencies such as a death, sickness, accidents, or something special for school nearly always require that the family pawn a possession, such as a watch, a pair of pants, a dress, or a bed. The four pawnshops are all owned by whites who live outside the town, and they charge 10 percent interest a month!

Misia* Juana, age thirty-four, is the mother of four children. She has had seven pregnancies. The oldest child is thirteen, the youngest five. A year ago she was abandoned by her "husband," who went to live with another woman who had only one child and a small *finca*, or garden plot. He is a cane cutter and supplies the family each week with basic but insufficient foods, such a rice, flour, potatoes, noodles, and cooking fat, all purchased in the company store. Juana has to supplement the food, pay the rent, and provide clothes, school books, and medicine. She works as a day laborer and after a harvest will glean with one or two of the children. She works intermittently because of her ill health and because often something needs to be done for the children. When she works, the five-year-old stays home alone because his sisters go to school. He is either locked in or out of the one-room house because of the fear of thieves.

Juana describes her childhood on the Pacific Coast where food was plentiful and nobody worked for cash. Their economy was subsistence farming and fishing. She came with her husband, José, to the *valle* to make money to buy some luxury items. Now, fifteen years later, there is no possibility of her returning to the Coast (where she has land) because she could never raise the capital necessary for the return journey and to support the family for the first few months. (Although she says that the latter objection is not so important, because on the Coast people help one another.) In the pueblo, nothing is given away. Of the separation of herself and her husband she said, "It is terrribly serious to lose your man, because then you live very badly. It is a sin against the children and it is very bad for me. I am left in the street when he goes to another woman. If we lived on the Coast, however, it would not be so bad."

With the strain of her responsibilities and the lack of food in the house (it is usual to hear one of the children crying after a meal, "*Mama, tengo hambre*" ["Mama, I'm hungry"]), she periodically goes "mad." She takes off her clothes and dances in the streets until someone catches her and takes her inside. If she does not recover she goes to the mental hospital in the nearby city, but she never stays more than a few days because she worries about the children.

She does not know what to do. She wants to buy a house so that at least the family will have a permanent roof over their heads, but

* The prefix *misia* is the lower-class equivalent of *doña* and carries the same connotation of respect.

working as a day laborer (and an irregular one at that) she does not make enough money. She talks of going to the city to work as a maid, but what would happen to the children? It would be difficult for her to find work, since she neither reads nor writes, and most employers want a literate person. Her chances of bettering her life seem dismal. Her ill health and disposition make it impossible to make the "best" out of day laboring. She has no capital to try anything else. Her life is a holding operation—against hunger, sickness, and sadness; yet she has a tenderness and gentleness for her children and other people that survives under extraordinary privation.

Miss Graciela, age twenty-eight, was born in the town and is the mother of three children. She has given birth to five, but two died at about nine months of age. She was brought up in a convent by nuns, who taught anticommunism as well as religion. Her parents are both dead, and what little land they owned has been dissipated among the inheritors, who over time have sold it to meet debts. Graciela owns the one room she lives in and the land on which it stands. Her children have all been fathered by the same man. He comes from the Pacific Coast, where he had a "wife" and children. He has another woman in the pueblo who also has a child by him. Graciela did not believe that Pablo had another woman until she saw her with him one day in the street, pregnant. She was very angry and jealous, not so much out of spurned love as out of pride and annoyance that his meager wages would be further divided. For they must now be divided among the woman on the Coast, Pablo's aging father, herself, her children, and the new woman and child. Their relationship had not been good for some time, and he had been seeing other women. He stayed out late at night drinking and dancing, and gave her little help with the children. One night she was sick and the baby was crying. After trying to console the baby she asked him to help, but he rolled over and went to sleep, saying, "It's your job, you're the mother, aren't you?" Subsequently she tried to keep him out of the room, and when he came home at 4:00 a.m. she barred the door. But this was ineffective, because he told her that if there was no intercourse, she would receive no money. Consequently, she became pregnant again. Piedad was born, and a month later the baby Cecilia died of pneumonia. The hut was damp, and there was no money for medicine. Then Pablo began working on a sugarcane plantation three hours away, coming back only on Sundays.

Since Graciela was dependent on him for money, she had to comply with his wishes. The money she received for herself and the children came irregularly and was barely enough. He would give her about $2.00 (U.S.) a week, but this only provided her with the most meager necessities (rice, the staple, costs 15¢/pound; meat, 40¢; a tin of powdered milk, $1.00). She has had several jobs but always finds it difficult to hold a job and care for the three young children, who are nine months, five, and six year olds. She has worked frying small things to eat in the streets, but that was not profitable. She had a job cooking at one of the plantations, but there were so many mosquitos and insects in the plantation-provided room that the children could not sleep. She then had a job living in, cooking and cleaning for an elderly grain merchant. However, he became sick and was frightened that he was going to die without kin in the house. On two days' notice he fired her. Her only solution was to return to her room and wait for her husband to come with money. The corner storekeeper gives credit, but on many items his prices are 10 to 20 percent higher than in the government-operated store.

There is little accord between members of her extended family, so child care cannot be taken care of collectively; nor does she have any security in case of an emergency, such as when she went to have a sterilization operation. The care of the children during her eight-day absence became a problem. She did not want to leave them with the sister she lives with; nor could she leave them with her childless sister. Finally she left them with her husband's lover, reasoning that she was the person who had the most obligation to look after them. The woman recognized her obligation, and the children were well treated.

Graciela can see few ways out of her situation. Her hope is to go to the nearby big city and work as a maid for a middleclass family for $20 to $30 a month. She would be unable to take the children with her and might leave them with the husband's lover or with a relation of his some two hours away. The separation from her children would be very painful, but she is matter-of-fact about the realities of her situation and her lack of choice. She tries to invoke magic in a half-hearted way to win back Pablo's affections so that he will give her enough money for her and the children's survival.

His life is not easy either, although he does not have the constant responsibilities of young children. He cuts cane and lives in a plantation camp three hours from the pueblo. He works under the hot sun, nine hours a day, five days a week. Saturday is a five-hour workday, after which the workers wait for two or three hours while the pay is given out. He suffers from back and eye trouble, and at thirty-three appears almost a physical wreck. On Sunday he puts on his silk shirt and dark glasses and tries to forget the canefields.

Unlike Graciela, Felipa is coping a little better with her life and has even been involved in some industrial strikes. She comes from the Pacific Coast and has no kin ties in the town. The wage she earns is not enough to support a family if they are to eat anything much other than rice. Hence, women like Felipa are under great pressure to work regularly, and to get their children into the work force as soon as possible. In contrast to country children, town children are frequently undisciplined, untrained in traditional customs, and likely to get involved in petty crime at an early age.

Felipa is twenty-seven and has three primary-school-age children. She lives alone with the children in one room, which she rents. She works as a day laborer and manages to do so fairly consistently, as she is strong and in reasonably good health. She makes one dollar a day and sometimes more. She has been involved in two strikes, although strikes among the women workers are rare. Other poor townswomen described the situation this way:

> We went to work at five in the morning. Don Juan, the *contratista*, offered us 15¢ per sack of corn that we picked. But we had heard that he was being paid 35¢ a sack. So we left and walked home, which was a good three-hour walk. There were no leaders; we were unanimous. The *mayordomo* of the hacienda spoke to him, and the next day he offered us 25¢. We weren't satisfied, but we need the money. If I don't work, we don't eat.

> One day we went to weed corn. The rows of corn were very long, as far as you could see. They were offering 20¢ a row, and each was about 400 meters long. We told the *contratista* that rows were worth 30¢, because besides weeding we had to drop pesticide on each plant

from a bottle. We have heard that these pesticides are very dangerous to one's health. He refused to raise the pay, so we left. We walked for one and one-half hours when the *contratista* caught up with us and offered us 25¢. We decided, reluctantly, to take the money. We all have children at home.

These examples are typical of the desperate situation. Whereas a peasant woman could combine farming and childrearing with a degree of emotional and economic stability for all, the poor towns-woman struggles to earn a living and to raise children as she would like to, that is, as *formal* ("polite") and worthy members of society. For peasants, especially the women, householding includes domes-tic work, child-rearing, and farming, and in a very real sense these are organically interconnected. For the townswomen, however, these basic aspects of life are structurally differentiated, and what is more, seem incapable of synthesis.

SORCERY

The new dependence on men induces competition between women that is dramatically illustrated in the use of sorcery and love magic. Sorcery (*brujeria*) is used to capture a man's affections, or to keep a straying man in line. It need hardly be said that it is more widely used in the town than in the country.

There are various methods women can use to capture a man's affections. Most involve some ritual use of potions, the ingredients for which are bought from the Amazon Indian traders in the local marketplace. The simplest *liga* is achieved by placing some of the special potion on the man's clothing. Others are more complex and ritualized. The commonly known recipes, or methods, follow.

Light and smoke a cigar about halfway. Take a candle (preferably bought with the money of the man you are trying to attract) and break it in half. Light one piece of it. Sprinkle sugar or pepper onto the burning cigar and puff very hard. Concentrate on the man. When the ash is ready to drop, let it fall and then stamp on it while saying three times, "So and so, *hijo de puta*" (son of a prostitute). It should be noted that this expression is a very common form of abuse, but normally it is used more often by men than women. It is believed that the smoke can penetrate the brain of the man.

Homemade *ligas* are also effective; two commonly used ones are as follows. Take some hair from the head, armpits, and pubic areas and mix them with the sperm of the lover. (The sperm is obtained after intercourse during which the woman does not have an orgasm, so as to maintain the purity of the sperm.) Place the ingredients in a bottle and mix them with alcohol. Then bury the bottle inside the house. For the second *liga* take some armpit and pubic hair, toast it, grind it, and mix it with the man's coffee. If the sorcery is strong enough, the man can be turned into a fool (*tonto*) and will forever "walk behind" (*anda atras*) the woman.

In the case of love rivalries and the tensions arising from a triangular relationship, it is not the male who is reproached for the affair, but the woman. It is commonly said that one of the women will try to use sorcery to harm or kill the other woman, or to at least terminate the relationship. It is supposed that she will frequently employ the services of a female sorcerer. Such was the case with Dolores and Julia.

Dolores had a husband who was having an affair with another woman. At that time she was working as a day laborer, and it was usual for the workers to eat a cooked lunch. One day she ate a lunch prepared by a friend, and from that day her stomach began to swell. At first she thought she was pregnant, but the swelling became very extreme and remained. Shortly after the swelling had begun her husband left her to live with the other woman. Two years later, Dolores was very sick, and the rest of her body was emaciated. She was sure that it was sorcery administered through the food. (Food is commonly considered to be a medium for magic; for this reason salt, for example, can never be borrowed.) Her old, blind mother became very angry upon hearing this and said that if the other woman should hear of her suspicions she would use more sorcery to finish her off.

Julia and Carlos have been married for ten years and have seven children. He has a photography business in which she helps occasionally. Their newly purchased television set seems to indicate that the business is going well. He comes from an agricultural family with little land, and she comes from the Pacific Coast. Carlos has a lover and a child by her. When he brought the "new sister" to the house one day, the children would have nothing to do with her. In spite of having a lover, he is extremely possessive of his wife and will not allow her to walk alone in the street. Recently he became very vicious toward her, and he beats her frequently. She is afraid, as are his brothers and his mother, that he will kill her but they feel powerless because they believe him to be bewitched. It is presumed that Carlos' lover is behind it.

Some time ago a strange woman came to the door and gave one of the children three beautiful oranges. Julia said they must be thrown away, which they were. Shortly thereafter the woman came again with more oranges, and this time they were put aside and stayed in the house until they began to go bad. From approximately this time Julia and Carlos' relationship began to deteriorate. They went to a curer, but Carlos refused to take the herbal remedies he prescribed. The situation worsened and Julia sent to the mayor's office to file a complaint and to take out a *caucion* against Carlos in case he should become more violent. The judge ordered them to see a psychiatrist (!) but neither of them wants to do that. Neither has any understanding of the workings of psychiatry, and they cannot imagine that a white, middle-class psychiatrist can help them.

Although women employ sorcery in questions of love, they do not employ sorcery as a means of directly improving their material situation. In contrast, some men working in the sugar plantations make a pact with the devil to increase production. The pact allows the worker to increase the amount of cane cut or loaded, but there are conditions attached to it—usually a time limit on one's life, and an unpleasant death. It is said that the money thus earned cannot be turned into productive capital and must be spent on consumer luxuries. A pig bought with the money would die, a business started with it would fonder. It is indeed devil's money, fit only for drinking and gambling. Like the townswomen, peasants (men and women) do not make pacts with the devil. The making of such a pact seems to be an expression of alienation from both land and work. The peasants do not suffer that alienation, and the townswomen cannot "afford" to, in the sense that to make such a pact would jeopardize their ability to provide food for their children.

In summary, it is important to note the role of sorcery. In a rapidly "modernizing" world, sorcery is not losing out. On the contrary, it appears to be patching up some of the gaping cultural, economic, and social holes produced by rural capitalism in its plantation form. Although it crosses racial lines (the most respected curers and sorcerers are Indians from the Upper Amazon), it does not often cross class lines; it therefore serves to unite lower-class people in some ways. Sorcery also unites women as a group, but in a complex way, because it both divides women, and serves as an acceptable rationalization of men's mistreatment of them. It contributes to their oppression, but is also one of their few sources of power.

CONCLUSION

In conclusion, it should be said that women in this modernizing situation have a difficult role and that they live it with great courage. Change in the mode of production works in this case to the disadvantage of women. Women have lost their economic independence while often retaining sole responsibility for raising their children. As peasants, women often choose to be singly responsible for their children, but it becomes very difficult to do so as proletarians or lumpenproletarians. This has resulted in women having to seek work wherever they can and under adverse conditions, as we saw in the case of the *iguazas*, the female agricultural laborers. We see also that tensions in interpersonal relations are exacerbated by an ambivalent acceptance of dependence on men, and an ambivalent reluctance of men to be depended on.

It is not so much the "sexist" culture that is the fundamental problem (although there is much sexism), but the new relations of production and lack of land that are disrupting the lives of both men and women, thus altering the function of traditional mating patterns that previously allowed great flexibility for both sexes.

The ability of women to change their lives for the better is seriously inhibited as they become increasingly dependent on men who now exercise a new power over them by virtue of the availability and nature of work. This new power arises from a fundamental and total change in the social relations of production: from a peasant mode of production to a capitalist mode. In turn, it is important to emphasize the growing dependence of the men themselves on these macroeconomic structures, and the declining control they have over their own lives. For women, the effect of this growing dependence on males might be more accurately described as a subdependence—a dependency merely mediated by the male wage laborer, which serves to bind women emotionally, economically, and often unwillingly, to men, and through them to the wider system.

3

Images of the Woman of Color in Brazilian Literature: O Cortico, Clara Dos Anjos, Gabriela Cravo E Canela, and O Quinze

Maria Luisa Nunes

The topic of the woman of color in Brazilian literature presents a certain confusion to the uninitiated and therefore requires some elucidation before it may be broached. Until abolition in 1888, there were enslaved and free women of color in Brazil. Of these women, some were black with no white admixture and others were *mulatas* (mulatto women) of varying degrees of white admixture. As one of the works we have selected will demonstrate, there is a marked difference in Brazil between the black and the *mulata*, especially between the enslaved black women and the free *mulata*. Within the Brazilian context, this is a significant factor since miscegenation has been a constant feature of the society. Although this phenomenon is extremely complex, the main point to bear in mind is that mulattoes have a great deal more social mobility in Brazil then blacks, consider themselves different from and superior to blacks, and are generally so regarded by the society.[1] In our study, we will attempt to show how the *mulata* is represented in literature as a symbol of Brazil and that she is the object of Brazilian society's rather ambivalent attitudes. Her sensuality is opposed to her innocence but she sometimes combines these qualities. Male writers view her differently from women. It is a very important consideration that the latter have always been an oppressed class with few rights in Brazilian society. It is this factor more than any other which has determined the role that the woman of color has played in Brazilian life.

The works we have selected for our study include many variables. Three of the authors who have written novels dealing with the question are men: Aluizio de Azevedo (*O Cortico*), Lima Barreto (*Clara dos Anjos*), and Jorge Amado (*Gabriela Cravo e Canela*). The fourth is a woman, Rachel de Queiroz (*O Quinze*). Of the four authors, Aluizio de Azevedo, Jorge Amado, and Rachel de Queiroz are white, Lima Barreto while one is a mulatto. At first glance, the limited number of nonwhite authors who have treated black themes seems odd, but in the Brazilian literary context, it is quite normal. In fact, most nonwhite Brazilian writers have not discussed racial themes. This, of course, is in sharp contrast to the situation in the United States where, historically, blacks have dealt almost exclusively with the problems of the color line. The near absence of discussion of racial themes by nonwhite Brazilian authors is simply an indication of Brazil's more complex racial hierarchy. The time sequence of the literature covered in this discussion ranges from the late nineteenth century, to the early twentieth century, to the twenties, and, finally, to the early thirties. The geographical settings of the works range from Rio de Janeiro to the Northeastern states of Bahia and Ceará. The geographical factor is important since it is from Rio north to Bahia and beyond that we find the greatest amount of Afro-Brazilian cultural influence and synthesis, while from São Paulo south we encounter the effects of European immigration in Brazil. Therefore, in discussing questions of race, it is important to take location into consideration. It is clear that all these variables affect the author's portrayal of his female characters, but because we are dealing with imaginative literature, artistry is of great consequence as well.

It is striking that in the three novels written by men, as opposed to the one written by a woman, the female characters cover a spectrum of symbols. These symbols include the black slave, the passionate *mulata*, the innocent young mulatto woman as victim, and ingenuous *mulata* as the personification of love. In Rachel de

Queiroz's novel, we find woman as a more complex human being. Such a judgment of the four works as this one is overly simplistic, however, and must be examined in the light of the variables we outlined above. Aluizio de Azevedo's slave and sex symbols reflect the author's vision of late nineteenth century tenement life in Rio de Janeiro. Although this is his personal vision, it also reflects some of the historical reality of the society. Lima Barreto's portrayal of the *mulata* as victim gives us firsthand insights into the status of women of color as seen by a man of color, a criticism of women in society, and a very subjective and personal view of the suffering of the nonwhite artist in Brazil. The Bahian Jorge Amado attempts to illustrate the cultural and racial fusion of the Northeast through his *mulata* heroine, Gabriela. The regional variable is most relevant in this novel if we are to accept Amado's glorification of Brazil's mulatto civilization. Rachel de Queiroz's novel perhaps comes closest to a depiction of a particular woman's interior life, but, apparently, traditional feminine roles have kept the author from dis— cussing important aspects of her character's existence.

Aluizio de Azevedo's *O Cortiço**appeared in 1890. An example of naturalist literature in Brazil, this novel portrays the life of a teeming Carioca**tenement of the second half of the nineteenth century. Its inhabitants are Portuguese and Italian immigrants and lower class Brazilians of all hues. As a backdrop for the main themes of the novel—the avarice and social ascension of a Portuguese immigrant, the accommodation to Brazilian life by another, and the sexual mores of the tenants—we see the racial integration of lower class life in Brazil. Directly related to these themes are two women of color: the black slaves, Bertoleza, and the *mulata*, Rita Baiana. In his essay "The Masters and the Slaves," Gilberto Freyre quotes an old Brazilian saying: "White woman for marriage, mulatto woman for f _____, Negro woman for work."[2] It would seem that Azevedo had this saying in mind while portraying of his female characters. In general, the novel lacks psychological penetration so that neither Bertoleza or Rita Baiana go much beyond stereotypes.

Bertoleza's role in the novel revolves around the theme of the ascension of the avaricious Portuguese immigrant. She is a black

---

*Translated as *A Brazilian Tenement*.
**Of or pertaining to Rio de Janeiro.

slave born in Brazil, a *crioula*, and belongs to an old blind man who resides in Juiz de Fora. As a vegetable seller in the city, she is able to bring her owner 20,000 reis a month and still have enough money left to buy her freedom. As the story begins, she has been living with a Portuguese who carried cargo in the city. When he drops dead while pulling a heavy load, Bertoleza takes on João Romão, another Portuguese, as confidant and asks him to keep her savings. He becomes her banker and bookkeeper and eventually manages all her affairs. He then proposes that they live together. João Romão uses Bertoleza's savings to expand his property. He promises freedom to Bertoleza and tells her he has bought it, but the documents he shows her are forged. In the interim, João Romão has told Bertoleza's owner that she ran away after the death of her man. Subsequently, her owner dies and João Romão is assured that the old man's irresponsible heirs will not come for Bertoleza. When João Romão wants to marry a rich white girl, Bertoleza becomes an obstacle to his social advancement. He wishes to get rid of the black woman by giving her a vegetable stand in another part of the city, but she objects, saying that she wants to enjoy what they have earned together and if he wants to marry, he should wait until after her death. He resolves the dilemma by giving her up to the heirs of her dead owner. When Bertoleza sees them coming, she commits suicide.

Bertoleza's characterization gives some insight into the stereotype of the black slave woman. First of all, she prefers white men. The narrator tells us that "she is happy to live with a Portuguese again because, like all black women, Bertoleza did not wish to subject herself to a black man and she instinctively sought a man of superior race."[3] It is not clear why Bertoleza did not wish to subject herself to a black man when the "superiority" of the white man consisted of exploiting and mistreating her in both the relationships mentioned. Nevertheless, there seems to be an indication of some moral commitment on the part of João Romão when Bertoleza tells him he must await her death before marrying. If she were simply in a master-slave relationship, she would presumably not have the right to make this demand. Azevedo does not give us, in the character of Bertoleza, enough material to understand the preference of the woman of color for white males, but he gives us a better indication in that of Rita Baiana.

In Bertoleza's physical characterization, she is repeatedly described as dirty, greasy, and grimy, and as João Romão sleeps beside her, she snores. She is fat, worn out from work, and reeks of a mixture of sweat, raw onion and rotten grease.[4] In short, the narrator informs us, she is ugly, wasted, dirty, and repugnant. She is João Romão's clerk, maid, and mistress, and works daily from 4:00 a.m., cleaning, cooking, selling, and mending. As a work animal, Bertoleza's characterization is somewhat bestial:

> She got up, with joints cracking, yawning, mumbling in her heavy sluggishness, and clearing her throat loudly.[5]

Bertoleza's slave mentality is part of her character drawing and predominates even after João Romão has repudiated her. Nevertheless, she loves him and subjugates herself to him:

> In her obscure condition of work animal, it was no longer love that the poor woman wanted, it was only some security for her old age when she could no longer earn her living. And she was content to sigh in the midst of her daily chores, cowardly and resigned, like her parents who allowed her to be born and raised in slavery.[6]

Azevedo's portrayal of Bertoleza seems to indicate that it is the slave's fault rather than that of the society that she is a slave. His logic in blaming Bertoleza's parents for bringing her into the world is faulty. Ultimately, Bertoleza's characterization is limited and corresponds to stereotypical beliefs about the role of the black woman. She is indeed the work horse who perpetuates her own enslavement to the European man without compensation. She is not sexually attractive so that she can never actually distract her companion from his goals, but she does represent a threat to his future social mobility.

The *mulata*, Rita Baiana, is important to the theme of the accommodation of the Portuguese immigrant to Brazilian life. We first encounter her as she returns from one of her frequent disappearances from routine in the tenement. As usual, she has gone off with Firmo, her irresponsible mulatto lover. Rita's relationship with him dates from her arrival from Bahia with her mother. When the older woman dies, Firmo began to take care of Rita, but they soon separated because of mutual jealousy. They continue to have a tempestuous relationship, punctuated by fights and separations, but always nourished by their reciprocal passion. Upon her return to the tenement, Rita meets Jerónimo, a Portuguese immigrant. Jerónimo becomes so impassioned by Rita that he fights Firmo over her, eventually killing him. He leaves his wife to live with Rita and ceases to meet any obligations to his child. Because of Rita, the Portuguese immigrant is transformed into a Brazilian. In the author's view, this is a negative attribute if we consider his comparison of the irresponsible Brazilian Firmo to the European immigrant, who is hard working and thrifty initially. Jerónimo becomes lazy, likes extravagances and abuses, and is lustful and jealous. No longer does he work hard, nor does he wish to get rich, and he gives himself entirely over to possessing and being possessed by the *mulata*.

Rita Baiana's characterization contrasts significantly with that of Bertoleza. The first thing we notice is that she is free in body and soul. This is evident in her sentimental life; she is reported to have at least one grand passion a year, not counting the minor ones. On the subject of marriage, Rita declares:

—Marriage? My father's daughter wouldn't fall into that. Marry? What for? To become a slave? A husband is worse than the devil, he immediately thins his wife is a slave! Not me, God forbid! There's nothing like living as mistress of oneself![7]

Rita is carefree, fun-loving, popular, and as the narrator informs us, volatile like all mixed blooded women.[8] Rita's physical appearance explains the sexual preference for the *mulata* indicated by the Brazilian folk saying. She dresses well, has thick shiny hair, and exudes the cleanliness of Brazilian women enhanced by a sensuous aroma of aromatic plants. Her bodily movements are provocative and as she smiles, a row of brilliant white teeth light her face with fascinating appeal.[9] Repeatedly, Rita's aromatic smell is evoked and at one point, Jerónimo, ill in bed, revives with her scent as she approaches him. When his Portuguese wife comes close, he notices her sour smell and suggests that she bathe more often. Rita's dancing has all the sexual attractiveness that the devil gave her, "the magic movements of a cursed snake: movements which naturally went with her scent and with her sweet voice, harmonious, arrogant, soft, and pleading."[10] When she sings, each verse is like the cooing of a dove in heat. For Jerónimo, Rita is the quintessential sex symbol. She is pleasure, voluptuousness, the bitter and golden fruit of the American hinterlands.[11] As for Rita, she becomes taken with Jerónimo once she sees his inclination for her, and the narrator informs us that "the *mulata*'s blood claimed its rights of purification and Rita preferred in the European the man of superior race."[12] Here is a clearer indication of Brazilian racial values and an explanation for the preference of the woman of color for the white male. Miscegenation is seen as a means of whitening the mixed race of Brazil. This point illustrates the Brazilian prejudice of mark as opposed to that of race. If a person looks white, by Brazilian standards he is white. His racial ancestry does not enter into the question as it would in the United States where known black ancestry causes the fairest skinned person to be classified as black. For the European, however, the *mulata* is the symbol of Brazil itself:

> The great mystery was in that *mulata*, the synthesis of impressions he has received upon arrivng here: she was the ardent light of midday; she was the red color of the siestas at the plantation, she was the warm aroma of clover and vanilla in the Brazilian forests which made him dizzy; she was the virginal and shunning palm tree which does not twist itself for any other plant: she was poison and sweet sugar; she was the sapota, sweeter than honey, and the cashew nut which opens wounds with its fiery oil; she was the green treacherous snake, the viscous caterpillar, the insect that drove him crazy, stimulating his desires, arousing his flesh slackened by homsickness, burning his blood, igniting a spark of that love in his veins, the notes of music made by sighs of pleasure, a larva of that cloud of beetles that buzzed around Rita Baiana and spread themselves through the air in an aphrodisiac phosphorescence.[13]

Rita then is the symbol of that tropical mulatto land, Brazil, and the means by which the European immigrant will be incorporated into it. Given the fact that he becomes so Brazilian in character that he has no further ambitions, the European's main contribution is, apparently, to "clean up the race."

Rita Baiana's stereotype is similar to Bertoleza's in that it fulfills the expectations and beliefs of Brazilian society in regard to the *mulata*. Both women of color have power over the European man. As we noted above, Bertoleza's mere presence at certain junctures of her consort's career is threatening. In her influence over the European, the *mulata* represents destructiveness. She kills all ambition in her companion by means of enticing him into a life of sensuality and moral degeneration. while Azevedo represents the *mulata* as a symbol of Brazil, his view of this situation is not positive.

Lima Barreto's treatment of the *mulata* in his novel *Clara dos Anjos* is a departure from that of Aluizio de Azevedo. The first version of *Clara does Anjos* appeared in 1904. The definitive version was published in 1923-24 in sixteen issues of the *Revista Sousa Cruz*. In the novel, Barreto describes the seducation and abandonment of a young mulatto girl by a more upper-class white scoundrel. Contrary to the image of the *mulata* as a fiery sex and earth symbol, Clara does Anjos is an overprotected daydreamer who has a very sentimental, idealistic notion of love. The striking feature of the scene of the novel, a suburb of Rio de Janeiro, is the free intermingling of individuals of all races and racial mixtures who are members of one lower middle-class society.

A mulatto himself, Lima Barreto reveals his identity *Clara dos Anjos*. Throughout the work, there are autobiographical references. One character, Leornardo Flores, is a mulatto poet who has suffered greatly because of his artistic aspirations as a man of color in Brazilian society. There are other characters who are alcoholic, as was the creator of Clara does Anjos, and among these figures there is always the fear of insanity which haunted Lima Barreto. His father was the keeper of a mental asylum and eventually died mad. Because of his personal experiences and his artistic concerns, Lima Barreto was able to create a convincing psychology for his character Clara while bringing under fire the role of women in Brazilian society. At the opening of *Clara dos Anjos*, Baretto quotes the historian João Ribeiro, *História do Brasil* (p. 103, 7th ed.).

> Some married them (the Indian women) others, almost all, abused their innocence, just as today is done to the mestizas, reducing them to concubines and slaves.[14]

The narrator of *Clara dos Anjos* maintains that all girls of color and humble origin are condemned, as are the rest of their people, in their efforts to elevate their social and moral condition. Although Barreto focuses on the tragedy of one mulatto girl, an overlapping of questions of class and color is apparent throughout. In reviewing Cassi Jones's affairs, the narrator informs us that the white seducer always got off free because the girls he dishonored were of humble social status and of all colors. Their status was a safety measure insuring that they didn't have any influential relatives to vindicate them. Cassi's mother, with her aristocratic pretensions, did not wish to see her son married to a black servant, a mulatto seamstress, or a white, but illiterate, washerwoman.[15] Race, however, is still the most important factor in social relations, according to the narrator. In the poor but integrated society of the Rio suburbs, the accident of color is a reason to judge oneself superior to one's neighbor.[16]

The portrayal of Clara dos Anjos reflects Brazilian shade consciousness as the narrator tells us that Clara was light skinned like her father and had straight hair like her mother.[17] The more important aspect of her character drawing is her psychology, however. One of the few outside influences in her life is that of the *modinha*, a melody conveying a simple-minded amorous sentimentalism. On the basis of the *modinhas* she heard, Clara built up a theory of love. Love conquers all. Because of it, there are no obstacles of race, fortune, or class; the amorous state is the greatest delight of our existence which should be enjoyed and suffered. Martyrdom gives it even more refinement.[18] Clara's vulnerability of Cassi Jones is heightened because he is one of the most famous *modinha* singers of the suburbs. In addition to the dream life in which Clara is immersed, she has no practical experience of life. Her parents love her and overprotect her to such an extent that she rarely goes out and has few friends. Her cloistering fosters the life of daydreams which are reinforced by the *modinhas* she hears. Furthermore, her curiosity about the outside world increases as a result of her excessively sheltered existence. Because of her lack of experience, penchant for daydreaming and fantasy, and her taste for the *modinha*, Clara becomes an easy prey for Cassi's attentions. Although she questions the racial difference between them, she concludes that it doesn't matter. Naively, she believes that even if Cassi's bad reputation were true, he would respect her father's house. Her lack of sophistication allows her to be carried away by Cassi's letters despite their spelling errors. She is convinced he wants to marry her, but her godfather, Marramaque, deflates that dream by telling Clara's father that Cassi would not choose a poor *mulata* if he desired to marry. After Marramaque is found murdered, Clara fears that Cassi is responsible, but she rationalizes the act as one of madness provoked by the seducer's love for her. Eventually, she allows him into her room when her parents are asleep and Cassi achieves his goal.

The moment of truth for Clara arrives after she has become pregnant and Cassi has run away. She realizes that her innocence and lack of experience blinded her. Cassi chose her because she was poor and a *mulata*. She fears ostracism and scorn from her family and friends and further exploitation by others even worse than Cassi. She envisions her end as similar to that of a local prostitute, suffering from shameful maladies and the excesses of alcohol. In the company of a strong-willed neighbor, Dona Margarida, Clara goes to Cassi's family. To Clara's appeal to Cassi's mother that he marry her, the older woman responds: "What are you saying, you nigger?" Clara's initiation into life is tragic and her final words in the novel are:

> —Mother, mother!
> —What is it my child?
> —We're nothing in this life.[19]

Interspersed throughout the story of Clara's seduction and abandonment are criticisms of women in Brazilian society. Not only are they overprotected and kept from real knowledge of the world, but they often forget their education entirely once they are married, as was the case of Clara's mother, Engracia. Furthermore, they have no desire to master any skill which might be useful to them and their families. They pass from the protection of father to that of husband and they have no aspirations for self-realization. The narrator's advice to Brazilian women is:

> What was necessary, as much for her as for her equals, was to train the character, acquire will, like Dona Margarida had, to be able to defend themselves against the likes of Cassi; and fight against those who opposed their social and moral elevation. Nothing made them inferior to the others except the general opinion and the cowardice with which they accepted it.[20]

Rather than propagating stereotypes, Barreto seems to be reacting against them and explaining the social conditions which give rise to the widely accepted belief in the moral corruption of the mulatto woman. Because of his own marginality in the society, he is able to enter into the psychology of the character with a great deal of sensitivity. We understand the victim's mentality and the social forces acting upon her. Although race and class are inextricably bound up in this society, Barreto makes it clear that race is the critical factor in the end.

In 1958, Jorge Amado published *Gabriela, Cravo e Canela*. The action of the novel takes place during the decade of the twenties in the Bahian cacau zone. Gabriela arrives at the town of Ilheus from the drought-stricken areas of the Northeast, becomes Nacib's cook, and from then on, the main plot of the novel revolves around their love story. Amado explores other themes related to love such as sex, fantasy, freedom, marriage, jealously, machismo, and women's rights. The question of race and class is present but subordinate to other themes. Gabriela, the mulatto heroine, is accepted by all in her role as cook, mistress, and eventually as wife to Nacib, the Syrian. When she encounters any semblance of discrimination, it is as a member of the lower classes who, through marriage, comes into contact with the upper classes. If this detail tells us anything about the tendencies of Brazilian society, it is that the lower classes are made of the nonwhites who meet resistance when they are socially upwardly mobile. Although Amado's treatment of class-race questions is understated, his heroine herself is a constant reminder of this subject.

Amado effects Gabriela's physical portrayal by means of other characters' brief impressions of her. Although she is covered with dust from the journey to Ilheus, Nacib notices Gabriela's shining eyes, and her clear and unexpected laugh. Another brief description sketches her as young, with childish features, a smile, the singing voice of the Northeast, a perfume of cloves, and the color of cinnamon. To Nacib, she is beautiful and desirable. To the townspeople, she is a beautiful "brunette." To the upper-class families she frequents with her husband, she is a beautiful but lower class *mulata*. This brief social commentary indicates that nobody forgets Gabriela's class and race, but it also shows the importance of personal appearance among the criteria for social moblity. Because of her physical appeal, Gabriela becomes a personification of love in the world of the novel. Everybody loves Gabriela and Gabriela loves everybody. As Nacib's cook, she brings trays of hors-d'oeuvres to his bar where she becomes a principal attraction. Men flirt with her and her presence makes the atmosphere more welcoming and inti-

mate. If there is any single basis of Gabriela's appeal, it is her love
for life:

> Gabriela loved the morning sun, cold water, the white beach, the
> sand, the circus, the amusement park the movies, fruit, flowers,
> animals, cooking, eating, walking in the street, laughing and convers-
> ing. She didn't like ladies full of themselves. More than everything
> else, she liked handsome men, making love. These things she liked.
> And Nacib. She liked him in a different way. Making love and really
> sleeping and dreaming of her cat, the sand on the beach, the moon in
> the sky and food to be made. She loved him so much.[21]

With sparse details and a sanguine approach, Amado evokes
Gabriela's past life. She likes happy thoughts, not sad ones. She
doesn't like to think of death, or her life with her aunt and uncle.
She likes to think of dancing, her mother and father before they
died, and her lovers, all except the first who was her uncle, old and
sick. Gabriela's psychic unwillingness to be touched by the sordid
realities of life explains her ethereal and freedom-loving spirit. For
the author and his male characters, she is a full-blown fantasy and
represents love:

> Love can't be proved, nor can it be measured. It's like Gabriela. It
> exists, that's enough—said João Fulgêcio. The fact of not understand-
> ing or explaining a thing doesn't finish with it. I know nothing of the
> stars, but I see in the sky, they are the beauty of the night.[22]

Gabriela's freedom-loving spirit includes sexual liberation accompanied by the appearance of innocence:

> She seemed like a child, thighs and breasts showing as if she saw
> nothing wrong in that, as if she knew nothing of those things, all
> innocence.[23]

Amado often tries to capture the essence of Gabriela's spirit in
metaphor. She is like a flower which remains beautiful and fragrant
on the bough but wilts and dies in silver vases. This observation
foreshadows the effect of marriage on Gabriela.

In another context, her nonchalance about sex is more than
disturbing to Clemente, a refugee from the drought with whom
Gabriela slept during the journey to Ilheus. He is in love with her
but she doesn't even say goodbye when she leaves the encampment.
Clemente's friend Fagundes explains that no man could be Gabrie-

la's master as he might be that of other women. A man could sleep with her and the next day, she would look at him like she looked at the others—as if the love-making made no difference. It would seem that if Gabriela demands this type of freedom for herself, she is also willing to give it—at least symbolically. She tames a half-wild tom cat, but the cat never gives up his nights of carousing. The male fantasy aspect of Gabriela's character drawing is never far from view.

Along with her spiritual and sexual freedom Gabriela enjoys freedom of movement in dance. This seems to be the one specified instance of black stereotyping:

> Immediately, he began to dance, he had the dance within, his feet inventing steps, his body loose, his hands beating the rhythm. Gabriela watched,—with her it was the same, she couldn't contain herself. She abandoned pots and pans, food, with her hand holding up her skirt. The two danced now, the little black boy and the *mulata* under the sun in the yard. At a certain movement, Tuisca stopped, he kept beating his hands on an empty pot. Gabriela turned, her skirt flying, arms moving back and forth, her body moving to and fro, her hips shaking, her mouth smiling.[24]

If in male fantasies, freedom and love are natural allies, Amado portrays the more realistic male reactions to a woman who claims them for herself. Nacib's predictable reactions are possessiveness and jealousy. He is afraid of losing his fiery *mulata* with whom he spends intoxicating nights. When Gabriela learns that Nacib is jealous, she wonders why, because she isn't. He could go with others if he wanted to. Furthermore, attentions from other men didn't change her and if she liked them, she slept with them in her imagination. For Gabriela, freedom is all important—she cannot become Nacib's possession. Nevertheless, he tries to make her his own by marrying her. Although Gabriela is the first to recognize their class difference, she is attracted by the idea of being able to appear in public with him. Once married, she hates the concomitant fancy clothing, tight shoes, expensive jewels, and obligations to appear in a society where she cannot be herself. She cannot walk barefoot, she must be a dignified married lady, and she must make people respect ner and forget that she was a cook who came to Ilheus as a migrant. Nacib's customers at the bar accuse him of putting Gabriela in prison after he has married her. This oppression naturally has an effect on Gabriela. With the straight jacket of conventions Nacib imposes on Gabriela, her love-making loses its ardor and her husband is unhappy. Although the couple discuss the problem together and seem to resolve it, Nacib's friends try to explain the difference to him between a wife and a mistress and urge him to frequent the brothels and nightclubs again. Eventually, Gabriela is unfaithful to Nacib with his friend Tonico. Nacib's mark of civilization is that he does not kill them. Amado gives a more solid blow to machismo through the ingenuous Gabriela's ratiocinations on the subject:

> The stupidest thing, without explanation: why did men suffer so much when a woman with whom they slept slept with sombody else? She didn't understand it. If Nacib felt like it, he could very well sleep with somebody else. She knew that Tonico slept with others, dona Arminda told everybody that he had a horror of other women. But, if it was good to sleep with him, play with him in bed, why demand that it be only with her? She didn't understand. She liked to sleep in a man's arms. Not anybody's. Of handsome men like Clemente, Bebinho, ah! Like Nacib. If the man wanted it too, if he looked at her asking, if he smiled at her, if he pinched her, why refuse, why say no? They both wanted it. That Nacib should be angry she understood. Only men had the right, women no. She knew, but how could she resist. If she felt like it, she did it without thinking it was forbidden. With the marriage over, why was Nacib still offended?[25]

Amado's plea for equality and his criticism of machismo is not limited to this rather unique heroine. A minor female character defies her father's authority to read the books she chooses, select her own lover, and when she is abandoned by him, goes to São Paulo where she lives alone and supports herself. While Amado is dealing blows to sexism, he also has a few for social pretentiousness as when Gabriela leaves a stuffy upper-class party and runs out into the street to join a folk festival, the Trio of the Magi. Followed by the young and rebellious members of the upper class, the entire party ends up parading in the streets with Gabriela at the head of the procession.

As we observed at the beginning of the discussion of *Gabriela, Cravo e Canela*, race and class are subordinate to other themes in this novel and if the depiction of Gabriela at first seems to be a male-oriented conception, Amado neatly does an about-face when his fantasy woman exerts her rights and upsets more than one social convention. Amado's artistry permits him to create a unique personality in Brazilian fiction. If he does not quite avoid the stereotypical, this is due to his having made Gabriela symbolize a free Brazil as well. Once again, the *mulata* represents Brazil, but in contrast to Azevedo's portrayal, Gabriela represents what is good about the country.

O Quinze Rachel de Queiroz's first novel, was written in 1929-30 and offers an interesting contrast to the three works discussed above. As a part of the Brazilian modernist-regionalist movement, Rachel de Queiroz's novel focuses on the drought-stricken Northeast of Brazil. More specifically, its principal theme is a modern young woman's quest for self-realization in an area where the traditional roles of women have been limited to marriage and childbearing. Rachel de Queiroz's white protagonist is a foil to the heroines of the male writers we have examined above, in many respects—race, class, attitudes toward men, reactions to women of color, and ultimate resolutions. The fact that Queiroz is a woman brings us closer to the reality of the subject matter even though her perceptions are not those of a *mulata* or of a black woman. In fact, her heroine completes the spectrum from black woman to *mulata* to white woman mentioned earlier in the essay and gives us a wider perspective than we might have gained by analyzing exclusively images of women of color in Brazilian literature.

Conceição, the protagonist of *O Quinze*, is a young woman of twenty-two. A native of the *sertão* (hinter lands) of Ceará, she is a member of a land-owning family of the region. She shares a very close relationship with her grandmother, Mãe Nácia, who represents the traditional woman of the Ceará *sertão*. Conceição is a modern woman, however, and has chosen to obtain a normal school education and become a teacher. Because she does not speak of marriage at her age, she says happily that she was born an old maid. Mãe Nácia, echoing the traditional view, believes that an unmarried woman is defective and that her granddaughter has odd ideas. Conceição is writing a book on pedagogy, scribbles poetry, and from time to time, cites Nordau and Renan. Her oddest ideas are a result of having read certain socialist authors.

Throughout the novel, we see a certain tension among Conceição's professional and intellectual goals, traditional roles, and human desires. Conceição and her cousin Vicente, a rancher, are attracted to each other and appear to be courting. At one juncture when Vicente comes to the city to visit Conceição, he is shocked to learn that she goes about all alone. Conceição explains that since she is an old school teacher, she must go to her job. A pretty young girl would not go out alone. Vicente responds that if he were in charge, he would let her go out only with a body guard. Conceição has radically different ideas as attested to by her choice of reading material:

> —It's about the feminist question, about the situation of women in society, about maternal rights, about the problem...
> Dona Inácia raised her hands, upset:
> —My daughter, why does a girl need to know these things? Do you want to have a doctorate, to write books?
> Again the girl's smile appeared:
> —Mãe Nácia! I read to learn and to become informed.
> —Is it only for this that you burn out your eyes, get thin.... reading al that nonsense?
> —Mãe Nácia, when a person renounces certain obligations, home, children, family, she has to have other things to think about.... If not, life is too empty.
> —And why do you distort your nature? Why don't you marry?
> Conceição looked at her grandmother with a mischievous expres—sion:
> —I never found anybody who would make it worthwhile.[26]

Despite Conceição's declarations about marriage, she is constantly preoccupied with the subject. She recalls the moment when she and Vicente baptized a child of Chico Bento, Manuel, and how pleased she was to see her name and Vicente's together on an official ecclesiastical document. Together, they were the spiritual parents. She considered their unity a good omen. On the other hand, an incident which we will describe below incites Conceição to think more carefully about this "unity." She begins to feel that Vicente is only good to look at like a beautiful landscape. In times of trouble, abandonment, or loneliness, where would she find the sure companion who would understand, complete her thoughts, and discuss her ideas? She wonders what kind of a couple they would make when, at night on the ranch, she would want to share something she was reading with him. He would murmur a distracted "Is that so?" from behind his newspaper, with complete indifference. His physical attractiveness would never breach that separation. At this point, Conceição's choice seems to be made. Nevertheless, the question of personal fulfillment haunts her up to the end of the novel:

> She would always be barren, useless.... Her heart would not nourish another life, her soul would not prolong itself in another small soul....a woman without children, a broken link in the chain of immortality.[27]

Ultimately, cerebral deliberations lead Conceição to reject Vicente as a future husband, but it is an emotional outburst which starts the process. A refugee from *sertão*, Chiquinha Boa, reports to Conceição that Vicente might be having an affair with a *mulata*, Zefa Bernardo. Conceiçã disillusioned and hurt as she relates to Mãe Nácia that Vicente spends a great deal of time talking to Zefa. Conceição believed Vicente to be indifferent to all other women. It was she who had aroused his heart. She comments:—'A *mulata*, a squaw, with kinky hair and rotten teeth."[28] Mãe Nácia, confirms that she had heard of Vicente's affair and dismissed it as boyish foolishness. Conceição is beside herself and exclaims:

> —Foolishness, no maam! Then Mãe Nácia, thinks it foolishness for a white man to go around dirtying himself with niggers?
> Dona Inácia smiled, conciliatingly.
> —But, my daughter, this happened with all of them
> —white men in the sertão.... there are always these stories. Besides, she isn't a nigger, she's a light skinned mestiza.
> —Well I think it's shameless.[29]

When Conceição confronts Vicente with her suspicions, Vicente's innocent behavior leads her to believe that he is a cynic. Mãe Nácia, might have put up with that sort of thing, but Conceição would not.

For the educated Northeastern woman of the thirties, the glorification of the *mulata* sex symbol had an entirely different significance than it had for the males of Brazilian society as portrayed in the novels discussed. The *mulata* was a nigger, an inferior, a threat, and above all, a humiliation to the white woman. If her grandmother's generation had passively accepted this kind of treatment from its men, it was time for a change. If at this time the white upper class woman was becoming more liberated, her decisive stand would have an effect on the entire society of the *sertão*. White men who wished to marry white women would be forced to abandon their double standard. With the liberation of white women, it is possible also that sexual mores would be relaxed so that the honor, i.e. virginity, of the white women, would not rest on the sexual exploitation of black women. We point this out in connection with Vicente's relaxed manner with women of color while he would prevent his white wife from walking on the street alone. We believe that the question is much more complex than these mores suggest.

From a modern perspective, Conceição's resolution of her dilemma is not entirely satisfactory. As a volunteer helping refugees from the drought, she encounters Chico Bento's family. She cares for his son, Manuel, her god son, and when the family moves to São Paulo, she keeps the child and raises him as her own. At the end of the novel, she rationalizes that despite her partial lack of personal fulfillment, she has raised a child and created a human atmosphere in her life. Her admission that all of this is so complex that she really doesn't know the answers indicates to us that Conceição is as perplexed as most modern women about the options and possibilities for true fulfillment.

In attempting to arrive at some general statement about the role of the woman of color in Brazilian literature, we are not surprised that male authors usually focus on the sexual aspect of women's lives. From our vantage point, it would seem that women have other preoccupations as well, witness Conceição 's spiritual and intellectual needs. It does occur to us that her creator is reticent about sexual matters and from the perspective of women in 1975, this seems odd. Queiroz's lack of emphasis on this subject is in sharp contrast to the male authors' obsession with it. However, while viewing women as sex objects, the male authors each bring an individual twist to their conceptions. Although he deals in stereotypes, Aluizo de Azevedo views the woman of color as a vehicle for social mobility for some European elements and as a means of incorporating others into the nation and its racial goals. As we noted above, he also sees her as a symbol of Brazil as well as a symbol of destructiveness. Barreto reacts to the stereotype of the *mulata* which connotes her essential immorality by depicting her as an innocent victim of a color-conscious society. Jorge Amado explodes a male fantasy by means of reversing traditional roles and in a humorous fashion, pokes fun at societal conventions while protesting the condition of women and offering up his *mulata* heroine as a symbol of what is good about Brazil.

Within the time sequence we have shown, there is a continuity of female symbols. In order to recognize the *mulata* as a Brazilian sex symbol, it is necessary to know something about black-white sexual relationships as indicated in social history and in literature such as Gilberto Freyre's *Masters and the Slaves* and the poetry of Jorge de Lima. Both these authors show that the tendency of Brazilian society has been toward miscegenation and an acceptance of its results. Miscegenation is not a taboo as it is in the United States, and its literary exploration is not accompanied by the bitterness, guilt, and violence exhibited in North American literature. What we have tried to show through the works studied is the individual authors' interpretations of a very highly nuanced society. To know why Lima Barreto goes to such lengths to depict the innocence of his heroine, it is important to realize that in Brazil, the *mulata* has an immoral aura about her. Regardless of a woman's color, if she is a potential homebreaker, or the woman that a man sees on the side, she is referred to as the "*mulata*." This gives some indication of how threatening the very idea of this woman is to the insititution of the family. Lima Barreto accordingly tries to explain the social causes of the *mulata*'s immorality. Simply by making Gabriela a *mulata*, Jorge Amado is playing upon the most vulnerable part of his country-men's fantasy life. In terms of continuity, the male authors are following a certain set of conventions. Rachel de Queiroz's heroine is the one who will possibly be most effective in modifying a social structure in which the conventions exist. Each artistic vision is, however, one artist's views and conceptions of the world around him which other views and conceptions may later add to and correct.

NOTES

1. For a full discussion of this question, see Carl N. Degler, *Neither Black Nor White* (New York: MacMillan Company, 1971).

2. Gilberto Freyre, *The Masters and the Slaves*, Trans. by Samuel Putman (New York: Alfred A. Knopf, A Borzoi Book, 1964), p. 20.

3. Aluizio Azevedo, *O Cortiço* (São Paulo: Martins, 1969), p. 20.

4. *Ibid.*, p. 128.

5. *Ibid.*, p. 145.
6. *Ibid.*, p. 213.
7. *Ibid.*, p. 72.
8. *Ibid.*, p. 221.
9. *Ibid.*, p. 71.
10. *Ibid.*, p. 89.
11. *Ibid.*, p. 187.
12. *Ibid.*, p. 187.
13. *Ibid.*, p. 89.
14. Afonso Henriques Lima Barreto, *Clara dos Anjos*, 3rd ed. (São Paulo: Brasiliense, 1969), p. 3.
15. *Ibid.*, p. 35.
16. *Ibid.*, p. 14.
17. *Ibid.*, p. 57.
18. *Ibid.*, p. 71.
19. *Ibid.*, p. 166.
20. *Ibid.*, pp. 165, 166.
21. Jorge Amado, *Gabriela Cravo e Canela*, 19th ed. (São Paulo: Martins, 1959), p. 401.
22. *Ibid.*, p. 402.
23. *Ibid.*, p. 190.
24. *Ibid.*, pp. 198, 199.
25. *Ibid.*, p. 400.
26. Rachel de Queiroz, *O Quinze* in *Tres Romances* (Rio de Janeiro: Livraria José Olympio Editôra, 1948), p. 101.
27. *Ibid.*, p. 120.
28. *Ibid.*, p. 49.
29. *Ibid.*, pp. 50, 51.

REFERENCES

Amado, Jorge. *Gabriela Cravo e Canela*. São Paulo: Martins, 1959.

Azevedo, *O Cortiço*. São Paulo: Martins, 1969.

Freyre, Gilberto. *The Masters and the Slaves*. Translated by Samuel Putman. New York: Alfred A Knopf, A Borzoi Book, 1964.

Lima Barreto, Afonso Henriques. *Clara dos Anjos*. 3rd ed. São Paulo: Brasiliense, 1969.

Queiroz, Rachel de. *O Quinze. Tres Romances*. Rio de Janeiro: Livraria José Olympio Editôra, 1948.

Select Bibliography on the Black Women Cross-Culturally

Compiled by
Filomina Chioma Steady

Africa

Adekogbe, E. "La Femme au Nigeria." *Perspectives de Catholicite*, v. 19 (3), 1960: 16-23.

Adibe, M.L., and A. Tessa. "Position and Problems of the Woman in French-Speaking Africa. II-Gabon." *Women Today*, v. 6 (3), 1964: 51-63.

"African Women Help in Rural Education and Training." *UNESCO Information Bulletin*, v. 22, Feb. 1966: 12-13.

"Africa's Food Producers: The Impact of Change on Rural Women." *Focus*, v. 25, January 1975: 1-7.

Aidoo, Ama Ata. *Anowa*. Harlow: Longmans, 1970.

_____ . *No Sweetness Here*. Garden City, N.Y.: Doubleday, 1971.

_____ . *The Dilemma of a Ghost*. Accra: Longmans, 1965.

Albert, Ethel M. "Women of Burundi: A Study of Social Values." *Women of Tropical Africa*, ed. Denise Paulme. Berkeley: Univ. of California Press, 1971.

Al-Shahi, A.S. "Politics and the Role of Women in a Shaiqiya Constituency (1968)." *Sudan Society*, v. 4, 1969: 27-38.

Aluko, Timothy Mofolorunso. "Polygamy and the Surplus of Women." *West African Review*, v. 21 (270), 1950: 259-260.

Ames, D. "The Economic Base of Wolof Polygyny" *Southwestern Journal of Anthropology*, v. 11 (4), 1955: 391-403.

Ames, D.W. The Selection of Mates, Courtship, and Marriage among the Wolof," *Bulletin d'Institute Francais d'Afrique Noire*, 18, nos. 1-2. 1956.

Andreski, Iris. *Old Wives Tales: Life Stories of African Women*. New York: Schocken Books. 1970.

Ardener, Edwin. "Belief and the Problem of Women." *The Interpretation of Ritual*. J.S. LaFontaine, ed. London: Tavistock, 1972.

Auber, J. "La femme dans les traditions et less moeurs malagaches." *Revue Madagascar* 22, 1955: 43-48.

Awe, Bolanle. "University Education for Women in Nigeria." *Ibadan*, no. 18, February 1964: 57-62.

———. "The Iyalode in the Traditional Yoruba Political System" in Alice Schlegel, ed. *Sexual Stratification: A Cross-Cultural View*. New York: Columbia University Press, 1977.

Awori, Thelma "For African Women Equal Rights are not Enough", *UNESCO Courier* v. 28 (3), March 1975:21-25.

Baker, Tanya, and Mary E.C. Bird. "Urbanization and the Position of Women." *Sociological Review*, v. 7 (1), July 1959: 99-122.

Barkow, Jerome. "Hausa Women and Islam." *The Canadian Journal of African Studies* v.6, (2) 1972:317-328.

Barthel, Diane. "The Rise of A Female Professional Elite." *African Studies Review*, v. 18 (3), Dec. 1975: 1-18.

Beidelman, T.O. *The Kaguru: A Matrilineal People of East Africa*. New York: Holt, Rinehart & Winston, 1971.

Beier, H.J. "The Position of Yoruba Women." *Presence Africaine* 1-2 (April-July 1955): 39-46.

Berger, Iris. "Rebels or Status-Seekers? Women as Spirit Mediums in East Africa." *Women in Africa*, Nancy J. Hafkin and Edna G. Bay, (eds.) Stanford: Stanford University Press, 1976.

Bohannan, Laura. "Dahomean Marriage: A Revaluation." First published, 1949. Reprinted in *Marriage, Family and Residence*, eds. Paul Bohannan and John Middleton, pp. 85-108. New York: Natural History Press, 1968.

Bohannan, P. and Dalton, G. (eds) *Markets in Africa*. Evanston: Northwestern University Press, 1962.

Boserup, Ester. *Women's Role in Economic Development*, London: George Allen and Unwin, 1970.

Brain, James L. "Less Than Second-Class: Women in Rural Settlement Schemes in Tanzania". *Women in Africa*, Nancy J. Hafkin and Edna G. Bay (eds), Stanford: Stanford University Press, 1976.

———. "Matrilineal Descent and Marital Stability: a Tanzanian Case," *Journal of Asian and African Studies*, v.4 (2), 1969:122-131.

Brandel-Syrier, Mia. *Black Woman in Search of God*. London: Lutterworth, 1962.

Brooks, A.E. "Political Participation of Women in Africa South of the Sahara." *Annals American Academy of Political Social Science*, v. 375, January 1968: 82-85.

Brooks, George E. "The Signares of Saint-Louis and Goree: Women Entrepreneurs in Eighteenth-Century Senegal", *Women in Africa*, Nancy J. Hafkin and Edna G. Bay (eds). Stanford: Stanford University Press, 1976.

Bunbury, Isla. "Women's Position as Workers in Africa South of the Sahara". *Civilizations*, v. 11 (2), 1961: 159-168.

Calame-Griaule, G. "The Spiritual and Social Role of Women in Traditional Sudanese Society," *Diogenes*, 37, 1962: 81-92.

Caldwell, John C. *Population Growth and Family Change in Africa*. Canberra: Australia National University Press, 1968.

Chilver, E.M., and P.M. Kaberry. "The Kingdon of Kom in West Cameroon," in D. Forde and P.M. Kaberry, eds., *West African Kingdoms in the Nineteenth Century*. London: Oxford University Press for the International African Institute, 1969.

Christian, Angela. "The Place of Women in Ghana Society," *African Women*, III, 3, 1959: 57-59.

Clignet, Remi. *Many Wives, Many Powers: Authority and Power in Polygynous Families (Abure and Bete, Ivory Coast)*. Evanston: Northwestern University Press, 1970.

Crane, Louise. *Ms. Africa: Profiles of Modern African Women*. New York: J.B. Lippincott Co., 1973.

Curley, Richard T. *Elders, Shades and Women: Ceremonial Change in Lango, Uganda*. Berkeley: University of California Press, 1973.

Davidson, Basil. *Black Mother*, 4th ed. Boston: Atlantic-Little, Brown and Co., 1966.

De La Rue, A. "The Rise and Fall of Grace Ibingira." *New African*, v. 5 (10), December 1966: 207-208.

Diarra, Fatoumata Agnes. *Femmes africaines en devenir: Les femmes zarma du Niger*. Paris: Editions Anthropos, 1971.

Dobert, Margarita. "Liberation and the Women of Guinea." *Africa Report*, 15, (7), 1970: 26-28.

———— . "Women in French-Speaking West Africa: A Selected Guide to Civic and Political Participation in Guinea, Dahomey, and Mauritania." *Current Bibliography of African Affairs*, v. 3 (9), September 1970: 5-21.

Dobkin, M. "Colonialism and the Legal Status of Women in Francophonic Africa." *Cahiers d'Etudes Africaines*, v. 8 (3), 1968: 390-405.

Donner, Etta. "Togba, a Women's Society in Liberia." *Africa*, v. 11, 1938: 109-111.

Dorjahn, Vernon R. "The Factor of Polygyny in African Demography," in Bascom and Herskivits, eds. *Continuity and Change in African Cultures.* Chicago: University of Chicago Press, 1959, chapter 5, pp. 87-112.

——— . "Fertility, Polygyny and their Interrelations in Temne Society," *American Anthropologist* 60 (5), 1958: 838-860.

Douglas, Mary. "A Form of Polyandry Among the Lele." *Africa* v 21: 1-12, 1951.

——— . "Is Matriliny Doomed in Africa?" *Man in Africa.* Phyllis Kaberry & Mary Douglas, eds. London: Tavistock, 1969: 121-135.

Dupire, Marguerite. "The Position of Women in a Pastoral Society." *Women of Tropical Africa*, ed. Denise Paulme pp. 47-92. Berkeley: University of California Press, 1971.

Earthy, E. Dora. *Valenge Women: The Social and Economic Life of the Valenge Women of Portugese East Africa.* London: Cass, 1968.

Eide, Wenche Barth and Steady, Filomina Chioma. "Individual and Social Energy Flows: Bridging Nutritional and Anthropological Thinking about Women's Work in Rural Africa: Some Theoretical Considerations," in Jerome, N., Kandel, R.F. and Pelto, G.H. (eds) *Nutritional Anthropology.* New York: Redgrave Publishing Company, 1980, pp. 61-84.

Ekejiuba, Felicia "Omu Okwei: Merchant Queen of Ossomari." Journal of the Historical Society of Nigeria v. 3 (4) 1967: 633-646.

Esike, S. O. "The Aba Riots of 1929." *African Historian.* (Ibadan), v. 1, (3), 1965: 7-13.

Evans, David R. "Image and Reality: Career Goals of Educated Ugandan Women." *Canadian Journal of African Studies*, v. 6 (2), 1972: 213-232.

Falade, Solange. "Women of Dakar and the Surrounding Urban Area." *Women of Tropical Africa*, Denise Paulme (ed.), pp. 217-230. Berkeley: University of California Press, 1971.

Fluehr-Lobban, Carolyn "Agitation for change in the Sudan," in Alice Schlegel (ed.) *Sexual Stratification: A Cross-Cultural View.* New York: Columbia University Press, 1977.

Fortes, M. *The Dynamics of Clanship among the Tallensi.* Oxford: Oxford University Press 1945.

Galadanci, S.A. "Education of Women in Islam with Reference to Nigeria." *Nigerian Journal of Islam*, v. 1 (1) Jan.-June 1971: 5-10.

Gamble, David. "The Temne Family in a Modern Town in Sierra Leone." *Africa* v. 33 (3) 1963: 209-226.

Gantin, Bernardine. "Christianity and the African Woman." *World Mission*, v. 13, Summer 1962: 13-22.

Gollock, Georgina A. *Daughters of Africa.* New York: Negro University Press, 1969 (reprint of the 1932 edition).

Goody, Esther N. *Contexts of Kinship: An Essay in the Family Sociology of the Gonja of North Ghana.* Cambridge: Cambridge University Press, 1973.

Goody, Jack. "Inheritance, Property, and Marriage in Africa and Eurasia." *Sociology* v. 3, 1969: 55-76.

Goody, Jack and Esther Goody, "The Circulation of Women and Children in Northern Ghana." *Man,* v. 2 (2), June 1967: 226-248.

Goody, Jack and Joan Buckley. "Inheritance and Women's Labour in Africa." *Africa,* v. 43 (2), April 1973: 108-121.

Gutkind, Peter C.W. "African Urban Family Life and the Urban System." *Journal of Asian and African Studies,* v. 1 (1), 1966: 35-46.

Hafkin, Nancy J., and Edna G. Bay, eds. *Women in Africa: Studies in Social and Economic Change.* Stanford: Stanford University Press, 1976.

Hamilton-Hazeley, Lottie E. A. "The Education of Women and Girls in the Provinces." *Sierra Leone Journal of Education,* v. 1 (1), April 1966: 20-23.

Hansen, Karen Tranberg. "Married Women and Work Explorations from an Urban Case Study." *African Social Research,* v. 20, December 1975: 777-779.

Harris, J.S. "The Position of Women in a Nigerian Society," *Transactions of the New York Academy of Sciences,* v. 2 (5) 1940.

Hastie, P. "Women's Clubs in Uganda." *Mass Education Bulletin,* v. 2 (1), December 1950: 4-6.

Hay, Margaret Jean. "Luo Women and Economic Change During the Colonial Period." *Women in Africa,* Nancy J. Hafkin and Edna G. Bay (eds), Stanford: Stanford University Press, 1976.

Hecker, Monique. "UNESCO and Women's Rights: An Experimental Project in Upper Volta." *UNESCO Chronicle,* v. 16 (6), June 1970, 257-265.

Hill, Polly. "Women Cocoa Farmers." *Ghana Farmer,* v. 2 (2), May 1958: 70-71.

Hoffer, Carol P. "Mende and Sherbo Women in High Office." *Canadian Journal of African Studies,* v. 6 (2) 1972, 151-164.

Ifeka-Moller, Caroline. "Female Militancy and the Colonial Revolt: The Women's War of 1929, Eastern Nigeria." Shirley Ardener, ed., *Perceiving Women.* London: Malaby Press, 1975: 127-157.

Izzett, Alison. "Family Life Among the Yoruba in Lagos, Nigeria." *Social Change in Modern Africa.* A. Southall, ed. London: Oxford University Press, 1961.

Jeffreys, M.D.W. "The Nyama Society of the Ibibio Women." *African Studies,* v. 15 (1), 1956: 15-28.

Jellicoe, M.R. "Women's Groups in Sierra Leone." *African Women,* v. 1 (2), June 1955: 35-43.

Jiagge, J.A. "The Role of Non-Governmental Organizations in the Education of Women in African States." *Convergence*, v. (2), 1969: 73-78.

Kaberry, Phyllis M. *Women in Grassfields: A Study of the Economic Position of Women in Bamenda, British Cameroons.* 2nd edn. New York: Humanities Press, 1969.

Kane, Malmouna. "The Status of Married Women under Customary Law in Senegal." *American Journal of Comparative Law*, v. 20 (4), Fall 1972: 716-723.

Keirn, Susan Middleton. "Voluntary Associations Among Urban African Women." Brian M. du Toit, ed., *Culture Change in Contemporary Africa. Communications from the African Studies Center*. Vol. 1., Gainesville: University of Florida, 1970.

Krapf-Askari, Eva. "Women, Spears, and the Scarce Good: A Comparison of the Sociological Function of Warfare in Two Central African Societies (Zande and Nzakara)." A. Singer, et al., eds., *Zande Themes*. London: Oxford University Press, 1972: 19-40.

Krige, Eileen Jensen. "Girls' Puberty Songs and their Relations to Fertility, Health, Morality and Religion among the Zulu." *Africa* v. 38 (2), April 1968: 173-198.

Lancaster, Chet S. "Women, Horticulture, and Society in Sub-Saharan Africa." *American Anthropologist*, v. 78 (3), Sept. 1976: 539-564.

Landes, Ruth. "Negro Slavery and Female Status." *African Affairs*, v. 52 (206), 1953: 54-57.

Landis, Elizabeth S. *Apartheid and the Disabilities of African Women in South Africa.* (UN Unit on Apartheid, December 1973). A. G. Bishop & Sons Ltd., Orpington, Kent.

Lebeuf, Annie M.D. "The Role of Women in the Political Organization of African Societies." Denise Paulme, ed., *Women of Tropical Africa*. London: Routledge and Kegan Paul, 1963: 93-120.

Leith-Ross, Sylvia. *African Women: A Study of the Ibo of Nigeria.* London: Routledge & Kegan Paul, 1965.

Levine, Robert A. "Sex Roles and Economic change in Africa." *Ethnology* 5 (2), 1966: 186-193.

Levine, Robert A., Klein, N.H. and Deven, C.R. "Father-Child Relationships and Changing Life-Styles in Ibadan, Nigeria." *The City in Modern Africa*. H. Miner, ed. New York: Praeger, 1967.

Lewis, Barbara C. "The Limitations of Group Action Among Entrepreneurs: The Market Women of Abidjan, Ivory Coast." *Women in Africa*, Nancy J. Hafkin and Edna G. Bay eds., Stanford: Stanford University Press, 1976.

───── . "Economic Activity and Marriage among Ivorian Urban Women," in Alice Schlegel (ed.) *Sexual Stratification: A Cross-Cultural View*. New York: Columbia University Press, 1977.

Little, Kenneth "Voluntary Associations and Social Mobility among West African Women." *Canadian Journal of African Studies*, v. 6 (2), 1972: 275-288.

Lloyd, Peter C. Divorce among the Yoruba. *American Anthropologist*, v. 70 (1) 1968:67-81.

───── . "The Status of the Yoruba Wife." *Sudan Society*, v. 2, 1963: 35-42.

Magbogunje, Akin L. "The Market Woman." *Ibadan*, v. 2, Feb. 1961: 14-17.

Magdalen, M.C., Sister. "Education of Girls in Southern Nigeria." *International Review of Missions*, v. 17, 1928: 505-514.

Marie-Andre du Sacré Coeur. *The House Stands Firm: Family Life in West Africa*. Trans. Alba I. Zizzamia. Milwaukee: Bruce, 1962.

Marris, Peter. *Family and Social Change in an African City: A Study of Rehousing in Lagos*. London: Routledge & Kegan Paul, 1961.

Marshall, Gloria. "In a World of Women: Field Work in a Yoruba Community." Peggy Golde, ed., *Women in the Field: Anthropological Experiences*. Chicago: Aldine, 1970: 167-194.

───── . "The Marketing of Farm Produce: Some Patterns of Trade among Women in Western Nigeria." *Proceedings of a Conference at the Nigerian Institute of Social and Economic Research*, Ibadan, 1962: 88-99.

───── . "Women, Trade and the Yoruba Family," Ph.D. dissertation, Columbia University, 1964.

Mayer, Philip, and Mayer, Iona. "Women and Children in the Migrant Situation." Part IV pp. 233-282. *Townsmen or Tribesmen*. Capetown: Oxford University Press, 1963.

Mbilinyi, Marjorie. "The Status of Women in Tanzania." *Canadian Journal of African Studies*, v. 6 (2), 1972: 371-77.

McCall, Daniel. "Trade and the Role of Wife in a Modern West African Town." A.W. Southall, ed., *Social Change in Modern Africa*. Oxford: Oxford University Press, 1961.

Mickelwait, Donald R., et al. *Women in Rural Development: A Survey of the Roles of Women in Ghana, Lesotho, Kenya, Nigeria, Bolivia, Paraguay and Peru*. Boulder: Westview Press, 1976.

Miller, Jean-Claude. "Ritual Marriage, Symbolic Fatherhood, and Initiation among the Rukuba, Plateau-Benue State, Nigeria." *Man* v. 7: 283-295, 1972.

Molnos, A. *Attitudes towards Family Planning in East Africa*. Munich: Weltforum Verlag, 1968.

Muhammad, Yahaya. "The Legal Status of Muslim Women in the North-
ern States of Nigeria." *Journal of the Centre for Islamic Legal Studies*, v. 1 (2),
1967: 1-38.

Mullings, Leith. "Women and Economic Change in Africa." *Women in Africa*,
Nancy J. Hafkin and Edna G. Bay (eds), Stanford: Stanford University
Press, 1976.

Mutiso, G.C.M. "Women in African Literature." *East African Journal*, v. 8 (3),
March 1971: 4-13.

Nasemann, Vandra. "The Hidden Curriculum of a West African Girls'
Boarding School." *Canadian Journal of African Studies*, v. 8 (3), 1974: 479-494.

Ngugi, WaThiong'o (James). *A Grain of Wheat*. London: Heinemann, 1967.

Nwapa, Flora *Efuru*. London: Heinemann, 1966.

O'Barr, Jean F. "Making the Invisible Visible: African Women in Politics and
Policy." *African Studies Review*, v. 18 (3), December 1975: 19-28.

Ogunsheye, F.A. "Les femmes du Nigeria." *Presence Africaine*, v. 32-33,
June-Sept., 1960: 120-38.

O'Kelly, Elizabeth "Corn Mill Societies in Southern Cameroons." *African
Women*, v. 1 (1), 1955: 33-35.

Okonjo, Kamene. "The Dual-Sex Political System in Operation: Igbo
Women and Community Politics in Mid-Western Nigeria." *Women in
Africa*, Nancy J. Hafkin and Edna G. Bay (eds), Stanford: Stanford Uni-
versity Press, 1976.

O'Laughlin, Bridget. "Mediating Contradiction: Why Mbum Women Do
Not Eat Chicken." M.Z. Rosaldo and Louise Lamphere, eds., *Women, Culture and Society*. Stanford: Stanford University Press, 1974.

Olmstead, Judith. "Women and Work in Two Southern Ethiopian Communities." *American Studies Review*, v. 18 (3), December 1975: 85-98.

Omari, T. Peter "Role Expectation in the Courtship Situation in Ghana."
Social Forces, vol. 42 (2), December 1963: 147-156.

Oppong, Christine. *Marriage Among a Matrilineal Elite: A Family Study of
Ghanaian Senior Civil Servants*. London: Cambridge University Press, 1974.

Oppong, Christine, and Okali, Christine; and Beverly Houghton. "Woman
Power: Retrograde Steps in Ghana." *African Studies Review*, v. 18 (3),
December 1975: 71-84.

Ottenberg, Phoebe. "The Changing Economic Position of Women Among
the Afikpo Ibo." William R. Bascom and Melville J. Herskovits, eds.,
Continuity and Change in African Cultures. Chicago: University of Chicago
Press, 1959: 205-223.

Pala, Achola O. "A Preliminary Survey of the Avenues for and Constraints
on Women in the Development Process in Kenya." Discussion Paper No.

218. Nairobi: Institute of Development Studies, University of Nairobi, March 1975.

———. "The Role of Women in Rural Development: Research Priorities." Discussion Paper no. 203. Nairobi: Institute of Development Studies, University of Nairobi, June 1974.

Pankhurst, Sylvia. "Ethiopian Women's Welfare Association." *Ethiopia Observer*, v. 4 (2), March 1960: 45-47.

Paulme, Denise. *Women of Tropical Africa*. Berkeley and Los Angeles: University of California Press, 1971.

Pellow, Deborah *Women in Accra: Options for Autonomy*. Michigan: Reference Publications, Inc., 1977.

Perlman, Melvin L. "The Changing Status and Role of Women in Toro, Western Uganda." *Cahiers d'Etudes Africaines*. v. 6, 1966: 564-91.

Pool, Janet. "A cross-comparative study of aspects of Conjugal behaviour among women of Three West African countries." *Canadian Journal of African Studies*, v. 6 (2) 1972: 233-259.

Razafyadriamihaingo, Suzanne. "The Position of Women in Madagascar." *African Women* v. 3 (2) June 1959: 29-33.

Richards, Audrey. *Chisungu: A Girl's Initiation Ceremony Among the Bemba of Northern Rhodesia*. London: Faber & Faber, 1956.

Ritzenthaler, Robert E. "Anlu: A Women's Uprising in the British Cameroons." *African Studies*, v. 19 (3) 1960: 151-156.

Robertson, Claire. "Economic Woman in Africa. Profit-Making Techniques of Accra Market Women." *Journal of Modern African Studies*, v. 12 (4), December 1974: 657-664.

———. "Ga Women and Socioeconomic Change in Accra, Ghana." *Women in Africa*, Nancy J. Hafkin and Edna G. Bay (eds), Stanford: Stanford University Press, 1976.

"Role of Women in National Development in African Countries." *International Labour Review*, v. 101, April 1970: 399-401.

Sa 'D Al-Din Fawzi. "The Role of Women in a Developing Sudan." *Women's Role in the Development of Tropical and Sub-Tropical Countries*. Brussels: Institute of Differing Civilizations, 1959.

Schapera, Isaac. *Married Life in an African Tribe*. Evanston: Northwestern University Press, 1965.

Schneider, Daivd M. and Gough, Kathleen. (eds.) *Matrilineal Kinship*, Berkeley: University of California Press, 1961.

Schlegel, Alice. *Male Dominance and Female Autonomy: Domestic Authority in Matrilineal Societies*. New Haven: Human Relations Area Files Press, 1972.

Schuster, Ilsa. *The New Women of Lusaka*, Palto Alto, Mayfield Publishing Company, 1979.

Simons, H.J. *African Women: Their Legal Status in South Africa*. Evanston: Northwestern University Press, 1968.

Siquet, M. "Legal and Customary Status of Women." *La Promotion de la femme au Congo et en Ruanda-Urundi*. Brussels: Congres Nationel Colonial, 12th Session, 1956: 197-251.

Smith, Mary F. *Baba of Karo, a Woman of the Muslim Hausa*. London: Faber, 1964.

Smock, Audrey C., and Giele Janet Z., eds. *Women: roles and status in eight countries*. New York: Wiley, 1977.

Southall, Aidan W. "The Position of Women and the Stability of Marriage in Tropical Africa." Aidan W. Southall, ed., *Social Change in Modern Africa*. London: Oxford University Press, 1961.

Spencer, Dunstan S.C. "African Women in Agricultural Development: A Case Study in Sierra Leone." African Rural Economy Working Paper No. 11. East Lansing: Michigan State University, April 1970.

Steady, Filomina Chioma. *Female Power in African Politics: The National Congress of Sierra Leone. Munger African Library Notes*, no. 31, August, 1975.

_____ . "Protestant Women's Associations in Freetown, Sierra Leone." *Women in Africa*, Nancy J. Hafkin and Edna G. Bay (eds), Stanford: Stanford University Press, 1976.

_____ . "Male Roles in Fertility in Sierra Leone: The Moving Target." in Oppong, C. et al. (eds.) *Marriage, Family and Parenthood in West Africa*. Canberra: Australian National University, 1978.

Steady, Filomina Chioma and Eide, Wenche Barth. "Individual and Social Energy Flows: Bridging Nutritional and Anthropological Thinking about Women's Work in Rural Africa: Some Theoretical Considerations," in Jerome, N., Kandel, R.F. and Pelto, G.H. (eds) *Nutritional Anthropology*. Pleasantville, N.Y.: Redgrave Publishing Company, 1980, pp. 61-84.

Stichter, Sharon B. "Women and the Labor Force in Kenya: 1895-1964." *Rural Africana*, v. 29, Winter, 1976: 45-67.

Strobel, Margaret. "From Lelemama to Lobbying: Women's Associations in Mombasa, Kenya." *Women in Africa*, Nancy J. Hafkin and Edna G. Bay (eds)., Stanford: Stanford University Press, 1976.

_____ . *Muslim Women in Mombasa*. New Haven: Yale University Press, 1979.

Sudarkasa, Niara. *Where Women Work: A Study of Yoruba Women in the Marketplace and in the Home*. Ann Arbor: University of Michigan Press, 1973.

Suleiman, S.M. "Women in the Sudan Public Service." *Sudan Journal of Administration and Development*, v. 2, Jan. 1966: 37-53.

Suttner, R.S. "The Legal Status of African Women in South Africa." A Review Article. *African Social Research*, v. 8, Dec. 1969: 620-627.

Touré, Sekou. "The African Woman." *The Black Scholar*, v. 4 (6-7), March-April 1973: 32-36.

——— . "The Role of Women in the Revolution." *Black Scholar*, v. 6 (6), March 1975: 32-36.

Uchendu, Victor Chikezie. "Concubinage among Ngwa Igbo of Southern Nigeria." *Africa*, v. 35 (2), April 1965: 187-197.

United Nations Economic Commission for Africa. "Country Report for Nigeria. Vocational Training Opportunities for Girls and Women." Addis Ababa: Economic Commission for Africa, 1973.

UN Economic Commisssion for Africa. Report of the Regional Conference on Education, Vocational Training and Work Opportunities for Girls and Women in African Countries. Rabat: UNECA 1971.

UNESCO *Report of the Conference on African Women and Adult Education*. Paris: UNESCO, 1962.

UNESCO. "Report of the Research Team Appointed by the Sierra Leone Commission for Education, Training, and Employment Opportunities for Women in Sierra Leone, 1974."

Urdang, Stephanie. *Fighting Two Colonialisms: Women in Guinea-Bissau*. New York: Monthly Review Press, 1979.

——— . "Fighting Two Colonialisms: The Women's Struggle in Guinea-Bissau." *African Studies Review*, v. 18 (3), Dec. 1973: 29-34.

Usoro, Eno J. "The Place of Women in Nigerian Society." *African Women*, v. 4 (2), June 1961: 27-30.

Van Allen, Judith. "'Aba Riots' or Igbo 'Women's War'?—Ideology, Stratification and the Invisibility of Women," in Hafkin, N. and Edna Bay (eds.) *Women in Africa*. Stanford: Staford University Press, 1976, pp. 59-85.

——— . "Sitting on a Man: Colonialism and the Lost Political Institutions of Igbo Women." *Canadian Journal of African Studies*, v. 6 (2), 1972: 165-182.

——— . "Women in Africa: Modernization Means More Dependency." *The Center Magazine*, v. 7 (3), May-June 1974, 60-67.

Wainwright, Bridget. "Women's Clubs in the Central Nyanza District of Kenya." *Community Development Bulletin*, v. 4 (4), Sept. 1953: p. 77-80.

Walker, Alice. "The Diary of an African Nun." *The Black Woman: an Anthology*. Toni Cade, New York: The New American Library, 1970.

Well, P. M. "Wet Rice, Women, and Adaptation in the Gambia." *Rural Africana*, v. 19, Winter 1973: 20-29.

Whiting, Beatrice B. "The Kenyan Career Woman: Traditional and Modern." *Annals of the New York Academy of Sciences*, no. 208, March 1973: 71-75.

Wipper, Audrey. "African Women, Fashion and Scapegoating." *Canadian Journal of African Studies*, v. 6 (2), 1972: 329-349.

_____ . "Equal Rights for Women in Kenya?" *Journal of Modern African Studies*, v. 9 (3), Oct. 1971, pp. 429-442.

_____ . "The Maendaleo Ya Wanawake Movement: Some Paradoxes and Contradictions." *African Studies Review*, v. 18 (3), Dec. 1975: 99-120.

_____ . "The Politics of Sex: Some Strategies Employed by the Kenyan Power Elite to Handle a Normative-Existential Discrepancy." *African Studies Review*, v. 14 (3), December, 1971: 463-482.

_____ . "The Roles of African Women: Past, Present and Future." *Canadian Journal of African Studies*, 6, (2) 1972: 143-146.

Women's Role in the Development of Tropical and Subtropical Countries. Brussels: Institut International des Civilizations Differentes, 1959.

United States of America

Angelou, Maya. *And Still I Rise*. New York: Random House, 1978.

_____ . *I Know Why the Caged Bird Sings*. New York: Random House, 1970.

Ashe, Christy. "Abortion or Genocide". *Liberator*, August 1970, pp. 4-9.

Beale, Frances. "Double Jeopardy: To Be Black and Female." *The Black Woman: an Anthology*. Toni Cade (ed.) The New American Library: New York, 1970.

Bell, R.R. "Lower Class Negro Mothers' Aspirations for Their Children." *Social Forces* 43 May 1965: 493-500.

Bell, Roseann P., Parker, Bettye J. and Guy-Sheftall, Beverly (eds.) *Sturdy Black Bridges: Visions of Black Women in Literature*. New York: Anchor Books, 1979.

Bernard, Jessie. *Marriage and Family Among Negroes*. Englewood Cliffs, N.J.: Prentice-Hall, 1966.

Billingsley, Andrew. *Black Families and the Struggle for Survival*. New York: Friendship Press, 1974.

_____ . *Black Families in White America*. Englewood Cliffs, New Jersey: Prentice-Hall, 1968.

_____ , and Billingsley, Amy Tate. "Negro Family Life in America." *Social Service Review* 39, Sept. 1965: 310-19.

Blassingame, J. *The Slave Community*. New York: Oxford University Press, 1972.

Bogle, Donald. *Toms, Coons, Mulattoes, Mammies and Bucks*. New York: Viking Press, 1978.

Bonner, Florence. "Black Women and White Women: A Comparative Analysis of Perceptions of Sex Roles for Self, Ideal-Self and the Ideal Male." *The Journal of Afro-American Issues*, v. 2, Summer 1974: 237-246.

Bracey, John H., Jr. *Black Matriarchy: Myth or Reality* Belmont, CA.: Wadsworth Publishing Co., 1971.

Bradford, Sarah Elizabeth. *Harriet Tubman, The Moses of Her People*. Reprint of the 1886 edition, New York: Corinth Books, 1961.

Braxton, Bernard. *Women, Sex, and Race*. Washington, D.C.: Verte Press, 1973.

Brody, Eugene B. "Color and Identity Conflict in Young Boys: Observations of Negro Mothers and Sons in Urban Baltimore." *Psychiatry*, v. 26 (2), May 1963: 188-201.

Brown, Hallie Quinne, ed. *Homespun Heroines and Other Women of Distinction*. Xenia, Ohio: Aldine, 1926. Reprinted, Freeport, N.Y.: Books for Libraries Press, 1971.

Browne, Rose Butler. *Love My Children: An Autobiography* New York: Meredith Press, 1962.

Burkhart, Kathryn W. *Women in Prison*. Garden City, N.Y.: Doubleday and Co., 1970.

Cade, Toni (ed). *The Black Woman: An Anthology*, New York: Signet, 1970.

_____. "On the Issue of Roles." *The Black Woman: an Anthology*. Toni Cade (ed). New York: The New American Library, 1970.

_____. "The Pill: Genocide or Liberation?" in *The Black Woman: an Anthology*. Toni Cade (ed). New York: The New American Library, 1970.

Carson, Josephine. *Silent Voices: The Southern Negro Woman Today*. New York: Dell, Delacorte Press, 1969.

Carruth, Ella Kaiser. *She Wanted to Read: The Story of Mary McLeod Bethune*. Nashville and New York: Abingdon Press, 1966.

Chisholm, Shirley. "Race, Revolution and Women." *Black Scholar*, v. 3(4), December 1971: 17-20.

_____. "Racism and Anti-Feminism." *The Black Scholar*, January-February 1970, v.1 (3-4):40-45.

_____. *Unbought and Unbossed*. Boston: Houghton Mifflin, 1970.

Copeland, E. "Counseling black women with negative self-concepts." *Personal and Guidance Journal*, v. 55, 1977: 397-400.

Cummings, Gwenna. "Black Women: Often Discussed but Never Understood." in *The Black Power Revolt*, ed. F. B. Barbour. Boston: Extending Horizons Books, 1968.

Dannett, Sylvia G.L. *Profiles of Negro Womanhood*. Yonkers, New York: Educational Heritage, 1969.

David, Jay. *Growing Up Black*. New York: Simon and Schuster, 1970.

_____, and Watkins, Mel, (eds). *Black Woman: Portraits in Fact and Fiction*. New York: William Morrow, 1970.

Davis, Angela. "Reflections on the Black Woman's Role in the Community of Slaves," *Black Scholar*, December 1971, 3-15.

Davis, Elizabeth L. *Lifting as They Climb: The National Association of Colored Women*. Washington, D.C.: The National Association of Colored Women, 1933.

Duster, Alfreda, M., ed. *Crusade for Justice: The Autobiography of Ida B. Wells*. Chicago: University of Chicago Press, 1970.

Epstein, Cynthia Fuchs. "Black and Female: the Double Whammy." *Psychology Today*, v. 7 (3), August 1973: 57-61.

_____. Positive Effects of the Multiple Negative: Explaining the Success of Black Professional Women. In J. Huber (ed.), *Changing Women in a Changing Society*. Chicago: University of Chicago Press, 1973.

Evans, Mari. *I Am a Black Woman*. New York: William Morrow and Co., 1970.

_____. *I Look At Me*. Chicago: Third World Press, 1974.

Fleming, J. "Slavery, Civil War and Reconstruction: A Study of Black in Microcosm." *Negro History Bulletin*, v. 38, 1975: 430-433.

Frazier, E. Franklin *The Negro Family in the United States*. New York: Dryden Press, 1948.

_____. *Negro Family in the United States*. abr. ed. Chicago: University of Chicago Press, 1966.

Giovanni, Nikki. *Cotton Candy on a Rainy Day*. New York: William Morrow and Co., 1978.

_____. *The Women and The Men*. New York: William Morrow and Co., 1979.

Gordon, Eugene. *The Position of Negro Women*. New York: Workers' Library, 1935.

Guffy, Ossie. *Ossie: The Autobiography of a Black Woman*. New York: Bantam Books, 1972.

Gump, J. "Comparative Analysis of Black Women and White Women's Sex Role Attitudes." *Journal of Counseling and Clinical Psychology*, v. 13, 1975: 858-863.

Gutman, Herbert G. *The Black Family in Slavery and Freedom, 1750-1925*. New York: Pantheon Books, 1976.

Hamilton, Kelly. *Goals and Plans of Black Women: A Sociological Study*. Hicksville, New York: Exposition Press, 1975.

_____ Lorraine. *To be Young, Gifted, and Black*. Englewood Cliffs, New ___ce-Hall, 1969.

Hare, Nathan, and Hare, Julia. "Black Women 1970." *Transaction*, 8 (Nov.-Dec. 1970): 65-69.

Harley, Sharon and Terborg-Penn, Rosalyn, eds. *The Afro-American Woman: Struggles and Images.* Port Washington, N.Y.: Kennikat Press, 1978.

Hedgeman, Anna Arnold. *The Trumpet Sound: A Memoir of Negro Leadership.* New York: Holt, Rinehart and Winston, 1964.

Hendin, Herbert. *Black Suicide.* New York: Basic Books, 1969.

Hernton, Calvin C. *Sex and Racism in America.* Garden City, New York: Doubleday, 1965.

Higgins, Chester. *Black Woman.* New York: McCall, 1970.

Hill, Robert. *The Strengths of Black Families.* New York: Emerson Hall Publishing Co., 1972.

Holiday, Billie. *Lady Sings the Blues.* Garden City, New York: Doubleday, 1956.

Holt, Rackham. *Mary McLeod Bethune: A Biography.* New York: Doubleday, 1964.

Hunton, Addie and Johnson, Kathryn M. *Two Colored Women with the American-Expeditionary Forces.* Brooklyn, New York: Eagle Press, 1920.

Jackson, Jacquelyn Johnson. "Black Female Sociologists." In *Black Sociologists: Historical and Contemporary Perspectives.* James E. Blackwell and Morris Janowitz. (eds). Chicago, University of Chicago Press, 1974.

Jackson, J. "But where are the men?" *The Black Scholar*, v. 3, 1971: 30-41.

Jackson, Mahalia and Whylie, Evan McLeod. *Movin' On Up.* New York: Hawthorne Books, 1966.

Jacobs, Harriet Brent. *Incidents in the Life of a Slave Girl, Written by Herself.* Edited by L.M. Child. Miami: Mnemosyne Pub. Co., 1969.

Jeffers, T. "The Black Woman and the Black Middle Class." *The Black Scholar*, v. 5, 1973: 37-41.

Jefferies, D. "Counseling for the strengths of the black woman." *The Counseling Psychologist*, v. 6, 1976:20-32.

Jones, R. (ed.) *Black Psychology.* New York: Harper & Row, 1972.

Jordan, June. *Fannie Lou Hamer.* New York: Thomas Y. Crowell Co., 1972.

────── . *Some Changes.* New York: E.P. Dutton & Co., Inc., 1971.

Kanno, Nellie B. "Comparative Life Styles of the Black Female in the United States and the Black Female in Lesotho." *The Journal of Afro-American Issues*, 2, Summer 1974: 212-217.

Katz, Maude White. "End Racism in Education: A Concerned Parent Speaks." *The Black Woman: an Anthology.* Toni Cade (ed.) New York: The New American Library, 1970.

King, M. "The Politics of Sexual Stereotypes." *The Black Scholar*, v. 5, 1973: 12-23.

Knebel, Fletcher. "Identity: The Black Woman's Burden." *Look*, 23 Sept. 1969: 77-79.

Ladner, Joyce. *Mixed Families-Adopting Across Racial Boundaries*. Garden City, N.Y.: Doubleday and Co., 1977.

———. *Tomorrow's Tomorrow*. Garden City, N.Y.: Doubleday, 1971.

Landes, Ruth. "Negro Slavery and Female Status." *African Affairs*, v. 52 (206), 1953: 54-57.

Lang, F. "Sickle Cell and the Pill: Birth Control Pills Dangerous to Black Women." *Ramparts*, (February, 1972).

LaRue, Linda J.M. "Black Liberation and Women's Liberation." *Transaction* 8 (Nov.-Dec. 1970): 59-64.

Leacock, Eleanor. "Introduction," in Frederick Engels, *The Origin of the Family, Private Property and the State* New York: International Publishers Company, 1972.

Lerner, Gerda. *Black Women in White America*. New York: Pantheon Books, 1972.

Lewis, Hylan. "The Changing Negro Family." *The Nations' Children*. ed. Eli Ginzberg. New York: Columbia University Press, 1960.

Lindsey, K. "The Black woman as a woman." In *The Black Woman*. Toni Cade, ed. New York: New American Library, Inc.; 1970, 85-89.

Locke, Alain. *The Negro in Art*. Reprint of the 1940 edition. Chicago: Afro-American Press, 1969.

Loewenberg, Bert J. and Bogin, Ruth, (eds.), *Black Women in Nineteenth-Century American Life*. University Park: Pennsylvania State University Press, 1976.

Lutz, Alma. *Crusade for Freedom: Women of the Antislavery Movement*. Boston: Beacon Press, 1968.

Majors, Monroe Alphus. *Noted Negro Women: Their Triumphs and Activities*. Reprint of the 1893 edition. Freeport, N.Y.: Books for Libraries Press, 1971.

Martin, Elmer P. and Martin, Joanne M. *The Black Extended Family*. Chicago: University of Chicago Press, 1978.

McDougall, Harold. *Black Woman*, New York: Saturday Review Press, McCall Books, 1970.

Milwaukee County Welfare Rights Organization. *Welfare Mothers Speak Out: We Ain't Gonna Shuffle Anymore*. New York: W.W. Norton and Co., 1972.

Minority women workers: A Statistical Overview, U.S. Department of Labor, ───'s Bureau, 1977.

───*ming of Age in Mississippi*. New York: Dell, 1968.

Mossell, Gertrude E. *The Work of the Afro-American Woman*. Reprint of the 1894 edition. Freeport, New York: Books For Libraries Press, 1971.

Moynihan, Daniel Patrick. *The Negro Family: The Case for National Action*. Washington, D.C.: U.S. Dept of Labor, 1965.

Naderson, Regina. *Who is Angela Davis? The Biography of a Revolutionary*. New York: Peter H. Wyden, 1972.

Negro Families in Rural Wisconsin: A Study of Their Community Life. Madison: Governor's Commission on Human Rights, 1959.

Noble, Jeanne L. *Beautiful, Also, Are the Souls of My Black Sisters*. Englewood Cliffs, N.J.: Prentice-Hall, 1978.

_____ . *The Negro Woman's College Education*. New York: Columbia Teachers College, 1975.

Porterfield, Ernest. *Black and White Mixed Marriages*. Chicago: Nelson-Hall, 1978.

Poussaint, Alvin F., ed. *The Black Family*. Washington, D.C.: ECCA Publications, 1976.

Reid, Inez Smith *"Together" Black Women*. 2nd edition New York: The Third Press, 1975.

Reid, Willie M. *Black Women's Struggle for Equality*. New York: Pathfinder Press, n.d.

Reiner, Béatrice S. "The Real World of The Teenage Negro Mother." *Child Welfare* v. 47 (7), 1968: 391-96.

Robinson, Pat & Group. A Historical and Critical Essay for Black Women in the Cities. *The Black Woman: an Anthology:* Toni Cade (ed); New York: The New American Library, 1970.

Scanzoni, John H. *Black Family in Modern Society*. Chicago: University of Chicago Press, 1977.

Shange,Ntozake. *For Colored Girls Who Have Considered Suicide/When the Rainbow is Enuf!* New York: Macmillan Publishing Co., 1977.

Shimkin, Demitri B. et al. (eds.) *The Extended Family in Black Societies*. Chicago: Aldine Publishing Co., 1978.

Sizemore, Barbara A. "Sexism and the Black Male." *Black Scholar*, 4 (March-April 1973), 2-11.

Slaughter, Diana T. "Becoming an Afro-American Woman." Special issue, Women in Education, *School Review* 80 (1972): 299-318.

Stack, Carol. *All Our Kin*. New York: Harper & Row, 1974.

Staples, Robert. *The Black Family: Essays and Studies*. Belmont, California: Wadsworth Publishing Co., 1971.

_____ . *The Black Woman in America: Sex, Marriage, and the Family*. Chicago: Nelson-Hall Publishers, 1973.

Sterling, Dorothy. *Black Foremothers: Three Lives*. Old Westbury, N.Y.: Feminist Press, 1979.

Stewart-Baxter, Derrick. *Ma Rainey and the Classic Blues Singer*. New York: Stein and Day, 1970.

Strodbeck, Fred L. "The Poverty-Dependency Syndrome of the ADC Female-Based Negro Family." *American Journal of Orthopsychiatry* 34 (Mar. 1964): 216-217.

Tanner, Nancy. "Matrifocality in Indonesia and Africa and among Black Americans." In Michelle Zimbalist Rosaldo and Louise Lamphere (eds.) *Woman, Culture, and Society*. Stanford: Stanford University Press, 1974.

Thomas, A. & Sillen, S. *Racism and Psychiatry*. New York: Brunner/Mazel, 1972.

Walker, Alice. *In Love and Trouble: Stories of Black Women*. New York: Harcourt, Brace and Jovanovich, 1973.

Wallace, Michele. *Black Macho and the Myth of the Superwoman*. New York: Dial Press, 1979.

Wallace, Phyllis A. and La Mond, Annette M. *Women, Minorities, and Discrimination*. Lexington, MA: Lexington Books, 1977.

Washington, Mary Helen. "Black Women Image Makers." *Black World* v. 23 (10) August, 1974: 10-18.

Watkins, Mel, and David, Jay eds. *To Be A Black Woman: Portraits in Fact and Fiction*. New York: William Morrow, 1971.

Williams, Bertha M. "Black Women: Assertiveness vs. Aggressiveness." *The Journal of Afro-American Issues*, v. 2, Summer 1974: 204-211.

Williams, Maxine, et al. (eds.) *Black Women's Liberation*. New York: Pathfinder Press, 1971.

Willie, Charles V. et al. (eds.). *Racism and Mental Health: Essays*. Pittsburgh: sity of Pittsburgh Press, 1974.

Women's Bureau, U.S. Department of Labor. *Negro Women in the Population and in the Labor Force*. Washington, D.C.: U.S. Government Printing Office, n.d.

Woodson, Carter G. "Emma Frances Grayson Merritt." *Opportunity*, 8 August 1930: 244-245.

Caribbean and South America

Bastide, Roger (ed.) *La Femme de Couleur en Amérique Latine* Paris: Editions
̱ ̱ ̱nos. 1974.

̱ ̱ ̱ *Structure in Jamaica: the Social Context of Reproduction*. New 1962.

Blumberg, R. L. with Garcia, M. P. "The Political Economy of the Mother/Child Family: A Cross-Societal View," in L. Lemtero-Otero, ed., *Beyond the Nuclear Family Model: Contemporary Family Sociology in a Cross-Cultural Perspective*. London: Sage Publishing, 1976.

Braithwaite, Edward K. *Wars of Respect: Nanny and Sam Sharpe*. Kingston: Agency for Public Information, 1977.

Castro, Fidel "The Revolution has in Cuban women today an impressive political force." La Habana: *Editorial de Ciences Sociales*, Ediciones Politicas, 1974.

Clarke, Edith. *My Mother Who Fathered Me*. London: George Allen and Unwin, 1957.

Cohen, Y. "A Study in Interpersonal Relations in a Jamaican Community," Ph.D. thesis, Xerox facsimile, Ann Arbor: University Microfilms, 1953.

Freilich, Morris, "Sex, Secrets, and Systems," in S. Gerber, ed., *The Family in the Caribbean*. Rio Piedras, Puerto Rico: Institute of Caribbean Studies, 1968.

Frazier, E. Franklin. "The Negro Family in Bahia, Brazil." Olen Leonard and Charles Loomis, eds., *Readings*. Lansing: Michigan State University Press, 1953.

Gonzalez, Nancy L. Solien. *Black Carib Household Structure: A Study of Migration and Modernization*. Seattle: University of Washington Press, 1969.

Handler, Jerome. *The Unappropriated People: Freedom in the Slave Society of Barbados*. Baltimore: Johns Hopkins Press, 1974.

Henry, Frances and Pamela Wilson. "Status of Women in Caribbean Societies: An Overview of Their Social, Economic and Sexual Roles." *Social and Economic Studies*, v. 24 (2), June 1975: 165-198.

King, Marjorie. "Cuba's Attack on Women's Second Shift, 1974-76." *Latin American Perspectives*, v. 4 (1-2), Winter-Spring 1977: 106-119.

Leyburn, James A. *The Haitian People*. New Haven: Yale University Press, 1941.

Makiesky-Barrow, Susan. "Class, Culture, and Politics in a Barbadian Community." Ph.D. dissertation, Brandeis University 1976.

Mathurin, Lucille. "A Historical Study of Women in Jamaica form 1655 to 1844." Ph.D. dissertation, University of the West Indies (Mona, Jamaica), 1974.

———— . *The Rebel Woman in the British West Indies during Slavery*. Kingston: African-Caribbean Publications, 1975.

Mintz, Sidney W. "Men, Women and Trade," *Comparative Studies in Society and History 13* (2): 247-269, 1971.

_____ . "The Employment of Capital by Haitian Market Women," in Firth, R. and Yamey, B. (eds), *Capital, Saving and Credit in Peasant Society*. Chicago: Aldine Publishig Company, 1964, pp. 256-286.

Moses, Y. "What Price Education: The Working Women of Montserrat," *Council on Anthropology and Education Quarterly*, vol. 6, 1975: 13-16.

Nash, June and Safa, Helen I., eds. *Sex and Class in Latin America*. New York: Praeger, 1976.

Ottorbein, Keith F. "Caribbean Family Organizations: A Comparative Analysis." *American Anthropologist* v. 67 1965: 66-79.

Pollock, Nancy J. "Women and the Division of Labor: A Jamaican Example," *American Anthropologist*, v. 74, 1972: 689-692.

Roberts, George W., and Sonja A. Sinclair. *Women in Jamaica: Patterns of Reproduction and Family*. Millwood, NY: KTO Press, c. 1978.

Rodman, H. *Lower Class Families: The Culture of Poverty in Negro Trinidad*. New York: Oxford University Press, 1971.

Simpson, George E. "Sexual and Familial Institutions in Haiti," *American Anthropologist* v. 44, 1942: 655-674.

Smith, Michael Garfield. *West Indian Family Structure*. Seattle: University of Washington Press, 1962.

Smith, Raymond T. "The Family in the Caribbean." *Caribbean Studies: A Symposium*, ed. Vera Rubin. Seattle: University of Washington Press, 1960.

_____ . *The Negro Family in British Guiana: Family Structure and Social Status in the Villages*. London: Routledge & Kegan Paul, 1965.

_____ . "Culture and Social Structure in the Caribbean: Some Recent Work on Family Kinship Studies," in Richard Frucht, ed., *Black Society in the New World*. New York: Random House, 1971.

Stoffle, Richard W. "Industrial Employment and Inter-Spouse Conflict: Barbados, West Indies." Ph.D dissertation, University of Kentucky, 1972.

Tuelon, Allen. "Nanny—Maroon Chieftainess," *Caribbean Quarterly* v. 19, 1973: 20-27.

Wilson, Peter, J. *Crab Antics: The Social Anthropology of English-Speaking Negro Societies of the Caribbean*. New Haven: Yale University Press, 1973.

General

Curtin, Philip. *The Atlantic Slave Trade*. Madison: University of Wisconsin Press, 1969.

Davidson, Basil. *Black Mother: The Years of the African Slave Trade*. Boston: Atlantic-Little, Brown and Co., 4th edition, 1966.

Emecheta, Buchi. *Second-Class Citizen*. New York: George Braziller, Inc., 1975.

Fanon, F. *The Wretched of the Earth*. New York: Grove Press, 1963.

Kilson, Martin L. and Rotberg, Robert I. (eds) *The African Diaspora: interpretive essays*. Cambridge: Harvard University Press, 1976.

Mintz, Sidney Wilfred. "Men, Women and Trade." *Comparative Studies in Society and History*, v. 13, 1971: 247-269.

Williams, Eric. *Capitalism and Slavery*. Chapel Hill: University of North Carolina Press, 1944. New York: Capricorn Books, reprinted 1966.

Some Useful Bibliographies

Cole, Johnetta B. "Black Women in America: An Annotated Bibliography." *Black Scholar*, v. 3(4), December, 1971: 42-53.

Davis, Lenwood G. *Black Women in the Cities, 1872-1975:* a bibliography of published works on the life and achievements of black women in cities in the United States, 2nd edition. Monticello, Illinois: Council of Planning Librarians, 1975.

_____. *The Black Woman in American Society: An Annotated Bibliography*. Boston: G. K. Hall & Co., 1975.

Indiana University. *The Black Family and the Black Woman: A Bibliography*. Indiana University Library and the Afro-American Studies Dept., Bloomington, Indiana, 1972.

Klotzman, Phyllis and Baatz, Wilmer, H., (eds). *The Black Family and the Black Woman: A Bibliography*. New York: Arno Press, 1978.

Kratochvil, Laura and Shaw, Shauna. *African Women: A Select Bibliography*. Cambridge, England: African Studies Centre, Cambridge University, 1974.

Murray, Jocelyn. *A Preliminary Bibliography, Women in Africa*. Los Angeles: Graduate Women in History, UCLA, 1974.

Contributors

Agnes Akosua Adioo, A Ghanaian national, is Women's Development Task Force Officer of the United Nations Economic Commission for Africa at Addis Ababa, Ethiopia. She has studied in Ghana, Canada and the United States, and holds a Ph.D. in History and Social Anthropology from the University of California, Los Angeles. She has held university teaching appointments in Ghana and at U.C.L.A. Her research interests focus on social change in African societies, and she has published several articles on the Asante.

Kenneth M. Bilby is a Ph.D. candidate in anthropology at the Johns Hopkins University. He received an M.A. from Wesleyan University in 1980. His interests include ethnicity, ethnohistory, ritual and music, and he has conducted field research in Jamaica and Sierra Leone. The topic of his field research was "Partisan Spirits: Ritual Interaction and Maroon Identity in Eastern Jamaica," and in 1979 he produced a film, *Capital of Earth: The Maroons of Moore Town*.

Laurence French has a B.A. (1968), M.A. (1970) and Ph.D. (1975) in sociology from the University of New Hampshire, and is completing a post-doctorate in psychological and cultural studies at the University of Nebraska—Lincoln. His major publications and research interests have been in the area of race and ethnic relations and multicultural education.

Nancie L. Solien Gonzalez was born in Illinois and received her graduate training in Anthropology at the University of Michigan, where she took her Ph.D. in 1959. She has done field work among Guatemalan Indian and Ladino populations, as well as among urban and rural groups in the Dominican Republic and in New Mexico. She has maintained a scholarly and personal interest in the Central American Garifuna (Black Caribs) since 1956 when she first visited them, and her most recent research is related to their migration to the United States. Dr. Gonzalez has taught at the University of California at Berkeley, the University of New Mexico, the University of Iowa, Boston University and the University of San Carlos in Guatemala, and is at present Vice Chancellor for Academic Affairs and Professor of Anthropology at the University of Maryland.

Josef Gugler is Professor of Sociology at the University of Connecticut. After an undergraduate degree in Economics, he did graduate work in Sociology in the Federal Republic of Germany and in France. In 1961-62 he carried out a study of urban-rural relationships in Nigeria. From 1964 until 1970 he was engaged in research and teaching at Makerere University College, where he was Director of Sociological Research at the Makerere Institute of Social Research. He held visiting appointments at the University College, Dar es Salaam, Tanzania, and the Université Lovanium, Zaire. During 1980-81 he will work in India on recent and current research on urbanization. He is coauthor of *Urbanization and Social Change in West Africa* (Cambridge University Press, 1978) and *Urban Growth and Underdevelopment*, to be published by Oxford University Press in 1981. His study of urbanization policy and its implementation in revolutionary Cuba appeared in *Comparative Studies in International Development* and the *International Journal of Urban and Regional Research* in 1980.

Darlene Clarke Hine received her B.A. from Roosevelt University, M.A. and Ph.D. from Kent State University, majoring in American History with a specialty in Afro-American History. She is currently Associate Professor of History at Purdue University, and previously taught at South Carolina State College. She is the author of several articles in the *Journal of Negro History, Negro History Bulletin,* and *The Southwestern Historical Quarterly* and is the editor of *TRUTH,* Newsletter of the Association of Black Women Historians. Her first book, *Black Victory: The Rise and Fall of the White Primary in Texas*, was published by Kraus-Thomson in 1979. She is currently working on a book-length study of blacks in the medical profession, and continuing research on the history of black women in nursing.

Irene V. Jackson is Program Director for the Center for Ethnic Music at Howard University. She received her Ph.D. in ehtnomusicology from Wesleyan University, and has taught at Yale University and the University of Connecticut. She is the author of a book on Afro-American music, and has published several articles on African and African-derived musical traditions.

Bennetta Jules-Rosette is Associate Professor of Sociology at the University of California, San Diego. She received her B.A. (1968) in Social Relations at Radcliffe College and her M.A. and Ph.D. (1973) at Harvard University in Social Relations. Since 1969, she has conducted a series of field studies in southwestern Zaire, (1969 and 1971-72) and in Lusaka, Zambia (1974-1979) on religious movements and more recently on popular African artists. This research was funded by the National Science Foundation and the National Endowment for the Humanities. Her major areas of interest are women's studies, African religion, and culture change. Her major publications include *African Apostles* (Cornell, 1975), *A Paradigm for Looking* (Abbex, 1977) and *The New Religions of Africa* (Ablex, 1979). She is currently completing a monograph on popular African art across the continent.

Joyce Bennett Justus was born in Jamaica and studied at the University of the West Indies, and at the University of California Los Angeles where she received her M.A. (1968) and Ph.D. (1971). She is currently Lecturer in Anthropology at the University of California, San Diego. She has conducted field research in Dominica on educational aspirations, in Los Angeles on female West Indian migrants, and in Jamaica on female sex role socialization.

Joyce A. Ladner received her Ph.D. in sociology from Washington University, St. Louis, has taught at Southern Illinois and Howard Universities, and is currently Professor of Sociology at Hunter College, and the Graduate Center, City University of New York. She has conducted research on the role of women in community development in East Africa, and is the recipient of several research grants. Dr. Ladner has authored numerous scholarly and popular articles, and her major publications include *Tomorrow's Tomorrow: The*

Black Woman (1971), *Mixed Families: Adopting Across Racial Boundaries* (1977) and an anthology, *The Death of White Sociology* (1973), and a forthcoming book on the changing South.

Richard Lapchick is a specialist on Southern Africa at the United Nations where he has worked for the Center Against Apartheid and the 1980 World Conference of the U.N. Decade for Women. He has taught at Virginia Wesleyan College. He is the author of two books and several articles, and has been an antiapartheid activist since 1970. He is a recipient of the Methodist Federation's Humanitarian of the Year Award (1978), and in 1979 received the Kenneth Kaunda Award for Humanism. He is the first recepient of the Martin Luther King Fellowship for studies in Race Relations.

Regine LaTortue was born in Haiti and holds a B.A. from Trinity College in Washington, D.C., an M.A. from the University of Illinois, and an M.Phil. from Yale University. She is a Ph.D. candidate at Yale working on "The Representation of Women in the Haitian Novel." She has taught at Yale and is currently teaching Black American, Caribbean and African Literatures at Brooklyn College in the Department of Africana Studies where she is also Deputy Chairperson. She has lectured and written articles on various aspects of black literature, and has published a book, with Gleason R.W. Adams, *Les Cenelles: A Collection of Poems by Creole Writers of the Early Nineteenth Century* (G.K. Hall, 1979) which focuses on Louisianan poetry.

Susan Makiesky-Barrow received her Ph.D. in anthropology from Brandeis University in 1976. She has taught at New York University and at the University of the West Indies. She was carried out field research on social and political change in Antigua and Barbados, and her research interests include the Caribbean, social inequality and culture, and sex roles. She is at present Senior Research Scientist in the Biometrics Research Unit, New York State Psychiatric Institute.

Sidney W. Mintz is Professor of Anthropology, the Johns Hopkins University. He has carried out field research in Puerto Rico, Jamaica, Haiti and Iran. His publications include *The People of Puerto Rico* (with J. Steward and others), 1956; *Worker in the Cane*, 1960; *Caribbean Transformations*, 1974; and (with Richard Price) *An Anthropo-*

logical Approach to the Afro-American Past, 1976. He is currently at work on a social history of sugar consumption.

Yolanda T. Moses is Associate Professor at California State Polytechnic University, Pomona. She received her Ph.D. from the University of California at Riverside in 1976. She conducted field research in the Eastern Caribbean in 1973 and 1974. Her involvement with the study of black societies in the New World, economic development and sex roles has led to an increased interest in women and world development, especially in the area of the politics of health.

Maria Luisa Nunes was born in Providence, Rhode Island. She is the descendant of Cape Verdean immigrants who settled in the New England area at the end of the nineteenth century. She holds a B. A. from Harvard-Radcliffe, an M. A. from Columbia and a Ph.D. from the City University of New York. Ms. Nunes has worked as an assistant political affairs officer at the United Nations and as a consultant to UNESCO. As assistant professor of Portuguese at Yale she also taught courses in Afro-American studies. At present she is associate professor of Portuguese at the University of Pittsburgh. Her publishing credits include books on Eca de Queiroz, Machado de Assis, and Lima Barreto, as well as an oral history on Cape Verdeans. She has published articles in journals and books in the United States, Portugal, Brazil and Africa.

Achola Pala Okeyo is a Kenyan national. She is Liaison Officer of the World Conference of the United Nations Decade for Women, and a former Research Fellow at the Institute for Development Studies, University of Nairobi, Kenya where she pursued research and evaluation of rural development and change in Kenya. She holds a B.A. from the University of East Africa, Dar es Salaam, an M.A. in Education and Ph.D. in Anthropology from Harvard University. She is also a founder-member of the Association of African Women for Research and Development, a research network and professional-technical association of African women interested in promoting women's advancement within the context of African development. Dr. Pala Okeyo is the author of numerous articles and monographs on women and development, and is the foremost authority on women in Kenya.

Kamene Okonjo is Senior Research Fellow at the Institute of African Studies, University of Nigeria, Nsukka. She has conducted field research on women in Nigeria, and written a number of articles on the subject. Dr. Okonjo studied in Nigeria, Germany and the United States, and is a leading authority of women in southeastern Nigeria.

Linda M. Perkins has a Ph.D. in the History of Education and Higher Education from the University of Illinois. She is currently a postdoctoral educational research fellow at the Mary Ingraham Bunting Institute of Radcliffe College. Her publications include, "Quaker Beneficence and Black Control: The Institute for Colored Youth, 1852-1903" in V.P. Franklin and J. D. Anderson (eds.) *New Perspectives on Black Educational History* (Boston: G. K. Hall, 1978); "Fanny Jackson Coppin" in the *Encyclopedia of Afro-American Education: A Concise Guide to the Historical and Contemporary Record,* M.R. Winston editor-in-chief (New York: Harcourt, Brace, Jovanovich, forthcoming). Dr. Perkins is at present writing a book on nineteenth century black women and their role in race "uplift."

Elizabeth Thaele Rivkin came to the United States as a political refugee from South Africa having spent two years in refugee camps in Zambia and Botswana. The article is one of many speeches she has given as a member of the African National Congress regarding the South African struggle. She received her B. S. and M. Ed. at the University of Rochester, and is currently a doctoral candidate in Sociology at Syracuse University. She last held the position of assistant codirector of Management, Development and Training at the State University of New York State at Albany.

Anna Rubbo is an architect from Australia with a longstanding interest in women in developing countries. After practicing architecture in Australia and England she went to Colombia where she spent four years. In addition to writing on women, she has written a doctoral dissertation on housing in the Cauca Valley, Colombia. Currently she teaches courses on architectural design and Third World housing in the Department of Architecture and Urban Planning at the University of Michigan.

Andrea Benton Rushing is Associate Professor of English and Chair of the Department of Black Studies at Amherst College,

Massachusetts. She holds a B.A. (Sociology) from Queens College, CUNY, M.A. (English) from Simmons College and Ph.D. (English) from the University of Massachusetts, Amherst. She has held teaching positions at Colby College, Harvard University, Simmons College and the University of Massachusetts, Boston. She has several publications on Black literature, including "An Annotated Bibliography of Black Women in Black Literature" (*CLA Journal*, 1978), and she has research interests in comparative studies of women in African and Afro-American fiction.

Ruth Simms (Hamilton) is professor of sociology at Michigan State University. She has a strong interest in Third World development and dependency relations; global racial and ethnic diasporas, and comparative urbanization. Her current research interests encompass the political economy of the African diaspora; economic development in urban West Africa, especially among women; and internal migration patterns in Ghana. She is a graduate of Talladega College, and the recipient of a Ph. D. from Northwestern University. Dr. Simms in Editor of *African Urban Studies*, and her publications include *Racial Conflict, Discrimination and Power*, and *Urbanization in West Africa*.

Carol B. Stack is Associate Professor of Public Policy Studies and Anthropology at Duke University where she is also Director, Center for the Study of the Family and the State. She holds a Ph.D. from the University of Illinois (1972) and specializes in urban anthropology, comparative national family policies, sex roles, cultural pluralism, and the rural South. He publications include: "Income Support Policies and the Family," (with Colin C. Blaydon) *Daedalus*, April 1977; "Who Owns the Child? Divorce and Child Custody Decisions in Middle-Class Families," *Social Problems*, April 1976; "The Urban Poor: the Dual Functions of Economically Cooperating Units in a Complex Society," (with John R. Lombardi) in *Anthropology and the Public Interest, P. Sanday, ed., 1976; All Our Kin: Strategies for Survival in a Black Community*, 1974; "Social Insecurity: Breaking Up Poor Families," in *Welfare in America*, B. Mandell, ed., 1974.

Robert Staples is Professor of Sociology at the University of California Medical Center, San Francisco. He received his Ph.D. from

the University of Minnesota, and has been a member of the faculty
at Howard University, Fisk University, and the University of Cali-
fornia at Irvine. He has lectured widely in the United States, South
America, and Europe, and serves on the editorial boards of *The Black
Scholar, Journal of Marriage and the Family*, and *Western Journal of Black
Studies*. Dr. Staples has published numerous articles in professional
and popular periodicals, and among his major books are: *The Lower
Income Negro Family in St. Paul* (The Urban League, 1967), *The Black
Woman in America: Sex, Marriage and the Family* (Nelson-Hall, 1973),
Introduction to Black Sociology (McGraw-Hill, 1976), *The Black Family:
Essays and Studies* (Wadsworth, 1978), and *The World of Black Singles:
Changing Patterns of Male/Female Relations* (Greenwood Press, 1980).

Filomina Chioma Steady is a social anthropologist from Sierra
Leone. She took a D.Phil. at Oxford University in 1974, and has
taught at the Universities of Sierra Leone, Yale and Boston. She is
currently Assistant Professor of Anthropology at Wesleyan University and Research Associate at the African Studies Center, Boston
University. Her publications include a monograph on women in
politics in Sierra Leone entitled *Female Power in African Politics*, and
several articles on women, health care, nutrition and urbanization.
She has traveled extensively and presented papers at several international conferences. She has been the recipient of a number of
academic awards and fellowships including the Ioma Evans-Pritchard Award at Oxford University, and a Social Science Research
Council Postdoctoral Fellowship. Dr. Steady has served as consultant on "women and development" to several international organizations, and was a consultant for the 1980 World Conference of the
United Nations Decade for Women. Dr. Steady is the 1982 recipient
of the Otelia Cromwell Distinguished Alumna Award from Smith
College, Northampton, Massachusetts.

Niara Sudarkasa (formerly Gloria A. Marshall) is Professor of
Anthropology and Associate Director of the Center for Afro-American and African Studies at the University of Michigan. Her publications include articles on African and Afro-American families as well
as on women, trade, and migration in West Africa. She is also the
author of *Where Women Work: A Study of Yoruba Women in the Marketplace
and in the Home* and of "Marriage: Comparative Analysis" in the
International Encyclopedia of the Social Sciences.

Constance R. Sutton, Associate Professor of Anthropology at New York University, received her Ph.D. in Athropology from Columbia University and her M.A. from the University of Chicago. She has recently completed eighteen months of fieldwork in Nigeria on a study that compares male/female social networks and perceptions of power and inequality among the Yoruba. Her previous work has been in the Afro-Caribbean region where she has conducted studies of plantation workers, migration, ethnic/racial consciousness, and gender relations. Her research interests include the impact of socio-political changes on gender relations, class relations and cultural ideology generally, both in the Caribbean and in West Africa.

Rosalyn Terborg-Penn is Associate Professor of History, and Director the Morgan State University Oral History Project. She is coeditor of *The Afro-American Woman: Struggles and Images.*

Stephanie Urdang is a journalist, researcher, and an editor of *Southern Africa,* a monthly news magazine published in New York. She has written widely on women in Africa, particularly Guinea-Bissau and South Africa. Her book, *Fighting Two Colonialisms: Women in Guinea-Bissau* (Monthly Review Press, 1979) is based on visits to that country, both to the liberated zones, during the war against Portuguese colonialism, and to postindependent Guinea-Bissau. She has taught on "Women in Africa" at Hunter College in New York, and is currently engaged in research on the effects of apartheid on African women in South Africa and the role of women in Mozambique, in addition to follow-up research and writing on Guinea-Bissau.

Kate Wittenstein received her B.A. from Bard College, her M.A. from Purdue University and is at present a Ph.D. candidate in the American and New England Studies Program at Boston University where she holds a teaching fellowship. Her research interests are in nineteenth century intellectual history and the history of women.